D1605858

The Selected Journals of
L.M. Montgomery

VOLUME IV: 1929–1935

Late in her life, L.M. Montgomery (1874–1942) expressed the wish that, after suitable time had elapsed, her handwritten journals be published. Montgomery—Mrs. Ewan Macdonald in private life—charged her younger son, Dr. E. Stuart Macdonald, with their care. Before his death in 1982, Dr. Macdonald turned over the handwritten volumes of his mother's journals and a much abridged version which she had typed, as well as her scrapbooks and photographic collection, account books and publishing records, personal library and various memorabilia to the University of Guelph.

The journals comprise ten large legal-size volumes of approximately 500 pages each—almost two million words—spanning the years 1889–1942. The first two journals deal with her early life in Prince Edward Island; the others deal primarily with her life in Ontario, at Leaskdale, Norval, and Toronto. This fourth Oxford volume is a selection of representative entries from the handwritten volumes 7, 8, and 9, showing her activities and preoccupations between 1929 and 1935.

The L.M. Montgomery Collection at the University of Guelph is linked to the University's Scottish Collection, the major archive of Scottish material in North America, and complements holdings in Canadian, women's, and children's literature. Other Montgomery materials are held in Prince Edward Island and the National Archives of Canada.

"Me, mineself 1932"

The Selected Journals of L.M. Montgomery

VOLUME IV: 1929–1935

EDITED BY

Mary Rubio & Elizabeth Waterston

OXFORD

UNIVERSITY PRESS

OXFORD
UNIVERSITY PRESS

70 Wynford Drive, Don Mills, Ontario M3C 1J9

www.oupcanada.com

Oxford University Press is a department of the University of Oxford.
It furthers the University's objective of excellence in research, scholarship,
and education by publishing worldwide in

Oxford New York

Athens Auckland Bangkok Bogotá Buenos Aires Calcutta
Cape Town Chennai Dar es Salaam Delhi Florence Hong Kong Istanbul
Karachi Kuala Lumpur Madrid Melbourne Mexico City Mumbai
Nairobi Paris São Paulo Singapore Taipei Tokyo Toronto Warsaw

with associated companies in Berlin Ibadan

Oxford is a trade mark of Oxford University Press in the UK and in certain other countries

Published in Canada by Oxford University Press

Canadian Cataloguing in Publication Data
Montgomery, L.M. (Lucy Maud), 1874-1942
The selected journals of L.M. Montgomery
Includes index.
Partial contents: v. 1. 1889-1910 – v. 2. 1910-1921 –
v. 3. 1921-1929 – v. 4. 1929-1935.
ISBN 0-19-540503-X (v. 1)   ISBN 0-19-540586-2 (v. 2)
ISBN 0-19-540936-1 (v. 3)   ISBN 0-19-541381-4 (v. 4)
1. Montgomery, L.M. (Lucy Maud), 1874-1942 – Diaries. 2. Novelists, Canadian
(English) – 20th century – Diaries.* I. Rubio, Mary, 1939- .
II. Waterston, Elizabeth, 1922- . III. Title.
PS8526.O45Z53 1985   C813'.52   C85-099705-4   PR9199.2.M6Z468 1985

3 4 5 6 - 02 01 00 99

Contents

Illustrations

Lucy Maud Montgomery's picture captions are in quotation marks.
Photo placement in the handwritten journals is bracketed.

Drawings

Acknowledgements

For this volume, E-mail, faxes, and CD-ROM have begun to supplement the telephone, mail, and on-site inquiries of earlier research. At the terminals of these devices we found indefatigable researchers, in particular Jennifer Litster in Edinburgh and Rosemary Waterston in Toronto. For this volume, we draw on research done over a fifteen-year period.

As our editions of L.M. Montgomery's journals move into the 1930s, we have been able to interview people who remember her. We are grateful to those who have shared their memories: Edmund and Bette Campbell of Haileybury, Ontario; Helen Mason Schafer in Kitchener; Isabel Mustard St. John, Elsie Bushby Davidson, and Wilda and Harold Clark in Leaskdale; Joan Carter, Joy Laird, Mary Elizabeth Coupland Maxwell, Marion Webb Laird and the late Anita Webb, and Elaine Crawford in Norval; Eric Gaskell in Ottawa; Violet King Morgan in Guelph; Linda Watson Sparks in Toronto; Jennie and John Macneill, George Campbell and the extended Campbell family in Prince Edward Island. We are especially indebted to the late Luella Reid Macdonald, of Brampton, who read the journals of her mother-in-law and gave us her own commentary on them, and to her daughter, Luella Macdonald Viejalainen.

For supplementary information, about Norval and environs: Kathy Gastle, Bob Crawford, Edward and Helen Mason Schafer, Gordon and Catharine Agnes Hunt, Kay and David Dills, Faye and June Thompson; about Brampton: Dr. Diana Brydon and Laraine Brydon Bigham; about Leaskdale: Allan McGillivray (Curator, Uxbridge-Scott Museum); about Montreal: Dorothy Waterston; about Sudbury: Brock Greenwell, of the Ministry of Northern Development and Mines; about Kentucky: Dr. Dennis Duffy; about PEI: Dr. L.B. Woolner, Doris Stirling Jenkins, John D. Kendall, Albert Middleton, and Constance M. Carruthers; about Winnipeg: Dr. Rex Richards, Dr. Margaret Morton, and the Rev. S.C. Sharman; about Bala and Northern Ontario: Jack and Linda Hutton, and Joanne Wood; about Guelph: Ian Easterbrook and Professor Gilbert Stelter; about Toronto: Fred Turner and Robert L. Woolner, L.L.B.

We thank the people working in archives: at the University of Guelph, particular thanks goes to Bernard Katz, Head of Archival and Special Collections, and his staff, Ellen Morrison and Darlene Wiltsie; at the L.M. Montgomery Institute in Prince Edward Island, Anna Macdonald; at the P.E.I. Provincial Archives, Harry Holman and Jill MacMicken Wilson; at the University of Toronto Engineering Faculty Archives, Professor L.E. (Ted) Jones; in Ottawa, Hillary Russell and Jane Waterston; in the Archives of the Law Society of Upper Canada, Marie A.E. Hammond; at St. Andrews College in Aurora, Sandra Scott; at the

Prince Albert Historical Museum, W.D. Smiley; at the Film Project, University of Guelph, Dr. Paul Salmon; in the Brampton Archives, Sharon P. Larade; in the Uxbridge-Scott Museum, Allan McGillivray.

Medical experts who helped us include psychiatrists Dr. Angus Beck in Charlottetown; Dr. Mary McKim and respiratologist Dr. Neville Lefcoe of London, Ontario; Dr. David L. Davison in Wolfville, N.S.; Dr. Ernst W. Stieb, Professor of the History of Pharmacy at the University of Toronto and Dr. Ruth Tatham, formerly of Homewood Sanitoriam, who each helped untangle the history of medications taken by Ewan and Maud Macdonald; Dr. Alexander Watt, formerly Head of Homewood, who made other earlier research possible; Dr. R.A. Cleghorn of Toronto; Dr. Steven J. Hucker and Dr. Zindel V. Segal of the Clarke Institute of Psychiatry in Toronto; Professor Don Kuiken of the University of Alberta. We have also drawn on earlier comments about his father's illnesses by the late Dr. E. Stuart Macdonald of St. Michael's Hospital, Toronto.

On Presbyterian ministry and missions, Dr. Ruth Brouwer of the University of Western Ontario, and Kim Arnold and Elspeth Reid of the Presbyterian Church Archives, as well as the staff of Knox College Archives; on women's material history, Virginia Careless of the Royal British Columbia Museum, and Anne Adams of Picton, Ontario; on meteorology, Morley Thomas; on the Institute of Literature and Letters of France, Sarah Waterston; on mining in the 1930s, Edmund Campbell, son of Nora Lefurgey and Edmund Campbell; on general historical questions, Dr. Ian Ross Robertson, Dr. Rae Fleming, and Dr. Michael Bliss; on Montgomery's quotations, the late Rea Wilmshurst, Glenys Stow, Professor Owen Dudley Edwards (Edinburgh), and Jennifer Litster (Edinburgh); on maps and roads of the 1930s, Professor Donald E. Irvine; on the radial railway system, Mel Andrews, Bob Crawford and Beverly Hayden; on Georgetown and the Eaton clan history, John McDonald; on Montgomery's books in Poland, Barbara Wachowicz and Krystyna Sobkowska; on the Macdonalds and clan migration in PEI, Dr. Mike Kennedy; for sharing supplemental research, Mary Beth Cavert of Minnesota; on some matters related to Montgomery's reading and comments, Dr. Catherine Kerrigan, Dr. Susan Brown, and Dr. Kevin McCabe; on the Cambridge Matriculation Exams, Dr. Bharati A. Parikh of Vadodara, India; on Montgomery's finances, Asim Masood; on legalities, the late James Innes (Hud) Stewart, Q.C., the Honourable W.G.C. Howland, and Evan W. Siddall of Toronto.

We also thank Dr. Carole Stewart, Dean of Arts, and Dr. Gerald Manning, Chair of English, who have given us much support for this project at the University of Guelph. We thank Madge Brochet and Paul Bradshaw for their technical assistance.

We owe a continuing debt to the Macdonald family, in particular, to David Macdonald and Ruth Macdonald, and to their solicitor, Marian Hebb of Toronto, who have all facilitated our work in helpful ways.

Those many students who have helped us include Jennifer Rubio and Rebecca Conolly, who did earlier work on proofing the text; James Conolly who did earlier work with identifying and processing photographs; and Kate Wood who has helped research, check data, and proofread.

For help with photographs, we express gratitude to Ted Carter, and especially to Edward Henley, of Florida.

At Oxford University Press, we have had excellent editorial help with this project from William Toye (who designed the volumes and edited the first two), from Phyllis Wilson, current Managing Editor of Oxford, and especially from Olive Koyama, our editor for Volume III and this Volume IV.

Last, we express gratitude to our husbands, Dr. Gerald J. Rubio and Douglas Waterston, who have given us unstinting sympathy and infinite support, as well as the benefits of their wide-ranging professional expertise.

The L.M. Montgomery Project acknowledges ongoing financial assistance of the Social Sciences and Humanities Research Council of Canada (SSHRCC), which has supported the research for this project from its inception, and from the University of Guelph, which has provided space and other facilities.

Mary Henley Rubio
Elizabeth Hillman Waterston

Introduction

After the immense success of L.M. Montgomery's first novel, *Anne of Green Gables* in 1908, a series of best-sellers established this Canadian writer as a world-famous author of popular fiction. By 1929, when this fourth volume of *The Selected Journals of L.M. Montgomery* begins, she was the published author of 16 books (including five sequels to *Anne of Green Gables*), more than 500 short stories and nearly as many poems.

Each new publication brought packets of admiring reviews from newspapers throughout the English-speaking world: from England, Scotland, Ireland, Wales, the United States, South Africa, Australia, New Zealand, British India. Her English-language sales were augmented by translations into Danish, Dutch, Finnish, French, Norwegian, Swedish, and Polish. She was read by men and women alike, erudite and unsophisticated, humble and prominent. For instance, in 1927 the Rt. Hon. Stanley Baldwin, Prime Minister of Great Britain, sought her out for a private audience when he came to Canada; every day the mail brought letters from fans in Hyderabad or Helsinki or Halifax. In this present volume of her journals, L.M. Montgomery confesses something she would never have admitted in public: "It is not a disagreeable sensation to be lionized" (Nov. 27, 1931).

Her fame and public success are only a small part of the record of life contained in this volume, however. In 1930 she wrote, "As a preacher's wife I cannot swear in public. But in this diary I do" (Nov. 19, 1930). As a passionate and judgemental woman, her strong emotions of anger and frustration needed a discreet outlet, and her journals served that function. "At the end of a disheartening day, I creep to this old journal for a bit of comforting. I need it." Here she vented her suffering and heartbreaks. But she wrote with equal passion about her pleasures: "I hate to think of all the lovely things I remember being forgotten when I'm dead," she wrote (July 11, 1931). This volume has many passages celebrating her love of nature, trusted friends, good books, story-telling, movies, cats, and tasty bites. She also writes of the joy in her visits back to her beloved "Island"—Prince Edward Island, where she was born.

Always keeping her personal journals under lock and key in her home, she regarded them as her "life-book". She had begun them in 1889 when she was fourteen, and she would continue them until 1942, the year she died. In her will she entrusted them to her younger son, Dr. [Ewan] Stuart Macdonald, for safekeeping and eventual publication.

In August 1929, when this fourth volume of *The Selected Journals of L.M. Montgomery* begins, she was 54 years old, the mother of sons aged 13 (almost 14) and 17, and the busy mistress of the manse in the village of Norval, Ontario, where her husband was the minister for two Presbyterian churches, at Norval and at Union, near Glen Williams. She was a highly observant woman who kept up on world events through newspapers and magazines. The world was in a tumultuous state, having emerged from the Great War (1914–1918/9) into a period of unparalleled growth through the 1920s. As this volume begins, it was poised for another disaster—the crash of 1929 and the Great Depression of the 1930s. Her first entry in this volume reads, "This morning, by way of variety, we had a little earthquake."

1929 began a period of general confusion. Canada's stock market had followed the New York and other world markets in a sudden plunge. Montgomery's journal shows the nagging anxiety about investments that beset her generation. The journal also reflects the wider-spread insecurity about work and income. In Canada, the sight of unemployed in Toronto matched news of the dole in Great Britain and arguments about the Works Program in the United States.

Montgomery's gold-chip investments evaporated overnight, her royalties fell off somewhat, and her husband's modest church salary was often in arrears, just as she began to worry about providing for her sons' university education, with costs of residence, tuition, books, and clothes. To make matters worse, a steady stream of supplicants sought help from an author they assumed to be wealthy, although in fact her finances had shrunk to the point that she had to type her own manuscripts for the first time since 1910. Loans she had made to various friends and members of her clan went unrepaid. In 1930 she made a trip to the western provinces, partly to try to call in some of these debts—a vain hope given the intensity of the Depression on the prairies.

The journal becomes a record of an era still within memory now, though not necessarily within contemporary understanding. This volume goes on to reflect the way the world Depression became ever darker during the 1930s as the threat of a second world war loomed so soon after the Great War. "What a mess the world is in!" she says in October 1931. Montgomery writes about the "Red menace" in Spain, the Japan-China War, and the rise of Hitler, elected both Chancellor and President of Germany in 1934.

Like so many of her generation, born and raised in the 19th century, Montgomery felt with discomfort the quickening pace of change in 20th century life. Her private world was inevitably shadowed by the outside world. Her journals are the catchment for both a life and a society seeking stability. In a moment of pique Montgomery writes, "Not even a cat would care to haunt so changed a world" (Nov. 25, 1933).

Against this international background of violent upheaval, Montgomery registers her own personal joys and traumas. Here is an access, via a fine writer's reports, to more than the world just before World War II. It is unique in that it is a reflection of feminine sensibility, a report on a woman's life in that world—a part of history rarely documented. Her self-revelation is tempered by the social mores of the time in which she lived. This is the record of a mature, intelligent woman, coping with both professional necessities and family demands, against the backdrop of history.

Her life in these years seemed to lurch regularly between glory and grief. This volume of *The Selected Journals of L.M. Montgomery* begins and ends with

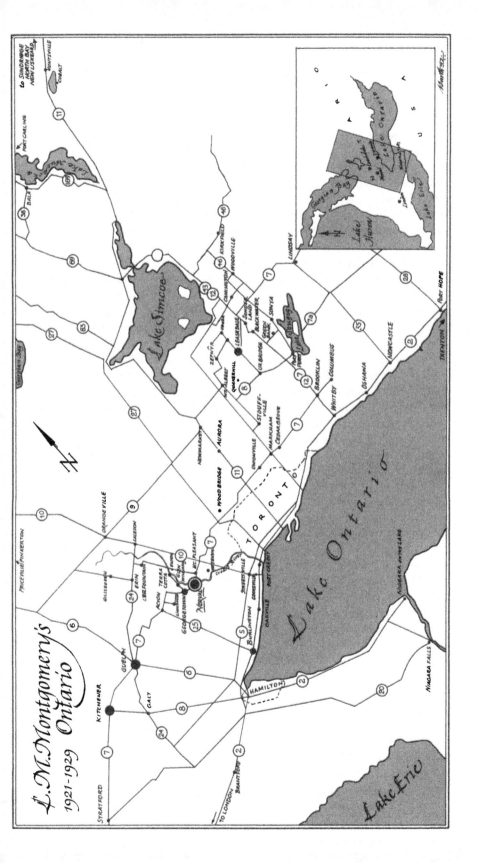

L.M.Montgomery's
Ontario
1921-1929

glorious experiences. Travels to Prince Edward Island and to western Canada brought warmth and friendship in 1929 and 1930, and 1935 opened the way to a new happiness and a move to a new life. But the period between these years was tumultuous. The literal earthquake which opens the volume prefigures her more personal ones.

The first disturbance to erupt into her life, early in 1930, was the intrusion of a young woman who declared a passionate love for the middle-aged Montgomery, calling her "a will-o-the wisp, elusive, exclusive, impulsively flitting here and there, leaving a trail of exotic sweetness that haunts one with a mad desire." Montgomery's account of Isobel, the young woman whose love-letters both repel and fascinate her, is painful and bewildering to read today when generalized attitudes towards homosexuality are so different. Montgomery picks up the language of the popular press of her era when she uses the term "sex pervert", putting it in quotation marks. She reads the 1930s medical texts in an attempt to understand homosexuality better; and while her comments may be offensive today, she is in fact far more open-minded than was the standard of her time. She is writing, remember, only 35 years after Great Britain tried and imprisoned Oscar Wilde for homosexual practices. Radclyffe Hall's novel *The Well of Loneliness*, an open treatment of lesbianism published in 1928, had resulted in scandal and a trial for obscenity. Despite the strong support of writers like Virginia Woolf, E.M. Forster, and Arnold Bennett, the book was banned and an appeal was refused. Nevertheless, a modern reader may find Montgomery's reaction to her obsessed and manipulative young admirer a source of some puzzlement, and will contemplate the various complications which kept her from responding, as most would, to unwanted personal attentions persisting in the face of rebuffs, whether the approaches were from a homosexual or heterosexual admirer.

The second "earthquake" began almost as soon as her older son Chester enrolled at the University of Toronto in the fall of 1930. Although he had always been a very bright student, Montgomery had other worries about Chester. Chester's first year was a disaster, his failure a terrible blow to his mother's pride. But a failed first year was not the only convulsion Chester brought into his mother's life. "There are many problems connected with Chester," she writes, "and I have to grapple with them alone" (July 2, 1932).

When the Macdonalds' second son, Stuart, entered medical studies three years later, his first results also brought disappointment. The reader—especially a mature reader who knows how difficult the late teenage years can be both for anxious parents and for their maturing and often rebellious children—can feel Montgomery's desperate anxiety and follow her concerns with sympathy. The reader may wonder whether her "secret worries" about both her college-age sons showed some of the over-reaction of a hypersensitive person. It is clear, however, that their family was living under intense pressure.

Among her close friends, several other women suffered enormous disappointment with and sorrow over their children. Mary Campbell Beaton's grown son faced humiliating public disgrace, and embarrassment to his family and clan, and this we are told about in great detail. However, her close friend Nora Lefurgey Campbell bravely and quietly faced another kind of sorrow—the devastating deaths of three of her four children. She lost one baby (Donald) and two half-grown children (Jessie and David)—Jessie to polio, and David, who survived polio but was badly crippled, to drowning when his iron braces pulled him under after a boat capsized. Montgomery had mentioned Jessie's death on October 4, 1925, when she wrote: "Yesterday I had a letter from Bertie [McIntyre]. I had asked her to inquire...[about] the whereabouts and welfare of Nora Lefurgey Campbell. It is several years since I heard of her. Bertie did and I was told among other things that Nora's only daughter Jessie, about twelve years old, died last spring of spinal meningitis. Poor poor Nora! She loved her children so intensely and was such a devoted mother. What is the meaning of these terrible rents and tearings of our deepest ties and feelings?" In this volume, Nora has moved back to Toronto, and she comes to Norval for frequent visits with Montgomery, bringing her only remaining child, "Ebbie". There is only cursory mention of Nora's great losses. Yet, with a storyteller's sense of drama and embellishment, Montgomery powerfully conveys her own heartache over her own two sons' failure to meet her standards.

Mothers bore primary responsibility for the training of children in this era, and in a time when public newspapers still carried reports about which university students were on "pass lists", a child's poor performance was a public humiliation. (In Montgomery's own school years, students' actual grade-standing for college entrance exams had been published in the newspapers.) We are also taken back to the time when "forced marriages" were a disgrace that affected a whole family, not just the couple involved: the couple's parents and the couple's children also carried the stigma and shame. Montgomery feels enormous anxiety over her sons' actions, watching for worrisome signs. She dwells at length on the humiliation of Mary Beaton's son, a charming and capable young man on the surface, who seems incorrigible in his leaning towards criminal activity.

It was midway through college that Chester hurled yet another explosion into his parents' lives. Montgomery reacted this time with such distress that she had to set aside her journal for almost three years. From 1933 until 1936 she was able only to scribble rough notes of daily events. It took three years for her to resume the task of polishing those sad notes into coherent entries in this journal which she intended eventually to be a public record of her life.

Chester caused his mother such extreme anxiety partly because he was so like his father in appearance and temperament, and she feared that his erratic behaviour might foreshadow a mental instability like her husband's. Indeed, the third "earthquake" in this period was a total nervous breakdown on the part of the Reverend Ewan Macdonald.

Ewan Macdonald had a long history of deeply depressed periods: as a boy moving into adolescence, as a college student, as a young man attempting advanced studies in theology in Glasgow, Scotland, which was then a world-famous centre for theological study. Maud Montgomery had not been fully aware of the seriousness of Ewan's troubles when she married him in 1911: they had actually spent little time together. His mental problems first disrupted their married life in 1919, when they were living in Leaskdale, Ontario. His depression had been so deep that she had taken him to Boston to consult the best "nerve specialists" in North America. He had slowly recovered and resumed his pastoral duties, and had moved, in apparent good mental health, to Norval. Here, in the handsome red-brick manse, the Macdonald family had again settled into relative peace.

By 1934, however, Ewan Macdonald was again in such bad shape that he had to be hospitalized. The world's financial collapse and the extended Great Depression were the background against which the Reverend Mr. Macdonald's nervous collapse and clinical depression occurred. While his mental prostration (as documented in this volume) was not caused by economic conditions, the general anxiety of the period undoubtedly added to his personal anxiety as a minister. Some readers of the earlier journals have speculated that Montgomery's own temperament may have intensified her husband's mental troubles. The present volume will add to that speculation.

His wife's concern over Ewan's nervous breakdown was that of a woman who had grown up knowing several families "tainted" by mental illness. She watched her growing sons with an anxious eye, noting her ongoing worries about them in this volume of the journals. As she observed her own family, clearly under great stress, she added stories about many other people who had been troubled with bouts of mental illness: Lizzie Stewart Laird, Jane Harker Macneill, Alec Macneill, her Uncle Leander Macneill, Ren Toombs, Tillie Macneill Bentley—all friends and relatives from Prince Edward Island. Her visit with deranged Tillie she builds into comedy. Of her former publisher and nemesis L.C. Page, she coolly remarks that he was never quite normal. She is surprised but not shocked when she hears the gossip that his brother George's mysterious death was suicide. When a young cousin seems to be rushing into marriage, she condemns the match because his family had always had a "bad streak of insanity" in it. And there is the ever-present Isobel, whose behaviour is so insistent and odd as to seem almost deranged. About her husband, the minister, with his recurring obsession about being condemned by God to damnation, Montgomery paraphrases Macbeth: "Who can minister to a mind diseased?" (June 11, 1934).

Her account of her husband's acute clinical depressions provides a touching insight for all of us, especially those involved in teaching, healthcare, and social work where untreated or uncontrolled mental illness still bedevils family units and unravels stable relationships. The journals also display the treatment of mental illness by health professionals, in and out of sanatoriums, in the early 1930s. Medications given to patients by their doctors often had a rebounding effect, making them far worse than they would have been without any treatment. We also learn that Montgomery—who reminds us that her grandmother made excellent red-currant wine (July 11, 1931)—also medicates with wine, an old-time remedy which could also act as a further depressant, as did some of the other drugs she mentions.

At times, Montgomery also became profoundly anxious about her own mental state. Her record of fluctuating moods becomes a precise case study with great interest for professional psychologists and for those who have suffered from mood disorder. Her records also provide the means to study marital interaction when two people both experience fluctuating moods. Freud's writings were bringing possible causes of mental disturbance under scrutiny. Montgomery read Freud and other medical authorities of the era. She also picked up terms from the popular press: "neurasthenia" is one which recurs frequently. Her accounts of her own mental state raise the ultimate question about the relation between mental instability and the mental intensity of a truly creative person.

Like a seismograph, the prose in the journals reflects her own level of agitation. Entries become shorter, to the point that they become minimal records of sleeplessness and illness and of remedies used to relieve distress. Then the prose expands and brightens, as Montgomery regains control of her own state of mind. She availed herself of the most up-to-date medical resources in Toronto, as well as in Boston, to try to understand the ancient scourge of clinical depression and affective mood disorder.

In comparison, when viewed a half-century later in a more secular time, the fourth earthquake recorded in this volume seems like a tempest in a teapot. Nevertheless the trouble in Norval Presbyterian Church brought radical changes in the Macdonalds' already disordered lives, occurring in an era when the church was beginning to lose its position at the centre of community activity. It also restored verve to Montgomery's narrative of events: there were causes to ascertain and villains to name. Her judgemental eye becomes very sharp as she analyses what has gone wrong.

As always in the record she had been keeping since 1889, L.M. Montgomery flicks in details about the way people interact in church groups and social activities, as well as in families. Her earlier volumes had described the insular rural life on Prince Edward Island before the Great War, and subsequently the quickening of life in the small farming community of Leaskdale, Ontario, north-east of Toronto. After the cross-Canada trauma over the matter of "Church Union", when the Presbyterian, Methodist, and Congregational churches voted on whether to merge into the United Church or to remain independent, the Macdonalds had moved in 1926 to Norval, a beautiful little hamlet set in a glen, with hills rising on each side of the forks of the Credit River.

Norval was a very small town, and the vote on "church union" had been divisive within the community. Life among the post-Union Presbyterians was not idyllic. Old controversies continued, exacerbated by the financial difficulties brought on by the Depression. Montgomery detected a new hostility of spirit in the Norval congregation and was at a loss to understand where it came from. In fact, the inability of the people to pay their minister's salary had led to serious misunderstandings, culminating in the dramatic climax of the period recorded in this volume of the journals.

Tension in the church led to a tragicomic battle, centred on the community's efforts to put on theatrical performances. Montgomery treated her husband's parishioners diplomatically in public, but her journal shows how her novelist's eye brightened as she regarded their foibles. Even though she feels herself to be the "toad under the harrow", she does not totally lose her sense of humour. She treats the little Norval earthquake with a mixture of farce and fury.

Even in the most disruptive phases of life in this period, Montgomery experienced moments of great exhilaration. Visiting Prince Edward Island, she found on an old Macneill farm a "secret field", whose beauty gave her the buoyant sense of a world of beauty always accessible to her. In Norval, about 30 miles west of

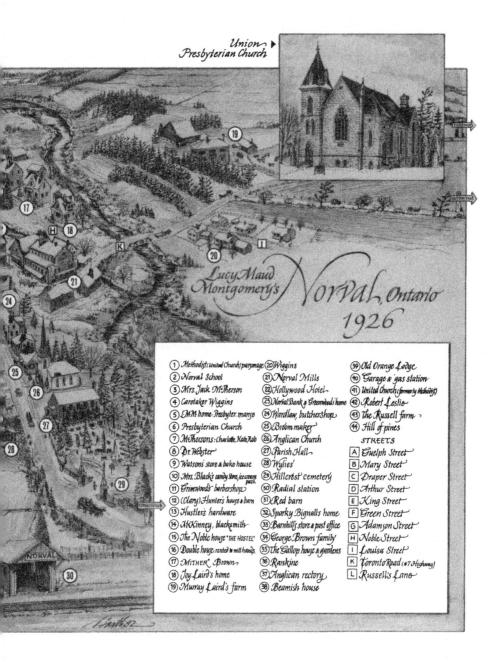

Union
Presbyterian Church ▶

Lucy Maud
Montgomery's *Norval*, Ontario
1926

1. Methodist (United Church) parsonage
2. Norval School
3. Mrs. Jack McPherson
4. Caretaker Wiggins
5. LMM home: Presbyter. manse
6. Presbyterian Church
7. McPhersons: Charlotte, Kate, Rob
8. Dr. Webster
9. Watsons' store & bake house
10. Mrs. Black's candy store, ice cream parlor
11. Grimwoods' barbershop
12. (Clary) Hunter's house & barn
13. Hustler's hardware
14. McKinney, blacksmith
15. The Noble house "THE HOSTEL"
16. Double house: rented to mill hands.
17. "MITHER" Brown
18. Joy Laird's home
19. Murray Laird's farm
20. Wiggins
21. Norval Mills
22. Hollywood Hotel
23. Norval Bank & Greenwood's home
24. Wardlaw, butchershop
25. Broom maker
26. Anglican Church
27. Parish Hall
28. Wylies'
29. Hillcrest cemetery
30. Radial station
31. Red barn
32. Sparky Bignall's home
33. Barnhill's store & post office
34. George Brown family
35. The Gallop house & gardens
36. Rankine
37. Anglican rectory
38. Beamish house
39. Old Orange Lodge
40. Garage & gas station
41. United Church (formerly Methodist)
42. Robert Leslie
43. The Russell farm
44. Hill of pines

STREETS

A. Guelph Street
B. Mary Street
C. Draper Street
D. Arthur Street
E. King Street
F. Green Street
G. Adamson Street
H. Noble Street
I. Louisa Street
K. Toronto Road (#7 Highway)
L. Russell's Lane

Toronto, sitting with her dear friend Nora Lefurgey Campbell on the banks of the Credit River, she felt a comparable sense of enchantment. Perhaps because these moments of epiphany were still available to her, in spite of all the earthquakes, she was able to continue her life as a writer.

L.M. Montgomery's journals had always suggested the ways a writer could transmute her "real" life into fictional equivalents. Volume I of *The Selected Journals of L.M. Montgomery* revealed the sources for the strength and charm of *Anne of Green Gables*, its early sequels, and *The Story Girl*. Volume II gave us the moving story of marriage and motherhood, illuminating the obliquities of such novels as *Anne's House of Dreams*, *Anne of the Island*, and *Rainbow Valley*. The disruption of the first World War and the changed world it brings is registered in *Rilla of Ingleside*. Between 1921 and 1929, the years covered by Volume III, Montgomery was torn between her urge to write and the necessity of fighting legal and parochial battles. She produced the *Emily* trilogy about a girl gifted with artistic power but thwarted by her family's lack of sympathy and by society's expectations of women. In the same period she also created *The Blue Castle*, that odd and fabulous romance about a woman who escapes from patriarchal and social oppression.

Now, reading Volume IV of the journals, we watch a more complex creative force at work. In this volume, we follow the author's day-by-day life during the time she was working on *A Tangled Web*, *Pat of Silver Bush*, *Mistress Pat*, and *Anne of Windy Poplars*. We recognize the symbiotic relationship between the everyday activity of a busy woman, beset with all sorts of problems, and the imaginative soaring of a productive, gifted author.

A Tangled Web presents the story of a cantankerous old woman's manipulation of her entire community. Even after her death, the content of her will ensures that she will dominate. Montgomery's touch remains that of the comedy-writer although her subject is the wayward passions of human beings, with a focus on greed, on the hunger for power over others, and on the vagaries of love. Herself aging and struggling to stabilize her own family, she can still create in her fiction a humorous portrait of a difficult old woman trying to control younger people. As she fixes her novelist's eye on the petty concerns of human beings, she shows her darkening suspicion that "all is vanity" in this world, even when she still makes comedy out of it.

Compared to earlier volumes of the journals, this volume is less directly revealing of the author's work-habits, her progress in current work, and her methods of composition. During 1929–30, the time of its composition, there is no consistent reference to *A Tangled Web*. During the early 1920s, she had recorded the periods of work on the *Emily* books. In this decade, she returns to her practice in the years of composing *Anne of Green Gables*. In the early years of the century, she kept her journalistic eye on "real" life, and kept mum about that other part of her existence, her immersion into an imagined life.

Yet there are oblique revelations still in this late volume of the journals. Very soon after completing *A Tangled Web* in 1931, she filled page after page of the journal with a meditation on her own tangled family history. Stories of the Macneills, the Campbells,and the Montgomeries were dashed off in her best and liveliest style, with ironic speculations about the realities of the partly mythologized past. She was gearing up for a new phase and for the intensities of memory caught in *Pat of Silver Bush* in 1932–33. In transcribing her journal entries for 1934, when she was composing *Mistress Pat*, she returned to annotations on the writing process.

The *Pat* books are in many ways the most interesting of all her compositions from a psychological point of view. The oddities of family relationships and the neurotic qualities in Pat herself fit in subtle and fascinating ways into the life story unfolding in the journal.

Pat of Silver Bush and *Mistress Pat* are set against the years of uprooting and debility and betrayal. They emerge as unpredictably poignant dreams of home and youth and love. The same snippets of poetry, each summing up some aspect of life, appear in the *Pat* books as in the journal. The charming young people in the *Pat* books show the persistence of Montgomery's vision of happy youth. "Jingle" in particular gains strength from the memory of Will Pritchard, a memory intensified during the trip out west to Prince Albert in 1930. In creating the character of Judy Plum, L.M. Montgomery found a way of defusing her present-day anxieties. Judy Plum is an aging and outspoken woman who debunks pretensions yet works to keep a beleaguered family together. In Judy Plum's comic speeches, L.M. Montgomery's wit releases some of her own tensions.

In *Mistress Pat* she registers her own distress over the rapidly escalating social change of her era, and the disappearance of the tranquil rural world of her childhood. In the mid-1930s Montgomery was still struggling to help her Prince Edward Island relatives cope with the problems of farming in a bitterly depressed region and period. Her journals contain sharply practical advice to her young cousins about how to survive tough times. The fictional "Silver Bush" lets her bypass modern stresses and recreate the good old times on the Campbell homestead at Park Corner.

Yet *Mistress Pat* ends in the destruction of that home. Pat's family members die or move out, and the home burns to the ground. Besides reflecting particular dismay at changes in rural Prince Edward Island, this story ties in with deeper personal troubles. Written as Montgomery watches her beloved small boys grow into less controllable young men, and as she contemplates the end of her husband's career and the probability of having to leave a home she adores, these books express her own sense of dislocation and change in her Ontario life, as well as the lost world of her youth in Prince Edward Island.

The mystery of creation remains, however, a mystery both solved and deepened by the account of life in the journals. Montgomery's sense of her own times, her response to the problems posed by her son, her reaction to her husband's growing mental disturbance and her awareness of her own tenuous state of mental balance, her yearning for her old home and the frustrations of her new social circle, her readings and her professional status: all these make the tangled web from which she cut her new novels. And all make, for us as readers of the journals, a literary work as rewarding as any novel.

The sales of the *Pat* books in 1933 and 1935 were disappointing. John McClelland, senior partner of McClelland & Stewart, her Canadian publisher, reported drops in sales and consequently in royalties. Was this the result of the economic depression, changing tastes in fiction, or readers' specific responses to some aspect of these books? Montgomery noted sadly in March 1935 that Hodder & Stoughton, the English publisher that had handled British editions of all her books, had turned down *Mistress Pat*. She found a reputable replacement in the Harrap company. But with two sons still depending on her to cover the costs of clothes, books, residence, and tuition, she fought to recover her market.

She began work on a new *Anne* story. She could build on the phenomenal success of *Anne of Green Gables*, still immensely popular. A new moving picture version made in Hollywood in 1934 was released with great fanfare. (A silent film had been made in 1919, but it was no longer in circulation.) Ironically, profits from the sales of *Anne of Green Gables*, and royalties from the new movie, went not to her but to her first publisher, L.C. Page of Boston. Determined to reap some rewards from the revival of interest in Anne, Montgomery prepared to respond to the demands of publishers and fans. The journals show her courting memories of the past to recall her own days as a novice teacher, and rereading her own early novels and journals in order to recapture the mood of energy and hope and fun. She meshed this "spade work" with observation of living young people—her own troublesome sons and their (to her) unacceptable girl friends, her cousin's children, and the young people she was now trying to wrestle into competence as Bible Class students or as amateur actors in church plays.

Anne of Windy Poplars, which she is planning at the end of this volume, lightly touches on the serious themes increasingly dominating the journal. The twin themes of nurturing friendship and neurotic attachment are played out as counterpoint throughout this volume. Male and female worlds were deeply separated in that era, and women who craved personal simple friendship and companionship outside of marriage were limited to close friendships with women. The language of female friendship had been effusive in the Victorian and Edwardian eras, and echoes of that language linger in Montgomery's prose. Her accounts of friendships with her cousins Laura and Bertie McIntyre, her anguished and loving reminiscences about her late cousin Frederica Campbell, her re-emerging contact with earlier friends Laura Pritchard Agnew and Nora Lefurgey Campbell, and her renewal of old and intense loyalties during joyful visits to Prince Edward Island are deeply pleasurable. On the other hand, her account of the young woman, Isobel, who expressed such a passionate attachment to her in effusive and explicit "love-letters", shows anger and frustration. Yet she allots a good deal of space in her journal, and in her life—though not in her fiction—to this neurotic relationship. Many of the women who relate to Anne in *Anne of Windy Poplars* adumbrate Montgomery's subconscious attitudes towards women's relations to one another.

Also running throughout this volume of the journals are the twin themes of match-making and misalliance. *Anne of Windy Poplars* may offer variations on courtship stories with happy endings, but the journal is more complex. In Norval, Montgomery was as busy promoting the romance of one adored young cousin, Marion Webb, as she was distressed over the romantic attachments of her own sons. (Marion was the daughter of the Webb family who lived in the

"Green Gables" house in Cavendish, Prince Edward Island.) Even though Montgomery almost always speaks with affection for her husband, Ewan, when she recalls her earlier romances she shows her awareness that her own marriage was a misalliance.

In this period, as always, Montgomery turned to books and remembered quotations for refreshment and solace. She reread perennial favourites, by Edward Bulwer-Lytton, Anthony Trollope, the Brontë sisters, and Marie Corelli, but she also was open to new books, including several controversial ones such as Sir James Jeans' *The Universe Around Us*, with its new-fangled ideas about the cosmos, and Emil Ludwig's *Son of Man*, an unorthodox story of the life of Jesus. She also read two current revisionist studies of unhappy marriages, Francis Hackett's *Henry VIII and His Wives*, and Ethel Mayne's *Life of Lady Byron*. She also developed a taste for tidy mystery novels, especially those by Agatha Christie.

Developments in film-entertainment offered her a new source for recreation—the movies produced in a golden age of cinema. Montgomery was very open to the flow of these new creations into her imaginative life. She made innumerable trips to nearby Toronto to see the movies, and also to attend plays at the Royal Alexandra theatre, to shop at the Eaton's and Simpson's department stores and to attend meetings of the Canadian Authors Association.

She was herself a public entertainer now, much in demand as a speaker, both locally and in Toronto or other Ontario cities. She undertook speaking engagements in connection with the appearance of each new book, and delighted audiences with her story-telling ability. At the Canadian Authors Association meetings in Toronto she met contemporary novelists and poets including Sir Charles Roberts, Virna Sheard, Wilson MacDonald, and Madge Macbeth, as well as critics and editors including Napier Moore and Hector Charlesworth.

Despite her fame, the many changes in public taste began to affect her own literary status. She had indeed been "lionized" earlier, getting favourable mention between 1910 and 1920 from literary critics, who fitted her into the category of regionalism and local colour, and from fellow writers like Mark Twain, who simply praised her ability as a writer. Her books had become bestsellers because of her skill as a humorist, as a storyteller, as a word-painter, and as an acute observer of human nature. However, the Great War had ushered in "Modernism": it prescribed a new way of evaluating literature and judging what subjects were appropriate for it. Her books, which looked back to a prewar society and drew heavily on the narrative skills of the oral story-telling tradition, came to be seen as old-fashioned. Fragmentation, angst, and disillusionment were the vogue, and Montgomery's novels, set in pre-war Prince Edward Island, appeared to be works of nostalgia and sentimentalism to the Modernist critical eye. There were tempests in her rural society but these were manageable tempests, and hence seemed trivial in a world which had seen the bloodbath of the Great War. And her stories were about domestic women at a time when the heroes of "serious fiction" were mostly male, and suffering males at that, carrying the mysterious wounds of a generalized psychic disturbance.

The men who dominated the book review pages of newspapers—powerful critics like W.A. Deacon in Toronto, Morgan Powell in Montreal, Arthur Phelps in Winnipeg—were calling for a new kind of Canadian writing: tough and hard-edged, exploring the seamy side of modern life. L.M. Montgomery realized how quickly tastes were changing. She read about Morley Callaghan's prostitutes with dismay and deplored the "pig-sties" of modern fiction. As a minister's wife, she was in any case limited in the amount of sexual activity or explicit depravity which she could put in her novels. She complains that she can't write openly of sex, given that she is writing about adolescents and young adults. As she finished the second of the *Emily* trilogy, she had grumbled: "The public and the publisher won't allow me to write of a young girl as she really is. One can write of children as they are; so my books of children are always good; but when you come to write of the 'miss' you have to depict a sweet, insipid young thing—really a child grown older—to whom the basic realities of life and reactions to them are quite unknown. Love must be scarcely hinted at—yet young girls in their early teens often have some very vivid love affairs. A girl of Emily's type certainly would. But the public—one of the Vanderbilts once said 'Damn the public'....I can't afford to damn the public. I must cater to them for awhile yet" (January 20, 1924). Her loyal world-wide readership was a mixed blessing: her readers supported her, but they also constrained her, as did her position as a minister's wife.

Nevertheless, Montgomery felt that her books would survive when others' would not. Out east in Prince Edward Island, she watched with amusement, and some distress, the way her books were transforming the rural Cavendish society. Tourists came to see all Anne's haunts, and the enterprising Cavendish wives set up tourist homes. When she went to the Canadian West in 1930, she was fêted as an internationally-known and much-loved author.

Perhaps because of the very pressure of ugly realities, of prosaic problems and unrewarding relationships, she had been able to create a long series of books that amuse, satisfy, uplift, energize, and inspire readers. She capitulated to her era's desire for happy endings in popular fiction, but her own energies and frustrations provide the serious undercurrents in her writing, while her tart Scottish sense of humour makes human foibles amusing, and thus diffuses the tension they create.

This volume records honours both national and international. For example, in 1931 she served on a committee with Canon Cody, Chairman of the Board of Governors of the University of Toronto since 1923, who would become President of the University in 1932; Judge Emily Murphy, one of the plaintiffs in the famous "Persons Case" that led to recognition of women as legal "persons" under the law in 1929; Nellie McClung, an equally powerful feminist and author; the distinguished artist Wylie Grier; and Col. Henri Gagnon, Managing Director of the Quebec City newspaper *Le Soleil*, Vice-President of the Canadian Press, past-President of the Canadian Daily Newspaper Association, active in the Canadian Legion, member of the French Legion d'Honneur, and decorated by the Pope. Montgomery served on this high-powered committee and, we may add, quietly dominated its decision. On the world stage, she received in March 1935 a major honour from France.

Despite the changing tastes in literature, she kept writing what she did best, portraying the society she had grown up in, putting in her usual slyly subversive and anti-authoritarian comments. But her muted tones, oblique approach, and increasingly sentimental longing for a lost world (as in the *Pat* books) turned her out of favour with the literary taste-setters. By the 1930s, her books—even an adult book like *A Tangled Web*—were being demoted to the children's shelves in book stores. There they filled a gap created by the need for juvenile fiction when the reading public expanded through universal education. Sadly, as her personal world moved into greater disarray, her critical reputation also was declining.

This journal also reflects some of the physical erosion brought on by aging. When the volume ends Montgomery is approaching her sixty-second birthday. She notes sadly how old friends are "dropping off" as her generation approaches the end of its lifespan. Her memory has always been vivid, and she relives old grievances. She comes back to the troubled times with her stepmother, forty years earlier, remarking bitterly that "the unpleasantness of it welled up today as I recalled it as bitterly and as poignantly as if it were yesterday" (Oct. 12, 1930). Yet her memory blurs now over the exact wording of quotations. She tended to quote not the classic poems she encountered in mature years, but the little jingles that lingered in memory from babyhood, or poems like "The Haunted Spring" that had affected her developing young literary sensibility (see Appendix C). Reconstructing her handwritten journal from notes, she scrambles things and repeats herself. (As editors we have removed duplicate mentions of the same events.) She sometimes mismatches the day of the week and the date, and she often does not bother to check spellings of names.

Either aging or a less formal society seem to have diminished Montgomery's earlier fastidiousness in language. She slips into contemporary slang: has "the willies" or notes that a friend is "a scream". She slides into a grammatical loose-ness markedly different from the school-teacherly correctness of earlier years: people get along "real well", and sentence fragments spatter the late entries. She also dredges up old localisms from childhood days, speaking for instance of having to "brisken up" and using old Scottish dialect words like "agley" for things gone all wrong, and "a grue" for a spell of shuddering. A remnant from the Anglo-India Raj period lingers in this post-colonial Canadian: Montgomery uses the word "tamasha", meaning a general commotion; the salty Irish maid Judy Plum in the *Pat* books converts the word to "tommy-shaws".

On the positive side, aging brought Montgomery some renewed friendships and a chance to travel. This volume includes fine glimpses of the Canadian west in 1930 and of Prince Edward Island, year by year, as changes mark the move-ment toward the 1940s. Old friends came to Toronto; new friendships developed; her garden, her books, and above all her cat revealed new delights. Most readers will smile when the jealous Isobel writes petulantly to Montgomery, "You love your sons, your cats, and I presume your husband" (February 11, 1932).

Journal references to physical erosions in an aging body permit a glimpse of medical practices. Occasional bouts of asthma are treated with strychnine tablets. A "bad chill" brings out a compound of arsenic. Montgomery catalogues the remedies she and her husband take for their "nerves". All shed interesting light on pharmaceutical remedies in pre-antibiotic and pre-antipsychotic drug days. Compounds made up in doctors' offices or local pharmacies led to some terrible mistakes, as in the "blue pills" administered to Ewan in 1934. Before the age of

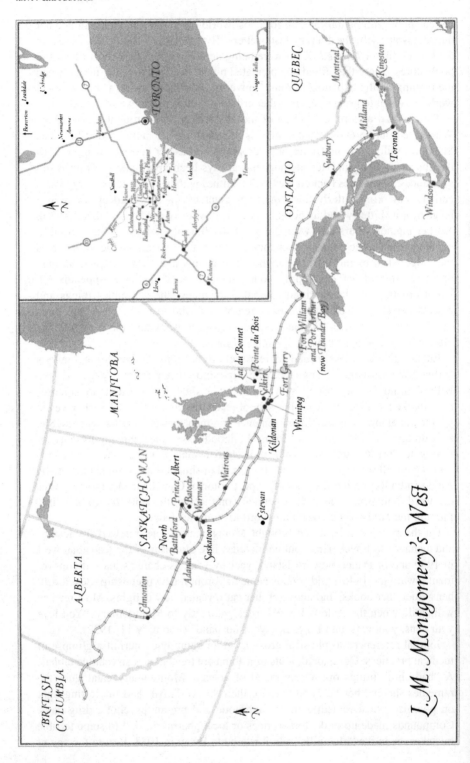

L.M. Montgomery's West

modern dentistry, abscessed teeth meant being put to sleep and having them all pulled—a dangerous process: she notes recent deaths in Toronto from the administration of ether in dentistry.

But it is hardly a sign of age or of forgetting when Montgomery fails to record the most troubling of her experiences at the time they first occur. It is as though she is protecting herself from admitting bad news and the journal from recording it. For example, in the record of the Christmas holidays of 1931 there is no mention of what was no doubt the most noteworthy experience: the receipt of a letter of warning from the University about Chester's inadequate performance. When in February a second letter comes and has to be acted on, the story is told in full detail; but of the first letter, no hint. The entries for those sad holiday times are filled with recountings of her dreams and notes about letters received from the Maritimes and the West. It is an interesting study of defensiveness—and an indicator also of the complex relation between the journals and their creator. She may dramatize events to heighten their effect once she decides to write about them, but she will also resist writing about deeply unpleasant events in her family until there is no chance of a reprieve or reversal.

Her evasions show another emerging conflict in her life, between her need of her journal as a release from anxiety she cannot talk over with her husband, and her growing perception of her journal as a permanent record that will eventually be published, exposing family privacies during her sons' lifetimes. She does not allow herself to express her worst fears about her family or her own deepest self-doubts in this journal. She tells nothing that she thinks will truly diminish her future reputation. She is always the patient wife and concerned mother. This volume of the journals appears frank and revealing, but yet there are subjects and events she clearly avoids. Consequently these late journals hold new fascination for those interested in the smoke-and-mirrors game of self-representation.

Montgomery's journals, as autobiography, remain partly enigma. Parts of them are as carefully written as any novel or poem. Parts are a tumble of unstructured responses to the immediacies of life. Parts are a revelation, honest and unsparing, of a woman's thoughts and feelings. Parts are a careful masking of fact, a cunning reworking of impressions for the sake of effect.

Whatever the delights and the torments in this volume, L.M. Montgomery maintains her rare ability of capturing them in words. Her tart expressions and whimsy keep her writing lively. Narrative and descriptive skills are made ever more enjoyable by her flashes of wit. She can be subdued or fired with rage, sentimental or cheeky. When she sank (as at times happened in these years) into a clinically depressed mood, she could still write, in simple effective sentences, about her despair (although we must always recognize the time-lag between the living through and the writing up of events). When life changed for the better (as it did near the end of this period) she could regain her old forceful style.

This volume presents great extremes of mood: she begins in high spirits, with her usual spunk, sinks into periods of despair in the middle of the volume, but returns to her characteristic energetic self, rising in indignation when she feels her family is badly treated. At the end of the volume we leave her looking forward with great excitement to a new life in Toronto where their family will live in their own home and she will have access to Toronto's cultural life. When they are faced with retirement, she does not consider returning to her roots in her beloved Prince Edward Island. The Island she loved is in her memory and in her books.

She was a word-smith always. In a passage written in Prince Albert, October 10, 1930, she speaks of the effect of looking at old photographs: "I felt as if I were looking, not *at* a picture but *through* it into an actual scene...and all as fresh and unfaded as if taken yesterday." Surely that is the effect that her word-pictures have on modern readers: we step through her descriptions into a world fresh and un-faded. But it is a world where there are always evasions. Secrets and untouchable topics are always hidden between the lines in this, her life-book. Yet, she keeps us with her, caught up in her life and living in her era.

Mary Henley Rubio
Elizabeth Hillman Waterston
University of Guelph
Guelph, Ontario

This volume is dedicated to the memory of Erich Barth, the artist
whose drawings of Cavendish, Leaskdale, and Norval have enhanced
The Selected Journals of L.M. Montgomery.

A Note on the Text

This volume of *The Selected Journals of L.M. Montgomery* contains material from the seventh, eighth, and ninth handwritten ledgers in which L.M. Montgomery transcribed her diaries. She was accustomed to jotting down brief notes every day or so, using whatever paper was at hand, and transferring these notes into her journal ledgers when she had larger blocks of time, and could polish and expand the entries. Usually she wrote up the entries as if the events had just happened, but sometimes she would write in retrospect. The time-lapse allowed her to embellish her journals by pasting in photographs, obituaries and other clippings from newspapers, greeting cards, and bits of material from former costumes. Simultaneously, she kept "scrapbooks" into which she pasted more memorabilia. The handwritten journals, the scrapbooks spanning her Ontario years, a shortened version of her handwritten journals which she typed in the last decade of her life, her personal library, her photograph collection, and much else are all held at the University of Guelph in the "L.M. Montgomery Collection".

As editors, we have used her original handwritten journals as our copy-text. The entries in this Oxford volume proceed in chronological order from August 11, 1929, until November 26, 1933. At that point, Montgomery broke off her established habit of writing up her diary regularly; she picked up the task again on September 16, 1936. From December 1933 on, the sequence of entries is interrupted by her 1936 interpolations, producing a dramatic flashback effect. We have followed her pattern here. Although we shorten her text, we have added nothing to what she wrote, nor have we rearranged any textual materials. This Oxford Volume IV covers from page 345 of her volume 7 to page 329 of her volume 9.

As in the three earlier Oxford volumes of *The Selected Journals of L.M. Montgomery*, we have dropped some entries or parts of entries that were repetitive or without general interest: entries, for instance, in which Montgomery recorded details about the weather or repeated notes about her husband's illness and her own ailments. For legal reasons, we have excised one surname. As in earlier volumes, we have exercised editorial discretion in order to make a volume of publishable length. There is, however, comparatively less material omitted from this volume than from the earlier volumes. A list of entries omitted or shortened appears at the end of this volume.

We have also dropped two long passages she transcribed from other sources. In this regard, we follow the principles established in Oxford Volume I to III of *The Selected Journals*. For example, we omitted from our published Oxford Volume III an artless diary kept by her cousin Charles Macneill, father of her friends Alec and Pensie and cousins. We also note the existence of another curiosity—a joint diary which Montgomery and Nora Lefurgey [later Mrs. Edmund Campbell] kept in 1903—which she did not copy into the handwritten journals which were our copy-text, but which only exists in the typed journals. Similarly, in this Oxford Volume IV, we have dropped from the text transcriptions of writings by two other people: family histories, one composed by her great-aunt Mary Lawson and one by her cousin George Montgomery. Because these accounts illustrate the tradition of passing down family memories in both oral and written form, and because they become the stimulus for Montgomery's own exercise in mythmaking and revisionist history, we offer them as Appendix A and B.

We also indicate in our volume where the beginning and end of her handwritten volumes occur. Montgomery's shaping instinct came into play as soon as she was faced with the empty pages of the ledger which would become her handwritten journal. Sometimes long reflective passages are used to fill out a volume, so as to begin the next one effectively. An illustration of this practice appears at the end of Montgomery's eighth volume (1929 to 1933), where a 19-page retrospective account of Laura Pritchard Agnew's life is used to round off the volume on an elegiac note, re-echoing the melancholy note on which she began that same volume. The last three pages of that handwritten volume include memorabilia associated with Laura: pressed flowers from her bridal bouquet and snips of fabric from her dresses. These material elements add interest and emphasis to the handwritten text which recounts the story of Laura's premature death in September 1932, but they are not reproducible.

We have included many of the photographs Montgomery has inserted into her handwritten journal ledgers, usually placing these pictures at the points she herself chose as appropriate. Her pictures are an integral part of her text, and sometimes they themselves become a secondary text which elicits verbal commentary from her. Occasionally we substitute a clearer picture of the same person or scene from another place in the journals, and we sometimes crop her pictures. With this volume we have been able to improve her photographs through new electronic scanning technology. We never add a picture to her record which is not in the original journals.

We have checked all her entries against a perpetual calendar, and we note at the end of this section where her dates do not conform with the actual day. There are an increasing number of mistakes in her dating as events in her life become more tense and as large chunks of time elapse before she writes up what has happened in her life.

We have regularized spelling and punctuation; for example, in her shifting spelling of "MacClure" and "McClure" in references to the same family. We have left errors in quotations in the text, in the belief that these minor slips form an interesting contrast to the accurate quotations in earlier volumes, when her memory was more precise. Such inconsistencies are referred to in our notes.

The notes also explain contemporary allusions. Our object is to provide a context for Montgomery's diary, both in a general sense of the period from 1929 to 1935 (the latter entries being written up in 1936), and a particular clarification of the lives and achievements of the people she mentions. We hope the Notes will add historical, cultural, theological, and social details, augmenting L.M. Montgomery's own vision (and version) of her life and times.

Mary Henley Rubio
Elizabeth Hillman Waterston

1929

Monday, August 11, 1929
This morning by way of variety we had a little earthquake. About half past six I awakened with the sensation that a big dog was padding heavily about the room. The whole house seemed to be full of knocks and queer noises. A dozen men seemed to be dancing on the zinc roof overhead. One of them was performing a *pas seul* on the bay window roof outside my room. An enormous truck seemed to be rumbling past. I sprang out of bed and drew up the shade. There was no truck—no dancer—no dog. Chester called out from his room to quit knocking on the door—that he was getting up. Then I suddenly realized what

Chester

it was. The noise and tremor lasted about twenty seconds. This is the third earthquake shock I have experienced since I came to Ontario. It seems to have been general all over the province of Ontario. In Brampton the paper on the walls was cracked.

Saturday, Aug. 24, 1929
The Manse, Norval
I have felt better this week and have been busy making up some glorious jugs of pickles. *Magic For Marigold* came from Stokes. Looks very nice. Also a letter from Fan Mutch who is coming up for a week at the Ex. and wants to stay with me! Of course I'm delighted to have her—but she couldn't have picked a worse week. Stuart has to have his tonsils out next Monday and Mrs. Mason is away. Nevertheless I have not forgotten how to cook a bite.

Thursday we had bad, and for Stuart, heart-breaking news. Mrs. Mills wrote that poor Dixie had been found by a neighbor chasing his turkeys and had been shot!

Poor little dog! He was always too fond of chasing things. I suppose the man can't be blamed, though he need not have been so hasty. I would willingly have paid for any damage Dixie had done. But he is dead and his loving faithful little dog heart has ceased to beat forever. Stuart and I had clung to the hope that some-time we could have him back again—next summer perhaps. He was so glad to see us every time we went up. And he *was* such a dear little dog. Is there any use

1

loving things? Wouldn't it be better to be like those people who never care for any little animal?

No, a thousand times, no. We *had* Dixie—and we have still a hundred charming memories of him. Nevertheless I had a very bitter cry Thursday night after I went to bed.

Monday, Sept. 2, 1929
This past week has been a wild one in many ways. I feel as if I had been riding a whirlwind. But there has been a lot of fun—old-time fun—about it too.

Not that Monday was very funny. In the morning we took Stuart to Guelph to have his tonsils out. I sat for a couple of hours shivering in the hall of the hospital. Ordinarily an operation for taking out tonsils is not a very serious thing. But in the past two months six children have died in Toronto under the chloroform while having tonsils out and there has been much talk about an impure anaesthetic and much newspaper discussion. So I was very cold and sick of soul until I knew Stuart had come out of the ether safely. Then we came home and, expecting Fan that night, and having a W.M.S. lunch to put up for the next afternoon, I at once started in baking and so filled up the afternoon. I was determined that I would have extra good meals while Fan was here for I have never forgotten those awful days of starvation at "Heart's Desire." I like Fan immensely as I always have done, and it comes natural to me to put up a good bite for my guests. And I just wanted to heap coals of fire on her head!!!

In the evening Chester and I drove into Toronto and brought her and her daughter Margaret out. Margaret is a nice looking girl but not a particularly fascinating guest. In brief, I don't like her. But Fan is a jolly congenial soul and we had a good week together. I would get up every morning at four, tidy the house, plan the meals and prepare them and then off we'd go. Chester chauffeured us and Ewan stayed home and looked after poor Stuart whom he brought home Tuesday, pretty sore and miserable. I hated having to go away and leave him so much but he was as ever a dear, unselfish, plucky little soul, and made no moan about anything.

Tuesday Chester took Fan and Margaret for a drive while I went to a W.M.S. meeting. Wednesday we went to Toronto, "did" Simpson's, had our lunch in the Arcadian court, our dinner at the Royal York and then took in a rather good "talkie." Got home and to bed about one, got up at four, did my work and left for the Exhibition right after breakfast. We had the usual strenuous day at the Ex. and stayed for the Grand Stand. I was atrociously tired when it was over and on the road home began to be obsessed, as over-tired people often are, by the thought of the mountain of dishes I knew were awaiting me, which must all be washed before I went to bed. I knew they could not be left till morning as we meant to leave early for Niagara. Ordinarily I would not have given them a thought, since washing dishes has never been any bug-bear for me. But as it was—

And when we got home, there in two trays on the dining room table was every dish beautifully washed and wiped. Darling Stuart had got up out of bed and washed all those dishes for me, miserable as he was!

Friday morning we went to Niagara. I have seen Niagara often but never too often. And I had a new sensation in the Cave of the Winds. I am not sorry I tried it but once will do. We certainly got a "kick" out of it. I did not see any "cave" about it but the wind was there all right.

We had a very pleasant day and left for home at dark. The drive back was rather flat after the exciting day, so to while away some long black miles we told tales and gave recitations. Chester spouted some in his best style, I did my bit and Fannie told a yarn so amusing that I copy it down here for its preservation.

Long, long ago (as all stories should begin, I believe) when Fannie was a girl on her father's farm in Milton, her step-sister Sarah MacKinnon lived there too. The said Sarah had a beau, named Lem McLean. And the said Sarah did not want a beau named Lem McLean. So the said Sarah turned the said Lem down one night, coldly and flatly and irrevocably.

Now, good industrious Mr. Wise had spent that whole day planting a hedge of young spruce trees up and down both sides of his long lane. It was a hard day's work and no doubt he surveyed the result at nightfall with pardonable pride—"something attempted, something done had earned a night's repose." But while Mr. Wise slumbered and slept the rejected Lem was walking down the lane, seething with impotent rage of soul. It *had* to be vented in some way. So Lem, as he stalked along, grabbed up a handful of the young spruces, first on one side and then on the other, all the way down to the road. No doubt it did him heaps of good. But when poor Mr. Wise arose in the morning, his nice little hedges were a series of gaps!

History does not record what Mr. Wise did—or said! It would probably not become a loyal daughter to reveal. He never found time to fill up the gaps. The trees grew up and are now, Fannie says, as big and tall as forty year old spruces can be. But every few yards there is a tell-tale space, reminiscent of that frenzied swain—who has been wedded for years to another lady and perhaps has completely forgotten how he wreaked his passion on Mr. Wise's spruce hedge!!

Saturday Mrs. Mason returned, much to my relief, so I had a couple of days of comparative leisure. Sunday evening Chester and I took the Mutches into Toronto to get their train. I miss Fan—she is good company. Today has been pleasant. Stuart is definitely better and able to eat and as I sit here writing, with a lapful of silken cat, I am at peace with my environment. I do not feel any mad desire to go out and yank up anybody's trees. But there have been times when I felt just like that. I can sympathize with Lem McLean.

Wednesday, Sept. 11, 1929
The Manse, Norval

A heat wave struck Ontario and we have been sizzling all the week—the hottest September weather since away back in the 1880's, so the weather man says. I am quite willing to believe it. I have been intensely busy getting the boys ready for school and preparing for my own trip to the Island. The boys went today. I am glad I am going, too. Otherwise the loneliness would be ghastly for awhile.

I have never seen the Island in its autumn coloring since I was married. I want to seek and haply find the old charm of "the fall," which used to have such a potent appeal for me. Will I find it again?

Tuesday, Sept. 17, 1929
Kinross, P.E. Island

On my dear Island again—feeling as if I had never left it—feeling that here only am I a complete being. No, I never *should* have left it.

I had a bad night last Wednesday night before I left home. Insomnia and blue devils! I have had too many of these nights this fall. Why, I don't know. I feel well and have no especial worries. I expect it is just nerve fag from overwork. But since I came to the Island I have slept like a top every night. I am home!

I left Toronto last Thursday evening and had a quiet uneventful journey eastward, mostly through gray rain. For the first time, I think, I knew no one on the boat as we crossed in the falling dusk. Then came the train ride to Charlottetown through the autumn landscape in the twilight. My Island looked a little sorrowful and forsaken, as if no one had loved it for a long time. Most of the harvest fields were bare but the leaves had not yet begun to turn. Here and there were great flocks of snowy geese in the dim sere fields—white as snow in the autumnal twilight. It was dark when we got to Hunter River and there was a light in the waiting room of the station. On the opposite wall thro' the door I saw a big poster— "Avonlea Restaurant, Cavendish Beach.".…One day this summer I understand there were all of two thousand people there. Desecration! I hate to think of it! But "the world do move"!

Well, I reached Charlottetown in a pouring rain and Fan and R.E. met me and took me home. It was just 6.30. I expected they would have waited tea for me and I was starving, having had nothing to eat since my dinner at noon at Sackville!

I think I recorded in this veracious journal an account of the slim meals Fan put up to us some years ago in "Heart's Desire." When she came up to visit me I heaped coals of fire on her head by providing the most lavish and delicious meals I could—heaps of good food. I really thought Fan might tumble to the difference between her table and mine and give me at least decent meals during my brief stay in her household.

Not a bit of it. They had had their supper before I arrived and when I sat down to the table this is what I saw. A cup of lukewarm tea. Three very small very dry half slices of bread. A bit of butter. And two stale shrunken pieces of what looked to be gingerbread dating back to the reign of Rameses I!!

I simply can't understand it! They are well-off—very well off and though both the families they belong to have the reputation of being "close," yet I have never heard that they were "mean with company." Perhaps Fan thinks starving her guests is living the simple life! Anyhow, there was nothing on that table I could eat hungry as I was. I choked down a slice of bread and drank my tea. The gingerbread I did not meddle with. It was really too prehistoric.

After supper Fan took me to a picture. I was not very keen to go out after my tiresome journey and the picture was poor stuff. The 50 cents Fan spent on this treat would have sufficed to give me a decent supper.

Sunday it poured rain all day until about four and I really felt a little blue and almost wished I was back in Ontario. Breakfast and dinner had been *very* sketchy meals—very indeed. For breakfast corn flakes (which I loathe) dry bread and tea—nothing more. For dinner rather poor cold meat and more bread and tea! Still, if one could have got enough even of that!

By supper time it had cleared up and we decided to go out to Cherry Valley—delightful name—to a Missionary concert which was being held there at which Fan was to read. When we sat down to supper I rejoiced. To be sure there was nothing but bread and butter and apple sauce. But the apple sauce was delicious and there was a big bowl of it and I thought I was going to get filled up satisfactorily at last. Alas, Fan announced that we would have to hurry to get off and down there before the meeting, for some reason or other. She and R.E. were through before I had well got started and I had to arise reluctantly from the table.

I have heard faddists say that one should always arise from a meal feeling hungry. Well, I complied with that dictum at every meal I had in R.E's house!

But the drive down to Cherry Valley was a sheer delight. The sun had come out and performed its usual miracle on those blue harbours and winding red roads. When it set, a great orange moon was rising over a field of wheatstocks. Lights were twinkling out here and there in the lonely pale, clear autumn dusk. Fan is excellent company. The concert was pleasant; and when we came out after it on the steps of the Cherry Valley church—which is "beautiful for situation"—I stood entranced. There before me was once more the beauty of a moonlit sea—the lovely Pownal Bay, a dream of silver and shadow. I just stood there and fed my soul on it while Fan talked to friends—and the boys were running around in the crowd cutting out their girls and steering them off to the waiting cars—just as in olden years, only it was buggies then.

But though my soul was sated my poor stomach was still dreadfully empty and I certainly hailed with joy the dictum of a certain Mrs. Mutch, a cousin-in-law of Fan's, that we were all to go to her house for lunch. Blessings on her hospitable heart! May her shadow never grow less! I think she saved my life. I think had it not been for her I should have been found cold and stiff in the morning and the doctors would have said I died of heart failure. We had oceans of lovely cake and ice-cream and I took a piece of every cake passed me—sometimes two pieces. They must all have thought me a greedy pig but I was past caring for that.

Monday was a gala day. I did not get much for breakfast but Fan gave a luncheon in my honor to some of her friends—and a very nice one it was. Chicken—scalloped potatoes—peas, cake, ice cream. Not too much of anything but enough. She *can* put up a decent meal if she wants to. Why then doesn't she want to? She had urged me to visit her—she had thanked me again and again for my "wonderful hospitality"—I know Fan really likes me and likes to have me visit her. And yet she starves me. Well, we all have our peculiarities. I, for example, *cannot* discard any piece of blank paper. I *must* save it to write on.

That morning I went down to Angie Doiron's little shop and got a darling dress of brown lace, with the long tail that is coming in. I wonder if long skirts will really come back. The designers are making a desperate effort to bring them in. I should like them for house dresses but never for the street. The new dresses are really charming after the above-knee horrors we have lately had to endure.

It was nice to see Angie again. But for the first time I see her looking old. She was a very handsome girl and a charming one. I fancy her life has been a tragedy. She was a French girl though one would never have supposed it. Her English was perfect—she had no trace of a French accent or of the peasant-like personality nearly all the Island French girls had. She was well-educated and clever. But there are very few French men on P.E.I. to mate with her—and of course no English man would. He would marry some stupid homely little English speaking girl but he would not marry clever, beautiful French Angie.

One of Fannie's guests at luncheon was Mrs. Arty Clark, who told me gravely that the Rev. Edwin Simpson had been to see her (Arty is his cousin) when he was on the Island this summer and was "dying to meet me." I hardly think it. I can't believe Ed is any more desirous of seeing me than I am of seeing him. He may have expressed a surface wish to meet me but I think it was a surface wish only.

After the luncheon guests departed I went up and said a few words to the girls of Prince Street School and then hurried off to what was the high spot of the day for me—the long-planned reunion between Mary, Nell, Ida and myself. It was held at Ida's and it was certainly a merry affair. And it was thirty-five years since we four had last been together. Then we were a light-hearted quartette of minxes at old P.W.C. with all our lives before us. Now we are all wives and mothers—and two of us are grandmothers!

We were not sober and serious as becomes aged folk. Instead we were wildly hilarious and revived all the jokes of our college year. I have not laughed so much—and so *real*-ly—for a decade. And Ida follows a different tradition of hospitality than Fan. Such a supper as she put up! There was enough on the table for forty. And everything delicious. I was absolutely ashamed of the way I ate. I laid it to the account of the Island air because I would not breathe a word against Fan.

We had a snap-shot taken—the result of which enlarged is seen on the opposite page—cheek by jowl with the one taken 35 years ago. It is hardly fair to compare the two since one is an untouched snap-shot and the other a finished studio photograph. But there is no blinking the fact that we have all changed! Ida has changed the least I think, Nell the most because of her white hair.

Time reverses many things curiously. In 1894 Mary was a far better looking girl than Nell. Mary was fresh and rosy with golden hair. Nell was sallow, old looking and always shabbily dressed. Her people were poor and she had had a hard struggle to get along as far as P.W.C.

Now it is the exact reverse. Nell with her snow-white hair, her shell rimmed spectacles, her rather ascetic face and a very nice black dress is absolutely a distinguished looking woman while Mary has gone terribly to seed.

In the evening I went out with Mary to Winsloe and stayed there till this afternoon. Mary is not a dainty housekeeper but she gives you enough to eat. Fan came out for me this afternoon and we went to a garden party at the Experimental farm where the tiny cup of tea, tinier sandwich and tiniest bit of cake were all I had to eat until I got to Kinross. Not that I expected or desired anything more at an afternoon affair but I *did* think we would have a bite at Fan's before starting for Kinross. Not a bit of it. Fan airily announced that we must start at once because R.E. wanted to get back before dark. So off we went. Had a delightful drive too

Nell, Mary, Maud, Ida in 1894 (clockwise).

Nell, Ida, Maud, Mary in 1929 (clockwise).

in spite of my empty stomach. Which, I may say Aunt Christie promptly and well filled as soon as the Mutches had gone!

Poor Aunt Christie! She is a sweet soul and she has had so much trouble in the past six or seven years. When we first began coming here sixteen years ago she had a husband and a family of eight. Now she has just Edison. All the rest are gone. Yet Christie is brave and sweet and cheerful still. I am very fond of her. She and Angus have always been my favorites in Ewan's family. But Angus has disappointed me. He has been behaving very nastily and unreasonably all summer over certain financial matters connected with Christie's troubles and hurling the most unjustifiable insults at Ewan and me. I am not going to waste valuable diary space going into the details of his kididoes but I am thoroughly disgusted with him. Christie and I had a long talk about it all tonight and cleared up several things that had been puzzling us. I expect Brother Angus' ears burned during our confab. I fancy that Edith, Angus' wife, is at the bottom of his behavior. Christie has no more use for her than I have. As for Ewan and me, Ewan *gave* Christie $600 five years ago and I loaned her $2,000 and have never asked her for a cent of interest and told her not to think of the principal at all until she was quite ready to pay it. So I think I have done pretty well by Angus' family and I say no thankyou to him for his ill-bred slams and insinuations. To be sure I think most of them were written while he was under a mistaken impression about certain things but when I wrote him a courteous letter pointing out the facts of the case he was not even man enough to apologize. To be sure he admitted grudgingly that I had been "very sporting" in my dealings with Christie but he did not say he was sorry for his insults to me and to Ewan. So Angus goes off my map!!

Cavendish, P.E. Island.
Sunday, Sept. 22, 1929

....John and Margaret Stirling came over and took me to Montague where I stayed till Saturday morning and had a most delightful visit. Margaret and I talked most of both nights—but under some circumstances talk does you as much good as sleep. I am afraid, though, that the Stirlings will not be long in Montague and then goodness knows where they will go. Well—"all life is bondage—souls alone are free." I found that in a volume of Lytton recently and at once copied it in my quotation book. At least, thank God for freedom of soul.

It is lovely to be on the Island in autumn again. I felt that I want always to come here in autumn after this. The brooding haunted peace is something that must be experienced to be believed.

Friday night Doris drove Margaret and me down to Lower Montague—a wonderfully lovely spot....Certainly the motor car has made travelling on the Island easier and pleasanter. But there is one thing I lament. In order to widen the roads for the use of cars every year more and more of the exquisite beauty of the tree-grown sides is being sacrificed. It is necessary but deplorable. However, in a few years new beauty will clothe the roads and there are still hundreds of dear "side roads" untouched of man, that are the dreams of idyllic loveliness they always were.

....Last night I went out to Winsloe and Mary had a gorgeous chicken dinner for me. Then after dinner Albert and Maud Middleton drove me up to Cavendish. It was a delightful afternoon and we had a merry drive. I had been telling Albert Fan's story about the Lem McLean who tore up the trees at the old Wise place and Albert declared he would make an excuse to call there on our way up and see if we could not see the trees—what was left of them.

We drove in to it by a new treeless lane. It is owned now by a family named Gillespie. The lady of the house came out to the car and Maud introduced us, winding up with the little flourish she can't help about "L.M. Montgomery."

No response appeared on Mrs. G's face. Poor Maud saw that her bit of lion parading had fallen flat and, not having enough sense to leave the thing alone, persisted,

"Haven't you read any of her books?"

Mrs. G. fixed me with a blank uninterested stare.

"No," she said. "*Is she a Baptist?*"

All the way to Cavendish we argued as to what she meant. I thought perhaps she was under a vow not to read anything save what was written by a Baptist. Albert opined that she thought nobody but a Baptist could write anything worth reading. Mary said it was likely she just thought I looked like a Baptist!

Albert told Mrs. Gillespie the story of the lane but, like Queen Victoria of blessed memory, she was not amused. She said they had closed up that lane last winter and cut all the trees down. So that was that.

We came up the old "Rustico road" and presently found ourselves on the road that led to the end of the world, as Stuart once called it. We drove up through Cavendish and turned down the "Big Lane." At its entrance were two signboards recently erected by the Provincial Government—one to "Avonlea Beach" the

The Webbs

other to "Green Gables"—i.e. Ernest Webb's place. It seems of no use to protest that it is not "Green Gables"—that Green Gables was a purely imaginary place. Tourists by the hundred come here and Myrtle turns an honest penny selling picture postals of Lover's Lane etc. etc. while no one will ever believe that Cavendish Pond is not "The Lake of Shining Waters."

Mrs. Allan Wyand, an enterprising lady of Mayfield, has started up a restaurant at the shore. This was the last Sunday of the season and only a few people were there. But a few too many for me. However, one of them, a rugged old Irishman who looked as if he had never opened a book in his life, came up to me and exclaimed, "Shure an' I niver dramed I'd have the honor of shaking hands wid you. I've read every book ye've iver written and I hope ye'll live for a hundred years and kape on writing them. Ye're the bright star of Prince Edward Island and we're all proud of ye."

It takes an Irishman to put the blarney over. He was quite a nice antidote to Mrs. Gillespie!

Oh, it is heavenly to be in Cavendish again. And I was beginning to think I loved Norval almost as well as Cavendish! Never!....

Tuesday, Sept. 24, 1929
Cavendish, P.E.I.
....This evening I had a "home" evening of the kind I thought had vanished from the earth. We all sat in the "sitting room" as it is still called there. The chill of the autumn evening was banished by a cosy wood fire. I did a bit of embroidery, Myrtle sewed, Ernest read, the girls wrote letters, the kittens frolicked—we talked when we felt like it and kept silence when we did not. And there was a friendly "kerosene" lamp on the table, casting a mellow glow over all.

"Webb Kittens and I"

I had expected to miss the hydro. I do not. I like the old kerosene lamps. They seem to fit into this life better than any modern illuminations.

Wednesday, Sept. 25, 1929

Today blew an autumn wind. But Myrtle and I went buggy riding. I haven't quite got used to the buggy yet. When I get into one I seem so dreadfully "high up"—there seems to be nothing underneath me. But apart from that weird feeling I love buggy riding. It is leisurely. You have time to see the beauty of the hills and fields—and such beauties as the road improvers have spared. We paid several calls and one of them was heartbreaking. We went to see Lizzie Stewart Laird. She was dreadful—dreadful. Her mind has come back to a certain extent but something of her—a very important something—has never come back. She looked like a toothless old hag of ninety. She was clothed literally in rags. She was dirty. Her house was filthy. And the tragedy of it was that she didn't mind—didn't care in the least. I looked at her and remembered a Sunday long ago when Uncle Leander, Uncle Chester, and their wives were in Cavendish church. Lizzie and Emma Stewart were on the green when we came out and my uncles stopped to speak to them. Lizzie and Emma were resplendent that day in new blue dresses and stylish little "lace straw" flower trimmed hats. After we went home uncles and aunts talked over the girls they had seen in church and decided that the "Miss Stewarts" were the "smartest" girls of the lot.

And now! Lizzie, too, used to be a perfect housekeeper and cook. But I shall be haunted for weeks by that terrible place. Poor, poor Lizzie. And why???

Thursday, Sept. 26, 1929

Tonight I gave a talk on Mammoth Cave to an Institute meeting in Mayfield hall. And for *the first time* I heard the Island hymn sung—the hymn I wrote over twenty years ago! I have never happened to be anywhere it was sung before.

And old Willy Moffat, who is 84, came up and shook hands with me and said, "I want to tell you that I once went home with your mother."

Poor mother! It's lucky he never went—or was let go—home with her again. If he had he might have been my father. I seem to have had some narrow escapes in fathers, judging from some of mother's old beaux! We howled over this in the house of Webb when I got home. It seemed like a bit of ancient history to us. And I have no doubt it seems like the other day to William Moffat—just as it seems the other day to me when Nate Lockhart or Chesley Clark "went home" with me from prayer-meeting or "Literary"!

Saturday, Sept. 28, 1929
Today was exquisite—warm, golden, dreamy—a typical autumn day. And I have drained it to the very dregs—only there were no dregs. It was all delicious.

In the afternoon I went over the fields to the old home. It is a terrible jungly sort of place now. And yet it is and ever must be hallowed ground to me. Everything I looked on had some memory of pleasure or pain. That old farm is very eloquent.

I found out a few amusing things recently. Uncle John is *very* sorry he tore the old house down. Very sorry indeed. And why! Because it has lately dawned on him that he could have made money over it. Crowds of people go there to see it— or the place where it was. One woman said to him this summer "I would give a hundred dollars to have slept for one night in the room where L.M.Montgomery slept." It was cheap and easy to say it, when the room was not in existence to call her bluff. But no doubt she would have given something and those lost dollars will haunt Uncle John to his grave. *Frank*, too, has been heard to lament the destruction. If the house were in existence his wife would come over and run a tea-room there in the summer for tourists! Mrs. Allan Wyand is full of a crazy scheme to *rebuild* the house, exactly as it was. And somebody else thinks the Government ought to do it and several people in Ch'town are reported to have said they would gladly contribute to it etc.

And I laugh in my heart and am well content. I am *glad* the old house has gone. It can never be degraded to the uses of a tea-room. It is mine—*mine*. I can see every room and line of it, every picture, every stick of furniture....

Uncle John has erected a black fox ranch in the jungle that was once the front orchard. But I found the old apple tree still there. It was just as it is now when I was a girl. It must be close on to a hundred years old. And it is still bearing apples. I brought two of them home and ate them. I had never dreamed of eating an apple off that tree again. And they tasted good. They were sweet apples, but they had a nice nutty flavor—quite different from the insipid sweetness of the "sweet apples" in the back orchard. I wished I had brought away more of them.

I found the old gray stone that always stood by the corner of the back orchard. When I was a child Grandmother used it as a weight for her cheese press. Boys coming for the mail on horseback used to spring on their nags from it. I wish I could have carried it away. It's a wonder some prowling tourist has not carried it off before now. Luckily it is rather heavy.

Some time ago I got an old faded copy of a picture Annie Clark took of the old home in 1895. I had a negative made from it and some pictures printed off. The view above is the result. The old apple tree is shown very clearly. Grandfather and Grandmother—Uncle Leander just home from the pond with a string of trout— Willie and Eric, two small boys dimly discernible in the boughs—and sitting on the stump of a branch of the old trunk—a girl. A girl with eyes and heart still full of the dreams of youth. Who was she? It doesn't seem just possible that she was I—or that I was she!

"1895" [Maud, Grandmother and Grandfather Macneill, and Uncle Leander in front of "the olde home" in Cavendish]

I prowled about there with my ghosts for a long time. The old juniper is still growing on the dyke. Beyond it to the South the hill fields are much the same....

When I had finally to tear myself away I went over to the spot where my dear ones are lying asleep. Mother's stone is very badly lichened. I think I must do something about it—or see if anything can be done.

I walked back by the school hill and over Pierce's field. Years ago, during my first or second visit home, I was aghast to find that Pierce had cut down an exquisite little grove of maple and spruce that had jutted out in one corner of this field. For years after it was a barren waste of stumps. And now it is beautiful again. New spruces and maples have grown up in it....

After supper this evening I slipped away for a solitary walk to the shore. It was the sort of an evening on which I love to wander abroad and alone—the gray, dull-silver brooding kind of evening I have never seen anywhere save in Prince Edward Island. Every step I took was a delight. I loitered. The fields were quiet and friendly and expectant—as if they loved me but took me for granted and were thinking a good deal about their own concerns. It was the mood I love best in them. And the pond was exquisite. It was not silver or blue or rosy or dark—it was simply translucent. An effect seen only on just that kind of an evening. The soul of the water was revealed. And away beyond it and beyond the dark rims of the dunes and the shadowy cup of the harbour was the winking star of the New London light....I lingered there for an hour—alone—all alone with my old love. There were no intrusive crowds that night—no raucous cars—no hot-dogs! It was my own darling solitude again, untouched, unspoiled with all its glamour and wizardry and memories. I owned the whole gulf!

I came home by the Big Lane. It was quite dark by now but not a spruce tree in that lane had forgotten me.

I think I shall dream of that shore many a time just as it was tonight—the splash of shining waves, the little misty hidden coves, the shadows and the silences. Beloved land!

Sunday, Sept. 29, 1929
Gartmore Farm
Today it rained—and Cecil Simpson motored Myrtle and Ernest and me to Tryon. I do not like motoring in a P.E. Island rain in a car minus chains, with a Simpson as a driver! For the first ten miles I expected we would skid into the ditch every moment. Then the road grew better and in spite of the rain I enjoyed the drive because of the magnificent colors of the maple groves along the way. Nevertheless I drew a secret breath of relief when we reached home at night. I don't like going away from home in a rain but I love to *come* home in a rain—to step in a moment from dark and chill and damp into light and warmth and welcome.

I could not stay long in it however for the time had come to leave for Alec's...

Wednesday, Oct. 2, 1929
....May and I set out after dinner for a long leisurely ramble to the back fields and woods of "Gartmore Farm." We went up the old brook valley where Pensie and I used to go for the cows on summer evenings of long ago, we went through a dear woodland lane of young spruces, through mellow old pasture fields where cows grazed and which were surrounded by golden and crimson maples, through another exquisite lane that led twistingly through woods to the very "back" fields that looked over Rustico Harbour. We just poked on and talked. "Mike," May's beautiful collie, went with us, sometimes keeping close to us, sometimes roaming afar after rabbits. We found a most exquisite little nook, shut all around with trees and full of frosted golden fern in which two darling little spruce trees grew, as

Gartmore Farm

"The Red Brook Valley"

shapely and perfect as only spruces sheltered from all rough winds can grow. We adopted them at once as our own particular trees, named them "Wood Queen" and "Fern Princess" and decided to tell Alec that never must those trees be cut down.

We explored light-heartedly a score of delicious nooks and groves and fields and corners. The woods had a beautiful mood on that day. A friendly mood. They welcomed us. And we, instead of being two grayish middle aged women, were young again—young with the eternal youth of the woods—young and happy and carefree. When it came time to go home we felt that we were leaving fairyland behind us. But it had been ours.

How this old life fits me like a glove always when I come back to it. As if I had never been away at all.

Thursday, Oct. 3, 1929
It poured rain all day. We welcomed it. It was badly needed. I sat and loved it— loved to look out and see the thirsty earth welcoming it—to hear the east wind booming at the window and the gulf roaring.

In the evening we went to see "Bob and Jennie," in their little old white house on the hill. The road was too slippery for a car so Alec "hitched up" the old mare and drove us over in old style—May and I on the seat and Alec standing on the— on the—what on earth did he stand on? I used to know the name well enough. Anyway he *did* stand on it, behind us, holding a lantern in one hand and driving with the other. We laughed all the way over. And then the five of us got together in a little room, which probably transgressed every canon of modern "good taste" but which nevertheless contrived to be a very cosy homelike little spot, and bandied jokes and insults all the evening, laughing till the tears literally ran down our faces. Every one of us *could* laugh. There are people who can't, nice people, lots of them, who smile and enjoy themselves but can never let themselves go in unashamed howls and yells of mirth. Oh, Bob and Alec and Jennie and May and I made whoopee all right. Jennie served us a good bite and we came away leaving Bob and Jennie laughing on the doorstep. I like to leave people laughing.

Saturday, Oct. 5, 1929
Gartmore Farm
Cavendish, P.E. Island
This was another type of autumn day—windy and fine but with great black clouds rolling up and over every now and then. I love their dark beauty.

I went to see Hammond and Emily and had tea with them and a good time. But my happiest hour was walking home by the cross-cut up Hammond's hill field and through by Bob's. Away over New London Harbour was one of those splendid panoramic autumn sunsets I have not seen for many years. I walked slowly, stopping every few minutes to savor it fully. It seemed like a harbour itself—a harbour of gold and orange sky, with purple-black clouds arranged about it like wooded hills. The illusion was singularly distinct. There were dark high headlands. Scattered little dark slits at the harbour's mouth. Further west a city not made by hands—with ramparts and towers. The New London light burning like a diamond spark against a golden sky. Over all a Valkyrie riding on a storm cloud.

And at exactly that hour next Saturday night I shall be in the dazzle and blatancy of the Toronto traffic, far far from this dear dark land of mine where only I can be a complete person.

Just back of Rob's barn I met a bull with a herd of young cows. They possessed the field corner where were the "bars" I wanted to pass. The bull did not seem inclined to move. I decided I would not try to make him. Possession is nine points of the law—and he had it. So I climbed into Rob's pigpen—his out-of-door pigpen—where the pigs were more friendly than the bull. I did not know how I would get out of it but luckily there was a panel by the barn with no barbed wire on it and I got over nicely and resumed my interrupted revel in the sunset as I went down Bob's lane.

My visit is almost ended. I go tomorrow. I hate the thought of it. I have had two such perfectly happy and delightful weeks in Cavendish. I have slept like a top in that cosy little upstairs room, waking in the mornings to see the maple splendor in the back fields where May and I roamed Wednesday. It has been too perfect. The gods don't give a gift like that for nothing. I shall pay for it—oh, I shall pay. But it is worth the price, whatever it may be.

The Manse, Norval, Ont.
Sunday, October 13, 1929
One lives a good deal in a week sometimes. And this week has been a curious mixture of pleasure and pain.

Last Sunday, October 6, was almost unmixed pleasure. It was a lovely day and Alec, May, Myrtle and I drove over to Park Corner. I hated to leave

16

The Haunted Wood

Cavendish and ate up every scene with my eyes as it slipped away behind me. When we called for Myrtle the sunshine was mantling over the woods back around Lover's Lane and the maple colored hills beyond. The dahlias and marigolds in Myrtle's garden were a poem of delight; and over the brook the spruces were talking gently together in what is now known, thanks to Anne, as "The Haunted Wood."....

We stopped at the old Geddie Memorial church and I went to Frede's grave!

We drove up after dinner to see Aunt Emily, taking Ella with us. Aunt Emily is beginning to look old. Well, she is old. But until lately she had retained an odd look of youth owing to her brown hair and rosy cheeks. Her hair is graying at last and her color has gone. She is the only aunt I have left on either the spear or the spindle side and it grieves me to see her failing.

Alec and May and Myrtle and I had our pictures taken together for a souvenir. The result as far as I am concerned is positively awful; but at least it will serve to recall a happy day.

The happiness ended when they had to leave for home. I felt wretchedly lonely and forsaken when they had gone. I am fond of Ella and the children and glad to see them but oh, for the faces of old.

Monday was gray and showery—a dear day in its way. But Park Corner is a house without laughter now. And it is beginning to have an *unlived* look about it. Orchards and farms and yards are grown up to a jungly appearance with seedlings and raspberry canes and weeds. It is not cared for.

"Four of a Kind" [May Macneill, Myrtle Webb, Alex Macneill, Maud]

I can see no hope for Park Corner. Jim, who has grown up into a very tall fine looking fellow, doesn't want to farm. Wants to go into a bank! He is foolish. With a splendid property like Park Corner—which Dan is quite willing to make over to him—he would be independent—and in a position to marry long before he will be in a bank. I try to tell myself that it will make no real difference to me. I would be rarely at Park Corner in future years, if at all. Jim would marry and his wife and children would be strangers to me. I would probably never come to it again. But it is in vain. I *cannot* reconcile myself to the thought that this beautiful old place, so long a part of the clan life, so beloved by Uncle John and Frede, must pass out of the name and family. It is *very very* bitter to me.

We went over to tea at Aunt Eliza's Monday afternoon. I like to go places with Ella for she has a Montgomerian sense of humor and we have many a laugh together. There have been times when I have felt very impatient with Ella for weakness and general foolishness. Yet I am really very fond of her and get fonder as years go by.

Aunt Mary was there too. Times change funnily. For years she and Aunt Eliza were not on speaking terms and never visited back and forth. Now they are quite good friends. I suppose as they grow old they are unconsciously banding themselves together against the younger generation who are just as unconsciously and inevitably crowding them off the stage. For that matter I am mellowing myself. Once I hated Aunt Eliza quite bitterly. Now I feel a fondness for her which is not disturbed at all by the odd speeches she always shoots off. Ella and I always have a good laugh over Aunt E's "felicities." She really produced very few this visit but she *did* drag in a reference to some girlhood friend of hers who had once declared she "would rather beg her living from door to door than be a minister's wife."

18

"Old parlor at Park Corner"

Aunt E. who belongs to a generation which held marriage to a minister to be the highest peak of feminine ambition, cannot quite forgive *me*, frivolous, novel-writing me, for having attained to such ultimate bliss. So she must give me a dig. Yet I am sure she is quite unconscious of this feeling.

Anyhow, we had a nice afternoon and a supper in keeping with clan traditions....

Friday was very fine and warm. At nightfall I found myself alone in the parlor, in the flickering firelight of a grate fire which Ella had kindled for company that was expected. I was suddenly overwhelmed with agony—so keen that I could only endure it by walking up and down. I spent an hour there with my ghosts....

> How strange it seems with so much gone
> Of life and love to still live on.

Wednesday the weather had changed and it was cold and windy though fine. I packed up in the forenoon and then sat down to what is quite possibly my last meal at Park Corner. Ella, poor soul, had got up a chicken dinner for me. I am sure the Island hens were glad when I left.

Ella drove me to Kensington with a horse and buggy. It is a long time since I have had such a long drive in a buggy and I liked it. It is a beautiful road, with the autumn trees aflame and the shadows of great clouds skimming over the hills. I went to S'Side on the train and was met by Herman MacFarlane, Helen Leard's son. We motored around by way of North Bedeque to Fernwood—or Sea Cow Head as it used to be called. I had rather hoped that I might cross by the old ferry and get a glimpse of the old Leard place on my way to Fernwood but it did not happen so.

But, in the autumnal gloom of twilight, we passed the Baptist church and graveyard where Herman Leard is buried.

For years Herman Leard has been—or has seemed—but a name and a memory to me. When the menopause took away from me the impulses and desires of sex, the thought of him ceased to have any physical influence on me. Sometimes I have even wondered incredulously if it could ever have been *I* who lived through that searing ordeal of passion and pain. I knew we would pass the graveyard but I did not suppose it would affect me at all. And then this thing happened:—

My heart turned over in my breast!

At least it did something which produced exactly that sensation. I have read of people's hearts doing this and thought it merely a figure of speech. I have found it is not. It is a real sensation and a very uncomfortable one.

And I had the oddest feeling that Herman Leard was *reaching out to me from his grave*—catching hold of me—drawing me to him. The feeling lasted only a few moments but it was gruesome and terrible.

Then we were past—Herman MacFarlane was talking unbrokenly on—he is a great talker—and I came to myself with a gasp.

The road therefrom down to Centreville was very familiar to me. What memories haunt it! At Centreville we turned into the Fernwood road and ere-long arrived at the old MacFarlane homestead, most charmingly situated on the shore of the strait—"beautiful of shituation" truly, as old Mr. MacFarlane, Helen's father-in-law, used to say.

As I walked up to the house I recalled with a spasm of inward laughter the last time I had spent an evening here. Herman and Helen and I had come over to a little party—Helen self-conscious enough because of her engagement to "Howie." Old Mr. MacFarlane was a man who would have passed the Old Testament test successfully, for he could not pronounce the letter S other than as "sh." This resulted in considerable embarrassment sometimes when he asked you to sit down. "Sit," pronounced as *he* pronounced it, had an awful similitude to a certain horrible word, used in the sub-vernacular to define a certain unbeautiful natural function. A word which I had heard all my life at school, although I had never used it and shrank from it as an unspeakable vulgarity. Fancy *my* feelings then when, before a whole roomful of company, half of them rapscallion boys, Mr. MacFarlane, anxious to be kind and hospitable, exclaimed, "Mish Montgomery, aren't you cold shitting away over in that corner? Shit nearer to the fire—shit right here in this rocking chair."

Poor "Mish Montgomery" accordingly "shat"—the past tense being irreproachable—feeling all the suppressed ribald mirth of those boys—and some of the girls indeed—behind and around her. I really almost died of shame!

I found Helen with white hair that once was gold but otherwise not very much changed. Helen and I were good surface friends that winter in Bedeque. We corresponded for a year or two, then the correspondence lapsed and I never heard from her until a couple of years ago when I wrote her a note of sympathy on her husband's death. I never was really very fond of Helen Leard. She had a bitter edge to her tongue when she was annoyed—which was frequently—and, if it had not been for a certain resolution which I made when I began boarding, viz. that I *would* not have any quarrel or trouble in any house where I was boarding, I fancy there would often have been wigs on the green. As it was, I gritted my teeth and let her speeches pass; so we remained on good terms and had lots of fun together.

Helen made my stay with her very pleasant and we had a good deal of fun recalling old times and acquaintances. And that night when I went to sleep I dreamed of Herman Leard—dreamed that I was again a young passionate girl, quivering with responsive ardor in his arms. And then—he was not there and I was seeking him helplessly through an endless succession of corridors and empty rooms until I woke, to see the coral clouds in the morning sky and the dancing blue waters of the strait below my window. Woke to realize that it was over thirty years since I had felt Herman's kisses on my lips and that for the most of them he had been dust and ashes in the North Bedeque burying ground.

I left Friday morning and had a very rough crossing—so rough that had it lasted much longer I would have been seasick. And I felt very down-hearted and depressed. Never have I yearned back so to my Island—never have I felt so sorrowful over leaving it.

My journey home was uneventful. I was almost frozen to death during my night on the train and thought wistfully of Helen's warm cosy puff which she had extracted from the spare room chest lest I be cold in bed. In Montreal, prowling about the magazine stall for something to read on the way to Toronto, I found a book with the cheerful title *Twelve Unsolved Murders*. I bought it—and half way through found the solution of a mystery that has long puzzled me.

In 1921 or thereabouts *Green Gables* was in the movies. Mary Miles Minter as Anne scored a tremendous success. It put her definitely on the map; the movie world was at her feet and everyone predicted a career for her rivalling Mary Pickford. Then, all at once, Mary Minter simply disappeared and was never heard of again on the screen. Not only that but every film in which she had starred likewise faded promptly out of existence. I often wondered over this but could never solve the mystery. Probably the Pages knew but for obvious reasons I could not seek enlightenment from them. So it remained a mystery to me until in this book it was solved.

William Desmond Taylor directed the picture. Taylor was a handsome and fascinating man, living apart from his wife, and had many love affairs. Mary Minter was infatuated with him. One morning Taylor was found dead on the floor of his bungalow in Hollywood. He had been shot. It has never been discovered who murdered him. I don't think the golden-curled Mary was suspected but when the police took possession of his bungalow several things were discovered which damned poor Mary in the eyes of the virtuous American public more fatally than even murder would have. Among other matters, a packet of letters from her to Taylor, proving conclusively that Mary had loved the handsome movie magnate not wisely but too well. This ended Mary Minter's career on the screen. The company that had a contract with her bought her off and all the films in which she had starred went into oblivion with her. One can't help feeling sorry for poor Mary, who committed the unpardonable sin of being found out.

I reached Toronto at 5.30, Ewan met me and we drove home in a drizzle. I was desperately homesick for my dear Island. I arrived here in the dark. Stuart was home for a week-end and I had been looking forward to being greeted by him. But he was out with friends. So there was nobody. But as I got out of the car, with a nasty choking feeling in my throat, there was a patter of little flying feet over the fallen leaves, a glad mew of welcome and then a soft vibrant furry body purring frantically in my arms. So I had my welcome home after all.

I found a nasty letter from Rollins. Page wants me to allow him to continue the publication of *Further Chronicles* and offers to pay me a "few hundreds." If I will not he threatens that he will publish the book from the 1919 MS.

Of course I will not give him the permission. And I do not think even he will dare to publish the 1919 MS. because it is expressly defined in the contract that the book could be published *only* in two certain years. But one cannot predict what Louis Page will or will not do. I shall never be safe from annoyance while he lives. Mr. Rollins says that Page, while cheering at a ball game, was stricken down with something from which it is not likely he will recover. Probably a paralytic stroke. However he can and does direct his business from his bed and evidently there is still enough life left in him to be malicious.

There was also a tremendous pile of letters from Australia. Some Australian girl—may jackals sit on her grandmother's grave—to whom I had written a letter, had published it with my address in an Australian paper. Hence this flood. I am too tired tonight to regard them philosophically.

Friday, Oct. 22, 1929
Norval, Ont.
We had the most glorious rain today. I just danced for joy when I heard it streaming on the garret roof. We have had practically no rain since August. For over a month our cistern has been dry—which was bearable—and our well has been dry—which was unbearable. Our bathroom was no use to us—we had no decent water to wash our faces in—we had to borrow some from the folks across the street to drink. It has really been dreadful. So no wonder we were crazy with joy when it began to rain this morning—when it kept on raining—when it changed from a drizzle to a pour—when darkness came down on a wet streaming world. Glory Be!

Today in a *Guardian* I saw the death of Edward McEwen of New London at the age of seventy. And a memory came to me. I changed. I was a girl of twelve sitting in the old Cavendish church of forty-odd years ago. Like everyone else in church I was twisting my neck to get a glimpse of the bride. Pensie Stewart had been married to Edward McEwen the preceding Wednesday and they were "appearing out" as the local saying went.

Pensie was a pretty bride. I forget her dress but I remember her bonnet. It had always been the old custom for a girl to put on a bonnet the minute she was married and wear a bonnet for the rest of her life. In my childhood the back of this custom had been broken. A girl had never flown in the face of tradition to the extent of having a wedding hat. A bonnet it must be. She wore it generally for a few months till the lustre of bridehood was outworn. Then it disappeared and she went back to hats. So Pensie wore a bonnet. A very pretty dressy little affair it was too, much much more becoming than the hideous "cloches" in vogue in this year of 1929. It was of "drab" silk with bows of "drab" ribbon, perched up on Pensie's head, with long "drab" strings tied under her rounded chin. "Drab" is a hateful sounding word, smacking of everything dreary. But it was really a pretty shade, half way between "fawn" and "silver gray."

Pensie did not know she marked the passing of an era. But she was the last bride to "appear out" in a bonnet in Cavendish. I do not remember who the next bride was but whoever she was she wore a hat. The grandmothers thought the end of the world was thereby foretokened; but somehow it continued to function.

I have forgotten Edward McEwen, whose obituary I read today. People were apt to forget him. He was a very insignificant looking groom—thin, pale, small. Beside buxom blooming Pensie he almost was transparent. But he has lived to be seventy. He begat sons and daughters who in turn have made him and Pensie grandparents. Grandparents! And it seems as yesterday that a small miss of twelve stole admiring glances at that bonnetted bride and wondered in her heart what kind of a bonnet she would wear some day as a—a—well, as a bride!

Tuesday, Nov. 5, 1929
Norval, Ont.
Last night I dreamed of Frede. I dreamed she was being married here in our church. And I was so happy. But I woke.

I am getting over being homesick. I am good friends with my house again and with my dear pine wood on Russells' hill.

But I have not felt at all well these past two weeks. I don't sleep well—I have

Maud

indigestion—something I never had in my life before. I feel slightly dizzy by times and my right ear bothers me a good deal—a sense of fullness—a buzzing—tiny needle-like pains. And my headaches are becoming more frequent. Whereas they used to be monthly affairs I have one now every two weeks. I don't like any of these indications. I remember that I am nearly fifty-five.

Sunday, Dec. 1, 1929
I feel, for the first time in my life, exactly like a senile crone. I have had all my teeth out!

They should have been out years ago I suppose. They were in bad shape. Several had abscesses at their roots. Pyorrhoea has played havoc with all my lower front ones. They were always ugly and uneven. But I hated the thought of getting them out. I clung to them as long as I could and spent a small fortune yearly having some filled—never to mention the torture of that infernal drill.

A week ago last Wednesday I motored to Toronto. I meant to take gas. And the day before the papers had been full of the case of a man who took gas to have his teeth extracted at the dental college and died under it. So I felt woozy. I got into the car that morning wondering if I would ever come back alive. And apart from that I had a horror of going into unconsciousness. Years ago I never dreaded that. I took ether to have several teeth extracted and always enjoyed the sensation. I do not know whether I ever recorded in this journal my first experience under ether. Dr. Bagnall of Ch'town was going to take out a tooth for me. I was in the chair with the cone over my mouth. Mary Campbell was sitting in the corner eyeing me with fascinated terror. To reassure her I began to wink one eye. Then found I could not stop winking—a newsboy calling a *Guardian* on the street below seemed to be shouting it in my very ear—I was gone.

As I came to I spoke—no, I *heard something speaking through my mouth*—some intelligence with which I seemed to have nothing to do; and this intelligence was saying, "Oh, doctor, heaven is so beautiful I'm sorry you called me back." Then with a click I was myself again—and just in the moment of that "click"—which was mental not physical—I had a vague flying impression that I had just had a perfectly wonderful and beautiful experience somewhere. Then it was gone—I was fully awake and Dr. Bagnall was laughing and saying, "I am glad you had such a good time. By the remarks most people make when they come out of the ether I should think they had been to the other place."

But it is fourteen years since I took ether and in the meantime I have come to dread any lapse in consciousness like that. However, I reflected that people do not die until their time comes. So I took the gas—and then I heard someone saying "Well, we didn't hurt you did we?" and I was firmly convinced that I hadn't a stitch of clothes on and that an icy cold wind from the pole was blowing over my naked body! Thankfully I came quite to myself to realize that this was not so. My clothes were still on but my upper teeth were gone.

Dr. C. would not take the lower ones out then. He said there was too much infection in them. All my teeth were infected or abscessed he said and I had really no business to be alive with such teeth.

I went home with Nora and went to bed. Did not have a pleasant afternoon to say the least. I came home the next day and put in a week on a diet of milk and eggs.

I have forgotten to record one curious little incident. When I arrived at the dental office it was ten o'clock. Nora had promised to meet me at 10.30 and my appointment was for eleven. I sat down to wait. So far as I knew I felt perfectly calm and not at all nervous, in spite of a few vague fears. Presently I glanced at my watch. It was 10.30. Nora had not come. I picked up a magazine and read a story—was so interested in it that I completely forgot my surroundings. Presently I recalled them and looked at my watch. It was eleven. Something must have happened to Nora. Then she came in. "You're a nice one to be on hand to cheer me up at a crisis," I said ironically. "Why, it's just 10.30," she said, And it was! In that hour my watch, hitherto perfectly reliable, had *gained half an hour*. There must have been a quite tremendous upheaval in some of my subconscious regions to affect my watch like that.

Last Wednesday I went in again and had the lower ones out. Thank heaven it is over. Once is enough in a lifetime. I did not mind the gas at all and felt no ill effects. Dr. C. said I was an excellent patient. But I do not recommend it to anyone as a "pleasure exertion."

I have been in bed ever since I came home with a very bad cold. And no doubt the shock to the system was very considerable. I hate to look at myself in the glass. As the gums are as yet unshrunken I do not *look* different. But I *feel* different. And when I smile—those toothless gums!

Grandmother Macneill never had a tooth in her head after she was sixty. Yet she did not look badly. She would not have any false ones in. Perhaps she was right, who knows! Anyway, she could eat anything anyone else could, even to beef ham!

An odd fact occurs to me here which I will jot down. Grandmother Macneill had *three teeth* when she was born. I have heard doctors say that this was indicative of sickly, short-lived children. Well, Grandmother was a very healthy woman and lived, as smart as a cricket, to be eighty-seven. Moreover, had pneumonia not carried her off she might have lived to the century mark for she was singularly smart and active with no signs of senility about her except some mental failings. No, *not* mental failings. Her mind was as good as her body. I should rather say some temperamental failings.

Dear old Grandmother! Of late years I have been thinking of her very often and very lovingly, as the difficulties of those last years fade in the distance. I would like to see her come in—I would like her to see Chester and Stuart—I would like to have a talk with her. In some ways she was a very wonderful woman. And in others—but it is best to let certain memories die.

Speaking of death—the *Youth's Companion* is dead, after a hundred years of life. I am sorry. When I was a child it was the paper par excellence for young people. And it was one of the first papers to accept and *pay* for my verses. For years I wrote poems for it. And then, all at once, it began to send them back. It wouldn't accept *anything*. A change of editors, I suppose, because the poems I sent in later years were assuredly far superior to my early attempts.

Perhaps that was why it died!!!

I suppose the taste of modern youth did not care for it—although it seemed to keep up with the times surprisingly well. Its time had simply "come."

Saturday, Dec. 14, 1929
The Manse, Norval
Ten days ago I got a temporary upper set in. After the first few hours I did not mind them and certainly the improvement in my appearance is quite amazing. It is a novel sight to see a row of pretty, even, white teeth in my mouth. They are of course not much use for eating purposes.

I have not felt well these past two weeks. My ear bothers me—buzzing, shooting pains and a sense of fullness. It keeps me from sleeping. And we have had such cold stormy weather. Nothing like it since we came to Norval.

Angus' wife is dead—died following an operation. I feel deep sympathy for Angus. The fact that he behaved so pettily this summer fades into the background—though it *is* a fact and perhaps it is mere sentimentality that belittles it now. He will be very lonely for he has no children to live for.

Saturday, Dec. 21, 1929
Certainly we have been living amid alarums and excursions of late. I knew when I had that perfect vacation in the fall that I would have to pay for it. Such things are not given for naught.

Wednesday was an abominable day of sleet and snow. I was very tired. I had been late at a trying rehearsal of the Sunday school Tuesday evening. When I did get to bed I could not sleep. In the forenoon I had to go to Georgetown and I spent the whole afternoon in the church schoolroom helping to decorate the tree, assort the gifts etc. At night the concert came off and in spite of the storm we had a good crowd and the children really did credit to our training. The usual hilarious scene of Santa Claus and giving of gifts followed. As I stood amid the shrieking crowd I suddenly had a vision. I saw a little woodland dell a thousand miles away with two darling little spruces growing up out of a foam of golden ferns while crimson maples flung banners all about them. I suppose that little dell is full of snow now but I was in the Fourth Dimension where there is no time—or where it can be any time you like.

Chester arrived home Wednesday afternoon. For the first time he got off a day earlier than Stuart so we wrote him to come home on the bus and leave his luggage. Ewan and I were to motor to Aurora Thursday and bring home Stuart and the grips.

Alas, on Thursday morning we arose to find the roads completely blocked. Ewan decided to go by radial and departed to take the ten o'clock car. Shortly after twelve a cutter drove up and deposited Ewan on the veranda. He limped in with many groans and a ghastly tale to tell.

The cars had been blocked by the snow. They waited in the cold station on the hill—waited until 12 o'clock. No car. Then came a car from Toronto and the conductor advised the waiting passengers to hop on and go over to Georgetown where the station was warm and they could wait comfortably for the eastbound car. They got on. Luckily Ewan's feet were cold so he promptly sat down in the "backest" seat by the stove.

And just about half a mile from the station the car collided head-on with a big snow-plough car coming from Guelph!

No one as yet seems to know why the snow plough was there. But it was and the result can be imagined. Three people were so badly injured that it is not known whether they will live or die and ten more hurt in various degrees. Ewan was flung to the floor and the iron work of a seat that had been sheared off by the plough struck him on the leg, bruising and straining his knee.

It might have been a thousand fold worse. Two minutes later and the cars would have met on the bridge that spans the west branch of the Credit. They would have crashed down to the bottom of the 60 foot gorge and probably not one of the passengers would have lived to tell the tale.

At first Ewan did not think his injury amounted to much but of course he could not go for Stuart. He insisted that Chester and I should go. There was, he said, a car going through at two and Stuart would be heartbroken if he did not get home that day. I did not want to go for I saw Ewan was excited by the shock to his nerves and would probably feel his leg much worse after awhile. I wanted him to send for the doctor but he scouted such an idea. Reluctantly I agreed to go and Chester and I set out. We got to the station at two. We waited there for three hours that seemed three years. It was bitterly cold. We almost froze, yet dared not leave lest the car come—for persistent rumors asserted continually that it would be along in a half an hour—a quarter of an hour etc. At five we could endure it no longer. We started home and had got to the bottom of the hill when we heard it blow. We turned and hurried up that terrible hill knee deep in drifted snow. I was out of breath when I got up but we caught the car and finally at a quarter to six we left. The trip in was endless—seemingly—for the car stopped at every stand to take in the milk cans—for the milk trucks were blocked and Toronto was in danger of a milk famine. It was nearly eight o'clock when we got in. There was no use in going to Aurora that night so we went to a hotel and I sank into bed with a sigh of gratitude for beds—but not to sleep. I was too tired and too worried to sleep. Friday morning Chester went out for Stuart and I went to see Dr. Royce about my ear. He could not find a thing wrong with it and the hearing was good. He said there must be some neuralgic or nerve trouble perhaps due to an old infection from the teeth and it might clear up after a time. I was relieved to find there was nothing serious—though it is serious enough to have something that annoys you all the time and keeps you from sleeping. I met the boys who turned up all right and we came home—had a terrible walk from the station—I froze an ear—but we all got home at last. To find Ewan in bed. He had to have the doctor after I left Thursday. Nothing was broken but the bruises were bad and he was to stay in bed for twelve days at least. His leg was very painful and his nerves were so bad he couldn't sleep. I was secretly afraid that the nervous shock might bring back his old trouble. But he seems better tonight and I hope he will sleep.

I feel very tired and rather downhearted—with that old feeling of imprisonment. It is rather a sad note to close a volume of my journal on. But many a gray dawn is followed by a sunny day. Perhaps 1930 will be better than its advent promises. And perhaps not. I don't know what is the price the gods put on that vacation!

The Manse, Norval, Ont.
Friday, Dec. 27, 1929
I find myself cringing a bit when I begin this eighth volume of my diary. I look over its bare 520 pages—and wonder what will be written on them—or if *anything* will be written on them all. I never began a new volume with just that feeling before.

Last Monday it snowed and drifted all day, giving me that nasty sensation of being a prisoner, which I felt so often in old days and in many Leaskdale winters but have never felt since coming to Norval. Chester was ill with flu and has not been well all the week. Ewan's improvement has been slow, too. But Stuart hustled out Monday in spite of the storm and got our Christmas tree. Nothing daunts that boy. We got it up in the dining room and he put on the decorations. It did look very pretty when he finished with its "icicles" and all its pretty colored balls. I *do* love those Christmas balls. They give me as much pleasure as if I were a child.

Wednesday was Christmas and after breakfast Stuart, as always, acted Santa Claus and distributed the presents. We missed "Dad." For the first time he was not at breakfast and dinner with us on Christmas day. Stuart made a valiant effort to carve the goose but had to have assistance.

I did one little thing Christmas day which had a significance to no one but myself. I hung up in my room above my bed a picture of the lane at Park Corner with Frede peering out around one of the trees.

Years ago I was at Park Corner one summer afternoon. Frede was spinning in the garret and I called her to come down and stand in the lane as I wanted a "human touch" in the picture I meant to take of it. She came: but as she had on only an old blue wrapper and was in her stocking feet—spinning with the big wheel meant much walking and was hard on feet—she insisted on screening herself a bit by one of the trees. The picture, taken with my old plate camera, came out well but sometime later it was broken and I had only two or three prints of it. So I took one to Eaton's where they do marvellous things with old pictures, had a film negative made from it, and had a picture enlarged and colored from the film. This was what I hung up today where I can see it everyday—and lie in the darkness feeling that Frede is watching just above me and that, if I just knew the exact magic to make, I could step up into the picture and clasp hands with her. And we could both slip away into the shadows and silences of that old wood behind her and find our way back to the Land of Long Ago.

I had a pitiful letter from Amanda yesterday. She has been very ill with an abscessed ear and is afraid she is going to be deaf in it. She is lonely and sad. I am so sorry for her. It is true enough what she says, "I have had such a dreary drab existence"—and though she brought that existence on herself by marrying a man she should never have married, yet am I exceedingly sorry for her. And I can do little to help her. I must send her some books and write her in an effort to cheer her up. Yet who could cheer anyone up who had to live with George Robertson?

Altogether I feel a little dreary myself. Yet I look out of my window and, beholding the fine and beautiful austerity of my pine wood on this gray autumn twilight, feel comforted. For where there is Beauty—there is God.

Monday, Dec. 30, 1929
Ewan managed to get downstairs today with the aid of a crutch, having religiously fulfilled his twelve days. And eight of us Norval Anglican and Presbyterian ladies have begun practice for a dialogue or rather a short play for our Old Tyme Concert in February. As we have all attained years of discretion I hope it will be easier to train them than the young fry. But I daresay I shall run up against other snags from which youth is free.

I am not well. My ear bothers me and my face. I have some queer eruption on it that comes and goes and burns and stings and does not seem amenable to any application. Between the two I am losing too much sleep at nights.

1930

Thursday, Jan. 2, 1930
The century is getting to be quite an old maid.

I had another sleepless night last night, not wholly due to face and ear. I got word yesterday that the Canadian Associate Co., a concern in which I have a heavy investment, has had to pass its semi-annual dividend owing to losses in the October stock panic.

This worried me. I was depending on that dividend to pay the boys' school fees for the term. It will inconvenience me. But I would not worry over that if I were sure the company's embarrassment is only temporary and that it is really in a sound position. I have too much in it to lose. I was foolish to invest so heavily in it. Yet there are good men at its head and I hope things will come out all right eventually. Nevertheless it cost me a sleepless night. Today I had a nice letter from Myrtle which cheered me up a bit as a letter from "home" generally does.

Sunday, Jan. 5, 1930
Ewan can now limp around with a cane. He took his own services today and went to the Glen House for tea from Union. Chester and I went over for him in the evening, the highway being still open for cars. It was delightful to be back there again. I lost the sensation of being a prisoner for a time at least.

Tuesday, Jan. 7, 1930
I have a little joke to record. It is really worth it.

I got a "fan" letter today from a teen-age girl in Wisconsin. It was the usual adulatory letter regarding my books but it contained this gem, "I know the Rev. Edwin Simpson and he tells me that Anne of Green Gables is a real person and that he knows her well—a Mrs. Webb who still lives in P.E. Island."

I should put here a whole line of exclamation points!

Poor Ed. He knows as well as I do that Myrtle Webb is not "Anne"—that she does not remotely resemble Anne, either physically, mentally or historically. But he wanted the "kudos" of being supposed to know all about "Anne" and he told that whopper, never dreaming that I would ever hear what he had said.

Really, it isn't safe to tell lies.

I did not mention the Rev. Edwin's name in my reply to that girl. But I said that Mrs. Webb was not in the least like "Anne" and I indulged in a few ironical remarks concerning "people who seem to have no conception of the creative power that is the author's gift and who must imagine that every character in her stories has some prototype in 'real' life." I hope she shows him my letter. I can picture his face.

Wednesday, Jan. 8, 1930
The boys returned to school today, leaving a lonely house. I took them as far as Toronto. Both have racking coughs and I feel worried about them. Stuart led his class in the December exams and made 100 in several subjects.

We had a magnificent ice-storm today and the pines along the road were amusing extremely. They were weighted down with ice and looked exactly like a lot of disgruntled old spinsters who had indignantly turned their backs on a derisive world.

Saturday, Jan. 18, 1930
This morning I got up, shivering with all the symptoms of another attack of flu. Nevertheless the Young Men's Bible Class were to meet here tonight so I plunged into preparations for them doggedly. Just about half through I got word that Mrs. Arthur McClure was seriously ill and of course her boys could not come. As Clarence was treasurer we could not have the meeting without him, so it was called off. After dinner I went to bed and am here still. I'm afraid I will not sleep. There is a certain nasty nervous grasshopperish activity in my brain that will prevent it.

Ewan is improving steadily if slowly. But another company I have some money in has cut its dividend in two and that is not a cheerful bit of news when one is sick and blue.

Thursday, Jan. 23, 1930
I have been dragging around all the week. My face and ear are troublesome and my head feels very queer by times. And the steady bitter cold and unrelieved grayness continues.

The Graphic Pub. Co. of Ottawa recently asked me to read and report on a MS. story for them—a story written by two girls in B.C. and intended for girls' reading. I had hoped to be able to report favourably but the book is trash—crude and dull and uninteresting. I feel that I wasted my time horribly in reading it.

Saturday, Jan. 25, 1930
The Manse, Norval
It is eleven years today since Frede died. I woke early in the dull gray lifeless winter morning, with the mercury ten below zero, and thought about her. To me she died yesterday.

Monday, Jan. 27, 1930
Yesterday when I came home from church I took a chill and had to go to bed with hot water bottles. I must go back to my old-time remedy of Bland's iron and arsenic pills. I certainly need something and need it quick.

Tuesday, Jan. 28, 1930
Last night the big old mill in Norval burned down. It is a bad blow to Norval for it was the only industry the small village had and several families got their living in it. None of our families are affected by it but nevertheless I regret the passing of the mill very keenly. Two beauties have gone out of Norval for me—the "mill

"Norval Mill from the East"

light" and the cowls and weather vanes on its roofs. The "light" burned all night like a beacon in a little open cupola on the top of the highest building. Four years ago, when I came to Norval for the first time and swooped down the big hill to the east I saw the light apparently poised high in air and asked the Barracloughs what it was. "We are in Norval—that is the mill light" was the answer. And ever since it has been a sort of beacon when we came home late. I shall miss it—but I shall miss my trolls of old mythology more. On the roofs of the mill were three chimneys with large cowls on them. And fastened to the cowls three weather vanes,

"Norval Mill from the West"

two large and one small, of a rather peculiar design. When these dark cowls and vanes came out against a sunset sky they had a most extraordinary resemblance to three little dwarfs, such as might have stepped out of some old Nordic fairy tale of gnome or kobold. They had a charm and mystery all their own—an old-world note in this little Canadian village that always gave me the keenest delight when I walked down main street or came over one of the bridges on a fine evening after sunset and suddenly saw my three Little Goblins of the Mill keeping their vigil a-top of the old red brick walls. And now I shall see them no more.

Tuesday, Feb. 11, 1930
The weather continues hard and very cold. I have been miserable most of the time, though I fancy myself a little better lately. But I'm certainly getting thin— or rather thinner which I can bear very well if it doesn't go too far. I am, however, sleeping better now.

Our annual Old Tyme Concert came off last night and was a big success. My dress was a lovely silk one, dark ashes of roses, over a huge crinoline, with dear little puffed sleeves and lace frills. It had nothing of the old world gorgeousness of my Queen-of-Scots costume last year but it had a dignity and grace all its own. I never wore crinolines of course, nor even a bustle, but I felt quite at home in the puffed sleeves. I wish they would come in again. They were the prettiest fashion ever was in sleeves before the puffs became too big and therefore ridiculous. The sleeves for the past few years, when there were sleeves at all, have been mostly very tight and plain.

Our little play went off very well. But such undercurrents!

Saturday, Feb 15, 1930
Thank God, I'm home again, even if it is below zero, with a sharp wind blowing and a house like a barn. We have such poor coal this winter we simply can't keep warm.

This has been a rather weird week. The unfeeling way in which day follows day when one isn't well is rather cruel. Wednesday night the session met at A. Giffen's and as usual the session's wives were invited to tea with them. As the road to Giffens' is impassable for anything but sleighs Albert Hunter took a double cutter and we, Mr. Wiggins and Albert's wife all went with him. I had been looking forward to a sleigh drive; it is four years since I had one. And no doubt it would have been pleasant enough had it been fine. But as we left it began to rain—the first rain of the year. And all those six heavy miles up to Giffens' it poured. I had to hold up an umbrella and I got chilled to the bone. An evening of boredom for me followed and then another wet drive home. I had been feeling much better the first few days of the week but something—the exposure or the nervous strain of bad roads and patches—pulled me down again and Thursday I was miserable with ear and face worrying me to death—buzzing and stinging. And Thursday night I had another weird drive.

Our Guild was going over to Union to put on a program for a social evening. As I was the president for the evening I had to go. Ewan and I intended to go in our small car, "Billy" being temporarily out of commission, and young Gray was to take all the rest of the performers over in his truck!! Among them was Mrs. Boyd the wife of the Anglican minister, toward whom I certainly have no very friendly feelings. She never returned my call and has always been very cool and distant. But she had a serious operation a year ago and I really thought to bounce over those iron-clad roads in Billy Gray's truck would not be very good for her. So I made her go with E. and I took my chance on the truck. I got there and back alive but I hanker not for any more truck drives. The night was fine and moonlit but bitterly cold. We were all perched high in air on the planks Billy had put across the rack. And as we tore along the Georgetown road I thought we would be blown into the fourth dimension—or absolute zero or something like that. When we dipped down into the Glen the wild rough roads compelled Billy Gray to drive more slowly. The cold became bearable and those white eerie hills all around us in that pale ghostly moonlight were very beautiful. Nevertheless I was a thankful woman when we got safely to Union church and still more thankful when we got home again....

Saturday, Feb. 22, 1930
The Manse, Norval
We have had a week of "false spring." Mild as May, constant thaw, nearly all snow gone and roads wild and weird as an opium dream. Tuesday night we went to Union to a Guild meeting over roads that were a blasphemy. I never was on the like of them in my life before—in a car at least. We passed safely over many dangerous places and then went into the ditch in a place that did not look at all bad. Fortunately we were going very slowly and the ditch was full of soft snow so neither we nor the car were hurt. But it took an hour or more to get a team to haul it out. Then we had to come home over those terrible hills between the Glen and Georgetown. I don't know how we got up one of them. As a result I have been very miserable again the rest of the week. Early on I felt better but now I seem as bad as ever. I get discouraged and in my blue moods imagine that there is something really serious wrong with me of which these annoying symptoms are the cause.

Saturday, March 1, 1930
I know I have been hovering on the brink of a nervous breakdown all winter and I realized it acutely when Mrs. Mason came in one afternoon this week and handed me *83* "fan" letters from Australia. In the last 3 weeks I have received over one hundred and fifty.

A girl in Australia last fall to whom I had written a letter, published said letter and my address in a paper—something she should never have done without my consent—and the deluge started. If I were quite well I could tackle or ignore it, but as I am it gets on my nerves. I hate not to acknowledge them. They are all nice letters individually and I know how badly the 'teenage' writers of them will feel if they never get a reply. But this last year or so my fan correspondence has become a nightmare. Every spare moment, when I might be reading or resting I have to write letters and though they are generally short and crisp, yet there is a certain outlay of time and strength on each and I have none of either to spare.

I have another problem on my hands—something quite different from anything I have ever been up against. Like most people I have met many problems of various kinds in my life and very few, if any, ever completely floored me. Someway or other I managed to solve them—or at least grappled with them until in time they solved themselves. But I am up against something now which is too much for me—and which nauseates me past all telling into the bargain.

When I came to Norval I got a letter from a girl...named Isobel...At the time I knew nothing of her but soon discovered that she was a school-teacher..., where she lived with her widowed mother and her sister...

The letter was too gushing and adoring; but some parts of it were very witty and brilliant and entirely delightful. I answered

"Isobel in Fancy Dress"

it briefly as I do all letters and Isobel kept on writing at intervals and as her letters continued to be brilliant I enjoyed them and occasionally wrote in return. Finally I met...[her] family—went up to...supper with them one night. I could no longer resist Isobel's fervent plea, especially as she was just out of the hospital after an operation. Yet even then I felt slightly uneasy. Her letters were a little—just a little—"too—too" it seemed to me. I do not like to have people kissing my feet metaphorically. Then, too, Isobel had taken to sending me occasional presents—rather too expensive presents. This I did not like.

I was surprised to find that Isobel was not overly young—almost thirty I should say. I had supposed from her gushing letters that she must be about eighteen. I was also surprised to find that she, who could write so brilliantly, was extremely dull company. She could not talk on any subject and she appeared to have read nothing—except my books! Her sister... was much brighter and pleasanter. And her mother was a very sweet and charming woman.

Ever since, Isobel has persecuted me with letters, gifts, invitations and phone calls. The letters I do not mind, the gifts are her own lookout. But the invitations! When I was finally driven to accept one, in the hope of getting some peace for awhile, I was bored stiff. They were like nightmares. But the phone calls were worst of all. She would ring me up, generally when I could least spare the time, and keep me at the phone for half an hour. She seemed to have nothing to say except that she was blue, lonesome, discouraged, etc. etc. etc. And I couldn't think of anything to say. There are very few people in the world I can't talk to but poor Isobel is among the few.

Last spring her mother died. Isobel begged me to go up for the funeral, the which I did, though as it was a private funeral with only family friends I felt rather *de trop*. Isobel seemed to get considerable satisfaction out of my being there however. And truth compels me to state that she did not seem to feel her mother's death very keenly.

[Her sister]..., who had long hankered for a missionary's life, now decided to go. Personally I think it was quite as much her duty to stay with her sister; but she evidently thought otherwise and departed for a training school in Toronto. The home was broken up; Isobel at first stayed with her married sister...but last fall she got a couple of nice rooms in a house and moved in. All these months the afore-said invitations, letters and phone-calls went on. I was in very truth very sorry for Isobel...She seemed to me a very lonely, pathetic creature, with no real interest, hope or ambition in life. She did not like teaching; and there was evidently no beau in the offing. In fact, as far as I can find out, Isobel never had a beau. I did not understand why then, for she is of average good looks, but I am afraid I understand it all too well now.

To repeat, I was sorry for her and felt I ought to do all I could to help her. Last August I went up at her urgent and repeated request and spent an afternoon with her and her sister in Rockwood Park. As usual, Isobel in my presence seemed incapable of speech or indeed of doing anything except walking like a silent shadow at my side. Personally I felt, as Sinbad must have felt, ridden by his Old Man of the Sea. I came home, drew a long breath, and hoped for a few weeks' respite.

The next week I got another letter from Isobel. She said that she thought she was losing her mind—that only I could save her—that she wanted very much something which only I could grant. She wanted to come down to Norval and stay all night at the manse—and she *wanted to sleep with me*.

The letter was so wild and distraught that it frightened me. And more than that it disgusted me. For at last I knew the truth about Isobel.

The subject of "sex perverts" has been aired sufficiently of late in certain malodorous works of fiction. I had learned of it in the cleaner medium of medical volumes. There was something in it that nauseated me to my very soul centre but I did not think of it as anything that would ever touch my life in any way.

From that moment I felt no doubt that poor Isobel was a pervert. Not to blame for it, I suppose. Born under the curse as another girl might have been born cross-eyed or mentally deficient. But nevertheless cursed and pariah.

I could not tolerate the thought of granting her request. Yet I dared not show her my repulsion and disgust. Who knew what the unfortunate girl might do? I wrote back telling her that I had a friend coming to visit me (it was luckily just before Fannie's visit) and that as my spare room would be occupied I could have no overnight guests for a time. And after my friend left I expected to leave for the Island etc. etc. etc.

I heard no more from Isobel until my return. Then she resumed writing and phoning. She wanted me to go up and spend a week-end with her. I put her off and off with no end of excuses—my teeth—Ewan's accident—my illness—etc. etc. etc.

Finally a specially piteous letter—she had been ill—she was so lonely—would I not come?

I surrendered and went. I was afraid not to—afraid that the girl would do heaven knows what if I didn't go. Besides, I had convinced myself that it was all nonsense to suppose Isobel a pervert. She was merely a lonely, neurotic girl who cherished a romantic adoration for me, thus filling a life that was otherwise piteously empty of everything that makes life worth living. And as such I wanted to help her if possible.

I went up Friday and returned Saturday. Isobel has two nice cosy rooms. Somehow I got through the evening, night and day. I even "slept" with Isobel. I hate "sleeping" with strangers but apart from that I had nothing to complain of, and I decided I had been a nasty-minded idiot to think of Isobel as I had done. She was as usual as quiet, shy, restrained as—as—the simile *will* come into my mind—as a girl in the presence of her lover. Only once did she say anything queer. At supper her landlady commented on her poor appetite—Isobel was eating nothing—and said something jokingly about her being happy. "I am perfectly and entirely happy tonight," said Isobel in a strange impassioned tone.

I have a feeling that Isobel did not sleep that night—indeed, she said after we were in bed—"I do not mean to sleep at all tonight. I mean to lie awake and revel in my happiness."

"Silly goose," I said. "What you want to do is get all the sleep you can and build yourself up."

Isobel said nothing. *I* did not expect to sleep but I did—for I had slept little the two previous nights. The bed was fitted out like a bridal one—exquisite sheets, pillows, coverlet, blankets and puff—all evidently brand new and purchased for the occasion. In the morning I got up, devoutly thankful the ordeal was over, and still inclined to think, in spite of Isobel's queer speeches and queerer intensity of manner and personality, that I had been utterly mistaken in my fears.

I put in a forenoon of boredom and made my escape after dinner, leaving Isobel crying on the radial platform.

Today I got a letter from her. I will copy it here. It will illustrate my problem better than any comment on it.

"My Darling:—

It really is quite delicious to write that. I ought to be washing a few things but it is really too romantic a night. But the sweet incense of your presence still broods around me like a dream from which I am only half awake.

Darling, I love you so terribly, I do. I have a suspicion that if my chronic indisposition were accurately diagnosed much of it must be pronounced "love." To say that I worship you is a most colorless statement of the fact. I can't tell you how much I loved having you. You are just as pretty as ever you can be with your lovely long braids and your sweet, sweet face, and the blue dressing gown, and I adore you. I want you again. I simply cannot endure not to have you again soon. It sounds quite ungrateful, I know, but I am suffering all the agonies of being in love. I have derived some comfort from sleeping in the precise spot you occupied half hopeful that some of the dear warmth might still be found to linger. But I crave something tangible. I want to hold in my arms what is dearer than life to me—to lie "spoon fashion" all through a long long night—to cover your wee hands, your beautiful throat and every part of you with kisses. I'm just mad with love for you.

Perhaps tomorrow I shall be sorry I wrote this. But it is true. I have a feeling that I have treated you unfairly.

And after this shameless confession don't you think I am a terrible creature?"

Is there any need for comment on such a letter? When I read it I flung it down, flew to the bathroom and washed my hands. I felt slimy and unclean.

And what in God's name am I to do? I can't talk this over with Ewan. He simply would not believe in "perversion" and would say Isobel was out of her mind. Perhaps she is. It would be better if she were. But I am at my wit's end. If I snub or scold her—if I ignore her—I am terrified over the possible results. The girl who would write such a letter as that is beyond help. Her concluding question seems to imply a slight realization of what she really is. I *do* think she is a "terrible creature."

Well, I can only hope that a merciful Fate will solve this problem for me, because it is beyond my solving.

A few weeks ago I decided to begin with *Anne of Green Gables* and read all my own books through. It is years since I read them and they seemed as new to me as if someone else had written them. I have just finished *Rilla*—much of which I had entirely forgotten. I don't know whether I should be ashamed to say that I found myself laughing and crying over my own book. And how clearly it reflected the atmosphere and background of those war years!

One evening recently I got out my scrapbooks of reviews and skimmed through them. They are amusing reading. The great majority are laudatory but an occasional one is contemptuous or venomous. But the amusing thing was their contradictoriness—if there be such a word. One critic makes a statement. Another flatly says the opposite. They cannot possibly be reconciled. Here are some bracketed specimens I culled in my hurried ramble through those dusty old scrapbooks. At times it is hard to remember that these "criticisms" could be about the same book.

Green Gables of course began it. I remember well the thrill which my first Clipping Bureau envelope full of reviews gave me.

"Anne is one of the most delightful girls that has appeared for many a day." / "Anne is altogether too queer."

"One of the most charming girls in modern fiction." / "Anne is overdrawn and something of a bore."

"An altogether fascinating child." / "We would leave the house if Anne lived with us."

"Anne is unconvincing." / "Anne is absolutely convincing."

"Quite too precocious." / "No more charming child was ever conceived by an author."

"The book is not without interest." (Oh, what damnable faint praise!) / "A charming story told in a charming way."

"It will find more favour with maids under 14 than with their elders." / "Old and young alike will fall beneath its charm."

"The first half of the book is the best." (I agree with this completely) / "The poorest chapter is the first one."

"L.M. Montgomery more than once falls into artistic temptation." / "A real literary gem!"

"There is no maudlin sentiment about the book." / "A book of sugary sentimentality."

Anne of Avonlea

"Sequels as a rule are unsuccessful but this one is an exception." / "The readers of *Anne of Avonlea* will suffer a keen disappointment. The story is crude and commonplace."

"Anne is not quite so fascinating as her smaller self." / "Anne, as described at Avonlea, is even more delightful and lovable than at Green Gables." / "Anne has not deteriorated."

"Light as the proverbial feather." / "Wholesome and brilliant."

"A lot of schoolgirl gush." / "A tender beautiful story full of humour, sentiment and pathos of the right sort." / "Wholly free from mawkish sentimentality."

Kilmeny of the Orchard

"Lacks the freshness and spontaneity of *Anne*."

"It is in every way as charming as *Anne*."

"Not up to either of the *Anne* books."

"Thin and sweetish. Doesn't keep up the reputation of L.M. Montgomery."

"A vivid, strong, interesting story."

"Miss Montgomery is one of the few authors who never disappoint their readers."

"The plot, if plot it can be called, is a very ingenuous one."

"The plot of the novel shows great constructive skill."

"The plot is of the slightest."

"A story is told with great dramatic strength in this weird little novel."

"Here is a plot that develops surprises."

"A plot not particularly novel."

"A sustained plot with a slightly melodramatic climax."

"Plot has unusual psychological interest.".…

Chronicles of Avonlea received fewer unfavorable criticisms than any of my books I think. I can find only one in the scrapbook.

"Miss Montgomery is not always at her best in these stories. Some of the sketches are rather too slight and leave no impression."

To offset this:—

"To say that one sketch was better than another would be to insinuate that the latter was not just as good as it could possibly be. Which would be insinuating something utterly untrue."

"One of the best books of short stories published in our country in years."

"The substance and style of Miss Montgomery's work may belikened to a miniature painting."

"A series of tales each one of which is a gem."

" 'Each in His Own Tongue' is one of the most beautiful stories in the world."

"Subjectively one feels that the men and women, boys and girls, the very cats and dogs of her stories are human and real."

"Each story is a real gem in theme and workmanship. Exquisite of coloring and touch."

The *Golden Road* got some heckling....

Anne of the Island likewise got slaps and caresses....

As for *Rilla*—
"This is a story better adapted to the youthful than to the adult mind." / "Its pages are rich in fun and pathos, with sentiment and philosophy of an unusual order."
"This is a tedious book." / "The story is a gripping one in many ways."
"A book not at all out of the ordinary."
"A book to read—a book that has distinction of an outstanding kind." / "The whole book is arresting and the authoress has undoubtedly scored another original success."
"*Rilla* is crudely handled." / "The authoress is a true artist. She gives just the one right touch."

When *Emily of New Moon* came out the criticisms were largely very favorable. There were ten "good" ones to one "bad" one. But a few "bad" ones did come.
"The characters are largely stock characters. No originality in either plot or character." / "The characters have moments of life but they don't live" may be contrasted with "The people in the book are all alive and interesting." / "Here is a beautiful piece of literary workmanship of a rare order, fine in artistry, delicately accurate and subtle in its psychology." / "The character studies are strikingly good." / "The book as a revelation of a child mind of an unusual and interesting type is charming." / "A series of fascinating character studies."
One critic says "a fantastic piece of fiction writing." Another says "The narrative gives the impression of having been lived—not merely imagined." Then comes, "An underlying sentimentality weakens the book" with its marked opposite, "Sweetness that never gets cloying and sentiment that never gets over the line into sentimentality." / "It is never over-sentimentalized." / "To read this book is like recapturing a vision of spring." / "L.M. Montgomery is a born story teller."

The Blue Castle provoked rather more diversity of opinion.
"The story is one exclusively for feminine readers." / "Equally suitable for masculine amusement." / "The best little yarn we have read in a year" (written by a male reviewer). / "The most charming book the reviewer has read in many years" (another man).
"A well-worn theme." / "A dash of originality in the plot holds the reader." / "Miss Montgomery displays lack of ingenuity in working out her plot." / "A charming idyll strongly constructed and worked out with literary and poetic grace." / "An unusual theme worked out unusually well." / "The story is fresh in conception with a constant flash of sparkling humor." / "A plot that can lay claim to originality." / "A none-too-new theme." / "An extremely good plot and a charming tale."

"A plot as threadbare as can well be imagined." / "The plot is ordinary, very ordinary, but the telling is good enough to make it seem unusual." / "Something new in novels and something worth while."

"A pleasant little sentimental romance." / "Extraordinarily well done with a fine balance of pity and humor." / "Obviously slight and artificial." / "The book is of no very great depth and may be described as saccharine." / "A most intriguing novel." / "The sentiment never cloys." / "This is without doubt the most captivating story Miss Montgomery has ever written. Even an utterly jaded reader will find it difficult to lay down the book in the middle of a chapter." / "An entirely innocuous and sentimental tale." / "The tale bubbles with humor." / "A strong vein of ironic humor." / "For sheer pleasure in reading a good story this novel is hard to beat." / "A really delightful novel—gay, brisk, entertaining and well written."

"A story that will cause impatience because it is so implausible." / "The varied scenes sparkle with reality. Knowing they are impossible we feel that they are real." / "*He* treats his problem with deftness and plausibility." / "Unconvincing but readable." / "The love-making is real and convincing." / "An incredible story."

"Entirely devoid of thrills." / "A book full of tingles." / "A thrilling story that abundantly sustains the reputation of the author." / "Surprising and thrilling." / "Plenty of unexpected quirks." / "A charming love story far removed from modernism." / "The theme is light, lively, yet modern."

"The setting is a small town in Canada but unfortunately the author is not successful in depicting local color" (this by the way was an Australian review.) / "Life in a small Ontario town depicted with skillful realism." / "Poignantly human." / "The characterization is rather well done." / "The characters are to be met in every town and hamlet." / "Peopled with beings drawn solely out of the imagination." / "A remarkable essay in character drawing. A masterly piece of work—an analysis of conflicting emotions." / "It hasn't any problems involving introspection and dissection." / "Lifelike and convincing characters." / "Another handful of mud flung at Main Street but a good story."

Of *Emily Climbs* it was said—

"Contains no great literary qualities." / "Tells a story with real artistry." / "The book has distinction."

"An exceedingly precocious young woman with a philosophy of life savouring more of forty than of fourteen." / "Emily herself is real." / "Emily will take her place among the immortal children of literature."

"The so-called entries from the journal are imperfectly fused with the general narrative." / "The extracts from Emily's diary are excellent."

"No such girls exist any more." / "The puppet characters who parade the walks of the bulk of new stories for girls are mere paper dolls beside Emily."

"The book is sentimental stuff." / "This is a darling book." / "Great poetic beauty, the dramatic instinct of the story teller, keen and delicious humor." / "A strangely endearing tale."

"Light inconsequential reading of the harmless schoolgirl type." / "Grown-ups as well as girls can read about her with real interest." / "The reader's interest in Emily does not fall off for an instant." / "A tale to delight old and young." / "Every page is embroidered and bejewelled by a high priestess of beauty." / "A substantial and satisfying story."

Of *Emily's Quest*—ditto.

"Those who have not read the previous books will find it none too pleasant at times trying to locate in their minds places and people to whom reference is made in retrospect." / "The novel is self-contained and any references to the past are perfectly clear and understandable."

"An old-fashioned sentimental tale." / "Profound in its every day philosophy." / "A delightful book."

"Emily is *not* a sugary sweet heroine." / "A book commended by feminine youth and masculine age can go forth to the world assured of a cordial welcome." / "No sickly sentiment."

"A bewildering and unintelligible character. The author has tried to make the most of a feeble plot." / "The book is admirably done in the way of characterization." / "It is teeming with youth and vitality—Emily's magnificent personality." / "The original and always refreshing Emily." / "Emily is a brick through and through."

"A mildly interesting, highly sentimental tale." / "The story has Miss Montgomery's quiet distinction of style." / "The beauty, the reality, the pathos of this love story puts the book far on the other side of the commonplace." / "A genuine treat." / "It abounds in human appeal and interest." / "Clean, human, wholesome and humorous." / "The story has much originality."

Well, there you are. What is one to make of so many contradictions?

One amusing thing about the reviews is the number of other writers I am likened to—Alice Hegan Rice, Kate Douglas Wiggin, Frances Hodgson Burnett, Miss Alcott, George Madden Martin, John Habberton, *Barrie*, "Gyp," *Lewis Carroll*, Miss Mitford, *Mrs. Gaskell*, *Jane Austen*, the author of David Harum, whose name just now has escaped me, Mary S. Wilkins, Zona Gale, Myrtle Reid, Kenneth Grahame, Sara Orne Jewett, Alice Brown, Mrs. Deland, Miss Wetherell and Annie Fellows Johnstone.

Then my name and initials suffer all kinds of indignities—L.W.Montgomery, L.C. Montgomery, *Lionel* Montgomery, *Louise* Montgomery, L.W.M. Montgomery, L.H. Montgomery, C.M. Montgomery, *T.*M. Montgomery, S.M. Montgomery, K.D. Montgomery, L.W. *Anderson*, L.B.Montgomery, *Laura* Montgomery,—while quite often I am referred to as "he," "his" and "him."

Geography is not a strong point with some critics. "The scene is laid in Nova Scotia"—"A girl adopted into a New England family"—"rural life in New England"—"The country of the novel is New Brunswick"—"The scene is Avonlea peninsula jutting out into the gulf of St. Lawrence"—"Life on Victoria Island near Nova Scotia. So far away one may doubt the actual existence of Victoria Island but one has the testimony of the geography to the existence of Nova Scotia"—(I consider the foregoing delicious. It was in an otherwise good review, showing that the reviewer must have read the book!)—"This detached portion of land near Newfoundland"—"A story of life in a Breton fishing village"—

"The scene is laid in *Scotland*"—"The scene is laid in Cape Breton Island"—"A Prince's Island college"—"A play of American farm life"—"*Western* Canada is a charming setting for this story"—"a story of American girlhood."

Some reviews were quite curious. One wonders what the critic who wrote "The author might have made more of her background for P.E. Island has not yet figured in fiction" thought life in P.E. Island was really like. A similar cast of thought is shown in, "What impresses the American reader is that the scene might as well have been laid in the United States, so like do these Canadians seem to our own people" and in "The Island has been little more than a name and a charming Black Prince on a postage stamp—the King in Highland costume." Certainly P.E. Island never had a stamp like that and I am almost equally sure Canada did not either. "Anne, aged 16 years and 6 mos. has charge of village school—one hesitates whether to wonder most at—the development of Canadian girls or the educational system of P.E. Island." Well, several girls I knew made very good teachers at sixteen and the educational system of P.E. Island turned out, among other things, Jacob Schurman, president of Cornell University.

" 'The Summons' is a good chapter" refers to a chapter in *Anne of the Island* which I thought a total failure. But the gem of all the reviews I have ever received is the following, published in an Oakland, Calif. paper. "Miss Montgomery must have invented her orchard as well as her modest mute. There are no orchards in P.E. Island. They are killed by the harsh salt winds that blow across the narrow strip."

Whenever I get blue I think of the foregoing and it cheers me up instanter.

Some reviews provide a chuckle for me.

"A suspicion that it (*Green Gables*) is more than half an autobiography in disguise of the gifted author." Not at all. "Miss Montgomery's home is in Cavendish, P.E.I., where she *teaches the village school.*" Not guilty. "From report Miss M.'s pupils had not a very strenuous time of it. Their teacher was more inclined to be delighted at their vagaries than proud of their scholastic virtues. When she found teaching uncongenial Miss M. retired from the profession and did a lot of thinking." This of course was all moonshine. One review said I had "written *Anne of Green Gables* for children and *Anne of Avonlea* for adults and was mistaken in both." I was not. I did not write *Green Gables* for children. And Avonlea was not written for anybody or any class but merely to carry on Anne's adventures for anybody who was interested in them. "It is said that this new story 'came to her.' " I forget what book this referred to but none of my stories have "come to me." "Her books would make a limited appeal to a modern schoolgirl" was an amusing extract from an Australian review. Amusing because of the deluge of letters I am always getting from Australian schoolgirls.

Sometimes people who "interview" me print a description of me. "Her figure is willowy and most graceful. Her features are classical. In conversation she is brilliant and epigrammatical." "Miss M. is petite with the fine delicate features of an imaginative woman." "Slight, pale and delicate looking, with pointy chin, small mouth and broad forehead. Her eyes are dark and deep and the heavy glossy black hair is something good to look at."

I have suffered much at the hand of interviewers. They get everything twisted and put in things I never said. One interview—to be sure it was a very flattering one—was a fake from beginning to end. I never saw the writer of it.

Some reviews make one wonder if the critic ever read the book under review at all, even in the most superficial way. *Kilmeny* was "the sweet sad story of an *Italian* girl" and her mother "quarrelled with her father *because he denied her some trifling request.*" *Blue Castle* was "another handful of mud flung at Main Street people." *Rainbow Valley* was "a story touching humanity at the preposterous angle of conventional piety"! Also "a rooster named Adam, pet of Faith Meredith and enemy of the entire parish. He is responsible for a large part of the humor of the book." "Adam" was not depicted as anybody's enemy and only one chapter in *Rainbow Valley* is concerned with his doings. Of *Anne of Avonlea* one critic wrote, "More matrimonial infelicity, satisfactorily solved by kicking over the traces." Echo answers, "Where?" Again of *Kilmeny*—"A rich young Canadian goes to a Breton village to teach school. There he chances upon a *blind* girl—the girl *recovers her sight* from a shock."

It annoyed me to have "Davy" called "a poetical little Yankee boy"—he was not poetical and he was not Yankee. It annoyed me to read the query—re *Kilmeny*—"Did some friend of keener insight and more dramatic turn suggest the story?" I never had any help from anybody, of keener insight or the reverse, in regard to any of my stories. Good or bad, such as they are, they are wholly my own. It annoyed me to read, "Miss L.M. Montgomery has become the wife of a minister. She will hereafter know what a real novel should be like." I have seldom read anything so asinine—unless it was the query "Why does she who wrote those beautiful poems, all distinguished for their originality and beauty, bother to write so ordinary a novel as *Anne's House of Dreams?*" Because, dear critic, I had to live and could not live on poetry. You knew that quite as well as I did. It annoyed me to read "Unfortunately the author is not skilful in depicting local color"—though it amused me to reflect that this was written by an Australian who couldn't have known much about Canadian local colour. But this was offset by another reviewer who said, "One would like to point out how inevitably and unerringly she handles the social background in all her stories." It amused me to read, "A near relative, Mr. D. Montgomery, the agent of the P.E. Island Railway at Georgetown, once assured me that most of Miss Montgomery's characters, in fact the principal that we make acquaintance with, are drawn from life." He added that he knew some of the characters in actual life and could vouch for the accuracy of delineation of them by his talented relative." Poor Cousin Dan! I'm afraid his desire for the limelight betrayed him that time. I don't suppose he ever thought I'd see it. None of my characters, except Peg Bowen and Miss Brownell were drawn from life but if they had been Dan could hardly have known it since the acquaintances we had in common were very few.

It amused me to read, "a picture of the old church where she met the Rev. Macdonald"—because said old church was pulled down long before I ever beheld the said Reverend. It amused me to read, speaking of my winter on the *Echo* staff, "It was there she learned the art of self-expression, the art of condensation and precise writing so necessary to a novelist." It more than amused me. I howled over it. I learned absolutely nothing in regard to literary skill while I was proof-reading ads and editorials for the Echo.

It also amused me to read *two* reviews of the same book in the same paper, a few weeks apart, one of which was *very* flattering and one almost abusive.

It amused me to read that *Kilmeny* "sullied in my (the critic's) mind the lustre of her (the author's) personality." I wonder if the writer of the sentence knew what she meant herself!

And it amused me to read that Uncle Leander was "the *Uncle Edward* of *The Story Girl*." I'll tell the world he wasn't!

It infuriated me to be called "a bright young *Nova Scotian* writer!!!"

And here and there among all the reviews and criticisms would come a note that would give me a special pleasure of my own, as if the writer thereof understood me and my work. It was not Mark Twain's far-flung letter "Anne is the dearest and most moving and delightful child since the immortal Alice," nor Meredith Nicholson's "A book to uplift the spirit and send the pessimist into bankruptcy," though of course these both pleased me. But here is a sample or two of what I refer to.

"Down by the sea listening by the moonlight to the surging waters of the gulf striking against the red cliffs, a young lady of P.E. Island conceives and writes a story which equals as a character creation the work of the masters of literature."

"A sigh of contentment at the first and a bit of sadness because the end comes all so soon."

"We can imagine that if she were ship-wrecked on a desert island with a pencil and a few quires of paper she would at once sit down under a tree and commence writing a most enchanting story."

Ah, well-a-day! All this has never meant very much of pleasure or pain, except superficially. I have written to please myself. It has not mattered much what anyone else thought. I have always tried to catch and express a little of the immortal beauty and enchantment of the world into which I have sometimes been privileged to see for a moment—the moment of "Emily's" "flash." Those who never have that glimpse cannot believe there is such a world. I can but pity them.

Sunday, March 2, 1930
Norval, Ont.

A few weeks ago I took a plate picture of the old home in to Eaton's to have a film made from it for advertising purposes. By mistake the first film produced was a "positive" in place of a negative. As it was of no use to anybody they gave it to me and for a whim's sake I had a picture printed from it. The result was rather odd. It is an exact reproduction of a snowy winter night in the old orchard.

It is just dark. The first snow of the year has come in late November and early December. The apple trees still have their russet leaves powdered with snow. The spruce tree boughs are heavy with it. The dead and dry flower stalks and heads stick up above the snow all over the garden. And there is a light gleaming in the kitchen window.

It is all so uncannily like what it would really have been had it been possible to take a picture under such circumstances.

Cavendish positive proof

Wed., Mar. 6, 1930
I have been very miserable much of the time lately. My ear and face trouble me much and I could growl a lot about them—but I won't. I could also growl over the fact that I got 28 more letters from Australia today. I vow that the sight of an Australian stamp will give me the "willies" for the rest of my life.

Something I was reading today in a farm magazine struck me. It seems that nowadays potatoes do not bear seed—at least in the regions whereof the writer wrote. And I don't believe they do around here. I wonder if they still do down home. I must find out. When I was a child potatoes always bore seed—great hanging clusters of "potato balls," which looked so much like green gage plums—but didn't taste like them—as too well I knew, having once—and once only—experienced in tasting them. I remember that a favorite sport of those days was to "shoot" potato balls by sticking them on the ends of long, limber switches and twirling them swiftly around our heads. I think I am sorry that potato balls have "gone out" of fashion.

Friday, March 8, 1930
The Manse, Norval
Today came word of Dan Johnstone's death in Calgary—from pneumonia. He was Ella's only brother and the last of her family. She will be broken-hearted, poor thing—she depended on him so much. It almost killed her when he moved west two years ago. I feel this death, too. Dan was one of the "old gang" at Park Corner years ago. A nice, good, quiet fellow.

It has brought back Frede's death, too. When I *realize* Frede's death, as I did today, I have a curious sensation of smothering. I want to push something off me—to gasp for breath. I have never been able to believe for any length of time that Frede *is* dead. If I believed it I could not live. It is like a moment of death when I have these dreadful seconds of believing it. I screamed aloud today when one of them came to me.

Monday, March 17, 1930
Death—and more death—

> There is no union here of hearts
> That finds not here an end.

Today two shocked missives came from May and Myrtle—each containing the news of the death of Hannah McKenzie—Hammond and Emily's only daughter. She was married a few years ago to Warfield Orr of New Glasgow and has left four small children. She died of flu-pneumonia.

There is no use asking why. That question is never answered.

When I read those letters I suddenly realized how long it was since I was young. And yet it seems but the other day that I was sitting writing at my room window in the old home. It was a lovely morning in early June. Suddenly I heard children's voices and laughter below. I looked out—and there was little Hannah McKenzie, about six, trotting along for the first time to school, with some older girls. She had no hat on and I can see her little buttercup head—literally "sunned over" with curls—shining along under the poplars and the white cherry trees and so on down the lane.

And now she is dead!

I keep rather miserable. Today I began the actual writing of the book I've been doing spade work on for a year. It has no name yet. It centres around the old Woolner jug and is to be a humorous novel for adults. But I can't get the time I should have for it. Oh, for a little real leisure!

And I got thirty more Australian letters today!

Wednesday, April 9, 1930
I was amused to read in a suburban department of a Toronto paper tonight that a few nights ago the Young Peoples' society of the United Church in Woodbridge had "The story of L.M. Montgomery's life" for one of their evening programs. Just the same, they know no more of my life than they ever did. Which is just as well—both for me and their illusions.

Today while doing some preliminary spade work for housecleaning in the garret I found in a trunk the old Teddy Bear that the boys used to play with—a most mistreated and depressed Teddy Bear, terribly patched, with only black boot buttons for eyes. Yet a Teddy Bear very dear to me.

He was new and handsome and debonair when Chester got him on a Christmas tree. Chester was very fond of him till he outgrew him and then he fell to Stuart. Stuart loved his "Teddy" very dearly. He must have him every night when he went to bed and when I kissed my boys good-night I must "kiss Teddy" too. So for the sake of those old evenings and those old kisses I cannot destroy poor old battered Teddy.

Stuart and Teddy

Another letter came from Isobel today, beginning, "My beloved" and continuing in that strain. That poor girl really turns my stomach. If she does not give up persecuting me I vow I'll open a vein. I am not well and I admit that today I have been blue-blue. But a volume of Marion Crawford's ghost stories cheered me up tonight. Ghost stories always do. There's no literature on earth I relish as I do a good ghost story.

Too, I've been reading lately Sir James Jeans' *The Universe Around Us* and several more of that ilk. Time was when I loved books on astronomy—and *understood* them. I can't understand the new ones—they seem to require a new language. When a scientist like Jeans tells me that a "quantum" of energy can "pass from one orbit of the atom to another *without crossing the intervening space*" I metaphorically turn up my toes. If this be true the materialists have their last prop knocked from under them. For that "quantum" must be something that is not subject to the laws of time and space and is therefore *spirit* not matter.

I accept the "quantum theory" because Sir James Jeans hands it out to me. But neither he nor anyone else can make me accept the "planetesimal hypothesis." To do so would be to agree that intelligent conscious life must be the exception in the universe instead of the rule—something I can never believe. If our planets were pulled out from the sun by a passing star such a thing could happen very seldom in the universe. And this would mean that all the uncounted millions of burning suns around us were created for nothing—exist for nothing—have no life bearing planets circling about them. My reason refuses such a conclusion. It would be absurd. God would not waste so many good suns.

Saturday, April 26, 1930
The Manse, Leaskdale. Norval
Rather a funny mistake that—I suppose because we have just got home from Leaskdale. Thursday came word of the death of poor Mrs. Horace Quigley. I felt shocked and sad for I had always liked her very much. We went up to the funeral today, leaving early in the morning. Had dinner at Geo. Leasks'—who haven't changed, either of them, in the last eighteen years.

We saw almost everybody at the funeral. Some look the same, some have changed much in the four years since we left. Mr. McInnis seems to be doing well but some don't like him and George Leask said, "I think most of us would be glad to have our old man back." The manse looks bare, with many of the trees, all the vines and the shutters gone. It was a mistake to take the shutters off. Those long narrow windows needed them.

"George Leask's house"

We had supper at Jas. Mustard's. Mrs. Jim was always a dear soul but we miss him. It was one of the first places where we spent an evening soon after I went to Leaskdale. I remember it well—a clear crisp autumn night. We drove in along the shadowy school road and along the high "sixth," had a good supper and a pleasant evening. As we were going away Mrs. Jim said to us, "I think you two should be very proud of each other." It sent us home with a good taste in our mouths—something we did not *always* take home from some of our visitations in Leaskdale and Zephyr. Well, that was a long time ago.

We have been housecleaning and the boys have been home for Easter holidays. Chester has only one more term to put in at St. Andrew's.

One day recently I found an old faded picture in a box. A picture taken over thirty years ago of Kate Macneill, Charlie Perkins (her beau) and myself on a rock on Cavendish shore. I had destroyed the plate years ago. So I took it in to Toronto and had a film made from it. Kate and Charlie are dead—and I am estranged from all Kate's family. But here in the picture we all sit happy and forever young. Happy? Well, no. No doubt Kate and Charlie were, but I had just come out of two of the bitterest years of my life and was quite sure I should never be happy again. I felt old and sad and disillusioned. Yet I don't look old in the picture, in spite of the high flat hat and long skirt of the period—after all I was only twenty three, though I *felt* so aged!

There are few things I regret more than the fact that kodaks were unknown in my schooldays. Even a plate camera was a rare possession then. What wouldn't I give for "snaps" of all my old schoolmates and their doings. I haven't even a "snap" of Nate who was my first beau—the first man (?)—heaven save the mark, he was just fifteen, a few months older than Stuart is now!—who ever said to me "I love you."

48

Rev. J.A. Mustard

Wednesday, April 30, 1930
The Manse, Norval

Apropos of what I said in my last entry about having no picture of some of my old beaus—well, here is one of the Rev. John Mustard. It really belongs back in 1891 and has no business whatever in 1930.

Mrs. Hugh Mustard and Mrs. Jim have been very good friends of mine in their way. It used to amuse me a bit to speculate what they would have thought if they had ever dreamed—as certainly they did not—that I might have been their sister-in-law. What funny kinks life does have.

Today I had again the experience of coming out of hell into heaven—or at any rate what seemed heaven by contrast.

Many years ago I had a "cancer" scare, as described in some part of this diary. These past two days I have had another one. Monday morning I found a certain thing which I thought *might* betoken an internal cancer. I went to Toronto with Ewan and the boys—who were going back to St. Andrew's—and spent the day in Simpson's store. It was like a nightmare. I was haunted by dread and that night I could not sleep. Nor last night. I was not so badly upset as I was years ago, nevertheless I have had two very hellish days and nights. And then this morning I discovered that I was entirely mistaken. The fatal "sign" had nothing to do with me at all—and everything changed in a twinkling.

But there is an old superstition that things go "in threes." Will there come sometime a third scare? And will it be a real one? I ask myself.

Another flood of Australian letters today. This runs it up into the hundreds.

Today in a magazine I found a picture of Judge Jeffreys—the villain of the *Bloody Assizes*. I had never seen a picture of him before. But I had formed a very clear one in my mind from reading Macaulay's account of him—an account which, however Macaulay erred in some of his portraits, has never been impeached as a faithful one of Jeffreys. I saw him quite plainly—the brutal countenance, the furious eyes, the merciless mouth. But his picture staggered me. The man was beautiful with an almost womanish beauty. He looks like a dreaming poet—an unfallen seraph. Did the painter flatter him? Perhaps. But even so, it seems impossible that this could be Jeffreys! This

Judge Jeffreys

is foolish of me. Many beautiful faces have masked hideous and brutal souls—just as many hideous faces have been mated with beauty of mind and heart. I have recently been reading Feuchtwanger's *Ugly Duchess*—a historical novel about Marguerite Maultasch, Duchess of Tyrol. Her picture, from a portrait by Da Vinci, was in it. I have gazed at it, fascinated. It seems absolutely impossible that a human being could be so hideous. Impossible and mournful. Yet she was a statesman and a patriot, a wife and a mother, though her husband did not love her and her children died. She could never have known happiness. Well, perhaps it was made up to her in her next incarnation. Or perhaps she was expiating some wickedness of a former life. It must have been some incredibly awful wickedness. Perhaps she was Salome, dancing the Baptist's head off.

Saturday, May 10, 1930
The Manse, Norval
Long ago I remember reading somewhere "One must be either very young or very happy to be able to endure the melancholy of a spring dusk." It is true. Tonight I have been alone and very lonely. The exquisite, brooding beauty of the May twilight deepened my feeling unbearably. I want to have my boy-babies again—the dear little chubby creatures who used to trot about Leaskdale manse and give me "Scotch" kisses and "bear hugs." And I want Frede. I am weary of hearing the terrible silence when I call for her. I want the fragrance of old springs and the laughter of old evenings. Do my dead dream of me tonight as I of them?

Saturday, May 24, 1930
The boys are home for the old "twenty-fourth." Queen Victoria picked a good time for her birthday.

Have been reading Emil Ludwig's *Son of Man*. Much disappointed. It has all Renan's faults without Renan's excellences. His treatment of the miracle of Cana is farcical.

Today in looking over some boxes in the garret I came across one full of point lace—rather exquisite stuff too.

When I was a child point lace was "in." Very few knew how to make it. Generally those who did kept the knowledge a jealous secret. Aunt Annie learned it from an old lady in Ch'town who made her living by it and only taught Aunt Annie under a solemn promise that she would not teach it to anyone else. Aunt Annie didn't keep that promise *wholly*—she taught Aunt Emily—likewise under promise of secrecy. I used to watch Aunt Emily do it with fascinated eyes. It seemed to me wonderful. By the time I had "grown up" point lace was "out." It came in again about 1900, arriving first as "Battenburg," a coarse variety. Everybody learned to do it. I got a book of instructions, braid and a pattern, and, being always "handy" with my needle soon learned the intricate stitches. I have still the first bit I did—a Battenburg doily. Then I began on point. I was engaged and decided to make several pieces of "point" for my "hope chest." I did, working evening after evening by lamplight. It was a wonder I had any eyesight left. I made a "bertha"—a "bolero"—a table centrepiece—two or three of them indeed—a handkerchief, several doilies and odd pieces. And then by the time I was married point was "out" again. It had got too common—at least Battenburg had. Everybody could do Battenburg—but few could do the real cobwebby point. Well, my pieces will do for heirlooms. They may have a value someday because "L.M. Montgomery" made them. Some of the pieces that were never used or washed are as cobwebby as when made. A few pieces which I used about the house when I was married have been laundered and thickened. One piece—a cushion top or centrepiece—was made by Frede. I wonder if the time we spent on them was justified. Perhaps so. A thing made by hand, with time and toil and patience, has a personality nothing else could have. No quickly-made machine product can take its place.

Wed. May 28, 1930
The Manse, Norval
A letter from Bertie today brought the glad news that she may come east next summer.

This afternoon when I was sitting on the veranda a car drove up to the gate and John Mustard got out. I went to the gate. He was on his way home from a Presbytery meeting in Georgetown but would not come in. He looked very old and ill—he is not at all well. And he seemed as ill-at-ease as he always does in my company—though that may simply be his manner with everyone. But he gave himself away at the last. As he turned to go he said, "Good-bye, *Miss Montgomery.*" I think he was quite unconscious of having said it.

Reading over a sketch of my life today in a magazine—written by one who knew very little about it—I came across the statement that I had always possessed a great deal of persistence and determination. Well, I daresay that is true; and it recalled a proud moment of my life that I have not remembered for years.

One day when I was six years old Aunt Emily was churning in the kitchen. It was winter and the butter was reluctant to come. She churned and churned in vain. Then Grandma took a hand and churned for a time that should have been sufficient for half a dozen churnings. They both gave up and decreed the cream to the pigs. But neither had time to empty it out just then so the old blue churn remained squatted on the table. I promptly began to churn, full of delight. I had always yearned to churn but had never been allowed, lest I "spoil the butter," for if you churned too slow or too fast the butter did not "come right." But now it did not matter so I was not molested and churned away happily. Eventually the churn grew "heavy" and the crank harder and harder to turn but I would not give up because I had always been told that I would "soon get tired" of it. I hung on like grim death. I must have churned for an hour at least. Then I had to give up. Aunt Emily lifted the lid, preparatory to emptying the churn, gazed for a moment, then exclaimed,

"She's brought the butter."

Yes, on the whole it was the proudest moment of my life!

Friday, June 6, 1930
Chester came home today. He is through with St. Andrew's. It is nearly five years since I took him there, a little chap in knickers—he leaves it a full-grown man in

appearance. He is to take his Honours Matric exams in Georgetown. They are expected to be very hard this year and he is doubtful if he will get through in them all.

Stuart writes me that he has won the Bronze Medallion and the Award of Merit in the Life Saving Class.

Monday, June 9, 1930
Today I found in an old scrapbook a certain article, clipped from a 1914 issue of the old and defunct *Presbyterian*. It is entitled "Right Resolving and Definite Doing" and was written by John A. Paterson, K.C., who was a Toronto lawyer, somewhat more interested in church affairs than lawyers are wont to be. The subject was Ewan's project of getting Leaskdale and Zephyr congregations to support a foreign missionary of their own. And to me, who knew the inside realities of the whole affair, that article was full of unconscious ironic humor which made me smile rather bitterly. I wonder how often there are similar ironic realities behind all the fulsome plaudits and sketches that are continually appearing in the press.

"My story is a simple one," wrote Paterson. "It is only a humble effort of heroic and unselfish enterprise by some ordinary country people of our church who 'do good by stealth and blush to find it fame.'" — A certain Mr. Forbes, a graduate of the University of Toronto and Knox College, was designated for the Foreign Mission field—and in the ordinary way he would have been sent forth by the Foreign Mission Committee and necessarily a charge upon the Foreign Mission Budget. However, that was not the plan worked out by the Eternal Councils—it was to be accompanied by an injection of missionary spirit into two country congregations. These two congregations and their minister became simultaneously obsessed with the conviction that they wanted a foreign missionary of their own whom they were not only eager to support but whom they regarded it as an honor to support. That minister and Forbes visited these farmers—and storekeepers—and women—and children; the money was raised—$1200 a year without any time limit—. Thus it was that the minister and Forbes returned with joy and reported to the sessions—"If we had the spirit of the men and women and boys and girls of Leaskdale and Zephyr the raising of our Budget would be as nothing" and so on.

Well, now for the truth behind all this. Paterson is right when he attributes a good deal of this to Ewan. He should have attributed it all. For from first to last it was Ewan's idea and no one else's.

Personally I did not think it a wise one. And events justified my opinion. I knew that Leaskdale and Zephyr were too weak to keep such a thing up, whatever they might do as a *tour de force*. But Ewan went ahead with his project. Between us we pledged $200 a year to the scheme, leaving $1000 for the two congregations to raise. As there were then about 90 families it should have been quite feasible but I knew too well what the most of those families were like. I fear the "Councils of Eternity" had very little to do with the affair.

Ewan—and Ewan alone—Mr. Forbes was not there and had no part in the canvassing—went to every family, explained the plan and asked them to pledge a certain amount every year for five years—for there *was* a time limit though Mr. Paterson says there was not. A very few—perhaps five families in all—entered into the spirit of the plan and promised to pay liberally and ungrudgingly. A good many more were *not* enthusiastic but they liked Ewan and agreed to contribute simply because he asked them. Many more agreed grudgingly because they were ashamed not to. And a few would not promise anything.

This being done Ewan asked the Foreign Mission Board to assign us a man and Mr. Forbes was told off to us. Ewan asked him to come out and stay a couple of weeks with us, visiting all the families and so getting well acquainted with the people who were sending him. I always have thought that had Forbes done this a real spirit of missions might have been worked up and the outcome might have been very different. But he did not—although he promised to do it. Then he sent word that he could stay only a week—there were several "receptions" and "farewell gatherings" in Toronto he must attend, forsooth. A week was a very short time to work in so many visits but Ewan remapped his plan of campaign to suit the new time limit. And then when Mr. Forbes did come he coolly announced that he could stay only three days as he had to be back in Toronto on a certain night for a "presentation" Bloor St. church was making him. As one of these days was taken up with the designation service this left *two* in which to get acquainted with the people. Of course this was impossible. Ewan and Forbes dashed madly about, calling everywhere—for nobody could be left out—and staying of necessity such a brief time that there was really no good accomplished at all.

We were unlucky in our choice of a man—or the aforesaid Eternal Councillors of Mr. Paterson's screed bungled things badly. Forbes was stiff and cold, utterly lacking in magnetism or inspiration.

From the first it was uphill work. Only the first year was the whole $1200 paid—and at that Ewan had to visit a third of them and collect it. Every succeeding year it was worse and worse. Forbes had promised to write a monthly letter to be read in the churches. He did not keep his promise but he did send an occasional letter. And I used to think it would have been better if he had not. They were the most pitiful apologies for letters—dull, dry, stiff, utterly uninteresting—and filled for the most part with whines about how slowly he was getting on with the language etc. Finally I made Ewan stop reading them. They were killing out what little real interest the people had in him.

Then he did a foolish thing. He enlisted and went to France. He got permission from the Board, which was all that was strictly necessary of course. But he did not trouble himself to consult with the people who were paying his salary and who should have been consulted out of courtesy if nothing else. He went and the first notification we had of it was his letter announcing his arrival in the trenches. This gave a good handle to the many who were tired of paying what they had reluctantly promised and they kept grumbling that he had deserted his post etc. etc. etc. There was some truth in this and we could not make them realize that the money was still being used on the foreign field in the work of missions. And by the fifth year, although Forbes was back in Honan, no more than half the year's salary was paid in. When the five years were up Union was looming in the air and Ewan did not make any attempt to prolong the term. He realized that he had made a mistake and that the whole thing had been a pitiful fizzle—owing partly to the fact that there was no real missionary spirit in the congregations of Leaskdale and Zephyr and partly to the kind of man Forbes was. So in view of all this Mr. Paterson's article reads very ironically now and his encomiums upon "those men who knew they could not take their money with them so were sending it ahead of them to bear rich interest *here* from the never insolvent bank of Love and to earn richer dividends *there* from the head office within the Everlasting Doors" make me give a twisted smile of derisive memory. James Lockie was one of those men—one of those "sessions" so highly lauded. And he and his wife told us that it was "that missionary scheme that had ruined Zephyr church."

Well, it is all over and forgotten now. But it is not a memory that gives either of us much pleasure.

Monday, June 16, 1930
The Manse, Norval,
At the end of a disheartening day I creep to this old journal for a bit of comforting. I need it.

One night last week I had a queer and abominable dream. I dreamed that I woke up in my bed and found *everything*, bedstead, pillows, sheets and spread, literally crawling alive with *bedbugs*. Millions of them! Inches deep! And I madly tried to scrape them off with my hands but could not get ahead of them. As soon as I scraped a few off their places were at once filled. All I succeeded in doing was to cover my hands with unspeakable, nauseating slime and blood and crushed bodies of vermin. I was tearfully trying to get it off my hands when I awoke.

The dream worried me because it was one of those clear-cut dreams that are always significant. Mrs. Mason, who is full of lore culled from "dream books," vowed that to dream of bedbugs meant illness. Well, the illness has come but somehow I am nastily afraid that the dream meant more than that. *Something* is coming and my soul has tried to warn me of it in such imagery as it could command. At least, such is my conviction. But it may only be because I'm blue and lonesome and ill and discouraged. I've had a dreadful attack of flu—the third since New Year's. That is too much.

Last Tuesday I began with a bad cold in the head. I tried all the remedies I knew for Thursday our "Missionary picnic" was to come off and I wanted to be well until it was over. Wednesday I felt miserable but crawled around making and icing cakes. Then Wednesday night I went to bed. I sent Ewan into the boys' room and proceeded to spend a ghastly night alone. Soon after I was in bed a racking unceasing cough started—and with it a very bad attack of asthma—just the same as I had in the spring of 1925 only worse. Of course I should have roused someone and had a doctor. But I always have such a horror of giving people trouble. I suppose it is a hangover from childhood when I had it well grained into me that I must not give trouble. So I stuck the night out, gasping in torture with every breath but hoping that the asthma part of it would disappear, as it had done in 1925, as suddenly as it started. But in the morning I realized that I must throw up the sponge. Mrs. Mason phoned for Dr. Paul—Kate MacPherson came in and looked at me, then fled home for strychnine tablets—she said I was so "blue" that

54

she was afraid about my heart. Dr. Paul came, gave me an injection—and in a few moments what a heavenly relief!

Of course there was no picnic for me that day—which was all to the good, except that I was to preside and had at the eleventh hour to get someone to take my place. Mrs. Buchanan, the missionary who was to speak, wandered in and told me it was all part of my Heavenly Father's plan for me. I agreed with her because I was too weak for argument but with "mental reservations." I *don't* think it was my Heavenly Father who tortured me all that night. I prefer to think it was the devil!

Chester went for Stuart Wednesday and brought him home Friday. Stuart has led his class and made an average of 91%—not so bad.

I crawled up Saturday but have felt rotten. I cannot sleep at nights for coughing and I cannot eat. And I don't want to eat. I don't want ever to get up again. I am possessed soul and body with the beastly depression that the flu leaves behind it. Nothing is of any use. I'm no good and nobody I'm connected with is any good. Nothing decent will ever happen to me again—and so on—and so on. My blues are not all imaginary. I have some real worries, a consequence of the way the stock market crash last fall has affected some companies in which I had large investments. They have not paid dividends and this makes things rather hard for me financially. But I would not mind this if I could only feel sure that the companies themselves would weather the storm eventually. In daytime I believe they will but in darkness I see them all on the rocks. Then some of my "friends" have borrowed large sums of money from me and don't seem to have the least intention of ever paying it back. All this "gets on my nerves" when I'm

"Chester 1930. Age 18"

ill. Then, too, Edmund Campbell had promised Chester a job for the summer, surveying a copper mine in Newfoundland which he is promoting. New York financiers were backing him and all looked bright—till the copper slump in May. The financiers tied up their money bags—the promotion won't go through this year—and Chester is out of his job. I am sorry, because there is nothing for a boy of C.'s age to put in the time at in Norval. There isn't even amusement or companionship. And C. is too big a boy now to lie idly around all summer. He and Ewan don't pull well. For one thing they are too much alike. For another Ewan has no understanding of youth and young men whatever. I have to act as "buffer state" between them and it isn't pleasant. Just now everything looks too difficult and the grasshopper is a burden.

Sunday, June 22, 1930
I'm in the mess my vermin dream foretold. And it's what I would call a hellish mess.

Last Tuesday morning I got up feeling rather better. It seemed possible to me that sometime I might even want to work again. I planned a quiet restful day. Taking it easy. Doing a little mending; catching up with some correspondence. And then in came Ewan with the morning mail—and my peace was smashed to smithereens!

There was a letter from a certain Mr. Agnew, *Barrister.* I tore it open with a nasty qualm and the heading, "Rex. Vs. Beaton" stared me in the face.

It was to the effect that Sutherland Beaton was in jail, having been arrested for stealing $500 from the Cabinet Tea Company for whom he was working. That he wanted me to put up bail for $1000 for him and that his trial was to take place in September.

And that was that!

It did not surprise me. I knew a good many things about poor Sutherland.

When Sutherland came to see me a year ago last New Year's I was quite taken with him. Apart from the interest I would feel in the son of an old friend, I found him an attractive youngster. He was nineteen, good-looking, gentlemanly, with quite a gift of the gab, fluent and plausible but not offensively so. He told me he had landed an excellent position with a firm in Toronto and had been appointed their representative in the Maritimes. The salary he mentioned rather amazed me. It seemed a large sum for an untrained youth like S. to get at the start. But it didn't occur to me that he could be lying. He also told me that he had to put up a bond for several hundreds of dollars and that this took all he had saved since he came to Toronto (he had been there a few months) and left him without ready cash to pay his fare east. Would I lend him a hundred dollars and he would pay it back in three months.

Of course I lent him the money. Even if I hadn't believed him I couldn't have refused Mary's son. And I did believe him, having no reason to do otherwise. Sutherland took his departure and I heard no more of or about him until one night late in February when I was called to the phone, Toronto speaking. It was the firm which had employed Sutherland and the manager wanted to know if I could give him Sutherland's address or his peoples' address. He said they had never heard a word from S. since he had gone east, except that he had drawn a check on them. He also said he had been greatly taken with Sutherland and thought him just the fellow for their work, etc.

I couldn't give him Sutherland's address but I gave him Archie's and then came back to bed in some alarm. I thought something must be the matter—Sutherland must be ill or something. So next day I wrote to Mary, asking her if anything was wrong.

She did not reply for a long time but eventually her letter came. She said her heart was almost broken and proceeded to tell me why. Then last fall when I was there she told me the full story. And a very miserable one it was.

They had wanted Sutherland to take an education. But he would not. When he was seventeen he left school and took a job on as agent for an insurance company.

Before very long there was trouble. He was caught forging names on the company's cheques and cashing them. He lost his job but was let off because his parents made good. He started for Toronto and at Borden did the very same thing again, cashing the cheque before he left the Island. All he had told me about the "bond" and the big salary was lies. He had no real salary at all—was merely working on commission. He went to the Maritimes but did no work and the company fired him. He then went home for a while. During this time his brother Roland was in the hospital having an operation for appendicitis. Roland had quite a bit of money in the bank and when he got out he went to get it to pay for his operation. He was informed that his account was already thirty dollars overdrawn! Sutherland had been forging Roland's name to cheque after cheque and had cleaned him out!!!

They hushed the matter up and kept it in the family. Sutherland came back to Toronto where he drifted from one job to another but took good care never to come near Norval manse, although I wrote to Mary and told her to tell him to come out whenever he liked. I heard and saw nothing of him till this letter came.

I was not fit to go to Toronto but go I had to. I did not know what to do about giving bail. As I had no real estate on which to give a bond I would have to put up a thousand in cash. I had only a few hundreds in the bank and would have to borrow it. But this would not have bothered me if I had been sure Sutherland would not skip his bail. He was quite capable of it and I did not feel I could lose a thousand dollars even for Mary's son. However, when I got in and talked with the lawyer I found bail was not needed. Agnew said he had decided that it was no use for Sutherland to wait till the fall assizes. It was just as well to have his trial at once because all the evidence was against him and he hadn't much chance of getting off. But he said the "Cabinet Tea Co." were a couple of crooks and he felt that since this was Sutherland's first offence he could get him off on suspended sentence if he pleaded guilty and *if restitution were made*. And he asked me if I thought his parents would make it. I said "Yes" unhesitatingly. I knew Archie and Mary would pay anything in reason to prevent their son from serving a penitentiary term. I said I would wire Roland to come to Toronto at once and if he could not I would appear in the courtroom at the trial and offer restitution. Agnew arranged for the trial to be next Wednesday and I came home almost in a state of collapse.

That night at eleven a wire reached me from Mary. Archie was too ill with heart trouble to come, Roland could not. Would she do? I wired that she would, though I dreaded the ordeal for her. And then I went to bed for a sleepless night.

Wednesday I went to Streetsville to attend a district W.M.S. I should not have gone for I wasn't fit but I had promised to take part in the program and hated to disappoint them. After my part was over I had to go over to the manse and lie down. Thursday I went to Dr. Paul and told him he must give me something to keep me from starving to death. I could neither eat nor sleep—partly from worry over Mary and partly from a terrible cough which racked me night and day. He gave me medicine but so far it has had little effect. I'm "all in."

Yesterday Chester and I motored in to meet poor Mary. She was in a sad state but bore up fairly well until this afternoon when Chester took her to Toronto and Mr. Agnew took her to see Sutherland in jail—where he has been, poor chap, ever since May 31st. They could only talk to him for three minutes and Sutherland wouldn't listen to reason. He refused to plead guilty and demanded bail and to have his trial put off till the September assizes. Agnew told him he would have no chance whatever if he would not do as he was told and Mary came home distracted. I cannot blame her. If it were my son I would be even worse than she is. But I am really not able to stand up to this just now. If Sutherland is sent to the pen I don't know what will happen to Mary. I think it will kill her. She has none too good a heart.

Monday, June 23, 1930
Neither Mary nor I slept last night. I got Dr. Paul to send her up a sleeping potion today. She can't go on like this. Ewan and I took her in to Toronto today to see Sutherland again. I had never been in a jail before and it was a ghastly experience when your friend is with you to see her son. When our turn came we were let in and saw Sutherland for three minutes behind the bars—a white haggard but jaunty Sutherland who wouldn't listen to anything we could say. We had to come away on that note, Mary nearly distracted. I sat down as soon as we got home and wrote Agnew, telling him to go and see the mad boy and get him to see reason. If he can't—what are we to do? Sutherland will certainly be found guilty—he has been passing cheques again besides taking money paid him by the customers of the company and no mercy will be shown him.

Mary is dreadfully upset tonight—almost beside herself. I don't know what to do with her. One can console—encourage—help in bereavement or natural sorrow. But this is a bitter thing to suffer or deal with. And how are we to put in the time of suspense till Wednesday?

Tuesday, June 24, 1930
Thanks to Dr. Paul's dose Mary got a little sleep last night and consequently I did too, but I take such dreadful coughing spells about three o'clock that I can't sleep the rest of the night. I am not picking up as I should. Today I phoned Agnew and got a little bit of good news (comparatively speaking) that helped us over the rest of the day. Sutherland has come to his senses and will plead guilty. Agnew is *almost* sure Sutherland will be let off on suspended sentence. That "almost" keeps us on the rack. Suppose we can't get Sutherland off. Well, we will know by this time tomorrow.

Wednesday, June 25, 1930
Ewan, Mary and I motored into Toronto this morning, met Agnew and went to the court with him. It was all like a nightmare. Mary broke down and began to cry. When Sutherland was brought in and placed in the dock she gripped me hysterically. "Maud, is that *my baby* there, is that my baby *there?*" I held her in my arms and tried to soothe her and as I did an old memory suddenly unrolled itself before me. A dark chilly wet autumn evening in the November of 1893. Two girls in their teens sitting in the dim twilight in the "parlor" of an old house in Charlottetown. The night is dull. They must make some fun for themselves. They begin. They tell stories and make witty speeches about everything and everybody in their small

world. Each spark kindles another. They laugh so much and so long that the tears run down their smooth rosy cheeks. They have two hours of undiluted merriment. Then they go up to bed, feeling that it is certainly a jolly old world, full of fun and good-times.

And now they were sitting weeping in a court-room, while the beloved son of one of them stood in a criminal dock!

It seemed to take ages but in reality it was over soon. Agnew made some request of the Judge—the Judge shook his head and repulsed with his hand—Mary uttered a groan and whispered "he is refusing—he is refusing"—my heart turned sick—Agnew nodded encouragingly—Sutherland said "guilty" in a strangled voice—then the Judge was saying—what *was* he saying—"oh, Mary thank God—thank God—he is letting him off—letting him off on suspended sentence for a year—listen Mary darling—it's all right—he's clear."

Somebody—a gray-haired man—grabbed Mary by the hand and said, "Is that your boy? Tell him to live with God and he'll come out all right." Well-meant—excellent advice—but knowing what I know of poor Sutherland rather ridiculous. I wish I could believe that Sutherland has got a good scare that will make him go straight the rest of his life. But I have my painful doubts. He doesn't seem to have any real understanding of his position or its consequences.

There was some red tape to be gone through with in regard to the probation officer, and then we brought him home. He is going home with his mother on Friday. Mary is almost happy in her relief at getting him off. I wish I could think it would be her last anxiety.

We hoped it would not get into the papers. But there was a half a column in the *Star*, giving an account of "George Beaton's case," and the "gray-haired mother" who wept bitterly as he stood in the dock. The creature who wrote it actually had the audacity to phone Agnew and ask him if they couldn't have a photo of Mary to run with it!!! He didn't get it; and he missed something else, too. If he had known that the woman who was with Mary was "L.M. Montgomery" the case would have come out on the front page with headlines, probably adorned with *my* picture, as all the papers carry a cut of it. I was very nervous all the time I was in court lest I be recognized and that very thing happen. The scandal would be horrible and our congregation would buzz like a hive. Thanks be to a merciful fate no one knew me. The other papers merely had an obscure paragraph. I have written to the Ch'Town editors asking them as a personal favor to keep all reference to the case out of their papers. But it will likely leak out eventually. Someone in Toronto will see that *Star* stuff and write it home.

Sutherland is not at all grateful to us for all we have done. He keeps telling his mother he would have got off if he had had his trial in the fall. How he could expect to get off I don't know. His story is that the manager of the Co. *told* him to take what he needed out of his receipts and report it to them. The trouble is he *didn't* report it. And they both deny that they ever told him. He hasn't a scrap of evidence that they did.

I should enjoy spanking young Sutherland!

Anyhow, we've saved him from the pen *this* time. But my poor Mary will go in an anguish of dread the rest of her days.

Friday, June 27, 1930
This was the day Mary and Sutherland were to have left for home and I am afraid I rather looked forward to it, because, what with coughing all night and eating nothing all day I am not fit to have "company."

But Sutherland has shown his hand. I thought his meekness in regard to going home rather too good to be true. He has got his mother coaxed round to leaving him in Toronto and she must stay till he gets a job. How he will get a job with this hanging over him I don't know. But Mary, in spite of all that has been, is as wax in his hands. Besides, I think she dreads taking him home, where Roland will have no great use for him and positions are hard to get.

Sunday, June 29, 1930
The Manse, Norval
Really, I think Sutherland Beaton hasn't the sense he was born with. He has been known in Toronto as "George Beaton" and that is the name under which he was tried and which was published in the papers. So Mary and I both told him that he must drop the George in future and be known as Sutherland, so that strangers would not connect him with the "hero" of the criminal court. This morning at breakfast I happened to call him Sutherland. Whereupon Mr. Grier, the minister who had come to preach our anniversary services, asked smilingly, "Do you always get the full name?" Sutherland replied: "I am called that at home but in Toronto I've always been known as George." I held my breath. Suppose Grier had read that report of "George Beaton's" trial and remembered it because of the "sob" stuff in it. But evidently he had not and the terrific moment passed away.

If I were Sutherland Beaton I would want to get as far from Toronto as possible and never see it again. But he seems to have no shame and no realization of his position.

Friday, July 4, 1930
The Manse, Norval, Ont.
On Wednesday S. went to Toronto and landed a situation. Certainly he did it with an ease that surprised me. It is with the *Hayhoe Tea Co.* where a friend of his worked. He says they know all about his affair and told him he was lucky to get out of the hands of that bunch of crooks!

Is he lying?

Mary seems quite satisfied. If I were in her place I would go to Toronto and see for myself but I do not like to suggest to her that there is anything fishy about her son's story. The joke is that he is not to start work for three weeks, when their present salesman is leaving. So I had to say Sutherland must stay here until then. I do not exactly like the position especially with a boy like Sutherland. He has no sense. Last Monday night at our garden party he was squiring Elsie McClure all around, treating her at the booth etc.—with his poor mother's money. If Joe McClures' knew he was a thief, out on suspended sentence, they would never forgive me. I shall be in constant terror lest someone in the congregation stumble on the truth.

Mary left for home this morning. Chester and S. and I went to Toronto with her. She carries a heavy heart home with her, poor thing, though matters might be worse. I felt ashamed of being rather relieved to see her go; but I do feel so ghastly most of the time—too tired to talk or hold my head up. I have done my best for Mary in her trouble: she told Mrs. Mason there was no one in the world she loved as she loved me and that she could never have got through with this dreadful experience had it not been for me. But I am ill and it has taken a tremendous lot out of me. Yet tonight I am lonesome. I miss Mary and I feel blue and tired of everything. Life and the world all seem farcical.

Sat. July 5, 1930
Had a very bad night last night. The asthma returned, also a night sweat. I cannot write and that unfinished book haunts me. A letter from Myrtle contained the bad news that Ren Toombs has gone violently insane and is in the asylum. Poor Minnie. No trouble could be worse—except Mary's.

Monday, July 14, 1930
I am not improving. Every night almost I have an attack of asthma and coughing about three which lasts for two hours, leaving me exhausted and unable to sleep. No medicine seems to help. In the day time I am fairly well but tired all the time. Today Ewan and I came in to Toronto, had dinner at Cuth's and met Bertie. She is unchanged and looks well. It was delightful to see her again. She will be out next week. I *do* wish I felt better. It is too bad that when Bertie can come so seldom that I should be like this when she does come. I really almost dread her visit. I don't feel myself capable of putting forth the effort to make it pleasant. I'm too tired to enjoy anything.

Somebody told me lately that Stuart is the cleverest boy at St. Andrew's.

"Together again"
[Group at Cuth's: Maud, Ewan, Laura Aylsworth, Bertie McIntyre]

Friday, July 18, 1930
Oh, for one good night's sleep. My nerves are in a terrible condition.

I had a letter from Mary. She says Archie and Roland were very much displeased because she did not take S. home and she wants me to get him to go home yet. S. refuses to go. What am I to do?

S. has been putting in a pretty good time driving about every day and night with Chester or Murray Laird and chasing all kinds of girls. I shall be very thankful when Monday comes and he departs to his job. I have got a

"Should auld acquaintance be forgot"
[Chester, Bertie McIntyre, Ewan, Maud]

nice and inexpensive boarding house for him with a Mrs. Leslie, a friend of Mrs. Mason's—having warned the poor lady in confidence not to lend him any money. I've told him to come out and spend a week-end with us whenever he likes. And if I ever get well enough again I'm going to find out for myself just what sort of a job he has got and all about it. At present I'm not fit for anything. I'm not getting any better either.

Saturday, July 26, 1930
Last Monday C. and I took S. in. I told him to go straight in future and make up to his mother for all she had suffered. He was very glib but I do not trust him. We brought Bertie out and she has been here all the week. And I have enjoyed it and have felt better. I believe all I need is rest and pleasant companionship. My nights have not been good but both cough and choking spells are becoming slighter. We have driven about everywhere and had delightful conversations as of old. We took B. to Toronto today and had lunch with Laura. Bertie is going down to the Island. If I could only go with her! But I can't leave home when the boys are home and in any case I'm not fit to travel. Tonight I am blue and lonely, missing Bertie. My head feels so queer. I can't describe the sensation. It may be only nerves—or it may be a symptom of some more serious trouble. I wish I could get up enough courage to go and have myself thoroughly overhauled. But I am a coward—just now at any rate. I only want to lie down and sleep for a hundred years. I would not mind the prick of the fairy's spindle. But I have put it on record that the next time I dream of *bedbugs* I shall just go down to the Credit and jump in. It would be cleaner and pleasanter!

Monday, July 28, 1930
The Manse, Norval
Saturday night I had a miserable night, coughing and choking but last night I had a good sleep. We are enduring a "hot wave" and today was the hottest yet. Perhaps because it was election day. I voted for the Liberal Gov't. and so did E. but we were not very sure if we were doing wisely. Sometimes it seems to me the Conservative policy would be best for Canada. So when we went to the Glen House and it became speedily evident that the Conservatives were going in with a big majority we did not worry over it. I sometimes wish I could pump up some of the enthusiasm I used to feel over elections. It was good sport.

Tuesday, July 29, 1930
I had a fair sleep last night, disturbed by a little asthma towards morning. I haven't felt very well all day. Ewan left for his vacation in Muskoka. I wrote in the morning and made raspberry jelly in the afternoon. But I seem to have a dreadful cold in the head tonight again.

Thursday, July 31, 1930
I really am discouraged. I had a poor night Tuesday night and was miserable all day. Then last night I had another dreadful night—not quite as bad as the one in June but almost. This afternoon I had to send for Dr. Paul. He gave me a hypodermic which soon relieved me. He says it is the asthmatic type of hay fever I have. I am not sure if he knows anything about it. I haven't much confidence in him.

We are having a bad drought, aggravated by the extremely hot weather. There has been no rain since the first of July, and my garden is dying, after all my hard work and its early promise. I dare not take any water from the well for it, because the well is going dry. We have to get our drinking water from a neighbor's and save what is in the well for the toilet. We had such a dreadful time last year. I hope things don't get as bad as that again.

I had a fine sleep last night and have felt real well all day. Which was fortunate because a very nerve-racking thing happened this afternoon. "Buster" Black, a young imp of evil who has been vacationing with his grandmother in Norval and two small Bignall girls came up here and went down into the vacant lot and deliberately started a fire! When it began to spread wildly the three young devils got alarmed and ran away. By good fortune another boy saw it and ran in to tell us. I was lying down but got up and rushed out. At my first sight of the lot I thought everything was lost. The lot seemed to be all ablaze as the fire swept through the dead and crisp grass. On one side it had almost reached the church sheds. On the other it was almost across to the MacPherson barn. And there was no water in the well, nor could I have carried it if there had been. I ran back to the house, called to Mrs. Mason to get help and seized a broom. This was not as vain a weapon as it sounds. By the time two men had arrived with buckets I had the fire beaten out on the shed side. They got water from MacPhersons' well and soon had it out on the other side. But in ten or even five more minutes the fire would have reached the church sheds which after this dry hot spell would have caught and burned like tinder. Our garage would have gone—likely the church and manse—not improbably the whole village. I have no strength or nerve for shocks like these and tonight I feel demoralized. I would like to turn young Buster over my knee and give him a good dose of the old reliable.

Thursday, Aug. 7, 1930
....A letter from Myrtle came today, saying that Ern Macneill's wife had a son. So perhaps the old place may remain in the Macneill name yet. I hope so anyway.

Friday, Aug. 8, 1930
Very hot. Head felt queer all day. Finished autographing the advertising cards Mr. McClelland sent me to do in May. There must have been over a thousand of them. Two letters today upset me. One was from Jean Leslie to Mrs. Mason containing what is to me a mysterious statement about Sutherland. He has "landed a new job"—"selling barber's supplies"—and Jean thinks he is "lucky to get it since it is so hard just now to get anything to do."

What does this mean? Something with the savour of bed-bugs I swear. I suppose I'll have to investigate for Mary's sake.

A letter from Ella says Jim is going to go in the bank at Kensington this fall. So farewell, Park Corner. I will write no more lest I write too much. It is too bitter to think of!

Monday, August 11, 1930
A welcome wave of coolness has come—but no rain. This morning C. & I took Stuart up to spend a week with the Mills who are living near Port Perry now. On our way through Toronto we saw the big R-100 afloat in the sky of morning like a huge silver fish.

I think I am really improving. I am sleeping and eating better.

Monday, Aug. 18, 1930
Haven't been any too well. Most nights I have an attack of asthma around 3, and cannot sleep even when it is over. Last night, however, I had a lovely sleep and it has made a big difference in my feelings and outlook. I have been very busy, too busy. Am trying desperately to catch up with my new book. I can't feel that it will be any good. Isobel...continues to pester me with love letters.

Today I was in Toronto and hunted up the Hayhoe Tea Co. The manager told me they had no such person as Sutherland or George Beaton in their employ and had never heard of such a person!

It was only what I had expected to hear. Yet this proof that Sutherland had told his mother and me such a string of utter lies sickened me. And what on earth am I to do? Write it to Mary? She will worry herself sick. Besides, he has a job now though heaven knows what kind of a one. I must get in touch with Jean Leslie and find out. There is no use asking Sutherland anything. He would not tell the truth.

I weigh only 131 lbs. Haven't been so thin for ten years.

Had another ghastly "love letter" from Isobel...today.

Saturday, Aug. 23, 1930

Wednesday Chester and I and the Barracloughs motored up to Midland and spent a couple of days with Ewan. We had a nice trip and a delightful motor boat excursion around the Georgian Bay. Not such a bad-looking lot of people!

"*Himself and Meself*"
[Ewan and Maud]

"*Chester and Eva Winfield*"

Thursday afternoon C. brought me to Toronto and I stayed all night with Nora and talked galore. Spent the day with Bertie, who was just back from the Island and was leaving next day for Vancouver. I came home today, feeling very blue. Will Bertie and I ever meet again?

I am finally committed to a visit to Prince Albert in October. I can't work up any enthusiasm over it. It is too long since I left it—thirty-nine years. Nothing there for me now, not even ghosts. Besides, I hate leaving home. If I were going east to my dear Island I would rejoice but the west is a stranger to me now. However, I daresay once I'm really off I'll enjoy it. It's the bother of getting ready that tires me. This summer has been like a nightmare.

"*Mr. B. and Mr. M.*"
[Ernest Barraclough and Ewan]

"*Mrs. Barraclough*"

Saturday, Aug. 30, 1930
Norval, Ont.

Recently I have been sleeping and feeling better but last night I had asthma all night. However, I have discovered what is causing these attacks. Nothing more or less than eating tomatoes! I suspected this when I had that dreadful night in Midland after a supper at which I had eaten tomatoes. I never ate them again until yesterday and had no trouble but did not really believe the tomatoes or their absence had anything to do with it. Yesterday afternoon at Eldred Macdonald's wedding in Union there was a piece of tomato on my plate about as big as a half dollar. I was feeling quite devilish and daring so I ate it defiantly. And last night was the result!

The joke is I've only grown fond of tomatoes in recent years. Before that I detested them. But Ewan was very fond of them—I was constantly meeting them in salads and sandwiches—and presently I found myself liking them. And now, having acquired a taste for 'em I must relinquish them. Really, this is a damn contrary world.

Tonight Chester and I went to Georgetown to see the movie *Journey's End*. I think it was foolish of me to go to such a play in the present state of my nerves for it was such a racking poignant thing that at some points I could hardly bear it and sat with set teeth and clenched hands. But it is a wonderful picture.

Recently I re-read, during a night when I could not sleep, Marie Corelli's *Sorrows of Satan*. What a commotion that book made when it came out over thirty years ago. And now I suppose nobody under thirty has ever heard of it. It was about as wild and absurd as any book could be—but Marie could tell a story. After all, I prefer the Satanic sorrows to the modern sex putridity. At least, one doesn't have to hold one's nose, in spite of the fair "Sybil's" awful awfulness and her naughty love for that indifferent devil.

Tuesday, Sept. 2, 1930

Sunday night I had a good good sleep and felt fine yesterday—which was fortunate in view of what happened. In the morning I finished my new book, except for revising and polishing and drew a breath of relief for this summer has been the hardest one I've ever known as far as finding time for literary work goes.

Then I helped Mrs. Mason get supper for two friends who were coming out from Toronto. Ewan was away and we planned a dainty table for the four of us. We had just sat down to it when the deluge came. A ring of the bell—I went to the door. There on the veranda, big, blowsy, red-faced was Bess Walker—the Bess Cook of old days. And with the said Bess were her husband, her daughter, two of her friends and their daughter—six in all. I had to ask them to have supper, never dreaming that they would stay. But they did. They had called just for that I firmly believe. Such a time as Mrs. Mason and I had, enlarging the table, hunting out more dishes and food, getting them all placed. I would not have minded if they had been friends of mine but it riled us a bit to have my friends' visit spoiled by a gang like that. The house seemed like a nightmare until they got away.

I have been re-reading of late all Laura's old letters in an effort to make her seem, after all these years, a real creature again. But they baffled me. They were the letters of a Laura I once knew—but she can't exist now. And those old days are so dream-like that I cannot realize they ever were real. I feel that I am going to visit a phantom.

Thursday, Sept. 11, 1930
The Manse, Norval
Last night Chester and Murray Laird left in the latter's car for a trip to P.E. Island. I shall not, of course, know a really peaceful moment until they return. There are so many things that *might* happen. Every paper I pick up somebody has been killed.

One must just fall back on predestination. There are times when it is a most comforting doctrine.

I am really improving and for the first time since mid-June am beginning to feel like myself. I am sleeping better and the mental depression I have suffered from so continually is leaving me. If I could get a real rest I think I would soon be well again. But Mrs. Mason is away on her other vacation week and I have had so much company. I have never had such a summer for "company" in my whole life. We have simply never been free from it for more than a day at a time. And, with but two or three exceptions, it was people who mean nothing whatever to me. I find that living so near Toronto has its drawbacks as well as its advantages. It is too easy for folks to get here.

September 30, 1930
Tuesday. Somewhere in the woods of Northern Ontario.
I have actually—once again—started for the west—something I really did not believe up to last night that I would do.

Yesterday I had planned to pack up and hoped to get a little rest. Rest! It is not in my vocabulary at all.

Sunday night John Stirling phoned from Toronto that he had been up to the General Council of the United Church and would like to see us before going back. Of course we wanted to see him, too, so cheerfully invited him out. But it *was* the worst possible time he could have picked. However, I contrived, by getting up early Monday morning, to get packed up before he came and we had a pleasant visit with him. In the evening Ewan took us all into Toronto—John to go to P.E.I., I to leave for the west and Chester to board at Knox College.

Chester and Murray got home safely last Sunday. Chester was vaccinated during the week and it is just "taking." He was quite miserable yesterday and I hated to leave him alone at Knox. Likely he will be all right in a few days—but suppose he shouldn't.

My train left at ten o'clock. Ewan said good-bye and left me. I sat down and recalled the last time I left for the west—forty years ago. That rainy morning— driving from Park Corner to Kensington with Grandfather Montgomery— young—excited—hopeful—never on a train in my life before—Sir John and Lady Macdonald in their special—the odd sensation as the train started that the *station platform* and the people on it were moving away from us—all life before me—father at the end of the journey. While I recalled it all my train started. I was again en route for the west.

I had a poor night as usual. I never sleep well my first night on a train and in addition it was most frightfully rough. Today has been the most tedious I ever spent while travelling. From dawn to dark we have journeyed through scrub woods—nothing but endless leagues of young spruces and birch, bare and autumnal. I was disappointed for I remembered the scenic beauty of the old C.P.R. route. The C.N.R. has nothing like that to offer.

I passed the day reading a bundle of "John O' Londons" Mr. MacMillan had sent me and working out the cross word puzzles in them. I adore cross word puzzles and only wish I had the time for them. At home I never have time. So I had a real devilish orgy today. And in addition I found a thing of beauty in a verse of Poe's I never remember having seen before. It was so exquisite it hurt me. And yet I can't explain why it was so exquisite. It was one of those verses which seem to hold for me some secret mysterious magic, quite apart from the ideas expressed.

> Now all my days are trances
> and all my nights are dreams
> Of where thy dark eye glances
> And where thy footstep gleams,
> In what ethereal dances
> By what eternal streams.

The magic is in the last two lines. I have repeated them over and over again and every time the thrill of spiritual ecstasy they gave me was so acute as to be almost pain. Why—*why*? Did *I* once share in some "ethereal dance" by "some eternal stream" and is it a pang of divine homesickness that rends my soul? At all events this couplet has rainbowed the day for me and will sing to me forever.

Wednesday Night, Oct. 1, 1930
Last night I had another poor night—because I was cold. There are few things more miserable than to be cold in a railway berth. I detest spending a night on a train anyhow.

This morning we travelled through the Manitoban prairies. They are considerably changed from older days. We reached Winnipeg and I had to spend the day there. So I phoned Harry McIntyre who is manager of a bank in Winnipeg and after office hours he came for me in his car and took me for a delightful drive around Winnipeg. I must of course revise all my old impressions of it. The greatest change I saw was in its trees. There are beautiful trees everywhere—beautiful parks—beautiful homes.

Tomorrow I shall be in Saskatoon—tomorrow I shall see Laura. I write that but I do not believe it. I shall see *some* Laura—but not the Laura I parted from at the Prince Albert station that sunny morning so long ago. Where is *she*? With the Maud who left on the train perhaps. But I shall not find her at Saskatoon.

I am afraid—shall I find some stranger—some woman I do not know—I was foolish to come—I should have kept the old memory unspoiled!

Thursday, Oct. 2, 1930
Saskatoon, Sask.
Why was I afraid?

This morning was foggy and we travelled through a very uninteresting part of Saskatchewan. But as noon approached the fog lifted and the sun came out brilliantly. As we pulled away from Watrous a porter went through the car proclaiming sonorously, "Time goes back an hour." It did—for me it went back forty years.

We reached Saskatoon at noon. I picked up my box and went out. As I stepped from the train I looked about a little bewilderedly at the crowd of people. The next moment a young man seized me—his face was vaguely familiar—the next moment I was in Laura's arms. Yes, *Laura's*—no stranger but Laura.

I suppose we made dreadful fools of ourselves. We were really quite mad—But

> There is a pleasure sure in being mad
> Which none but madmen know.

We would embrace and kiss—draw back and look at each other—embrace again. I don't really know how long we kept this up. Time had ceased to have any meaning for us. I have never in all my life felt so extraordinary and overwhelming an emotion as I felt then. And Laura says she had the same experience. We laughed—we cried—I would not exchange those moments for the Koh-i-noor. I knew then that love was immortal.

Patient Willard—Laura's oldest son who is principal of a Saskatoon Collegiate—finally disentangled us and got us into his car. Laura and I sat in the back seat and gazed at each other. "Maudie, is it *you*?" said Laura. "Laura, is it *you*?" said I.

It was, just the same dear Laura I loved years ago. Not outwardly. Laura is greatly—almost terribly changed. She looks far older than even a woman of 56 should. Her hair is almost white—her face lined and wrinkled. Her life for the last twelve years has been very hard and full of worries. I do not think I would have known her if I had met her unexpectedly. But under all the outward change the old real Laura was there and came out again in expression as soon as the bedazzlement of change wore off. On this page are two pictures, one of Laura and me standing together at her door—very poor ones, too—and one of us standing together, picnic-bound before the manse in Prince Albert thirty-nine years ago.

Only one thing I cannot get used to—the fact that Laura is so much shorter than myself. I did not think I grew after I was sixteen—but I must have. I have no remembrance of being taller than Laura in P.A. In fact I am sure I was not. So I must have grown.

Our brief insanity passed but we have been revelling in each other all day and in this amazing re-birth of our old friendship. Willard took us for a drive around Saskatoon in the late afternoon. The air was full of colors and Saskatoon—which was a station house, a post office and about four houses when I last passed through it—is a rather amazing place. We looked at all the "sights" but really *saw* little but each other. It seemed impossible to catch up with 39 years talk in two hours but we accomplished it after a fashion, leaping from year to year with incredible agility. In her cosy home we *talked*.

"Autumn 1930" [Maud and Laura]

"Spring 1891" [Maud, Laura, and Alexena]

Andrew Agnew has changed very little. He is a good fellow, a kind husband and father, but I have never felt acquainted with him. I never did that P.A. year when I saw so much of him. He remains a stranger. But he and Laura are very happy together in spite of their financial troubles, and the fact that their home is overrun with the mob of university boys poor Laura has to board to make both ends meet.

Laura's oldest daughter Christine, and her two younger sons are at the coast. Eleanor, her youngest daughter, a girl of about fifteen, is home. A very sweet and charming girl. Not, to my disappointment, one particle like Laura. She "takes

"210 Clarence Ave. Saskatoon"

after" the Agnews, with glossy black hair, dark eyes and oval olive face. A genius with the violin.

But I can't get used to Laura being the mother of a grown-up family. It knocks me out every time.

Willard looks like his mother and quite a bit like Will P. He is a dear boy, old for his years because of the war. Thirty-three years ago I was starting for Charlottetown one May day with old Mr. Crewe and as I went I read a note from a friend of Laura's in P.A. telling me that the baby had come safely and all was well. It doesn't seem very long ago. Yet what a changed world.

Tonight Laura and I sat together on the sofa and *talked*—as we talked years ago in our walks through faint blue twilights in the lost years of this sad lovely world. It is not quite possible that it is only about eleven hours since we met. It rather seems that we have never been separated. I find still that, as I wrote in this old journal years ago, "I can tell Laura anything—the thoughts of my inmost soul." Very few have I found of whom I could ever say that. Emerson's definition of a friend as "one before whom we can think aloud" is a counsel of perfection more or less. I have many dear friends before whom I could never think aloud. But it applies to Laura. I could think aloud before her with no difficulty or self-consciousness. And the chords of our natures are still perfectly attuned.

Our friendship was no gradual growth, as others have been. I was rather prejudiced against Laura before I met her. Annie McTaggart and my stepmother both seemed to hate her and were constantly saying nasty things of her. As I did not like either of them I took their remarks with a very large pinch of salt—nevertheless it left some impression. I did not feel conscious of any wish to meet Laura Pritchard. And then one night, around the first of December we met—and from our very first handclasp loved each other. There was never any question of it—never any doubt. Each soul recognized its own. And tonight as we sat together hand in hand before her open fire we realized what we had lost out of life in all these years because we had been separated.

Well, the gods do not like perfect things. I have found that out.

Friday, October 3rd, 1930
Saskatoon
Last night I found out again what a good friend a bed is.

Laura and I *talked* all the forenoon. I notice two things in Laura that were not of her in the old days. One is her faculty of mimicry. I suppose she always have possessed it but I never knew her to exercise it. She is a "scream." When she begins to imitate the peculiar and unforgotten dialect of "the breeds" I writhe helplessly with laughter.

And Laura is something of a religious devotee. There *were* traces of that of old I remember. She has a firm conviction that "the Second Coming" is very near, even at the doors. But said conviction does not prevent her from shrieking with laughter over a good story, even one with a slightly *risqué* flavour, nor does it prevent her from worrying a bit over some of the matrimonial designs of her boys. I have learned the kind of remark that sets her off on her pet theory and I shall avoid making it. And we have too many things to talk of to waste time on any second coming but our own. Dear Laura—she is so dear and sweet and lovable that nobody minds her theological vagaries. She is a wonderful mother. Her children arise up and call her blessed. I shall not hurt her dear heart by letting her suspect that I do not believe in the second coming or a literal garden of Eden. It would grieve her dreadfully. And no one could endure grieving Laura.

This afternoon I spoke to the Women's Canadian Club here and had a nice time. But the real fun of the day came this evening when Laura and I and a friend of hers, Mrs. Fraser, foregathered in her kitchen and from eight to one o'clock made sandwiches and told stories. I haven't laughed so much since the night at Bob McKenzie's last fall. The gem of our collection was undoubtedly the yarn Laura told of an old character in the early days at Kildonan, Manitoba—where her mother and father were "raised"—named "Skilly" MacLeod. The said Skilly was noted for his "Spoonerisms" and tales were always being told of him in this regard. One stormy spring night a flood swept away a mill dam pertaining to his brother Angus. The next morning the bishop happened to call and found old Skilly rushing around in wild excitement. "Oh Good Lord, my morning, Good Lord, my morning. Ye'll excuse our being all upset here. My dam brother Angus burst in the night."

This is priceless. I must work it into some book to preserve it. I capped it with one about old Dicky Pillman of French River but the only chance this story has for immortality is in my journal for it would not "do" anywhere else. Old Dicky was talking to Uncle John Campbell one day about a recent robbery and remarked indignantly that it was no wonder there were robberies when "the weemen" were getting so careless. "Why," said old Dicky, "I came home the other night and the door was in bed and Veny was wide-open!!"

Monday, Oct. 6, 1930
210 Clarence Ave., Saskatoon
Saturday we were all busy getting ready for Laura's reception. I wore my new "long" dress—for long dresses are "in" again—at least for parties. It feels exceedingly funny to have a skirt trailing about my feet again and having to lift it in front when I mount the stairs. But I like it—in spite of everything I like it. Because it deludes me into feeling as if time had really turned back. When Laura and I were last together long skirts were worn—anything else for a girl out of childhood would have been thought indecent!

I hardly think long dresses will remain "in" long. Yet there is no knowing what vagaries fashion will take.

Saturday was a beautiful day. As I was out in the morning taking some snaps of the house Willard glanced up and said, "The air mail is two hours late." There was the plane—soaring through the blue sky. I realized then that, in spite of long skirts, many a year had passed since I sojourned in the "great lone land." There is no "great lone land" now.

A strange little incident happened Saturday morning. Someone, I know not who and could not discover, phoned Laura to ask her "if Miss Campbell were with Mrs. Macdonald." It must have been someone who had known Frede in that year at Red Deer and had never heard of her marriage—or her death. The thing gave me a curious sick turn. Alas, no, "Miss Campbell" was not with me. Where she lingers—

In what ethereal dances
By what eternal streams

I know not, but the banks of the Saskatchewan know her not nor ever shall.

The reception was like hundreds of others. A very successful function. I was bored to death—and beginning to be annoyed by a nasty little cough. Moreover, I resented the waste of time during which Laura and I could have been alone together. But some things are not done. Laura's friends would never have forgiven her if she had not given them the opportunity and I could not put her in such a position. So I smiled gallantly but was very glad when all was over and Laura and I were sitting together on a sofa before her dreaming fire—just talking.

Sunday morning I found myself with a bad cold. I went to church with Laura but felt so miserable I was glad when we got home. I went to bed—at four had to have a doctor to give a hypodermic for asthma! Is this to be my lot henceforth whenever I catch a cold?

This morning I was better but spent the day in bed. In one way it was a gain because it furnished an excellent excuse to refuse invitations to several functions. And Laura sat by me all her spare time—and we *talked*!

And this morning I had a letter from—Edith Skelton!

The way the past has been giving up its dead of late years is almost uncanny. Edie and I corresponded for a few years after I left P.A. Then our letters ceased. I never could get in touch with her again although I heard she had married. She is now living in Adanac, Saskatchewan, and when I go to Battleford I shall try to get to see her. She married a Mr. Wheatland and has a grown-up family. I should like to see Edie. She was a sweet girl and we had no end of fun together in our brief association.

Tuesday, Oct. 7, 1930
I got up today and feel all right except that I have a bad cough. Laura and I had a good day together and planned to have a walk together tonight. We have not been able to have one yet, and we are leaving for P.A. tomorrow night. But our plans miscarried. George Gunn suddenly appeared!

This *is* positively uncanny. Thirty-nine years ago George Gunn was in P.A. a young divinity student, and dancing attendance on Laura. She had no use for him, of course, but he never quite saw that. We used to make fearful fun of him. I have never seen him since. Laura hadn't seen him for over thirty-five years. And tonight he bobs up and "we three meet again."

Of course, these things are foreordained. They couldn't happen otherwise.

He has just come to Saskatoon to take charge of a church. He is still a bachelor. A clever, quite fine-looking man with a kink somewhere in his make-up—perhaps because of his Indian blood. One of his grandmothers was a Squaw. He spoiled our last evening together but I forgave him for the fun I got out of his and Laura's heated discussion over the Second Coming. George pooh-poohed it. And when Laura cornered him rather neatly with a New Testament prophecy he responded airily that that was merely "a frill of the Evangelist." Laura nearly died of horror on the spot.

Friday, Oct. 10, 1930
Prince Albert, Saskatchewan

Once again, with curiously mingled emotions, I write those words at the top of an entry in my journal. And amid those emotions something that I can call by no other name than "homesickness" predominates. I never was homesick for Prince Albert before. But ever since my arrival here and in spite of the jolly time I've been having I have felt in the deeps of my soul a curious nostalgia for the old Prince Albert which—as I have long known but only now realize—has long since vanished from the face of the earth.

Wednesday was a nice day until evening. After dinner Laura and I cut loose from all responsibility and proceeded to "do" Saskatoon. We walked all over it, scorning street cars, and poked into all the stores. Then we had our suppers at a down-town restaurant. And while walking and poking and eating we *talked*. We took the train from Saskatoon to P.A. at about seven. I was sorry it was too dark to see the country. But Laura and I *talked*. We reached P.A. about nine in a pouring rain. The station is not where it was when I was here before. It is further east, just across what used to be called "Church St." and which is now Central Avenue. Alexena and Fred met us. I got out and I looked around me. I could see nothing familiar. The old Church St. with its scant sprinkling of houses and its many vacant lots was now a long, solid, brilliant street of stores and business places. We got into Fred's car and he drove us down to the end of the street by the river. The corner where father's house was is occupied by a chain drug store! Not one old landmark could I see.

Then we turned about and drove "up the hill." There is a fine new court house where the old one used to be and a war monument in front of it. Fred drove up to it to show it to me—and got into some P.A. mud which has not lost its "gluey-ness" in all the years. He couldn't get it out and had to go off and phone for assistance. Very much annoyed was Fred but I was secretly glad. I sat there and saw ghosts. Just beyond and behind the court house was "the old McTaggart house." One old landmark at least that was unchanged. Its windows were lighted up, especially the big "bay" in the east corner, just as I had seen it lighted one similar rainy night nearly forty years ago. It was a Sunday night. Father and his wife were away and were prevented from returning home by a thunderstorm in the early evening. Annie McTaggart was down with me—probably as a spy for Mrs. M. since I had no wish for her company. Will P. was there having tied his nag at our front gate. I was going up the hill for the night. When we went out Will's horse was gone! Only the bridle was left. We walked up the hill through the mud. There were no paved roads or cement sidewalks on Church St. then. And no electric lights. As we went up the hill the McTaggart house—it was the *new* McTaggart house then—was all alight just as I saw it Wednesday night. Will said good-night and left on the trail that led out to Laurel Hill farm. I went in and found George Baker and Min Wheeler sweethearting in the parlor. Tried to joke then but was silenced by George's retort concerning Will P.

Alexena and Fred Wright's house

Now, Will is dead and Min is dead—and George has another wife—Fred came back with a garage man and I came back from my eerie flight through time.

The whole hill is built up now. Alexena's home is a very charming one, built on the hill a good bit west of the court house where we used to pick hazel nuts long ago. It is a very delightful home. Fred is wealthy and they have every luxury and convenience.

Time does queer things. Laura and Alexena were married within about two years of each other. At that time Laura was supposed to be making by far the best match from a financial point of view. He had a good position in his brother's store and a fair salary. Fred was a clerk in a jewelry store and hadn't a penny. And today Andrew is a clerk in another man's store in Saskatoon and poor Laura has to keep boarders to eke out. And Fred is a wealthy man with one of the finest jewelry stores in the west, a luxurious home and oodles of money.

But—they have only one son and he is stone deaf! His deafness began to come on gradually when he was nine and in a few years was absolute. Everything has been done. They have spent a fortune on him and to no effect. That is their heart-break and it is a bitter one!

Alexena is also greatly changed—but in a way for the better. When she was a girl she was rather sallow, with jet black hair and

"Alexena and Fred Wright"

River Street, Prince Albert, Sask.

large brown eyes. Now, although she is only three years older than me, her hair is white as snow but she is a strikingly handsome woman. Tall, imposing, beautifully dressed, with her brilliant brown eyes under her snowy hair.

I saw a good deal of Alexena that year in P.A. and we were very good friends, although I did not say much about her in my journal of that time. Our friendship was not the deeply passionate attachment which bound Laura and me together, but it was a very pleasant affair as girl friendships go and we have never lost touch with each other. It is good to see jolly, warm-hearted Alexena again.

I had never met her husband before. He had come to P.A. after I left. I am greatly taken with him and felt as if I had known him all my life—far better than I know Andrew Agnew. He is kind, hospitable, jolly and fine looking. He and Alexena are very happy together. It's nice to realize that there are a few decent marriages in the world in spite of everything.

Thursday morning Alexena took us for a drive and we made whoopee—enjoyed everything—and *talked*. We drove over the river first. River St. is the only one left in P.A. that seems at all natural to me. The old low buildings of 1890 are replaced by bigger and more up-to-date ones but the general effect is the same. On the river side, where once nothing but the tassels of prairie grass grew there are trees and seats. The general effect of the view up and down the river is the same as of old, save for the bridge that spans it now.

The Saskatchewan seems to me to have *shrunk*. It hasn't, of course—its banks are just where they always were. But I seem to remember it as twice as wide. I must have got its old memory overlaid with later impressions of the St. Lawrence. The water in it is very low just now which of course helps to make it *look* narrower. But even so, it is no longer the lordly river of my recollection. On the further side where in my day was naught but a great forest, with one solitary trail winding from the river far into the wilderness, are now houses, roads and railway tracks. *Then* one could not look on the river without seeing "dug outs" crossing here and there, full of Indians and squaws and the streets were full of them. I have not seen an Indian since I came to P.A. And I miss them!!

When we came back from across the river we drove out to the golf links and through streets where I used to pick strawberries on the "flats." The "bluffs" are almost bare now, although here and there one gleams out jewel-like in the same pale perfect poplar gold I remember so vividly of that autumn in P.A.

We came home in time for dinner. A right merry meal in Alexena's beautiful dining room, under the brilliant lights. Alexena's table traditions are of the race of Joseph. No starvation rations here!

Then we went to the Empress Hotel where I was to speak to the Canadian Club after dinner. There was no "Empress" hotel in my time. Nothing then but the old "Queens" which was kept by the Obans, who had Indian blood in their veins and kept a rather dreadful hostelry from the point of view of cleanliness and cuisine.

In all the gathering there was only one person I knew—Mrs. George Will who was "Benie" MacGregor, Alexena's sister. But her husband who came to P.A. just after I left it and knew father well, came up and said, "Hugh J. Montgomery will never be dead as long as you're alive."

Ah, but he *is* dead. And I thought as I stood there and spoke to that audience, how proud he would have been if he had been there to see—as he might quite credibly have been since he would have been no more than 89 if he were alive today. How his blue eyes would have shone to see his "little Maudie" thus honored.

And I recalled the last time I had stood before a P.A. audience—at a March concert in the old Presbyterian church. A young girl of fifteen with her life before her and her dreams still in the dreaming.

I often wonder what my life would have been if father's second wife had been a lovable woman. I liked P.A. tremendously after my first homesickness wore off. I enjoyed every minute of my life there that was not lived under Mrs. Montgomery's eye. The "lure of the west" was strong for me. Had I liked her and she me I would probably have stayed there—lived my life there. And whatever it would have been, one thing is certain—it would have been an entirely different one. I suppose I would have written books—I had to do that—but they would not be the books I have written. I might have married—but the men who came and went through my years would not have been the same men. *If—if—if!* It was not to be.

One of the speakers at the banquet told a funny tale. Before my arrival the P.A. paper informed the public that "Mrs. Ewan Macdonald, better known to some of our readers as Miss *Lucy* Montgomery, is to be the guest of Mrs. Wright etc. etc." An old timer who knew father wandered into the speaker's store the next day and remarked, "I see that there Miss *Lucky* Montgomery is coming to town."

I wonder about the "Lucky."

We came home and went to bed. Laura and I slept in a cosy upstairs room. It was the first time we had slept together since that night in old "Southview" shortly before I left for the island. The processional years rolled back. We were girls again—laughing—telling stories—wondering—no, no, no, *not* wondering about the future. We *knew* all that now, for good or ill. We talked only of the *past*—so we were not really girls.

But we almost forgot we weren't.

This morning we again drove over the river to visit the new Provincial Sanatorium which is built in the pinewoods, just about opposite the spot which used to be called Goschen—and just about on the spot where the old Indian encampment used to be and where Laura and I picked—or tried to pick blueberries—one memorable day long syne. But those forests have changed. The huge pines have gone—burned down in the fires that swept the country many years ago. And all the country now is covered with a secondary growth of young pines. It must be quite lovely there in summer. The Sanatorium is a wonderful place and we had luncheon with the superintendent, Miss Montgomery, who is no connection of mine.

We drove all the afternoon and finally wound up by going to afternoon tea in one of the houses on the hill. It was one of the old haunted autumn twilights of Prince Albert I remember so well and so lovingly—a twilight now starred with the electric lights, and far beyond the hill we saw other hills and bluffs growing purple with night.

I thought of Will—he and I used to prowl about together in those old winter dusks. He has seemed so near me—and so *alive*—ever since I have come back. I feel as if I would meet him around any corner, with his crooked smile and his twinkling hazel eyes. Only somehow—I never do—he has always just passed.

This feeling was intensified by what happened tonight. It was after another of Alexena's delicious dinners. We were sitting around the fireplace in the living room, talking of old times and somebody recalled a certain Bible Class picnic. "I have the picture of it," said Alexena. And she went up to the den and brought it down.

I have hung over that picture for an hour. It fascinates me indescribably. I remember that picnic so well. We had all met at the front door of the manse that fine summer morning and a photographer came up and photographed us. Laura

Picnic party, 1891

and I were standing together. I *did* so want one of those pictures. I timidly asked father if I could get one—timidly, because I knew poor father was terribly hard up for money that summer and Mrs. M. had just been having several expensive photographs of Kate and Bruce taken. Father said rather shortly, "That will be another fifty cents" and I dropped the matter instantly.

And now, nearly forty years afterwards, I saw the picture again. I suppose if I had had a copy and had looked at it occasionally during all these years, it would not now have such an effect on me. But it had a tremendous effect. I felt as if I were looking, not at a picture but *through* it into an actual scene—as if, could I but step through it, I would find myself back in my lost youth—back in the old Prince Albert—back among my old friends. There they all were. *There* was the Laura I had loved, the slim schoolgirl with her unlined face—there was *Will* sitting in one of the trams full of life and hope. And all as fresh and unfaded as if taken yesterday. Yet some of those people were dead and all of us were old.

The dresses! We thought we were dressed in the very tip top of the fashion that morning. Long skirts—the beginnings of puffed sleeves—ribbon trimmed hats on the top of our heads. Laura had on a pair of lace mitts and was very conscious of them. And we all had waists where waists should be and were all young and happy and sure of ourselves. If anyone had appeared before us dressed in the fashions of today we would have screamed with laughter at her. The poor creature—a hat like an old bonnet without strings pulled down round her face—no waist *at all*—no *hips*—and showing her legs, the hussy. From what asylum had she escaped?

The men look quite up-to-date. Male garments have really changed little. Mr. McTaggart had a beard and one or two of the younger men had heavy moustaches. But they would none of them have looked much out of place in a photograph of today.

Alexena says I may take the photo home and have a copy made from it. It seems odd to find a wish granted after forty years. If father had known how much I wanted that picture I know he would have bought one for me. But it meant so little to him and he did not understand how much it meant to me. And I am to have one after all.

Will *all* our wishes be fulfilled sometime—somewhere?

Suppose—for a silly fancy—I *could jump into* that picture—and be fifteen again with life before me! *Would I*?

No, a thousand times no! If I had to live my life over again just as it has been. Nothing could induce me to do *that*. But if I knew it would be different—even though I knew it might be hard enough in its way—well, I think I'd take a chance on it! I would not face the same old tribulations but I might do with a new tribulation. And life *is* an interesting thing, no matter what happens in it.

Well, one can think and guess as one likes. The fact remains that I can't jump back into the past.

Saturday, Oct. 11, 1930
Prince Albert, Sask.
Alexena "received" today and most of the P.A. women came. It was the usual boredom for me but it was a successful function of its kind and Laura had a

delightful time because it was a visit home for her. She knew most of the people so well.

We had a drive around town this morning and I found a couple of old landmarks. Miss Baker's house! It was just a couple of doors from us. Lucy Baker, a missionary to the Indians, lived there alone—a quaint little old lady who liked the society of the young. Many an evening long ago I used to have supper with her. She always had the most delicious chocolate cake. I was very fond of her. Her house was a snug little clapboarded and white painted place. It is still there but so pitifully shabby and outlived. Looking so much smaller by reason of the big buildings around it. Forlorn—forsaken. It hurt me to see it. And the old manse! It has come down in the world terribly too. Half of it has been torn down. The other half is used as a garage. The old church is gone of course; and not only that but the "new" church, the corner stone of which I saw laid and which was about half-built when I left P.A., is the "old" church now and is also a garage.

It seemed strange to see those two ghostly old houses—strange and sad. It hurt me to see them.

I heard two funny things at today's party. One lady, whose husband is a school-teacher, told me her husband told her to be sure to tell me that one time in a school examination paper in English history he asked the students to name the wives of Henry the Eighth. One boy included *Anne of Green Gables* in his list!!!

The other was curious. In *Magic for Marigold* the scene is laid in Harmony and the clan of which she is a member are "the proud Leslies." Of course I meant "the proud Macneills" in so far as I meant anybody. As for Harmony I got the name off a P.E. Island map. I know nothing of the place and never knew anyone who lived there. But this lady had lived there when a child and she told me there actually was a family of *Leslies* there *who were noted for their pride.*

What a devilish coincidence!!

Sunday, October 12, 1930
More ghosts. Many of them.

This was a dull gray day. I certainly have had no sunshine since I came to P.A. We went to church this morning but it meant nothing to me in especial—a new church and no one I knew. But this afternoon Fred and Alexena and Laura and I went for a drive—to Maiden Lake and "Laurel Hill Farm."

I wanted to see Maiden Lake again, for the sake of that gay old picnic day there. And I am half sorry that I did. It hurt me, too.

It was much smaller. This is not my imagination. All the lakes are smaller. Some of them have dried up altogether. The poplars about the lake were dead or leafless. It seemed a sad blighted place. Perhaps in summer it is beautiful still but today it seemed horribly desolate.

On our return we visited Laura's old home. I remembered the last time I went to it—that Sunday afternoon in the year 1891. Will called after Bible class and took me out. I remember how furious Mrs. Montgomery was. Laura had asked father if I might spend a week with her. Father consented willingly but when he told Mrs. M. what he had done she made a scene. It meant she must do her work and look after her own two children for a week. This was intolerable. Poor father had to yield and ask me if I would mind going for only a couple of days instead. I was bitterly disappointed but for father's sake I agreed. He told Mrs. M. this and I knew he told her. So when I came downstairs that day with my valise I was quite amazed to hear her say, in that indescribable tone she reserved for offenders of all kinds, "Where are you going Maud?" with a kind of icy amazement as if she had no idea whatever where I was going. The unpleasantness of it welled up today as I recalled it as bitterly and as poignantly as if it were yesterday. I have never in all my life known a woman who could infuse as much venom and insult into harmless words as she could.

But once away I drew a long breath of relief and gave myself over to happiness. It was a lovely day: Will was with me, a jolly, Josephian comrade: the prairie was green and gold and flower-starred. And as we drew near the hill on which the Pritchard house—a new, snug, white-washed log house—stood, Will laughed and said, "Look at Old Crazy." Laura was flying down the hill waving her hands madly. She hopped into the buggy—we hugged and kissed enthusiastically—

No, no, that all happened 39 years ago. Today the bluffs were bare and the prairie dark and sullen. And as we drove in at the gate we saw a name "The Ochils" on the arch that spanned it. No longer "Laurel Hill." There *is* more in a name than Shakespeare thought. I felt a chill over my spirit like new fallen snow.

The family living in the house welcomed us warmly and were quite overcome because "L.M. Montgomery" was under their roof. But I paid very little heed to them or their raptures. I was in the grip of some tremendous emotion—far more so than Laura who had spent years in it to my two days but had been back frequently since leaving it. So it did not overwhelm her as it did me. I could not talk. I wanted to cry. There was the old parlor where Laura sang to Andrew Agnew that Sunday evening, while Will and I sat together on the sofa and—well, flirted a bit. Anyhow we held hands and he "stole" the little ring I wore—the little ring I wear yet—the ring that is never off my hand day or night. It is an amazing thing about that ring—it was a mere thread of gold when Aunt Annie gave it to me when I was twelve—it was a still slenderer thread when I gave it to Will—and when it came back to me after his death. It has never been off my finger since. And it has never worn out. I would not know my hand without it. I want it on my hand when I die—when I am buried. It is a symbol of something—I hardly know what—but something old and sweet and precious and forever gone.

It was almost a relief to come away—it was all too nerve-shaking and heart piercing. An agony—yet a wonderful agony. It is wonderful to feel so deeply, even if the feeling be half pain. One *lives* when one feels like that. Its illumination casts a glow over life backward and forward and transfigures drab days and darkened paths.

And *Will* seemed to be there—"the skirts of that forgotten life, Trailed noiseless at my side." I felt sure he was in the other room—out in the hall—coming down the stairs. He was as real as Laura and Alexena and Fred—more real, for *they* have changed and *he* has not. He is "forever young."

I don't know if I were most sorry or most glad when I came away. I would not have missed that experience for anything—and yet it was very terrible. Too near something that is of eternity, not of time.

I was there only once before—I shall never be there again. But we live in "heart-throbs, not in figures on a dial" and that lovely hill means more to me than houses where I have spent years. Because it holds forever something of my youth. It is, for me, haunted.

When we came back to town—*not* behind old "Courtney" with Will driving— we went over the river and had a long pleasant drive through the autumnal pine woods. The sunset effects up the river were lovely as we came back—as they used to be long ago. And as we drove up a different street home another bit of the past popped out for me—a building with a sign "Royal Hotel"—in other words, the old High School. Quite unchanged—in better preservation than the manse or Miss Baker's. It has been painted and kept up and looks as if it belonged there and were not merely a stranded derelict. I thought of Mustard—and Will—and all the High School boys—and I laughed. The memories of the old High are not ghostly or sentimental or romantic. They are just amusing. But I am glad to have seen it. I could see myself, a slim schoolgirl, going home from it on winter evenings with Will beside me carrying my books. Will—Will—how he haunts Prince Albert for me. He and father. They are everywhere.

Monday, Oct. 13, 1930
Prince Albert, Sask.
Today was the first day of sunlight since I came so I took some snaps, especially of "we three." Here we are smiling at fate and the years. We do not look half as sober as we did in that picture of almost forty years ago. Why should we? We were young then with tremendous life and all its problems before us. Verily, it behoved us to look sober. But now the greater part of that life is lived—its problems solved or outgrown. We can afford to laugh.

We drove away up the river today— where Will and Laura and I used to drive of old. We went to afternoon tea with Mrs. McLeod, the wife of the warden of the penitentiary, and had a very nice time. Then we came home— laughed and told tales around Alexena's table—and then spent a cosy pleasant evening at home talking to each other. We needed no other amusement.

Tuesday, October 14, 1930
I had another very heart-stirring experience this morning. We drove out to the cemetery and I stood by father's grave. Laura and Alexena wandered away and left me alone with my dead. It was a damp misty morning, with moisture dripping heavily from the trees. Before

"1930" [Maud, Alexena MacGregor Wright and Laura Pritchard Agnew]

me was the plot and on the gravestone was father's name. I was wrung with unspoken and unspeakable emotion. I could not even cry. There separated from me by a few feet of earth was what was left of father—of the outward man I knew. I might call to him but he would not answer. Yet I felt so tenderly, preciously, dreadfully *near* to him. As if, under that sod, his great tired beautiful blue eyes had opened and were looking at me.

I turned about and there was Will's grave. By a strange coincidence the plots are side by side. There was Will's name on the family headstone. And he had been dead for thirty-three years. Yet I felt him, too, near me, living.

It is strange what an influence the memory of Will has over me—how dear his memory is to me. I was never in love with him—I never fancied myself in love with him. At that time sex meant nothing to my unawakened body but I never felt for him even the passion of sentiment which at that time I thought was love and which I had already felt for more than one boy. But I *liked* Will Pritchard better than any boy or man I have ever met in my life. With no other have I ever felt that realization of *perfect comradeship*—of complete and utter congeniality. A simple, old-fashioned expression which Will once used in a letter to me describes this feeling better than pages of attempted definition could do. He wrote, "I always felt at *home* in your company." Ay, that was it. At *home*. A mysterious bond between spirit and spirit with which sex or sense had nothing to do. And so it has lasted, as things of the spirit must and do last, when the passions of the flesh have long since faded out into oblivion or repulsion. Changeless and immortally young. And that is why I stood by Will's grave today and felt as if our friendship was a thing of yesterday, still vital and beautiful—nay, not of yesterday but of today.

I could have stood there for hours between those two affections. It seemed to me that I could not tear myself away. Father, I cannot leave you again—Will, we must nevermore be parted. Such, in its essence, was what I felt—what my heart said.

I thought, too, of my mother's grave—so far far away. How far sundered sleep those two who shared one bridal bed.

Father's gravestone is a pitiful little affair. Surely his wife might have put up something with more dignity. She retained father's position as jail warden until she gave it up for real estate dealings and it could not have been a question of money. If her name were not on it, too, I would see that it was replaced by something more suitable. But as it is I cannot. Her children would probably resent it.

At last I had to come away. But it seemed to me that soul and spirit were almost torn in twain in the coming.

Could I have had my wish I would have gone home and spent the rest of the day in solitude and communion with my dead. But it was not possible. We had promised to go to luncheon at the Empress Hotel. It was a very smart affair with a delicious menu. But it was only my outward form that was there. *I* was still between those two graves on that misty hill.

Wednesday, Oct. 15, 1930
This morning we woke up to find it snowing. And it has snowed all day. Alexena's home looks like a Christmas card. I must confess I had not expected a blizzard in

October. I knew it might come in November. Laura cannot remember anything like it before. It must have been staged for my benefit.

We were out at a "tea" but have had another jolly evening at home. Yet am I sad. Tomorrow we must go—Laura to Saskatoon—I to Battleford. This will be our last night together. And we have had such jolly ones ever since we came.

Forty years ago I was a very young girl with little worldly wisdom or experience. But I knew how to do one thing—I knew how to choose friends. I made no mistake about that.

I wish now that my visits with Laura and Alexena are over that I could go home. I really feel very little interest in the rest of my itinerary. I am going to Battleford because I promised the Webers I would—I am going to Edmonton to find out for myself just how Irv Howatt is doing and if there is any chance of his ever paying me back the money he borrowed from me—and I am going to Winnipeg to see Kate and Ila because it wouldn't do not to. But I am very indifferent to it. It will all seem horribly flat and savourless after these two weeks of perfect comradeship and jollity—with their strange undercurrent of pain and seeking and longing for vanished things.

Again for me comes a "last night" in Prince Albert. Thirty-nine years ago I passed one—a summer night. Laura was with me—and Will. The next day I was to leave for "home" and the joy of that overcame the "parting pain." And tonight—I think it is really a last night. For somehow, in spite of promises and plans and talk of motor trips in days to come I do not think I will ever come again to this little northern city between the river and the poplar bluffs.

When I left P.A. before I remember I wrote a poem of "Farewell"—father had asked me to. I shall not write a poem of parting this time. I shall only in my heart echo the concluding line of that old poem—truer now perhaps than it was then—

> Friends, prairies, forest, river—all I bid you
> One last, one long farewell.

Sunday, Nov. 2, 1930
Norval, Ont.

Really, the best part of a holiday is getting home. I might not have thought this so whole heartedly if I had come home from P.A. but after the boredom of the past two weeks I do.

On the night of Wednesday, Oct. 16th, Laura and I had our last night of laughter together. We woke to find the blizzard still raging. At first it seemed that we would not get away from P.A. that day. Trains were uncertain—taxis all but impossible to get. The one we finally secured could get only within two blocks of the house. There in snow to our knees Alexena bade us good-bye. I hated to leave her. She is a darling—and we may never meet again. But one cannot linger over parting embraces in a western blizzard. The train was late—and just after we started we stopped again and sat there for nearly an hour while a snowdrift was shovelled through. By an odd coincidence the train had stopped right by the house to which Laura went as a bride thirty-three years ago. It was new then, built for her. It was old and shabby now. I felt as if it had been a part of my life, too, for I remember Laura's description of it and my keen interest in it.

84

I remembered, too, the last time I had left P.A.—that fine September morning in '91. Of all that watched me away that morning Laura was the only one with me now. Father's face was not there to see me off. He was sleeping quietly in that snow-covered grave over the hill. My emotion, when I thought of it, was so poignant and terrible that I felt as if it must tear my heart in pieces.

We crawled along through the stormy afternoon and early falling night so slowly and with so many delays from drifts that I soon realized that I could not possibly get into Saskatoon by the time the Battleford train was scheduled to start. So I cheerfully accepted the fact that I could have another night with Laura after all. We were having a good time. Alexena had given us a *roasted wild duck*, bread and butter and cake, so we ate it up together and enjoyed it. We were quite cosy and contented when—a whirlwind swept us apart. At least that was the impression left on my mind by the events of the next fifteen minutes.

The train had stopped at Warman. The conductor came through the car calling out, "Anyone wishing to go to Battleford get off here and take the train from Saskatoon." Something gave me the impression that one must hurry if one wanted to get that train. I stood up, grasped my hat box, flung my arms around Laura with a choking good-bye kiss, plunged off the train—and was simply swallowed up in the fury and blackness of a prairie blizzard. Never have I experienced anything like that wind. In spite of the fact that I was weighted by a heavy hat-box I was blown along that platform like a leaf and if I hadn't blown into a man I'd probably be blowing over the prairie yet. I held on to him—hard—and gasped out, "Where is the train from Saskatoon?" "Not in yet," he said coolly. "You'd better go into the station and wait." I thought I'd "better" so I stumbled through a snowbank to my knees and managed to get in. My first thought was of Laura. Could it be possible we had really parted? I ran to the window in hopes of waving one last farewell to her at her window but all I could see was the tail-light of her train disappearing in the darkness. I watched it out of sight. A horrible line of Byron's flashed into my mind. "All farewells should be sudden when forever." Surely ours had been sudden enough. But I passionately refused to believe that it was forever. It could *not* be! Laura and I could not have seen each other for the last time!

I went to the agent and asked him when the Saskatoon train would come. He replied that the said train was waiting in Saskatoon for some delayed eastern train and that I might just as well have gone on to Saskatoon and got on her there!!!!

No, I did *not* swear.

I went and sat down drearily. The station was badly-lighted, badly-heated and very dirty. Full, too, of French half-breeds. Everything was so depressing that I couldn't even lose myself in dreams—my old escape from unpleasant or boring realities. The hour passed however, as all hours do, no matter how endless they seem. At last the train was announced. I picked up a loitering boy to carry my box and went out, expecting to see the train by the station. To my dismay it was an eighth of a mile away, diagonally across a town block, to be reached by a long narrow board walk. The station agent, with a lantern, and the box boy started ahead, calling back a warning to "look out for the drift." There was no need to "look" for it. It loomed up before me breast high with no track through it but the holes made by the feet of the aforesaid boy and agent. I tried to negotiate it by putting my feet in those holes. But it was no use. Down I floundered, snow to my eyes. My shrieks of despair brought the two males back to my rescue. They dragged me out. I took hold of the boy with the box and said politely but firmly, "I shall not let go of you again until I am safely on that train." There was no more snow but there was a terrific wind. I thought we'd never get across. But of course we did and eventually I found myself sinking with a gasp of relief into a seat.

I hope I'll never see Warman again anyhow. Ugh!

The drive to Battleford was dreary. Outside was darkness. The train was full of French for the most part. I was lonely and tired and disgruntled. I berated myself for ever promising to come to Battleford. I had done so partly because Mr. Weber was very insistent, but more because father had lived there for a few years before going to Prince Albert and I wanted to see it because of him. But now I wished myself back by Alexena's cosy fireside.

In due time we reached North Battleford. Mr. Weber met me full of apologies. The blizzard had tied up traffic. It was impossible to get his own car out and no taxi would venture on the four mile drive between the new and the old towns that night. The only way of conveyance was to go in the mail courier's sleigh. Could I?

Seeing that I had to I could. But it was no joke. Mrs. Weber had sent a fur coat but I had to sit up on high, on a board laid across the sides of the sleigh and the wind blew through everything. But the snow had ceased, the world was bathed in pale moonlight, and the scenery was rather beautiful and weird. I can't say I enjoyed the drive—it really seemed endless—but it was less unpleasant than I had feared. In due time we really did get to Mr. Weber's house and stumbled into it out of the snow and wind.

I stayed there until Saturday morning but found the visit only tolerable. Mr. Weber writes interesting letters but personally he is not nearly so interesting. He and Mrs. Weber were kind but after Alexena's hospitality—well, I found myself in a very different milieu.

The house was cold and I was cold all night. As I cowered chillily under the blankets I thought wistfully of twenty-four hours before when Laura and I were snuggled down under Alexena's cosy puff, shrieking with laughter, and Alexena stealing in to share the fun. I was homesick—homesick for P.A. and homesick for Norval. The sight of the latter name on the map in my time table nearly made me burst into tears. But I was afraid the tears would freeze on my face so I choked them back and said, "Cheer up, two weeks from tonight you'll be nearly home."

By Friday the blizzard was over and the day was fine but very cold with a high wind. It was hard, looking out on the snow-bound world to realize that it was only the middle of October. During the day a Mr. and Mrs. Clouston called—they had known father intimately during his years in Battleford. It is always wonderful to me to meet anyone who knew father. It seems to give him back to me again for a little while. At night I gave a talk to the pupils of the schools.

I had another cold and half sleepless night and was not sorry to get away in the morning. Mr. W. managed to get his car out so the drive to North B. was much pleasanter than the first one had been. The scenery around Battleford must be quite beautiful in summer. I had a tedious drive from Battleford to Edmonton. Nothing but snow-covered prairies. It was rather gruesome to see hundreds of acres of

"Daisy and Mineself"
[Maud and Daisy Williams McLeod
in Edmonton]

wheat in stook, each stook a pyramid of snow. We reached Edmonton at night and Daisy and her husband Mr. McLeod met me. Daisy has changed little from the Bideford days. A little plumper, more matronly and grayer but quite recognizable. She has an extremely pretty daughter. I always liked Daisy and I enjoyed my visit with her but I was homesick all the time. Did not feel especially well either. The high altitude probably disagreed with me. I could not sleep at night and kept thinking that I was 2000 miles away from home. But there was one delightful thing for my first evening there. Letters from Stuart and Ewan were awaiting me. My, but they tasted good. Darling Stuart. It was dreadful to think I was so far away from him.

On Monday I went to see Irving Howatt. Found him as shabby as a singed cat occupying a shabby office. He is doing nothing and never will. I came away bidding farewell to my four thousand dollars. I shall never see a cent of it. And it would educate Stuart. Well, it can't be helped. I lent it to him because Stella begged me to. I have been entirely too obliging to my relatives for my own financial good.

I lunched with Jim McIntyre who lives in Edmonton and in the afternoon my old pupil Bertie Hayes, who is a Mrs. Arnett, took me for a drive around the city. Edmonton must be a nice town in summer. I spent Monday night longing for Thursday morning when I would start home. Tuesday and Wednesday were taken up with "teas." Tuesday night we dined at Jim's. Uncle Duncan is still there at 87, but feeble and rather childish. Curious. He drank heavily for two-thirds of his life and made his family wretched. Yet here he is, alive, when so many loved and useful folks have passed on.

Thursday morning I turned my face definitely eastward. Daisy had been most kind and I had had some very pleasant hours but I was secretly childishly glad to be going home. I had a nice restful day and at six we got to Saskatoon where we stayed half an hour. And darling Laura was there and we had a darling half hour together, saying our good-byes decently and in order. It wiped out that horrible parting at Warman. Really, I had felt as if I couldn't go back east without seeing Laura once more. As the train pulled out she stood waving and smiling after me as she had waved and smiled that sunny September morning 39 years ago. Shall we ever meet again? God knows. And why have we, who were so formed to be congenial companions had to spend our lives apart? I don't believe even God knows *that*.

Friday morning I reached Winnipeg and spent till Sat. afternoon with Kate and her husband. I had not seen Kate since that day in Beaverton when she was so dull and inane. I have concluded that she must have had something on her mind that day which prevented her from taking an interest in anything because she was very different during this visit and was very nice and kind. I could never feel as much at home with her as with Ila but I am glad the impression of that former meeting was erased. I hated to feel that way about any of father's family. Kate looks very old and careworn but that has intensified her likeness to father. She looks far more like him than any of us. It gives me a strange feeling to see father's very eyes looking at me from her face. Her husband Sinclair McKay is a very nice fellow and I liked him very much. But he has poor health—he was overseas—and I think they have a hard enough struggle. Bruce, Kate's little boy, is a very pretty, clever but rather spoiled child.

I spoke to the Press Club Friday afternoon and Carl came to dinner that night. He has grown fat and bald and lost his resemblance to father almost totally. But he is a dear chap and I love him. He works in the Grain Exchange Building and Saturday morning he took us to see the "pit." "Pit" is an excellent name for it I think. As I stood in the gallery and looked down I wondered what the Nazarene would say of it, supposing He came in and stood there!

Saturday morning a friend of Kate's drove us about and took us out to see old Kildonan church and graveyard. I was interested in it because I had heard Will P. talk of it often. His grandparents lived there and in his childhood visits he had attended Kildonan church, where the service was still in Gaelic. Apart from my personal interest, it is a very interesting old spot.

I was at a luncheon in the afternoon and sat near a Mrs. Fitzgerald, daughter of Archbishop Matheson and a second cousin of Laura and Will. She talked of Will, saying what a dear, charming fellow he was and how much they all loved him.

At five that afternoon I started for the Pointe du Bois woods where Ila is living, while her husband builds the new power plant. I had to go to Lac du Bonnet in a stuffy train crowded with French and I was extremely tired. Ila met me at Lac du Bonnet and we went out to the Pointe on a little electric railway which has been built through the woods to carry supplies to the plant. There is no other road of any kind. Pointe du Bois is really an interesting place. Nothing but woods, rocks and rivers. But as the old power plant is there they have literally "hydro to burn." The houses are lighted and warmed by electricity and the little paths through the woods are all lighted up o'nights. It's really the most curious mingling of primitive conditions with the most up-to-date equipment I've ever seen. Ila has a very cosy little home and I really had a pleasant visit. But I kept on being homesick and fairly counted the hours till Monday night when I could really start for home—home—my own comfortable bed—the boys—and a little cat with jewel eyes.

There was no snow there and it was a pleasant change after four days of seeming winter. Sunday was fine and we took a trip on the radial to Slave Falls where the new plant is being built. "Bill" MacKenzie, Ila's husband, is a nice chap but I did not "take" to him as I had done to Sinclair. Ila has three well-behaved kiddies, none of whom, however, has the charm Bruce has, in spite of his "spoiled condition."

I was all right in day-time and enjoyed myself. But no sooner did I go to bed than I was submerged in homesickness. And, strangely enough, not only home-sickness for Norval—but for Cavendish—for *old* Cavendish. One night I count-ed up the people in Cavendish who had been in Cavendish when I came home from the west before. There were only *thirty*. And this made me cry.

At last Monday evening did come. I packed with secret joyousness. My heart sang "Going home—going home—going home." Ila went up to the station with me. It was a hard gray twilight with a wild, weird western sky behind the dark trees. The world seemed dead—but my soul was spring-time because I was start-ing home. I had had a nice visit—pleasant company—delicious meals. Ila is a cook by the grace of God and not by rule o'thumb. But I was full of joy to be going home.

Ila went to Lac du Bonnet with me where I said good-bye and got on the bus for Winnipeg. I rather enjoyed that strange dark drive to the 'Peg. Arriving there I spent the night at the Royal Alexandra and the next day with Kate, driving out to Fort Garry and "doing" the Winnipeg stores. Was rather bored all the time and drew a long breath of relief when I found myself alone on my train at 5.40. Thank heaven I wouldn't be expected to talk to anyone for at least 30 hours.

I was really woefully tired. I had been "going" constantly for weeks and felt worn out. My visit west was anything but a rest and that is what I need. I was too cold that night to sleep and Wednesday was a dreary day, spent entirely in travel-ling through "pulp" woods of Northern Ontario which were white with snow—endless acres, only varied now and then by the cold virginity of a northern lake, black-gray amid its untrodden woods. But Thursday morning we pulled into good old Toronto and I met Ewan and Chester at Simpson's. Ewan and I drove out to Aurora for the Prize Day ceremonies. How good it was to see my boys again. Stuart got his first prize for general proficiency and is rosy and happy. It seemed

Lucky

like coming back to summer again for the day was warm and fine, the grass green and many of the trees still wearing their golden leaves. We got home at 7.30 Thursday night and I had the first really good sleep I've had since I left P.A.

So my western visit is over. The Saskatoon and P.A. part of it was sheer delight but the rest I could well have spared. It was pleasant in spots but I could have enjoyed myself just as well at home with less expenditure of nerve juice. However, I'm glad to have seen the west again and realize the changes it has undergone in these years. It is good to know one's own country.

Lucky met me with warm purrs, all velvet and silk. Darling puss!

But yesterday and Friday were not sheer enjoyment. Several business letters were to be read and some of them by no means pleasant reading. One was to the effect that a certain company in which I had invested over three thousand dollars has gone to the wall, as an aftermath of the stock market crash last fall! This is bad enough, but if another company does not follow suit I will not complain. I should have had more sense than to put money in such a concern so I must pay the price of my folly. But I didn't sleep much last night.

Monday, Nov. 3, 1930
This morning a wire from Al Leard said that his sister Helen had died suddenly on Saturday!

The news gave me a shock and I have felt downhearted all day. Helen has not meant anything in my life for many years but when an old tie is broken there is pain. And a nasty feeling that one's contemporaries are beginning to slip away. It was rather strange that Helen and I should have had that "re-meeting" so to speak last year. Ay di me!

Tuesday, Nov. 4, 1930
When I was in Edmonton I met Judge Emily Murphy who was sure another war was pending in Europe. Her bankers had told her so. Mussolini is waiting his chance to pounce. But a salesman who was here today thinks it will not come. I hope so. The very mention of another war drives the blood to my heart. The world is in a shocking enough mess at present without more war. What is to be the outcome I know not, with Red Russia looming ever more and more menacingly on the horizon of the east. At three o'clock at night I always feel that I cannot go on enduring it. But one just must—till God gets tired of it!

My ear is bothering me again this fall just as it did last. I went to a specialist then and he could not find anything wrong and did me no good. In the winter it got better of its own accord and has been all right till lately. It worries me especially when I lie down at night, with a faint buzzing, a sense of fullness and occasional needle like pricks of pain. It may be a hangover from the infection surrounding my teeth before I got them out.

I was amused and nettled at something I heard Sutherland Beaton had said the other day. The said S. is not doing much—has only a badly paid uncertain job and won't have it after Xmas. Jean Leslie asked him what he would do when he had no work—would he go to Norval. "Not much," said Sutherland. "I nearly died of its dullness in the summer. I can't imagine what it would be like now."

Hum! Well, I suppose Norval *is* dull to a boy of Sutherland's type. But at that I should imagine it would be a little livelier than Toronto jail.

Have been re-reading Shaw's *Back to Methusaleth*. I enjoy Shaw. But he doesn't know just when to stop. And most of his stuff is brilliant fireworks, not a permanent coruscation. Still, he tastes good.

Friday, Nov. 7, 1930
After a certain dream I had not long ago I was not surprised to read in today's paper that Marshall Pickering was dead. He died of complications resulting from his diabetic condition. I wonder if his heirs will try to make trouble for us. They

may make one more attempt—it will only be one more—but one more is too much. I feel as if I couldn't endure any more worry along that line. My ear continues troublesome and spoils my nights.

Sunday, Nov. 9, 1930
I had a good sleep last night and had I been able to have my usual quiet and restful Sunday afternoon of reading I might have felt much better tonight. But it was not to be.

After S.S. this morning Mr. Reid called a meeting of the S.S. executive to discuss the S.S. concert. For the past two years Margaret Russell, one of our girls who teaches school in Toronto, has trained the children in the musical part of it. She is a crank and a terror but she knows her work and trained them well. A week or two ago Mr. Reid—who, as superintendent, has the right to do this—asked me to ask Margaret if she would train them again this year. I did so—Margaret agreed—and I so reported—at this meeting.

It was plain at once that Mrs. George Davis' dander was up at this. Mrs. D. is the wife of an Englishman who runs a poor little farm near Norval. She is English born herself and very much the type of lower class English. But she is a good singer. I have felt sorry for her and have always tried to do what I could for her—giving her books for her children and asking her to sing whenever possible. She dearly loves to sing and be in the limelight. I heard she wanted to be in the choir and I asked them about it but the project was at once squashed. I was told she had been in the choir before her marriage and had made no end of trouble, trying to "run" everything and they would not have her back on any terms. So I gave that up and got her in as Secretary and Treasurer of the S.S. A mistake, as I see now.

Mrs. Davis wanted to train the children for the S.S. concert but Mr. Reid said it couldn't be thought of. In the first place she was so unpopular among the children that they would not listen to her and in the second place it would be an insult to Margaret Russell to pass her over after her hard work the past two years for Mrs. Davis.

When this matter of the music had been settled I moved a committee to see to the *rest* of the programme—recitations, dialogues and drills. I and Elsie McClure, Luella Reid etc. were put on it and I moved Mrs. Davis be put on also. I had my reward. When the question of presents came up it was decided that we would this year get only presents for the children who actually came to S.S. Hitherto we have been buying them for all the children in the congregation. And then Mrs. Davis piped up, "And the presents should be *suitable*, also."

This was a flat insult to me and Charlotte MacPherson. We have always done the buying and tying up and addressing and a lot of worry and work it is. It is a job nobody has ever wanted and it has always been shuffled off on me. I was really quite stunned at Mrs. D's insolence. I never had anything like this happen to me before in all my years of church work. I think I am as capable, at the least, of judging what presents are "suitable" as Mrs. Davis is and I think we always made a very good selection. It is no easy matter to buy a present for fifty or sixty children of all ages, at our limit of 15 cents. I would not of course take any notice of

Mrs. D's remark but Charlotte said sharply, "We did our best to get suitable presents." Mrs. D. did not let on she heard and the meeting dissolved.

This afternoon just as I had settled down to read the phone rang and Margaret told me that she was not going to train the children as "there were too many too anxious to tell her what to do." I did not know what had happened but I did know Margaret was frightfully touchy and it was up to me to find out what was wrong and right it if possible. So I sighed, got my wraps and walked up the hill to Russells'.

I spent two hours there smoothing Margaret's ruffled plumage. I didn't wonder she was peeved. Mrs. Davis had called in there from church and had told her a deliberate lie. She said that she, Mrs. D., had been appointed to "assist" M. in the musical part and then she proceeded to lay down the law. The children were to be taught hymns, "not those silly songs etc." A less touchy person than Margaret would have been annoyed. Eventually I persuaded Margaret to overlook this and go on with the matter without paying attention to anyone. But I came home tired and down-hearted. The work of getting up that annual concert is hard enough without complications like this.

Monday, Nov. 10, 1930
Norval, Ont.
Our guild started up tonight with an opening social. Had a letter from Ella Campbell tonight. Maud has had her tonsils and adenoids removed at last. For four years I have been trying to get Ella to have this done, telling her I would pay for the operation. She has put it off and off until finally Maud could hardly speak plain. At last she has done it—much to my relief, although, with poor Ella's usual felicity—she picked the very time I am financially straitened. What with no book out this year, two boys at college, and nearly three thousand dollars cut from my income owing to the passing of various dividends it is a long long time since I had to be so careful of my expenditure. I count every cent and spend absolutely nothing that is not necessary. I had meant to buy a new winter coat for my old one is decidedly shabby but now I shall have to make it do and use the money to pay for Maud's operation.

I am not feeling especially well and get very blue, especially in the wee sma's when I cannot sleep. Some nights I do not sleep at all.

Tuesday, Nov. 18, 1930
Have had a very busy crowded week with one thing and another, but have on the whole felt better and slept better than for some time. But occasionally that queer feeling in the head that bothered me last winter and last summer after the flu comes back. I can hardly describe it. It is a feeling of tightness and heaviness across the forehead. It may be only nerves—I never have it when I am out in company or in cheerful surroundings—but it is very annoying.

Shaw's *Joan of Arc* has been giving me pleasure at stolen moments this week. But I get so little time to read. Einstein says in a recent pronouncement that "Time-space is eating up matter." Perhaps he knows what that means. I don't. But I think something is eating up time.

Wed. Nov. 19, 1930

Drat Mrs. George Davis. No, away with all squeamishness. As a preacher's wife I cannot swear in public. But in this diary I do, in emergencies. This is one of them.

Damn Mrs. George Davis!

I had a letter from Margaret Russell tonight. Mrs. Davis went there again last Monday morning and was so "bossy" that Margaret told her that she had better take over the management of the whole thing. Mrs. D. alertly agreed, saying that two people could not run the music. She also informed them that *I* had no business to ask Margaret to take over the training before the executive meeting!

Then after Margaret went back to Toronto Mrs. D. had a change of heart, wrote M. that she wanted her—M.—to "assist" her and M. was to get music and bring it out!

But Margaret will have nothing to do with it. Well, I shall not coax her to. I think she has let us down very meanly. She knows quite well what Mrs. Davis is and she ought to be above taking notice of her. Neither should she have told me what Mrs. D. said about me. It does not do any good and it makes my relations with Mrs. Davis more difficult because I cannot help feeling bitterly towards her for such conduct after all I've done for her. And I foresee no end of trouble in working with her during the concert practices. "Oh, for a lodge in some vast wilderness!"

Saturday, Nov. 22, 1930

Last night we had our first S.S. practice and Mrs. D. "acted up." When she found that Margaret Russell had dropped out she flew off the handle, said Margaret had *asked* her to help her—which was another falsehood—and flounced off home, leaving Luella Reid and me with all the children on our hands. We could do nothing from a musical point of view but we got some dialogues going. I could not sleep last night and today has been dark and dull and dispiriting. I am not well and everything worries me.

Sunday, Nov. 23, 1930

Today in Sunday School—Mrs. D. not being there—the Session asked Elsie McClure and Luella Reid to train the children in music for the concert. So we are going on with it but the whole thing is poisoned for me.

I had however a nice restful quiet afternoon for once and spent it reading *Joan of Arc*—Shaw's play. It took the taste of Mrs. Davis out of my mouth!

Thursday, Nov. 27, 1930

I have been feeling a little better and sleeping a little better but life is full of pinpricks. Mrs. Davis is trumpeting her "wrongs" everywhere, especially to the United Church people and accusing *me* of getting Luella to train the children because, forsooth, Chester "goes with" her. I had nothing whatever to do with it—the Session decided it wholly. However, I can take no notice of Mrs. Davis. I cannot stoop to defend myself to such a person. Luckily everyone knows her and her record pretty well. One tale of her reveals her pretty thoroughly. She "had to get married," as the old phrase goes, having got into trouble with her uncle's hired man. Her baby was born a few weeks after her marriage. Mr. Patterson, the minister, heard she was ill but did not hear about the new arrival, so he went up to see her. When he went into her room Mrs. Davis laughed and said, "I've got a surprise for you Mr. Patterson"—and proudly showed him the baby!! Poor Mr. P. was so dumbfounded he never knew what he said or did.

I have begun preparing a one act play for Old Tyme night in February. Mr. Greenwood—Garfield McClure and his wife—and myself. So you will perceive it is an "all-star cast." Mr. Greenwood, Anglican manager of the Bank of Nova Scotia here, is the best amateur actor I ever saw in my life. The play is the old one *None So Deaf As Those Who Won't Hear.* Twenty-four years ago Alf Simpson and I drove into S'Side one autumn evening and on our way back stopped at St. Eleanor's to attend a concert. This play was put on and I thought—and still think—it was the most amusing farce I ever saw in my life. Four years later in Cavendish I tried to get it up for a local concert. But we had only just got started when word of father's death came. I had to drop out and no-one else would take it on. And now I'm going to have another try at it. It means work and time, of course, but somebody has to work to make that Old Tyme concert a success.

Tuesday, Dec. 2, 1930
I knew we would at least hear something from the Pickering folk. This dull, gray cold day a letter came—not from Greig but from his partner Littlejohn. Probably Greig feels that his epistolary powers are exhausted as far as we are concerned. At least the letter was not like his threatening and insulting ones. It was quite a mild appealing letter, pointing out that we ought to pay "a widow" an "honest debt" and asking us to let him hear from us.

The point is, it was *not* "an honest debt." If it were it would have been paid long ago. It was nothing but a "frame-up" bolstered on lies and perjury. As for the "widow" she is not in need and has plenty to live on and a family of grown-up children to look after her. Littlejohn feelingly reminds us that Mr. Pickering "had to sell his bonds" to pay the costs of the trial. But did we force the trial on him? He went to law of his own free will in an attempt to extort money from us, and won his suit by perjury. Let him and his take the consequences therefore.

Nevertheless, this letter was not a pleasant incident in a bleak, cold day. It stirred up too many bitter and humiliating memories.

Wednesday, Dec. 3, 1930
We had S.S. practice tonight and it went quite well but I was so terribly tired, not only in body but in mind and *spirit*, that it seemed an endless nightmare to me.

I see that Cronan, the head man in the company, Insurance Investments, that failed has been arrested for fraud in connection with the company's operations. I felt sure there was something like that at the bottom of the affair. But punishing him won't restore their lost money to the shareholders!

Saturday, Dec. 6, 1930
This was a dismal day of fog and rain with no good news and several bits of minor bad news. Nevertheless I am sleeping better and feeling better. If I could only get a *real* rest I believe I would soon be all right. But that seems impossible.

"Marion and Chester"

We had a pleasant evening Wednesday—supper at the Glen House and the High School commencement with the Barracloughs also. An evening like this always picks me up.

Thursday afternoon we drove into Toronto to meet the Montreal train and bring Marion Webb out.

For the second time in my life I am trying my hand at match making!

The first time was years ago when I tried to forward a match between Oliver Macneill and Campsie Clark and, failing that, between him and Lucy MacLure. I had no better success with that and the only result was that ill-will in several quarters was my portion for a time. So I sensibly vowed never to dabble in the like again and have up to this time kept the vow.

When Marion was here on her visit four years ago Murray Laird, a very nice chap, well-off, nice looking, quite the pick of the Norval young men, seemed quite taken with her and drove her around quite a bit. I thought of asking Marion to prolong her visit but several considerations prevented me. I was not sure how Myrtle and Ernest might regard it. I was not sure that Murray meant or ever would mean anything but a little flirtation with a new girl. And, finally, had I not vowed never again to attempt the role of matchmaker?

So I said naught and Marion returned home.

When I was down home in 1929 Marion was going about with a young Elmer Fyfe of Stanley Bridge and the affair seemed pretty well advanced. Cavendish gossip was that they were soon to be married. Then last September Murray took that sudden notion of another trip to the Island and went. I rather smelled a rodent. Murray has not gone with any girl in particular in these four years and he needs a wife, owing to conditions at home. I had a "hunch" that he was going down to spy out the land and see if there was any chance for him. I, knowing by this time, that Marion was engaged to Elmer Fyfe, thought there wasn't but said nothing and cogitated the more.

Then just before I left for the west I had a distracted letter from Myrtle. Marion was very unhappy. She had always loved Murray but thinking there was no chance of his ever caring for her had decided to marry Elmer whom she liked and who was a nice boy but with no particular prospects, having a father who was a "driver" and kept everything in his own hands, etc. etc. etc. Myrtle asked no favors but I knew what was back of it and sacrificed my vow on the altar of friendship. When I came home I wrote and invited Marion up for the winter. She wrote back accepting. She said, very nicely, that she was fond of Elmer but after Murray had come she "felt like a prisoner"—what an echo of my own old experience that was! How well I knew that feeling!—and had realized that she could never marry Elmer and be happy. So she had broken her engagement and, though she had no reason to think Murray cared for her or ever would—she wanted to get away for the winter, until the buzz of gossip and wonder should die down!

So she came yesterday. She looks pale and ill and has evidently had a bitter autumn of it, poor girl. What a tangled web life can be!

It seems only the other day that Marion was a little golden-haired toddler down in Cavendish. Now she is a woman with all a woman's pain and problems. I have always been very fond of Marion and I would like to see her happy. The gods be gracious unto us!

Monday, Dec. 8, 1930
Yesterday morning when I sailed into church and down the aisle with Marion sedately behind me I fancy a young man in the choir got the surprise of his life. I had never let slip any hint to anyone of Marion's coming. The echo of the benediction had no more than decently died down than Murray was springing down from the pulpit platform and rushing up the aisle to our pew. I am sure all the old Norval gossips—and there are plenty of them—got their crawsful of excitement. I did not know whether Murray would be down this evening because his father is very ill with a heart attack but come he did and he and Marion are in the parlor at this very moment and I am in the study, licking my chops with satisfaction.

Sunday, Dec. 14, 1930
There has been hardly a day this week that something nasty didn't happen. And nothing pleasant has occurred. It has just been a series of mosquito bites and gnat stings.

Chester came home last Tuesday with a hurt leg. Another boy had accidentally run the sharp brad on one of the legs of his theodolite into Chester's leg. I think it must have tapped a vein—it has bled so badly and repeatedly. The doctor was afraid of lock-jaw so gave him serum treatment and I think that danger is passed. But Chester is losing time. I can't find out how he is getting on with his subjects. He never tells anything or talks about them. He has always been like this. I am not just easy about him or his progress at college some way.

Andy Giffen, one of our elders, is brewing up a desperate row in the church over something the Ladies' Aid did that he doesn't like and he is threatening to leave the church. He is one of those men who insist on having their own way in everything or there is no getting along with them. We cannot afford to lose him however and Ewan is doing his best to smooth matters over. Ewan is good at that but Andy is a hard proposition, and we are continually worried about it. Mrs. George Davis is spreading all kind of lies everywhere about the S.S. concert especially among the United people who will want to believe them. What that woman wants is a right good spanking. Really, I think God must get very tired of some people.

My nerves have got so bad I can't sleep at nights and my head bothers me a good deal. Just a nasty feeling in it—not a pain.

Monday, Dec. 15, 1930
Mr. Giffen was here again today. Ewan was away so I had to bear the brunt of his ravings. I kept my temper beautifully and was as courteous and reasonable and placatory as possible but if dear Brother Andy had known what I was thinking about him behind my suave exterior I imagine he would have got an unpleasant shock. Of course he has nothing against Ewan or me but we have to bear the unpleasant effects for all that. He is very absurd in some of his contentions. There is insanity in his family I understand and really his recent kididoes are not those of a rational man. If he only knew how funny he is! He spoiled the whole day for me and I won't sleep tonight. I would like to chain him and Mrs. Davis together for a month. I think *that* punishment would fit the crime!

Stuart, Ewan, Chester

Wednesday, Dec. 17, 1930
Stuart came home today for the holidays and I found I was still able to laugh a bit. Lately I have been feeling as if I could never laugh again.

Stuart has "begun to grow." He is almost as tall as I am now. I was afraid he was going to be small, and I do not think he will ever be very tall, but I am in hopes now that he will be of medium height. He has, of course, lost his seraphic childish beauty but is not a bad-looking chap.

We had our last S.S. practice tonight, thank heaven. It was a sort of nightmare and nothing seemed any good or done right. But I am all nerves and frayed edges, and perhaps things are not as bad as they seem. But tonight I feel as if I had been pulled thro' a keyhole. Selah.

Thursday, Dec. 18, 1930
I worked the whole day getting ready for the concert and fixing up the school-room for it. Chester came home for the holidays. And the concert came off at night and wasn't too bad after all, though I was so tired after it was over that I felt I would rather stay in the church all night than walk home.

Two things embittered the evening for me. One devilish, one a bit cruel.

The devilish one was that those who had tied the presents on the tree did not tie on the mouth organ we had got for Bobbie Davis. And after the presents had been distributed Mrs. Davis came up to me and smugly remarked that "poor Bobbie" had not got anything. Of course it would have to be Bobbie out of the whole school that this would happen to! That is the everlasting cussedness of things. I said "Well, I got something for him" (she didn't believe me of course!)—"but it must have been mislaid." Charlotte and I hunted frantically. It couldn't be found. In desperation we snatched a ball that had been labelled Bruce Ismond. Bruce wasn't there and it had been put aside for him. Something else could be got for Bruce—we gave this to Bobbie Davis. Then of course, after it was all over, the mouth organ turned up in a box on the table!

And yet there are people who say there is no devil.

The other thing was a personal matter and I am foolish to feel hurt over it. But I do.

For fifteen years I got up Sunday School concerts in Leaskdale, working slavishly for two months to do it and nothing was ever put on the tree for me, not even a card. But as I did not expect it, it did not hurt me. It had never been the custom. When I came here I did not expect it either, so it came as a very pleasant surprise the first concert here when both my Bible Class and the Sunday School at large put a gift on the tree for me. They have kept it up and so, to tell the

"Chester, Dec. 1930"

truth, I had come to expect it! This year there was nothing from either—not even a card. It has been a hard year financially of course for everyone in the church but I don't think that was the reason. I think it was simply that nobody thought of it or took the responsibility of seeing that it was done. When I came home I couldn't help a few tears. It was not that I cared for the value of the gifts but one does not like to be totally forgotten, after toiling for two months to get up the concert especially this year when it has been so hard and unpleasant. However, it is all of a piece with the rest of the pricks and stings of this unpleasant fall and in itself is not worth a thought.

Saturday, Dec. 20, 1930
Word came today of Ren Toombs' death. He has been ill for some time. I feel very sadly. There is another home where I have always been a welcome guest and always had good times which will never be the same again. Poor Minnie! Three years ago she was so ill it was feared she would not recover and Ren seemed quite well. Now she has recovered and he is gone.

I felt quite sure last Wednesday morning that we would hear bad news from Ren. I dreamed that I looked out of the dining room window and saw a procession of women coming across the church lawn, with Minnie Toombs and Lily Bernard at the head. I hurried to the door to meet them exclaiming, "Oh, why didn't you phone me you were coming? I haven't anything to eat in the house." "That does not matter," said Lily sadly. "We do not feel like eating." I woke then and told Ewan my dream, adding that I knew it meant ill news from the Island.

I remember so clearly the day Ren and Minnie "appeared out" in church after their wedding. A young, smiling happy couple, just beginning life. It seems impossible that it can be so long ago.

Sunday, Dec. 21, 1930
Andy Giffen was out in church today after an absence of several weeks. I think Ewan has got him smoothed down and the danger of his leaving the church is averted. But he impresses me as being loaded with disagreeable potentialities yet and just on the point of explosion. We dread the annual meeting. Andy, we hear, is planning to break loose there and tell the world what he thinks about everything.

Monday, Dec. 22, 1930
Tonight a huge turkey was left at our door by Garfield McClure with "From the Sunday School" written on it. But that doesn't quite remove the sting. I know what has happened. After the concert Garfield (who was Santa Claus) and the MacPhersons awoke to the fact that I had been totally forgotten. They thought this terrible and I know Garfield and the MacPhersons just clubbed together and got this turkey and that the rest of the Sunday School had nothing to do with it. However, the turkey won't have any the worse flavour for that.

Sunday, Dec. 28, 1930
We have been on the go the whole week, out late at nights etc. and I am so tired.
    Christmas was last Wednesday. Stuart got our tree as usual and we had a fairly nice time. I have been sleeping poorly and my nerves are bad. The only bright spot in the week was Stuart's splendid report. On it one of the masters wrote "a brilliant pupil" and opposite a couple of papers, "These could hardly be improved on."

Monday, Dec. 29, 1930
I slept very poorly last night and won't sleep much better tonight. We were over to the S.S. executive meeting at Robert Reid's tonight and it was not pleasant. Mrs. Davis came boldly down and asked to go over with us. Then she spent the evening telling everybody how they ought to do things and exasperating certain people who are edgy enough now. Sam McClure and his wife are acting up and both refuse to teach longer in the Sunday School. They have heard something somebody has said—we can't find what—and are as "touchy" as so many people in this church are.

Tuesday, Dec. 30, 1930
I didn't sleep all night, not even though I took a bromide. But I felt better today perhaps because Laura Aylsworth and her son Mac were here in the afternoon and it heartened me up to see some of my own house of Joseph again. Mac has quite grown up and is a nice-looking chap.
    I had a card today from Willard Agnew announcing his marriage. Poor Laura. She and Andrew were bitterly opposed to it and she was worrying about it while I was there. The girl Willard had fallen in love with was not at all the kind of wife he should have chosen. Too young—poorly educated—no background. It is a pity. Willard is a fine, nice, clever fellow. But it may turn out better than Laura fears. I hope so anyway.

1931

Wednesday, Jan. 7, 1931
Norval, Ont.
I wonder if 1931 will be as hag-ridden as 1930 has been. It has not begun very auspiciously. For the most part I have been very miserable—sleepless—lifeless—no appetite—waking up every morning—if I have slept at all—to dread the nasty thing that is reasonably sure to happen. Just now, my conception of heaven would be life without fear. But I suppose if I were not so run-down things would not worry me as they do.

I did have a pleasant day yesterday. We were in to Toronto and had lunch at Cuth's to meet Jim MacIntyre who has been east, taking the body of his father for burial in Charlottetown. Poor Uncle Duncan has gone at last at 87. He drank his youth and prime away, ruined his wife's life and did absolutely nothing for his children. And his reward was length of days and tender care to the end! Hum! Laura was there too and we had a pleasant time. Then I had a good hour with Nora. All I need to set me up I verily believe is some pleasant companionship and some real rest.

Stuart went back to St. Andrew's today. I miss him sickeningly. But I wish I felt as easy about Chester as I feel about Stuart.

Today I began to read the *Iliad*—that is, Pope's translation of it. Strange to say I have never read it—although I have had a copy of it for seventeen years. I just can't say why. Yet I am not wholly ignorant of it. In childhood I read a series of papers on it in a children's magazine. They gave an outline of it and many quotations, which I learned by heart and have never forgotten. But I'm going to read it now and perhaps I shall forget a little the worries and annoyances of my present existence in the battles of three or four thousand years ago.

Friday, Jan. 9, 1931
Today I had to go to Georgetown to take part in one of those "prayer services" with which the church of today is being cluttered up. I disapprove of them wholly and consider the theory of them absolutely vicious. It is as if you said "God won't hear your prayer in the solitude of your home or even the entreaties of a few faithful souls at your regular monthly meeting. But if you get a lot of women from different societies together for a big 'prayer fest' thus He may grant your request." However, being the minister's wife, I went, though I would have served God much better by going to bed. After the service I had to be "judge" in a Mission Band speechifying—something I detest at any time but which was peculiarly distasteful today when I was so tired and nervous. Then Mrs. Dick of Union

came up and coolly asked me if I wouldn't take a class in Union Sunday School! I really gasped. This is what it implies—I would have to go over to Union at 10 o'clock, teach said class, sit through a sermon, come home, snatch a hurried bite of dinner, teach my Bible class here, and sit through the sermon again. I would have absolutely no rest on Sunday, the only day in the week where I do have an hour or two to myself. And yet Mrs. Dick knew I had not been well for weeks.

Of course Mrs. Dick is not renowned for her common sense. I am sure nobody else in Union would have dreamed of making that request. There are plenty of girls over there to teach that class. I told Mrs. Dick very decidedly that I couldn't possibly do it and she seemed very much aggrieved. What do they pay the minister a salary for, if his wife won't work all the time for them?

But I had one bit of satisfaction today and it really did me heaps of good. Mrs. Sinclair, who had asked me to be the judge and literally *made* me be it against all my protest, came up to me and said, when I stated that I wasn't well, "You'll have to *give up writing*, Mrs. Macdonald."

Really, I almost boiled over. Half my worry this winter is that I can't find time to do my own work. I glared at the little fool and permitted myself the luxury of a biting retort.

"No, Mrs. Sinclair, I shall not give up my writing. But I do intend to give up running all over the country doing other people's work for them."

Oh, I can tell you I licked my chops over that.

But I had some more discouraging business letters today. What is to be the outcome of certain affairs I do not know—but I "guess and fear."

Wednesday, Jan. 14, 1931
Last night the annual congregational meeting came off. Ewan and I have been dreading it for weeks for we had received several intimations that it was going to be a stormy one. Andy Giffen was reported to have said he was going to air all his grievances, etc. We went over in fear and trembling—and the whole meeting passed off as smoothly as cream. Nevertheless, it might easily have burst into flame. I sat the whole evening as on the crater of a muttering volcano. Andy kept very quiet but I think it was Garfield McClure held him on leash. A few words Ewan said when he opened the meeting also had their effect. I came home when it was over, devoutly thankful but so nervous after the evening's tension that I could not sleep all night. And my head has been bad and queer all day. Moreover Margaret MacPherson came in this evening with a tale of woe about Mrs. Law, a Scotch widow who has been living in Norval for a couple of years and comes to our church. Mrs. Law is ill with an internal trouble which can be cured only by an operation. She cannot work and has neither food nor money. Of course we must look after her, as it is certainly our duty as human beings to do. And I am ready to do my share. But I suspect that I will have to do a good many other folks' share also and "run" the whole affair. And just now I really don't feel as if I were quite up to it.

Thursday, Jan. 15, 1931
The executive of our W.M.S. met here this afternoon and among other things I brought up the matter of Mrs. Law. Some were not any too ready to move in the

affair. They said Mrs. Law had given her son Lewis seventy dollars in the summer to make a payment on a motorcycle which he did not need at all and which he lost later by reason of not being able to keep up the payments, and they thought she did not deserve help when she threw away her money like that. I pointed out that the woman was ill and destitute and couldn't be allowed to starve no matter how foolish she had been. Eventually it was agreed to ask everyone in the congregation for a contribution and Miss MacPherson and I were appointed a committee to administer the fund for Mrs. Law's benefit. Also, to ask the managers to let her have the house she lives in rent free—it belongs to the church—until she is able to work or until her son gets a better job. He is at present working on a farm at Cheltenham for winter wages of $10 a month. The said Lewis is a strapping youngster but reputed to be not over fond of work. She has also a daughter Violet, a girl of thirteen, who goes to school.

Monday, Jan. 19, 1931
Today, after a bad night of nerves and asthma, came another of those bits of bad news that have been so plentiful this winter—the news of Hammond MacKenzie's sudden death from heart failure. It made me feel very wretched. Hammond and Emily have always been such good jolly friends of mine and their home a pleasant one to visit. I suppose from now on, as long as I live, this is how things will be—old friends dropping off here and there every little while. This is one of the things that "growing old" means.

I got a photo of Edith Skelton and her husband today—a good-looking elderly couple. In the matronly woman of the picture I can see nothing of my old slender P.A. chum—except for something about the dark eyes. This Edith is a stranger. I think I would almost rather not have seen the picture.

Edith wrote of how much happiness her life in Prince Albert was after I went there. She had had a hard time of it with Mrs. Montgomery who treated her in a wholly unjustifiable manner, for Edith was a nice, well-behaved hard-working little girl with whom not a fault could be found. Poor Mrs. Montgomery. I have lived with a great many different women at one time or another in my life and never have I known anyone with the disposition she had. I can never get over my bitterness in regard to the way she used me. And I had gone there prepared to love her and anxious to please her. I tried so hard to please her, especially for father's sake. But everything I did was wrong in her eyes. She was determined to put me in the wrong in everything and stuck at nothing to do it. She even told lie upon lie about me after I had left there—outrageous lies with not a vestige of truth in them. My indignant friends in the west wrote to me of this but I took no notice of it for father's sake. And it did me no harm in the long run for nobody seems to have believed her. One of her lies was that I "pricked" her children! I never touched one of her children! Bruce was a darling baby and I loved him and waited on him and took care of him while she gadded about town. No, I can never forgive her and the less I think of her the better. I haven't thought of her for years until this P.A. visit and Edith's letters have brought her back to my mind—and the old resentment as well. Just now, when I am nervous and depressed and ill, all these old troubles and bitternesses seem to return upon my soul and I cannot cast them out.

Saturday, Jan. 31, 1931
The Manse, Norval
This has been a miserable month. Not a single night of wholly good sleep or a day of feeling wholly well in it. The weather has been cold and gray almost continually. Church worries and troubles ditto. I just wish childishly that one nice thing would happen—just one *real* nice thing to hearten me up a bit.

I think heaven would be life without fear.

I dread the seventh of February. Perhaps it is foolish of me. We shall see.

Last July I had a worried wakeful night over several matters. At last I fell into an uneasy slumber, wondering when the end of the business depression with its consequent dangers and dreads would come. And in the moment between sleep and waking I had one of those "visions" I have often had. But it was cloudy and vague—I seemed to waken too quickly to catch it in its fullness—but I wakened with the conviction that I had been told that "Feb. 9th" would mark the beginning of a brighter era in business but there was something—I could not tell what— connected with "Feb. 7," and that something was unpleasant. Ever since I have dreaded "Feb. 7th." Will it mark the "crash" of Canadian Associated Cos. or Gibson & Taylor—or both? If so, I am ruined.

Sunday, Feb. 1, 1931
Today's "little unpleasant thing" was that Chester had to leave the car on the highway last night because it "acted up" and our two good rugs were stolen!

I felt fairly well all day but all the evening my head and ear have troubled me. I say "head" but it is really a nasty, queer, *woolly* feeling across my forehead.

Monday, Feb. 2, 1931
Last night I had the first good sleep in weeks and have felt well all day and able to work. Went to play practice at hall tonight and came home through a very cold brilliant moonlit night. Its beauty soothed and heartened me. The loveliness of Nature is eternal. And the pines on the hill were asleep, their shadows on the moonlit snow more beautiful even than themselves.

Tuesday, Feb. 3, 1931
A wretched night—nerves bad and an attack of asthma at four. It was fifteen below zero this morning but we went to Toronto. The landscape after an unusually heavy white frost was a miracle—a dream of loveliness. The frost on the twigs was nearly an inch deep. In spite of everything I enjoyed the drive.

Put in an application for Marion at Eaton's and Simpson's. There does not seem to be much prospect for her, owing to the terrible business depression that has weighed the country down like a wet blanket for over a year.

Poor Isobel...is ill and writes piteous letters. She "gets on" my raw nerves considerably.

Fri., Feb. 6, 1931
I had a queer nasty dream just before I wakened this morning from a fair sleep. Someone was holding a platter to my mouth with food of some kind on it—food that I did not want to take. I woke without taking it.

This dream is not good. Tomorrow is the fatal seventh. Is there any connection? I do so dread any fresh trouble. I feel I haven't the strength to stand up to it this winter.

I couldn't write this morning—nervous restlessness too bad. I seem to be waiting for some blow to fall. The customary bit of bad news was not wanting. Jas. Bentley is dead—Tillie's husband. He was an old man, so it is only in the nature of things, but I am sorry for poor Tillie. She is not well herself.

Two ladies called about an Institute Valentine Social in the Parish Hall. Would I help? Another phoned about the "World's Prayer Service"—another of those prayer-fests. Then there was a Guild Social at night and all through the programme, which was put on by a visiting society, I felt that I could *not* sit still another moment. *And* there was another letter from Isobel today, full of yowls because her rooms have been messed up owing to hardwood floors being put in below. One would think it a catastrophe of the hugest dimensions.

The customary bit of bad news was supplied by a letter from Can. Ass. Co. They are going to "re-organize." Probably this means a shrinkage of capital at the best. I wonder if this is the bad news for the 7th. No, it does not seem quite bad enough. There is something else.

Stuart came home today for the week-end. It was so good to see him again.

Sunday, Feb. 8, 1931
Well, it came! And a bitter bitter thing it is.

I had just laid down my pen Friday night when Stuart came in with the mail. There was a letter from the Secretary of the Varsity Council on Delinquency, informing us that Chester had been reported to the Council for poor attendance and poor work in the Dept. of Engineering Surveying and Drawing—*and advising us to withdraw him from the university.*

I have been worried about Chester ever since he went to Varsity. In the first place it seemed to me that he had chosen a profession he had no real fitness for. I urged him to take up something else—for instance law for which I think he has considerable fitness—but nothing would move him. All the fall term I felt sure things were not right. He came home too often and seemed to be doing nothing. I could get nothing out of him about his work or studies or anything. Then during the Xmas holidays we got a letter from the Council of Delinquency, saying that his work and attendance had been poor and that if he did not pull up he would find himself in a bad position at end of year. We gave Chester a serious talking to and he promised he would settle right down to work and make up for lost time. I could not get any satisfactory explanation from him as to why he had not attended his classes. It spoiled the whole Xmas season for me.

At that time it was a bolt from the blue. I had not felt easy in regard to Chester over some things. He makes a great fool of himself where girls are concerned. He is bone-lazy. And financially he has even less sense than his father. But he has brains and I never dreamed that he would fall down in his work and classes.

Since New Year's he has not come home often and I thought he had settled down to work. So this letter almost drove me mad. I walked the floor half the night. It was all so terrible. The abject *humiliation of having him come home because he had not made good*, before our congregation. How certain enemies of ours would gloat! I suffered the tortures of hell. Ewan was no help or consolation. About all he could utter seemed to be the four most unpopular words in the English language—"I told ya' so." He did not like Chester coming home so much and going to see a certain girl when he was home. But if I couldn't stop that why didn't he—or try to? He never made any effort or did anything beyond torturing me with his endless fault finding about it. His behavior made me feel very bitter. And in the middle of my anguish that miserable Isobel...had to ring me up on the phone and hold me for minutes that seemed years pouring out in a flood of woes avant the fact that her landlady had been putting in hardwood floors below stairs and as a result Isobel's rooms and furniture had been covered with dust!!!

When Isobel finally hung up I went to bed. I knew I would not sleep without some assistance and I felt I must have sleep, to face the next day. Yet I dreaded sleeping. It would be so hideous to wake and remember. I took two codeine pills—and they had no more effect than water. I lay awake all through those dark wretched hours wondering if dawn would ever come while Ewan slumbered as peacefully beside me as if he hadn't a care in the world.

In the morning I got up and dressed. I knew I looked ghastly and that everyone could see I had been crying. This was a time I wished passionately that we had no outsider in the house.

Saturday was a *hellish* day. Ewan and I started for Toronto after breakfast. It was a cold gray stormy day, snowing and blowing. The drive in was like a nightmare. I have been through nothing so bad since our drive home after the Pickering trial. We found our way to the office of the Council where the secretary Mr. Wilson and the chairman Prof. Allcut were. It was a humiliating interview. I was too crushed for any initiative and Ewan does not shine in an interview of that kind. I suppose I am hardly in a position to be just to those men but I thought them abominable. Supercilious—unsympathetic. Chester was so far behind in his work he could not catch up now. They said that since New Year's his attendance had only been 50 per cent. I *cannot* understand this. He promised so earnestly he would attend his classes. "We are not *sending* him home," said Mr. Wilson condescendingly. "We are only advising." I *did* spunk up a little at this and said rather sarcastically, "I shouldn't suppose a boy *would* be sent home simply because he has fallen down in one subject out of about fifteen. I think that would be a rather extraordinary thing."

We-ell—they didn't want us to blame the university if he failed!!! And Mr. Wilson said it wasn't only in Surveying and Drawing—he had been talking to Prof. Wright a few days before and the Professor had told him that Chester had never handed in his essay on Technical English and that he was the only one in the class who had not done so.

In one way this was the worst thing yet. I knew Chester had found the Drawing very hard. It was such an entirely new thing and he has never been any good at doing things with his hands. I could understand his getting discouraged over it. But if he had not written his essay—something he could easily do—the whole thing was hopeless.

I told those top-lofty men that Chester had done well at St. Andrew's, that his headmaster wrote that he was "a boy of exceptional ability" and that he had passed his Senior Matric with honors. But they listened to it all with a superior smile, enduring the fairy tales of a foolish mother. It is no use—those men were neither considerate or helpful. Allcut is an Englishman and his manner was detestable. They would not allow a ray of hope—Chester was so far behind he couldn't possibly catch up.

"Well, we are not going to take him away from college," I said decidedly. "If he loses his year he loses it but he is going to stay here."

It was a relief that they did not refuse to accept this. I had had a terrible secret fear that there was *something* more behind their advice to withdraw him. I could not understand them advising us so, merely because Chester had slumped in one dept. There were no bad reports from any other. And I cannot understand it yet. But there was nothing else, so my worst fear was groundless.

It is curious that so often while one is enduring some very bitter thing that a mere minor accident or mischance happens and has a curiously exaggerated effect on the whole matter. As I was talking to them the string of my pearl bead neck-lace suddenly broke—half the pearls cascaded over the floor, the other half slipped down my back and kept dropping every time I moved. I had to scramble about the floor picking them up—for the pearls though only beads were very good French ones and the necklace had been expensive. This silly thing was the last straw. I have never felt so utterly *insignificant*.

I wonder if those men had known I was "L.M. Montgomery" if they would not have been a little more considerate. I have often seen it work out so. But I took good care they should not know. I shall always remember just how they behaved to plain, obscure, countrified Mrs. Ewan Macdonald. *She* received only the scant-iest courtesy from them—verging on contempt because she tried to show them that her son was not altogether a brainless nincompoop.

We finally got away and went to Knox College. The campus was full of boys, coming and going. It seemed to me as if *everybody* knew our errand and pitied us. Chester was out at a class so we went to his room to wait and I broke down and cried. When I finally saw him coming across the yard much of my bitterness and resentment went out of my heart. All at once I remembered him as the dear little baby I had welcomed so passionately, vowing in my heart that he should have every chance—the chances I had wanted so much in youth and could not have. It had all come to *this*—but he was still my son—my dear son.

We showed him the letter. He went a little white when he read the conclusion where we were advised to withdraw him. But his reaction puzzled me.

"Mother, they're crazy. I admit I did make a fool of myself last term. But since New Year's I have missed only two classes in Drawing because I had headaches. And just the other day Blank '——' (one of the demonstrators. I forget what

Chester called him) said to me 'Last term we did not think you were a good student but this term you've certainly pulled up'."

"But there's the report," I said drearily. "And you've never handed your technical English Essay in."

Chester looked amazed.

"Why, mother, I *did*. I handed it in five days before it was due."

I felt sure his surprise was genuine and that in this at least he was telling the truth. We had a long talk. Chester promised that he would get up at seven in the morning for an extra hour's drawing and go back for half his lunch hour. He is going to try his best to catch up as far as possible—if he can be depended on. I can't think what has got into the boy. Did he imagine he could get through college without work? He will lose his year and we lose all the money it has cost us. And the humiliation of his failure! But perhaps it will wake him up. He seems to have needed some drastic treatment.

I came away heart sick. I hated to leave him to his dejection and solitude—even though he had brought it on himself. After all he is young and we are not all wise in everything. At least one's mother should not be too hard on one. But this thing has made us old—old. I feel as if I could not stand up to life anymore.

We had dinner in a restaurant—I could not eat much—and then drove home through the wild afternoon of wind and snow. This evening I looked over Chester's records at St. Andrew's—records I had been so proud of. Well up in his classes—high marks in almost all subjects—"thinks well and reasons clearly" one master had written opposite Mathematics.

My dream regarding "Feb. 7" is "out" with a vengeance.

Last night I was so exhausted I slept well—but the waking was terrible. I did not see how I was to get through Bible class and church. But I got along better than I feared. We can always do what we have to do. Bible class was endurable because I got more or less interested in the lesson and momentarily forgot my worry. But to sit through the church service immobile was hard. After supper Ewan took Stuart to Aurora. Poor chap, his week-end home has been spoiled by this.

Tuesday, Feb. 10, 1931
Another hard day got through somehow. Compelled myself to routine tasks. Went to play practice tonight but had no heart for it. The whole world has gone stale for me.

Wed., Feb. 11, 1931
Today things were a bit better—fortunately, for my nerves had about reached breaking point. A letter came from the complacent Mr. Wilson. He was mistaken about Chester's Technical essay. He had "got the impression" from Prof. Wright that Chester had been the boy who hadn't handed it in. Was "sorry for the misunderstanding" etc. He may well be. He had no business to make such a statement without knowing what he was talking of. "Impression," indeed! He has inflicted the keenest torture on me with his "impression."

My relief was tremendous and I found myself able to work again. Not of course that this makes the real deficiency any better. But it was the worst thing—the thing that had worried me most. Was Chester lying about it? Or was the essay lost, leaving us with no proof that it was ever handed in? These questions have tortured me night and day. But Mr. Wilson "misunderstood" so it is all airily dismissed, bless him! It is a pity that the effect it has had on me cannot be so lightly removed.

Another little bit of good or rather relieving news was a letter from Gibson & Taylor to the effect that they are going to amalgamate with the Can. Ass. Co. This threatened bankruptcy will be thereby averted. Mr. Taylor called me up on the phone and told me the amalgamation would be to our great profit in the long run. I hope so sincerely. Meanwhile that is one great worry almost removed.

Thursday, Feb. 12, 1931
A dull gray day—a bad sort of day for a sore heart. But I am thankful I can work again. A letter came from Chester today. He has had a long talk with Prof. Wright of the Draughting Dept. and there is a better understanding on both sides. Prof. Wright told him that, since he understood the matter better, he would never suggest his withdrawing from the college. This is a great relief.

Sunday, Feb. 15, 1931
I went to Toronto yesterday, having promised sometime ago to read a chapter from my new book to the Authors' Association. I had little heart for it but I found that I enjoyed the evening for all. A little incense does hearten one up! And a little conversation with people who are interested in something besides local gossip. (Not that I don't find local gossip a bit thrilling sometimes myself. But one likes it as a relish, not as a dish.) To be sure, poor old Garvin came up with his perennial yarn of advising that mythical Toronto firm to "take on" *Green Gables*. I can't remember how many times he has told me that.

I am taking a cold and I shiver with fear that it will bring back my asthma. Oh, for spring! This winter has seemed interminable to me.

Wednesday, Feb. 18, 1931
Monday night we were at the Dolson golden wedding, held at Sam McClure's. I had dreaded it because I have no heart for such things just now. But I enjoyed it. The general excitement stimulated me and for a time I "forgot because I must." We had a very delicious dinner, I made a toast speech that seemed to "take"—and after dinner I danced a quadrille for the first time in over twenty-five years!!

All the older folks were dancing. The bride and groom of fifty years led off. I was watching the dancers when Mrs. Sam insisted that I must dance one set before I went home—so for a joke I went out with Sam. I had expected to find I had forgotten all about it. But presto hey! The music suddenly tingled in my feet—I found myself floating over the floor as lightly as thirty years ago—and the pattern of the dance was still woven in my brain. And in my heart was suddenly a burning wish to dance—dance—dance the night away.

But I came home demurely. My dancing days are far in the past—what there was of them. It was one of the minor tragedies of my youth (and I did not think it a minor one then) that I loved dancing so passionately and got so little of it. In all my dancing years I don't think I was at more than twenty dances all told. The first time I ever danced was one night at Ren Toombs when I was a girl of fifteen. We danced an old eight hand reel to the music of a jews-harp a small French hired boy played. I danced with Stanton Macneill—he is dead now. And Ren is dead. And the other dancers are scattered the world over.

Nor have I any longer a dancing heart!

Friday, Feb. 20, 1931
I was in Toronto today, giving readings at Jarvis St. Collegiate. Wrote 200 autographs after it and got a corsage bouquet! This evening I went with Murray and Marion to see *The Cat Creeps*. I haven't been to a movie for ages but I wanted to see this one because *Saturday Night* said it was extremely weird. It was—so much so that Marion couldn't endure it and had to go out. But I enjoyed it—its "creepiness" just gave me some delightful thrills.

I am feeling better these past few days. My head and ear are not bothering me so much. But I never feel really well. What I want is a real *rest*—from worry and monotonous duties and mosquito bites. But these are ever present in this year of the black cat. For instance just now a fight in the choir has brought about a situation in which it looks as if we were going to lose one of our best families. These recurring worries have embittered the whole winter. No sooner does Ewan soothe and patch up in one case than somebody else breaks out in a new quarter.

Friday, Feb. 27, 1931
....Last night I had my first experience of being "on the air." I was in Preston giving an evening of readings and before the concert I went to a broadcasting station and read a couple of my sea poems. I felt as silly and self-conscious as ever I did in my life when I was talking into the microphone. But I think if I had been absolutely alone I would not have felt so. There were a few people with me and a few people always have a bad effect on me though I do not mind a crowded auditorium in the least.

Chester came home tonight. I cannot extract very much from him about his progress in "catching up." But I think he is trying.

Sat., Feb. 28, 1931
Today Ewan took Mrs. Law to the hospital for her operation and Violet came here to stay while her mother is away. Nobody else would take her. Ordinarily I would not mind having her but just now it worries me to have strangers around. It makes just a little harder my efforts to "carry on" and keep a brave face on me. Besides, I'm not overly fond of Miss Violet—nobody is, poor kid. But she has to be looked after while her mother is away. And who but the minister's wife has any responsibility in the matter? However, Marion and I got a bit of fun out of it all. Thank Joseph, Marion is sealed of his tribe.

Monday, Mar. 2, 1931
The Manse, Norval
Had a nervous sleepless night for no reason except just nerves. Felt miserably depressed and as if the best of life were over—as it probably is, but when one

does not realize it too keenly one can forget it and carry on. Nothing pleasant happened today. But something not pleasant did. It is of a piece with this winter's pattern that Mrs. Mason should tell me today that she was to be married in June and wanted to leave the last of March.

It wasn't a surprise at all. I knew she was engaged and would be getting married some time this year. But from something she said not long ago I had thought she would not be going until the fall. So far then, the news was a surprise and an unpleasant one.

We both cried. Mrs. Mason and I have got on very well together and have had four very pleasant years. She is the best maid I have ever had. Neat, competent, a good worker. Never "forgot" things. Was interested in everything. Perfectly healthy. Good company. I haven't a fault to find with her—except that she really was a terror to dishes, breaking them and chipping them. My good dinner set is chipped terribly. But it was a pleasure to work with her and I feel lost at the thought of her going.

When she came I think people thought I was crazy because I took a woman with a young baby. And I knew it was a doubtful experiment. But it turned out successfully. Helen has always been a good, well-behaved quiet child....

I do think Mrs. Mason might have stayed till after housecleaning. It is the worst possible time to take on a new maid. I suppose I must advertise. There is certainly no one around here I would care to have in the house.

I have finished the *Iliad*. Had I been able to read the original I should probably have enjoyed it. But I got very tired of the unending gore and slaughter, especially in Pope's smooth, monotonous rhymes. However, I feel a certain satisfaction in having at least achieved the reading of it. And I got one good chuckle when I came across the lines—

A mighty stone, such as *in modern days*
no two of earth's degenerate sons could raise.

The italics are mine! Here, nearly a thousand years before Christ, was old Homer lamenting the degeneracy of "modern days!!" Just as folks are doing now!

Monday, March 9, 1931
I don't think there will be much of me left when this winter gets through with me. I have been in bed ever since last Tuesday with one of the worst attacks of flu I have ever had. I felt despairing when I realized it was coming on for I feared my asthma would come back with it but strangely it did not. However, I was sick enough without it and had a dreadful cough. The doctor gave me serum to prevent the disease getting worse. If it *did* prevent it I am thankful he gave it, for I was bad enough as it was. I crawled up today but feel exactly like a caterpillar someone has stepped on. And the look of me!!

One little gleam of sunshine came this week. Chester wrote that he had at last caught up with his drawings. That is good news as far as number goes. But how about the quality?

Also *Anne's House of Dreams* is being translated into Polish.

We have had a terrible blizzard and roads are blocked everywhere. There has been nothing like it in Ontario for years. For the first time since we came here Ewan could not get to Union on Sunday.

Saturday, March 14, 1931
I haven't liked myself one day this week. I cough all night and all day am a victim to that odd feeling of not belonging to this—or any world—that so often follows a bad spell of flu. This feeling is intensified by the state of being storm-bound. We can't even get our car out of the garage. Marion went to Preston last Saturday to visit friends and has never been able to get back and I miss her terribly.

Mrs. Mason had a letter from Jean Leslie this week saying that Sutherland Beaton had left there, leaving a board bill of thirty dollars unpaid! And we found Violet Law out in a series of the most barefaced lies. I can't go into details. It was all sickening. And after all our kindness to her while she was here! Fortunately her mother came back from the hospital the same day we discovered it and Violet went home. I really couldn't have tolerated her in the house after that. There was not the slightest excuse for her lying, either. There is not much use in trying to help that class of people. They are incapable of gratitude. But I feel badly over it. I was sorry for Violet and wanted to help her.

Sunday, March 22, 1931
Well, I am through with match-making!!!

All this winter the one bright spot has seemed to be what I took for the happiness of Murray and Marion! Ever since Marion came here Murray has apparently been devoted to her. He has taken her out constantly, he has had her visiting his home and all his relatives, he has spent evening after evening here till all hours. Marion bloomed like a rose and I had a certain vicarious happiness in looking on at them. I even felt a little wistful envy now and again. It seemed such an ideal match. Both young, happy, in love with each other. So it seemed to me and, I may say, to everyone. Everyone in the church seemed to view it as a settled thing. I have had lots of hints about it. As for me, I was as pleased and full of plans as if Marion had been my own daughter. It would be jolly to have someone of my own living so near me, in that beautiful home beyond the pine hill. I even had the wedding gift I was going to give Marion picked out!

Well, we have all been fools together!

For the first two months of Marion's visit I know she was perfectly happy. Like everybody else, she thought her little romance was developing just as we hoped. This past month I have thought at times she seemed a little dull but as Murray was as apparently devoted as ever I did not connect it with him but put it down to the fact that she was disappointed over not getting the place in Eaton's or Simpson's we had tried to get for her. The business depression is so acute that they are not taking on any new clerks. Marion was anxious to get a place. Times are hard at home and I imagined she was anxious to earn some money to provide her own trousseau when the time came for it.

Then came the bolt from the blue!

Last night when I came home...on the 12 o'clock radial Murray and Marion met me in his car and brought me down. They had been spending the evening together. At the gate I slipped out and in, leaving them to say good-night alone. A few minutes later as I was in the kitchen Marion came in, walked straight through the dining room and upstairs without a word or a glance at anyone. This was so unlike her that I was rather disturbed. But this morning at breakfast she mentioned the fact that she was going up with Murray after church to have supper there, as his brother Mac and his wife were to be there for a visit, so I supposed everything was all right. After service friends of Marion came from Toronto and she could not go up to Lairds but said Murray was coming down in the evening. Everyone was out this evening but Marion and me. We were sitting here in the dining room writing letters; Marion was writing one to her mother. When the door-bell rang she got up and handed me the letter she had been writing. "I want you to read this, Aunt Maud. You'll have to know it sooner or later."

That speech told me at once that something had gone wrong. With a nasty premonitory chill I went into the library and read the letter. Here it is—at least, the part of it concerned with the affair:—

"I think I warned you a few letters ago that Murray and I would never be anything but the best of friends. Well, we had it out last night and that is all we ever will be. I've known somehow for over a month or so but the subject was never brought up in real earnest until last Wednesday night. He knew I cared for him a good deal and so far as being friends goes—well, it goes pretty deep; but under the circumstances I could not be happy as his wife. He has realized that for some time but don't think less of him because of it—he is just as fine as you think he is but it was not an easy subject to tackle for him. The main reason—there is more than one—is that a home for me means little ones and since Murray practically hates them—well, there's only one thing to do. He can't help it or understand it. As for getting over it he has tried hard enough—tried to love Mac's and Mercedes' wee one—but the loathing is still there.

Well we've had a happy winter. It will soon be over now. Murray has certainly been very kind to me. I guess he *has* spoiled me. He has been a great pal and will still be."

I read this letter—and felt suddenly old and feeble and silly and foolish. I curled up on the lounge and cried. I could not have felt more bitterly hurt and disappointed if Marion had been my own child. Something that had seemed beautiful entirely now was spoiled and tawdry and repellent.

And I felt resentful! Nobody asked Murray to come after Marion. I never even mentioned to him last fall that she was coming up, for fear he might think I attached some significance to it. To everyone else I said Marion was coming up to try to get something to do in Toronto. So Murray was under no compulsion whatever to run after her as he has done.

As for this curious obsession of his about children:—I remember that a couple of years ago Chester, who had been up at Lairds, came home and remarked at the supper table, "Gee, mother, I never knew anyone who detests kids as Murray does." "Nonsense," I said. "He doesn't detest them." "Yes, mother, he does. He says he hates them." "He'll get over that when he has some of his own," I said. I really did not attach any importance to it. I have heard several self-conscious lads declare they couldn't stand kids. But it is evidently something deeper with Murray. I can't understand it. He is such a nice, gentle chap—the very type of man you would expect would love children.

Murray did not stay very long and after he left poor Marion came out and we had a cry together and a long talk. Marion feels dreadfully. But she is a pretty brave girl and will not let it spoil her life. She says, in spite of everything, she is glad she came because now she *knows*. If she had not come she would have been haunted all her life by the question "If I *had* gone would things have come right?"

I feel this, too. In my first bitter reaction I wished I had never meddled in the matter at all—never asked Marion to come up. But if I hadn't Marion would always have felt dissatisfied, Myrtle would have resented my not giving her a chance, and I would always have felt remorsefully that, if I had, it might all have been as we hoped. So after all I don't regret it. All the same, as I said in the beginning, I'm through with match-making for all time.

I do not know what the "other reasons" Marion referred to in her letter are. I asked Marion plainly, "Does Murray really *care*?" She buried her face on my shoulder and murmured, "He cares—*some*." That told me all. Murray *doesn't* care enough. If he did, all difficulties could be smoothed away, even the matter of his obsession regarding children. And this is why I feel bitter against Murray. He should not have come after her at all unless he loved her. She would not have been led on to care so deeply then—but what boots it to discuss? I suppose Murray cannot love to order any more than anyone else. I can't understand why he doesn't love Marion. She is such an attractive girl. They seemed made for each other. Marion is a girl in a thousand. Murray will never find anyone who will make him the wife she would. Well, I may be able to see all this in a different light sometime but just now it seems to me the last straw of this intolerable winter.

I should not try to help people. I do not bring luck to anyone. I have seen this before, more than once and thrice.

Marion felt as if she ought to go home. I have dissuaded her. There is nothing there for her. In a few years Keith will be bringing in a wife. I have told Marion just to stay here until there is an opening in Toronto as there is bound to be sooner or later. Then she can take a business course in the evenings and fit herself for a really good business position. This is what she wants to do, I know.

I hate to go to bed. I shall not be able to sleep. Everything seems *ugly*. It is years since I felt so bitterly disappointed over anything. It seems to pierce to the very core.

Monday, March 23, 1931
I did not sleep well of course—cried half the night like an idiot. But one cannot help being an idiot. If one could life would be a simpler affair. This has been a blue day all through. That nothing might be lacking for discomfort a letter came from Chester this morning saying that he had been laid up for a week with flu and so lost much valuable time. I suppose it means that his last chance of saving his year has gone.

Tuesday, March 24, 1931
I had a good sleep last night and feel abler to go on today. But I cannot take an interest in anything. Somehow, I feel bitter and unfairly treated—like a hurt child. Marion is brave and cheerful but I know she is not sleeping well. Her nights must be hard, poor child.

When I knew Mrs. Mason was going away I wrote to Jennie Harrison to ask her if she would come. She wrote me that she would like to but her sister Edna's health was so poor that her mother was not willing for her to take a permanent situation. I was disappointed for Jennie is a wonderful cook and housekeeper and a girl I like. But Mrs. Shier when she heard of it wrote me and said there was a Mrs. Thompson in Zephyr who wanted a place and she thought I would be very well suited with her. She had a baby girl a year old and had left her husband because he was "such a brute."

I was not overly enthusiastic. I had hoped to get a maid without a baby. The experiment had turned out all right in the case of Helen, who was a very good child. But the odds were against its being so successful another time. Then, too, I did not like the husband-fact. You know where you are with a dead man! But a living one may turn up any time and persuade a wife to return to his bed and board. And finally the very name of Zephyr sticks in my nostrils.

On the other hand, I did not like the idea of advertising and taking up again with a perfect stranger. Mrs. Shier knows what I need and her recommendation carries weight. So I wrote Mrs. Thompson and had a letter from her today saying she would come.

Wednesday, April 1, 1931
Yesterday I wasn't well but today I have felt better than for a long while—perhaps because darling Stuart came home last night for the holidays. But the day's unpleasantness was not to seek, for soon after breakfast a wire came from Mary Beaton telling of Archie's sudden death. Archie Beaton's death means nothing to me for I never liked him. But I am upset because of Mary. He did not make her life happy. He was queer in his mind for several years—which was not his fault—and drank heavily until very recent years—which was his fault—so that altogether Mary's existence with him has not been an enviable one. Nevertheless, no doubt she will feel his death keenly and she is in no shape to endure worry and sorrow.

Mary is the first of our old "quartette" to be a widow. Of course Archie was fully fifteen years older than she is. And it seems but the other day that I danced at her wedding.

Saturday, April 4, 1931
I have been sleeping a little better of late and so feeling better in daytime. But I wonder if I shall ever again feel glad just to be alive.

Tonight however I had a good laugh—for which I thank whatever gods there be. I was re-reading Mark Twain's *Roughing It* and came on his account of "Tom Quartz"—the cat who was blown up in a mine. I have read that a score of times and every time I read it I simply double up in spasms. Tonight I laughed until the tears came into my eyes. Old "Tom" did me more good than all the rotten medicine I've been taking this year.

But I would like to get away from *everything*—just to be alone and quiet for years and years—in some green land where I need never hear the name of a missionary auxiliary or a Bible class or a choir or a board of managers!....

Tuesday, April 7, 1931
....We had our "Banquet" tonight, closing the Guild for the winter. I had a rather good time—on the surface. But oh, I'm so tired.

Wednesday, April 8, 1931
This morning Ewan and I had to go to Toronto. And I bid Mrs. Mason good-bye for she was going in the afternoon and would not be here when we returned. We met Mrs. Thompson and her baby "June" and brought her home. I never trust first impressions so will defer all expressed opinion on her until she has been here sometime. When we came home I *realized* that Mrs. Mason had gone. I was very tired and this, coupled with bad news about Mr. Greenwood, broke me down and I made a fool of myself. Couldn't eat any supper—couldn't stop crying. I *hate* crying before people.

I have been utterly depressed tonight. Marion had bad news of her mother—too. She is very ill with a bad attack of jaundice. I rather think her disappointment about Murray has brought this on—jaundice is often induced by unpleasant emotional disturbances and Myrtle is of the type in which such effects follow. On the whole this has not been a heartening day.

Monday, April 13, 1931
Things no better. Still coughing, sleeping badly, nervous and down hearted. Mrs. Sam back in choir, but Mrs. Davis is acting up again. No cheerful mail—Myrtle very miserable—poor Marion in the swither as to whether she should go home—June Thompson crying night and day. But this afternoon I had a temporary escape. Went to lunch with the Hodgins in Brampton—very nice intellectual people—and read a paper to the Literary Society there. Came home cheered up and far less nervous.

Tuesday, April 14, 1931
"Here hath been dawning another blue day." The first delightful thing was a man calling while we were at breakfast with a summons for Chester for "driving negligently" on the public highway! I was amazed for Chester has really always been a good driver. Of course this spoiled the day. As Chester could not appear in person E. had to go to Mimico and see the magistrate. It turned out that the young idiot had been driving *too slow* (with his arm around Luella Reid!!!) and did not have his permit with him when the "cop" demanded it. Ewan had to pay fifteen dollars fine! And this on a spring when every cent counts!

Ewan went to see Prof. Haultain in Toronto. Haultain is the man who gets the boys places in the mines for summer work. He had told Chester he had no work for him because of his poor record in college. But E. interceded and Haultain relented and gave him a letter to the Frood mine in Sudbury. I am glad because it will be better for C. to be away and at work. He and his father don't get on well when he is home—which is not *all* Chester's fault by any means—and there is little for him to occupy his time with. It is a great relief to me that this is arranged. It has been one of my recent worries.

Then tonight another blow fell. The Bank of Nova Scotia here has been closed!

I really feel badly over this. All my life till I came to Norval I have been inconvenienced by not being near a bank. It has been so convenient here. And now I am back to the old inconveniences. The bank has been going behind ever since the mill was burned down. That really killed Norval.

Then, too, this means that Mr. Greenwood, even if he recovers, will not come back to Norval. And he will leave a huge blank in our social life and in our Guild.

Stuart's report came today and *was* a bright spot. But then Chester used to have excellent reports at St. Andrew's too....

Thursday, April 16, 1931
Last night we all went to Aurora for a drive when we took Stuart back. And it was delightful—through a green, mystical twilight, under soft sunset skies. Marion is ideal company for a drive—interested in everything. I enjoyed it so much that I came home rested and cheered and had the best night's sleep I've had for weeks. I think all I need for recovery is rest from work and worry. But that seems difficult to get just now.

Saturday, April 18, 1931
Tonight Marion got word that Myrtle was very ill with an attack of peritonitis and they wanted her to go home at once. She will go Monday....

Monday, April 20, 1931
This morning E. and I drove Marion in to Toronto and saw her off on the Montreal train. I felt wretched. If Marion had been going home, the fiancée of Murray Laird, to prepare for her wedding I would have been as happy as a lark.

It was a lovely day and when we got home the daffodils were in bloom in the front yard. But nothing cheered me up and while I was restoring the room Marion had occupied to its guest-room status I felt so lonely that I couldn't keep the tears back. Then tonight, a man called and asked for Mrs. Thompson. A little later when I went into the kitchen he was there and she calmly introduced him as her husband!!!!

He stayed till eleven! Now, what is in the wind? I suppose he is trying to get her to go back to him. A nice state of affairs. But what else would one expect this fiendish year?

However, I have gained three pounds these last two weeks, so perhaps I am on the up grade physically....

Tuesday, April 21, 1931
Chester came home today. He thinks he passed all his exams but two. If this is so, he will not lose his year, although he will have to take supplementals. But it is the

lab work I am afraid of. In that he passes or fails on the year's work, not in exams, and I fear he did not make the grade. The suspense is abominable. One can face what one knows. He is very glad he has got work for the summer and is determined to make good in it at least.

Sunday, April 26, 1931
This has been a devilish week—of course. Luck has had double pneumonia!

Last Wednesday morning when I got up I found Luck sitting on the rug in front of my mirror looking very stodgy. He had been out in the night—getting out through a broken cellar window—and had evidently gorged himself on something for he was as full as a tub. I thought he was feeling sick from over-eating, as happened before, and left him alone most of the day as we were very busy housecleaning. In mid-afternoon I grew uneasy. He was lying on the sofa and his little flanks were heaving tumultuously. I did not like it so I phoned the vet. He said it was likely only stomach trouble and advised a dose of castor oil. I gave it to him but before long he vomited it up.

He grew worse rapidly—could not get his breath and half sat, half lay with his mouth open. After supper I decided he had been poisoned and phoned Dr. Nickell to come up. The vet came—prodded and squeezed poor Luck—who gave some piteous cries in the process—and then said "Your cat has pneumonia. One lung is full and the other nearly so."

I felt despair fill my heart. I had known of many cats getting pneumonia but I had never heard of one recovering. The vet gave me tablets to give Luck every three hours and said to keep him covered up warm by an open window where he could get the fresh air.

This was easier said than done. It was no easy matter to keep Luck covered. I dared not leave him and I could not stay in too cold a room myself—the weather had turned very cold—so I took him into the only vacant room—the guest room,—covered him up on the foot of the bed by the open window and sat up all night with him. It was a hard night. The poor cat suffered so. He could not get his breath and his eyes followed me so pitifully as if to say, "Can't *you* do something for me?" I felt broken-hearted. Luck has been such a dear little chum and companion and this hard winter and spring in especial he has been such a comfort to me. I put in that wretched night, while the rain poured down outside and my poor little pet fought his battle for life, trying to picture and so discount life without Luck. No Lucky— no gray puss galloping across the lawn to meet me whenever I came home—no cat beautifully folded up for slumber on the spare room bed and looking up half guiltily, half pleadingly as if to say, "I know I shouldn't be here but am I not beautiful? Have you the heart to send me away?"—no pussy lying across my stomach in the wee sma's—no little hunter proudly bringing his kill to my bedside at dawn—no ball of furry stripes on the cushioned library chair—no cat appearing from nowhere whenever I went to work in the garden and insisting on helping me—no cat galloping upstairs as soon as I begin writing, to curl up on my papers and go to sleep— no delighted purr every time a kind look fell on him or a kind finger touched him—in short no lovely, loved, lovable Luck in existence at all—nothing but a pitiable little rack of fur and bones buried somewhere under the trees on the lawn.

Luck had captured the vet's heart. He said he had never seen such a nice cat and he came up in the morning on his own bat just to see how he was doing. The report was none too encouraging. Luck was no better. On the other hand he was no worse. I was not much good all that long, dark, cold wet day. But at night I thought Luck seemed to be breathing a little easier. I sat up another night with him, dozing fitfully with my head on a pillow. By morning I was sure he was better. He could breathe with his mouth shut. And when I saw him trying feebly to wash his face I knew he had the turn for the better. I really cried with joy.

Since then he has slowly improved. But today was the first time he ate a little....

Monday, April 27, 1931
It is still bitterly cold. I have been busy today getting C's outfit ready. A letter from Marion today does not paint a very bright picture of her mother's condition. Luck seems pretty well but the poor cat has gone to a shadow. Still, he is alive!

Saturday, May 2, 1931
There is another row on in the choir—this time started by Mr. Capps, the trainer, a very indiscreet and peppery man. Ewan is almost discouraged and so am I. There has been nothing this whole winter but these petty church squabbles.

But we have had a few pleasant days away from it all. Thursday morning we started for Sudbury, to take Chester up and made the whole 320 miles in one day, getting to Sudbury at ten at night. The last 80 miles were through a Dantean landscape lighted by a full moon.

Sudbury is a town of some 20,000 surrounded by hideous bare hills wherein hides precious bane. Chester went to the mine, passed no end of red tape, re doctor examinations and so forth, and was told to report next morning. We got him a nice boarding house—only it was No *13* Lorne St. I don't like that. No, I *don't*! I don't care who laughs at me. No good will come of it.

When the time came to leave Chester I felt dreadful. My baby—away up there in that rough country—with all kinds of temptations. Well, he must learn to face them. So far, Chester though he has let us down in some ways, has never shown any inclination to riotous living. Nevertheless, I left him with a heavy heart.

We had a nice drive home taking it more leisurely, and got here in mid-afternoon. The house seemed terribly lonely—Mrs. Mason—Marion—Chester—gone. But thanks be to some pitiful god Lucky is still here and came to meet me with joyful purrs.

Monday, May 4, 1931
Norval, Ont.
We had a letter from Chester this evening. He likes Sudbury—but the letter was not reassuring. He said he went to work Sat. morning and his first job was to roll heavy stones and break them with a hammer. Naturally, he was not very expert at it—and the "boss" fired him on the spot! But the men said he hadn't had a fair chance and got another boss to give him a different job.

This worries me. Surely they can't expect a boy who has never done any hard manual labor to keep up with old hands from the very first. It is absurd. Prof.

Haultain told Ewan they did not send them underground at first or expect them to work hard the first summer. But this does not look like it.

Friday, May 8, 1931
This has been a nasty week. I haven't felt well and every evening I walked down for the evening mail, dreading a letter from Chester. None came till tonight. He got on all right at his second job but it lasted only a day and a half and then he was set to shovelling "muck" into a car and unloading it elsewhere. He does not say much about it but somehow the letter left me vaguely uneasy.

There is more trouble in regard to the choir, too. Really, this sort of thing can't go on. It's wearing us both out.

I have been housecleaning—and hating it. Generally, I like housecleaning—it is nice to get all the winter grime and dust out and everything freshened up. But this year I can't put any heart in it. I'm not well—I'm worried—I'm down-hearted.

I wonder if I will ever again feel glad just to be alive.

Saturday, May 9, 1931
This morning the Engineering pass lists were out in the paper—and Chester's name was not among them!

It's what we were expecting of course. But this did not make it less bitter. Somehow, I couldn't help *hoping*—he thought he passed in all but two.

It has been a wretched day. I wanted to get away and cry but had to keep up appearances. But I have felt very very bitterly. I have not deserved of Chester that he should let us down like this.

Sunday, May 10, 1931
A bad night—tearful and sleepless. And then to go to church, feeling that every-one knows. Worse—there was a C. Macdonald on the civil engineering list who passed and some people think this was Chester and congratulated us. And then we have the humiliation of confessing that it was not.

A Miss Ferguson came this afternoon to speak at our "Open Missionary" service tonight. I had to entertain her smilingly and talk about a hundred things when I felt little like it. Oh, well, this sort of thing can't last always. One comes to the end in time.

Monday, May 11, 1931
The Manse, Norval, Ont.
It's rather a curious experience to hear of a compliment having been paid you thirty-seven years after it was uttered. Fan Wise sent me a copy of a recent P.W.C. magazine. In it was an article by Dr. Ramsay who was in my class at P.W.C. Writing of Dr. Anderson, he drew a picture of the old Doc when he was delivering himself of an opinion on something. In this especial instance it was the first issue of our college paper, for which I had written a sketch entitled "The Usual Way,"—a skit on two girls studying. "A work of—ah—eh—*genius*."

I could see Dr. Anderson as he delivered this pronouncement. But I never knew at the time that he even read the sketch. He never mentioned it to me.

Dr. Ramsay's article made me *homesick*.

Tuesday, May 12, 1931

Ewan and I were in Toronto today and we went to the college and got Chester's marks. It is far worse than we thought. He failed in *nine* subjects out of fifteen! *How* could he have made such a mess of things?

We had a bitter drive home. Everything seemed tarnished. I feel as if I couldn't look anybody in the face. There are some who will be glad of this!

This evening I got out all Chester's St. Andrew's reports and looked them over—crying bitterly all the time. I had been so proud of them. Not a bad one among them all—lots of marks in the 80's and 90's—"good student"—"reasons well"—"thinks clearly"—"this mark (82!) not worthy of his ability"—"has unusual reasoning powers"—an average of 80% on his five years record! How comes it that a boy with this record fails so disgracefully his first year in college? Just pure laziness, that is all. One may as well look the unsavory fact in the face. And it is not only that he has lost a year in college. It is what is going to become of his whole life?

Wednesday, May 13, 1931

A sleepless night. Mr. Taylor was here in the morning. The situation regarding Gibson & Taylor is not very promising yet but the Can. Ass. Co. matters are cleared up and that was my biggest worry.

This afternoon Nora and some of her friends—old Island folk—came out and had afternoon tea. In one way I enjoyed it—it is always so good to taste the Island flavor—but in another it was torture, for I was afraid they would ask awkward questions about Chester. Still, their visit did me good—pulled me out of myself a bit.

We are putting in the garden now. I compel myself to do it but all my old joy in it is gone. Everything seems so *tarnished* this spring. It is dreadful to be unhappy in *spring*. The world seems so happy—so out of tune with one's unhappiness.

Saturday, May 16, 1931

I slept better last night and feel a little better in all ways today. In the *Guardian* that came this morning was an account of the burning down of father's old store at Clifton. I am sorry. It was one of the old landmarks of my past.

Monday, May 18, 1931
Norval, Ont.

This morning I picked up a *Guardian* and read in it a paragraph announcing the death of Edwin Simpson's wife in the hospital in Washington State.

That the death of a woman I never knew should throw a cloud of depression over the entire day for me is a psychological puzzle. But it did. I suppose it was partly because it brought back that bitter spring thirty-four years ago—*thirty-four* years!—and partly because it is not a pleasant thing when one's contemporaries or the wives of one's contemporaries begin to pass off the stage.

Ed is pastor of the Baptist church in Yakima, Wash. He has wandered all over the continent, never remaining long in one place. I wonder why. He was always a restless, nervous mortal. He will be very lonely now. But I suppose I am being quite hateful and cynical when I say that if Ed is not married again within three years it will not be for want of trying. Not that he is to be blamed for that!

Tuesday, May 19, 1931

This has been another dreadful day. This morning I was helping Mrs. Thompson stretch the curtains on the lawn when I heard her give an exclamation. I looked up—and there was Chester.

I took him into the house and heard his story with indignation. I have never tried to excuse Chester for losing his year. That was all his own fault and he admits it. But this is not. He has not had a square deal.

He was ill three days out of the first week. They told him men were often like that at first when they went underground but that it would pass. It did and he was not troubled with it again. Monday of the second week he twisted his ankle— something that might happen to anyone—and was laid off for a day and a half. Wednesday he went back to work. Thursday the boss told him he was not getting out as much ore as he should and must do better or he would "fire" him. Chester tried his best and he says he got out quite as much as the fellow who was working with him. But Friday they paid him off and told him to go. Moreover, he found that the boss had told them on *Wednesday*—before he spoke to Chester at all—that they were to "give him his time."

I simply can't understand it. Do they expect a college boy who has never done any such hard work, to be able to hold his own with the old experienced workers? If so, it is most unjust. *Anyone* would need at least two weeks to get used to it and acclimated to the underground. It would be fair to dock their pay until they could do full work but to discharge them before they had got fairly started is outrageous. It is not as if they had to keep them on permanently.

So, I can't understand it at all and I don't blame Chester for this. But the whole situation is intolerable. If Chester had done well in college it would not matter. Or if, failing in college, he had made good all summer, it would have helped. But now everyone will believe that he was fired because he was no good and his professors will believe it—and it will make everything far harder for him next year. Besides, how will he ever get another chance?....

Thursday, May 21, 1931

There is no use thinking you can't endure things. You *have* to—and you *do*. But these past three days—and nights—have been very bitter.

There was a bit of good news in Marion's letter yesterday. Her mother has taken a definite turn for the better. Will it last? One must hope so.

Tonight when a phone call came I heard a voice say "*Mr.* Macdonald of Aurora" wants to talk to you. They were speaking of *Stuart. Mr.* Macdonald! My baby!!

Tuesday, May 26, 1931
Norval, Ont.

This house is always strangely empty when Stuart's laugh has gone out of it. He has been home for the week-end and Victoria day.

I have settled down to writing and routine work again but my heart is always very heavy. Worried, too, with several annoying little physical ailments—one of them being eczema on neck and arms.

Mrs. Thompson went away—or went home—for the holiday. Her *husband* came and took her! I can't fathom the situation. But if he shows up again I'm going to ask her just what she means to do. I have to know. As it is, I can't feel settled or make any plans for the summer. Not that I *want* to make plans. I've no heart for that. But certain matters must be arranged for.

Rev. Mr. Paulin of St. Andrew's called here last night. He said Stuart was "a very popular boy."

This afternoon I led a W.M.S. at Mrs. Humphrey's and tonight I have a headache. An aspirin will cure that probably—but what will cure a heartache?

Sunday, May 31, 1931

Have just finished reading—for the second and probably the last time—Holt's *Cosmic Relations and Immortality*. It has left me firmly convinced that there is nothing in "spiritualism." Of course I admit there are many strange and mysterious things which nobody can fully explain but I can never believe the "spirits" of our dead do them.

May is finished. A beautiful month as far as weather and the outward world go. A hellish one as regards my life.

Monday, June 1, 1931

At last the name of my new book is decided. For four months we—Stokes, McClelland and I have been wrangling over it. Well, wrangling is too hard a word—but we have had a time over it.

When I finished the book I found myself unable to decide on a name that really pleased me. So I put a list of tentative titles on the first page and told the publishers to select what pleased them. The titles were, *The Quest of the Jug—Darks and Penhallows—The Fun Begins—A Tangled Web* and another one I have forgotten. They liked none of these. Then I suggested *Aunt Becky Began It.* That didn't please them either—it was "too long" but they wanted to call it *Aunt Becky.* This was absurd because "Aunt Becky" dies in the first section and the book is not about her at all. Stokes wanted to call it *The Moonman* and I countered with *Crying For The Moon* which would have been a very suitable title indeed. But Mr. French thought that "didn't sound like a Montgomery Book" and suggested *Rose of Love* or *Ribbons of Moonlight*—nice sentimental blue-and-pink, sweet-sixteen titles for a humorous novel mainly about middle-aged people! I got plain mad finally and told them to call it any darned thing they pleased. So tonight came Stokes' letter and catalogue. They have decided on *A Tangled Web* after all. I am glad it is one of my own titles. After all, I wouldn't like a book of mine to bear a name of someone else's choosing. Thank God, it escaped *Rose of Love.*

122

Another letter from Isobel...! Pleading to be allowed to come down and "hold me in her arms for a whole night." I am to write and tell her I love her! Otherwise she cannot live.

Love her! If the poor girl knew how I loathe her! I shall have to write very plainly and tell her I cannot tolerate this sort of thing any longer, be the consequences what they may. I cannot be pestered in this fashion any longer, no matter what she does. In this letter she speaks in a veiled fashion of suicide. This is what I have always been afraid of. But come what may, I must escape from this sort of thing. She might as well be dead as living the unhappy life she does—a life in which no one can help her because she is not helped by the things which appeal to normal people. If her sister...had stayed home and companioned her instead of going to Japan to teach heathens who don't particularly want to be taught I think she would have been doing God more real service...Miss Ferguson told me when she was here that when...[she] was in the Training Home she was more trouble than all the rest put together. For one thing she had to be given a room by herself because no girl could put up with her on account of her insisting on *praying* from ten to eleven every night when her unfortunate roommate wanted to sleep!!!

I have no appetite—I sleep poorly—I feel a dreadful nervous unrest all the time. Everything unpleasant hurts and worries me out of all proportion to its importance. What I need is a good long absolute *rest* away from all problems and worries and work. But I cannot get it, so must just crawl on.

Tuesday, June 2, 1931
Today I was looking over two short sketches, one of the Macneills, the other of the Montgomerys; it occurred to me that it would not be a bad idea to copy them both in this journal to ensure their preservation against any accident.

The Macneill document is in the form of a letter written by Aunt Mary Lawson to some nephew of hers who had asked for information about the clan....[*See Appendix A.*]

"*Aunt Mary Lawson*"

There are, in Aunt Mary's account of her family, many gaps, some of which I can fill from other sources, many of which I cannot. The nephew to whom she wrote the letter was a Harold MacDougall, whose mother Emma was the daughter of Great-Uncle William Macneill. She was considered a great beauty in youth but her marriage did not turn out successfully. I think she left her husband or he left her. They lived, I think, in California.

Aunt Mary is mistaken in saying that John Macneill came to the Island with the *first* Chief Justice Mr. Stewart. Dupont was the first Chief Justice and Stewart was the second, coming to P.E.I.—then St. John's Island—in 1775. This John Macneill seems almost a mythical personage to me. Aunt

Mary says he came from Argyllshire but does not tell the parish although one would think she must have known. It has always seemed to me a curious thing that we have absolutely no documents either in the Macneill or Montgomery families connecting them with the relatives they left behind in the Old Land. There must have been letters exchanged, even if they were few and far between. But there is not a trace of any such. To all seeming, when those families came to Canada they were cut off at once and forever from all connection with the friends they had left behind. One only tradition has been handed down—that Hector Macneill, the minor Scottish poet who wrote "Come Under my Plaidie etc" was a first or second cousin of John Macneill. I think there is no doubt of the truth of this. Aunt Mary's father told it to her, receiving it in his turn from his father. Besides, all our Macneills had the literary strain in them and some of them composed poetry quite as good as Hector Macneill's.

John Macneill came out in 1775. The family of William Simpson came out in the same year, I think in the same vessel and that it was on the voyage that John Macneill met his future wife, Margaret Simpson, then a girl of sixteen. As their eldest son was not born until 1782 it does not seem probable they were married much before 1781 but I do not know the date of their wedding. This marriage was the first of the long line of intermarriages between the Macneills and Simpsons. They were hardly to be blamed. It was not easy to find suitable mates in those days. There were very few families on the Island, apart from the French. And a good many of the emigrants who came out then were of a type very inferior to the Macneills and Simpsons. When a Macneill or Simpson wanted a bride his choice was restricted almost to his own clan. The result was that good and bad qualities were reproduced and intensified to a marked degree. Whatever the Simpsons and Macneills were, they were not colorless or negligible.

It may be in order to copy here the birth register of the said Simpson family and the certificate of character they brought with them....

It must have required a tremendous amount of courage for William and Janet Simpson to emigrate with such a family to the wildwoods of North America, crossing a limitless waste of seas. Perhaps it was the courage of desperation, seeing nothing ahead of their large family but pinching poverty. But I wonder what Janet thought about it when she left. Sixteen year old Margaret took it more lightly, I expect. It would be an adventure for her. I wonder what she and John looked like and if they walked together on the ship and talked of the strange new land to which they were going. The "certificate of character" is couched in the stilted language of an older day. And note the Scotchman's caution. He is not going to come out flat-footed and say that William and Janet are fit, really fit, to be received into any community of society. No, no, he will not commit himself so far. All he will say, is that he "knows no reason" why they shouldn't be!

Well, John and Margaret got married. They must have lived in Charlottetown at first for their oldest son, William Macneill, my great grandfather was born there. I have often heard my grandfather say that his father was the first English male child to be born in Charlottetown. A female child had been born before him.

As Cavendish was not settled by the "Simpsons, Macneills and Clarks" until 1790, John Macneill must have lived elsewhere until then. I am not sure where but I have heard it was somewhere east of the Island. Nor do I know what finally induced them to move to Cavendish but move they did in 1790, and lived in a little log house near the shore. I do not know how old John Macneill was when he died but as he lived long enough to beget nine sons and three daughters he must at least have attained to middle life. Then one day he suddenly took ill with what was called inflammation of the bowels. There was no doctor nearer than Charlottetown and Charlottetown was at the other side of the Island to be reached only by a narrow bridle path through the woods. So John got on horseback and Margaret mounted behind him and so they rode to Charlottetown. It was their last ride together. Nowadays John would be promptly operated on for appendicitis and probably go home safely with his Margaret in a motor car in two or three weeks. But nobody knew anything about appendixes then. John died. It was impossible to take his body home for burial over a bridle track. So he was buried in the old "Malpeque Road" burying ground just outside of Charlottetown. No stone ever marked the spot and the last resting place of John Macneill is unknown.

Margaret managed to bring up her family; and then in old age she made a sorry break. She outraged her family by marrying some old man, poor and of a lower social class. I have heard his name but have forgotten it. I know it was not a pretty one. Eventually he died or left her. She lived to be ninety years and ten months old—really, one couldn't kill the women of those days with a meat axe! She was buried in Cavendish graveyard and her grave is marked with an old slab of the Island sandstone on which is recorded that she was the wife of John Macneill. No mention is made of the second husband. Neither Simpsons nor Macneills were proud of *him*.

Of the twelve children of this marriage, apart from my Great grandfather William—I remember hearing of only four—"Uncle" Malcolm, Uncle Neill, Uncle David, and "Aunt Effie." Uncle Malcolm married a Sally Campbell, sister of Uncle John Campbell's father. He built the house where Amanda lived in her girlhood and it was such a palace in those days that it was always called "Government House." Malcolm had the renowned Macneill temper. Neill was a black sheep to some extent, got his housekeeper "into trouble" and married her. The other Macneills froze them both out. Aunt Effie married a Simpson—of course—and their son William Simpson whom I knew well in childhood was always called "Will Effie." There were so many William Simpsons they had to distinguish them in some way.

The only one of John and Margaret's family I ever saw was my Great-great-Uncle, David Macneill. He was a very old man when I was a girl but not so very much older than Grandfather. He lived where Myrtle and Ernest live now. He was a very brilliant old man intellectually and marvellously well-read with the famous Macneill memory as well as their temper. Uncle David made the mistake of not marrying a Simpson. Instead he married a Mary Dockendorff from North River, of Dutch descent and of good family. But all the Dockendorffs were "queer" and the queerness came out very strongly in Uncle David's family. There was an "odd streak" in them all. So I think he might as well have stuck to the Simpsons.

It gives me an odd sensation to reflect that I knew well a man who was the son of Margaret Simpson Macneill who was born in 1759.

The mention of the Dockendorffs (we called it Duckenduff) touches a spring in my memory and two more sons of John and Margaret pop into remembrance—Great-great "uncles John" and "James." They both married "Duckenduffs"—three brothers marrying three sisters. And there was an old romance connected with the marriage of John. The lady Dockendorff had sent him word to come to her home on a certain day to be married. There were no regular mails or post-offices then, of course. Somehow the message was twisted or misunderstood and John Macneill thought it was the day after. Came the wedding day. Bride ready—guests there—but no groom. One wonders what Miss D. felt like that night. One can imagine. For when John arrived next day, all agog to be married, he was speedily sent to the rightabout. No excuse availed.

But thirteen years from that very day they were married. I state the fact—I cannot fill in the hiatus. Perhaps it took thirteen years for a Dockendorff to forgive. Or perhaps she had found out by that time she couldn't get anyone else. The "John and Jane Macneill" and the "Big George" of my childhood were the offspring of this marriage, as well as several others.

I always chortle with glee over Aunt Mary's sly statement that "the Simpsons always strongly believed they were above the common herd." Aunt Mary Lawson never really liked the Simpsons. But the Macneills were supposed to have a little of the same conviction. What is more I think that both they and the Simpsons were quite correct! The "common herd" of those days were very "common" indeed. It was an old by-word in my youth— "From the conceit of the Simpsons, the pride of the Macneills and the vainglory of the Clarks Good Lord deliver us." But at that they had something to be proud of!

I think Aunt Mary was quite right in saying that her father was the most talented of the family. At least he made the most mark. It meant something to climb as high as he climbed on a P.E. Island farm in those days. Intellect—perseverance—driving power—"hands that the rod of empire might have swayed"—Great grandfather Macneill had them all. Faults, too—"the Macneill temper"—and he let his farm go to seed while he hob-nobbed with politicians in Charlottetown. But there is a tradition that he would have been knighted for his services—everything was in train to make him "Sir William,"—but the jealousy of his brothers, headed by Malcolm, prevented it. How, I do not remember—I heard Aunt Mary tell the story when I was very young—I think they prevented his re-election or something of the sort. Jealousy was a Macneill characteristic as well as pride, as I had bitter reason to know. However, "Old Speaker Macneill" no doubt sleeps as peacefully in the old Cavendish burying ground as he would do if "Sir William" were chiselled on the gravestone at his head and we, his descendants, are not burdened with living up to a title!

William Macneill married Eliza Townsend, who was said to have been a beauty in her youth. Her grandmother was the Elizabeth Townsend who is buried in the old private graveyard on the banks of the pond at Park Corner. It was of her the story was told that she was so bitterly homesick when she first came to the P.E.I. woods that she would not take off her bonnet for weeks. I wonder if it was from her I inherit the agonizing nostalgia that has gripped me so often in life.

They came out in 1775. Their son, Captain John Townsend, was the father of Speaker Macneill's bride. Who her mother was and when and where she died I do not know. Captain John was evidently an adventurous blade and lived a colorful life. Uncle John Campbell's farm was part of their original "estate" and they gave it the name of Park Corner. Like all the rest they seemed to be cut off from the old land. There are no stories or memories of friends in the old country. They were English people so William Macneill flew in the face of two traditions when he married the fair Eliza but in his case it turned out well.

I do not know where the original painting of Capt. John is, or who has it. I never saw it but I saw a copy made from it at John C. Clark's one time. I think I must try to trace it some day.

William Macneill was a busy and useful man. I have heard Grandfather say that his father in his prime knew every man, woman and child in P.E. Island. I think there is a portrait of the Speaker in the Legislative building in Ch'town. He and his Eliza settled down in Cavendish and proceeded to have one of the large families that were a matter of course then. It was William Macneill who built the old home in Cavendish.

The mention of Captain John Macneill rouses a dormant memory of *another* son of John and Margaret—"Uncle Charles" who was moved to emigrate to "Upper Canada"—now Ontario—which was equivalent to going to the other side of the world then. He had owned a mill at New Glasgow before going and nearly died of homesickness in Ontario. Like many others of the clan he poured his agony into verse and I have often heard Grandfather quote from it some stanzas that represented "Uncle Charles" dreaming he was back home but I can recall only a stray line here and there.....

.....Aunt Mary's oldest brother John married a Simpson. Her next brother was "Uncle William" whom I knew very well, as he lived in Rustico. He, too, was a poet. But all I remember of his poetry is a line or two from a little skit he wrote upon some of Sir John A. Macdonald's political dodges—the first two verses.

> Hey, Sir John, what's wrang the night
> That ye hae ta'en sic hasty flight
> Fleeing awa wi' all your might
> Across the sea in the morning?
>
> Down in the east there's an unco din
> And mebbe ye did weel to rin
> Although it winna save your skin
> As ye'll find oot some morning.

Uncle William introduced a new blood strain by marrying the daughter of a Welshman. "Aunt Ann" was a great beauty in her youth and had some very handsome daughters. I remember her only as a very old wrinkled little woman. She lived to be nearly a hundred—at least her body did. For ten years her mind was dead. She forgot everything, even her own children. I used to look at her and pray "Oh, never let me live to be like this."

"Uncle Tom" I saw frequently in youth but he and Grandfather were not especially fond of each other. Perhaps because he married a Simpson. Grandfather had
such a rabid horror of the Simpsons. "Uncle Jimmy" lived next door to us in
Cavendish and was what was called in the vernacular "a character." We young fry
thought him half crazy but it was probably only the eccentricity of thwarted
genius. He would probably have made a good sailor but as a farmer he was a failure. He had the family gift of verse-making and as he sat and watched "pigs' potatoes" boiling on the long autumn evenings he composed hundreds of poems—
satiric and mock-heroic—on local events. Not a line of them was ever written
down which was a pity because they were capital. I can just recall two lines of a
poem he once composed upon a local feud in New Glasgow:

> Round Houston's corner now the battle raged
> And every man was busily engaged.

Uncle Jimmy's marriage was a tragedy. He did not marry a Simpson but it
might have been better if he had. He was the only one of the boys who made a
mesalliance. One can read that between the lines of Aunt Mary's guarded reference "daughter of an honest Scotchman." Nothing much could be said of old
George Harker than that he was honest. The Harkers were very "poor trash"
indeed and the Macneill pride got an awful jolt when Jimmy Macneill married
Jane Harker. Jane's mother was no better than she should have been. She was
married to George Harker just after they "came out" but the child that she bore
soon after arriving here was not her husband's but the son of the captain of the
vessel on which they came. George never acknowledged the youngster as his
although it bore his name but he forgave his wife and begat sons and daughters of
undoubted legitimacy. I known nothing more of George Harker except one thing
and that one thing always made me feel friendly to him. Aunt Jane once told me
of the day when her father took her and her little brother to the school for the first
time. Old George thus addressed the teacher, "Dinna be hard on the bairns, master. I'll no blame you if they canna learn."

I think that would be imputed to George Harker for righteousness when he
came to the Hall of Judgment.

But it was not Aunt Jane's low origin that made her life and the lives of all connected with her a tragedy. I remember Aunt Jane only as an old woman with an
incredibly wrinkled face. But she was a fresh, apple-cheeked girl when Uncle
Jimmy lost his heart to her and all might have been well had it not been for the
fatal strain of insanity in her. Off and on all through her life she had these "spells"
combined with suicidal tendencies. In old age she was not exactly out of her mind
but she was so peculiar and queer that her family had a miserable existence. They
never dared cross her for fear she would do something terrible. She wrecked
George R's life. He was a brilliant fellow and under a happier star might have
been a successful man.

It is no wonder poor Aunt Jane had attacks of insanity. Aunt Mary says she had
a family of two sons and two daughters—one of the sons dying in boyhood. But
Aunt Mary does not say that besides these poor Aunt Jane *had eight dead babies.*

Grandmother told me this. Surely enough to drive any woman insane. What tragedies lie behind the dry records of births and deaths in old families. Fancy going through the Valley of the Shadow of Eve eight times only to grasp Death as a reward in your hand!

They were all lovely babies, too—Grandmother said—beautiful plump little waxen creatures who never opened their eyes to the light. Poor, poor Aunt Jane!

Aunt Mary says Uncle Jimmy was "saved." Just why she singles him out for this statement I do not know, unless it was because he had never gone to church for many years before he died. This was a terrible thing in the eyes of his generation and perhaps Aunt Mary wanted to throw a defiance in the teeth of anyone who might infer from it that his future fate was dubious. A Macneill *must* be "saved" even if he were not wholly orthodox!

It is very curious what a different impression Aunt Mary had of her brother Alexander,—Grandfather Macneill—to what I have. To me—and, I am sure, to all his grandchildren—Grandfather seemed a stern, petulant, "touchy," unjust and arbitrary old man. We were all afraid of him. To Aunt Mary he was the affectionate congenial brother and friend. And I do not doubt that both of us were right—from the angle from which we saw him.

I think modern psychology would explain Grandfather Macneill as a man who was, quite unconsciously, *jealous* of youth. He was jealous because we could do, be and feel as he no longer could. We had life before us—we could laugh and enjoy the future with no thought of lengthening shadows. He resented the fact that he no longer could do this and he visited his resentment on us. I remember how furious Grandfather was one evening when Grandmother was away and Lucy was over. As we got the supper we were constantly laughing and joking—perfectly harmless mirth and jokes, yet it aggravated Grandfather unbearably. He was writing to Grandmother and curtly shortened up his letter by stating that Maud and Lucy were "acting such fools" that he could write no more. That was his typical attitude to youth's light-heartedness. I remember one incident of that same evening which hurts me even yet. I was broiling some beef ham for supper on the old gridiron whose wires were stretched so far apart that it was difficult to keep the slices of ham in when it was turned. As I turned it one little piece slipped through and fell on the coals. Grandfather turned on me with as black a face as if I had done something truly dreadful. "Your Grandmother," he said, harshly, "could have cooked that meat without letting a particle of it fall"—and he glared at me savagely. Perhaps she could—being more expert than I was; yet at that I had seen the same thing happen with her and so had Grandfather. But I was cut to the heart. Grandmother was away—I was a child of twelve trying to do my best in her absence and all the thanks I got was a speech like this.

But to Aunt Mary and many other of his contemporaries he presented an entirely different face. I remember Aunt Mary telling me once that there had never been a boy more idolized by his mother and sisters than Grandfather was—and my secret amazement over the statement. I daresay that very worship spoiled Grandfather in later life when he was unconsciously still expecting it from everyone and resentful because it was not forthcoming. Yet if Grandfather had been a little kinder—a little juster—a little more considerate of children's feelings—we would have all given him whole-hearted adoration. Instead of which our entire memory of him is punctured with cruel, unjust speeches and blighting looks. And yet it is of this man that Aunt Mary says she never found in him "a deed ungentle or a word unkind." Verily, human nature is a queer thing. No wonder biographers and historians can never arrive at ultimate truth about anybody or any event. Oliver Wendell Holmes brings up this point in his Breakfast Table Series when he speaks of all the different John Smiths in one man—John Smith as John Smith sees him, John Smith as his neighbor sees him and John Smith as God sees him. He might have increased the John Smith's ad infinitum for every "neighbor" would see a different John Smith.

Aunt Mary's reference to Grandmother is cool. I don't think Aunt Mary was very fond of any of her sisters-in-law. Certainly she never cared for Grandmother, although they always preserved a friendly attitude to each other. Why she speaks of Grandmother being "educated in England" I don't know, unless it was to increase the family prestige a wee bit. In a sense, of course, Grandmother got all the education she ever had in England. She went to some school there until she was twelve, when she came out to Canada.

I remember Aunt Mary's oldest sister Margaret, but I remember her only as an extremely old woman who had completely lost her memory and knew not one of her children—did not even remember the existence of her husband. She was bent, wrinkled, querulous; and yet Aunt Mary once spoke of "Margaret dancing for joy around the cradle of her first baby." Ah me, what things life does to us!

I remember "Aunt Ellen" too, as Aunt *Helen* was generally called. Also an old woman in a cap, beauty and brain long gone, but with a friendly twinkle in her eyes as she teased me about some schoolboy sweetheart.

"Aunt Jane" I never saw. Anne Macneill died of measles when she was 26. To a woman of Aunt Mary's age that might seem early youth. She is buried in Cavendish churchyard. Oddly enough Aunt Mary forgets to mention one of her sisters—"Aunt Phemie." Perhaps she really did forget her. Or perhaps she did not want to tell her nephew what the Macneills regarded as a family skeleton. Aunt Phemie had married some man—I can't remember his name—who turned out a scalawag. He left her—or she left him. She went away to her sister Jane, obtained some education and made her livelihood teaching school in some American city. She never came home—I suppose the Macneill pride was too strong in her—but she sent Grandfather her picture once and a very fine-looking woman she was. She was alive when Grandfather died but she must have died, too, long ago.

Aunt Mary herself was a wonderful woman. She might say Aunt Ellen had the brains of the Macneill girls but Aunt Ellen could not hold a candle to Aunt Mary. If she had been educated she would have been an intellectual queen. But nobody ever dreamed of educating girls in those days. And I daresay they were just as happy.

All the eleven children of William and Eliza lived to old age, except Anne. But they are all gone now. All in all, in spite of human faults and shortcomings they were a fine race and I need not be ashamed of my ancestry.

The Montgomery sketch was written by George Montgomery—Uncle John Montgomery's brother, and, like the Macneill's sketch, is full of burned-out emotions between the lines of sober facts....[*See Appendix B.*]

For a wonder George Montgomery does not say that the "family tradition" also asserts that our family were descended from a cadet of the Earls of Eglinton, whose family name was Montgomery. There is nothing to prove this but there are two bits of circumstantial evidence which go to bolster it up a bit. Grandfather Montgomery, in early life when he first began to attend the sessions of the Local House went to a ball at Government House. When he entered the ball-room a titled lady who was present, Countess of something I forget what, fainted. It turned out that she had once been engaged to the then Earl of Eglinton but for some reason the match was broken off. When she saw Grandfather coming into the room she thought it was her old lover, so striking was the resemblance. Grandfather's daughter, Aunt Mary McIntyre, told me this.

Another time Grandfather was walking on the street of some American city when a young man ran up to him in surprise and said, "Why, Uncle, I didn't know you were on this side of the pond." It turned out that he was a nephew of the Earl of Eglinton.

So there may be something in it and there may not. It doesn't matter anyhow.

George says that Hugh Montgomery and his wife Mary MacShannon (who ought to have been Irish from her name) settled at Princetown in 1769. But he does not tell how they came to settle there. They had been bound for Quebec. But poor Mary Montgomery had been most desperately seasick all through the long voyage across the Atlantic. In the gulf of St. Lawrence the ship was short of water and the captain anchored off Prince Edward Island and sent the men on shore for water. And he told Mrs. Montgomery she could go too and stretch her legs on land. Mary went; and when she got to land she vowed that she would never set foot on a ship again. Her husband had to land there also with his goods and chattels. There is no tradition of how he took it and whether he was willing or unwilling. Fox Point is where Uncle John Montgomery and Aunt Emily lived. The old Montgomery homestead was there. It is a very beautiful spot but must have been wild and lonely enough when Hugh and Mary set up their roof-tree there.

"Donald Montgomery married Nancy Penman." A laconic statement, giving no hint of the colorful romance behind it.

The Penmans lived at Port Hill. I remember Grandfather Macneill telling me that the Penmans were U.E.Loyalists. But this cannot be harmonized with George M's assertion that they came to P.E.I. in 1758 with Lord Rollo. Probably George is right. At any rate, the Penmans were poor but the daughters were of such transcendent beauty that they married into all the good families of the North Shore. Nancy was the handsomest of all the handsome Penman girls and she was wooed by David Murray of Bedeque and Donald Montgomery of Malpeque. One stormy winter day Donald was alone in the house at Fox Point when David arrived along on his way from Bedeque to—Donald strongly suspected—Port Hill. The Montgomerys were nothing if not hospitable; and hospitality in those days meant treating your caller to a glass of good Scotch. Donald did this; moreover, he plied his

"Old homestead at 'Fox Point' "

guest so strongly that David imbibed much more than was good for him, loosened up his tongue and told Donald that he was going over the bay to ask Nancy Penman to have him.

Donald was a bit flabbergasted. For some reason unknown, he feared that the "first man" would win. Perhaps Nancy would not dare to trifle with a bona fide offer and would say "yes" to David's wooing, lest no others should come. So the crafty Donald plied the unlucky David still more hospitably, the upshot being that David fell most unromantically into a very sound very drunken sleep. Donald went out, took David's equipage and hied him over the bay. David's equipage was not romantic either. It was a rough wood sleigh drawn by a sturdy steer.

Donald got to Port Hill and lost no time in proposing to Nancy, who accepted him without demur. But Donald had no wish to linger in the Penman household until his enraged rival should come, so next morning he persuaded Nancy to go away with him for a visit and when David arrived in a very bad temper—having galloped over the ice on a young unbroken colt he had found in Donald's stable— the bird had flown. While David was storming around Betsy Penman came in and told him he was a great fool to be making such a clatter. *She* was as good-look- ing as Nancy and *she* would take him gladly. David cooled down and did what was expected of him. And it was one of our family traditions that David and Betsy were the happiest couple that ever lived.

On second thought, the reason why Donald had been afraid David would get his girl may have been because he knew old George Penman favored David Murray. At any rate he did not favor Donald, for the latter had to steal his Nancy away after all. He sent his brother John for her and Nancy slipped out of the house one night and drove away with John. "Oh, what will I do if Donald doesn't marry me after all?" she made moan. John gallantly assured her that if Donald wouldn't *he* would. "And I would have died sooner than marry John Montgomery," the ungrateful Nancy told Eliza Townsend afterwards.

Donald was only too glad to marry Nancy and they settled down at Fox Point, where they had *seventeen* children. No race suicide for Donald and Nancy. They had one hundred and eighteen grandchildren. It actually makes me dizzy.

Sixteen of their children grew up and married. One wonders about all those marriages. Were they all for love: or were some of them contracted because people had to get married in those days—girls, anyhow? No other career was possible for them. Mary's at all events did not end happily. George says the Rev. Mr. Pidgeon she married was a Presbyterian minister but the person who *told* me the tale said he was a congregationalist minister. Which agrees better with the statement that he was sent out by the London Missionary society. No Presbyterian would have been sent from London in those days.

According to the tale I was told he was pastor of the only congregational church on the Island. And said congregation was split up and totally destroyed by the said Pidgeon's scandalous goings on with some woman of the same. His wife left him and betook herself and family to her brothers in New Brunswick. Mr. Pidgeon was cast out by his church and lived for years in a miserable little hut in or near Long River. One Sunday afternoon he went to service in the Geddie Memorial church at Springbrook and during the service fell dead in his pew. As his hut was such a mean place the undertaker brought the coffin to the church, prepared him for burial there, and there the funeral service was held. He was buried in the old cemetery there and I think there is one of the old-fashioned horizontal slabs over the grave although I do not know who erected it.

This is the sordid outline of the story. One wonders about it—was it as sordid as it seems? Was Mr. Pidgeon all to blame or was he swept off his feet by some sudden temptation? Was "the woman in the case" a common vamp or was she the innocent victim of a Don Juan or of an overwhelming passion? Was it a cheap intrigue or a great love? Was Mary Montgomery partly to blame or was she not? What were the reverend outcast's reflections during the rest of his life? Nobody now knows or ever will know.

"Donald Montgomery"

The Rev. George Pidgeon who played such a prominent part in the Union disruption is a grandson of Mary's. Loyalty, whether to church or marriage vow, does not seem to be part of the Pidgeon equipment.

As for the little Margaret who "died young"—how young was she and why did her girlish eyes close so soon?

Grandfather Montgomery—"Big Donald," partly because he was a tall broad-shouldered man and partly to distinguish him from his cousin "Little Donald"—was, beyond all doubt, the handsomest man I ever saw in my life. I remember him only when he was old. If he were any handsomer in youth God help the girls of his day! No only was his face handsome but his presence was stately and impressive. He was said to resemble the beautiful Nancy very strongly—which doesn't exactly harmonize with the Eglinton story! As I knew him he had magnificent thick snow-white hair, a deep dimple in his chin—which only one of his grandchildren inherited and none of his children—and the magnetic, dark-blue heavy-lidded eyes which many of us inherited.

His first wife—my real "Grandmother Montgomery"—was his own first cousin, Annie Murray, daughter of David Murray and Betsy Penman. She died of "consumption" in her early forties. There is no picture of her and I have no idea of what she looked like. One only thing do I know of Grandmother Montgomery—and that is very sweet. Let me write it here as a memorial of her.

Aunt Margaret Sutherland told it to me. When a small child at school she was persuaded one day when school came out to go down to "the Cove" with some of the children instead of going home. Presently some irate sisters or brothers arrived in search of her and informed her that "mother" was going to "give it to her" when she got home. The little Margaret went home trembling with fear. But when she got home "mother" just took the fearful little guilty mite up on her lap and cuddled her in her arms, rejoicing to find that she was safe. Dear Grandmother Montgomery, dead these seventy-five years, I think I would have loved you.

I do not know how long Grandfather remained a widower. He eventually married a Charlottetown widow, a Mrs. Gall, *née* Louisa Cundall. She was "Grandmother Montgomery" but I never felt any affection for her, though neither did I dislike her—which I think was the attitude of most of her stepchildren. She was quite a "great lady" and her dressy "caps" were the wonder and admiration of the young fry. She was a strict "Church of England" woman and always went to her own church, never having aught to do with the Presbyterian church where Grandfather was a staunch elder. She had a son "Willie Gall" by her first marriage; he died when a young man. She bore one son to Grandfather, but he died while a baby.

One of Grandfather's first family, "Christie," died when she was only sixteen. Young as she was, she had lived long enough to know love and was engaged to some young McKay of Clifton. All the Montgomery girls were a bit precocious. But it was the fashion then for girls to marry young. And they are all gone now—that handsome, virile family, so full of the joy of life. None of them lived to be very old. Perhaps Anne Murray handed down a certain delicacy of constitution.

I used to be at Grandfather Montgomery's very often when I was a child and a visit

"Mrs. Donald Montgomery"

there was a great delight to me. They lived then in the old house—a quaint old spot. I remember a certain old "back hall" leading from the kitchen to a part of the house "Grandmother" claimed as her own. On one side of this hall the wall was lined with cupboards where all kind of things were kept. At its end there was a big grandfather clock and a short flight of steps leading up to a room where Grandmother sat and entertained her friends. Beyond it two or three more steps led down again into her bedroom. It was in that old house I took and nearly died of typhoid fever.

I was there the summer they built the new house and a certain small black-haired girl, the daughter of the housekeeper—for "Aunt Louisa" did not do any "menial" work—and I had great fun picnicking in the big "bay windows" before they were boarded up. I must have been very small.

I knew only three of the sons and daughters of Donald Montgomery and Nancy Penman—Grandfather, "old Uncle Edward Montgomery" of Malpeque and "Aunt Elizabeth" who was Uncle John Campbell's mother and Stell's and Frede's grandmother. Uncle Edward lived quite near Uncle John Montgomery and was a very old man when I saw him. But "Aunt Elizabeth" lived at Park Corner until I was quite a big girl and I remember her quite distinctly. She was a very old lady then, had been very handsome in her youth, and was a fine-looking old woman still, with very large sunken eyes.

Her husband James Campbell was twice married. His first wife was "Elizabeth Montgomery," a sister of "Little Donald." She bore him at least two sons and died. Then he married "Elizabeth Montgomery," sister of "Big Donald!" One wonders what a man feels like whose two wives bore the same name! Would their identity become so mingled in his consciousness that they would seem like one? And would not the second wife feel a bit ghost-like? Elizabeth Montgomery, No. Two, evidently inherited her mother's fecundity for she, too, had *seventeen* children. And four of them died in one week the summer the "black cholera" came to P.E. Island, brought thither by a negro on a ship. Elizabeth Campbell was ill in bed at the time, giving birth to another child. And when she rose from her bed it was to be told of the death of four of her children.

One wonders *how* any human being could endure a blow like that!

Perhaps Elizabeth was as strong emotionally as she was physically. I have often heard Aunt Annie tell this story. "Aunt Elizabeth" was seventy. It was a hot summer day and she walked down to the pond spring and carried up two pails of water. Then she sat down.

"Annie," she said, "I have a very strange feeling. I never felt it before. *I think it must be what you call tired*!!!"

Verily, there were giants in those days. This woman had given birth to seventeen children, had brought them up and had done the work of a primitive P.E. Island farm. And yet, on the day she was seventy, she had her first experience of "feeling tired."

My Aunt!!!

Although I never saw Great-Uncle James Townsend Montgomery (Uncle John Montgomery's father) I remember his widow "Aunt Rose" very well. I used often to be at Malpeque after Aunt Emily went there and Aunt Rose was living then.

She was a sweet-faced old woman who always wore a close-fitting frilled white cap, not at all like Grandmother Montgomery's dressy head-gear. Aunt Rose was what we called "very religious." The Montgomerys were certainly not that. They were decent, God-fearing folk who stood by their church as became them but I fear John Wesley would have considered them as little better than brands yet unplucked from the burning. But Aunt Rose's brand of piety was not repellent. She was a really good Christian woman. And every Sunday she and I together read a chapter of the *Bible*. I remember reading the book of "Esther" so for the first time. Aunt Rose kept a pocketful of juicy raisins and whenever I read a verse she gave me a raisin. Bible reading with Aunt Rose was really very delightful. To this day I cannot hear or read of Esther and Vashti, of Mordecai and Ahasueras, without recalling dear, pink-cheeked old Aunt Rose and her raisins.

Of a very different type was her sister "Aunt Matilda" who lived there too. Miss Matilda McGary (or McCary—I am not sure which) was the typical old maid of fiction. I shall never forget her beady black eyes flashing under her cap rim. For Aunt Matilda too wore caps but while Aunt Rose's fitted softly and snugly about her cheeks Aunt Matilda's flared out militantly around her head. She was not beloved and had a very bitter tongue. But she never used it on me and in fact I rather liked Aunt Matilda and she seemed to like me. She used to tell me exciting tales of how the Roman Catholics persecuted her father and his family while he was a minister in Ireland.

Ah, well, they are all gone now, those old Montgomerys and their brides. Aunt Emily's son James lives at Fox Point, a queer odd mortal with no children. So the old homestead of Hugh Montgomery will pass into other hands with this generation. Well, there are not I daresay many Canadian farms that have remained in the same family for one hundred and sixty years.

So passes the glory of this world—and the loves and hates and hopes and fears of it. And nobody cares now whether Donald Montgomery cut David out with Nancy Penman or no, and no tears are shed over the four little Campbell children who died together in that black week. Elizabeth Montgomery's tears have been dried long since and Grandfather Montgomery's stately figure walks among the ghosts.

Monday, June 8, 1931
The Manse, Norval
....I have been reading a very fascinating book—*Henry VIII And His Wives*, by Hackett. It is so well written that it is enchanting—and the subject matter would make any book interesting. My own troubles seem very slight beside Katherine of Aragon's and Anne Boleyn's. Henry is one of the enigmas of the race. One simply cannot believe that anything like him happened.

Monday, June 15, 1931
I had a lovely time tonight. For a few hours I was young and happy. We went with the Barracloughs up to the private fishing ponds owned by a club to which he belongs. It was a most beautiful spot, to which we went through little back roads where nobody ever goes and where there are such delicious things to see. The day

was burning low behind the dark hills and the ponds were all velvet and shadow. While the men fished the lower pond Mrs. B. and I walked through the pines to the upper one. I re-discovered the fact that I have always been next of kin to the woods. We sat for an hour on the bank of the pond, rimmed round with its pines. It was so deliciously quiet—and I read about bluff King Hal and his unhappy, far-off brides. I was loth to come away and leave that enchanted place.

Tuesday, June 16, 1931
I am afraid my asthma is returning. I do not know why, for I have no cold and am perfectly well in the day time. Perhaps it is the strawberries. If so, I choose the asthma!

Word came tonight that Stuart has won the Isabelle Cockshutt prize in history—$25—as well as the first General Proficiency Prize in his class. I wonder if I dare rejoice a little over this.

Saturday, June 27, 1931
The Manse, Norval
I have been having a very good time but between much gadding and an hour or so of asthma every night I have come home rather done up. I went into Toronto last Monday and stayed at Cuth's at nights. There was a reception at the Art Gallery that night for the visiting lions and I had a rather interesting time. One lady came up and said, "I am sure almost everything has been said to you about *Anne of Green Gables* that can be said but I am going to tell you something I am quite sure nobody has ever said before. Did anyone ever tell you that Anne of Green Gables helped to alleviate the pains of confinement?" "No," I said feebly. And she went on to say that during her first labor her husband sat by her bedside and read *Anne of Green Gables* aloud to her and they both laughed so much that it wasn't nearly as hard for either of them as it would otherwise have been!

"Your husband was a hero," I said, more feebly still. *What* a yarn! He was an Englishman—naturally. Nobody but an Englishman would or could do a thing like that.

I drove home in company with Marshall Saunders who, as usual, talked of nothing but the Pages and their doings. She has them on the brain. Louis, it seems, is now confined to his bed but is still directing things. Also, she told me something that solved an old mystery—that telegram from L.C. in which he informed me that Mrs. George Page had never recovered after her husband's "shocking death." As it was officially given out that George Page had died from heart trouble I could

"Cuth's House"

not see anything peculiarly "shocking" in that, apart from the fact that any sudden death is of course a shock to the survivors. But Marshall Saunders says that George Page really shot himself. She was told this by someone who knew all the facts of the case. This was truly "shocking" enough. But neither of those men were quite normal and probably George was unbalanced mentally when he did it.

Tuesday, besides attending the sessions of the Association and meeting several old friends—and alas, missing several who will come no more—I was a guest at a luncheon given by the Optimists' Club. A dinner at Hart House that night followed, given us by the Government. The dinner itself was good but for the rest I have been at funerals that were far more fun. Three men made three seemingly interminable speeches which we at the far end could not hear at all. *Why* will after dinner speakers talk as if it were the first, last and only chance they ever had or hoped to have at public speaking? An after dinner speech should be short and snappy.

Almost all the women smoked or apologized for not doing so.

At the next morning session a Mr. Luckovich—a member of Parliament from the west—gave an excellent address on "Our New Canadians and Literature." Fifty years ago his Ukrainian parents came to Canada, poor and ignorant people. Now their son is a member of Parliament and very enthusiastic regarding Canadian ideals and laws. There is hope for the "melting pot" yet when one generation can travel so far. The only sign of his extraction was his very marked "inferiority complex"—the result I suppose of his childhood and youth when he was made to feel inferior by the Canadian children around him. *His* children will not have it. It came out in his repeated apologies for giving his opinions on literature before "such an audience." His opinions were excellent and correct but he had no confidence in them.

I went to the Toronto Hunt Club to a luncheon given by Mrs. Sheard, a lady who writes good poetry and very poor fiction. I enjoyed myself but was tired out by the high-pitched chatter of the women. I notice the difference even in five years. They all seemed to be talking feverishly, as if trying desperately to say all they wanted to say before somebody interrupted them. Mostly it would not have been any loss if anyone had. When we were waiting in the lounge of the Royal York for the party to gather, a Miss Dennis from Halifax and I happened to be sitting together. "Since we have to wait I am thankful I am with you," she said. "One can be quiet with you. You are not talking desperately all the time. I don't feel as if I had to talk, too, to keep up with you."

I think that is the nicest compliment I've been paid for many a moon.

At night the dinner was at the King Edward, given by the City. Again a good menu followed by another fearfully boring long-winded program. Luckily I had agreeable table companions. Wilson Macdonald, the poet, was on my right hand. I liked him. I also like his poetry very much. But his naïveté is amusing. When the main course was served the waiter brought Macdonald a plate full of very prettily arranged vegetables—"only that and nothing more." "Are you on a diet?" I asked teasingly. He gravely informed me that he never ate meat—it was not a fit food for "genius." Tagore and Whitman had said so. I hid a smile. Wilson writes very charming verses but he is not a "genius" and never will be, even if he lives on vegetables for a hundred years. As for me, I am not suffering from any delusions of being a genius so I eat all the good things I can get hold of and I ate the city's good menu, thankful that my appetite is beginning to be what it was.

As we could not hear half the speeches Wilson amused us by sleight-of-hand tricks at which he is very expert. He put a cent on the table, put his hand on it, lifted his hand palm upward, showing nothing. The cent had vanished but a moment later he coolly extracted it from my sleeve. In spite of all this we were frightfully bored. When the men finally got through, two ladies got up and made speeches of about two minutes each. "I'll never again say that women are the talkative sex," groaned Wilson Macdonald.

I hurried away as soon as I could but not before Mr. Luckovich had come up and told me how much he had enjoyed my books. He was very nice but his origin came out again in the sunflower compliments he paid. No subtlety there. "You are very good-looking," he said. "One does not expect a writer to be so good-looking." However, his sons will have learned how to pay compliments more gracefully.

Two more big pi-jaws the next day finished the convention. Between times I went to a Press Club luncheon and an afternoon tea. Met Napier Moore, editor of *Maclean's*, at the latter. He wants me to write a serial for *Maclean's* but I can't write serials. I spent Thursday evening at Cuth's talking to Laura. I had a much more interesting time than at the dinners but had a real bad attack of asthma that night. I came home yesterday and ever since have been reading the proofs of *A Tangled Web*.

Thursday, July 2, 1931
We have had two really dreadful days and nights of intense heat and humidity. I don't think I ever experienced anything like it before. I could not sleep at nights and had to drive myself to work. Today I did up twelve jars of strawberry jam. It turned out excellently but by evening I was a wreck. We went over to the Glen House. Mr. B. and Ewan went to preparatory service in Union. Mrs. B. was talking to another guest on the veranda. I lay down in the swing chair, intending to relax for a few moments. I fell asleep—and slept soundly for three blissful hours in the fresh cool air. I felt like a new creature when I woke up. It is the loveliest house in the world—and the loveliest people. I can go on now again even if tomorrow is as today.

Friday, July 10, 1931
Norval, Ont.
I am one of the judges in the Canadian part of the great International Kodak Co. Competition. The others being Nellie McClung, "Janey Canuck," Wylie Grier, artist, Canon Cody, and Lieut. Gagnon of Quebec. Today we met at the Royal York to judge the children's pictures. Only three of us could be there—Mr. Grier, Lieut. Gagnon and myself. We had a very smart and delicious luncheon and then proceeded to "judge." As I knew there had been 35000 entries in the children's section alone I did not see how we were to get through them all in one afternoon. But I am very green in such matters. I have ripened suddenly. The Kodak Co. had "weeded out" all they thought couldn't classify and as a result there were only about 150 pictures—21 to each province—to be passed on! It was not difficult for

the winning pictures almost leaped to the eye. At least the first and second prizes did. We had little disagreement on them. The third one was more difficult to choose. There were so many that seemed equally good. In most of the cases I agreed with Mr. Wylie's opinion. In a few I did not although I yielded to his artistic judgment, merely reserving my secret right to my own opinion. I also wonder about the vast number we did not see. As the pictures were to be chosen, not for technical excellence but for beauty and interest I daresay many were rejected that we might have thought even better. But perhaps not. It is surprising how few really interesting or beautiful pictures of children one sees.

However, I've got a very enjoyable day out of it. The drives in and out were charming. The country is looking its loveliest with waves of roses breaking everywhere.

I have been re-reading Macaulay's *Life* by Trevelyan. I read it first that winter in Prince Albert. Found it delightful then and found it just as delightful still. But most of its charm is due to Macaulay's letters. One criticism the writer of the introduction makes is that Macaulay's letters show nothing profound in his nature. Very likely. Very likely—nay, almost certainly—had they been profound they would not have been delightful. The ocean depths are profound—but I prefer a sunlit meadow for my strolling. Anyhow, I should like to have got letters from Macaulay.

Saturday, July 11, 1931
Made red currant jelly. It looks like rubies and tastes as good as it looks. Red currants always make me think of Grandmother and her currant wine. I love making jellies and jams and nice things to eat generally. If I had not been a poor devil of an author I think I would have made an excellent cook.

Tonight I cut all my lilies and put them in the church. A great basket of Madonna lilies and one of regale lilies—the latter have bloomed this year for the first time and are most wonderful. I could stand before them with all the ecstasy of worship.

Hodder and Stoughton have written that the new book can't be called *A Tangled Web* in England because last year they published a book _The_ Tangled Web. So it is to be *Aunt Becky Began It* in England. Surely this would be the end of the tamasha about the name of that blessed book!

Do we ever forget anything? I think not. This afternoon I was rummaging though an old notebook to find an idea for a story I had promised *The Chatelaine* to write. I read one over—and in a moment nearly forty years had become as naught. I was back in the winter of 1892—I was sitting by the east window of the sitting room at Park Corner. It was the early evening of a stormy winter day. The snow was sifting under the sills, fine as sugar. The wind was roaring outside—and how cosy it was to hear it in that warm fire-lighted room, with the delicious odors of one of Aunt Annie's suppers seeping in from the kitchen. I was alone—I had been working my "stint" of arithmetic and it had grown too dark for it. So I laid down my pencil and slate—slates were still in use then—leaned dreamily back, and looked out of the window—as so many eyes had done before me. I saw a landscape of spruce-dotted hills with the wind blowing over it and fields where there seemed to be a winter dance of goblins. There was one austere old hill that sometimes warmed briefly to a glow of sunset; and half way up this hill, I think by the line fence between the Cuthbert Montgomery's farm and his neighbor's, was a group of tall spruce trees—three of them, growing closely together and marked out from all the others in my vision by an oddity of outline which made them look like three tall women huddled together, whispering. Of what were the trees talking? I began to weave a story around that question. The trees were talking of and watching a story that was being lived in the house I sat in. For years it went on and the trees had a part in it—always watching, always whispering, as joy and sorrow, tears and laughter came to the house they loved. I had a very happy hour of creation there before it grew so dark that the trees were swallowed up in the storm wrack.

Afterwards I wrote the idea of the story in my little notebook. Someday I would write it, I thought. But I never did. I don't think now I ever will. It is too slight and fairy-like for the robust appetite of today. I am a little sorry, too.

From that time I seemed to have a particular interest in those three trees. They and I shared a secret. Always when I was at Park Corner I looked across to them and they seemed to wave their arms to me and whisper "Is it written yet—*our* story?" I saw them the last time I was there. But they had grown very old. Half their boughs were dead. They were beaten to death by the winds of so many years. They were only old crones who had been young green maidens when they whispered that tale to me on that stormy winter evening of long ago.

I hate to think of all the lovely things I remember being forgotten when I'm dead!

It is curious how old memories bob up. A phrase in what I have just written— "the odors of supper seeping in from the kitchen"—makes me remember our old "cook house at home." This was a little building at right angles to the kitchen, with a plank platform between. It had been, I recall being told, the porch of the "old" church in Cavendish—that is of the church that preceded the "old" church I went to as a girl. I think it was the first church ever built in Cavendish and judging from its porch it could not have been a very imposing building. I used to picture the porch in the days before it came down in the world, when the old Scotch men and women of the early 1800's came into it and the lads waited for their lasses at the door. I daresay it was steeped in romance and theology.

Every spring the cookstove—first the old "Waterloo" and then the coal stove— was moved out to the "cookhouse" and all the cooking done there for the summer. It must have meant a great many extra steps for the cooks but it kept the main house cool and free from flies—which was a desired thing in the days before screens. Many a good bite was cooked in that old spot. The shelves all around the walls were used as a pantry. Grandma kept her dried hams in a big box of oats in the corner and bunches of garden herbs and "shalottes" hanging from the beams. Grandma made her cheese curds there, too, and put them into the "hoops" which were then carried out to the cheese press at the corner of the orchard fence where a big gray stone served as a weight. Grandma was a "master hand" at making cheese. It is a lost art as far as individuals are concerned. All cheeses nowadays are made in factories. And as a result they have not the flavor of the cheeses

Grandma made. Something is lost when things are made *en masse*. I wonder if there is a single woman in Canada today who can make a cheese—unless it be someone in the "foreign" colonies.

The mention of cheeses wakens another memory. It is evening. Grandmother and Grandfather are adjusting the cheese hoop under the press. I am standing by watching them and drinking in the loveliness around me. June was walking over the fields. The sun had just set and I saw that loveliest of all created things—a young moon in an amber evening sky.

And the lambs were playing in the pasture field by the house.

Do lambs play like that now? I suppose they do, only I never have a chance to see them. But what gorgeous times those lambs did have at their evening games while their placid old mothers nibbled on around them. In a drove they tore from one end of the field and back again, the noise of their small hoofs like mild thunder. They would run those races until dark fell—seemingly just for the joy of running. I never saw such happy creatures.

Today I heard someone use the expression "see stars." I wondered if she ever had "seen stars" as she meant. For many years of my life I was well acquainted with the expression "it made me see stars"—had indeed used it myself. But I believed it to be merely a figure of speech, conveying the idea that one was rather knocked out or dazed. But one night I had an experience that convinced me of its literalness.

It was a cold winter's night. I had undressed shiveringly and hopped into bed eager to draw the blankets close around my ears and snuggle down. But whoever had made the bed had tucked the clothes rather too far and firmly down at the foot. I gave two or three gentle tugs but apparently made no headway. I must have loosened them however, for when I suddenly gave a hard, impatient tug they came away without the least resistance and my doubled right fist which had been clutching the top edges flew up and struck me a whacking blow on my right temple.

Stars! I saw a whole constellation. There was one tremendous star as large as my fist and around it a galaxy of smaller stars all dancing madly against a dead black universe. I fell back on the pillow half stunned, dazed; the next morning I had a yellow and purple bruise on my maiden brow and a sore spot for weeks. But I had "seen stars."

Why do devilish things always happen to the things we prize most? When the "loot" of the blue chest was divided at Park Corner I got a couple of glass plates, one very small, the other about six inches across. I have prized it all these years—and last year I broke it in the silliest, most incredible way. Broke it badly, too. I cried for an hour about it. Then I took it to a place in Toronto where they do wizard work and really they patched and rivetted it wonderfully. But it is only a flawed plate, for all, and will always have to be handled as such. I had a dozen other glass plates recently bought and if they had all been smashed I would not have greatly cared. But it had to be this prized old plate of story and old tradition!

Yes, there *is* a devil!

We had our first apple pie of the season today. It was good. But where oh where are the apple pies of yesteryear—or rather the apple turnovers? Grandmother was a crackerjack at making apple turnovers. She always made me one when she baked the pies—a delectable creation with fluted edge where the "turned over" crust was pinched together, full of juicy spiced apples. To run in from outdoors on a crisp cold autumn dusk and eat a hot, spicy, juicy apple "turnover" was to pity the gods on high Olympus with nothing to eat but ambrosia.

So, one doesn't forget anything. The other day something recalled to me an old poem, "The Haunted Spring," which I learned for a Friday afternoon recitation when I was about ten years old. I haven't thought of it for years, but I found I could go through it without a line missed—and I suppose I will always remember it with a thrill of its old charm until time gets through with me. I do not remember the name of the author. It was no famous name. The poem was in an old anthology that was lying around the house....[*See Appendix C.*]

Of course, with my love of dramatizing everything, the "Haunted Spring" was the old fir-shadowed spring down in the school woods and the hills back around Lover's Lane were the "hills so green" where the lost hunter dwelt with his fairy bride. When I loitered in the twilight meadows of our old farm and repeated that poem over to myself I ached with the beauty of it, as if some supernal musician had swept my soul with his fingers and evoked some ethereal harmony. Some other world drew very near. Back among those darkening hills shadowy ladies were beckoning lone wanderers to goblin banquets. Little ghosts of laughter seemed to drift to me over the valleys. I, too, drank from the waters of paradise— I too kept tryst with mystic lovers by the little brooks back in the hilly land—and was never quite the same again. One cannot be who drinks even in imagination from such a magic cup. One has stepped ever so little a way over some strange, impalpable barrier which forever must intervene between one and the realities of existence. Which is both a blessing and a curse.

It seems that my new book cannot be called *A Tangled Web* in England because last year Hodder & Stoughton published a book *The Tangled Web*. So mine is to be called *Aunt Becky Began It* in England. I don't like having two names for it but it cannot be helped.

A letter from Ella contained worrying news of Alec Macneill. He has not been well all spring—his old stomach trouble—and now they say he is melancholy. This may only be distorted gossip of course.

Thursday, July 16, 1931
The Manse, Norval.
We took Chester to Toronto today. He has got three weeks' work as janitor of a Toronto school during the caretaker's vacation. He will get about a hundred dollars for it which will help out a bit.

Then I had the delightful experience of having a boil in the canal of my ear lanced. It has been aching for several days and nights. So I went to a specialist and he found the boil. He used a local anesthetic but still it was painful enough. The injection of the anesthetic was very painful. And for two hours afterwards the aching in my ears was almost unendurable. He said it would not affect the hearing. I hope this is so. I have always had a bit of dread that I might inherit Grandfather Montgomery's deafness. He was very deaf as long as I can remember him.

Saturday, July 18, 1931
The Manse, Norval.
I had to go in again today to have my ear treated. Very painful—but it is progressing favorably. The doctor does not think there will be any more. When he first saw it he said there might be two or three more. I am obliged to him for his change of opinion.

Wordsworth remarked in one of his poems,

> What fond and foolish thoughts will slide
> Into a lover's head—

Well, fond and foolish thoughts will slide into anybody's head. Where do they come from half the time? This evening I was coming up the street in the dusk, feeding my soul on the dark loveliness of the pines on the hill when I suddenly thought, "When the time comes for Stuart and Chester to die—as come it will however soon or far—will there be anyone to watch by their dying pillow and soothe the pain of passing?" Somehow, the thought filled me with anguish. Suppose—suppose—there would be nobody—suppose they died forsaken and alone—my little lads whom I have loved so much and tried to care for! This is morbid, no doubt. But when one is run down nervously as I have been for some time, one thinks queer things....

Sunday, July 19, 1931
The Manse, Norval.
....Mr. Greenwood died today. I do not recall any death, outside of my own personal circle, that has affected me so much. Mr. Greenwood has been a friend ever since we came here. He was the finest amateur elocutionist I ever knew. He has been such a help in the Guild that I don't know how we will run it without him. He added color to every life he touched. It seems impossible to think that he *is* dead, he was so full of vigor and life. It is only a few months since he and I and the Garfield McClures were getting up a play for Old Tyme Night and having such fun over it. Mr. G. as old deaf "Mr. Coddle" was the funniest thing I ever saw in my life. He brought down the house.

Thursday, July 23, 1931
We had a very boring "missionary picnic" today. The address was tiresome and I did not listen to it. Instead I amused myself tracing out cloud pictures in the blue northern sky. There were some wonderful ones—a Titanic "Jove" for instance with sweeping beard and hair of living white. An ancient Greek might have thought that he really did see the Father of Heaven.

Tonight at the Glen House we were talking of something that recalled a rather absurd experience of mine years ago. Frede was teaching in Stanley and boarding at Ross's. I walked up one morning in early spring to spend the day with her and very foolishly put on a pair of new shoes. They did not hurt me but when I had finished my 6-mile hike I found I had blistered heels. I spent the day in

Frede's slippers but when I put on my shoes for the return at evening I found it utterly impossible to endure them. I was rather in a quandary. Frede had only one pair she could lend me—an old discarded pair. I put them on and started. But Frede "went over" notoriously on her heels. The shoes were so badly warped I simply could not walk in them, my ankles ached so. I tried the experiment of putting them on the wrong feet, whereby the "slant" was in the opposite direction. Thus, I managed to hobble half the distance. But by the time I got to the bridge at Bay View I could not have taken another step in them to save my life. My ankles and muscles ached intolerably. I took off those boots of torture and hurled them savagely over the fence into the woods.

After my first wild spasm of satisfaction and relief passed I faced the thought of walking home three miles over a rough road which had thawed into mud during the day and was now freezing rapidly. Well, I did it. And it was not so very dreadful. Of course my stockings were soon cut into ribbons which left me with practically bare feet on frozen mud and ice. But I had no more pain and all I dreaded was that someone would come along and offer me a "lift" and I would be obliged to explain my predicament. It would be a local joke for a month. Luckily nobody did. The frozen roads were my friends for nobody wanted to be on them after night. Nearly home I met a truck wagon going the other way but it was too dark by then for the driver to see my feet! That was one walk down through Cavendish which I did *not* enjoy. Mighty thankful was I to get home. I expected to have a bad cold as a result but nothing of the sort happened. I was never a penny the worse for it!

Tuesday, July 28, 1931
The Manse, Norval.
E. left for the Island today. Stuart took him to the station. S. is learning to drive the car this summer so I am going through all the agonies I went through with Chester. He is getting on very well though.

Stuart has grown a great deal this summer. He is taller than I am now. And the other day I found a letter on his table from a girl.

There was no harm in the letter or the girl. But it gave me a pang because it made me realize that I am no longer the only woman in my baby's life. It is a far cry from the days when Stuart was so worried because he might have to get married sometime and leave his mother!

I wrote an article today for *The Chatelaine* on "What the Minister's wife expects from the congregation" to companion one from Nellie McClung on "What the congregation expects of the Minister's Wife." I wrote nothing but the truth but I did not write the *whole* truth. I yearned to—after twenty years repression—but it would never have done!

Thursday, July 30, 1931
Ewan is on the Island tonight. It makes me feel lonely and homesick to think of it. I want to be there too—my heart is aching for the sea—for the shadowy pond by

the dunes I loved—for little fir trees in moonlight—rain over the gray harbour—
little sunset hollows with white violets in them—trees I grew up with—lovely pink
sand-hills—white birches that used to try to catch me with ghostly hands—brooding motherly old houses. I should be there, too!

Sunday, Aug. 2, 1931
About a year ago it seemed to me that, as I could leave this journal to only one
boy, I should make a typewritten copy of it for the other. So every Sunday I type
a few pages and lately I have been copying the entries concerning Herman Leard.
The slowness of the process allows the details to "sink in" to such an extent that
I seem actually to be *living* them all again. Tonight after I had finished I was so
deeply in the grip of that old emotion that I could not remain in the house. I went
out and walked about the dreaming streets of the little village, with the misty
summer night all around me. But I was not *here*. I had gone back over thirty years.
And I wanted to *stay* back there—with Herman and youth and *life*.

I have often vainly wondered what was the secret of the irresistible fascination
Herman Leard had for me. He was only moderately good-looking, he was
insignificant, he had absolutely no brains or culture. On the other hand, I was no
silly, impressionable girl, ready to fall fathoms in love with the first man who
kissed her. Neither kisses nor men were any novelty to me. I was twenty-two and
had had beaux galore ever since I was fifteen—nice boys who made nice love to
me. Most of them had kissed me occasionally. And a very boring and silly performance I thought it at best and at worst very nauseating. Six men had asked me
to marry them. Edwin Simpson, one of the handsomest and cleverest men I have
ever known, had tried his best to make me love him and had failed. I had tried my
best to love him and had failed. And yet the first touch of Herman's lips on mine
made me his forever, as I have never been any other man's, not even the man's
whose wife I have been for twenty years and whose children I have borne. *Why
was it*? Four hundred years ago it would have been called witchcraft. People have
gone to the stake because of it.

There are, I believe, people born with this power and gift, just as some are born
with the gift of music or pen or brush. It has nothing to do with their brains or
their beauty or their social status. They may be quite unconscious of possessing
it. Looking back and realizing its potency I think I did well to resist it and escape
it as far as I did—thanks to the powerful passions of pride and ambition that were
my birthright.

As I am writing of the past I will put here a picture belonging to that past. It is
not a sea-nymph who has come out of the cave behind her to keep tryst with some
expected lover.

It is myself in the bathing costume of the period—*my* bathing costume at least.
Nora Lefurgey and I had no regular bathing dresses. Nobody in Cavendish had,
but on that lonely shore what mattered it? We generally put on "combination"
suits and very fine things they were for it. One evening I "took" Nora in hers and
she took me in mine. We hid the pictures away in terror lest anyone should see
them. We would have been disgraced forever!

Maud at Cavendish Beach in 1903

I came across the plate in a box in the attic the other day and had a picture printed off. I think it is quite charming—and quite up-to-date. The bathing dresses in which the girls of today publicly disport themselves are far scantier!

Wed. Aug. 5, 1931
I was in Toronto today and went to Mac's office. Found Mr. Stewart there, for the first time since his illness. He has recovered wonderfully, although he will always have to be careful. It was nice to see him there again. I always liked him very much.

Stuart has passed the four matric exams he took.

Everyone in the house but myself has been ill with flu and I have had a strenuous week. But I read *Dr. Thorne* this evening and was consoled. The world is upside down. All our cherished beliefs and traditions have gone by the board. Red Russia's shadow lies darkly over all. But thank God it is still possible to read *Anthony Trollope*!

Friday, Aug. 21, 1931
The Manse, Norval.
Today my copies of *A Tangled Web* came from Stokes. I do not like the jacket they have on it. It is well enough in itself but the figure in poke-bonnet and crinoline on it will suggest a sentimental novel of the Victorian Era, which is the last thing I want people to think it. I intend to speak my mind to Stokes. I did not think they have been doing what they might for my books this past five years. They do not bother "pushing" them at all but are content to let them drift along on my reputation.

I dedicated it to Fred and Alexena Wright. I am running a little short of people to whom I can dedicate my books. I cannot bring myself to put on the title page of my books the name of any person who has not meant something to me in the way of inspiration and friendship. People have wondered why I have never dedicated one of my books to Grandfather and Grandmother Macneill. *I could not.* I can never forget how Grandfather fought against my getting any education at all, beyond Cavendish school, and how, until I began to make a little money by it, Grandmother sneered at my passion for writing as a silly waste of time. I owe them a great deal in many ways but *nothing* as far as my success in writing goes. And therefore I cannot dedicate a book to them. If they had ever said but *one* encouraging word to me when I was a young struggler it would be possible. But they never did.

Monday, Aug. 31, 1931
I had a big day of making pickle and jelly today. I like doing this. It is delightful when all is finished to look at rows of translucent rubies and ambers on the table. But I was tired when the day ended and yearned for a quiet evening reading *Framley Parsonage.* I remember the first time I read it. I was a girl of fourteen and Uncle Leander had bought one copy of it for his summer vacation. I had never read a novel of Trollopes before. I sat on the back porch steps all one golden summer evening and read it—and loved it. Nor has my love ever faded. Times without number have I read it since then and always with the same delight. I wanted to spend the evening with my dear old unchanged friends—Lord and Lady Lufton, Mark and Lucy and Fanny Robarts, the Grantleys, not forgetting Griselda, Miss Dunstable, the Harold Smiths, *and* the inimitable Mrs. Proudie. And instead I had to go and spend it at a U.F.O. Meeting.

I wonder what Griselda Grantley would have done at a U.F.O. But Mrs. Proudie would have been quite at home.

Today a letter from Mrs. Jim Mustard informed us that Will Cook had married Lily Meyers!! It has always been expected he would but I could never bring myself to believe it. He has committed social suicide. The worst of the poor creature is that she is such a liar. I don't know how he could have been so mad but I suspect, from something in Mrs. Mustard's letter, that there is the usual scandal behind it.

Talking of marriages. I don't know if I ever happened to mention in this journal the fact that Rob Anderson was married a couple of years ago—and *not* to Elsie—to some Irish girl in Toronto. I admit I would like to know just what broke it off between him and Elsie. They were engaged when they left here....

Sunday, Sept. 6, 1931
The Manse, Norval, Ontario
Cuth and Ada and the Sutherland girls who have been here to supper have just gone. The "Sutherland girls" are Betty and Margaret, the daughters of Jack Sutherland. I haven't seen them since they were tiny tots. They are very nice girls with whom I felt at home at once. We sat long around the table and laughed uproariously. I told them the tale of *Earl Grey* and the Macphail unmentionable and also May Macneill's wild adventure with the Duke of Devonshire. I don't believe I've ever written the latter in this journal and it

148

would be a pity not to. It is too delicious to be lost. I only got it at second hand but it lost little in May's telling.

A few years ago when the Duke of Devonshire was our Governor General he visited P.E.I. and announced that it was his lordly pleasure to visit Cavendish, which had been named after some cadet of his house who was interested in the early settlement of P.E. Island.

This set Cavendish by the ears of course. Committees of entertainment were hurriedly formed. It was decided to hold the levee on the grounds of the then vacant manse and a committee of ladies fitted up a room in it for her Grace the Duchess. Carpet—curtains—couch—water—basin—towels—soap—mirror—hairbrush etc. For all emergencies save one did they provide. I suppose that one never entered their heads. Probably they imagined that vice reines were not as common clay in this respect.

The Vice Regal party arrived on a dusty summer day. The duchess and her attendants were convoyed to the room where they removed the stains of travel. Then one of the duchess' ladies appeared in the lawn rather vague and anxious. May Macneill, for her sins, was the one to whom she addressed herself. The duchess etc. etc. Where could she go?

Poor May almost dropped dead in her tracks. There was only one place *to* go—the old watercloset behind the barn, cheek by jowl with the manure heap, the only way to reach which was to go through the horse-stable. Poor May with crimson face led the way, the Duchess meekly following behind. They went over the lawn and through the stable. May's hand was outstretched to open the little door of the holy of holies—when the door suddenly opened and the Duke stuck his head out warningly!!!

May and the Duchess went outside the stable and stood there until the Duke got through!

Betty Sutherland told me a bit of family history I did not know when I was writing the Montgomery history in this journal a short time ago. It is too picturesque to be forgotten. It seems that Mary MacShannon Montgomery *bribed* the captain of the vessel with a *bottle of whiskey* to set her on shore that day of days!

After all, prohibition may not be an unmixed blessing!

Thursday, Sept. 10, 1931
The Manse, Norval, Ontario
Stuart returned to St. Andrew's today. He has grown up this summer. The accompanying picture is not good of his face—he is really a rather good-looking kid—but shows him up as a youth.

I feel lonely and forsaken tonight. Tired, too. That rascal Luck woke me up at four last

"Age 15½" [Stuart]

"Corners in our Norval Library"

night, shouting all over the house that he had got a mouse, and I could not get to sleep again.

Stokes have got a new jacket for the book after all. They have gone to the other extreme and the design looks like a head-on collision between two comets. However, it is much more "striking" than the other and better suited to the book.

This has been a frightfully hot week. The weather seems bewitched—the hottest September weather since 1898, they say!

Sunday, September 13, 1931
The other night I tried an experiment—taking some indoor pictures with a time exposure by electric light. The result was quite successful. I must try it with all our rooms.

"Corners in our Norval Library"

Today was about 93 in the shade. For this and several other reasons it was a kind of nightmare.

I have been reading Ethel Mayne's *Life of Lady Byron*. All the mysteries that intrigued us so in youth when we were studying Byron's poems at college are definitely cleared up. The whole tale is sordid and terrible—and ununderstandable. Lady Byron's character is almost as much of an enigma as Byron's—nay, more so.

One of the mysteries is—*how* could such a man as Byron write "The Isles of Greece" or "There was a sound of revelry by Night" or "Roll on thou deep and dark blue ocean, roll." Well, it is only explicable if we look upon Byron's brain as on some subtly fashioned violin which some supernal musician picked up and played on, saying, "This violin is so constructed that it serves as a medium to express my divine melody. I care nothing if its owner is vile and depraved and outcast. It is only the violin that matters to me."

Of course Byron was abnormal. He would be a case for a psychiatrist today. There is no use in judging him by normal standards. Annabelle Milbanke was the last woman in the world he should have married. She had no earthly idea how to handle him. No woman could have been happy with him. But some women could have managed him and made him toe the line to some extent. Byron knew this himself as is shown by some of his statements to his intimates.

The Life of Lady Byron is the most fascinating book I have read for many a day. But such letters as she wrote! And how people seemed to keep every note and scrap in those days.

Speaking of keeping letters. I have recently been "weeding out" my fan letters ruthlessly and burning them, keeping only the best. Hitherto I have kept them all but space at last rebels. I have burned thousands of enthusiastic school girl letters these past few weeks—and there are thousands more to burn.

Wednesday, Sept. 16, 1931
Today I went to Guelph and bought me a new hat—with an ostrich feather curling around it! It made me feel queerly young again. It is years since feathers were "in." Many of the new hats are very pretty. For years hats have been hideous in themselves and unbecoming to anyone past first youth.

Thursday, Sept. 24, 1931
Tonight I learned again the meaning of moonrise in September. Ewan and I went out to make a call. The call was nothing—but the drive there and back was ecstasy. It was through a night of silver following a day of gold. We went along a lonely road where great pines cast pools of shadow here and there on the radiant road. There was a hint and sparkle of frost in the air. Such a night always makes me yearn to be young again—a girl with a beau in the offing. Very seldom do I feel so. I am generally thankful that all the strain and stress of passion is over. But when I realize that there is still moonlight in the world I am swept by a sudden mad longing for my lost youth. To be young again—on the Cavendish hills or the shore meadows! Oh!!

Sunday, Sept. 27, 1931

I have been haunted all day by a nasty dream I had this morning just as I was waking—I heard a voice or read the words out of a letter, I could not be sure which—"L.M. Montgomery—*five* or *six* years longer." I seemed to get the impression that this was how much longer I had to live! Perhaps I am mistaken in that—the whole thing was rather blurred except for the phrase itself. But if it does not mean that I am sure it means some great change in the year 1936 or 1937.

Tuesday, Sept. 29, 1931
The Manse, Norval, Ont.

Yesterday we took Chester to Toronto to begin his college course over again. Last year we saw him off with high hopes and confidence. Today only with doubts and fears.

Then I went to the Royal York for the final day's judging of the International Kodak Competition. The full tale of judges were there this time—Mr. Grier, Colonel Gagnon, Canon Cody, Judge Emily Murphy, Nellie McClung and myself. We had a very interesting day. There were six classes of photographs—Animals, Still Life, Architecture, Scenery, Informal Portraits and "Games, Pastimes and Occupations." In all, 180,000 entries had been made but they had been weeded down to about two hundred. Even then it was difficult enough. The pictures were all very beautiful and well taken. We had to decide the three prize pictures in each class. Then, out of all the first prizes, the big $1000 prize for all Canada was to be chosen. Finally we got all the exhibits finished except the "Games, Pastimes and Occupations." There was considerable difference of opinion in regard to these and the rest of the judges had about decided on a certain picture for first. But my eye had been caught by a small picture down in a corner which nobody had noticed at all. I looked at it closely and then asked the manager to let me see the enlargement—they had enlargements of all the exhibits there too. He brought it and set it up on the easel.

"There," I said, "is what I call a perfect picture, both as regards technical excellence and heart interest."

Wylie Grier looked at it and agreed. They all agreed. The Prospector got the first prize in its class.

Then came the tug of war. The first prize enlargements were put up in a row and we all sat gravely before them to decide on the first prize. Wylie Grier wanted a study of a boy with his father's sword. Mrs. Murphy and Mrs. McClung were determined to have a portrait of an old man reading, Canon Cody wanted something else and Colonel Gagnon

"The Prospector"

held his tongue—an art in which he excels. Nobody even mentioned the Prospector. I got up.

"See here," I said inelegantly but forcibly, "all these other pictures are charming pictures—but they might have been taken in any country in the world. This one of the Prospector could have been taken only in Canada. It expresses the very essential spirit of pioneer Canada—the immortal quest—beyond the hills of dream—the 'something lost behind the ranges.' That is what you want to send to Geneva, with the cachet of First Prize for all Canada on it—a picture that will interpret Canada to the world."

My burst of eloquence persuaded Wylie Grier. He surrendered—"You are right, Mrs. Macdonald." The ladies held out a bit but I fought tenaciously—in the end there was a unanimous vote for my choice as first prize. And I licked my chops privately in satisfaction as we sat down.

The funny part was that when we went upstairs to prepare for luncheon Mrs. Murphy and Mrs. McClung were quite wild with excitement. "Oh, I'm so glad *we* got that picture chosen," cried Mrs. Murphy. "It's just *Canada*."

I could have howled—but I didn't. I had got my way and that was all I cared for. A picture which, but for me, would not have received even Honorable Mention in its class has captured the all-Canadian prize and goes to Geneva. That's enough.

We had a wonderful luncheon with a corsage of orchids and roses for each of the ladies. I sat by Hector Charlesworth, the noted musical critic of *Saturday Night* and found him a very nice man in spite of his bushy-beardiness. After lunch Mr. Morgan asked us to go back to the Exhibition room to see a new moving picture camera working—a new process for taking and reproducing pictures in colors. They were certainly very wonderful and we were all exclaiming in admiration when our mouths were temporarily stopped by the manager's calm announcement that the company was going to present a camera and reproducer to each of the judges as a mark of gratitude for our services!!!

Really, it seemed rather too good to be possible. The full outfit must cost about five hundred dollars. Of course, like everything in my life, it comes to me *too late*. If I could have had this when my boys were small. How wonderful to set up a screen, touch a button, and see them playing on Leaskdale lawn as they did fifteen years ago! Then—the joker in the affair is that the films are frightfully expensive. Still, I expect to get some pleasure out of this. And I expect the boys will be thrilled. The Kodak Co. has "done us proud."

Saturday, Oct. 10, 1931
The Manse, Norval, Ontario
One paragraph in a very good review of *A Tangled Web* in this morning's *Globe* made me very cross. It said I must have spent many hours talking to the old folks in P.E. Island, getting the incidents and droll sayings!!! Gods, must I put up with this?

There are just two anecdotes in *The Tangled Web* that I got from anybody. The rest is purely my own invention—incidents, dialogue and plots. G-r-r-r!

I suppose, however, it is a compliment in a way! I must have made my characters and their conversation very lifelike if it is supposed I copied them from old wives' tales of reality....

Thursday, Oct. 15, 1931

I was rather blue for various reasons all day but coming home from a village call at night I saw something that heartened me up. Over the dark pines on Russells' hill October was wearing a slender new moon like a ring. It was such an exquisite sight in itself—and made me think of so many old, loved, unforgotten things. It did me good like wine.

The papers are full of rumors of war between China and Japan. War—the very word makes my spine crawl! And we are all waiting breathlessly for the election in Britain—which will, one thinks, decide the fate of civilization.

What a mess the world is in!

Wednesday, Oct. 21, 1931

This afternoon we went to Aurora for prize day, taking the Barracloughs with us. It was a delightful day of summer warmth and we went across country by new roads where the autumn maples were blazing in crimson and tawny. Just before we got to Aurora we saw a pretty sight—which I had never seen before and yet which was strangely familiar to me. I had visualized it often when reading English novels. The Aurora Hunt was out—before us men in the "pink" were jumping the fence into a field—a field that was filled with lovely dogs. Everything was charming and the dogs were adorable. We sat and watched until the last horse had gone over the bars.

Stuart got his prizes and was happy and sunshiny.

Thursday, Oct. 22, 1931

Edison is dead. "A prince and a great man has fallen this day in Israel."

I suppose Edison and Henry Ford have done more to change the world and life in the world than any other two men since the birth of history. Only the unknown man who first conceived the idea for making a sign stand for a word on the shoulder blade of a deer can be classed with them.

Stuart

I am sorry Edison is dead. It seemed somehow that he could not die. But it matters more to me just now that my garden is dead—all its color and personality gone from it. And it was such a good garden this year—and such a delight and comfort to me. And one always wonders—now—if there will be another spring for me and my garden together.

Saturday, Oct. 31, 1931
The Manse, Norval, Ontario
My head has been better this week. It has troubled me a good deal all this October off and on—just simply a "queer feeling." I had it last fall and in the spring.

The National Gov't was returned in Britain last Tuesday. For the first time in years England has a strong gov't. Let us hope it will be able to extricate her from her troubles. But as long as she carries on the "dole" system I fear she will never stand on solid ground.

A letter from Marion says Myrtle has had another very bad spell.

And I have begun to drill the Union Dramatic Club in a play!! We practice four nights a week in an endeavor to get it up quickly and out of the way. It's all right for the club. But for me! Well, it's my kismet.

Sat., Nov. 7, 1931
My "movie" camera etc. came Thursday. They have sent a full outfit. I wish I could get up a little enthusiasm over it. They sent four films so I shan't have to waste money learning it.

This afternoon Ewan and I went to Toronto to the opening of the new mining laboratory. I enjoyed the day. Also my mind is relieved on one point.

Last Tuesday Ewan met Prof. Haultain at the college and the latter asked him how Chester got along in the Frood last summer. Ewan told him the whole story. Prof. H. was very indignant. He said they had never fired a student before, because they (the mining Faculty) had an understanding with them. He said he would write about it and if they could not give a satisfactory explanation he would never send them any more men. I wrote C. at once to go to Haultain and tell him the whole story. He told me today he had done so. I feel now that Prof. Haultain will know just what happened and not hold it against C.

C. is doing better this year I think. He seems interested in his work and has got good marks in his tests and drawings so far. Altogether I enjoyed the day and feel less discouraged about some things.

But it has been a terribly full week and I am very tired. Monday night practice. Tuesday night practice. Wednesday afternoon WMS at Union, Thursday afternoon a meeting of the local Institute at which I had to give a reading. At night I drove 32 miles to Aberfoyle where I gave an address to the Puslinch Institute. Friday afternoon, the Anglican Bazaar and practice tonight. Friday the trip to Toronto. Today was pleasant but all the rest was—duty!!!??!

Monday, Nov. 9, 1931
The Manse, Norval
I had a letter from Margaret today and a note from Marion saying her mother was to be operated on for gall bladder trouble Saturday. So it is over by now but it will

be a few days yet before I hear of the result. I await it with bitter anxiety. I so fear the doctors will find some internal trouble more serious than they think.

I had not heard from Margaret for a long time and welcomed her letter. But she is not very happy. They left Montague last summer and went to an old Methodist circuit near Alberton where they are living in an old "parsonage," seven miles from the station with no hydro or sanitation. It is a burning shame that John Stirling should have dragged Margaret to such a place at her age. He "thought it his duty to go there"—forsooth! I suppose he owes no "duty" to his wife, who is no longer young. I like J.S. but there are times when I could cheerfully immerse him in boiling oil.

Today came the news of Lucy L. Montgomery's death—my namesake writer and correspondent of long years. She was 85 and had been ill for some time. I shall miss her letters and the news made a dreary day seem a little drearier.

Tuesday, Nov. 10, 1931
The Manse, Norval
Had a very curious dream last night of being pursued by a black bull but finally escaping him! The black bull is an old Scottish symbol of death. Had it anything to do with Myrtle? Tonight, just after I had come home from the (wearisome) play practice at Union I was alarmed by a phone ring. A phone ring at eleven is a very rare thing here. Was it a wire of bad news from P.E.I.? My legs trembled so that I could hardly stand as I took the receiver down. But it was only some Toronto idiot calling to ask me to address some idiotic society or other. How I enjoyed saying "no" with polite viciousness!

I must now gird up my loins and apply myself to the S.S. concert program. Remembering last year and the hullabaloo Mrs. Davis kicked up I dread the whole thing richly. But it has to be gone through.

Thursday, Nov. 12, 1931
Today was one of those dark fuzzy days Ontario seems to have a monopoly of in November and December. We had to have the hydro turned on most of the day. I did not sleep very well last night after that 'phone call—it doesn't take much nowadays to shake my nerves. But there was a welcome bit of good news in the mail—a note from Marion saying the operation was over and the doctor's considered it a success. This is a relief. There are so many anxieties and worries of one kind or another this fall.

Wednesday, Nov. 18, 1931
November drags on in a succession of dark, dull, though very mild days. The openness of the season is amazing. Marigolds, scabiosa and lupins are still blooming in the garden.

I had another nasty shock this morning—a call to the phone—a telegram for Mrs. Ewan Macdonald—I turn sick—from Webb, of course! No, *Montreal*! A business wire. But I was upset for the day. And a worrisome letter about another business matter haunted me. In these days of "depression" and failing dividends most of my business letters are depressing or worrisome. I did so hope the Can.

Associate Co. in which I have a heavy investment would have been able to pay a dividend, Nov. 1, but it is not going to do it. It would have made the difference between comfort and pinching this fall and winter.

Sunday, Nov. 22, 1931

I picked a bouquet of marigolds and lupins in the garden today. Many self-sown seeds are coming up all over it—lettuce, gypsophila etc. "Two springs in one year" is no good sign I'm told. But there are no good signs just now it seems to me. This afternoon was dark and gloomy. As I sat alone I was haunted by remembrances of old Sunday afternoons at Leaskdale when my maid went home and I was alone with my two little lads, playing pirates about the floor or sprawled on it reading. I had few lonely Sunday afternoons there. But now—the boys are gone and even when home have other resorts for Sunday afternoon. This had to come—but that doesn't make it any the less bitter.

Friday, Nov. 27, 1931

On Monday night I went to Montreal and stayed there until Wed. night. I had an absolutely delightful time—felt perfectly well—and enjoyed every minute. Really, all I need is a little pleasant companionship and some release from monotonous, never-ceasing "parish" duties.

I stayed with the R.N. Taylors. Mrs. Taylor was Marian Sutherland of Ch'town....She was one of the Island beauties then. The first time I ever saw her was when I was at Uncle Robert's on my way west and she was there, too. I thought her the prettiest creature I had ever put my eyes on. There is but little of her beauty left—it was largely a matter of coloring. But she is a "nice looking" woman and has a delightful home. I succumbed to her luxury and took my breakfast in bed Wednesday morning—something I really don't enjoy, however. It makes me feel sick or lazy. Tuesday I was at an enjoyable luncheon given me by the Press Club and a tea given by the directors of the Maritime Club. In the evening I spoke to the Maritime Women's Club and had a delightful evening. Met several old friends and daughters of old friends.

And among the women who came to speak to me was a face I knew—Miss Phelps of Macdonald college. The last time I saw her was when Frede died. How it all came back and tore at my heart amid all the pleasures of the evening!

We had a drive around the mountains Wed. morning and I went to lunch in the Sun Life building where Florrie Sutherland has worked for 24 years and is in charge of a department. Some man missed a good wife. Had lunch with the great T.B.McCaulay himself, President of the Sun Life, and was shown all over the building which is really a wonderful place where they breathe air that has been washed and scrubbed, and where there are hospitals and rest rooms and gymnasiums and lounges and cafeterias and butcher shops etc. etc. for the 3000 people who work in the huge hive.

The Montreal Branch of the Authors' Association gave a tea for me Wednesday afternoon and it was like all other such functions. But I enjoyed it. After all, it's not a disagreeable sensation to be lionized!!

I came home last night and had to hurry off to play practice at Union. And this morning the mail was full of depressing letters. One brought a new problem of worry and humiliation—I can't go into details. Then another company has passed dividends—my English royalty of $750 came whittled down to $469 by exchange and income tax—Joe McClure, one of our best men has had a stroke or something like it—one of our Georgetown friends has been in an auto accident where he killed a man and is under arrest for criminal negligence—and not a single cheering item to set against all this. I have spent a most unhappy, bitter day and will not sleep tonight—especially after S.S. practice.

But—the things one dreads don't always happen. The S.S. practices are going smoothly on, with no friction or disturbance of any kind and Mrs. Davis is helping amiably and angelically after all her tantrums of last year. So one must be thankful for small mercies.

Saturday, Nov. 28, 1931
The Manse, Norval, Ont.
A hard day of bitter unrest,with nerves on edge and boring company to entertain. The weather was abominable—cold, dark, raw—the furnace wouldn't burn and the whole house was chilly. I slept none at all last night and felt haunted and desperate. I think I must have been born in the wrong time of the moon!!

A letter from another friend I lent money to. Can't pay the interest this year. Nobody can. I have lent over ten thousand dollars to various friends and they won't even pay the interest. As for the principal they evidently look upon it as a gift! If I had never lent a cent I would not be counting my pennies as I have to do this fall.

Will Cook has married Lily Meyers who has been keeping house for him since his wife's death. There is a child expected any day. I always knew what would happen. Will really did well to hold out so long. He has been "melancholy" ever since the wedding and won't work. Consequently he, too, can't pay me the interest on the money he borrowed!

His family are broken hearted over it. What a mother to give his young daughters! I could laugh satirically over it all—I, who know Lily so well. She is, however, a worker and if Will gets out of his slump should be a help to him along that line. But the poor creature can't speak the truth even when she tries.

Tuesday, Dec. 1, 1931
The Manse, Norval
My nerves have been very bad all day. Market news was bad—Mary Beaton has been operated on for gall stones. But *this* should be good news if she recovers. She has been a martyr to bad attacks for years and has feared to have an operation because of her bad heart.

I am going to play practice four nights out of the week!!!

Friday, Dec. 4, 1931
My nerves continue bad. It isn't quite so unendurable in day time though curious burning and stinging sensations in my face vex and harass me all the time like gnats, but at night the nervous unrest becomes so bad that I can hardly endure

158

lying in bed. Last night, as I could not sleep, I read *The Wind In The Willows* and it helped. Thank God, I can still enjoy fairy tales. And it is one of the most delightful of its kind.

The days go on in a dreary routine with all kinds of "little bad news" and nothing cheering or pleasant to offset them. I have been fighting off what started in to be a bad attack of flu and have conquered. Thank heaven, I have found a remedy that heads these attacks off. For the past few years I have had three or four every year and I attribute the state of my nerves to the poison with which these attacks filled my system. The remedy is simple enough. At the first symptom of cold stir 1/2 tsp. soda into juice of a lemon, fill glass half full of water and drink while fizzing. If lemon is not handy 1/4 tsp. cream of tartar will do as well. Repeat every two hours until symptoms cease, then be careful of exposure for a few days. Its results are almost magical with me. I hope it won't lose its power by repetition. So many remedies and drugs do.

The whole world seems to be wanting to borrow. I have had half a dozen people writing to me for loans. Some I hated to refuse. But I haven't it to loan and had to say no—luckily, perhaps, for I have found that it is poor business to lend money to *friends*.

After supper I lay down for a few minutes with Benson's delightful *Miss Mapp* to read and darling Lucky purring on my breast, occasionally giving me a kiss on the chin. I longed just to stay there cosily the whole evening with Lucky and *Miss Mapp*. But I had to get up and go to practice at Union....The practice was a nightmare to me. It isn't a pleasure at any time. There is one young idiot who giggles all the time and tries to make everyone else giggle. It is of no use to ask him not to. I know the night of the play he will be as grave as a judge and do quite well but he holds everything back by his foolishness. Tonight it was doubly hard to be patient. I felt like throwing down the book and saying acidly, "Young people, I am not coming here night after night to train you for my own pleasure or welfare. I think the least you can do is to take the play seriously and get it up without acting the fool continually. If not, I'll go home."

But of course I didn't. I have attained to a wonderful <u>outward</u> patience in my life!

Friday, Dec. 11, 1931
The Manse, Norval, Ontario
I could not sleep "one wink" last night. Nothing helped my nerves. But strangely I felt quite well today—better than for a long while. Which was providential because I had to go to Toronto to buy the presents for the S.S. tree. I loathe the job. It poured rain all day so we did not even have a pleasant drive. I also bought such slim presents as were possible for the family. It is the first Christmas I have had to pinch to do even this. God knows where all this will end. No end to the world depression is in sight—on the contrary things seem to loom more bleakly than ever. Nobody knows what is going to happen in Germany and no improvement is possible until it is known. Germany ruined the world in 1914 and she is likely to ruin it again in 1932. Yet the foolish, blind Peace of Versailles is as much to blame as she.

Sunday, Dec. 13, 1931
I have had two *good* nights' sleep and feel so much better. I believe all I need is enough sleep. But today is our third dark drizzling dreary Sunday and my soul rebelled over various things. But tonight I read *Lady Into Fox* and was amused by it. It is quite the craziest thing but surprisingly well done for an insanity.

Saturday, Dec. 19, 1931
Thanks be, the hardest week of the fall is over. Monday I worked all day, getting ready properties for the dress rehearsal of the play. Tuesday afternoon we had the annual business meeting of our W.M.S. and Tuesday night we put the play on. They did well and it went off excellently. But I was too tired to sleep when I got home at one. Wednesday night we held the dress rehearsal for our concert. Thursday I found time to write a little and Thursday evening Charlotte MacPherson and I labelled the presents. Yesterday afternoon the boys came home and Chester's "Gee, mother, you're *pretty*" as he kissed me was the only pleasant thing that happened this week....

However, Australia has turned out the Labor government that has got her into such a mess and that is another step to righting the world.

Good heaven, how tired I am!!

And yet there are still cats in the world—dear round fat purry pussy cats. Praise be!

Saturday, Dec. 26, 1931
I am glad Christmas is over. It has been for me a dreary one and the whole week has been dreary. I have not been well—and I seem to be haunted night and day with fear of something—I know not what. I am horribly afraid of life—of everything. This is all plain neurasthenia. I have not had an attack like this since those dreadful winters down home years ago.

I think Chester has done better this term than last year. He seems to have done well in all his tests, save one, and that one he passed in last year anyway. He seems to be taking a real interest in and getting a real grasp of his studies. But last year robbed me of my *confidence* in him and I cannot recover it. I think a part of my "fear complex" is caused by an unreasonable dread of getting another letter from the Delinquency Council such as we had last year. My nerves are in poor shape, so that every little worry casts an exaggerated shadow over everything.

My nights of late have been nightmares—not able to sleep and not able to think—or to escape from *reality* in waking dreams—just dreadful unrest of body and mind! I am going to give up writing in this diary as long as I continue like this. There is no sense in a continuous record of blues and worries with nothing interesting or pleasant or even humorous to lighten the shadows.

1932

Saturday, Jan. 2, 1932

Never mind wishing anybody a happy New Year. It sounds too much like a mockery.

I said I was going to give up writing in this diary as long as things remained as they have been of late. But I can't do it. I'm so much in the habit of writing here that I can't omit it without pain. Besides, what other outlet or companionship have I?

Monday night I entertained the Bible class as I annually do. And Tuesday night we *did* have a delightful time. We were all invited over to the Glen House for supper as it was Mr. B's birthday. We had one of the banquets Mrs. B. always puts up and a lovely evening to follow. Stuart was gracious and attractive as always—"what a lovely manner he has," said Mrs. B.—and Chester seems to be finding it easier to be friendly and easy than before. Altogether it was a green oasis in the desert of the month and life tasted good again. But of course the bill was presented Wednesday when something nasty happened that spoiled the day for me and prevented any sleep. Thursday evening Mrs. T. went home for New Year's—and Friday, Jan. 1, 1932, we awoke to find a pretty state of affairs. Really, I don't know when we're had a more *hellish* day then yesterday. Here's hoping it isn't a symbol of what 1932 is going to be. Let us pin our faith to the old saw, "A bad beginning, a good ending."

We awoke as aforesaid to find Old Man Ontario in the grip of one of the worst ice-storm of years. Trees—wires—fences—everything coated with ice and a pouring, freezing rain persisting. At ten o'clock just as I put our New Year's dinner in the oven—pop went the hydro. It has never come on since—and the days have been almost as dark as the nights. We make shift with two old coal oil lamps and candles. But we have had a New Year's dinner of boiled eggs!!

We have an old coal range but the oven is rusted out and quite useless. We can cook on top of it, of course. But—it was New Year's. The shops were shut so nothing could be got. Accordingly—eggs!! Thanks be, we had plenty in the house!

But with the hydro went toilet and water facilities also, since the engine couldn't work. We were glad to have the old pump to fall back on. My head was queer all day and I have never passed a drearier New Year's. The phones are out, too, of course, and likely to remain so for awhile judging from the newspaper account of the damage done. One of the big maples on our lawn split in two and fell—luckily away from the house.

One day this week the Island paper had an account of the death of Bayfield Williams in Vancouver.

I went back in thought thirty-seven years. I was stepping off the train one summer afternoon at Ellerslie. A smart young man steps up and hands me his card—E. Bayfield Williams. Then he introduces his companion—a pretty golden-haired slip of a girl—Edith England. We have a merry drive to Mr. Miller's. Edith and I are dear chums from that day.

And now—they are both dead!

Poor Bayfield. He had every chance and bright prospects. He was clever—well-educated—popular. But he threw everything away—ruined his life—broke Edith's heart through drink.

He was killed by being struck by an auto. Edith was drowned. It seems strange that they both died violent deaths.

Saturday, Jan. 9, 1932
The Manse, Norval, Ont.
The hydro came on last Sunday afternoon after over 48 hours of absence and I danced with joy. But both phones have been out all the week and it has made things hard in a great many ways. Chester went back to Toronto Monday. I think all through the holidays I was really half expecting every day to bring a letter saying that he would not be allowed to go back. This was absurd because he seems to have really done quite well this term—had good tests and seems much more interested in his work....

Stuart went Wednesday and since then life has seemed drenched in the cold gray light that sweeps over the world before a snow squall in November.

We have begun to practise a play for Old Tyme Night. I have no heart in it. We miss Mr. Greenwood so terribly. But then I have no heart for anything just now—and there is so much to do—Guild papers—the Old Tyme Concert—a W.M.S. concert—various presentations of our Union play in other places—special prayer fests—God being more inclined to grant a prayer made at a special gathering of three or four societies than one made quietly in one's own Auxiliary!—an executive meeting of the local Auxiliary to be entertained and lunched—I grow distracted at the thought of it. If I were well I could dovetail and plan for them and polish them off in a jiffy. But as it is I feel that if I live through January and February nothing can kill me or drive me crazy. I ought to have a six months rest—where I could cry or laugh or swear just when I felt like it—and I can't even get a six hour one. Selah.

Sunday, Jan. 10, 1932
I was much amused lately in reading Kate Douglas Wiggin's autobiography, *My Garden of Memory*, to find that she had had an experience with a school teacher very much like mine with "Izzie" Robinson. The description she gives of her might have been written of the said "Izzy"—"the instructress of this time was thin, sallow, censorious. The glance of her cold blue eye pierced one's very marrow; her lips were too thin for sweetness."

This teacher was guilty of treatment which Kate resented. In after years when the latter was a successful writer Miss "X" crossed her path again and addressed "Kate dear" with "a honeyed inflection I had never hitherto observed in her voice."

But Kate had a little more spunk than I had in a similar situation. She treated Miss X to a small, polite Parthian shaft which must have avenged several ancient grudges.

And she met Earl Grey too—when she was a judge in some competition of plays he was fathering. She spent a week at Rideau Hall. But I don't think she sat with him on the steps of the family watercloset. At least she does not say so.

Tuesday, Jan. 12, 1932
The Manse, Norval

A gray, east-wind day—and bad news! Mr. Taylor was here—the new President of Canadian Associate Co. Things there are in bad shape. God knows how it will come out. It may mean financial ruin for me. It is due, indirectly, to the stock market crash of '29. I remember at the time I thought it meant nothing to me because I hadn't been dabbling in stocks!

Everyone thought Mr. Dawson, the former President, such an able man. And he has been worse than a fool and has got the company into a fearful mess.

After Mr. Taylor left I was useless for the rest of the day. Had to go to Devotional Guild in the evening and affect composure. At the P.O. I got a letter from Chester which I was too much of a coward to open. I knew it might have news of the exam in Mineralogy he had taken when he went back and I dared not read it lest it upset me past sleeping. But I might as well have for I didn't sleep anyhow—had a dreadful night of nervous restlessness. Everything seems so hopeless in the dark.

This morning I opened Chester's letter—and it had good news. He feels quite sure he passed his exam all right and besides he made 95 in a test.

Then, too, a company I have been shivering about declared its usual quarterly dividend and that is much just at present.

Sunday, Jan. 24, 1932
The Manse, Norval

Dull gray rainy fuzzy days—sleepless nights—worry—constant efforts to do a hundred things—a funeral—a barn burned—play practices—nerves all agley—hopeless—resentful—Red menace in Spain and Germany—such is the week in retrospect. And nothing cheering or pleasant.

Well, perhaps hardly *nothing*. I re-read *The Bonnie Brier Bush* and *Auld Lang Syne* some of those sleepless nights and forgot my worries in the old charm. What delightful books they are! What a *good* taste they leave in your mouth! You feel after all that there are some decent people in the world—that folks are not all "Elmer Gantrys."

It is odd to imagine "William Maclure" and "Elmer Gantry" in the same world. Yet they both exist. But it is a good deal pleasanter to read about Maclure.

These tales of Scottish rural life have oddly the same flavour as the Cavendish of my childhood, the memory of which is like a silvery moonlight in my recollection. The atmosphere was the same, the background very similar. And as I read the book I went back—back—back to a world where there were no Reds or static or war debts or Hitlers.

I read recently a statement to the effect that a man or woman who was born in 1830 and died in 1913 would have lived his entire life in what was the happiest period of the world's entire history to date. True! I have often felt a certain envy of the women of my mother's and grandmother's generation. They lived their lives in a practically unchanged and apparently changeless world. Nothing was questioned—religion—politics—society—all nicely mapped out and arranged and organized. And my generation! What have we not seen? Everything we once thought immoveable wrenched from its pedestal and hurled to ruins. All our old standards and beliefs swept away—our whole world turned upside down and stirred up—before us nothing but a welter of doubt and confusion and uncertainty. Such times have to come, I suppose, but woe to us whose kismet it is to live in them.

Sunday, Jan. 31, 1932
The Manse, Norval

A very gloomy, worried, unhappy January is over. I suppose February will be the same. "Forward though I canna see I guess and fear."

Re-read *The Way Of All Flesh* this week. It always rather puzzles me that I can enjoy a book like this in its way, as I enjoy the *Bonnie Brier Bush* in its way. But then a liking for good maple syrup and griddle cakes doesn't prevent one from liking a cocktail, too, now and then. "To each saint his own candle."

The week has been monotonous with a nightmare Wednesday evening for variety. We were to put on the Union play at Erindale. Jack Cooke offered to take me and as I knew Ewan was sick of seeing the play and didn't want to go I agreed. Jack was to call at seven as we wanted to be there by 7.30. He did not come till 20 to 8. Billy Cooke and Will Townsend were with him. We tore up the highway at a break neck speed to make up for lost time. At Brampton Jack stopped for gas and discovered some screw or nut missing from a wheel. The garage man tried to hunt up a nut to fit it. Nothing doing. They tried on nuts for half an hour and had to give it up. Put a *nail* in to hold the wheel. All this time I had been writhing in concealed impatience. It was twenty to nine when we got away—fourteen miles still from Erindale and the play billed for 8.30! We whizzed, and my thoughts about that wheel held on by a nail were not a panacea for tortured nerves. I expected every moment we would land in the ditch. But such was not our kismet and we reached Erindale at nine, to find an impatient audience and a half-frantic cast who couldn't think what on earth had become of us.

Followed wild bustling to get ready—a bitterly cold passage to stand in the whole evening to prompt—a very poor sort of lunch after the play—and another drive home with that nail still faithfully holding the world together. At twenty to one I crawled up stairs to find Ewan cosily snuggled in bed. "You will take me wherever we put on the play after this," I told him with ominous calm. "Not for a gold brick would I undergo another night like this."

War has broken out between China and Japan—which will not help to settle a muddy world any. No wonder certain simple souls believe we are living in the last days. Well, in a sense we are—the last days of the system under which the world has functioned for several centuries. It is tottering to its grave. After all, it had its points. What will follow it no man knows.

Today I read Mary Rinehart's *Tish* books and laughed so much that I felt far less neurasthenic. Besides, I had another of my strange symbolic dreams last night—a *good* dream, *if* my interpretation is correct. There is where the doubt comes in which prevents me from relying on it wholly. But it has cheered me up. The dreams of ill-omen have been fulfilled. May I not "believe them when they augur cheer?"

Sunday, Feb. 7, 1932
The Manse, Norval, Ont.
I have wound up a busy week with a nasty cold which was not helped any by a visit yesterday from Isobel...She has been wanting to come all winter and I have been putting her off on one excuse or another for I felt that in this worried winter of neurasthenia and anxiety she would really be the last straw. But I had her yesterday and put in a day of miserable boredom aggravated by symptoms of cold. I should have been in bed. I tried my best to give her a pleasant visit but it was up hill work. She can't talk about *anything*. A whole day of this nearly gave me the jitters. I could not help breathing a devout prayer of thankfulness when she finally left on the evening bus. That girl is becoming a veritable Old Man of The Sea to me. I wish I dared give her a dose of rude truths. But I am really afraid of the consequences. I don't think it would take much to send her over the borderline into insanity—or suicide. Haven't I enough worries of my own to bear without having this inflicted on me?

Wednesday, Feb. 11, 1932
Today brought nothing to encourage or cheer. Quite the reverse. Edgar Wallace is dead. No more "thrillers" to hearten a weary world and make it forget its suffering for a little. I have a sense of personal loss.

Then there was a letter from Isobel. Here it is, as a proof to my descendants that I have not exaggerated my problems.

Feb. 8, 1932
Dear Mrs. Macdonald:—
Since this is the last letter I am going to write you I will try just this once more to tell you something you will never know.

It is that I love you. With all my soul I love you. All Eternity would be too short to manifest my adoration. And I cannot understand why, when, for a whole year, I have lived and worked and endured for that glamorous, too-sweet day when I should have you, I should come from it with a heart wherein are only tears and tortuous disappointment. Why, after all this time, should I be further from you than at the beginning? Why, after worshipping you from tiny girlhood, should I not be rewarded with a little genuine love?

You say you love me. I don't believe it. I doubt that you love anybody but your boys and your cat, and, I presume, your husband. Though, to tell the truth, when I think of a husband, my imagination always becomes entangled in the stars and never goes any further. You love your cat; he knows it. You have a kiss—two kisses—for every creature in creation but not one speck of love for a hungry heart that has pleaded for it too long. You are like a lovely scintillating jewel whose radiant heart is cold and cruelly hard.

You are lovely. I had such an eye feast. You really are a beautiful woman. You are more beautiful now than you have ever been before. You have beautiful eyes, and hair and skin, and a sweet sweet mouth and a face as pretty as a flower and the whole ensemble is one of exquisitely dainty grace. And such a rich personality. You are so lovely that you are heartbreak to me.

You were considering about me. I could have told you and do now that all the restorative I need, to make me blossom as the rose is held in your two little restless hands. They are such darling fascinating little hands. I adore them. And I know that all I need is just a few good doses of you. If I am happy I am well. Love is a most terrible, a most restless net. It makes us helpless slaves and ensnares all our own personality and submerges it in the dominating power of the thing beloved. You make me nervous, awkward, self-conscious; and I'd love to be your friend. I have always worshipped something in you. I know you are really the very stuff of which my soul is made. But I never can be a friend while I am under the power of this terrible love for you. And I really believe in my soul that the only help for it is a little indulgence and satisfaction.

I do not know for what I am asking but I do know that it is nothing unnatural; that it is only what love has always demanded through all the ages of history. Just a little recognition, just a little meeting of this cursed hunger for you that haunts me day and night.

Everybody loves you, admires you, craves a little something from you—and turns with it on his way rejoicing. But I have never been able to turn away. We were taught rigidly to recognize worth and to me you are the loveliest thing in all the universe. Did you see what a former Brantfordite, a minister who visited you one Sunday afternoon last summer, wrote about you? Do you think he would have gone, do you think he would have written as he did if he had not been in love with you? Why, every word was a caress, though a reverent one, embedded in yearning.

I understand somewhat why these so-called freaks turn to you from sordid, disappointed lives. It is because of something for which you stand, which they long for and have not.

I don't know just what it is I want and I am too tired to try to ferret it out. But I'm quite sure it is to be found some where in the world. I know people—I am thinking of one in particular, some one lovely—who, I know, would meet every advance three quarters of the way, would more than satisfy every desire, so that I should be happy and without a pang. Absolutely, the only relief for hunger is to feed it.

But it just isn't in you. You are a will-o'-the-wisp, elusive, exclusive, impulsively flitting here and there, leaving a trail of exotic sweetness that haunts one with a mad desire. You are extremely unselfish with your time and your things and beautifully unspoiled by fame. But you really do not want any love. For it you have an outright or veiled disdain. And it seems to me that if you would accept just a little of the adoration that lies so heavily on my heart that it would dispel or greatly lighten its load. For it is a load that exists despite reason or scorn.

I know, if you do not, that Saturday was just a bore to you, a waste of precious time, a something that could be got-over not to be endured again for at least a year. A year is a long long time and it is a long long time till spring. And then you will come up for a day and I'll have to share you most of the time with other people and it will be more stupid for you than anything has been yet and I just can't bear it.

I know how a person becomes invested in another's eyes with beauty and glory they do not possess and all that; and how one always comes to view with eyes serene the very pulse of the machine but I cannot help it. You're the dearest thing in all the world to me. There is nobody else like you. I'm just mad about you. I suppose I should be psychoanalyzed and need shooting or something but I cannot help it and am not going to try any longer.

I thank you for my visit and I do appreciate all your letters and the many precious things you have given me but somehow in spite of it all I feel just heartbroken. As I said in the beginning I am not going to write any more to you. I've loved to write you. But I'm too tired to try any more to have you understand and too sore to care to write about anything else.

I'll die without you. You've always shone like a golden star in my life but now a mist veils the light and I must stumble on alone.

To die for love of L.M. Montgomery! That would invest me with glory and beauty and fame and I should have forever from the hearts of the world what I craved from you and you denied.

You must think I'm one dashed fool. And I think you're the sweetest thing in the world. But it's no use to tell me not to love you too much because I do. It's just the age-old pitiful tale of a heart consumed with love for one who has none to give. Nor could I accept one tiny sacrifice on your part.

And so I will end this, my last letter to you, part of which was written in school in the light of day, I being in my right mind, calm and unperturbed by the seething mass of humanity around me.

Sincerely
Isobel...

So much for my effort to give her a little of the "happiness" she declared she craved—"seeing me." She is quite right in saying she bored me, although I thought I had not let her see it. I suppose she felt her own deadly dullness *must* bore anyone. I *must* escape from this incredible morass. I shall write Miss Isobel a letter that will bring her up with a round term. I wish to heaven she *wouldn't* write me again but I have no hope of such devoutly-to-be-wished good luck. Not a chance of it. I have been trying all my life to suffer fools, if not gladly, at least patiently. But I haven't any of that kind of patience left this winter of constant worry and dread.

So I "cannot love." Can I not, Frede? Answer from the grave.

But not with the love Isobel...wants, I admit. I am not a Lesbian.

Yet she is very absurd. How she loves to dramatize herself. "To die for love of L.M. Montgomery." There is not much fear of her doing it, luckily. Well, in my youth I had some men rave rather wildly of loving me—though I don't recollect any of them ever actually threatened to die for me. But it has been reserved for me at the mature age of 58, to inspire poor Isobel with this desperate passion!

Faugh! The whole thing is too nauseating to be purified even by ridicule.

Last night I beguiled some sleepless hours by reading Nate's letters, having come across the box in which they were during an attic rummaging. While I read them I was strangely happy, bewitched back into the past.

But when I had finished I nearly died of *homesickness*. I wanted, not Nate or his schoolboy devotion, but the life I lived in the years those letters were written—that life comparatively free from care, full of simple yet thrilling pleasures, with no threatening clouds in the background—full of hope and laughter and zest. Those letters, or, rather, their background, brought home to me with a sort of despair the awful contrast between that life and the one I am living now.

As for Nate himself, he seems something like a dream, so entirely has he receded into the past. Yet I remember one night in 1890 when I lay awake all one night and cried bitterly because Nate and I had had a tiff!

Perhaps the things I lie awake and worry over now will turn out to be as little worth wailing over!!

I have always been sorry that I could not have retained Nate as a *friend*. I liked him so much; we were so congenial intellectually. I thought I had it all nicely set at one time—but it was not so written.

I always liked Nate from the first day he came to school—"the new boy"—"the new Baptist minister's son"—which he wasn't—with all the glamor of novelty about him. He was about nine or ten and not at all handsome. Nate was never handsome, though he had a strongly cut face with a whimsical smile and expressive eyes. That first day he was a pale freckled lad, with a habit of sticking the tip of his tongue between his teeth when he smiled—a habit he was always ragged about.

At first Nate's advent meant nothing to me. He was a Baptist. I was Presbyterian. Between us was a great gulf fixed.

The feeling between the two denominations was still very bitter at that time. The Baptist church in Cavendish had its origin in bitterness. Originally, of course, all the Cavendish people—Macneills, Simpsons, and Clarks—had been Presbyterian. Three Macneill men had married three Dockendorffs from North River who were Baptists—and remained Baptists at heart in spite of outward attendance. I am not sure just how the recession movement started. One Simpson family had for some reason taken up the Baptist "heresy." Dr. Isaac Murray of the Presbyterian church had a genius for antagonizing people. Then "the resurrection of Lazarus" brought all the smouldering disaffection to a head.

One day at dinner hour in school a group of Bright Young People decided to "play" the burial and resurrection of Lazarus. Dr. Murray always blamed the suggestion on Ernest Macneill, son of Great Uncle David Macneill. Great Uncle David (who was one of those with a Dockendorff bride) retorted that the idea had first been hatched in Johnny Murray's head. At all events Johnny Murray was *Jesus* and Ernest was Lazarus. A shallow grave was dug and the whole story "played out," to the admiring wonder of the assembled school children. But when the said children carried the tale home—well, there were some doings in old Cavendish.

Had there not been already some rankling bitterness—had there not been three Dockendorff wives—had the old Macneills and Simpsons had a little plain common sense that would have seen in the whole prank nothing but a childish love of a dramatic tale which should have been passed over with a mild rebuke for dragging sacred subjects down to the level of amusement—there would never have been any Baptist church in Cavendish. But there *was* bitterness—and Dockendorffs—and a disposition to take children's kididoes very seriously. Dr. Isaac and Great Uncle D. both flew off the handle—Uncle D. stopped going to church—the disaffected Simpson family seized the psychological moment to bring in an evangelist to expound Baptist theology—a number of families listened—believed—pulled out and founded the Cavendish Baptist church. A little building was put up in the maple woods at the beginning of the Cavendish Road and a minister was called—the Rev. Mr. Freeman, I think—a Baptist of the Baptists, who said roundly that no one but an immersed person could go to heaven. The Baptists and Presbyterians had nothing to do with each other but the Baptists, not to have too dull a time of it, soon started a lovely shindig in their own church. I don't know what it was about but "Big" George Macneill and Arthur Simpson were the leaders of the two factions and remained bitter foes all their lives, despite the fact that they were brothers-in-law. Mr. Freeman sided with Big George and politely referred to Arthur as Mr. A.(S.) S., bestowing an entirely gratuitous initial on the latter.

I have no recollection of Mr. Freeman but I dimly remember Mr. Woodland who succeeded him. A young man with a pretty bride, not so narrow and bigoted as Mr. Freeman. When he went away the Rev. Mr. Spurr came from Nova Scotia, with his wife, his baby daughter and his stepson Nathan. Nate was called Nathan Spurr at first and called himself so, until he was about fourteen when he suddenly began to use his own name.

His mother was the heroine of a romantic tale. She had been a little Nova Scotian school teacher and had married Nathaniel Joseph Lockhart, a young sailor. They had a few happy months together and then he went on what was to prove his last voyage, on a ship bound for South America. Off Hatteras in a terrible storm he and the captain were both swept overboard. At least that was the story the crew told on their return. But "Pastor Felix" wrote me that the truth was never known but they had too much reason to suspect foul play of some kind.

Meanwhile Mrs. Lockhart was expecting Nate's birth and went home to her mother's for it. On the train she picked up a paper and read in it an account of her husband's death!

Nate had a book of poems written by his uncle—which also invested him with a halo of romance in my eyes....

Mrs. Spurr did not look in the least like the heroine of a romantic tale. She was a trig, bustling, capable little woman. Plain but merry of face. Most of the Baptists liked her except a few who wanted to "run" her and found they couldn't. I liked her very much—I came to know her quite well later on as I took music lessons from her. Mr. Spurr was a nice man, rather broad in the beam but a terrible misfit in the pulpit. It was really painful to listen to him. But he was a good pastor and probably that was the most flourishing period of the Cavendish Baptist

Church—a church that is almost defunct now. During his pastorate the younger Presbyterians began to go to the Baptist church Sunday nights, looking upon it as a social outing. It was long before I was allowed to go. Grandfather thought I was headed for perdition because I wanted to. I loved to go to it—not because of any theological bias or interest—or religion either it must be admitted. I liked to go because it was in such a beautiful spot. I loved to sit in the corner of one of the pews by the windows and look out into that lovely maplegrove—purple in summer twilights, silver-laced in summer moonlights, crimson and gold in autumn afternoons, white-aisled and glamorous in winter evenings. I was always perfectly happy there at any time. Later on, I admit it didn't spoil it at all to know that Nate was sitting in the choir and stealing sly glances at me over his hymn-book—much to the wrath of the fair Baptist maidens who resented bitterly his straying from the fold.

But all this was still far in the future when "the new boy" came to school and I wrote that night in my diary, "The new Baptist minister's son was in school today. His name is Nathan Spurr. He is freckled but I like him."

Well, I always liked him. But for the first years I had little to do with him. One thing I soon discovered, however, my leadership was endangered.

Up to this I had had no rival in class or exams. I had always led easily. Now I found that I would have to work to retain my laurels. Nate was a brilliant student and he was out to win. From that day there was always a keen though perfectly friendly rivalry between us. We were pretty well matched. Sometimes he came out a mark or two ahead. Sometimes I did.

And then we—suddenly and all at once as it seemed—found out how congenial we were in everything. We loved books and loved to talk about them—we were ambitious and liked to talk about that—we had the same taste in jokes—and we were both just beginning to hear the first siren notes of the call of life. We took to walking about together at recess and talking—writing letters to each other every night—walking home together from Literary—exchanging significant smiles in company—thrilling tremendously when Nate warbled the bars in a popular school song

> And oh, how perfect, how divine
> To think her virtuous charms are thine

—and looked straight at *me* when he sang it!

The Baptist girls of that generation have never forgiven me to this day!!

Nate soon was—or fancied himself—in love with me. I was romantically intrigued by him although I was not in love. But it was wonderful to find I was possessed of a power that could send Nate scowling into a corner if I ignored or snubbed him—and flush his cheek and brighten his eye if I smiled on him or sent him one significant glance.

Yes, it was quite wonderful. I would give much to be able to feel that thrill again.

Then came the time when he asked me to tell him which of the boys I liked best in Cavendish. I confessed I *liked* him best. This was the simple truth. I liked him tremendously. The trouble Nate seemed to take if for granted that I meant more than liking—that I meant I loved him. Whereas I had meant nothing of the sort.

I smiled a little over his note tonight—that little screed written in red ink in which he said he not only liked me best but loved me. I smiled a little—but not much. One could not smile much. I remembered the school girl of 15 down in the school woods that winter morning under a big gray maple blushing over that note, and I cannot smile at her. No, to tell the truth I envy her.

"Feb. 18, 1890," I wrote in my diary that night. "I am sure I shall never forget this date." But alas! If my memory had not been refreshed by the said letter I am afraid I could not have recalled it.

But I paid for that moment of thrill and ecstasy. Paid for it in the loss of a friendship I wanted and the acquirement of a lover I did not want.

I tried to think I wanted him. When I found out how seriously Nate was taking it I tried hard all that winter and spring to persuade myself that I loved Nate and would be willing to marry him in the years to come.

It seems very laughable and absurd now to recall how I worried over this and the sleepless nights I spent over it, trying to persuade myself I loved him and knowing quite well even than that I didn't. Why, I detested having him kiss me! Walk home with him under starlit summer skies—moon around garden gates and whispering leaves and sunset shores—talk—talk—talk—oh, delightful. But when it came down to the plane of the physical I knew that never in any year to come could I marry Nate Lockhart—Nate Lockhart who was then fifteen—almost two years younger than my son Stuart is now!!

And while I was worrying in this fashion and losing much sleep over it—it *did* seem so tremendously important then—and who shall say it wasn't? Isn't it just that I've lost my sense of proportion when I think it so trivial now?—the Baptist folks were saying I was "crazy about him"!!

Nate had been very jubilant for awhile after our exchange of confessions. And then he began to realize that I was holding back—retreating. He was a proud lad—nothing was ever *said*—but he accepted the situation gallantly. We parted that summer as friends merely—I went west—he to Acadia College. New interests came into being for both of us and widened the distance between us. We corresponded. I did not keep many of Nate's college letters—I don't know why—I have only a few of them. I enjoyed our correspondence very much when it was conducted on a friendly basis—I thought I had succeeded beautifully in my attempt to convert Nate into a friend. And I'm quite in the dark yet as to the precise reason why he ceased to be.

He was in Cavendish in the summer of '91 but I did not get home from the west until he had returned to Acadia. We corresponded that next year and in the spring of '92 he wrote me the last letter I was ever to get from him, just before we left for home. As he was to be on the Island almost as soon as his letter I did not answer it. He was in Cavendish only a few days before he left on a summer agency. I saw him once or twice—but the old comradeship was impossible. We no longer met every day in school—we belonged to different churches and "sets"—there was no possibility, situated as I was, of asking him to call. And if I could have done it—well, all the Baptists would have said I was "trying to get him back"—Nate himself might have thought so. Then he went away and was not home again before going back to college.

I suppose I should have answered his letter then but after the summer silence I somehow "didn't like to." I thought he would write again—and I suppose he thought I owed him a letter. At any rate that was the end of our correspondence. I was sorry—but not sorry enough to make an effort to keep it up. I was afraid if I did he might think things I didn't want him to think.

I saw him once for a few moments at the Baptist church the next summer of '93 or '94 and he walked home along with me and Lucy after service. The last time he was in Cavendish was in '96 when I had a brief chat with him at a school examination. That fall the Spurrs left Cavendish. And the next time I saw Nate was in the late autumn of 1901 when I turned my head at the Dalhousie "Break-up" and to my amazement saw Nate among the crowd of boys at the door. He saw me at the same moment and recognized me with the old comical uplift of eyebrows. I smiled and waved my hand at him. And when I went out I looked for him, never doubting that he would have waited to speak to me. But he had not. And I still think it was abominable that he had not. To tell the truth, it hurt me a bit.

Along in February I met him on the street one day and he turned and walked to my boarding house with me. I asked him to call sometime. He said he would—but did not.

I have never been able to understand it. We had been friends for six years after our schoolday romance. We had parted on the best of terms that day in '96. There was no reason that I could think of why he should not have been friendly.

Then, too, when *Green Gables* came out I thought Nate might have written me a line of congratulation. I had attained the old ambition I had used to talk over with him. I think he should have sent me a work of good-will. But no word has ever crossed the "gulf of change" between us.

Well, it makes little difference. Only as I said in starting, I am sorry I could not have retained his friendship.

Nate practised law in Sydney for a time—didn't do much at it—there were too many lawyers there I fancy—then he married a Miss Mabel Saunders of Wolfville and went to Estevan, Sask. I have never heard anything about his success there. John Laird was once conductor of a train that ran to Estevan. The first time he came home he told me he had seen Nate occasionally at the Station but had never been at his home. A few years later I saw John again. I asked him if he had ever met Nate's wife. He said no. Then added a queer thing. "I don't know what came over Nate when he went west. He seemed to get a swelled head."

I suppose this means that Nate had not invited John to his house. This was odd. John was his best pal in Cavendish and they had sat together at school for years. But I am sure the reason was not "swelled head." Nate was not that sort of a boy.

Why am I scribbling on in this idle fashion? Just because I am lonely and homesick and like to write and think of events and people of those early happy days. I suppose Nate's life has been like my own—like everybody's—compact of failure and success, joys and sorrows. He had one terrible sorrow, poor fellow— that tragic shooting of his favorite son. I remember how that hurt me when "Pastor Felix" wrote of it. The boy might have been *my* son—if only I could have loved his father. I have always been sorry I couldn't—because Nate *was* such a jolly comrade. Why, is it that all through my life the men I've *liked* best were the men I couldn't *love?*....

Thursday, February 25, 1932
Norval, Ontario
Of recent years there has been a great deal written and published concerning the folly and the horror of war and the necessity of doing away with all the possibility of it if civilization is to be preserved. Not long ago I read an article in a prominent review in which it said that it was to *youth* the world must look for the abolition of war.

As a commentary on that statement I record what I heard a young girl of about 18—to whom of course "the war" is only a matter of history—say tonight.

We were over at Fred Lyon's to one of those never-ending play practices. I was talking to Mary Lyons about the Chino-Japanese turmoil and Mary asked me if I thought it likely to spread and involve other nations, especially the States. I said I thought not. She said, "I do hope it won't."

"Oh, you selfish thing!" cried young Margaret Leslie. "Do you grudge us a little excitement?"

Well, I must not be too hard on Margaret. The war is to her only a name. And I recall, with shame, my over excitement one day in 1897 when I opened a paper and saw by the headlines that the U.S. and Spain were at war! Why, I was thrilled!

No, it is not to youth the world must look for the abolition of war. If this generation—the generation that lived through that awful conflict—does not abolish it that desired consummation is still afar off.

It is my opinion that war should be abolished. It has become too awful and hellish a thing to be allowed—no longer a clean swift conflict between man and man but a hideous revel of mechanical massacre. It must go. But when it goes certain wonderful things will go with it. There will be no more great literature—no more great art. These things were either given by the gods as a compensation—or are growths whose roots must be watered with blood. We will not have them when war ceases.

Friday, February 26, 1932
The Manse, Norval
I had that rare thing this winter—a good sleep—last night—which was well, for the powers that have been sticking pins into me this year gave me another job today. Came a very vexing letter from Ella Campbell concerning one of the matters which have been worrying me all winter. Speaking of worries I have been hounded by no less than seven distinct and separate ones. It is any wonder I'm insomniac? Chester's progress at college—his prospects of getting mining work next summer—the predicament of two companies in which I have heavy investments—my own health—Myrtle's condition—and the condition of affairs at Park Corner.

The last, indeed, should be no worry of mine but is dumped on my shoulders notwithstanding. Briefly, the state of affairs is this.

The farm was left to Aunt Annie. She in turn made a will, leaving it to Donald with the proviso that he always support his mother and educate the other children. When Aunt A. made this will Donald was only a small boy and we all hoped he would make good. Before Aunt Annie's death she had begun to realize that Dan would never make a farmer. He was rather wild, extravagant and *not* fond of work. He would take no advice or suggestion from old experienced farmers but she died without altering her will so Dan was to come into the property at 21 and in the meantime guardians were appointed. Stell took Dan away with her. He has never amounted to much, drifting from one poor job to another, and I think Stell is sick of her bargain and anxious to dump it on someone else.

The farm was rented and all the stock sold. Ella and her family—with my help—I have dressed Maud—contrived to get along on the rent. I will say for Ella that with all her weaknesses, she is a good and thrifty manager where money is concerned—something that no one at Park Corner, except Frede, ever was. Jim has grown up—a fine fellow everyone seems to think—good-tempered, industrious, a good manager. I had always hoped that Dan would give Jim the place with its responsibilities and he always talked as if he were quite willing to do so, as soon as Jim came of age—which would not be till December, 1933. But Jim wanted to go in a bank. He always said that Dan talked differently to him than to me—which I daresay is quite true for I have found out that Dan is not wholly truthful—and that he did not believe that Dan would ever give him the place. But Jim, although he tried the entrance exams twice could not pass it. This finished his chances of getting in a bank and he had now grown so big and tall that he did not feel like going to school any longer. Last fall Ella wrote me in a great fluster. Heath Montgomery, who had rented the farm, would not rent it again. Nobody else would offer enough rent to live on. But Dan had written Jim he would make the farm over to him if he would undertake to farm it. Ella said Jim was quite excited and eager but it would need at least $700 to start with as all the money had been used by the executors to pay for repairs. Would I lend her $700?

Now, I was "fed up" with pouring money out on Park Corner. Before George's death I had, at Stell's urgent request, lent him $2000. When he died I knew Aunt Annie could never pay the interest so I had a mortgage drawn up, by which it became due in 1938 but no interest was to be paid. So I have already lost by this $1400, besides all I *gave* Aunt Annie plus Ella.

Moreover, I have—I admit it—grown *superstitious* about any place I love or try to help. I seem to bring it bad luck. It never prospers, no matter what is done. Even if I had had the $700 to lend I would not have wanted to risk it in any further enterprise at Park Corner. But I simply did not have it. Poor Ella has always thought I was made of money and that they had only to go to "Aunt Maud" in any emergency.

Nevertheless I could not shake off my old love for Park Corner and my memory of the kind old hearts that once beat there. I simply could not bear the thought of it and all its ghosts being sold to strangers. It were sacrilege. Yet there was no other alternative. Dan could never come home now and farm successfully on P.E. Island even if he would. So, ill, weary, discouraged as I felt, I roused myself for old sake's sake to make one more effort to cheat the devil.

I wrote to Stell asking her if she or Clara could not lend the $700 and I wrote to Ella and told her to try to get it from someone on the Island and I would join Jim's note for it for three years.

Stell wrote back the usual screed of wails—she had no money—Clara had no money—Dan was out of work and she thought he'd better go home and take the farm.

I was angry. Stell had said, times out of number, that she knew Dan would never make a farmer. She took him away and spoiled him and now she wants to get rid of the trouble and worry of him. I wrote her a rather plain letter, pointing out to her that it was folly to think Dan could make good at P.C. after eight years of a totally different life etc. and I asked where he was to get the money for a start. I said plainly I would not venture any more money on him but I would try to help Jim.

Well, Ella's letter of today says that after all Dan refuses to make the place over to Jim but offers to give him a fifteen-year lease of it. In fifteen years, if Jim has made good, he is to have the place. Jim says—and I don't blame him—that he will not stay on those terms. So poor Ella turns to me. What is she to do? I'm sorry for her. Naturally she doesn't want to leave her home and go out on the world at her age. And I see she is frantic over the thought of Dan, with his extravagant notions, coming home to try to farm—she says she can keep house for Jim who is used to the plain ways they live but she could never do it for Dan etc.

Well, I must see what can be done, though I suppose the net result will be that I shall reap ill-will on all sides and probably Park Corner will go to the dogs anyway. Jim is a good fellow. But he has no capital and little experience. All of his neighbors are discouraging him from attempting it—because forsooth, as we very well know, they all want to buy that splendid farm cheap for their sons. I fancy this is what is really behind Heath's refusal to rent. Jim will be a marvel if he can make good in the face of all that. But it seems a shame he can't have a chance, when he is willing to try.

I have written to Dan as follows:—

"Dear Donald:—

I have received your letter this morning and also one from your mother. I would very much rather not have been involved in this matter at all. I have enough worries and responsibilities of my own at present. And it has been my experience that one seldom gets much thanks for trying to settle affairs of this kind. In the long run one is so apt to get ill-will from both sides. But since you ask my advice in the matter I will give it and if I employ a bit of *plain speaking* you will have to take it in good part. I am actuated in all I do or say in this matter by a sincere wish to do right by all concerned and help Park Corner to get back where it used to be. I love the old spot better than any place on earth and I have done more than you may realize for it. After your poor father died (up to his ears in debt owing to his inability to be thrifty and *do without* things) it was I who came to the rescue: I *gave* Aunt Annie two or three hundred dollars a year until she died and paid two thirds of her funeral expenses. Then I arranged the mortgage so that no interest need be paid on the $2000 your father borrowed from me from 1918 to 1938. That is, for 20 years, and that means exactly $2000 in interest that I have given to Park Corner or will have given by 1938. So you cannot accuse me of being grasping or out for my own interest.

Now, the best way is to look *all round* the matter, exactly as it is. In the first place Jim says emphatically in his letter that he will not attempt to work the farm unless you make it over to him but will get out at once to find something to do for himself. And from what I know of Jim I feel sure he will stick to that for he knows his own mind and is a determined fellow. *And I do not blame him.* You and I cannot expect, Donald, that a boy of Jim's age, who must soon decide what he is to do, would tie himself down to working hard and *living hard* for years on a farm that isn't his own and might never be his own. Suppose he worked for ten years and was beat out. He would have *nothing* and be too old to start afresh at anything worth while, because he would have no training or education for anything. Even five years would leave him handicapped in this. You can see this for yourself I am quite sure. At best, Jim would have a hard enough row to hoe but I believe he could and would do it if the farm were his, but he cannot be expected to do it unless he is sure of his ground. Anyway, he says he will not, so that is that.

Then there are three courses open—either for you to go home and farm, make it over to him, or sell it.

As regards the first—now for the plain speaking. I do not think, Donald, that you would make a successful farmer. This is no disgrace to you. It is not everyone who has the qualities of a farmer. I think you are an unusually smart bright boy and have qualities that will win success in a great many paths of life but you have not the ones necessary for a farmer. If you started farming on P.E.I., especially as things are now, the odds are that in a few years you would be hopelessly in debt and there would be nothing left. You would still have to support your mother and educate Georgie. You would have to hire help part of the time for Jim would not stay home.

On the other hand suppose you sell it. Prices for farms are low now. When my $2000 was paid to me out of it (as it would have to be for I could not afford to lose it altogether. I am not young and my hard years of mental work are beginning to tell on me) how much would be left and how long would it support your mother and Georgie? Ask yourself that question very seriously. Besides, Jim couldn't be sent off with nothing to start him.

Now, Donald, I honestly believe that what I am going to recommend is the best course and fair to all concerned. I may be mistaken for no one is infallible. But this is what I advise. Make the farm over to Jim. Perhaps you could put in a provision that in five years time if Jim feels he can't make a go of it and wishes of his own will to throw it up it would revert to you. I can't see why this would not be possible. Then, you are *free.* You won't have any further responsibility for your mother or anyone and will have *no one but yourself* to provide for or worry over.

And I do not think you would be making any great sacrifice. As I have already said, if the farm were sold (at a loss as it would have to be today) what would be left after my $2000 came out of it and how long would it last, supporting your mother etc? Not very long, believe me. In a few years at most it would be all gone and you no better off. So you are not giving up very much, you see.

Again, I am quite sure Jim could start up on $700. You say a thousand, but, my dear, your ideas are just a little *too big* for P.E. Island. That has always been a *Campbell failing* and was the main reason why your father couldn't make things go. Prices are low now—good cows can be bought for $35—and $700 would be plenty to start in a modest way. Jim and your mother are very economical and Jim has, I have noted, a good business head on his shoulders. They would have to live very sparingly for a few years but they are used to that, whereas you are not, and your mother can make a dollar go further than anyone I know. So $700 would be plenty. I can help Jim out to the extent of $700 but I could not go good for a thousand. I haven't even the $700 to lend now for the "depression" has struck me the same as anyone else and the boys' school bills are heavy but I would join his note if he could get the money on the Island or borrow it for him here if he couldn't— I have confidence in Jim because I have been observing him very closely every time I have been home. If he can't make a go of it nobody can. But I think he should have a chance. You will be free then and need not give him or anybody another cent. I feel sure Amy could and would pay the $49 interest for a few years' as her share in helping to put the old place on its feet and surely the rest could at least get their living out of it. Jim is shrewd and I don't think anyone is going to get away with cheating him in a bargain.

This is the only advice I can give and it seems to me the best plan. And if you decide to follow it, it should be done at once. Jim must start right away if anything is to be done this year. They can't rent the farm and it would be folly for them to leave it idle for a year and them with nothing to live on. I suppose the legal steps would take some time, as red tape always does, but if you would write Jim giving him your word to sign over as soon as it can be arranged I think he would be willing to start right in.

You see, Donald dear, whoever takes that farm will have to *live hard* for the first ten years. Make no mistake about that. *No luxuries*—no cars, not even a fancy driver, no amusements, the barest necessities in clothes and a very plain table. *You* don't know how your mother has economized in the past six years but *I do.* When I would be at P.C. she would get little luxuries for the table on my account (which she shouldn't have done) but I know how they live when they are alone and would have to live for the first few years. Jim has known nothing else so it will not be so hard for him but how would you like it? If you let Jim have the farm I will do all I can to help him out because I have confidence in him, knowing him as I do. You see, you can't really expect Jim to hang on there any longer with no prospects. He has his own way to make in life with no assistance.

I would like to see Park Corner restored to what it once was—the best farm in P.E.I. But it will be no easy matter to do it and I think since Jim is willing to try he should be given a free hand. He does not need another man *all* the time. One man is plenty for the work there except an odd time or so as in harvest etc. Indeed, no one could afford to keep a steady hired man on that farm for the first few years. That is why I say it will be hard sledding at first. I really do think you would be horribly discontented and unhappy there after the life in Los Angeles.

Now, I have told you plainly what I think as you have asked me to do. If you don't like it you are not obliged to do as I suggest but I have the interests of Park Corner and your family truly at heart and am doing this from the purest motives. If I thought only of myself I would say sell the farm and pay me my $2000. If I had $2000 to invest today in some good stocks that are ridiculously low I would treble it in three years time. But I am *not* thinking of my own interests.

To sum it all up, I think if Jim had the farm he would put *his heart into it* and make it go—your mother would be happy to stay on in her old home with a son who is used to her ways, and you would be free of all worry about it, with no further drag on you."

This letter was as much for Stell's benefit as Dan's, since I am quite sure she is behind his doings. No doubt she will be furious but I do not care. She can't say much since she owes me thousands she has never been able to pay me even a cent of interest on.

But the whole matter has "thtirred me all up" and I foresee no sleep tonight.

Monday, Feb. 28, 1932
Norval, Ont.
No single pleasant thing has happened lately. Life seems like a landscape on the moon. I have bad nights of nervous restlessness and queer indescribable feelings in my head much of the time. I need a long absolute *rest* but it is vain to wish for it.

I have been reading Crozier's *Letters of Pontius Pilate* tonight. Fiction but remarkably well done. Probably Pilate's letters, if he wrote any, were very much like these, though probably not so epigrammatic. One passage of fine unconscious irony amused me much. Pilate, who is having a hard time trying to make the Jews pay for his aqueduct, says he is determined it shall be finished. He depends on it to preserve his name to future ages, or words to that effect.

Well, Pilate's name has been preserved but not by his aqueduct!

Jesus he dismisses as an innocent reformer who might become a handle for his (Pilate's) enemies to make trouble for him in Rome. So, as he is very unimportant, he is best out of the way. It really doesn't matter to anybody!

A letter from Marion brought no good news of Myrtle. Must I lose this friend, too?

Thursday, Mar. 17, 1932
A letter from Dan today. My epistle seems to have knocked some sense into his—or Stella's—head. He agrees to all my suggestions and says he will give Jim the place.

And now, if Jim doesn't make good, everybody will blame me!!

Well, one thing is certain. Jim *may* fail but Dan *would*!

I've written Jim and Ella to go ahead and prepare for spring work and if Jim can't get a loan down there I'll try to raise the $700 in some way. I'm a fool, I know, financially speaking. But I can't see Park Corner thrown to the lions and that family turned out on the world.

Sunday, Mar. 24, 1932
Last night E. and I went in to Toronto to see the Gymnastic contest at the Central Y for the Junior Medal and championship of Ontario. Stuart had entered as the St. Andrew's competitor. He warned us not to expect him to win as he said he hadn't the ghost of a chance and indeed I never thought of such a thing. The evening was very interesting as both Junior and Senior contests were held. There were four tests—high bar, horse, parallel bars and mat. And Stuart won the medal and is Junior Champion of Ontario at sixteen years.

It's the first "nice" thing that has happened to me this winter! I was so pleasantly excited all the way home that for the time being I escaped from my drab world and felt young and light-hearted again.

But payment will be demanded. Stuart has been giving his time to athletics instead of to his studies. For the first time since he went to St. A. he did not lead at Christmas and did not lead his year. This is a disappointment to me but Stuart would rather be champion because that "brings honor to the school."

Wednesday, March 30, 1932
Chester and Stuart have been home for Easter. Chester and I had a long interesting talk Thursday evening. He seems to be getting on well this winter but he says he is a little afraid of the chemistry and may be conditioned in this. I really can't bear it if he is. If it were his first year it would not be so bad but to be conditioned in *anything* in a "repeated" year will be such a black mark against him in his professor's eyes that he will never convince them he is any good.

Our Old Tyme Night came last night and was a success, although I and a few others had to work like slaves to make it so. I wore a darling dress of flowered muslin over a crinoline with a lace shawl and a pork-pie hat of pearls and flowers, and for a little while forgot my worries and heartaches and enjoyed the evening.

Thursday, Mar. 31, 1932
Norval, Ont.
Stuart went to Toronto today for the Inter-scholastic contest and won the Parallel Bar Championship for Ontario over sixty competitors and picked up another medal. As for me I had a depressed letter from Jim and Ella. They have not been able to get the money down there. I went to the bank and borrowed seven hundred, feeling as if I were a criminal! Besides, as things are, it may land me in a nasty predicament.

Saturday, April 2, 1932
Stokes' report came today and one item was a pleasant surprise—an unexpected five hundred for the reprint of *Marigold*. This disperses my financial worry for the rest of the year. I'll have enough to get along on if nothing unforeseen turns up.

I began to write my new book today, *Pat of Silver Bush*. I like the idea of it I have in mind. But how can I write a book when I am worried and nervous and insomniac? And can get only dribbles of time and leisure for it? The world and market news continues bad and there seems no break in the clouds anywhere. No good news from any country, far or near.

One amusing thing is that we are all hoping Hindenburg will "get in" in the forthcoming German election. Yet in 1918 how we were cursing him! *What* ironic Power is running the universe and delights in standing us on our heads?

Saturday, April 16, 1932
The Manse, Norval
....My head feels so queer all the time—as if a tight band were round it. Some days I can't write. It is the first time in my life that I haven't been able to lose myself in my writing and so gain some respite.

When I can't sleep I sit up and read Flora Klickmann's delightful *Flower Patch* series. They soothe and rest and cheer me temporarily. I feel as if I had "got home" when I go to her "Flower Patch." If *I* had a retreat like that! If I could just get away some place where I needn't *see* anyone or talk to anyone for a month!

Wednesday, April 20, 1932
Today the blow fell which I have been dreading for two months. The Simpson Co. passed its dividend. This means nearly a thousand dollars more cut off my already pinched income. I had expected this and budgeted without it, so that I would not worry so much if I thought they would get on their feet again after business picks up. But they may go on the rocks completely and I have $14,000 in them. It was thought a gilt-edged investment when I made it....

Saturday, April 23, 1932
The Manse, Norval
Chester came home today. He thinks he has passed his exams. We will have three weeks of anxiety waiting for the news. This would not be so hard by itself but in connection with everything else—

Simpson's shares are down to $12 on the market. My $14,000 is worth just about $1680 at present.

Everywhere we go we hear nothing but "the Depression." It gets on the nerves. What good does it do to talk about it? We all know too well that it exists. It *must* pass but to hear people talk you would think it never would. And when you hear this reiterated continually you get hypnotized and begin to think perhaps it never will and that there is nothing but ruin ahead.

Saturday, April 30, 1932
I have never had time to take up the moving picture camera I got last fall but I let Chester have a reel to practice on. Every time he was home all winter he took a few pictures. Recently he completed it and had it developed. I really expected nothing of it. But today he called me into the parlor and ran the reel off. And it is just capital. I was so amused and tickled that for a time I forgot all my woes. There was one scene of Ewan and me walking on the lawn that made me feel spookish. We were so life-like and natural that I had an eerie feeling that I had just got out of my body and was looking at it as a ghost might.

And there was the cutest one of Lucky marching across the lawn.

We ran the film backward, too, and it was too funny for words. I have at one fell swoop become a moving picture crank and only fear that since we are all so desperately hard up we can't afford many reels if any.

If there had been something like this when I was a girl! If I could go to a box and take out a film, put it in the kodascope, adjust a lever—and see Grandmother coming smiling out of the old kitchen door—father walking down from the barns—Amanda and I prowling along our lanes—the "old gang" playing ball on the school playground—Uncle John Campbell welcoming us—Frede and Stell and Clara running down under the birches—Nate whistling along a silver road of new-fallen snow—old friends gathering roses in lost gardens—Well, Dave and I building our playhouses or racing the chargers of the foam along the sandshore—mayflower picnickers marching down the road with bouquets and wreaths—the old "quartette" passing along a Charlottetown street—myself lingering along Lover's Lane—Laura running down the prairie slope at Laurel Hill—old loved pussy cats, Topsy, Lady Katherine, Max, Pussywillow—the Daffies—kittens that have been dust for half a century, prowling around the yard or scampering up apple trees that have long ceased to bloom—Pensie and I scrambling over the rocks—fishing boats coming in to shore—well, it sounds like a fairy tale. But the next generation when they are old will be able to do it. And yet—perhaps, after all, it might not be so delightful. There might be more sorrow in it than pleasure.

Speaking of playing "ball"—what fun we had. The game was somewhat complicated. It was not baseball nor was it like any of the ball games played today. Perhaps it is no longer played anywhere. But this was the game as we played it on the old school playground in the last decade of the 19th century....[See Appendix D.]

Sunday, May 1, 1932
The Manse, Norval
I had a fair sleep last night and a peculiar dream about Mr. Taylor, which seemed of good omen in so far as I can interpret its symbolism. I dreamed he gave me a ring with two large diamonds in it. As I went away down the street one fell out. I took it back to him. He said, "Oh, we will stick that in again," —and did so. I left the office thinking, "Now, if these diamonds are real all will be well."

Mr. MacMillan, a missionary, was here today, speaking at Union's open missionary meeting tonight. He had a friend with him named *Godbole*.

Well, what's in a name? *Pace* Shakespeare.

I wrote Isobel a letter today that ought to instil a little common sense into her—if that be possible. But is it?

Monday, May 2, 1932
The Manse, Norval
I had a perfectly *hellish* night of nervous unrest. Today my head was better until I began to write letters and then the "queer feeling" returned—as if a tight band were bound round it and as if my eyes were being drawn out of my head. After supper the feeling vanished completely and I felt perfectly well. A heavenly feeling like rain after burning drought.

Tuesday, May 3, 1932
I had a good sleep last night and so enjoyed my day in Toronto. Called at McClelland's and saw Mr. Stewart who is back at work. It was nice to see him there again. He has always been my favorite of the two partners. He has only one working lung but the T.B. seems killed and if he is careful he may live for years. In the afternoon I attended a meeting of the Ministers' Wives Association and gave them a talk. Had a nice time. But *such* a lot of homely women!

I had a talk with Mrs. Stewart whose husband was minister of...[Isobel's church] for fourteen years...She says Isobel has always been queer. She fell in love with one of the ministers who preceded Mr. S. and persisted in going to the manse to see him until his wife put a stop to it. The fair Isobel seems to have a knack of falling in love and apparently it matters little with which sex!

Yet am I sorry for her. It is appalling to be cursed as she is.

Mr. Stewart (of McClelland's) gave me Agatha Christie's new novel *Peril at End House* and I shall read it tonight and forget my woeses for a space. Thank God for a good clean interesting yarn where the author is *not* intent on saving humanity by turning it inside out and displaying the intestines....

Wednesday, May 11, 1932
One worry has vanished—for this spring. Chester has passed all his exams without any conditions.

I have been waiting in sickening dread for the results. This is partly why I have slept so badly of late. As day by day drew nearer to the time we might expect them there were moments when I felt as if I could not endure the suspense any longer. Last year the results were out on May 12 and we did not expect them any earlier this year. This morning Chester brought the mail up just as we rose from breakfast. I opened the paper and saw it contained the science results. As we were just going into the library for prayers I dared not glance over them until I could be free to get by myself. I don't know what Ewan read. The quarter of an hour seemed an eternity. Then I went into the parlor and shut the door and with shaking hands opened the paper. I saw Chester's name—with no conditions attached!

The relief was almost painful. He has not done badly for exactly half the pass list had conditions.

Of course this does not do away with all the problems connected with his course. Indeed, perhaps it complicates them further. It might conceivably have been better had he failed again and then he would have to turn to something else. But at least we are all saved the humiliation of last spring and perhaps the other problems will arrange themselves in time.

I have had some slight asthma these past few nights. I hope it is not returning. I have felt weak and good for nothing ever since my April spell of flu and have no appetite.

Friday, May 13, 1932
The Manse, Norval
A letter from Myrtle today was in one sense encouraging, in others not. She says the doctor was there and told her there was no danger of her having cancer. But

he seemed rather surprised that she had not developed the symptoms of it and I don't like that. It is as if he expected it. I know that there is a widespread impression that she has cancer and it has worried me so that in so far the letter was good news. But she is very miserable—has chills and fever every few days and is not gaining. Whatever it is, I fear she will not recover now.

Well, we must face these things.

Today, too, came the hideous news that the Lindberg baby has been murdered. Like all the world we have been following the developments of the case for many weeks. It is a hellish thing and were I Lindberg I would cast from my feet the dust of a country where such things could be done to me with impunity. That poor mother!

And what about God?

I am still housecleaning and gardening. The former tires me unreasonably and I cannot find any solace in the latter.

Monday, May 30, 1932

Last Monday Ewan and I and Mrs. Thompson and June motored up to Leaskdale. I really didn't want to go. It is odd—but as the years pass I seem to develop a keener dislike to the thought of going back. It is as if all I suffered there rises up and drowns out all the good with its bitterness and Leaskdale is so linked with it that I cannot separate the two. But neither Ewan nor I have been getting on well since our April flu. I am weak and nervous and Ewan has a persistent hoarseness. We thought, now that housecleaning and gardening are over, that a trip might do us good. And it did. I ate and slept well all the time we were away—despite the awful beds we encountered. Why well-to-do farmers with every comfort in their homes, cannot have better beds has always puzzled me. But then my own bed has always been so comfortable that it has spoiled me for other couches.

On the whole I enjoyed the trip. The drive up was pleasant, through blossoming orchard lands and young spring woods with a hundred different shades of green. Most of the folks talked of nothing but the depression and poor prices; but some few were cheerful and told us some good juicy scandals, which I, no longer under the necessity of being A Good Example in Leaskdale, rather enjoyed, especially as they concerned some folks we had no reason to love. Mrs. Wm. Sellars has been having a hard time with her hubby who seems to have strayed sadly far from the strait and narrow path. Yanking him from his old Presbyterian moorings and towing him over to the United Church pier hasn't been good for his morals. Rumor has it that Mrs. Sellars had to pay several thousand dollars out to save him from jail, the girl in the case being under "the age of consent." As it was said that she went over to the United Church because her father had told her that she would not get a cent from him unless she did, this seems to me a bigger spot of poetic justice than is often seen in this topsy turvy world.

We spent Monday night at Mrs. Jim Mustard's and Tuesday night at Geo. Leask's. After I went to bed at the latter place I lay and watched the lights of the old manse through the window and felt very queerly. What joy and agony I had felt in that house. We called there next day. The lawn is neglected. No flowers.

My old peonies looked forlorn but the spirea bush I planted twenty years ago is a huge shrub now. We came home Thursday night in a dreadful combination of rain and fog. Rain by itself is an honest thing. Fog is lovely and eerie. Together they are horrible.

For welcome when we came home was a notice that the Bell Telephone had cut its dividend.

On Friday Chester and I went into town and brought Eleanor Agnew out. She is studying violin music in Toronto. She went back tonight. She is a sweet girl and it was strange and lovely and a little *unreal*—to have Laura's daughter a guest in my home.

I am writing a series of three articles on Mary Slessor of Calabar, Joan of Arc and Florence Nightingale for a book of "Famous Girls" McClelland and Stewart are going to bring out. I detest it but it will bring in some extra money and that will help out. I have to

"A poor picture of Eleanor" [Agnew]

do it in the evenings because I can't take the time from my book—which is getting on very slowly. And in the evenings my head is generally queer.

Sunday, June 5, 1932
The Manse, Norval
I had a disagreeable experience tonight. I went out of courtesy to the Anniversary services of the Norval United Church. A certain Mr. Robb preached—the same Robb who was in Beaverton the time of the Union fracas, having come there from the west with a very unsavory reputation in regard to certain matters. He made himself very obnoxious *re* union and Ewan and several other ministers of Presbytery administered a figurative and well-deserved spanking to him. Of course he has hated Ewan ever since and I suppose he thought it a good chance tonight to get square. He was speaking of St. Andrew, who "suffered from being the brother of a distinguished man," and went on to illustrate it by saying that he was "like the husband of a distinguished authoress"—he is always referred to as "the husband of So-and-so."

Although he did not mention names he might as well have done so. The congregation knew what he meant and—like minister, like people—a riffle of laughter went all over the church. My face burned with anger. But why be angry with such a creature! The man who would stoop to that would stoop to anything. The United Church is welcome to such a representative.

As for the sermon it was an amusing lecture. He seemed to be trying to do one thing—make the people laugh—and he succeeded to perfection. Seldom have I seen a jollier assemblage. Every few minutes a gale of laughter swept over the audience. But it was mostly the visitors and young people who laughed. The older people looked rather grim. Even in the United Church there seem to be some who are outmoded enough to think that the place for a low comedian, amusing as he may be is not in the pulpit of a Christian church. But I suppose I cannot be an impartial judge of Mr. Robb's brand of humor.

Friday, June 10, 1932
Head and hands queer all day but I managed to write my stint.

I had another exasperating letter today from Isobel..., full of reproaches and yowls of complaint from beginning to end. She is full of indignation because in my last letter I hinted to her what the world would call the sort of love she vows she feels for me. This is amusing in a girl who wrote to me, "I want to hold you in my arms all night—I want to cover your face, your neck, every part of you with kisses etc."

Of course, I believe she is quite unconscious of her Lesbianism—or rather, that it *is* Lesbianism.

But I am completely out of patience with her and have written her as follows:—"My dear Isobel:—You must forgive me if I say candidly that I think it is wiser that this unsatisfactory correspondence of ours should cease for a time. All winter and spring I have been nearly distracted by several pressing worries and problems of my own, coupled with my anxiety over the lingering illness of a beloved friend and your letters of reproaches because I cannot be some person whom you have created out of your imagination and called by my name—a person utterly unlike the practical elderly woman I am—have really been the proverbial last straw.

If the time ever comes when you can feel contented with what contents my other friends—a sane friendship with an occasional friendly visit or letter I shall be very glad to respond. Until then I think it better for both of us that this unhappy condition of affairs should cease."

I hope this will make her so angry that she will leave me alone forever. She has been a veritable Old Man of The Sea to me for the last two years.

I met Mr. Bull on the street tonight—an adherent of the United church in Norval. He asked me what I thought of Mr. Robb!!! I replied coolly that I did not care for a preacher who was too amusing. Whereupon Mr. B. said, pounding a handy gate-post with his fist, "After that man preached in the morning I went up to him and told him that we didn't need any more of that kind of preaching in this church."

It is to laugh! But Mr. B's disapproval evidently didn't worry Mr. Robb much, if the sermon in the evening is any criterion.

But I feel that I am not wholly unavenged!

Lucky is purring on the table as I write and looking at me with bright round eyes. How dreadful it would be *not* to love a cat! How much one would miss out of life.

Monday, June 24, 1932
Norval, Ont.

A letter from Isobel today.

"My beloved darling:—

Yes, indeed it must stop for I, neither, can stand any more. I have been so bitterly heartsick.

Let us forget it all and be real friends. I love you so. Please believe me that it is not an imagined creature, but your own dear self I love.

Can't there be a few times this summer when I may have you. Perhaps you will come up to my Aunt's early in July. And perhaps I may go down to see you once in a while—please, try to understand my special need for you. This I am sure is the cure for all my feverish longings and festering wounds"—and so on and so on, winding up with a promise to be content with "friendship" and a postscript that undid it all. "Not all the fiends in Hades can tear you from my heart."

I understand her "special need of me" only too well—much better than she understands it herself. It is the horrible craving of the Lesbian. I doubt if she will keep her word to be content with simple friendship. If she does I will try to help her as far as possible to endure life. But such is the horror she has filled me with these two years that I actually *dread* seeing her or spending an hour in her company. When I am nervous or depressed I feel fairly hag-ridden by her.

Saturday, July 2, 1932
The Manse, Norval, Ont.

I have had a good week—heaven with a little spice of hell in it—a dash of cayenne. And I have felt better in every way. All I need, I really believe, is a bit of cheerful companionship.

Last Monday Nora and Ebbie came out and stayed till today. Nora and I drove and made strawberry jam and went for long delightful walks together and *talked*. Oh, how we talked and how good it was! One afternoon we went up to the Y camp and came home through the woods along the west Branch of the Credit. We picked and ate wild strawberries for an hour. I had never seen a wild berry since we came to Norval. We found a corner full of wild honeysuckle—we saw three cute baby skunks—*saw* them only!—we told stories and ragged each other and shrieked with laughter. This seemed good to me. I thought I had forgotten how to laugh—really laugh.

"Ebbie" [Nora and Edmund Campbell's son]

I discussed with Nora the problem of Isobel. She warned me in horror to cut her off completely.

"If you don't you may get involved in heaven knows what dreadful scandal some day," she said.

"I may get involved in a scandal if I *do*," I said wretchedly. "She has made veiled threats of suicide before now."

But I have been reading Andre Thedon's *Psychoanalysis and Love*, lately. His chapter on "Unconscious Homo-sexualism" might have been written about Isobel, even to the very wording of the letters. Although Nora declares that the girl who wrote me that she wanted "to hold me in her arms all night and kiss every inch of my body" is *not* an unconscious Lesbian but a fully conscious one. I disagree with her here, however. Isobel is too unsophisticated to realize what her curse is.

We have been having fun galore with moving pictures.

Today Chester drove us all in to Toronto. Nora and I insulted each other from the time we left until we got in. If Isobel...had heard us she would have thought us insane. (And we think her insane! "All the world is queer etc.")

Nora and I have always possessed the knack of "ragging" deliciously. I have never met anyone but Nora with whom I could play such a game. It requires an unfailing touch—the slightest over-emphasis would be fatal. For years we have joyed in it and never once have there been hurt feelings. It is quite untransferable to paper—one might as well try to paste a gossamer in a scrapbook. I should love—I should dearly love—to play that game of fence with Isobel...for an audience. It would give her an entirely new slant on friendship!!

On our way home from Toronto, Chester and I had a long talk on various things. I am thankful at least that I have been able to keep his confidence. But there are many problems connected with Chester—and I have to grapple with them alone.

Friday, July 10, 1932
The Manse, Norval

Today was dark and wet and on such days my nervous unrest is always intensified. I could hardly sit still in church. I don't understand these spells. I never had anything just like them before. They are very dreadful. Yet I seem to be quite well physically.

I suppose the day I spent Friday didn't help my nerves any. I spent it with Isobel...in the hope of pacifying her for some months. She was visiting an aunt in "Crewson's Corners," a sleepy little hamlet on the Guelph highway. I dreaded the day for I did not know what I would do if I had to sit alone with Isobel all day. I rather thought I could end up by howling like a dog!

But for once Lady Luck was on my side. Her married sister was there and she and the aunt sat in the same room with us. So I contrived to make conversation although it was terribly boring. Neither the aunt nor the sister are at all interesting. Isobel never spoke until spoken to—just sat there and nursed her Lesbian longings. At least, I, recalling the confessions in her letters, supposed that was what she was doing. We all went for a walk in the afternoon along a remote tree-fringed road where wild strawberries grew. Alone with the wind, or with someone like Nora such a walk would have been the keenest delight. As it was, it was only one degree better than the stuffy parlor. I *felt* all the time that Isobel, who stalked along looking like the wrath of God, was *furious* because I wouldn't indulge her horrible desire for physical caresses. I could barely suppress a sigh of relief when after supper Chester and his lady friend came for me. Isobel presented me with a big bouquet of sweet peas when I left. They were lovely and, if they had been the offering of a normal friendship, they would have given me pleasure. As it was I hated to take them.

Yesterday my head was queer and I wrote at *Pat* with difficulty.

My madonna lilies are out. They are beautiful. There is no trail of the serpent over them.

Our colored movies are really quite beautiful. It is a pity the films are so very expensive and the pictures fussy to take.

Thursday, July 14, 1932
The Manse, Norval
Laura Aylsworth has been out for a few days. What a pleasure to have one of the race of Joseph handy! We had plenty to talk of. Laura's daughter Pat is to be married in August, to Kenneth Langdon, a young lawyer of Georgetown. And I am to be matron of honor!

I think the mere idea of a woman of my age being matron of honor to a young bride like Pat is absurd. But Pat has set her heart on it, coolly explaining that all the girls she knew would be wild with envy if she had "L.M.M." for matron of honor. I have yielded to please her, although for more than one reason I don't care for it. Laura and I have had some fun, however, planning out the details of the wedding. It is to be a very simple one in Knox college chapel and Ewan is to marry them.

It doesn't seem long since Bertie wrote me that Laura had a little daughter. And now she is marrying. Pat is a pretty bit of fluff. Ken is a nice creature, stuffed with sawdust. They are very well matched and should be happy enough as long as life is good to them. I should not care to bet much on either of them amid the swellings of Jordan.

Monday, July 18, 1932
This morning came a letter from Myrtle with the most surprising good news. She is *much* better. Hasn't had a chill or a temperature for six weeks, is eating well, and able to go out and pick berries. I can hardly believe it. Everyone in the spring wrote me the dreariest predictions about her. And now this burst of sunshine! If it only lasts!

The good news went with me to the Sunday School picnic and sustained me through the boredom of the day. In the afternoon I made my escape and in a corner of the lake among the pines read Benson's new book on Charlotte Brontë. A fascinating volume. But I do not think Charlotte was in the least like the domineering little shrew he pictures her, any more, perhaps than she was like the rather too saintly heroine of Mrs. Gaskell's biography. I doubt if anyone knows, or knew, or ever will know the real Charlotte Brontë. I do not put any faith in Benson's theory that Branwell wrote parts of *Wuthering Heights* and inspired the whole. There is no foundation in the world for it beyond the assertion of two of Branwell's cronies that he read the first few chapters of it to them and told them it was his own. They *may* have been telling the truth but I would not put the least confidence in any statement of Branwell's. He was entirely capable of reading someone else's MS. and trying to pass it off as his own. No doubt he was more in Emily's confidence than Charlotte ever knew and had got possession of her MS. in some way.

Benson blames Charlotte for her unsympathetic attitude to Branwell. I imagine that an angel would have found it rather difficult to be sympathetic under the circumstances. Benson cannot understand a proud sensitive woman's heart, that is all. I love Charlotte Brontë so much that I am angry when anyone tries to belittle her. But I *will* admit that she seemed to have an unenviable talent for disliking almost everyone she met—although she often revised her opinions on further association. Charlotte had no gift for suffering fools gladly. And the things she says about the man she afterwards married!

Thursday, July 21, 1932
The Manse, Norval
Tuesday we motored to Kingston with the Barracloughs as he was going to a meeting there of the Grand Lodge. We returned today after a delightful trip during which I felt perfectly well.

On Wednesday we had a very enjoyable boating trip through the Thousand Isles. How much our enjoyment of any place is conditioned by our state of mind at the time! When Ewan and I came through the Islands in 1919 I was disappointed in them. But I was then racked with worry over Ewan's condition and could not enjoy anything. Moreover the day was hot and hazy with a violent wind blowing. The Islands were parched under the suns of a dry summer. This time everything seemed changed. Air crystal clear, islands green and flower-hung. It was all *nearly* as lovely as I had pictured it in childhood. It couldn't have been absolutely as lovely. No place could.

I enjoyed the trip. But now I am back again, feeling tired and discouraged about many things.

Saturday, July 30, 1932
The boys and I were in Toronto Thursday (Stuart has to go in to practice at the gym for the contest at the Exhibition) and we brought Eleanor Agnew out for a week-end. Ken, who had been in to see Pat also came out and we were a very jolly crowd. Stuart could keep a crowd going himself. He has more than a bit of my own old knack of keeping up a round of jest.

It is very lovely to have my Laura's daughter as a guest in my home—lovely and a bit incredible. And Eleanor is such a darling. She does not look like Laura in the slightest degree but she is like Laura in her manner. I see this resemblance more strongly every time we meet.

I have been absolutely *hungry* for Laura ever since the renewal of our friendship two years ago.

Saturday, August 20, 1932

I have had a most wonderful week. Nothing like it has been in my life for years.

I have been *young* again.

On August 4th Mrs. Thompson went home for her vacation. For the first week I was alone and liked it, the only untoward thing being that that wretched Isobel kept writing, imploring me to go up for a week-end with her. This persecution is really becoming unbearable. I thought when I spent that day with her she would give me peace for awhile. But no sooner is one visit over than she is begging for another. If I could but be free from her! But unluckily as long as she keeps her promise of being content with friendship (only she is not really content—only pretending to be) I must endure her.

On Friday August 12, Nora and Ebbie came out. Eb camped out with the boys by the river and Nora and I went on a voyage to some magic shore beyond the world's rim.

We did all the work together in the day time—and such fun as we had! We joked—and talked beautiful nonsense—and did things just for the fun of doing them—and tried dozens of new recipes. And we laughed. Oh, how we laughed— and laughter as I have long been a stranger to. I thought I had forgotten how to laugh like that.

And every evening after the supper dishes were finished, we walked four miles, in a lovely ecstatic freedom under a harvest moon, up the "town line road" to the station and back.

I hadn't believed there was anything like those walks left on earth. From the moment we found ourselves amid the moon-patterned shadows of that road every particle of care and worry seemed to be wiped out of our minds and souls as if by magic. Hope was our friend again—we were no longer afraid of tomorrow. We just loitered on and on under the old old stars that had looked down on our

"The Tent by the River"

girlhood rambles by a far-off sea, through the faint enchanted moonfire. In daytime that road is a very commonplace one but steeped in moonlight it is magical.
The trees along it seemed to stand in an exquisite silver bush and beyond it beauty seemed shimmering over the fields. The air was full of cricket song. The far
hills and valleys were compact of some mystery and charm as old as time.

Sometimes we talked. Sometimes we merely walked in silence, tasting our own
wild joy. When we did talk we said whatever came into our heads. We discussed
every subject on earth from the lightest to the most profound. When we exhausted earth we adventured the heavens, to the remotest secrets of "island universe."
Sometimes we quoted poetry. Nora would voice the first line of a couplet and I
would finish it. Once in this alternate way we recited the whole of Wordsworth's
"Ode on the Intimations of Immortality," lingering over the lines, "Our birth is but
a sleep and a forgetting etc." Our minds seemed to strike sparks from each other.
It was so easy to be witty and brilliant. We opened doors of memory long closed.
We looked again on faded joys and dim old griefs that had once been agonies.
Once we stopped beside a field gate and stood there in absolute silence for a
whole hour, uttering not one word, in a kind of divine trance, just drinking in the
loveliness of a sunset sky of rose and dark gold against which trees shaped themselves in eternal repose. I have never met anyone in my life, not even Frede, to
whom nature means as much as it does to me, except Nora. We are of

> those who feel the thrill
> Of Beauty like a pang.

We could walk for a day through fields and woods and be perfectly happy in
our indescribable perfect communion with some great Over spirit that seems to
take complete possession of us.

The views of the Credit by moonlight!

Nora said one evening that something had come back into her life that had been
lacking since her daughter died. And I knew that something had come back into
mine, however fleeting, that had never been in it since early girlhood.

One night we returned about ten from our ramble. As we came up the walk we
heard a voice floating through the open veranda door and I said to Nora, "If this
were Cavendish I would say that was one of the Simpsons."

And when we came in—there was Milton Simpson, Ed's youngest brother! He
was motoring to Muskoka on a vacation trip—he teaches in some U.S. college—
and had called.

When I taught in Belmont Milton was at P.W.C. and came home for vacations.
I liked him very well then—he was a nice looking child and did not have the craze
for talking which possessed the others. But he seems to have developed it. On this
particular night he talked from ten to twelve with hardly a pause for breath—and
with that odd Simpson peculiarity of asking you a question and giving you the
vivid impression that he is not listening to your answer at all. When he had gone
I said to Nora, "Milton Simpson will be a radio in his next incarnation and someone will shut him off and that will be the worst punishment possible."

And yet I was glad to see him! Somehow, he brought some of the old Island
flavor with him—a whiff of "the days that are no more."

"Nora and Ebbie"

He said Ed was very miserable—had had a complete nervous breakdown and had had to give up his work. His poor wife died of internal cancer after twenty-one operations. Horrible! This is what youth and hope and ambition must end in—or if not in this in something else just as pitiable.

One night Nora and I varied our itinerary and instead of going up the Town Line, we went up to the Norval graveyard, through it, and sat on a pile of lumber on its further side for hours. This sounds queer and morbid and eccentric but it is not. From that side of the graveyard there is a view of the moonlit Credit that was exquisite. We looked at it as we talked. All around us were pines against a sky washed white in moonlight. The whole place was "abandoned to the lonely peace of bygone ghostly things." But the glimmering spectral monuments behind us

"View of the Credit"

meant nothing to us. Our dead lay not there. Had it been Cavendish graveyard, looking out on the old gulf and the silver pond, I, at least, would have been too beset with spiritual presences to have talked at all.

One day I had Isobel...down. Nora was full of curiosity concerning her. I, on my side, had promised to have her down and had been dreading the martyrdom of a day spent alone with her. So I invited her to come on Wednesday when I would have Nora to take the edge off her.

Wednesday morning was lovely and Isobel came on the bus. I suppose she had been looking forward to being alone with me for a whole day and was bitterly disappointed on finding Nora here. For the first few minutes I really thought the girl was going to cry. At first Nora and I both tried to draw her out and keep going a general conversation. It was of no use. Isobel would not be drawn out. The utmost we could extract from her was a sulky yes or no. Nora and I finally reacted nervously and the spirit of perversity came upon us. We began to do what we had sworn we wouldn't do—rag each other before Isobel. We certainly did it. Isobel sat and listened to the insults and reproaches we hurled at each other as if she couldn't believe her ears. I'm sure it was a weird revelation to her of what friendship with me might be!!

At dinner we must have further horrified her. The boys bandied jests as Nora and I did and hardly a sensible thing was said, but oh, we were witty and satirical and amusing.

Isobel never smiled.

After dinner, in desperation, I proposed a drive over to the Georgetown greenhouse for a fern Nora wanted. All the way over and back Isobel sat in sulky silence and spoke only once, although Nora and I dropped our ragging and conversed normally.

We got home just in time to escape a raging thunderstorm and Nora and I put in two ghastly hours until we escaped to get supper. After supper Chester drove us up to...[take Isobel home]. Isobel drove the whole way in a silence that was more than sulky—that was simply a smouldering fury. Everyone felt it, even Chester. I gave up trying to include her in our conversation and talked to Nora. I was simply very angry with Isobel. She had pleaded to be allowed to come down. I had asked her to come—given her the privilege of meeting one of my best friends, a brilliant woman of the world whom anyone should enjoy meeting. I had received her into the intimacy of my family circle. And all her thanks was this behavior. I would dearly have loved to have taken Miss Isobel across my knee and administered a sound and salutary spanking by way of giving her a lesson in elementary good manners, common sense and ordinary decency.

Thursday, August 25, 1932
The Manse, Norval
Pat Aylsworth was married to Kenneth Langdon in Knox College chapel today.

I was matron of honor—and didn't look too grandmotherly. I wore a navy blue hat, dress of navy blue georgette and lace, and a bouquet of tea rosebuds. Pat was very pretty in brown, with velvet hat. As I stood beside her I recalled two other occasions when I had been one of the principals in a wedding group. I had been

Pat's Wedding

bridesmaid for Bertha McKenzie—and Bertha was dead. The second was my own wedding, in the parlor at Park Corner. Well, it is almost certain that this will be the last.

Just at this point of writing a green fly alighted on my hand. I paused to examine it. It was about half an inch long and so incredibly slender that it reminded me of the old geometrical definition, "length without breadth." And yet it was just as incredibly beautiful. The most exquisite pale green with a tiny enamelled pattern in white along its back. I never saw one like it before. What Power fashioned that tiny thing so perfectly and wasted (?) on it so much beauty and skill? No eye but mine ever saw it or appreciated it. To what end was it made so lovely? And why has the Power that made it so made so many hideous human beings and so many bitter and ugly human lives?

In revising my typewritten copy of the first volume of my journal today I noted especially the record of a certain Sunday long ago at Park Corner—a typical Sunday of those days. Clara, Stella and I got up Sunday morning and found if we wanted to go to church we must walk, the roads being those of early spring, impassable for either wheels or runners. We *did* want to go to church—very badly, indeed! But not, I am afraid, through any excess of religious zeal or spiritual urge to worship. But we wanted to see our friends. Church was, in short, a social function—almost our only social function—and we were not going to be deprived of it. Accordingly we all walked through to Long River preaching. It was 4 miles there and four miles back—8 in all. The day was fine and sunny, the ground hard from the night's frost. We enjoyed our walk. We may even have enjoyed the sermon, although I must candidly admit I recall nothing of it. We asked two girl friends home with us to dinner. They came—and we had all grand appetites for a Park Corner dinner—a Park Corner dinner—ay di me! "Them was dinners as *was* dinners."

After dinner we walked down to Sunday school at French River—2 miles there and 2 miles back—and ate a Park Corner supper. Then, in the cool delicious spring evening we walked down to the "English Church"—as the Anglican church was called then—at Springbrook. Four miles there and four miles back. At every gate some more girls and boys would join us, until we were quite a crowd—a very jolly crowd, albeit I think we all behaved circumspectly for Sunday and were never noisy or frivolous. Going home we did not go *en masse*. We "paired off." Arriving home we had a Park Corner lunch. Then we called it a day and went to bed. Our young legs had walked twenty miles that day.

I wonder if anyone in P.E. Island and Ontario does that today. Perhaps not; but they would if they had to. Sometimes I think it is a pity they don't have to. There is very little walking done nowadays—at any rate around here. The cars have spoiled that and youth is the loser.

Friday, August 26, 1932
The Manse, Norval
Tonight I have been looking amusedly over my three illustrated volumes of *Green Gables*. The original edition of 1908, the new edition of 1925, made from new plates, the original plates having been worn out, and the *Mary Miles Minter* edition, illustrated with photographs from the moving pictures.

Novels are not "illustrated" nowadays. *Green Gables* was the only one of mine that was, though most of them have "frontispieces."

In the first edition the pictures are, of course, old-fashioned now. The odd thing is, they do not look half so old-fashioned now as they did five years ago when skirts were at their shortest. Now, when skirts are long again, and "puffed sleeves" are coming in, the old frontispiece (awkward word!) in *Green Gables* would look quite up to date were it not for the high collars and unbobbed hair.

I do not think I like the "new" frontispiece quite as well. Being brought up to date and by another artist it does not seem to have as much of the real *Green Gables* atmosphere about it as the former picture. The skirts are shorter, the necklines low, the belts are around the hips instead of the waists. The old picture on page 33 of Anne's arrival at Green Gables I like better, too. Marilla is much more in keeping in the old one. In the new she is far too young and jaunty, looking more like a girl than the grim and angular spinster of my conception.

Matthew was better in the old one, also. Anne is fairly good in both but I like her better in the old. So I do in the picture where she insults Mrs. Lynde, although in neither is she good. Marilla and Mrs. Lynde are much better in the old but the later artist is right in drawing Mrs. Lynde with a bonnet. She came for a call, not a visit, and would not have removed her hat. I like the new picture of Anne going to Sunday school better than the old. It was distinctly stated in the story that Anne found the other girl whispering about her in the *porch*. Yet in the old picture they are shown sitting about in seats, evidently in the church itself, with open books in their hands.

The slate-smashing scene is better in the old. I do not like either Gilbert or Anne in the new. The roof-walking episode is practically the same in both but there were no tall chimneys like the one in the new on P.E.I. kitchen roofs in my day—nor even today as far as I know.

The old picture of Anne clinging to the bridge pile always annoyed me. The incident took place soon after Anne had had her hair shingled and when it was in short curly ringlets. Yet in the picture she has long hair. Neither of the Annes are in the least like *my Anne* but the new one is the poorest. Anne never was such a doll as that. The "old" Gilbert was better, too.

The last picture in the old one, where Gilbert meets Anne on a twilight road was another exasperating one. In the book it was distinctively stated that it was long past sunset. Yet Anne is pictured as carrying an open parasol! Again, it is stated that Gilbert lifted his "cap"—but in the picture he wears a dapper straw hat. And both Anne and Gilbert are as stiff and stilted as if they were part of a 1908 fashion plate.

The new one is much better—more natural—more as I thought of them, but the boys of Gilbert's time never wore "plus fours" or golf stockings—at any rate in *Avonlea*.

The Miles Minter edition is, of course, in a class by itself. The profile of the lost Mary as a frontispiece is good—very much as I had pictured Anne but Anne had no such long curls, though her hair was wavy. Anne waiting at the station is good but Matthew's is absurd, being clean shaven, whereas his long beard is featured in the book. For the most part Anne is good in all the pictures but her valise is *not* a carpet bag. Marilla is poor in some scenes, good in others. The scene with Anne and the *hen* in her bedroom is absurd because there is nothing like that in the book. Marilla is excellent in the scene where Anne kisses her. The picnic scene is poor, being too artificial and Anne and Diana walking to school are absurd.

In the scene where they dramatize *Elaine*, there are seven girls in the picture and only four in the story.

On the whole the tale owes nothing to the illustrations in the "new" editions.

Saturday, August 27, 1932
The Manse, Norval
Today a letter from Isobel. I had been dreading it for I knew she had been bitterly disappointed in her visit and, remembering the epistle evoked by a similar disappointment last winter, I apprehended a similar outburst. But this letter was a comparatively sane epistle and she informed me that she had had a "surprisingly delightful" day. Well, perhaps she had. But she hid the fact of her delight very successfully while here.

Nevertheless, she put in considerable of the "adoration" which I had forbidden. And she coolly asks me if I won't go up and see her before I go. She wants to "kiss me good-bye" before I go east in October!

When she was here she heard Nora ask me if I could spare time to go in and visit her before I left. She heard me respond that it was absolutely impossible—I had to finish my book—get the boys ready for college etc. etc. etc. And yet she has the presumption to imagine that if I would not go to Nora's I could go *to her*....

196

Wednesday, Aug. 31, 1932
A day of extreme heat with a 9/10 eclipse of the sun. It was very interesting. We watched it through smoked glasses. I recalled a similar one at home in the early years of the century—or the later years of the last century. Grandmother and I were cutting potato sets on the kitchen steps as we watched it. The same phenomena were repeated—the peculiar livid blue—the eerie light over all the world—the fading, attenuated shadows—and in the last stages the crescent shaped splashes of light on walls and lawn through the trees. What a horror an eclipse must have been to primitive men who saw it for the first time. To stand helplessly and see the sun literally eaten up, fearing that it had gone forever!

Tonight an owl was hooting most delightfully through the starlit velvet night up in the pines on Russell hill. I sat on the veranda, amid shadows as deep and still as a pool at night, and listened to him, wishing Nora were with me. There is something magical about an owl. His very name is predestined. An owl *couldn't* be called anything but an owl. Just as a frog—that funny, dear, charming, absurd word—couldn't be anything but a frog!

Friday, Sept. 2, 1932
The Manse, Norval
We all went to the Exhibition today since Stuart was to compete in the gymnastic competition. He won the gold medal for the high bar, the silver one for second place in the all-Canada championship. Not bad for a 16 year old.

Monday, Sept. 5, 1932
I had a very strange dream last night. I was at the old Cavendish hall with Mollie. We were girls again. We had just come out of the hall and were standing in the

"Veranda, Norval. 1932"

crowd in the moonlight. Nate and Jack were there—a little space away but I did not go to speak to them. There did not seem any reason why I should. We were all young again and belonged there. Presently Nate walked out to the road and stood by a *car* that was parked there. I heard someone in the crowd say, "Poor old Nate—he is finished." Instantly I seemed to realize that it was years since I had seen Nate and that I ought to go and speak to him. I started over and then he turned, with his hand on the car door and looked at me. He was pale and wrinkled—his hair was white as snow—tears were streaming down his face.

The dream broke—dissolved—I was walking down the moonlit road with Amanda. And she was trying to tell me some very bad news about some friend of mine—I could not find out who, or what the news was, before I woke up. Yet the dream has haunted me all day.

Sunday, Sept. 11, 1932

Nora came out last Tuesday and stayed till today. We have had another delightful time. Thursday night we walked to the station again and coming back saw the most exquisite moonlight effect on Norval dam. Tuesday afternoon we took a daylight hike. Having found the gravelly roads hard on the soles of our feet, clad in thin soled shoes, Nora put on a pair of Eb's and I a pair of Stuart's. The appearance of our feet was very weird and we were terribly conscious of them as we went down Norval street. But once over the bridge and in the autumn sunlight of the town line we thought no more of our feet and their looks; for our "soles" ceased to trouble us and there was nobody to see. We went about half way to the station, then down across softly golden fields to the woods, prowled and explored, and came home by the river. On our way along it we discovered an apple tree growing out from the bank among the maples and the pines—an apple tree grown from some bird-dropped seed, loaded with apples which were wasting their sweetness on the desert air. They were deliciously tart—just the thing for making pies and Nora and I vowed we would come back by moonlight and gather a basket apiece.

Then we crossed a pasture field and got our dresses and hose literally plastered with "stick-tights"—fiendish things that grow in Ontario. They are not what we used to call stick-tights down home, but are tenfold worse and simply ruinous to silk hose. But we had had an afternoon in "the wind, the sun, the golden day," that was cheap at the price.

In the little violet-blue hour that precedes night we again set off, each with a basket. This time we went through the Hostel yard to avoid stick-tights and eventually found our tree. We had such fun getting those apples down and picked up that we nearly died in spasms. Then we hid our baskets in the bush and went on up the river until we came to a place so breath-taking in beauty that we sat on a tree trunk for over two hours and just looked at it. We hardly spoke in all those two hours. Never had I felt so close to the love of all beauty—so *one* with it. It was enough just to sit there and drink in that loveliness of sound and sight—the moonlit lustre on the water—the shadows of the trees across it—the silver laughter of that river underneath the moon. When we had to drag ourselves away we both felt that we had captured one of those things even time cannot destroy.

"Where We Sat"

We came back to earth with a jolt when we reached the Hostel yard with our baskets of apples. There we had what was simply the funniest adventure I ever had in my life. It would take too much time and space to explain it or the why-ness of it, so I shall not attempt it. But when it was over Nora and I simply *reeled* down the long tree-shadowed lane of the Hostel, drunken with laughter—or with the silver wine of the night. In "life's unlit December"—if we ever come to it— we will recall it and see two jolly ghosts laughing under the moon.

As for the apples, we had a pie of them for dinner yesterday and it was the most delicious apple pie I have tasted for years.

"The View Across from Our Seat"

"Group at Laird Wedding"

The apples on the market today are never tart enough for real good pies. For an apple pie you want positively *sour* apples with any amount of sugar. They have a flavour no sweeter apples ever have.

I remember Grandmother's pies. They were "scrumptious," especially when she made the crust with cream instead of shortening, and she generally made me a "turnover" for my own special commissariat. Yum-yum—I am tasting them now.

Yesterday Ewan and I were at a pretty local wedding of one of our girls—Bessy Laird. And again in the evening Nora and I walked to the station—had another divine meal from "the bread of friendship" and lighted the landscape with the colors of our talk, while the evening hills drew their purple scarfs about them.

I had a letter today from Nellie Dingwall—who has half a dozen grandchildren!—She said she had heard that Myrtle was much improved in health and they are beginning to think she will pull through after all. I can't help feeling a little more hopeful, though almost afraid to. How wonderful it would be if Myrtle should really recover!

Nora went home this morning. I watched her drive out of the yard, feeling as if youth were going again with her. It has all been a little *too* wonderful—too delightful. What price will the gods exact?

Monday, Sept. 12, 1932
The Manse, Norval, Ont.
A lovely night of moonlight and silver. I was lonely for Nora.

Maud Campbell is going to P.W.C. having passed her entrance in the summer. I must squeeze out enough to pay her expenses there because I have always promised her enough education to enable her to earn her own living. If she gets through she will get the home school and be able to help them all a bit. But it comes at a hard time for me.

I had a letter from Myrtle and she is really much better and hasn't had a temperature for a month. It seems "too good to be true." I have grown so distrustful of hope.

Wednesday, Sept. 14, 1932
The gods have presented their bill. I knew it would come.

Last night a letter came from Eleanor Agnew, telling me that her mother had died a week ago. She was buried last Friday and was in the cerements of the grave when I was sitting with Nora by the moonlit river, feeling so happy!

It is dreadful. If this had happened before my visit west two years ago I would not have felt it with this keenness of agony. But during that visit all my old deep love for Laura burst into a second blooming—and ever since she had filled her old place in my life and has seemed so very near and dear to me. I *cannot* believe she is dead—she so bright, so full of fun and life, so much beloved, so much needed. I cannot believe in a world without Laura in it. It is incredible.

I *knew* when I parted with Laura that stormy night at Warman junction that we had parted forever. And those few minutes in Saskatoon on my return trip did not remove the conviction from my mind. I recall her as she looked in my last glimpse of her—walking along beside the train which was moving so slowly that she could keep up with it—waving to me—smiling! Laura—Laura!

She was only 58. We were born the same year—she in February, I in November. Poor little Eleanor! How terrible this will be for her, far away from home, among strangers. She was so devoted to her mother—they were more like sisters than mother and daughter.

> There is no union here of hearts
> That finds not here an end....

Thursday, Sept. 15, 1932
A disgusting letter from Isobel was the highlight of today. In my present mood of bitterness and sorrow I have less patience than ever with her meanderings.
"Mrs. Macdonald, Dear,

Listen:—

You are you know a dear dreaming thing who doesn't always listen to what is said to you. And the significance of this plea is not literally that you should listen but that you might rather comprehend."

Humph! I "comprehend" a good deal more than Isobel thinks I do. I am not a "dreaming" thing at all, but this is evolved, no doubt, by the fact that I *ignore* so many things in her letters that are distasteful to me.

"I love you so terribly. It isn't a bit of use to try to do anything else. Nor, I think, should it be necessary. It's like telling myself a lie."

I forbade her to write me any more "love letters" and she promised she would not. "Terribly" is right. "Disgustingly" would be righter.

"My dear, don't you see that I need you more often than your other friends."

"I hope you realize under my bland exterior an undercurrent of fierce burning resentment. Can't I arouse in you the tiniest spark of pity for my languishing condition?"

How can she know my other friends "need" me less than she does? And I *do* in full realize the "undercurrent of resentment." Nobody who was in her company that day she was here could fail to realize it. I wonder how she would justify her resentment. The only thing she could complain of is that I will not give her physical caresses. As for "pitying her" I am afraid pity is very far from my thought of her....

Yet she lives on and my Laura is taken! What a ridiculous and tiresome world it is!

Sunday Sept. 18, 1932
The Manse, Norval
Poor little Eleanor came out yesterday. She said she felt that she must come to me. She is broken-hearted but I think her visit here helped her. It helped her to talk about her mother to someone who knew and loved her, too.

When Laura was married she sent to me an orange blossom from her bridal wreath, telling me to wear it in mine when I was married. My wedding was not to be for many a day but I always kept the little bud and when I was married I twisted it in my wreath. Tonight I took it, twined it with a spray from my own wreath and gave to Eleanor, telling her when she married to wear both in her wreath. I have no daughter to wear it and Eleanor has the next best right. She is such a sweet child. But Laura's daughter couldn't be anything else.

Laura is dead! I think, *if I could believe it*, it wouldn't hurt me so much. I might accept it and resign myself to it. But it seems so foolish to be asked to believe it.

"There are no fields of amaranth on this side of the grave; there are no voices that are not soon mute however tuneful; there is no name with whatever emphasis of passionate love repeated of which the echo is not faint at last."

Mr. Hammond, editor of the *Globe*, and a party of his friends were here this afternoon, taking photographs of me and of the old Woolner jug.

I was always told by Grandmother that Harriet Kemp's sea-captain lover had the jug made specially for her in Amsterdam on his last voyage. But one of Mr. Hammond's friends was a

Maud and the old Woolner Jug

lady who is a collector of old china and she says the jug is positively old English "Sunderland" ware. Grandmother must have got things mixed. Probably the lover gave the jug to Harriet *before* he went on his last voyage.

Tonight I crossed Laura's name off from a little "birthday list" I keep, to facilitate the sending of birthday cards. I think the pen made a scratch on my heart.

Wednesday, Sept. 21, 1932
The Manse, Norval
Tonight I had a letter from Alexena with particulars of Laura's death. She really died of peritonitis, following the bursting of an abscessed gall-bladder. Her life might have been saved if the operation had been 48 hours earlier. "If—if—if—" Alexena says truly that Laura gave her life for her children.

It was to educate them that she slaved at boarding University students. It ought not to have been. Laura was just tired out.

Tuesday, Sept. 24, 1932
Chester returned to college today to enter the second year in mining engineering. I cannot feel easy about him in spite of the fact that he made 73% last year. I have a persistent feeling that he has made a mistake in choosing this profession and it will not "down" for all my reasoning. I doubt if he is fitted for it. If he were I would be well enough pleased for, in spite of its dangers and drawbacks, I believe it is one of the "coming" professions. But he is determined to go on with it seemingly. What a serious, anxious business it is, this of getting two boys started in the world. I was so happy with them when they were small delicious creatures, safe under the care and protection of home. But now!

I re-read *Ardath* the other night when I could not sleep and wanted something to distract my thoughts. Poor forgotten Corelli could tell a story. In spite of its many crazinesses *Ardath* holds you. *How* forgotten she is! And thirty years ago her books were the most talked of and written about and berated and belauded of any in the world. *Sic transit* earthly fame. In thirty more years nobody will know who L.M. Montgomery was either. But what does it matter? What does *anything* matter?

I leave on Monday for my Island. I really oughtn't to afford it. But I *must* see it. It is three years since I've been home and I'm hungry for it. I want to hear the winds in the groves of birch and spruce again—I want to sniff the tang of a fir wood—renew my friendship with the sea and see the moon rise over Rustico Harbour as in the olden years—I want to walk on a dim blue shore and hear lost whispers while the stars sink over the sand-dunes. *And* I want to hob-nob with old friends—listen to some good juicy scandals and some real spicy devilish gossip. So I have scrimped and pinched and am going to take my lunch with me and do without a sleeper. For home I must go or I can't face the winter. One month of freedom!

There is of course, no such thing as real freedom in this kind of a world nor ever can be. "To be free," I read in a book many years ago, "is just to change your master." This is true, but some "masters" are better than others.

Sunday, Oct. 2, 1932
The Manse, Norval
I had one of my now-frequent nights of nervous unrest last night. I don't know what causes them. But today was lovely. Nora and Ned came out and Nora and I had a walk up the river. It was pleasant but the magic of those moonlight nights was gone. I kept thinking of Laura and the gracious autumn day was full of sadness.

I leave for "the Island" tonight—motoring to Toronto to catch the Montreal train. I don't like leaving home on a dark, early falling autumn night like this. It is a dreary thing to do.

Sunday, Nov. 13, 1932
The Manse, Norval, Ontario
Back again—in body at least. Spiritually I am still on my Island—where I spent a happy month. A whole month of happiness—what a treasure! It was not the gay and buoyant visit of three years ago, although in pattern it was curiously like it. But

> Nothing in earth or heaven
> Comes as it came before.

In comparison my sojourn this time was "as moonlight unto sunlight and as water unto wine." Moonlight, however, is very lovely, with a charm that sunlight lacks. I had in the main a beautiful time. I seemed to leave all care and worry behind me and for that month was a girl again....

One afternoon I went over the brook—where there is still a vestige of the old "log" bridge—and through the spruce grove out to what was once "Pierce's field." It is MacCoubrey's field now I believe. No matter, it is really *my* field, because I love it!

Until I was married the northwest corner was filled by a beautiful grove of maple and spruce. Soon after my marriage it was cut down and I recorded my opinion of Pierce Macneill for doing so in this journal. On this afternoon I realized with a stab of delight that it had grown up again—again the corner was filled with maples and spruces. And in my first reaction—for it seemed "only the other day" when I was heart-broken over its murder—I said wonderingly "How soon it has grown up!"

And then I remember that it was twenty years since it was cut down! So it is no wonder it has grown up again. I had never hoped to see that bit of beauty restored. Yet lo, there it was. I wonder if Lover's Lane will ever be lovely again. I fear not. The only pretty spot in it now is the upper bridge with its bushes, not one of which was there twenty years ago.

There is another change in Cavendish. The school has been moved over the road into what was once the little field below our front orchard. No doubt it is for the best. There is room for a proper playground. But the old site looked so desolate and it hurt me.

Most of my nights were fine but one night it rained hard and Myrtle and I sat in her cosy living room and read and talked and did fancy work, with a couple of cats to do our purring for us, while the rain splashed against the panes and the wind made wild music and afar off the gulf boomed. Even a wild wet night like this was delightful on this beloved farm. It all tasted good—all the sweeter because I feared last spring that it would never be so there again. Myrtle's recovery is little short of miraculous. It seems the doctor told Ernest last fall when he operated that she had cancer of the pancreas and could live only a few months. And the same doctor now admits she is perfectly well and with care may live out her days.

When Myrtle was ill I persistently "healed her mentally" according to the suggestions in that old book *The Law of Psychic Phenomena*. Every night before I went to sleep I commanded my subconscious mind to cure her.

Did it?

No, I cannot really believe it. I have become such a fatalist. Everything is predestined and we can neither help nor hinder it. That conviction has been unalterably forced upon my mind and will always possess it.

I hated to leave Webbs'. I always hate to leave a house where I have been happy, if only for a day's visit. Happiness is so scarce and precious. But I had another delightful visit at Alec's....

We went down to "spend the afternoon" with Minnie. I do like that old phrase. It sounds so deliciously extravagant and luxurious to "spend" a whole afternoon!

It was my first visit there since Ren's death. I missed much his jolly, friendly presence. But Minnie was there and two of her married girls were home for the occasion. And we had our planned walk. It was a heavenly day, with the distant sea shimmering in an azure ecstasy and we went through the woods to the birch-rimmed fields with their borders of brown spicy ferns, that are so often hidden away at the back of P.E.I. farms, utterly unguessed at by the prowling tourists, and came home by another wood lane and enjoyed every golden moment. And then Minnie's son Will took us for a drive around the old "shore road" to the harbour, and we all climbed up to the light in the lighthouse and saw the white riders of the foam careering up the sands.

And on the way home I encountered—but did not laugh at—one of those ironic jokes that old cynic Time loves to play.

We passed Will Houston's house and one of the girls proposed we drive in for a moment because he would be so pleased. I assented. For the first time since Tillie went to sleep so many years ago I drove up the lane to the little white house. It was not the trim place it was in her day—corroding change had been at work everywhere. It was shabby and untidy, with a littered yard and gray uncared-for barns. We found out that Will was not at home but up in the turnip field on the hill beyond. So we drove up—and Will came over to the car to speak to us.

I had not seen him for twenty years. Then he had been a handsome, well-preserved man of late middle age. Now he was old—very old. I had been told that he had "failed greatly" of late years, but I was not prepared for the reality. Old! I would never have known him. He is frail, shaky, bleached, senile. I looked at him as he clung to my hand and talked childishly and vaguely. And I remembered that I had once actually been *afraid* of this man at times.

And it seemed very ridiculous.

Well, I may be old and bleached and senile, too some day and men may say, looking at me, "Can *she* ever have been desirable in a man's eyes?"

Is life more beautiful than cruel—or more cruel than beautiful?

But it had been a good day. And the next was better. It, too, was a golden day. And Alec and May and I went back and saw the Secret Field.

Three years ago, when May and I spent that afternoon back in the woods we hunted for it—Alec had told us of it—but, though we found many lovely fields and corners, we could not find it. So this time Alec went with us to show us where it was. We took the car back through his fields to the wood line. Just before the wood-path swallowed us up—those wood-paths, with their pockets of sunshine here and there, are so full of magic I am never quite sure of coming back to the world again, once I trust myself to them—we turned to look at the gulf—the one thing in Cavendish that has not changed—far down below the fields, its unfenced acres darkly, gorgeously blue. Ontario lakes don't know what real blueness is.

Then we plunged into the woods—which as ever were full of secrets they were always on the point of whispering to us but never quite did—and Alec piloted us to the Secret Field.

I never saw anything like it. It possessed me at once and forever. I shall always belong to it.

It is a small field of about two acres, long and narrow. It seems that a MacLure family in Rustico began to clear a field in the woods back of their farm on what they supposed was their land. A new survey was run and it was discovered to be on Alec's land. As Alec had already more cleared land than he could handle he did nothing with the field and it is grown over with feathery bents. And it is *totally* surrounded with woods, without one solitary break in them—this was its unique charm. Spruce and maple, birch and beech in a thick unbroken wall all around it. What a place for fairy revels!

I stood there—and saw it in early spring when the trees were all shades of living green—I saw those dream-like moonlit trees on a summer night and caught my breath at the vision—I saw it in the splendor of autumn—I saw it after a winter snowfall in a winter twilight. And I loved it terribly—so terribly that I've been dying of homesickness for it ever since. I see it as I write, dark and still and full of secret wisdom, encircled by its firs and leafless maples, with my own old stars shining down on it.

It won't live long. Already its bents are feathered with tiny spruces and in a few years the woods will have taken it back.

But I have seen it and it is mine forever.

We visited our "Wood Queen" and "Fern Princess" and we went through maple lanes with their silky whispers and glamorous shadows. I was young again—I am always young in the woods. And then we went home, full fed of delight.

Wednesday was windy and cloudy, but soft and mild. I walked down to the old house by the shore that was once Hammond's. A sad visit. Emily is old and bent and frail. There was no laughter. And though we spent the evening at Bob's there was no laughter. We must have laughed ourselves out that evening three years ago. It could not be repeated.

There were other visitors there, strangers—alien to our jokes and memories, and we had a pleasant evening—no more. Bob is not well and looked—as so many of the C. men did this time—frail and blanched and old. Very little like the jolly Bob of years agone. Oh, the things time does to us!

But there was laughter the next night despite the downpour and the chill and the sweep of gray rain over gray sea. For the Stirlings came down and we had a glorious evening. And just when they left the next day Alma came. She is legally Mrs. Adrian MacLure but to me she is simply Alma Macneill. I had not seen her for twelve years and at first I was shocked at the change in her. The golden hair was snow white, the blue eyes faded, the wild rose complexion gone. But her smile was as sweet as ever and we had a regular talk-fest.

Strange that after all these years of marriage and motherhood and sojourn in a strange land, when I go back to "the Island" it all seems to vanish and that is again my home.

But that night was a bad one. Always, on every visit since my marriage, my last night at Alec's has been a bad one—and a little worse every succeeding visit. Because I am always leaving Cavendish the next day and wondering if I will ever see it again—ever sleep another night under the roof of Gartmore Farm. I felt abysmally sad. Dreadful pangs of loneliness tore my soul. The wind wailed around the house. "The future like the gathering night was ominous and dark."

Well, after an hour of tears I slept. And next day was fine and Alec and May and Myrtle and I had another drive uncannily like the Sunday of three years ago. Only—we did not laugh quite so much. We drove over to Park Corner, had a duck dinner in the Park Corner tradition, then went up, along our glorious blue gulf, to see Aunt Emily. Alec and the two M's went home after supper and left me feeling old.

Yet, it was pleasant to see Park Corner come alive again—cows in the stalls, little calves running around, the carts going and coming. Jim has had a very successful first year and a good crop. If only he could get anything for it. But times are as dreadful there as anywhere else.

Yes, Jim has done well. But I have grown very superstitious regarding anything I back or love or am interested in. I am not a lucky person. I do not bring good fortune to any person or place associated with me. I have realized this for many years. And so—I can't feel hopeful over Park Corner.

Stell has acted very strangely too, and I am completely disgusted with her.

Tuesday night Ella and I were to supper at Heath's and after supper we all sat around the open fire in the big parlor where everything is still exactly as it was in Grandfather's time, even to the pictures on the walls and the curtains in the windows and the big mirror over the mantel. We told stories of old days. Even yet, life at Park Corner has its moments and this was one of them. I did not like Aunt Eliza overly well years ago, nor she me, but of late we have grown fond of each other. With all her oddities she is a lady in the old Montgomery tradition and I have not found many traditions better. She is over 80, but her black hair is untouched of winter and her mental faculties have not failed. Yet I may not see her again. Heath's wife, a kind vulgar creature, will never take her place. With Aunt Eliza, when she goes, will go something that has been in that home for over a hundred years—"the custom of our caste.".....

My last night on P.E. Island was spent in Kensington and was simply a dreadful one. Never shall I forget it. And yet it is to laugh. To laugh and sigh. For truly it was as sad as it was laughable.

Tillie Macneill Bentley (who is now a widow and living in a very cosy little bungalow in Kensington) had written to Amanda soon after I reached Cavendish telling her to tell me that I must go to see her before I left for home. So I wrote her I would spend my last night on the Island with her. Heath drove me up to Kensington on Wednesday night and we reached there about seven o'clock. I knocked at the front door, which had a storm door on and after quite a while I heard somebody fumbling at it and groaning and oh-dearing in a very lamentable tone of voice. Finally she got it open and I stepped in with an offhand, "Well, Tillie, how are you?" Whereupon she fell on my neck, groaning and shrieking. "Oh, Maud—I'm dying—I'm dying. I can't entertain you—I can't get any breakfast for you in the morning—oh dear—oh dear!"

I realized in a moment that she must have gone off her head again as she has several times in the past so I said, "Well, never mind, Tillie. If you don't feel up to having company I'll spend the evening with you and then run down to the hotel." Here I was interrupted by a fearful yelp. Oh, that would never do—I must stay but she was afraid I wouldn't be warm enough and she knew she would be no good in the morning and who was to get my breakfast, all in a high-pitched hysterical voice and gripping me by the arms. I told her she needn't worry about my breakfast as Ella had given me plenty of lunch. This calmed her for the moment and I was able to disentangle myself and get out into the kitchen where there was a fire. Tillie staggered to a chair and poured out her woes. She had had a complete "nervous breakdown"—she was dying—she had falling of the womb and high blood pressure and "bladder trouble" etc. etc. etc. Really, in some ways, the whole performance was darn funny. I could hardly help laughing outright in spite of the dismay I felt over the predicament in which I found myself. How in the world was I to get through the evening and night with Tillie in this state? Luckily a caller arrived—Alf Macneill, an old schoolmate, who had heard I was coming and wanted to see me. Alf never meant anything to me but I could have fallen on his neck and hailed him as a long-lost brother! He stayed two hours and, as he was a fluent talker, time got away. Tillie had collapsed into a chair and punctuated our conversation with groans and "oh dears," with an occasional whoop of anguish when her feelings got the better of her. She was big and fat and looked the picture of health and admitted she hadn't "an ache or a pain" but she was dying and she knew I would be cold in bed and she thanked the Lord she had seen my face once more.

At ten she got herself into the pantry and started to get a lunch. Alf and I both protested vigorously but oh yes we must have a lunch and she didn't know whether she could get it or not because she was dying but she would try. I then begged her to let me help her but this appeared to be the final insult. She shut the pantry door—and such groaning and weeping and "oh dearing" as went on in that pantry for a full half hour. Alf and I sought comfort in each other's eyes but dared not interfere. Finally the "lunch" appeared—a buttered biscuit, two cookies, a bit of cheese and a glass of raspberry vinegar—a decent little bite but why such an unearthly fuss over getting it ready? Alf and I ate it. I had had a tremendous supper at Lula Montgomery's before I left P.C. but I dared not leave a crumb. Then Alf went. I really never thought I should feel such heartfelt regret at the departure of any of "old Cyrus' sons." Then Tillie poured out another flood of woes, going over the same ground. "You see I'm telling you the truth—there is no use trying to hide it—I'm dying. Oh dear, oh dear, I'm dying." I wanted her to let me get a doctor but she said the doctor would say it was only her nerves and wanted her to have an operation for the womb trouble but she knew she would die under it. I pointed out as diplomatically as possible that she thought she was dying anyhow and why not be a good sport and take a chance. But Tillie was not taking any chances. Personally, I think it is the womb trouble that brings on her attacks of neurasthenia.

However, I began gossiping about old days and friends and presently Tillie forgot all her woes, laughed with real laughter and was quite all right. "Oh, Maud, you're doing me so much good but when you're gone I'll be as bad as ever." We kept this up till one o'clock, when Tillie finally decided she must let me go to bed. But oh dear, how was she going to get me my breakfast in the morning! Finally I got to bed. Tillie had *three* flatirons and a brick all boiling hot for me. I took the brick but positively refused the flatirons. Tillie had piled enough quilts and puffs on the bed for three beds and everything reeked of mothballs. *She* took some sleeping dope the doctor had given her, went to bed and slept like a lamb but I never closed an eye until after five. After such a nerve-wracking evening I was simply a wreck. About five I dropped off but was aroused at six by Tillie falling out of her bed—just across the hall—with a thud that jarred the house. I rushed in but she had got up and was staggering around the room and falling against the wall. I noticed, however, that she carefully avoided the furniture so I concluded her staggers were only a form of hysterics. She was groaning "Oh dear, how could she ever get the fire on and get my breakfast?" I implored her to go back to bed and I would be on the boat at nine, in plenty of time to get my breakfast—but nothing availed. Down she went and all the time I was dressing I could hear her terrible groans. As she had admitted she hadn't a pain or ache of any kind I knew her groans were purely neurotic but they were none the less gruesome to hear. When I got down she had the fire on, tea made, bread and butter and a nice mould of potted meat on the table. If I had been hungry it would have been a good meal but as it was I just had to force every mouthful down. I couldn't induce Tillie to have a cup of tea with me. She just sat by the stove and groaned and cried. She was dying and she would never see me again. Of course I wasn't silent during all this. I tried to reason with her—pointed out how comfortably she was situated and that she had often recovered from these attacks before. No use. Tillie was determined to die. Every now and then she would get up and stagger around until the wall brought her up. I thought this sheer hysteria but I was afraid she might be really dizzy and have a stroke or fall on the stove. I was determined I would not leave her alone in such a state so I said I would go out and get a neighbor to stay with her. So I did. It was not quite light and fearfully cold. I had to go quite a distance to the house of the woman she wanted and as I was turning in at the gate in the dim light I caught my foot on a loose board and fell headlong on the hard frozen earth, bruising my face, twisting the nose-clip of my glasses so that they were of no use to me on the way home, and tearing a hole in the elbow of my practically new travelling dress. However, I was lucky to escape without a broken collar bone or arm! Then I had to pound on the door for what seemed endless ages before I could wake Mrs. Evans up. It was really only about fifteen minutes but that is long enough on a bitter cold morning in a high wind. Eventually she wakened and went back with me. Then came the awful scene of parting with Tillie. She was groaning and shrieking "Oh, Maud, I'll never see you again." I told Mrs. Evans to send for the doctor and literally tore myself away and hurried to the station. What an ending to my pleasant visit to P.E.I.

I fairly ran to the station through the crisp autumn air and drew a huge sigh of relief when I got on the train. And yet I was really horribly sorry and grieved over poor Tillie's condition. We have always been good friends of a sort—she is linked with many sweet old memories of dead days. It is terrible to see her like that, with no one to look after her properly.

I had an uneventful journey home and have been busy ever since picking up dropped threads....

Friday, Nov. 18, 1932
The Manse, Norval

Stuart came home for the week-end and had a narrow escape. He came with some of the Brampton boys—five of them in a car. The roads were icy and just out of Brampton the car skidded, turned over twice and went into the ditch. Luckily no one was badly hurt. Two boys had scratches but Stuart was not hurt at all. They might have been killed or seriously injured. I did not know of it until Stuart arrived home, smiling and brisk. Even so it was a nasty shock.

But I forgot it and all else when I went into the parlor and ran through the kodascope the moving picture film I took on the Island. It came out splendidly—and how homesick it made me. For I seemed to be looking through a window right on P.E. Island. It seemed to me if I called out the folks there must hear me. For there was Myrtle walking along the shore with the waves splashing high on the rocks around her—there were the trees waving in Lover's Lane—Marion and Pauline giving the five cats their dinner—"Lindy" perking up her saucy gray head—Marion and Anita walking towards me down the Whispering Lane—Alec ploughing in the field by the house, with the gulf beyond him—May and Alec by our little spruce trees—May and Alec in the Secret Field—the Park Corner gang coming around the curve of the lane. When the film ended I came to myself with a spiritual jerk as if I had at one bound crossed a thousand miles. I wish I could have afforded a dozen films when I went down.

Tuesday, Nov. 22, 1932
Norval, Ont.
I wrote Isobel today as follows:-

"My dear Isobel:-
I am afraid you will consider this an unkind letter. It is not. It is written after much serious thought, as the only way out of what I am sure you must feel as I do has become a rather unbearable situation for both of us.

I told you last spring that all intercourse between us must cease unless you could be contented with such measure of friendship as is possible between a woman of my age and experience and a girl of yours. You promised me that you would be. But your letters of August and September have convinced me that you either cannot or will not be satisfied with what I can give. You persist in asking for what I cannot give.

You call this "love." My dear, it is nothing of the sort. It is simply an obsession, as any psychiatrist would tell you. Their records are full of just such cases, even to the wording of the letters, as you would realize if you had studied as many of them as I, in the pursuit of my profession, have done. And such an obsession almost always ends in misery and unhappiness for its victim unless it is removed by the removal of its object. Some day you will suddenly awaken to the fact that you have recovered from it and are *free* once more. Then you will realize that this letter has been the truest kindness.

Your letters show plainly that these visits back and forth are worse than useless. By your own confession you are always more unhappy after them than before. Therefore it is best for you that they cease. In the future, when you have escaped from the tyranny of your fixed idea, you will see clearly that all I have said is true. And then we may be able to have the friendly acquaintance we had at first and which is all you should ask or I can give."

Of course Isobel will think this a very "cruel" epistle but she has driven me to it. I cannot tolerate her dreadful craving any longer. It is for her good as well as my own that it must stop.

Thursday, Dec. 1, 1932
Norval, Ont.
A letter from Isobel came last night but I did not open it until today. One faces things like it better in the morning.
And it was distinctly a letter to be faced!

Dear Mrs. MacDonald:-
All of the things you said are very likely true, except one. And, if you give me credit for any ability of judgment at all, please try to understand that I cannot submit to what you term the removal of the object. Please, let us work this out together. It will not take very long if we both bring to it a reasonably tolerant and understanding heart. Please show me patiently what is meant by friendship and love and I'll try sincerely to learn. If you are my friend please don't forsake me when I need you. Don't shut me out alone in the darkness of despair. To have nothing more to do with me till I get this out of my heart when the taking hurts

so, to leave me groping without a ray of light, seems so damnably awful I can't even conceive of anything so heartless and cruel. And I think it is only fair to tell you that I won't be able to stand it. Your attitude of condemnation will soon break my heart.

To cut me off entirely from you even for a time will accomplish its purpose and that right speedily. But it will bring such bitterness that I don't believe God himself could ever wipe it away.

Please, Mrs. Macdonald, come to see me soon. I'll try to think of you only as a friend and be sensible. I've been wanting to be as you desire me but it is really hard. Please try it anyway and your promise will bring me happiness again.

When one reflects that this is a letter written by a woman to another woman the nature of my problem is apparent. On this one point the girl is not sane, so the rules and decisions which would apply to sanity do not hold here. It is this which makes my problem so difficult.

I suppose Isobel will conclude that I have not "a tolerant and understanding heart." Alas, I "understand" the situation too well and I have been "tolerant" too long.

The letter has worried me frightfully. But I have decided to ignore it. It seems harsh to refuse the plea it contains but I *know* nothing save unpleasantness can come of our association if Isobel will not tear this Lesbian horror from her heart. I *must* be firm. She will be far happier after the pain is over. She will probably turn round and hate me but that will really be much more comfortable for both of us.

Saturday, Dec. 3, 1932
Norval, Ont.
Today I finished *Pat of Silver Bush*. It has been a desperate struggle to get time to write it. Shall I ever have a little real leisure for writing again? I cannot see any prospect of it. If I had not found it so hard to get time for it I would have loved writing *Pat*. It has a setting after my own heart and "Pat" is more myself than any of my heroines. I have put Alec's Secret Field in it and the Webb cats and "Silver Bush" is so real to me that I feel I have lived there myself.

I was very well for the first two weeks after coming home but now my nervous unrest and odd feelings in head have returned. And so many things are worrisome and disheartening. I feel bitter somehow. Life shouldn't be like this.

The "Depression" shows no sign of lifting. Wheat is the lowest in price for 400 years so it is said—markets are dead—crude oil has crashed—my poor investments dwindle daily. One that was worth $14,000 dollars three years ago is worth today exactly $840.

Somehow, this has been the darkest and dreariest day since coming back. And I must go to S.S. concert practice tonight. G-r-r!

For that matter I am running to some kind of a practice all the time. We are getting up a play for Old Tyme night. But I rather enjoy this. We have a bit of fun at the practices and forget our daily dozen of worries.

I had a nasty dream last night. I am sure it foreboded bad news of some kind.

"Clara" [Campbell]

Tuesday, Dec. 23, 1932
Norval, Ont.

Yesterday came a wire from Stella saying that Clara had died, following a too late operation for appendicitis!

In these recurrent agonies of sorrow I pay the price exacted by the gods for my gift of friendship! I have not seen Clara for nearly a quarter of a century but we were like sisters all through childhood and girlhood. Clara went to Boston in my twentieth year but our old affection has never been broken in all these years of separation. Last night I lay awake and remembered all the fun and laughter of our youth when life was singing in our hearts. I always loved Clara. She was a girl of sweet disposition and affectionate heart, with a keen eye for a joke. How those dark blue eyes of hers could shine with mirth. She had, like myself, the "Montgomery eyes" which grew dark at night owing to the enlargement of the pupils. What jolly times we had together year after year, sharing all our little secrets and love affairs! And now she is dead by the shore of an alien ocean. Everyone of that family gone save Stella—Uncle John, Aunt Annie, Clara, George, Frede. All that merry jolly laugh-loving circle that used to sit around the table while Uncle John carved to the manor born and Aunt Annie smiled as she dispensed gravy and "stuffing." And three of them went in their prime.

Well, what is there to say? Nothing—unless I repeat what I have said so often in this diary!

The past two weeks have been dark and cold. I have not been well and I have been too busy and very bitter. Christmas is only two days away but there is nothing of it in my heart. It is getting to be such a ghostly world for me.

1933

Tuesday, January 6, 1933

I finished up with *Pat* today. In twelve days I have typed 100,000 words. I have not typed the MS. of a book since *Anne of Avonlea*. But it would cost fifty dollars to have it done and this year every cent counts so I did it. I am very tired but that would not matter if I had peace of mind. Several worries dog me. And I have not been well at all—long nights of nervous unrest—queer tight feelings in head—all the symptoms that were absent during my visit home have returned. Of course worry aggravates them.

Friday, Jan. 13, 1933
The Manse, Norval, Ont.

Today I took the MS. of *Pat* to Toronto and Mr. McClelland, Mr. Ford and Mr. Boyd celebrated it with a lunch in the Round Room in Eaton's. It was pleasant and I felt a little cheered up. Mr. M. had brighter reports of western wheat.

Sunday, Jan. 22, 1933

This has been a hellish week. On Wednesday I was in bed with flu and though I broke it up with soda I have just been dragging around the rest of the week, blue and worried and hag-ridden. And I had two *awful* letters from Isobel.

A few days previously I wrote her, after a letter from her in which she *again* promised to be content with friendship. I felt that I simply *had* to make it exactly clear to her just what kind and degree of friendship was possible between us.

"My dear Isobel:-

You say you will be content with such measure of friendship as I can give you. But *will you*? I very much fear that you live in a world of dreams and are unwilling to face unromantic facts. One of these facts is that for any real or satisfying friendship some things are absolutely necessary—and are just as absolutely lacking between us. These things are, approximately equal age, approximately equal experience and a certain number of mutual interests.

I am a woman of 58. At that age one does not form deep new friendships with anyone, even with those of one's own generation. I have many so-called "girl friends." When I first became acquainted with you and your sister I thought our association would be such as I have with those girls. They are satisfied with an occasional visit and two or three letters a year. If this will content you it is yours. If it will not I have no time in my overcrowded life for more."

Then, having thus made it clear to her that I could not be running up...every few weeks and writing continually, I finished up with some pages of friendly chat.

Thursday night came a reply from Isobel. Anything like it I have never received in my life before. And on Friday night came a second, likewise reeking with insults!....

If the thing were not so horrible it would be funny to contrast these letters with the reams of nauseous adulation she has poured out to me. She has made my life miserable for two years with her whines and reproaches but when *I* try a little plain speaking I am "cruel" and "unfair."....

Well, it all serves me perfectly right for even tolerating her attitude as long as I have done. I am glad she has written these letters for she will never have the face to write me again. I am *free* at last, thank heaven. It has been a horrible experience. The girl is not sane and I deserve all I have got for being fatuous enough to think I could help her or guide her back to normalcy.

But this has not added any pleasure to a dark depressing week of worry, little unpleasant happenings that sting and fret, and illness.

Saturday, Jan. 28, 1933
The Manse, Norval, Ont.
....I re-read Guadalla's *Palmerston* this week. Very fascinating. What lives those English of the "upper classes" led in Palmerston's day! As nearly ideal as possible one would think, at least as far as pleasure and interest went.

Of course, most of the men wore side-whiskers!!!

Another company cut its dividend in half this week. But that is getting to be a commonplace....

Sunday, Jan. 29, 1933
Norval, Ont.
Something bad is going to happen. I *know*. I had a dream last night.

I was driving our car myself and the road was blocked by a car in front. But I got around it—and then ran at full speed into a *barred door*. I got out, thinking "This is the end. The car is ruined and I can never get through that door." But the car was very little hurt—merely the bumper bent. Then the barred door opened without difficulty and I drove through and into a garage safely.

The latter part is a little reassuring—but what is going to *come first*? I cannot imagine but I know it is dreadful.

Sunday, Feb. 5, 1933
It has happened. It is too cruel and hideous and unexpected to write about. I have spent two days in hell. I cannot see how I am to go on living. I have suffered so dreadfully that I feel as if I were going insane. And I have had to keep up a face to the world when something in my soul was bleeding to death.

This is what the dream foretold. And I cannot find any comfort in the second part. I have never had to face anything like this before. And I cannot understand it. It is all a hideous puzzle to me.

Today in church I coughed incessantly and a pain tore at my side. A girl in front turned to me when service was over and said, "If you were one of us"—she is a Toronto teacher—"you would be sent to bed with a nurse."

Would that heal a broken heart?

Monday, Feb. 6, 1933
Norval, Ont.

I had a terrible night last night and as bad a day. I have not slept since Friday. Oh, I *haven't* deserved this. I *can't* understand it. And then tonight, on top of all else, came a letter from Isobel! I had never dreamed for a moment that she would dare to write me again. But I suppose when she found I was not going to answer her letters she determined she would compel me to take some notice of her. She writes thus insolently:-

Dear Mrs. Macdonald:-

I am coming down to see you quite soon. Not for a visit of course—though I imagine that this time we may have a topic of conversation of great mutual concern—but for an interview. And, as I realize that in your overcrowded life I might go a hundred times and not find you perhaps you would be tolerant enough to let me know when it would be convenient. It will be useless to deny any convenience because I have to come and I am going to. Possibly Saturday night or Sunday night, whenever there is a convenient bus.

What a composition! I shall decline to be "interviewed," and I do not feel that I shall be very tolerant. Note her sneering repetition of my phrase "my overcrowded life." The poor fool has no conception of what my life really is. I am sure my blood boiled when I read that letter. I could hear it bubbling in my veins.

That this should come when I am already half crazy with bitter worry!

Tuesday, Feb. 7, 1933
The Manse, Norval

I took veronal last night—and slept an hour. The rest of the night was hag-ridden by Isobel's letter which in my present condition I could not shake off. But I simply cannot have her come here. I cannot endure it—or endure getting another letter from her. I have today written a letter that *must* open her eyes. I am sorry that I have been compelled to write such a letter to a fellow creature but there are some things I cannot bear. I told her plainly at last that her passion for me is Lesbian, abhorrent in the eyes of all decent people. I told her that she had "heaped insults on a woman old enough to be her mother—a woman who, from the time she had first introduced herself into my life several years ago had been consistently kind to her—who strove to give her such friendship as was possible under the circumstances, and who never refused her any favor she had asked except—a fatal exception, of course—the satisfaction of her Lesbian craving for physical caresses. I told her I felt under no obligation to expose myself to further insult and catechism of any sort and that I had been "tolerant" too long. Finally I wound up by saying: "Take my advice. Accept with some dignity and restraint the situation you have brought on yourself. Cease to persecute me. If you do this I will try to forget the nightmare of this past year and remember you only as you seemed in the beginning of our acquaintance when you and your sister appeared to me as two nice young girls with whom I could have the simple pleasant friendship I had with many young girls and when your letters, apart from their personal paragraphs, were brilliantly written and enjoyable. If you come here I will decline to see you because no good purpose could be served by any such 'interview.' I have been sincerely desirous of helping you, realizing the form of perversion from which you suffered and hoping that, if you could be persuaded to take a sane and normal view of friendship between woman and woman it might help you to overcome your maladjustment. But the attempt has been vain and I was foolish to have made it."

Surely—surely—this will convince this mad girl!

Thursday, Feb. 9, 1933
Last night was the coldest night in Ont. for 6 years. All my nice ferns froze. But what does a thing like that matter now? Yet it hurt me. They had been so beautiful—and now they look indecent. They are like my hopes and dreams.

And then a letter from Isobel. Am I *never* to escape her? She grovels and weeps and implores. It is all a misunderstanding. Can I be "divine enough" to forgive. She didn't mean a word of those two letters and she can't live without my forgiveness etc., etc., etc., her "tortured heart" will burst—she loves me more than ever—she has "learned a lesson," etc.

No, there is no escape for me. I can't set my foot on a writhing worm. I can't let a human being suffer so when I can prevent it. Am not I suffering hideously, with no one to comfort me and no prospect of any relief. And yet—it *is* weakness on my part because I feel sure she will never be content with friendship. I thought I was free of her. Now she is on my back again. And in my present wretchedness of worry and heartbreak it seems to me I *can't* bear any more of her.

I have written her as follows:—"If after all that has taken place you really wish to try to resume the old friendship we had in the beginning I am willing to, although I do not know if it is a wise thing for either of us. I can of course, forgive, and even forget in the sense of ceasing to cherish any resentment: but to forget in the sense of actually wiping out memory is not in anyone's power and I fear the memory of those two letters of yours will be, for a considerable time at least, in the background of my mind, causing reserve and self consciousness. And I rather fancy that after your agitation has calmed down some of my plain speaking will rankle in your memory and poison any relationship between us.

"However, if you wish it, we can try. But you *must* recognize the limitations of such a friendship and not prepare fresh disappointment for yourself. It is exactly as I told you—only a limited friendship is possible between two people so far sundered in age and experience as we are. It is not my fault or yours that there is this unbridgeable gulf between us but it remains a fact and you must accept it and its consequences, or you will always be disappointed and keep me worried. You must be contented with what I can give."

And yet the whole thing is so grotesque—so devilishly grotesque!

Stuart came home tonight for a week end. It was a bit of comfort to see him—he is always sunny and cheerful. And yet I have a secret worry about him too which frets and gnaws and teases. Perhaps I am foolish and will laugh at myself some day. But I know what can happen in this world. And I have seen all my other hopes crushed to death. Why should this one survive? It would be too kind of Fate to leave me *one* comfort—one unflawed thing.

Saturday, Feb. 17, 1933
....I have been reading the proofs of *Pat*. It is well I finished the book before this came—I feel now as if I could never write again. But I have felt like this before— and when the raw agony passes into a dull ache I have been able to go back to my dear work and find comfort and escape in it.

There have been several play practices—a Y.P. meeting—I have been fighting off a cold. A letter from Isobel, though comparatively sane, added no pleasure to the week. But I do not ask for pleasure—now. I would be thankful and satisfied with just relief from pain.

Among the many disagreeable things these years is the number of begging letters of all kinds I get. I can't check up on them all—and it is impossible to help all. Some are so very pathetic. And yet I did check up on the most pathetic of all and found it a tissue of falsehoods. Then so many elderly women write me asking me "how to get their stories accepted." They *must* make money and this is the only way they can think of. Poor souls, it is pitiful. They do not seem to have the faintest realization of the long years of hard work, stern training and bitter disappointment which must precede literary success—or of the fierce competition they are up against. They think if I would only share my magic formula with them they could make money right off by "writing." Alas!

I can bear up in the day. But at night things become unbearable.

Sunday, Feb. 26, 1933
My unpleasant symptoms of head and eyes have returned this week and have added a little quite unnecessary wretchedness to life. Our Old Tyme concert came off Thursday night. Amid the general excitement I partially forgot my secret pain temporarily and enjoyed it. I had rented a pretty dress of flowered muslin with a still prettier hat of the old poke bonnet style, pink and green, and we had a good crowd and everyone seemed pleased. Friday night I had "the session" to supper and gave them a better feed than some of them deserved.

I have been dreaming of Cavendish tonight—of the old sandshore—the "long sandy beach" of the Indian name, "Penamkeak." Somehow, I want to be back there—alone between the ocean and the dunes—with the wind blowing from the salt seas—the light on New London Point shining over the harbour bar—and peace and forgetfulness.

Sunday, March 12, 1933
Norval, Ont.
Two pleasant things *did* happen this week and heartened me up a bit amid the general drabness. Mr. McClelland writes that Hodder & Stoughton are "very much pleased with *Pat*."

Gymnasium Team, 1932

And Stuart won the Junior Championship for Ontario again.

It was *not* pleasant however to hear of the serious earthquake in Los Angeles yesterday. I feel a bit worried about Stell but hope she is not in the zone where it is most severe.

Wednesday, April 8, 1933
Life crawls on. I perform all my little household rites which once meant so much to me but the heart has gone out of them.

Sometimes a few moments of forgetfulness come—as in the evening we spent at the Glen House. But the fresh remembrance is so terrible that one would almost rather not forget.

I cannot sleep and spend half the night in tears. And it must all be hidden from the world. It is not a grief or a worry one can tell.

One day we motored to Kingston with the Barracloughs. Normally I would have enjoyed it. Even as it was it sweetened life a little. But the ache was always there. For the rest most of the days have been dull and gloomy. I have gone to socials and play practices and missionary meetings—I have suited my talk to my company—I have suffered from headaches—I have re-read Laura's letters, which opened certain ghostly gates for me and made me *hunger* for the far, far past—I have helped the Union women make an autograph quilt—I have read British proofs of *Pat*—I have housecleaned—I have received begging letters—*and*, worst of all, I have gone up to...[visit] Isobel.

Of course it was awful. She met me as I got off the bus and we greeted each other with countenances carefully adjusted to the occasion as Tacitus remarked a couple of thousand years ago. It was raining, so we could not go for a walk. We went to her boarding house and to her little room. There I had to sit and try to talk while she sat opposite me and devoured me with her eyes. They were dreadful— the eyes of a tortured soul. After supper we went to see *Grand Hotel*. It was good and I enjoyed it when I could forget Isobel, sitting tensely by my side and thinking God knows what.

I've been reading old Froissart. What a rare old fellow he was! And what a lot of history has been made by fools! Perhaps that is why they exist. History would be dull without them.

Wed., April 19, 1933
The Manse, Norval, Ont.
Minnie Toombs is dead. The news was a bitter shock for I had not known she was seriously ill. Another dear old friend gone. This is what growing old means. And it seems but a few years since I saw her a bride "appearing out" in old Cavendish church. Alec will feel this. She was his favorite sister.

But Isobel...is left to the world!

Sunday, May 7, 1933
I have been sleeping a little better and the anguish of the last three months seems subsiding into a dull bearable ache. But the sore spot is there and so many innocent things and remarks press on it and hurt.

And I have a new little gnawing worry about Stuart which haunts me unquietly. I had to write him a serious letter. I hated to write it. In all his life I have never been worried about him before. There is nothing bad—he is just in danger of making a dreadful mistake.

I have been housecleaning and find it hard to take my old interest in it. For lighter recreation there have been missionary meetings. I have suffered from the nervous restlessness which has tortured me for three years and which is aggravated by worry.

Wednesday, May 10, 1933
Today was lovely and we went to Toronto with the Barracloughs and saw *Cavalcade*. It is the first thing I have *really* enjoyed for a long while. I am frightened to enjoy *anything* now. It seems like a defiance to *Some Power* that is torturing me and which will be freshly enraged by my daring to escape for even an hour from the torture. This is absurd, I suppose—but it's the way I feel.

Yet *Cavalcade* made me sad. I seemed to be reliving so much of my life since it began with the Boer war. What a thirty years it has been! I think the world never passed through thirty more terrible ones. And at present war clouds lower over Europe again.

Last night I dreamed of Frede. She was alive and we were together. I dream of her so seldom—and I so wish I could.

Thursday, May 11, 1933
I knew I would pay for my day of escape. Today Mr. Barraclough called with news of his brother's sudden death in England. This may mean that he may have to go to England to live. I cannot bear to think about it.

There has been no nice mail—and no letter from Stuart. Is he angry or alienated because of mine? It makes me sick to think so. Alienation from Stuart is something I cannot bear. And yet I *had* to warn him. There is no one else to do it.

Friday, May 12, 1933
The Manse, Norval, Ont.
I am very tired but much happier. (Hush, hush! *They* may hear!!)

We went up to Leaskdale yesterday to attend the funeral of Mrs. Marquis—an old friend of ours whose death saddened me. We were often at her home when we were in Leaskdale. It was one of the very few homes I really enjoyed being in. The family—at least, the mother and girls—had a Josephian flavor.

The old manse looked forlorn and deserted. It is yet vacant and the congregation is feeling the effects of the depression.

When I got home I found a letter from Stuart. He seems to have taken my letter in good part and said he did not wish to cause me sorrow or annoyance and would respect my wishes. I must believe this and trust him. But with my knowledge of the world and its pitfalls for youth and ignorance I cannot even yet feel quite easy. But at least the sting is taken out of this particular worry.

We are getting our garden in. At first I thought I could not take any interest in it this spring; but when I began work in it the old charm seized me and comforted me and poured a certain soothing balm on my aching hurts. I am so thankful for just a little relief from ceaseless pain.

CHURCH CELEBRATES CENTENARY

Union Church celebrates centenary

Sunday, May 28, 1933
Today Union congregation celebrated its centennial in the usual way—old ministers preaching, special music, crowds of people—quite as much a social function as a religious one. The pleasant part of it for me was after the evening service when the visiting ministers and wives were entertained at the Glen House with one of the suppers Mrs. Barraclough knows the secret of—the lost Park Corner touch. It was

delightful—with an underache of worry for me over the possibility of the Barracloughs going to England. They are certainly going this summer for a visit at least. Will it be only a visit? Mr. Barraclough doesn't want to live in England— he prefers Canada. But he may have to.

There were some references to the "next centennial" of Union church. I wonder if there will ever be another. I doubt—I very much doubt it. It is quite possible the building itself will be there "a hundred years to come." It is a very substantial gray stone construction. But I feel quite certain that there will be no congregation to worship in it. In a hundred years—if Sunday services are held at all—they will not be held in little country churches. There will be just a few central churches in large cities and the services will be broadcast from them. Country people will sit in their homes, press a button and hear and *see*. Union church, if it still exists, will be given over to owls and bats and wandering winds. A pity, perhaps. But there will be something to take its place. Human nature will always find—or create—something to supply its needs—feed its hunger, material or spiritual.

Thursday, June 15, 1933
The Manse, Norval, Ont.
We have had an unusually warm June so far—oppressively so. The stock market has boiled up after a year of bearishness and I have made a few hundreds out of it. This means that I can keep my head above water financially for this year anyhow, and so removes one gnawing worry. But there are so many left.

Today I went to Toronto and Nora and I went to the museum. It was wonderful. I must go again soon—and I must go alone. I want to stand before certain things and look at them till I am satisfied.

There were tablets from Ur, written before Abraham was born—children's shoes that some mother had tied on little restless feet before Moses led the Hebrews out of Egypt. There was the mummy of a young girl who lived 3000 years ago. It seemed to me sacrilege to look at her—and yet I looked. Who loved her? What man kissed those shrunken lips and whispered love words in her ear? What mother adored her? What hopes, fears, dreams, passions burned and shone and smouldered in that skull? She is hideous now—was she beautiful then? Why did she die young and whose heart broke when she died? And how often has she lived since then and has she ever come and looked at her own mummy?

Monday, June 19, 1933
Stuart came home today. He led his class, won the Lieut. Governor's Silver medal and the Etienne medal for French and tied for the Latin prize. He has finished with St. Andrew's. It doesn't seem possible that it is five years since that morning he went away, a little lad of twelve, saying, "There is something *romantic* in going away to a boarding school." He has changed from child to man in those years—I wish I could have my chubby blue-eyed little lad back. It is a silly, futile wish—but every mother wishes it with an aching heart.

The Canadian Authors' Association is going to England—leaves Wednesday— at least most of them. I wanted to go too, more than I've wanted anything for years but several reasons made it impossible. Well, it does not matter. If I were only free from constant worry I would not feel bitter about the mere loss of a pleasure. But what a pleasure it would have been!

The heat continues. The nights are very oppressive. We have not had anything like this for several years. And no rain. The drought is becoming serious.

How oddly old memories sometimes rise to the surface of consciousness! Tonight while I was working in the garden weeding a row of parsnips I suddenly recalled a comical old incident and laughed, for a moment of forgetfulness before I sighed.

I was back at Park Corner—the old jolly Park Corner of '92. It was an early spring evening. "Amby" Warren, an old local vagrant, had come to Uncle John's and asked Aunt Annie if she could let him have a few parsnips. His system required parsnips. Aunt Annie—who never refused a bite to a mortal creature told him to go out to the garden and help himself to her parsnips, mellowed and sweetened by the winter frosts. Clara and I were laughing in the parlor—Clara who is sleeping by the far Pacific. We happened to glance out of the window. There in the twilit garden we saw an odd sight. Ragged old Amby, in his red woollen sweater, was squatted on his haunches by the parsnip bed, busily digging therein, while a stick or something he had thrust in his pocket stuck up behind him exactly like a stiff tail.

> Did you ever see the devil
> With his little wooden shovel
> Digging 'taties in the garden
> With his tail cocked up?

giggled Clara.

The quotation was so apt that we shrieked with laughter and Aunt Annie slipped in and enjoyed the joke, her eyes twinkling with mirth. They are all dead now. Ay di mi.

"The Garden"

Tuesday, June 27, 1933
The Manse, Norval, Ont.

I had an unpleasant little experience last night—of an utterly new kind. And it has hurt me a bit. Because I have never before, that I can recall, been publicly insulted by a woman who has been something of a friend and whom I liked.

A year or two ago Dr. Howard and family came to the Presbyterian church in Georgetown. She made quite a fuss over me when we met—a wee bit *too* much, indeed—re my books and we have been quite friendly. She was a jolly looking lady, with twinkling brown eyes and a bosom like a shelf and I have liked her very much and always enjoyed meeting her.

Tonight Ewan and I went with the Barracloughs to a garden party at Limehouse, the country section of the Georgetown congregation. About 700 other people went, too. The drawing card for us all was Agnes Macphail, M.P. I had never heard her or seen her and although I do not think very highly of her as far as statesmanship goes, still, curiosity is probably the last passion to die.

The program, like that of most "garden parties," did not start until nine. The first part consisted of music and speeches from various ministers, lasting till ten. Then we all fondly hoped Miss Macphail would come on. Everyone was already tired of sitting on hard planks, made damp by an afternoon shower, listening to very third-rate speeches and equally third-rate music. But up pops a "girl orator" whose name was also on the program. She was in her teens and she had been blessed—or cursed—with a remarkable fluency of utterance. Also, with an extremely "good conceit" of herself. For one solid hour that child, who knew nothing of life or its problems, laid down the law on every possible point. She told mothers how to bring up children and children how to behave to parents. She told husbands and wives how to use each other, lovers how to choose each other and governments how to govern. It would have been pitiful had it not been so boring. Everything she said was a platitude—something she had read somewhere. There was not one single original thought in what she said—unless it was the concluding "allegory" which was so crude and jejune that she probably made it up herself. And tired, hard-working people who had come to hear Agnes Macphail had to sit for an hour and listen to that. Everybody in my vicinity was as bored as I was, judging from their remarks. "I didn't come here to listen to piffle like that," growled one man.

I really felt disgusted as well as bored. It was an insult to our intelligence. But everything comes to an end, even the vaporings of immaturity and she finally finished at 11 o'clock.

And now, we thought, for Agnes!

Not a bit of it. Dr. Howard genially announced a "recess" which lasted for half an hour, during which more people ate and drank at the booth, and presumably rested a certain portion of their anatomy which—judging from my own—must have been rather numb. During this lull Dr. Howard brought Miss Macphail to me and introduced her. She sat beside me and we had a chat. She was pleasant and flattering but I found no reason to change my opinion of her. She is very egotistic—and I imagine pretty hot-tempered. However, I did sympathize with her in her fury over the way her speech had been postponed. I had said to her,

"Of course at these affairs it is the usual thing to keep the best for the last but I think it is a mistake. And they certainly overdid it tonight."

"Entirely too much so," snapped Miss M. "If I had known there was to be another speaker I would not have come. It is 11:30 now. I shall feel that everyone is tired and wishing I would get through so that they could get home to bed."

But at last Dr. H. remounted the platform and introduced Miss Macphail. Whatever one may think of her political and economic views she is a very entertaining speaker. She left politics alone and spoke on "Life as an Adventure" and was witty and sensible and human. But it was 12:30 when she finished and I felt as if I had been sitting on that hard plank since time immemorial.

As the Barracloughs and I stood in a group Mrs. Howard came up, expansive and gushing as usual and asked how I liked the program. I replied truthfully that I enjoyed Miss Macphail's speech tremendously and—rather less truthfully but not wholly mendaciously—also the music especially the band. I said no more, for although I did not suppose the "girl orator" was anything to Mrs. Howard, I was not going to volunteer any criticism of the program at a garden party given by one of her churches. But Mrs. Howard said, "And what did you think of the little girl?"

I did not see any necessity for telling polite fibs in regard to her so I said, laughingly, "I think before she gets up and tells the world how to run itself she ought to go back to school and learn how to pronounce her words properly."

And then up popped the devil! The words were hardly out of my mouth before I realized that I had put my foot in it. Mrs. Howard's black eyes suddenly flashed fire.

"What words did she mispronounce? *I* didn't notice any."

Her tone was so insulting that I was a little nettled. "I noticed some," I said quietly and tried to drop the subject. But Mrs. Howard was not dropping anything. "What *were* they?" She persisted. So I let her have it. "She called 'duty', '*dooty*' and 'constitution' '*constitootion*' a dozen times." I did *not* add, as I might have done, "and she dragged in several French phrases by the scruffs of their neck and murdered every one of them."

"She is only in her teens," flashed Mrs. Howard. "She is one of our Simcoe girls and *I* thought her wonderful—*and so did everybody else.*"

With that, the angry lady whirled about and made off without even saying good-night.

By this time I was pretty nearly as angry as she was, though I did not make an exhibition of it before the public. If the girl was one of Dr. Howard's former congregation Mrs. H. had no business to ask me what I thought of her without informing me of the fact. She had asked for my opinion and had no right to be in a fury when she got it.

Well, why should I be upset because Mrs. Howard behaved like a fishwife? After all, she is really nothing to me but a superficial acquaintance. Nevertheless, I do not like being insulted in such a fashion before my friends and I do not think I am under any obligation to take it lying down. Ever since coming to Norval I have been doing favors to the Georgetown congregation, going over to concerts and missionary meetings to give readings and talks, so I think I have a right to courtesy from their minister's wife. And besides I do regret a pleasant friendship spoiled—for I shall never feel that I want to be in her company again. And I am so depressed just now that a thing like this hurts me out of all proportion to its real importance. I have never hurt any human being's feelings purposely and if Mrs. Howard had given me any hint that the girl was a friend of hers I would have passed her question off politely by saying she had a wonderful command of language or something equally true and meaningless. She told me nothing—she asked for my opinion and slapped me in the face for giving it.

Thursday, July 6, 1933
The Manse, Norval, Ont.
With what bitter suddenness one's mood can change from almost happiness to sorrow. Last Friday morning the long desired rain came and I danced for joy, forgetting all else for a little while and being really happy all day. I should have remembered that this is not permitted to me. At night came word that Mrs. Robert Reid had taken a serious turn for the worse in Toronto General Hospital. She was operated on early in the week and thought to be getting on nicely. Saturday night word came that she was dying and I went in with the family. It was all bitter and dreadful. Mrs. Reid was one of the few women in Norval congregation to whom I have been really attached and certain family reasons made her death one of peculiar significance to us and created certain complications. The poor thing flung her wasted arms about my neck and asked me to be a mother to Luella. I promised to be so, as far as was in my power. She died at noon next day. Since the first of last September four dear friends of mine have died. This is what growing old means.

Well, they are at rest. Worry—disappointment—heartache—pain—sorrow are ended for them. They sleep well. I can find it in my heart to envy them.

But Isobel...is left! Last Monday a letter came from her. I had never heard one word from her since...March and I had hoped this silence meant that she had really got it into her head that I meant what I said and that it was useless to torment me longer. My already depressed heart sank lower at sight of her detested handwriting. And the contents, though mercifully brief, were unpleasant. She *cannot* keep her pen away from the forbidden topic. For example:—"In reading not long ago I encountered this:—'Whosoever loveth a genius is out of luck with his devotion, except he beareth all things, endureth all things, suffereth long and is kind.' And alas, it is but too true. It seems to me that a devotion which, spurned and buffeted can from the very floor of murder and suicide, still rear its head, deserves applause and the right at least to existence."

And again:—"I should stop now—not that I have nothing to say. I have too much. But everything I think of seems to be precisely the thing I should not say. Why, I don't know. The fact that you told me very plainly that I am nothing more to you than a stalk of rhubarb might have a little bearing upon this peculiar reticence. Oh, yes, you did."

I told Isobel she must not write me love letters. And I have decided to ignore in my reply to her all these personalities and deal merely with her request that I go to see her soon again. But if I did not ignore them I think I should write her somewhat as follows.

"I am not a 'genius'. But in regard to your quotation I would say that I think a person who persists in forcing an unasked and unwanted 'love' on *anyone* is asking for disappointment. And as for the bearing, enduring and suffering long, I think that has rather been on my side than on yours."

If the poor girl but realized it she is nothing so innocuous to me as a stalk of rhubarb. Deadly nightshade, rather!....

I have just been out for a breath of air on the lawn. Little night winds were gossiping among the dark pines on the hill over which there was a most glamorous effect of silver clouds in a moonlit sky. I drank it in with the eyes of my soul and in spite of many secret worries which I have no one to share, it soothed and healed my heart and gave me a little inspiration to go on with.

After all, there is nothing like being alone with the night. "From the cool cisterns of the midnight air, my spirit drank repose." There *are* things "above the smoke and stir of this dim spot that men call earth." There must *somewhere* be a source of that beauty and some time we may find it.

I wish I could stay out of doors all summer, down by the river bank, in a tent like Stuart's, and just rest. I am so tired I feel like a bit of chewed string.

Friday, July 7, 1933
Norval, Ont.

This is Chester's 21st birthday. I was very happy this day twenty-one years ago. I was a mother—Frede was with me. It seems incredible that it can be twenty-one years ago. I wonder what it would be like to feel as happy as that again. The sensation seems to belong to some other world. And compared with today! But what is the use of writing about it?

I went to a "Missionary Picnic" at Georgetown church today, per a general invitation which it would have been discourteous to ignore. Mrs. Howard came and spoke to me at the end. She was very polite and decidedly self-conscious. I was equally polite and splendidly null. My disagreeable sensations of "that night in June" have passed like the snows of yesteryear and her behavior matters nothing now. But our friendship will not be renewed. It was not worth putting up with insults.

Saturday, July 15, 1933

The drouth continues. Our lawn is like a burned blanket. I water the garden every night with a hose but it does little good. The hard well water is really worse, I think, than none at all. I have had lovely peonies and lilies—the spring rains were sufficient for them—but my annuals were nothing worth. I do not remember so hot and dry a summer since I came to Ontario. Almost every day rain promises but comes not. We do not have even a thunderstorm in spite of the awful heat.

Anthony Hope is dead. I feel as if I had lost a personal friend. He has written nothing for many years. But in the 90's his *Prisoner of Zenda* and his *Rupert of Hentzau* were read by everyone. I get them out every two or three years and read them over and enjoy them as much as ever. I would not give one of them for all the reeking sex novels or "cross sections" of life on the market today. After all, it is fairy tales the world wants. Real life is all the "real life" we want. Give us something better in books.

Tuesday, Aug. 1, 1933
Two weeks of intolerable stifling heat. Some nights the feeling would sweep over me that I could *not* endure another day of it. And gnawing worries, such as are my constant portion, become more intolerable still in such weather. But we had a lovely rain a night or two ago. I lay awake and listened to it with an insistent delight. Since then the heat has not been so bad.

Ewan left for the Island today. I am not taking a vacation this year—cannot afford it. But I mean to have a kind of one while he is away. I am not going to "write" or "visit" or do any more things I don't like doing than I have to. I mean to read a good deal and do a bit of fancy work and *dream*.

Pat of Silver Bush is out. I wish Frede had lived to read this book. It would appeal to her, for she loved her home with the passion I had for mine. Somehow, I love *Pat* as I have not loved any book since *New Moon*. It seemed to me such an "escape" while I was writing it.

Friday, Sept. 1, 1933
The Manse, Norval
We were in Toronto today and Stuart won the Gold Medal in the C.N.E. contest thereby becoming Junior champion of all Canada. He takes it coolly. I am still weak and appetiteless but I have been sleeping beautifully at night. That is such a blessing.

Coming down the steps of one of the Exhibition buildings I met Mrs. Howard coming up. She was quite gushing again and I was polite. One may as well be on civil terms with a neighboring minister's wife, but the said Mrs. Howard will never have the chance to insult me again. I shall never say anything *real* to her again. My conversations with her hereafter will be as innocuous and lifeless and uninteresting as an *Elsie* book. Selah.

Saturday, Sept. 2, 1933
I had an amazing and quite exciting letter from Marion tonight. She wanted to know if she might come to Norval for a visit. *Murray* had been intending to go to P.E.I. but his father's health prevented. But some matters had to be settled and *he* wants her to come up.

I was much surprised. I knew they had been corresponding after a fashion since she went home and last summer I rather thought that something was going to come of it after all. But last winter Murray began to go about with Anna Linklater, one of the Norval teachers, a quite pretty girl. Murray seemed quite devoted and several people spoke to me as if they thought a marriage was imminent. I supposed that the end had come between Marion and Murray so that this letter came like a bolt from the blue.

Of course I'll be glad to have Marion come, and in any case I could not refuse. All the same, I hardly like the situation. Suppose Marion comes—suppose she and

Murray can't adjust their problems. She goes home—Murray returns to Miss L— gossip exults. Ha, ha, Mrs. Macdonald brought Marion up in a last desperate attempt to secure Murray and failed! I know enough of human nature to know exactly what they'll say. And—I don't like it.

Sunday, Sept. 3, 1933
The Manse, Norval.
Twenty-two years ago last March I played the organ in Cavendish church one Sunday and left the platform never dreaming but that I should play the next Sunday and many Sundays more. Since that day I have never touched an organ before an audience until today.

We have plenty of women in Norval church who can play but for the past two years we have found it impossible to get an organist. So an outsider from Georgetown has been playing and being paid $150 a year for it. Last year—at that terrible annual meeting which I can never forget, when everything was behind and in debt as a result of "the depression" and everybody seemed discouraged— I proposed a plan. Nobody wanted to be tied down for a whole year but if three of the women would play for three months each I would take my turn for a quarter. To this they agreed.

I knew I could play as well as one of them at least. So ever since I have been practising up my old church music. The organ is a half pipe with a narrow keyboard and at first I found it difficult to get used to it. But as time went on I picked up and even enjoyed it. Today I took the plunge. I was pitiably nervous but I don't think I showed it and unless people told terrible lies I got on well enough. What I dislike most about it is sitting in the choir facing the congregation during the sermon. For certain personal and perhaps foolish reasons this is very distasteful to me.

This evening I went up to the Y camp where a band of C.G.I.T.'s are week-ending and gave them a talk around their camp fire under the pines. I really enjoyed it and forgot for the moment what a melancholy business life has been of late. There was some fairy charm in the surrounding shadows and the old pines—and the girls were eager and enthusiastic and delighted.

Friday, Sept. 12, 1933
Tonight I feel happier and more at ease than I have felt for a long time. A way has been opened up through what seemed an *impasse* and an acute worry of the past week has been dispelled. I feel as if a millstone had rolled off my shoulders.

The past week has been very busy and in some ways very hard. But then everything seems hard when one is worried. I had three days of a nasty illness. I had the Union W.M.A. here one afternoon—I had to go to Toronto to give the "Scripture Reading" at a Presbyterial meeting—I had play practice at Union—I had to preside at a corn roast at Garfield's last night, in aid of the Sunday School (!!) with a heart gnawed by worry all the time. Oh, that is the trouble. All these things would have been quite endurable and some enjoyable if it were not for underlying worry and disquiet. But now that this is removed I think I shall pick up a little heart and courage again.

Saturday, Sept. 23, 1933
The Manse, Norval, Ont.

I dared to be a little happy last week for a few days and that is not permitted. Since then another hideous thing has come and a new worry. I feel broken and can neither eat nor sleep. Something in my life that has always been beautiful and perfect—the only unspoiled thing I had—has been spoiled and smirched. And this worry may last for years. I have gone through nights of hell this week.

I have been told that as you grow older things ceased to hurt so much—you ceased to feel so keenly. I am nearly sixty and this mercy has not yet been vouchsafed to me. Instead, I think I feel *more* keenly and hideously. And I have not the hope of youth now—I have not the years ahead when things may be better—there is no tomorrow for which I can endure today.

I feel as if something in me has been hurt to death.

Marion came last Saturday night, Murray bringing her from Toronto. I was so wretched I couldn't even be glad to see her.

Nora came out Tuesday and we went up the river. I could not enjoy it—but her visit helped a little—numbed the gnawing agony for a time. She had much to tell of her trip to the Island this summer where she opened some ghostly gates after her absence of twenty years. That is too long to neglect our Island. It has its own way of taking revenge. I wish I could have gone with her and roamed together over its misty green hills once more. But I suppose that will never be.

There was a bit of gossip, too. Among other items she met and had a long talk with Edwin Simpson. She says he is a very handsome man, with snow white hair—I can't see *that*—quite well physically but a complete nervous wreck. He cannot sit still for a minute and insomnia has him in its clutches. It is pitiable. He was always very nervous and excitable of course but this is a real break-down.

One thing did amuse me. He remarked to Nora, "I have read Maud's last book from cover to cover and I cannot see one thing in it."

Nora thinks this is an expression of jealousy. I don't, because I don't think Ed is jealous of another's success, whatever else he may be. Of course, he may feel a certain resentment that anyone who didn't appreciate *him* sufficiently, should have stepped into the limelight. No, I think Ed was speaking the simple truth. He has absolutely no sense of humor, so the humor of the book would not appeal to him. He has not the least appreciation of the loveliness of nature, so that would leave him cold. He does not care for children or understand them in the least, so the simple story of a child's unfolding would mean nothing to him. And there is nothing else in *Pat* that would appeal to a mature mind. The odd thing really is that he should make such a remark to the Campbells, knowing them to be friends of mine and quite likely to repeat it to me. Also quite likely to know of my old affair with him and to ascribe his remark to the venom of a rejected suitor. I'd have thought he would have been more canny than that.

He also told Nora he thought it was a pity that the name and idea of God could not be blotted out of the consciousness of humanity! An odd thing for a minister to say! Let us charitably ascribe it to his neurasthenic condition.

Nora, who has never lost her impish vein, asked him to go to see her if he happened to be in Toronto and promised him she would bring him out to see me! He said he would. But he will not. And I certainly do not want to see him.

In a review of *Pat* which came today one sentence amused me. " 'Judy' must be a person the author has known long and well."

"Judy" is purely imaginary. I never knew anyone in the least like her. But I suppose the assertion is really a big, if unconscious compliment.

I was over to Dr. Paul this evening, taking Stuart to be vaccinated. Dr. Paul looked at me and said sternly, "You are working too hard."

But it is not hard work that is the matter with me—it is worry.

Tuesday, Sept. 26, 1933
The Manse, Norval, Ont.
Things are a little better. Some of the soreness has gone out of my soul. But I feel tired and *bruised*.

Today Stuart went to Toronto to attend the University. In one way it hurt me to see him go—my darling! In another it was a relief. For I fear so horribly that he is going to be roped in to making a terrible mistake and get himself entangled in a fashion that would be ruinous to him. He is so young—not yet eighteen, poor child, and thinks he knows exactly what he is doing—as any young inexperienced lad thinks. Stuart is all I have to live for now and if he fails me I am done.

Then, too, I am not easy about his career. He has a brilliant intellect but he doesn't seem to have any leaning to *anything*, except sport. When he told me a few years ago that he had no idea what to go in for I suggested medicine. I think Stuart would be successful as a doctor, with his brains and personality. He fell in with the idea readily. But what if he doesn't like the work and doesn't succeed? I talked to him seriously before he went and pointed out that he could go in for anything he liked if he did not care for medicine. But he said he liked the idea as well as any other. But men do not succeed brilliantly in a profession if they care no more for it than that. These worries ought not to be wholly mine. They should be shared—but they are not.

Oh, for a little rest from bitterness of soul!

Wednesday, Sept. 27, 1933
This was a rather dreary day—but dreary days must be lived through. But—when there are so many of them.

Yesterday in an old box in the garret I found a little "valentine" Stuart once made for me. It brought tears. And in the same box I found an old picture clipped from a magazine years ago and always kept—why? Because some boy—and I can't even recall who it was—said that the girl in it looked like me!!

Well, it is a long time since I stood tiptoe to watch for life like that. But the picture has some charm of old days in it that makes me love it still. So I am putting both it and the valentine in this volume, so that they may not be lost.

This evening Murray and Marion went to Brampton to see *Rasputin and the Empress* and took me. I would have enjoyed it if I could have risen above my worry. There were even moments when I did. Lionel Barrymore as "Rasputin" was very eerie. I am sure I shall never forget his face as he sank below the water of the river. Coming home the moonlit autumn hills were calm and peaceful under the old stars. Murray and Marion seemed very happy. I brought them in and gave them tea and sandwiches. And then I was glad to get away by myself where I need not pretend to be bright and carefree. It is sometimes a great thing just to be alone. One gets so tired of pretending....

Saturday, Sept. 30, 1933
Marion and I did have a laugh tonight. A letter came from Isobel. It was so fat I beheld it with dread. But it turned out to be an account of her relations with the Bennies on their trip east! Such a screed! Bennie certainly is in her black books. She abused him without stint or reason. We knew Bennie of old, when he was in Uxbridge, and he is by no means an admirable character. But he is hardly as sooty as Isobel paints him. She must, it seems, go to the most violent extremes in everything—hate as well as love. But Marion and I certainly "got a kick" out of her spiel. I wish all Isobel's letters were as entertaining. I would rather read abuse of Bennie any day than adulation of myself.

Tuesday, October 10, 1933
....A few years ago I wrote in this journal that I wished puffed sleeves would come in again. Very few of my wishes have ever come true but this has. Puffed sleeves are in—the veritable old "leg of mutton" of the 90's. And I don't care a hoot! They don't look so smart as they did long ago some way—because, I imagine, they are not set on "linings" as formerly and so held up firmly and perkily. They look limp and apologetic.
But I seem to care nothing for fashions now. The ceaseless changes seem absurd. Women should wear a uniform after they are fifty.

Saturday, Oct. 14, 1933
The Manse, Norval
This morning Marion ran into my room, blushing, and showed me *her ring*. A beauty—two diamonds and a sapphire. Murray certainly did the thing well. We laughed and cried together and for a little while I was almost as happy and excited as Marion herself.
Marion *is* very happy. I could almost envy her. Because I never had *that* happiness.
I don't know how they have got over the "baby" question. Probably it solved itself when other problems were solved. I rather think the real snag before was the fact that, owing to his father's health, his parents couldn't retire as parents do in Ontario. He felt he couldn't ask Marion to go in with them and while he was very fond of her was not so violently so as to demand some arrangement from them. They have, I think, come forward with a suggestion themselves, the whole clan being very eager for the match. And so things have been smoothed out for Marion. The house is to be divided. It is big enough for two families. Marion

didn't tell me all this but I have picked up bits here and there and I think I understand the whole situation pretty well. I think, too, they will be happy. They are suited to each other. Murray is a lucky chap for Marion is a lovely girl.

So, after all, my bit of matchmaking has not been the failure I once thought it, and quite a lot of tears and grief were wasted. Perhaps my worry of this bitter fall will prove to be as idle. At any rate I am calmer now and at times life has some pleasure in it again. Dawn still comes beautifully over Pine Crest Hill—cats still guard mystic secrets and two adorable squirrels have been our visitors once a year, coming to get the nuts from the big walnut in front of the church. A black one and a gray one, the latter with the longest plumiest tail I ever saw on a squirrel. The black one isn't perfectly black—I am afraid his mother was no better than she should be—but the gray is without a flaw. I love those two little creatures.

I have been re-reading *Puck of Pook's Hill* for the umpteenth time, and forget all my worries while under its magic. And there are critics who say Kipling is "outmoded." It is to laugh. I would not give the tale of the "Captains of The Wall" for all the reeking sex stuff of the past twenty years.

Tuesday, Oct. 31, 1933

Today Ewan and I and Murray and Marion went to Aurora for Prize Day—for the last time. We have been there many times and I am sorry it has come to an end, for it has always been a pleasant and stimulating affair. Today the drive was very pleasant, with the lombardies like great golden candles all over the landscape as we rolled along. Marion, too, is a delightful companion for an outing. I like a patch of excitement like this about once a week.

Lord and Lady Bessborough were there. Lord B. spoke—quite well, as all these Englishmen seem able to do but with no outstanding merit. Lady B. is nice-looking—as a countess she is called beautiful—with lovely eyes. Gossip has it that they are not the most harmonious couple in the world.

How bored they must both have been. And how well they hid it.

I felt very sad when we came away. I shall not likely be there again. Everything passes.

But Marion and I had the delight of talking everything over. That is half the fun of an outing....

Wednesday, Nov. 8, 1933
The Manse, Norval, Ont.

Today Ewan drove me over to the Union W.M.S. The day was mild and brooding, with gray valleys and purple distances. I dared to feel a little happy again—not only with outward happiness but with inward—my own strange happiness, as if I were drinking from some deep, still, lucent pool in my own soul. I don't know exactly what Jesus meant when he said, "The kingdom of heaven is within you," but I know what I mean by it—that very experience I had today—that realization of a life apart from this harried life of earth—that sense of being *One* with Eternal Beauty itself. It is so long since I experienced it—and it was once a daily, hourly thing. I won courage from it—"the fountain of perpetual peace flows there."

Saturday, Nov. 11, 1933
I spent a dreary day with Isobel. An hour of her practically lays me out. The whole thing was as usual. Isobel gave me a cushion cover and a very pretty plate she brought back from her trip for me. I do wish she would cease showering gifts on me. I am afraid to refuse them lest she take a spasm. Yet I hate to accept them.

Ewan came up for me and we came home through the drear November night, full of driving snow. The thought of winter gives me a grue.

Tuesday, Nov. 14, 1933
I had a letter from Marion. She says she "never dreamed seven weeks could be so happy" as those she spent here and she "owes it to me." Poor child, I am glad she had those seven weeks. The gods themselves can't take them from her, no matter what comes after.

It is curious to reflect that those seven weeks which were so happy for Marion were among the bitterest and most wretched I have ever lived through.

Friday, Nov. 24, 1933
....Lately I have been having a debauch of George Bernard Shaw. Today I reread *Androcles and The Lion*. Shaw is very brilliant. I think he must be a reincarnation of Voltaire. And yet—satirically true as he is, his writings lack the essential truth after all. And he is too conscious of G.B. Shaw. He is always saying in effect, "Oh, am I not clever. You *must* think me tremendously clever. You can't deny it. Listen to this and this."....

Saturday, Nov. 25, 1933
The Manse, Norval, Ont.
Something today recalled to me old Caroline Macneill's black satin bonnets. I can see them—or it—as distinctly now as I could forty years ago when I sat behind her in church. No trimming, but row upon row of glossy shirrings, and fitting snugly around her head like a cap. They were outmoded even then but still thought quite suitable for old ladies who had outlived the tyranny of fashion. Two years ago a girl in Norval wore a little brown velvet hat which, except that it lacked strings, was an exact replica of Caroline's satin bonnet. And yet it looked utterly different from it. I wonder if Caroline's bonnet had set trimly around waves of golden hair, framing a blooming youthful face instead of Caroline's sunken eyes and face of a thousand wrinkles, it would have looked as funny as it did. No, I do not wonder. I know it would not. It would have looked quaint and bewitching, just as Margaret Townsend's brown velvet hat did.

In an old book today I came across the phrase "the new woman"—and smiled. It is so dead now—nobody would know what you meant if you used it. Yet it was a world-wide slogan in the 90's—and meant a woman who wanted "equal rights" and dared to think she ought to vote. To some it was a dreadful epithet; to others a boast. And now the new woman and the old woman are gone and the eternal woman remains—not much changed in reality and not, I am afraid, any happier.

I wonder does anybody make "pot-pourri" now—or is it as pre-historic as the new woman. I came across a recipe for it in my old "household hints" book today.

A jar of pot-pourri was part of the regular furnishing of any reputable parlor in my youth. I compounded many of them, saving up roseleaves all summer, wherever I could get them, drying them carefully on newspapers spread on the floor of the old "look out" upstairs. Then, when they were properly dried, they were put into bowls with all kinds of spices and sachet powders and anything that would smell nice. The final result was a mystical magical odor suggestive of Arabian nights and the gardens of Haroun Al-Raschid. I think it rather a pity "rose jars" have gone out.

Today in one of Ewan's books I happened to pick up there was a chapter on "answers to prayer." Some of them were a bit ludicrous it must be confessed.

I have prayed many prayers in my life. Few of them were answered. I have lived to be thankful some were not. Some were answered after a fashion. I prayed only one prayer in my life that was answered absolutely by the book.

One day during the winter I spent with Aunt Emily in Malpeque Uncle John brought home a stray dog he had found and tied it up in the barn, saying that, if no owner turned up, he was going to take it down to Grandpa (our old "Gyp" was dead.) This worried me terribly. I had never been able to keep a cat as long as Gyp lived and this dog was a big black sleek-looking fellow who was evidently no friend of cats either. I had left a beloved kitten at home and the thought of this dog after it filled me with anguish. For several days I was a haunted creature. Then a day came when Uncle John took me and Aunt Emily up to an examination in the school and left us there while he went on an errand. I knew he meant to go to Cavendish next day and take the dog. Desperately I prayed "Dear God, please let Uncle John tell me on the way home that a man has come for the dog!"

Uncle John returned. Aunt Emily and I climbed into the pung and started home on the Malpeque winter road that ran through every man's field and back yard. As we skimmed across a field below the school Uncle John turned to me and said, "A man came for the dog today"!!!

Looking back to some of the prayers I heard in childhood it is a wonder they did not forever give me a "scunner" of public prayer. Well, perhaps they did. When I was a child the only people who "offered prayer" or "led in prayer" in our church were the Simpsons. They fondly believed they had "the gift of prayer." George Simpson, the "red elder," did pray fairly well—at least, he did not make himself or his prayers ridiculous. "Elder Jimmy" prayed invariably the same prayer which he had learned out of a book. We young fry knew everyone of his conventional phrases by heart and could have prompted him if he had ever forgotten. He always pitched his voice in an unnatural sing-song at the start and kept it up all the way through. It really got on people's nerves, as did the prayer of Junius Simpson, who had to clear his throat with such frequency that nobody ever knew what he was saying. As for Howard Simpson's prayers they were a farce and the ministers should never have asked him to "lead." But of course Howard would have been offended if he had been neglected. He could not pronounce the letter "r" and his invocations to the "Holy Spilit" were hard to bear. The irreverent boys in the back seats didn't bear them. They openly sniggered.

I often hear ministers today lamenting the absence of men in their congregations who can "lead in prayer." But such prayers as those the Simpsons offered up were better unprayed.

These latter days I am much pestered by "fans" sending me their autograph albums to write in. Two came all the way from Australia the other day. The revival of the autograph album vogue is curious. A few years ago a girl wouldn't have been "found dead" with an autograph album in her possession. Now they are fashionable again. Well, God forbid that crinolines and bustles ever return. Puffed sleeves and pork-pie hats are in—though worn with a difference.

I read an article recently on "The Ifs of History." After it I sat and thought of the "ifs" in my own life.

If mother had not died.

If Uncle John Campbells had been living next to us instead of Uncle John Macneill.

If I could have stayed out west.

If my application for the Lower Bedeque school which I sent in when I left P.W.C. had been accepted.

If I had been able to take an Arts course.

If Edwin Simpson had been a man I could love.

If Anne of Green Gables had been accepted as soon as it was written.

Probably any of these "ifs" would have changed my life beyond all recognition. But there are no "ifs" in predestination—in which I have come to believe absolutely. We walk our appointed ways.

In glancing over an old volume of this diary the other day to settle a question of dates, my eye caught the line, "No cat can ever be to me what Daff was." And I smiled and sighed. For I believed that when I wrote it. And yet Luck is, and always has been, from the moment I first saw him frisking across Alec's yard in the sunset light, dearer far to me than even Daffy. For Daffy, though he was beautiful and elfish and delightful, did not love me. He never wanted to be petted—he "walked by himself." Luck *loves* me. He loves to be loved. His purr when he is petted and stroked and told he is lovely, is a joy forever. If you do not pay him a compliment every day he will sit under the sideboard and look at you with heartbroken eyes. He loves to snuggle against you all night, with his dainty silver paws curved inward under his velvet breast. In short, as Marion says, he is "chummy." And not his best friend could ever call Daff chummy.

But he was an old duck of a cat for all that. I wonder, does he ever haunt Leaskdale manse. I wonder if, on some moonlight summer night, a gray cat rises from his grave in the corner of the lawn and creeps into the old white-brick house—to look for his cushion in the parlor—or the chair in the sewing room—or the puff on the boys' bed—or perhaps for the old welcome and the old laughter—for Frede— for me—or for two laughing-eyed roguish little lads. But the little gray ghost will find none of them—and so I think he will be glad to creep back to his sleep in the vine-hung corner. Not even a cat would care to haunt so changed a world.

Oh Frede, Frede! Daffy had for me one charm Luck can never have—he was beloved by you.

Something that was said at play practice the other night—a casual jest bandied about among the players—about some one who had "slept in the bush," stirred up an old memory of the first and only time I ever slept in the woods—in reality, though I have done it a thousand summer nights in imagination.

"Daffy"

It was soon after I went to Bideford. One golden Sunday afternoon in September, I was alone in the parsonage and I went for a walk to a maple grove in Mr. Williams' field. It was a lovely spot and the day was warm. I sat me down in a ferny hollow, cupped by the roots of some flaming maples. I was drowsy, having been out late for two nights. I pillowed myself on the spicy ferns—and fell asleep. I slept for two hours and wakened only when the late afternoon began to hold an autumnal chill. I wonder what anyone would have thought if he or she had come upon me there. I daresay it would have been a pretty picture enough. I remember I wore a pretty beflowered challis blouse and I was—not ugly—myself then and I somehow like to remember my sleeping there, like a wood nymph or a dryad on my couch of fern under the crimson maples waking, as one woke then, to laughter and high hope and tempting ambition. Ah me, I waken so sadly and heavily now. And if I ever dared to fall on sleep in a September wood—God help the rheumatism....

Sunday, Nov. 26, 1933
The Manse, Norval
Sometimes I almost wish that I had never gone out west in 1930 and met Laura again. Had I not done so there would not have been that strange resurrection and renewal of a love that had been overlaid by the years and I would not suffer as I do over her death.

But no—those two weeks with Laura were worth any after pain. There was about them something strange—haunting—*fated*. They "cast a glamor"—they were a direct gift from the gods and such a gift can never be unwished.

During recent weeks I have been reading over Laura's letters, living over again year by year and month by month our long friendship. *I have been with Laura.* As I worked she shared my

"Laura, the Matron"

task and I talked to her. When I walked down the street she was beside me. Ere I fell on sleep her head was on my pillow and we were girls again, chattering of boys and balls....*[End of Volume 8]*

"Journey's End"
Sept. 16, 1936
I wonder if it *is* "Journey's End"! I hope so—or would hope it if I dared any longer to hope anything. But I dare not. I have no courage left—nothing but a dull determination to *endure*, and make the best of things since they cannot be changed.

I have not written in this journal for nearly three years. I could not. But I can no longer live without it. I *must* have a confidant of some kind—I *must*, once more, write things out. It will help a little—it always did and I need all the help I can get, even to endure.

Luella Reid

Nearly three years! And oh my God, *what* a three years!

My last entry was on Sunday, Nov. 26, 1933. A short time before this I had had a dream which I felt sure predicted something very nasty. I was afraid, too, that it concerned Chester.

This feeling was right. On Saturday afternoon, December 2nd, Chester and Luella Reid came to me and confessed that they had been secretly married in Nov. 1932!

Before going on I may as well fill in certain hitherto unwritten records regarding Chester. Perhaps a little of the festering bitterness will leave my soul if I write it out. Hitherto I could not—I *could not*—bring myself to do it. But this old journal has been the receptacle for all my sorrows and this may as well go into it, too. The bitter record may as well be complete.

Up to the time he left St. Andrew's Chester really gave us very little anxiety of any kind. His record at St. Andrew's was more than creditable and we never

"Chester"

had any complaints of any kind about him, either in regard to studies or behavior. His reports were sprinkled with "Excellents" and "Very Goods," with such comments from the masters as, "Has done extra work in this subject"—"Thinks clearly and reasons well"—an 82 mark was "not worthy of his ability"—"Knows his work very well"—"Has unusual reasoning powers"—"Good work" etc. The only criticism was that his writing was poor. It was a just one for Chester had always been a poor writer. His early teachers were much to blame for this. Once a master wrote, "He does not do himself justice in exams." Yet he very rarely did not make a good mark. In his first year he was 4th on the Honour list. The second year he was 3rd. The third year he led his class and took a special prize in general proficiency and the Ashton medal in English. The fourth year he was second in the Honour list and while in the last year he was only 6th on the list, his marks were generally in the 80's and 90's. His conduct was invariably excellent and very good and when he left St. Andrew's this was the "character" Dr. Macdonald gave him.

"This is to certify that Chester C. Macdonald attended St. Andrew's College from Sept. 1925 to June 1930, writing on his Honour Matriculation this June.

Macdonald is a boy of excellent character and exceptional ability. Each year that he has been at St. Andrew's College his name has appeared on our prize list and he has done very well on both the Middle and Upper School examinations."

With all this I think we were justified in feeling easy regarding his college course—or at least in not entertaining any very serious apprehensions regarding it.

Chester like all boys began to take notice of the opposite sex but in this regard he did not give us a very great deal to worry over. He had a friendship for awhile with a certain Helen Watson who was a connection of some of our Union people. This affair lasted for a year or two and then ended. As she seemed like a nice, sensible girl I was rather sorry when this faded out of the picture. One summer I was a bit worried because he seemed to be hanging about a girl in Union congregation who belonged to a family very low in the social scale. Moreover, in his position as the "minister's son," this made a lot of underground gossip which made me uncomfortable. But when I spoke about it seriously to C. he gave up having anything to do with her. Then he began to chum with Luella Reid, the only daughter of Mr. and Mrs. Robert Reid of Norval church. Mrs. Reid was a very sweet woman whom I liked. Robert Reid, though one of our elders and a man of good family, was an uncouth and self-opinionated man whom I did *not* like. Luella herself did not attract me particularly. She always made me feel that she did not like me. Perhaps this was only shyness on her part, but she certainly did not have an attractive social manner. At any rate when I realized that Chester was becoming serious in the affair I was not wholly pleased because I thought he was far too young at nineteen to know what he really wanted in the way of a wife and that his choice might be very different if he waited for a few years. Luella was a year older but neither of them were old enough to decide definitely so important a question. But when Chester told me they were engaged I felt the only thing to do was accept the fact and hope for the best. At all events, it was something to know that Chester would be in little further danger of getting entangled with some girl of whom we could not approve at all. As I began to know Luella better I concluded that quite possibly things were better as they were.

Chester decided to go in for a course in mining engineering. I did not feel easy over this because I did not think he had any real fitness for it, except in his brilliance in mathematics. But I had always believed in letting young people choose their own profession—*if* they were quite sure they knew what they were doing. I was not at all sure that Chester *did* know. I strongly suspected that what attracted him to mining engineering was the "romance" of it—living in wild places, the chances for travel, and the belief that riches were easily acquired in that profession. But he was quite determined on it. I consulted several business and professional men and they all said, "Yes. The day of white collar jobs is past. There is a future in mining engineering. Let him take that course."

Chester in mining clothes

The result of C's first year I have already recorded. In so far as *that* was concerned he had only himself to blame. But he was *not* to blame for the strange conclusion of his brief experience in the Frood mine. We have never wholly solved that mystery but we have discovered that another boy was "fired" the same day who had also failed. Probably they were both dismissed simply because their names were not on the pass list. But if they were not willing to *give* this as the reason it must have been because they had no business to send them away on account of that. We have a good deal of reason to believe that Haultain, the head of the Mining course, had something to do with it but of course we will never know.

Chester repeated his first year and did well. He must have been at least third and perhaps even first in his class, below the "Honours," as I worked it out from his report. He was within a point or two of the "Honours" list. So when he went back for his second year I felt reasonably at ease, for I thought he had learned his lesson. There was no complaint from the Council at Xmas, about his attendance or anything else. But one thing worried me. From several small things, each too petty to enumerate but considerable in cumulative effect, it was evident that Haultain, the head of the Mining School, had a "down" on Chester.

After the Xmas holidays Chester returned to college. He had not then heard any word regarding the four exams he had taken at Christmas. Ewan and I went in to the city on February 3rd. He went to Knox to take Chester his laundry. Then he came back to pick me up at Simpson's. When I got into the car I naturally asked how Chester was getting on. Ewan's answer was to hand me a letter which Chester had just received that day from the Council telling him briefly that owing to his failure to attend lectures properly since Christmas he was not to be permitted to finish his year and was to leave at once!

Ewan *might* have evaded my question and kept this letter back until we got home, especially as we had with us the two MacPherson girls who had gone in with us. It would have made it a little less terrible for me. As it was, I had to drive 26 miles that bitter gray winter evening trying despairingly to conceal my agony and talk occasionally to the MacPherson's in the back seat as if nothing were wrong. They were such avid and malicious old gossips that I could not endure the thought of their suspecting my misery. I managed to control my voice but my tears I could not. They flooded my eyes and ran down my face in the concealment of my high fur collar all those interminable miles. It seemed to me I would *never* get home and get to my room, to hear the whole story from E.

Ewan had gone to Prof. Haultain but had not got much satisfaction. Haultain brusquely said that Chester had failed in all of the four exams he had taken at Xmas and had not been attending his classes and he had told the Council to send him home. It was evidently all Haultain's doing and he did not deny it.

Of course we believed Haultain. Even when Chester came home and said that he had only missed 3 classes because of headache—Chester has been subject to bad headaches all his life—and that he did not know why he had failed in all the exams as he was afraid of only one, we still believed Haultain. But since then we have found out that Haultain *lied* to Ewan—and he must have lied deliberately. This past year Chester accidentally met two of the professors on the engineering faculty at separate times and each of them asked him why he had left in the middle of the course. Chester said he had been told he failed in four exams.

"Well, you did not fail in the exam I gave," each of them said to him!

It is even possible that he did not fail in the other two. But if he did, to fail in two did not mean that he could not get his year. The exams were not finals and in any case a student is allowed two sups. But Haultain had evidently made up his mind to get C. out.

I had caught Haultain out in a lie before. One morning last November I came in to Toronto from Montreal and went up to Knox to see Chester. He was hurrying to see Haultain before class about something and having overslept a little he had not waited to shave so as not to be late for his appointment. Apart from that he was all right as I, looking him over very critically, saw. His shirt and collar were fresh and clean, though faded, and everything else was all right. But in a letter to Ewan a few days later Haultain said Chester had come in with unblacked shoes and "a filthy collar." He did not know that I had seen Chester just as he was going in and would know that this was absolutely false. I did not take the matter up with Haultain as I did not want to antagonize him to C. still further as would certainly have happened if I had let him see I knew he was telling a falsehood. But this was not as bad as his telling the Council what was not true in regard to C's exams. If we had known this at the time we would have appealed and I believe we would have won out. But perhaps it is all better as it is though I was far from seeing or feeling this at the time.

I can never forget the pain and humiliation of that week. Chester came home the next Tuesday. He felt badly enough—worse than we knew, I think, for *he* knew what we did not—his foolish secret marriage—and I did not add to his suffering by any reproaches. I had had time to check the matter over calmly and come to a conclusion.

We told Chester we would give him one more chance. I had let him go in for mining engineering against my better judgment, because of my opinion that children should be left free to choose their own careers. He had made a mess of it. Now he should try my idea. I had always believed that he would do well in law if he set his mind to it. Of course the profession of law is overcrowded—but so is every other. I told him I would back him once again if he would make an honest effort. He agreed and we set about the matter.

There was this difficulty. When C. took his Honour Matric he had had Mining Engineering in mind and had taken the studies required for that. Three that he did not take were required for entrance to the law school—British and Can. History, French Grammar and French Literature. How was he to get them? Go back to High School or study at home. He decided to do the latter. He studied hard all winter and spring at home and in June he went to Georgetown and wrote the exams with the students of the High School.

The pass lists were not out till late in August and we had weeks of suspense, although he felt sure he had passed. But I had one bad night. I was ill in bed with flu the evening the results came out in the *Telegram*.

Chester's name was not on the pass list! The despair of that night!

The next day a letter came for Chester telling him he had passed. As he was not a student at Georgetown High his name had not been included in the Georgetown lists.

The next thing was to get a lawyer to take him into his office. The new rules required a student to work in a law office for two years and then attend the law school in Osgoode Hall for three years as well as work in office. We had a hard time to get him in anywhere because the offices were already filled with boys who had applied in the spring as soon as their Matric results were known. Time after time we were disappointed. The days passed in dreary suspense. Eventually he got in the office of a young lawyer named Ernest Bogart. We knew nothing about him but he was Hobson's choice.

Chester went in the last of September and began work. In a short time we felt he liked it and was beginning to feel an interest in it. I recall bitterly one night in October when we had been in to see both boys, Stuart just starting in his medical course and Chester seeming happy and satisfied. Ewan said, "It is a long time since I felt so happy and contented as I feel tonight"!!!

It was all right in October. But all through November I was worried and uneasy. I sensed trouble somewhere and feared it was in the office but he kept assuring me that all was well there.

Then came the revelation of December 2nd! For the first time since the summer following my year in Belmont I could no longer "write things out" in my journal. And I have never been able to attempt taking it up again till now. For misfortune and trouble followed in breathless succession and these three years have been a nightmare. But I kept a sort of brief daily record in a notebook and from these entries I shall try to "write up" after a fashion these lost years. The

242

record may as well be made complete in all its bitterness and humiliation and disappointment.

Sun., Dec. 2, 1933
The Manse, Norval
This has been a day in hell. I don't know how I survived the night. It seemed to press upon and stifle me all through the endless hours. I had to go to Bible Class and church as if nothing had happened. I sat there, thinking of next Sunday when everybody would *know*. Because amid all the horror looms out one thing —this marriage must be announced in the local papers at once. It is the only way to avert a flood of scandal. There will be much in any event. I shrink as from a scorching flame from all the gossip that will roll like a torrent over the countryside. I shrink from the torment and ugliness of it all. If Ewan were not a minister it would be far far easier. But in our position it is terrible—terrible. How can we bear it?

"Luella Reid"

But if the marriage is announced with the name of the minister and the date of the marriage, people cannot say that it is a case of their "having to get married"—though I suppose some will say it anyhow. Oh, how could Chester bring this on me! But there is no use in asking such questions. No use in writing about it more than must be. The only thing to do is try to make the best of it and be thankful it is not worse. I tried to warn Chester when I sent him to St. Andrew's and then to the University of all the mistakes a young man might make. But I never warned him against marrying before he was through college because I never supposed he could be fool enough to do it. He has already broken my heart and disappointed me bitterly but this—this!!

After church we went over to Robert Reid's. Chester and Luella had told him that morning. I dreaded it more than words can say. He is not a man I like and the humiliation was bitter. But it was not quite as hard as I feared. He did not reproach us—I suppose he felt he could not. Luella is older than Chester and should have had more sense. I think he was really a little relieved that we did not blame her. He agreed with us that the marriage should be announced at once. Luella and Chester did not want this. Their idea was to get a little flat and live in Toronto and then write her friends, telling them of the marriage. Poor idiots, they don't realize what gossip would say and people believe. The only thing to do is announce it openly and prove that they have been guilty of nothing else than sickening folly and selfishness. Yes, that is the right word for it. They have both been utterly selfish. They never thought of other people's rights and feelings. Of course the air of all the colleges is full of this disgusting talk of "companionate marriage."

This all means extra expense for us and we are having it hard enough financially as it is. But that is the least of the horrible situation. It is their keeping it a secret that hurts the most. I wish I could die. Death would be a welcome relief from this intolerable anguish and worry. At times I am filled with such a terror of the future that I cannot face it.

Monday, Dec. 4, 1933

Last night I took veronal and got a little sleep. Chester went back to Toronto this morning. The day has been awful. I go around in a daze of misery but I could not work or think. Most of the time I have shut myself in my room and walked the floor. Ewan is no help. In many ways he makes it harder for me.

I had to go to Georgetown this afternoon to see Kenneth Langdon about some law matter and had to tell him of Chester. This telling people is such a bitter thing. He said, "What a tragedy! He'll never get through his law course now with this on his mind."

This is part of my worry. But I have made Luella and Chester both promise that he will go on with his course. His life must not be ruined by this. But it will make everything a hundred fold harder and is it not hard enough? When Ken said that I could hear all the world saying it. And may they not be right?

There are moments when I think I must go mad. I am like some miserable writhing worm that has been trodden on but cannot die. I have not deserved this at Chester's hand or Luella's either. It is cruel—cruel.

Tuesday, Dec. 5, 1933
The Manse, Norval

I got a little sleep last night. But the wakening! Will there ever come a time again when I will not dread the morning?

We went to Toronto. It was a dismal drive. I did some necessary shopping as in a painful dream. The whole world seemed a mocking show in which I was bound to a stake of torment. I saw Stuart and had a little talk with him which helped a little. I was so tired when I got home but I had to go to a play practice at Union Church. It was a dreadful ordeal. All those gay young people laughing and joking as *I* did once. Next practice night they will know all and how will I be able to endure it? I kept up an outward show of composure until at a late hour the practice was over but when I found myself alone with Ewan in the car I broke down and cried bitterly all the way home. Crying does no good but it is a little relief to strained nerves.

Wednesday, Dec. 6, 1933

Last night I had a fair sleep from absolute exhaustion. But today has been very dreadful. I know again what it is to be hungry for death. I passed the forenoon in spells of doing necessary work alternated with spasms of despair. In the afternoon I had to go to a W.M.S. meeting in Union. It was a hellish ordeal. The announcement of the marriage was out in the Georgetown *Herald* but I could not tell if any

244

of them had seen it. Of course I knew no reference would be made to it in my presence. I managed to maintain outward composure but at the cost of another breakdown in the evening. I have cried until I am sick. I feel so *alone*. There are no friends near to whom I can go for sympathy or advice. And the last three years have been such a nightmare of worry and disappointment. But nothing—nothing compared to this. I am "a prisoner with no hope of release."

Thursday, Dec. 7, 1933
I wonder how many more days like this I can live through.

I lay awake most of the night trying to look certain facts in the face. At three I took veronal, realizing what a day was before me and that I had to do something to make it endurable. I had a few hours of drugged unconsciousness to suffering. When I rose I wondered how I could get through the day. The Norval Institute was meeting here. It was a bright sunny morning—such a contrast to my state of feeling. I spent the forenoon preparing the house and keeping a rigid rein over myself. The women came. And some people who are not members and had never been here before. I knew why *they* came—out of cruel curiosity to see how I was taking what had happened. I met everyone with a fixed smile and came and went and talked like an automaton. The *Herald* came today with the announcement in it—and I knew everyone had seen it. Of course no one *said* anything about it but here and there were groups whispering who hushed when I came near. I knew what they were talking about. Luella came. It was the best thing for her to do I suppose—but it made it harder for me. There were times when I felt I could *not* bear it another moment—that I must scream aloud before them all. I must have looked like death.

At last—at last—it was over and they were gone. Then in the evening after this dreadful day I had to go to play practice. It was hard and bitter but not so awful as the afternoon. But there were so many passages in the play that seemed to have a devilish significance in regard to Chester's marriage. As the players spoke them I writhed, wondering if they saw the significance as I did.

Oh, it is all so cruel and unfair! I never neglected my boys—I tried to teach and train them properly as best I could—I have worked like a slave to give them every chance and a fair start in life. And now!!

> This day that seems so strange, so sad, so bitter,
> Will soon be some forgotten yesterday.

No, I am too old to find comfort in that. Such consolations are only for the young.

The whole countryside will be in a flame of gossip and sneers tonight.

Friday, Dec. 8, 1933
The Manse, Norval
I slept a little better last night. We had to go to supper at Arthur McClure's this evening. The whole evening was anguish. I did not know if they knew. They do not see the Georgetown papers. The announcement would be in the Brampton papers today but I did not know if they had yet seen it. I tried to talk—even to laugh.

One can endure a worry if there is any prospect of its end. But to live in misery for years—perhaps for all the rest of my life—never to know another moment's real peace! How can I face it?

My dear pussy, Luck, seems to *know* I am suffering. He follows me about and sits on the table or chair beside me and gazes at me with round soft eyes that seem full of sympathy. He is the only thing I have to comfort me.

Saturday, Dec. 9, 1933

I had a bad night—no sleep till late. It has been a hard hard day. Bitterly cold—the house was cold all day as it always is in cold weather. I shivered from dawn till dark—and this did not make my mental misery any easier. There was no nice mail of any kind. I had hoped Nora would get out as we had planned. She is the only creature I could talk this over with—but she could not come. At dark I could endure no longer. I walked the floor and cried. I feel that I *cannot* bear this. And how can I bear to go to church tomorrow? If there had been a death in my family I could stay home. But *this* must be braved out as if it didn't exist. To stay home—to show misery—might make people think things are even worse than they are. If only tomorrow were over!

Sunday, Dec. 10, 1933
The Manse, Norval

It *is* over. But such a day exacts the toll of years.

I slept a little last night. Nora came this morning and a long talk with her gave me a little of the courage I needed so badly. I taught my class and it was torture. And the church service was a hideous ordeal. I would rather die than endure the like again. There were outsiders there—come to see and gloat, I know.

Ewan preached well but it was very hard for him, too. In the evening we went to the Glen House. The Barracloughs are the only people in the congregation we can talk to about this. It helped a little. But nothing can help much or long. While the anguish is momentarily dulled one feels it is still there and will devour again when the drug wears off. As soon as I got home the old despair surged over me again.

Monday, Dec. 11, 1933

This has been the most hideous day of my life. Last night just as we went to bed we discovered that the marriage notice in the Brampton paper gave the date as November of *this* year.

I had written out the notice plainly and when Ewan handed it in he told them he wanted it printed *exactly as it was written*. In spite of this some unutterable fool had changed 1932 to 1933.

Coming on top of a day of miserable strain like yesterday I could not endure it and broke down. Of course we can have it corrected. But people will see the first notice who will never hear of the correction and when the baby is born in May they will think it was a forced marriage! I did not sleep at all and in the morning I simply could *not* get up. I stayed in bed and gave myself up to despair. Chills shook my body. I could not eat. A letter came from Stell, very depressing in its tenor. Of course she did not know what had happened but her growls seemed the last straw. I could not see a ray of light and I wished for death.

Tuesday, Dec. 12, 1933
We had no veronal in the house so yesterday Ewan went and got some. I took a tablet and slept blessedly. As a result I felt calmer and more composed today—fortunately, as I had to go to a W.M.S. It was very difficult. The hardest thing in all this is the false position it puts us in. We can't talk of it or claim exemption from anything because of it. We just have to go on as if nothing had happened when we know everyone is talking of it. We know when we go anywhere everyone is thinking of it and *nobody* speaks of it.

I went to play practice tonight but only five were there and it was a miserable affair. I was too hopeless to care to try to pull them into shape. All heart has gone out of me.

When Chester was born I was so happy! And now! Well, I am not the first nor will I be the last. But what comfort is there in that? "Never morning wore to evening but some heart did break," is true but does not help the pain any.

Wednesday, Dec. 13, 1933
I had a fair sleep last night. But the awakening is always so terrible. Charlotte MacPherson and I had to make out the lists for the Sunday School concert gifts today. Then we went to Brampton to see *The Sign of The Cross*. We could not get out of going as it was a preview for ministers and we had promised to go. I could find no enjoyment in it. Afterwards we went to Georgetown Presbyterian church to the "fowl supper." We did not stay for the concert—could not. We came home as soon as we had choked down a little of the supper. It was hard to meet and talk with all those gay happy people and hide the gnawing worry and humiliation underneath. If only I need not go anywhere—see anybody—talk to anybody! If I could creep into some dark corner and hide until the pain had become endurable!

Thursday, Dec. 14, 1933
The Manse, Norval
I rose at 6.30 this damp bitter cold morning and Ewan took me and Charlotte MacPherson into Toronto to buy the gifts for the S.S. tree. This has been put on me every year since I came and this could be no exception. It is a task I have always disliked and it was more distasteful than ever today amid all those gay crowds. Then came a cold dispiriting drive home. Yet getting home cheered me a little temporarily. I was tired and cold and hungry and there was warmth and food and rest—and Luck's purr. A parcel of books from Mr. McClelland, too. For the first time since that dreadful Saturday I could read a little this evening....

Friday, Dec. 15, 1933
This has been a dismal day of sleet and fog and gloom. Ewan had to be away and there is no nice mail. I worked doggedly all day—one forgets a little when one works. An old village gossip calling made a reference to Chester's marriage! It cut me like a burning whip. I *can't* talk of it to people. They would like me

better—feel more sympathy with me if I could, I suppose. But I *cannot*. It hurts too horribly.

Sunday, Dec. 17, 1933
The Manse, Norval
Another dark and gloomy day. Chester came home and he and Luella sat in my pew at church. I held my head high and hid my feelings but it was a bitter ordeal. And as yet I can only feel bitterly towards them. I cannot yet forgive them the deception—the humiliation.

Luella came over from church and was here for supper. I talked to them both very seriously and they seemed both very sorry for what they had done and seemed to realize a little of what they had made us suffer. Nothing is settled yet as to the future but it soon must be.

This is our third hideous Sunday but the worst is over now. I don't know how I have lived through it. If Ewan were anything but a minister it would not have been anything like as hard.

Monday, Dec. 18, 1933
I had a letter from Myrtle today—a comforting one. I had written and told her. That is one of the bitter things about this—my friends have to be told and it is so hard to tell them. It will drag on for months—every week or so a letter will have to be written and the whole miserable story repeated. At every facet of my life this affair confronts and tortures me.

Thank heaven, I can read again. I am reading Grote's *History of Greece* and this evening I went back 2400 years—I shared the Retreat of the Ten Thousand and was present at the death of Socrates. It minimized my tragedy in perspective. But now that another day has been got through I am so terribly, so ghastly *tired*. Will I ever feel rested again?

Wednesday, Dec. 20, 1933
A dark day with sleet and snow. Robert Reid called about the Sunday School concert and seemed quite chipper and cheerful. He evidently does not feel this very deeply. I went over to the church and helped decorate the Xmas tree. The concert came off tonight. I had dreaded it but it was bearable. I think I am beginning to be a little numb.

Thursday, Dec. 21, 1933
The mockery of Christmas cards is beginning. Every one hurts me. I went down to the post office tonight for the evening mail—the first time I have had the courage to go down since December 3rd. It was a dark lonely walk down the street and I felt like an exile. I knew as I came out of the office that the loafers would talk about me and about my son.

Tuesday, Dec. 22, 1933
Last night I crawled into bed at eight just to escape from things. But I slept little all night. Was miserable with the nervous unrest that has tortured me so many

nights of late years. Chester and Stuart came home on the bus. They looked well as they came up the street together, but that could not give me the old thrill of pleasure. It was the first time I could not be glad to see *both* of them come home for Christmas. Christmas! What kind of Christmas can we have this year? But when I was in bed, tired and dispirited, dear Stuart came in and made toast and brought it up to me. It was a little comfort—one sweetening drop in this cup of bitterness and humiliation I am being forced to swallow.

Saturday, Dec. 23, 1933
The Manse, Norval
It is bitter to waken on these dark dreary mornings. We put up the Christmas tree today and I did up my presents without any heart or joy in it. Our old pleasant Christmases are gone forever.

I read *Poor Splendid Wings* tonight—a biography of the Rossettis and their circle. What mistakes mortals make! And how they suffer! It is better not to have wings. If you do not fly you never suffer the agonies of having to crawl, bruised and beaten, after flying.

Sunday, Dec. 24, 1933
The fourth hard Sunday—a dark dismal day—is over. Will they ever grow easier? I suppose so—everything does. If things would just get *bearable*!

Luella was here to tea and she and Chester and I had a long talk. We have decided that the best thing for them to do is to rent a little flat in Toronto and live there till the baby is born....

Monday, Dec. 25, 1933
The bitterest and most unhappy Christmas I ever spent is over. I had Luella here and tried to be pleasant but how my heart ached. I thought every morsel of dinner would choke me.

After dinner Ewan and I had to call on Mr. and Mrs. MacKinnon, the United minister and his wife, who were celebrating their golden wedding today. We made the proper gestures and came away, knowing that as soon as we were gone the other callers would be mouthing over our misfortune. Then I called at the MacPhersons. But such calls are dreadful now because there is one thing I cannot talk of and yet everyone is thinking of it.

Tuesday, Dec. 26, 1933
This cold and snowy evening we went to supper at the Glen House and forgot our situation for a little while. We can talk things over with the Barracloughs because they understand and sympathize. But I had another anxiety and bitterness tonight of which I could talk to nobody and which seemed unbearable on top of all else.

Thursday, Dec. 28, 1933
We have had two bitterly cold days. The house was so cold I really suffered from it. And I was so broken-hearted and worried I could not find relief in work.

Friday, Dec. 29, 1933
The Manse, Norval
Another horrible day. It was 22 below zero this morning—the coldest night for 19 years according to *The Globe*. The house was like a barn and my heart ached until I could have welcomed death. But I was able to work a little and for the first time since December second I have been able to escape from reality into a world of fancy and come back with some strength and composure obtained there, which helped me through the day, despite a gushing letter from Isobel to her "beloved." Such a letter at such a time is almost unbearable. I don't want to hate her—I don't want to hate anybody—but when she torments me so in my misery how can I help it? There are moments when I feel I hate everyone. But when I can get into my dream-world I forget it—there is no hatred there—and when I come back to reality it seems a little less bitter and hatred vanishes....

1934

Monday, Jan. 1, 1934

At the stroke of 12 last night Stuart came in and wished me a happy New Year. It sounded like mockery though I loved his doing it. It must be the most unhappy New Year I have ever had. And I can see no prospect of ever being happy again. I can see nothing but worry and constant dread in all the years to come. But I have been unhappy for so long that I have ceased to rebel against *that*. All I ask is enough relief from pain to be able to work. It is so dreadful to begin some little task and then drop it from my trembling hands because a flood of wretchedness overwhelms me.

But I have lived through one day of 1934. So I suppose I can live through them all one by one.

I winced when Stuart came in to wish me a Happy New Year. Because I knew that it could only be a miserable one. But if I had dreamed of the horror and misery it held for me, beyond what I had foreseen! Could I have borne it? No, not in prospect. I should have gone mad. 1934 was to be the most hellish year of my whole life without any exception, not even that terrible 1919. Everything about that winter of 1934 was hard and it was not made easier by the roads and weather. It was as far as weather goes one of those winters that are dated from. It was the coldest winter in 35 years—week after week of *wicked* cold. And the roads were like nothing I had ever experienced. Ice—two or three feet deep—over all the concession roads. And we had to be out on them somewhere almost every night. The strain of driving on them was so great that I do not wonder it proved too much for Ewan. It seemed to me again and again that everything conspired to make our intolerable situation harder.

Monday, Jan. 2, 1934
The Manse, Norval

Chester went back this morning and Stuart on the night bus. So we are all alone again. But I am beginning to get a grip on myself at last—I am able once more to set my teeth and say "I will see this through—and do what is right and best as far as I can see it—no matter how hard it is."

Tonight I went to the play practice at Union. It was hard. One of the cast acted the clown as usual and kept all the others in shrieks and giggles most of the time. I felt they simply wasted the evening as far as getting the play up was concerned. They are really a nice bunch of young people. I like them all. But they need to be pulled up with a round turn for all that and I can't do it. I can't afford to antagonize them and in any case just now I am too spiritless to call them to order. I've just no heart for it. I seem to see everything through a gray drizzle.

As usual, owing to all this, it was past eleven when the practice was over. We came home by the Glen road and had a very nasty experience with the car turning around on glare ice and coming to a standstill in such a position that it seemed the slightest movement would send it into a very deep and steep ditch. After a long time a truck came along and with the driver's assistance we got on the road again and at last blessedly home to bed and a good read. I find myself able to read again and in the hour's oblivion from pain thus gained there is a chance for torn nerves and bruised feelings to heal.

Wednesday, Jan. 3, 1934
After such an evening as last I am always miserably tired the next day. Today was snowy and cold. I made cake and sandwiches, for I had the Old Tyme practice here. We had a good practice—how I would have enjoyed it if it had not been for my sore heart.

Saturday, Jan. 6, 1934
This mild gray day Ewan took Luella and me into Toronto and I got Chester and Laura Aylsworth and we went house-hunting. I have decided to rent a small flat for Chester and Luella, put some necessary furniture in it and make them a sufficient allowance to live on. I can't as things are just now give them very much.

It was a very hard day. We went to place after place that was advertised. Some were hopeless. Some were too expensive. At last we found a three room flat on the upper floor of a respectable place on Shaw Street. I think it will be quite comfortable when it is fixed up. Then we had tea at Laura's. I had been feeling exhausted—"You look dreadfully tired, mother," Chester said remorsefully—and it heartened me up a little. But when I got home at nine my nerves that had seemed partly skinned over were raw again. I shall not sleep tonight—I am too tired—and too unhappy. My life seems to be uprooted and withering. Yet when I came in the beautiful curves of a contented pussy cat basking on a radiator rested me a little.

Sunday, Jan. 7, 1934
The Manse, Norval, Ont.
A gray *starving* sort of day. As usual church and Bible Class. The torment of it is growing bearable. I do not feel quite such a target for gossip and surmise. One *feels* when these things slacken.

Monday, Jan. 8, 1934
I went into Toronto today on business. Saw Mr. McClelland. I thought he looked old and tired. Then I went to Nora's. Ned was home and *he* looked old and tired. Or is it that *I* felt so old and tired that everybody seemed so. Nora and I went to the Can. Lit. Club as long before this wretchedness came I had promised to give them a talk tonight. As I sat waiting my turn my heart went like a trip-hammer. I never felt like that before a speech in my life. It seemed to me I could *not* get up and talk there. But I did.

Wednesday, Jan. 10, 1934
I managed to sleep a little last night but have a cold. Went to W.M.S. at a Union Home. It was hard—as everything is hard now. I have always enjoyed the Union Missionary meetings but today I was thankful when it was over. In the evening I went to Old Tyme play practice. Another day lived through.

Thursday, Jan. 11, 1934
Slept poorly. This morning Luella and I went to Toronto and I bought enough furniture for their little flat. Once I dreamed of furnishing Chester's house for him when he should marry and start home-making. I meant to do that much for him by way of a wedding present. I did not think it would be like *this*....

Monday, Jan. 15, 1934
Today I began work on a sequel to *Silver Bush*. I am beginning to get a grip on myself at last. I must arrange my life, however bitterly, with this new set of facts. Since we can't escape life but must live on till our time comes the only thing to do is to accept it and endeavor to make it bearable.

Tuesday, Jan. 16, 1934
Today I wrote a little poem "The Night." And as always it was an escape. While I was writing it I was free from pain—free from fear. But I had to go to Union play practice tonight and it was hard for my nerves were terrible and the whole evening seemed one of torment. But life is all torment now. There are just shades of difference in its intensity, that is all.

Saturday, Jan. 20, 1934
On Thursday I had the W.M.S. Executive meet here. I suppose I caught a relapse of cold Wednesday night for I was ill all day with chills and sore throat. I kept

Frede under trees [at Silver Bush]

up—talked—helped plan the programme—and then when they went I crept off to bed where I had to stay till today.

I had a letter from Chester Thursday. He and Luella seem quite happy now they are away from it all. It is I who am left to bear the brunt of heartache and gossip. Well, I do not wish them to be miserable. There is enough pain in the world. But I wish I had something to help me bear mine.

Last night I had a fair sleep and got up today. I cannot bear staying in bed. My mind preys on itself and my thoughts and fears torture me. When I can get up and do some work it makes things bearable.

Tuesday, Jan. 23, 1934

I felt better today and able to go to the W.M.S. at MacPhersons'. But I was glad when practice was called off tonight because of the illness of some of the cast. Not that I was glad they were ill!! I have spent the evening in bed reading. I am thankful I *can* read again and forget for a little while.

Thurs., Jan. 25, 1934

It is fifteen years today since Frede died. If I could talk my trouble over with her I think I could face it, perhaps as gallantly as I used to face things long ago. Well, perhaps I shall meet her again in the dawn of some eternal day and all the bitterness of these several years will be forgotten. If I could have died, too, that awful morning at Macdonald, what anguish I would have been spared.

Sunday, Feb. 4, 1934

This is a cold bleak night—such a night as long ago in Leaskdale manse I liked to slip into their room to see if my little boys were tucked snug and warm in bed.

It has been a hard dreary week of intense bitter cold. The days in this sad, laughterless house have been nothing but ghosts. Struggle as I will—and do—I cannot feel anything but sad and heartbroken.

There were two play practices and the roads were dreadful. Covered with solid ice—every minute one feared the car would slide into the ditch. It was very hard on nerves that were already worn almost to breaking point. Thanks be, the Thursday night one was the last for the Union play. I shall be so relieved when it is over.

Sunday, Feb. 11, 1934

This has been another bad week. The cold has been almost unendurable. We could hardly keep warm even in bed.

We had the dress rehearsal of the play in the hall Tuesday night. Everyone was cold and I felt absolutely discouraged over the result. But dress rehearsals are usually discouraging.

Wednesday night Ewan and I had a terrible experience. We went in to Toronto in the morning, attended to business and went up to have supper with Chester and Luella in their little flat. Then we started on what proved a ghastly drive home. Our clutch began to misbehave. We called at a garage and the mechanic said he had fixed it so that we could get home. But half way between Cooksville and

Brampton—about the worst spot it could have happened—it broke down. By this time it was snowing thickly and bitterly cold—28 below zero. Ewan had to walk half a mile to a house to telephone while I sat in the car and got colder every minute. Ewan came back, nearly frozen, and we sat there and waited for the towing car. Every minute seemed an hour. Finally we were towed into Brampton and got a taxi to take us home. We arrived at twelve, half dead. I got warm drinks and hot water bottles and got into bed, too exhausted to think of anything but getting warm. I expected to be ill after such an exposure but I was none the worse. It was Ewan who suffered—he has had a bad bronchial cold ever since.

Thursday morning it was 30 below and remained at 30 until mid-afternoon when it began to grow colder. Thursday night was the night set for our play and I had been hoping to get it off my shoulders at last. The night was fine and brilliantly moonlit but it was the coldest night Ontario has experienced in 85 years. We had to call the play off. Not a soul would have come out. Cars would have frozen up. So after it was settled I went to bed and had a *lovely* sleep—the first real good sleep for weeks.

Today our water pipes were frozen—something that has never happened before. We had to melt snow for use. Yesterday was bitter cold in the morning but by night had moderated. Such a relief! Our pipes started to thaw out by tea time. I lit a fire in the parlor and spent the evening there. I had a letter from Mr. Macmillan to read and as I read it life seemed to regain a little of its old flavor. He writes such delightful letters. I read it over four times to get every bit of its savour, like a dog polishing up a plate. That's not a poetic simile but it exactly expresses my feelings. Then I studied a new seed catalogue and found surcease of pain in thinking about my garden. After all, spring must come even in my tortured life....

Sunday, Feb. 18, 1934
Another dreary week—but are not all my weeks dreary this winter? I have not felt well. I cough a great deal and sleep poorly and my head has that queer tight feeling so much of the time. It has been very cold, too—15 below zero almost every night. We had two play practices; but our play is certainly under a jinx. We have had to postpone it again because two of our cast are down with mumps. It is disheartening. I do so want to get it over and off my harassed mind.

One of the bitter things about going anywhere now is that people who used to ask me, "how are *the boys* getting on?" now ask only about Stuart. I am thankful they do *not* ask about Chester and yet the very fact that they do not—or cannot—hurts me.

Yet life has had, even this dreary week, a moment or two of sweetness. Tuesday I wrote a poem and was happy while I wrote it. Ideas are beginning to come to me again. My mind, so long numbed by pain and humiliation, seems to be waking up. Wednesday was Valentine's day and Stuart sent me such a nice valentine. He never forgets. And I am beginning to be able to take pleasure again in Lucky's beautiful curves and stripes. He is stretched on my bed as I write, a purring object of charm and grace.

And then last night after sunset—for a wonder there had been a clear sunset—I looked out of the front door glass on going upstairs and saw a thin silvery green ky behind the snowy winter pines on the west-branch hill. Instantly the old nchantment of life returned for a moment. It was as if some ancient spell had ıeen worked whereby I escaped through some door of dreams to far secret mead-ıws by rivers where there was peace and among blue hills where there were parkling fountains. It lasted only a moment—but I seemed, as always, to get trength from it. Life has not seemed so bleak and bitter today.

'unday, Feb. 25, 1934
'he Manse, Norval

n a letter from Myrtle this week she told me the fact of C's marriage was all over 'avendish now, someone in Toronto having written it to someone in Charlotte-own. Of course I knew it was only a question of time until this happened but I vrithe as I think of the gossip it will occasion and how it will be mouthed over xultantly by certain people who are no friends of mine. This is bitter—but after ll it is the least of the trouble.

Albert of Belgium is dead. He was "the" hero of the Great War. One can never orget *Punch*'s immortal cartoon of the Kaiser sneering at Albert, "You have lost ll." "Not my soul," replies Albert.

Peace to his ashes.

Bacon says somewhere, "To die is as natural as to live." Of course. Death vould never have become the thing of horror it is considered if it had not been for he sadistic imaginations of fanatics and mad theologians.

It is a rather strange thing that I have never in all my life had any fear of death ıs death. I feared—still fear—the physical suffering that may precede death but ıothing else. While life still ran like a pleasant golden river for me I did not like he thought of death because it seemed to me a sad thing to *stop living*—to leave his beautiful world—to go away from faces beloved and scenes known.

I remember the first time that the thought of death presented itself to me as a 'omforting one. It was one night in one of those dreary years after Grandfather's leath when I was beginning to find life sad and hopeless. I had come home alone n the dark of a summer night from some meeting in the church—I felt friendless ınd forlorn—youth was passing—there seemed nothing before me but dreary ınloved years of toil and frustration. As I opened and closed the old gate leading rom the barn yard into the green before the house I leaned against it for a few noments before going in to the darkened house to face emptiness.

Above me the old stars of a summer night blazed down. The air was full of faint urf-thunder on the faraway dunes. A little night-wind brushed my face like the :iss of a ghost. And with it came the thought, "But this cannot go on *forever*. ıome day there will be an end—some day death will save me."

And at once the thought of death became a *comforting* one. Death was no foe—leath was a kind and friendly thing. I went in calmly—even happily. I have never orgotten that moment.

The early part of this week was a little milder but it is cold again. This morn-ng it was 20 below. Tonight a bitter gray wind is blowing up from the river, and omehow I have been thinking of Park Corner—of the old orchard there with the ıpple bloom in full snow—of the old bridge where we walked with the murmur of the sea in our ears—of the old grove with the sun dappling the ferns—of Aunt Annie's supper table—of Frede's laughter—can I not hear her laughter still?

Renan in one of his books says:—"If, even as we are, we could once a year at odd moments see the loved ones we have lost long enough to exchange a few words of greeting, death would be no longer death."

True, oh, true!

Sunday, Mar. 11, 1934
The Manse, Norval
I have had a bad cold and have been unable to write. Had to have another of those abominable play practices this week. It has kept cold and the soft water cistern has frozen up. This is a serious thing when our well water is so very hard. But spring can't be very far off now.

After service this afternoon Ewan and I drove in to have supper with Chester and Luella. The little flat is quite cosy and I would almost have enjoyed the evening had I been alone. But Ewan always finds it impossible to adapt himself gracefully to any situation he finds uncomfortable. So I was rather glad when we came away. Everything is so different from what I had once dreamed it would be when I went to visit Chester in his own home.

Sunday, Mar. 18, 1934
The Manse, Norval
Another of the nightmare weeks of which this winter seems full. It has been so bitterly cold and the house has been cold. I wish drearily—for my wishes have lost all their color and brilliancy—that I could hie me away to some far fair land where it is always summer.

Then I was sick all the week with a cold so bad I think it was flu. We had a final(?) play practice on Tuesday night, driving to it through an eerie snow-blanketed land and I spent Wednesday in bed. Thursday I stayed in bed till noon, then got up and in the evening went to the Parish Hall where at long last we put that play on. And it was a wow. We had a packed house and all the cast did well. As for me, standing behind the screen, prompting, I was so sick there were moments I thought I could not stand there another moment, but I stuck it out, came home utterly exhausted and stayed in bed all day Friday. I could not lift my head but I thanked God for a world with pines in it. When I looked out on the pines on the hill I took courage.

I am better today but have a very gray feeling. Life seems ugly and empty. There has not been one pleasant thing this week to balance the cold and illness and worry.

I was very thankful that the play was over at last for it had been even harder work than usual to get it up. Yet if I had known that night that it was the last play I would ever train the Union Dramatic Club in I would have been very sad. In spite of all the difficulties I have enjoyed my work among those young people and some of them have rewarded my efforts. Jack Cook in especial is a wonderful actor. He really should be on the stage. Instead, he will be a farmer and, I suspect, an indifferent one. It is a shame to see such talent wasted. What a world of square pegs in round holes it is!

Thursday, Mar. 29, 1934
These past ten days have generally been cold or stormy, filled with a lot of routine duties. I find it hard to put any heart in them. But yesternight, after enduring a chilly house all day I hied me to bed with a new book—Benson's *Brontë*—and forgot the world and its worries and heartbreaks for a few hours. The book is very fascinating. But he is too hard on Charlotte and his idea of Branwell's helping Emily to write *Wuthering Heights* is simply silly. What a fascination that strange family exercise on the world! Every year fresh books, filled with fresh guesses about them, pour from the press. How furious they would have been had they dreamed how every action and motive of their lives would be thus raked over and held up to the world, with all sorts of absurd interpretations and suppositions.

Saturday, Mar. 31, 1934
Today *at last* I managed to begin work on my second *Pat* book. This winter so far has been very barren from a literary point of view. I could not get down to writing, try as I would, and even yet I have no heart in it. But it will be an escape.

Friday, April 6, 1934
On Wednesday night the Old Tyme concert came off with its usual acclaim. I am thankful it is over. I am so weary of going out to practices. Yesterday I was not only very tired but quite ill with stomach and bowel trouble. However I went to Toronto with the Barracloughs because we had planned it. The day seemed endless and I was so exhausted I did not see how I could endure the drive home. When I got here it was so lovely to get into my own delightful bed and *rest*. Oh, night is very welcome to me now. And there was a joyful pussy purring out his rapture over my return beside me. What a comfort a nice cat is! I wonder if all the spirits of all the pussy folk I have loved will meet me with purrs of gladness at the pearly gates. Ah, I am afraid they sleep forever, those little ghosts of gray and white and black that pad softly through the years. But I hope there will be cats in whatever galaxy my future incarnations may lie.
    Are there, I wonder, actually cats purring at this moment in some planet circling round Sirius?

Saturday, April 7, 1934
I had a good sleep last night and was able to write today. The robins are strutting all about the manse and church grounds these days—big, sleek fellows winking impudent eyes at us. I am glad I can find a little pleasure in them—it helps.

Sunday, April 8, 1934
Again I slept well. After service this afternoon Ewan and I went in to have supper with Chester and Luella. They seem happy and Chester certainly seems interested in his work. Had I been alone with them I would have enjoyed the evening but I felt the strain of Ewan's attitude. He is not unforgiving but he does not feel at home in their company just now.
    The drive home was hard on racked nerves. The Sunday night traffic is always heavy and those endless glaring lights were abominable. I longed for the old days

when we drove along in the soft darkness behind a nice horse. But then, if we had had to drive a horse we would not have been able to go into Toronto and out again tonight at all.

Something in Bible Class today brought up the question "What is Sin?" I tried to get the boys to define sin in a modern way but could not extract much. If they had an idea they could not put it into words. One boy produced the old catechism answer: "Sin is any transgression of or want of conformity with the law of God."

Very good—very true—*if* we knew exactly or even approximately what the "law of God" really is. What some theologians *say* the law of God is is a very different matter.

My own definition of sin is, "Sin is anything that does any harm, physical, mental, spiritual, to ourselves or anybody else."

It is not an elastic definition, but I think it is a reasonable and understandable one.

Monday, April 9, 1934
The Manse, Norval
I suppose I was overtired last night after the long drive and the dazzling lights for I had a very bad night of nervous sleeplessness. The rats of worry gnawed me without surcease. All my problems snarled around me like wolves. But as soon as I got up and went to work I felt better. In the afternoon I went to a meeting of the Travel Club at Brampton and had such a nice time that it cheered me up and I came home feeling like a different person.

Tuesday, April 10, 1934
New worries seem to pop up as soon as the old ones are conquered. Ewan has not been feeling quite well of late—never has seemed so since that night in the winter when we were stuck on the road that bitter night coming from Toronto. I thought he was run down and urged him to see a doctor. He did but instead of going to our own regular doctor, Dr. Paul of Georgetown, he went to see Dr. Williams. Why, I cannot say. He described his symptoms to Williams who coolly told him they were symptoms of a serious heart condition and, *if this were so* he might "go out like a candle any moment."

I cannot understand how a doctor could say such a thing to a patient of whom he knew nothing and when he had not made any kind of an examination. And even if he were sure it was true he had no business whatever to tell Ewan so. He should have come to me and told it.

I am worried—not because I think there is really anything wrong with Ewan's heart—it has always been a little weaker than normal and is slightly enlarged but I think the symptoms of which Ewan has been complaining are simply due to his nerves. He has had the same ones often all our life together. But I *am* worried as to the effect of Williams' statements on Ewan's mind. He is always very easily alarmed about himself and thinks every trifle serious. Dr. Williams did tell him to go into Toronto and have a tracing made of his heart action which would show the truth but to get Ewan to go is a different matter. He does not seem to be worrying over it yet and I hope he will not.

Wednesday, April 11, 1934
The Manse, Norval
I spent most of the day in bed ill with a bad cold and feeling discouraged. I lay there and looked out of the window on a dreary world of rain and snow. By times I read *Wuthering Heights*, which was a very poor choice for such a day and such an illness. There is not one agreeable character in the book—no one who seems really sane. Yet it has a wild, indescribable, inescapable charm....

Friday, April 13, 1934
This has been a bad bad day. I was not well. The world was all a cold gray. A bitter east wind blew and the trees cringed before it. My nerves were in a dreadful condition. In the evening I had to go to another play practice in Union church because we have been asked to put the play on in Glen Williams. I felt really dreadful coming home—as if I hated everybody and everything. I am *not* this sort of a person—it is only the result of being half ill and worried on a dozen counts. I wish I could get away for a complete rest and change for a week or two. My ragged nerves might heal up and I could get a grip on myself again.

Monday, April 16, 1934
This was another rainy day but cleared in the evening. After several days of misery my cold is better and consequently my nerves. We had a play practice in the Glen which was the usual nightmare but after it was over we went up to the Glen House and had a refreshing visit. What would we do without the Barracloughs? They have to go to England again this summer. I am sick with fear that they may decide to stay.

Tuesday, April 17, 1934
Tonight we put the play on in the Glen Hall. It was hot and stuffy behind the scenes and as I am not yet quite over my cold I spent a wretched evening. But the play went well and we had a good audience.

Wednesday, April 18, 1934
The Manse, Norval
We began housecleaning today by doing the garret. I am tired—but I love housecleaning the garret—I love being up there. I have often toyed with the idea of fixing up a little writing room there by the dormer window that looks out on the river and the west branch hill. But it wouldn't do. It is too hot in summer and too cold in winter. I could use it only a month or so in spring and fall.

In the evening we went with the Barracloughs to see *Little Women*. It was good—Katherine Hepburn made a fair Jo. And at last I understand why "Jo" could love Professor Bhaer. The P.B. of the film was not the bearded Santa Claus of the illustration in my book but a very delightful person with whom any girl might fall in love.

Friday, April 20, 1934
Ewan and I went to Toronto today and had a very pleasant time though it was spoiled for me by seeing a poor cat who had probably been loping happily home-

ward after a night of adventure or love and had been caught by a car and left a thing of horror to affront the spring morning. I had at last persuaded E. to have a graph made of his heart motion, so while he was at the hospital I went up and had a good pi-jaw with Nora. I always find when I am with Nora that I have not forgotten how to talk—as I sometimes think I have when I go for days without hearing or uttering a word of real conversation. And we both always feel better after a gab-fest—we can give each other rest. But apart from this the day was tiring and as always I breathed a sigh of relief when we were out of the city at last where there were wide gray hills, tree-misted, all around us.

Saturday, April 28, 1934
Had a very interesting letter today from a Mohammedan girl in Hyderabad, India, who has read and loved my books. She writes in excellent English with a quite modern outlook but the names of herself and her sisters sound like something out of the Arabian nights. Her father is evidently very liberal in his views for he does not make her wear the veil *at home* and she has been allowed to take the matric exams to Cambridge University. So even in India the day is breaking for women.

Another letter from a correspondent in Hollywood tells me that *Green Gables* is to be made into a talking picture. Page has got another large sum for the talking rights of which of course I can't get a cent. It *is* a shame. But it is my own fault, if that is any comfort. Mitzi Green is spoken of as "Anne." I know nothing of her—but any girl who would permit herself to be called Mitzi—!!

Monday, April 30, 1934
The Manse, Norval, Ont.
Today I opened all the windows to let in the spring. It was a lovely day—really, our first wholly decent day since last October. The winter is on record as having been the coldest for 84 years.

My cold and cough still hang on but I got the garden ploughed today and so hope soon to have the comfort of gardening again. I need some comfort for my life is full of several discouraging things, all too petty to mention but potent for misery. A black fly is a very tiny thing—but a cloud of black flies!!!

Somehow or other the terrible winter had been lived through. I began feebly to hope that the worst was over and that I might have a summer of comparative peace and freedom from worry and humiliation. I needed it, for I was badly run down after such a winter. If I had known what was before me for the next twelve months—well, we do not know the future and so we can struggle on.

I should have known the days were hastening to something unbearable—I had my warnings. One night in April I had a nightmare—something I rarely have. It was horrible beyond description. I *was alone in the universe*. Not another living creature but myself existed. The agony of it cannot be put into words. Ever since that night I have known exactly what a lost soul would feel in the endless starless night of eternity. I awoke, sobbing wildly, "I cannot bear it—I cannot bear it."

A few nights earlier I had had, not another nightmare but one of my clear-cut dreams. Ewan and I were in the car driving over a terribly rough road. There was quite a stretch of it in front but beyond that a clear road to the horizon. In the back seat a man was sitting, a stranger seemingly, a small dark man who complained of the roughness of the road. "But see," I said comfortingly, "when we are over it the rest of the road is clear and free."

I wakened, knowing that it was a warning but of what I could not see. Somehow I never thought of Ewan's malady. This was strange because, in all the years since his last light attack in the spring of 1927 I had never felt really easy concerning it. There was always the haunting fear in the background.

But I *hoped* he would never have any more. I knew that, though in his earlier years the attacks were brought on by some slight worry or depression, I also knew that the long stretch from 1919 to 1927 was the result of a psychical disturbance corresponding to the menopause in women. And that being over I let myself hope that he would be exempt from further attacks of melancholia, since the first one of all came about the time of his awakening sex life.

And then, on May 4, as suddenly as in that hideous spring of 1919, the lurking horror pounced again. Ewan had been secretly worrying over his heart and this was the result.

Friday, May 4, 1934

I am sick with horror tonight. Waking early this morning I missed Ewan and found him in the spare room. He had had a "nightmare" and could not sleep. My heart stood still. And when, during the forenoon, he came in from the garden and said he was "too weak" to do any work just exactly as in 1919—I went up to my room and cried aloud in despair, "Must I go through *that* again?"

Yesterday Ewan received the "graph" of his heart action. He now declared he was going over to Dr. Paul to have it read. He came back saying that the graph showed his heart action to be quite normal. Dr. Paul told him that there was nothing the matter with his heart, except a slight enlargement which was not dangerous as long as he did not do any heavy lifting. This was all to the good and if left at that might have relieved his mind of the worry induced by Dr. Williams' statement. But Dr. Paul spoiled it all by taking his blood pressure and telling him it was up to 180 when it should be only 150. Ewan has an exaggerated dread of blood pressure and though Dr. Paul told him it was not dangerous he came home in a state of almost panic over it.

For my own part I felt much relieved to find there was no serious heart affection. As for the B.P. Ewan's was quite normal not long ago and I fancy the present rise is the result of his recent worrying and will pass away with the removal of worry. I try to be hopeful but Ewan's condition tonight alarms me. The Barracloughs came and took us for a drive. Ewan did not want to go—a very unusual thing for him—but we urged him and he seemed better when we came back.

I cannot go through the old horror again. I cannot.

This is what my dream meant.

Saturday, May 5, 1934

Ewan had a good sleep last night—much better than I. Cough and dread kept me awake. *What* would I do if Ewan were going to have a serious attack? I could not take him away as I did in 1919—so many reasons make it impossible—and Norval would not be the patient congregation Leaskdale was. Nor would it be easy to hide Ewan's condition here.

Ewan has seemed dull all day. Mrs. Thompson and I housecleaned the closet, the hall and Stuart's "den." I worked doggedly trying to hope for the best—trying to feel glad over the return of the robins who nested in our veranda last year to their old nest. Normally this would have filled me with delight.

I feel so *lonely*—so shut off from help or sympathy. And I can do nothing but *wait*.

Sunday, May 6, 1934
The Manse, Norval
I had another bad night of coughing. E. seemed very dull all day and kept talking of his "weakness"—the same old symptom. He preached fairly well, however, and I taught my Bible class with my hidden worry gnawing at my heart. Oh, God have mercy—not again—not again—and not after such a winter as I have had!

Monday, May 7, 1934
A night of horror. Ewan was quite "off" again—could not sleep and I had to listen to all the old jargon I heard so many hundreds of times in the old years. He was "lost"—he was "doomed to perish"—he had "become a fatalist"—"God hated him" etc. etc.

I went about my tasks all day with a heart of lead. My only hope is that if Dr. Paul can get his B.P. down to normal Ewan will get all right. But when once an idea takes possession of his mind I know by bitter experience how impossible it is to eradicate it. And besides his worry over his "lost" condition will aggravate the blood pressure.

There was a U.F.O. meeting at Stirratt Leslie's tonight and we had promised to go. Ewan talked and played games—I don't suppose anybody noticed anything out of the way—but I, watching him, saw that he never smiled and that he pawed at his forehead with his hand almost constantly—the old gesture that has chilled my heart so many times.

Tuesday, May 8, 1934
This has been one of the old "days of hell." Ewan could not sleep and all his phobias have returned in full force. I spent most of the day in our room with him trying vainly to convince him of the foolishness of his fears. For a few moments I would succeed—then they would roll back over him like a flood.

He is in bed now and I have given him veronal. He must have sleep—he must not be allowed to spend another such night as last.

Wednesday, May 9, 1934
Ewan slept after taking the veronal but has been very bad all day. I made him go to Dr. Paul. The B.P. was down to 160 and Dr. Paul gave him some "sedative" tablets. I know just how much effect sedatives have on him. Dr. Paul, of course, thinks it is just an ordinary case of nerves and insomnia. Ewan tells him nothing

of his phobias. I wonder if I should see Dr. Paul privately and tell him. But he doesn't impress me as being likely to be of much help. And I do not trust his son, the younger Dr. Paul, because he drinks. Young Dr. Paul would probably tell it all over the country that Ewan had religious melancholia.

We cleaned the library today. In the evening I went to a play in the hall—it was advisable for certain reasons that I should go. I got Ewan to go, too, thinking it might divert him. I remember how a movie of Mary Pickford we once saw in Boston made him laugh and feel better the rest of the day. But he was very restless and inattentive and went home at the end of the second act....

Thursday, May 10, 1934
The Manse, Norval
As I slept alone last night I had a fair sleep. Ewan slept till 2.30 and then took one of Dr. Paul's sedatives. He seemed better this morning but drowsy all day.

After supper he lay down on his bed and "talked out" all his phobias again. He seemed better after it but spent the evening with a handkerchief tied round his head. *Nothing* gives even temporary relief to those headaches.

The Institute met in the hall this afternoon and I gave a reading and tried to seem as usual. Murray Laird brought me down some mayflowers Marion had sent him and he and Ewan had a chat while I sat on the veranda and sniffed their fragrance—and tried to remember what I had felt like in the days when I picked mayflowers in P.E. Island springs.

Ewan *as yet* can talk to people in a fairly normal way. If only he doesn't get worse!

Friday, May 11, 1934
Ewan slept well and naturally last night from 9.30 to 6. He seemed better all day and worked at his sermon. But at supper he suddenly became restless and took one of those odd nervous chills he used to have before. I got him into bed with a hot water bottle. Again he talked out his phobias and got temporary ease. But it is dreadful to have to listen to him.

Last night I wakened at four with a cough and asthma and went into Chester's room. A thin, clear, pale dawnlight was whitening over the river below the trees. Very early morning is a sad time, somehow. The splendor and rapture of dawn does not come till later. At first the world is tired and afraid and sad. Today was cold with a high wind. We cleaned the dining room. A letter from Stuart worried me. He is afraid of the chemistry exam.

Sunday, May 13, 1934
Today came a longed-for rain. Ewan slept till 2.30 then took Dr. Paul's sedative and slept till five. He read his sermon for the first time in years and did fairly well but I, sitting taut in my pew, could see how harassed he felt. He went to see Dr. Paul after Union service and the B.P. was still lower. He was *much* better when he came home. Perhaps it will all pass when he no longer need worry about himself. But fear is with me night and day.

The River

Monday, May 14, 1934
Ewan slept only four hours after the sedative but we went to Toronto and he seemed almost normal all the way in. As of old, when he has his hands on the wheel of a car he is a different creature. I wonder if it is because it gives him a certain sense of adequacy and mastery which banishes his phobias for a time. Or does he feel that he is "escaping" from them as the car flies along the road?

Stuart thinks he got through in his chemistry. I do hope so. If he were to fail and lose his year on top of all that has happened!

Wednesday, May 16, 1934
Ewan slept for five hours without "dope" as he calls it. But he had a very wild spell after dinner and wanted to go away. I bound a wet towel about his head, which he said was "burning up" and presently he grew calmer. But I felt very sick at heart.

I am trying to get my garden in. Ewan will not help—he is "too weak." Of course his "weakness" is purely imaginary or hysterical but he believes it is real and resents the fact that I am not alarmed by it. It is useless to point out that he felt just the same time after time years ago. He has forgotten all about that.

Monday, May 21, 1934
On Thursday morning, May 17, Chester 'phoned out that Luella had been taken to the hospital. I had promised to go in. She has no mother. I did not think it right that she should have to face her ordeal with no woman friend near her and I had promised her dying mother that I would be a mother to her child.

Ewan drove me in. He had had a very poor night and I dreaded to leave him as he was. He seemed fairly well, however, on the way in. It was a lovely morning with spring sunshine sifting through young green leaves—but my heart was very heavy. Ewan left me at the hospital and went home. About two o'clock a baby girl was born. The birth of a first little granddaughter ought to have been a joyous occasion but it seems that everything in my life that should be beautiful normally has been made ugly or bitter by some circumstance. Nevertheless I felt a little thrill of interest and excitement as I looked down at the tiny face. And it seemed so short a time since I had been looking into Chester's baby face.

Luella was very well so I went up to the little flat with Chester and got his supper for him. Afterwards I went to see Nora and had a heartening talk with her. What I would have done without her this year I cannot imagine. She knows the truth about Ewan's malady. She is the only person I have ever told it to. It helps so much to talk it over with her. But even Nora has no real conception of what he is like when these spells come on. No one could have who has not experienced it.

I could not sleep that night—partly from worry, partly from a cough and all day Friday I was blue and haunted. Saturday I came home on the bus, dreading intolerably what I might find. But Ewan seemed pretty well and almost normal when we went out to make a "sick call" in the evening. He took no interest whatever in the news of the baby but I do not fancy he would have been keenly interested in any case. In many ways Ewan is a very odd man, even when he is well, and never seems to have the reactions to anything that normal men have.

We both had a good sleep and I hoped he would get through Sunday all right. But he broke down in the middle of the sermon and had to stop the service. As I found out later he suddenly felt half way through that he was *doomed* for daring to enter a pulpit when he was not fit for it! It was all very humiliating. It must have made a great deal of talk. I explained as best I could that his nerves had gone back on him etc. There were two people there, too—outsiders whom I specially hated to have see him break down.

But his fit passed and he went to Union and preached the same sermon there all right. And he seemed quite well in the evening when he went to Barracloughs'. But my own nerves were all frayed and I found it very hard to sit quietly and talk. *What* will the outcome of it all be? His malady is so unpredictable. He may get well as suddenly as he often did before; but if he does not!!

Last night he slept from twelve to five and has seemed perfectly well all day except that he cannot stay any length of time in the same place.

I wrote the "Christmas" chapter of *Pat II* today and lost myself for a few blessed hours in "Silver Bush." I haven't been able to do anything at it since he broke down.

Tuesday, May 22, 1934
The Manse, Norval
E. slept well last night and as I went to Chester's room I got a much needed rest also. I like that room because of the lovely river view from both windows. There is something so lovely about the silence of the early dewy mornings and the pale golden dawns—the unbelievable colors on the dreaming water and the great willows. How lovely is the world even to my aching sleepless eyes.

In the forenoon Ewan went to see Dr. Paul while I waited, sick with dread. He came home and said, "I have good news for you." His blood pressure was down to normal. He seemed quite cheerful and normal. We went to the W.M.S. meeting at Myrle Early's and all through lunch he was laughing and talking with the ladies at his table. Can it be possible that now that his worry on this score has gone he will recover? I am afraid to indulge the hope but it has made such a difference in my feeling tonight. I wrote another *Pat* chapter and got my vegetable garden finished. The air was full of the perfume of my white narcissus and I felt like a recently tortured creature unbound from the rack.

Thursday, May 24, 1934

....Ewan slept only 2 ½ hours last night and woke with nightmare. Sick at heart, I gave him a sedative and he slept till 8. He seemed well through the forenoon and we drove into Toronto and saw the baby. I can't help loving the darling but E. showed no interest in it. Tonight his head has bothered him again. I am worried—worried—worried. But he is not nearly so bad as before Tuesday.

Friday, May 25, 1934

Ewan had a poor night—had a nightmare of *suicide*. This is even more terrible to me now than it was in his former attacks. Because since then his brother Alec, who lived in Butte, Montana, became melancholy just like Ewan, told his wife he meant to do away with himself—and then disappeared. This was several years ago. They have never found any trace of him and there is little doubt that he carried out his threat. Knowing this, it makes me cold with horror when Ewan talks or dreams of such a thing. He was none too well all day but seemed better at night. I could not write so filled in the day with routine work of all kinds.

Saturday, May 26, 1934
The Manse, Norval

E. had a poor night. He went to Scarboro in the afternoon where he is to preach for Mr. Burch who preaches for Union anniversary tomorrow. I reproached myself for sighing with relief when he had gone but I could not help feeling it. It was a pleasant sensation being alone. He is like a cloud of gloom in the house. I got some writing done.

Monday, May 28, 1934

A hard day. Ewan had a very bad night and stayed in bed all day—which was bad for him, but he wouldn't get up. I could not write. I am worried, too, awaiting the results of Stuart's First Year exams. I do not think he is any too sure of passing. This is not as it should be if he had worked as he should.

In the evening Ewan had one of his spells of wanting to "go away." I can't see how it can be managed. He is not fit to go alone and I cannot, for several complicated reasons, get away just now to go with him. Besides, past experience has proved that it never did him any lasting good.

Tuesday, May 29, 1934

I had a dreadful night. Even chloral gave E. only an hour's sleep. He talked continually, declaring he was "done"—"lost"—"dying," etc. He was very dull all day but calmer. I went to see old Dr. Paul and told him a good deal of Ewan's case. I can trust him as I could not trust any of the Uxbridge doctors. But he was no help—just said E. was "too much given to introspection."

This afternoon I managed to write a chapter in agony of mind. At four Ewan was off again—he was "dying" and was "afraid to meet his maker." I talked—argued—explained—the old story all over again as in those Leaskdale years. And with no effect save a temporary relief to him. He seems to believe what I say for an hour or two. Then the phobias return.

Wednesday, May 30, 1934
Ewan slept all night but was very restless and "twitchy" in his sleep. He seemed dull all the forenoon but able to read—something he has not been able to do of late. I had to go to a W.A. Sectional meeting in Georgetown in the afternoon, as I was on the program, and had to talk to a great many ministers and their wives and answer endless questions re Ewan. He came for me but would not come in. I saw he had a bad spell on and he was very bad for the rest of the day. In the evening we went to the Glen to bid the Barracloughs good-bye, as they were leaving to spend the summer in England. Oh, if only they were not going. Ewan seemed sunk in a gloomy reverie all the evening....

Thursday, May 31, 1934
The Manse, Norval
Ewan slept naturally until 1.30. Took a bromide and slept till 7. He seemed fair when he awoke but slumped after breakfast and had a very bad forenoon. I tried to write but could not concentrate my tortured mind on it. Bad as the forenoon was it was nothing to the afternoon. Ewan was simply wild and then ended up in a burst of tears. Very soon after he was quite better and remained better all the evening.

One anxiety was removed today. Stuart has passed his exams. I have been very worried about it for he was not at all sure he had passed—which was not as it should be. I am afraid Stuart went in more for a good time last winter than for study. He is very popular and his popularity is, as I have always feared, a snare to him. I have dreaded every morning to open the paper lest I see the list with his name absent. But I was spared that torture this morning for before the paper came up a friend called up on the phone and told me the good news. It was such a relief....

Saturday, June 2, 1934
Ewan had to take a sedative last night and slept till 8 but this has been a hard day. Smothering hot—94 in the shade. The heat affects E. and he was in bad case all day. In the evening I went up to the Y. camp and gave a camp-fire talk to the girls. It was pleasant under the silent pines with the stars beyond. I forgot for a little while. But the waking from these moments of forgetfulness is always very bitter.

Sunday, June 3, 1934
A very hard day. Ewan had a poor night and so, consequently, had I. He got through his sermon fairly well, reading it. I always feel exhausted after the strain of it, sitting there in my pew and watching every glance and turn of expression fearfully while preserving a calm exterior and smiling to folks afterwards.

The day was hot and dry. In the evening we went in to Toronto as I hoped the drive might do him good. He seemed very well on the way in but got bad as soon as we got in and was terrible all the way home. It was a nightmare and I almost cried with relief when we got home without an accident.

Monday, June 4, 1934
This has been another day of dreadful strain. E. took chloral and slept fairly well but was very bad when he woke—"must get away" etc. Later on he grew calmer and spent a passable day. He has had to keep a wet cloth on his head most of the time but his mind seems easier.

Mrs. Thompson went home for a visit and I was alone and thankful for it....

Wednesday, June 6, 1934
A hot night. I slept little but Ewan slept nearly ten hours without drugs. On the whole a fair day but his mind seems more disturbed than yesterday. It was very hot and great thunderheads rolled up in the sky but passed without a drop. To add to our troubles our cistern has gone dry and that is a serious thing. The well water is so hard it is unusable for anything but drinking and cooking.

It seemed cooler at night which was a blessing. I had to go to a Union W.M.S. this afternoon. It might have been pleasant except that several of the women spoke of the baby. There is no reason why they should not but as yet the sore spot in my soul is unhealed and every touch on it makes me wince.

Saturday, June 9, 1934
....A letter from Luella today says she is coming home to her father's as the city heat is too hard on the baby. It is no doubt the best arrangement but I shall be worried over Chester again. Well, one worry more or less is all in the day's work for me.

Sunday, June 10, 1934
The Manse, Norval, Ont.
The night was horrible and Ewan was very bad. He is always worse the night before Sunday. After the chloral had put him to sleep I broke down and cried. He got through the day all right however and seemed much better when he came home from Union.

We had a thunder shower this afternoon. It was delightful to hear the rain pattering on the garret roof. But it was too brief to do any real good.

I am, as always, so thankful that Sunday is over.

Monday, June 11, 1934
I had a poor night. E. slept fairly well after a bromide. He was very dull all day, haunted by all the old bogies. In the afternoon he went to Brampton and Dr. Brydon gave him an electric head treatment. I don't think they do him a bit of good—indeed, I think they do him harm. He is running around to all kinds of doctors but as he does not tell them the truth—merely complains of headache and

sleeplessness—they can do him no good and I doubt if they could supposing he did tell them. "Who can minister to a mind diseased?"....

Tuesday, June 12, 1934
A miserable night and still more miserable day. He was very bad all the forenoon and in the afternoon he took the worst spell he has had yet. He lay on the bed and groaned. He was going to hell—his end was near—only a few days more—he had *heard a voice* saying "He died this morning."

After talking it all out he grew rapidly calmer and was able to read the rest of the day. But I am exhausted.

We had a lovely rain today. I tried to write some of *Pat II* but found it almost impossible. I had to go to play practice at Union tonight. Stuart took me. It was the usual thing—endless giggles and inattention. I felt like throwing my book away and stalking out on them.

Wednesday, June 13, 1934
E. slept well and was pretty fair all day, though dull. I had the Missionary Picnic to look after today and was so busy there were moments when I forgot. I could not be with Ewan and was gnawed by worry. A very boring woman gave a very boring address and Stuart and I took her back to Toronto tonight. It was such a relief to see the last of her. I dreaded the return home but Ewan was reading calmly and greeted me with a smile.

Mrs. Thompson was impertinent to me tonight without the least provocation. She has never been guilty of this before though she has often taken sulky spells. This hurt me more than it should.

Thursday, June 14, 1934
The Manse, Norval
....I wakened at eight and went in to find that Ewan had not slept all night. Nothing he took had had any effect. He was in the worst state I have seen him in since 1924. He was going to die in a few days and go to hell—he was done for—all the old hauntings to a word. He refused at first to get up but I made him because I knew he would be better and I gave him a sedative. He lay on the bed all day with wet cloths on his head but was calmer and slept an hour in afternoon. I could not write but worked doggedly all day to keep from going mad myself. I painted floors—I sewed—I gardened—and tried to feel my old delight in my green rows of young lettuce. No use. My heart lay like lead in my breast. There was no nice mail. I had nothing to help me.

I went to play practice at 9 but as only 5 turned out, owing to a dance somewhere, we did not have it. I was relieved for I did not see how I could have stood up to it.

Ewan suggested calling at Reids' on our way back. We went but he was very dull and stupid all the time. Little Pussy-girl is really sweet but there are too many things to spoil my enjoyment of her.

I have decided that if Ewan is not better by July 1st he must go to Homewood Sanatorium in Guelph. It is frightfully expensive and I doubt if it will do him any real good but I realize that I cannot bear this alone any longer. Somehow we must give him a few weeks there. This will give me a rest that will enable me to carry on. Otherwise I shall break down.

Friday, June 15, 1934
Today was bearable. Ewan slept naturally for ten hours. He had a quiet day, reading on the veranda in the forenoon and on the bed in the afternoon. I compelled myself to write a chapter of *Pat II*. In the evening Ewan and I drove to Brampton and home around by Huttonville. As always in a car he seemed fair. He spoke of how long it had been since he laughed.

Saturday, June 16, 1934
Ewan had a bad night, sleeping little and that little as a result of chloral. He was quiet all day with no restless spells but complained of his head continually. I talked to him about going to Homewood. He seems to be willing, much to my relief. I had been afraid he would not be. I typed an old Leaskdale sermon for him to read tomorrow....

Sunday, June 17, 1934
The Manse, Norval, Ont.
Ewan slept from ten to 12.30 but I could not sleep. At 2.30 I saw a light in his room and went anxiously in. I found him like a terrified baby—he had had "an awful nightmare"—"oh, it was awful." He groaned and grovelled—literally grovelled. I got into bed beside him and read aloud for ten minutes until his mind grew more composed. Then he fell asleep and slept till 8.30. I slept a little but not comfortably. He was dull all day but not restless. Got through his sermon quite well. I had decorated the church with flowers and played the organ, my turn beginning again. I used to hate this long ago but, oddly, I find myself rather liking it here. Ewan preached at Union and went to tea at Verne Thompson's. He came home at eight and seemed really cheerful. Talked and read. At 9.30 he fell calmly asleep. Hope rises in my heart again in spite of all.

Monday, June 18, 1934
Ewan slept well with no nightmare but seemed dull all day—haunted and headachy. I woke at five to the music of a pouring rain. We had a magnificent rain all day—so much needed that I rejoice at it even though we wanted a fine evening to put our Union play on at Vaughan. I felt very tired and hopeless all day and in late afternoon felt so terribly nervous that I went to the spare room and indulged in a fit of crying. This helped me. After tea I dressed and went to Vaughan in Jim McKane's car with a gay load of young people. Jim is a very reckless driver and on those wet slippery roads I was almost sick from fright....

Tuesday, June 19, 1934
The Manse, Norval.
E. slept till 7:30. He was dull all day and worried—but about *sane* things—his work, memory, etc. I don't mind this as I do his terrible religious terrors. His

memory certainly is very bad just now—he forgets everything he should remember. But he was like that in 1919 and it will likely be all right when—and *if*—he recovers sanity.

I have got through the day without a breakdown but I feel very nervous.

Wednesday, June 20, 1934
E. woke after an hour's sleep and had to have chloral. I had a wretched night myself. Rose early and Stuart took me into Toronto. It was a lovely day but my heart was too sad to respond to it. The day seemed like a nightmare of shopping and worrying. Ewan is no better this evening. His head is bad. Chester came home for a few days.

Thursday, June 21, 1934
E. had a bad night. Took chloral but slept only one hour. It has lost its effect with him. He had, however, a fair day. I went to Georgetown and saw Dr. Paul, having him sign a certain necessary form for Ewan's admission to Homewood. In the afternoon Chester took me to Guelph. Homewood is a very nice place and Dr. MacKinnon to whom I explained E's case as fully as possible was nice and fairly encouraging though vague. Ewan seemed better this evening and we had a drive.

Friday, June 22, 1934
E. had a good sleep and seemed much better all day—perhaps as a result of the fact that he was "getting away"—perhaps not. In the afternoon Chester and I took him to Homewood. I felt very strangely when I came away and left him there. Yet it was the only thing to do. I *must* have a rest before I can take up the burden again. And they *may* help him.

This evening after supper I went across the west branch bridge and picked a cupful of wild strawberries in the ditch of the pine-clad hill. The tide of relief that swept suddenly over me as I realized that my burden was lifted at least for a time drowned every other worry temporarily and though I was in the ditch physically, spiritually I was in Arcady—back in the golden age—young with immortal youth, feeling as I used always to feel in that far-off girlhood. The world was lovely around me. Still, golden hill pastures stretched beyond. The sky was blue and opal. Then the twilight came, first gold-green, then emerald. Gracious living seemed possible once more. Every wind of the world was a sister. I was in a mood to hear the morning stars singing for joy.

If I could have gone to bed on that note! But John Ismonds were having a party for the Old Timers and I had to go. I spent hours of boredom, feeling strangely isolated from the merry-makers. And there seemed to be pinpricks everywhere for me. I was thankful when Chester came for me at twelve though nobody else dreamed of going home that early.

I feel terribly desolate tonight. The house seems as if there had been a death in it. How is poor Ewan?

I shall be in my own bed again. I am always glad to get back to it. But shall I sleep?

Saturday, June 23, 1934
I did fairly but have felt terribly tired all day. I did routine tasks and wrote a chapter of *Pat* but at five I felt utterly played out. I had company for supper, wrote some letters and put flowers in the church. Oh, how is Ewan?

Sunday, June 24, 1934
The Manse, Norval, Ont.
I could not sleep till late and woke early. The day was fine and warm. The United Church minister, Mr. McKinnon, preached in our church, as the vacation arrangement begins today. The day has been hot and long and I don't feel well. Stuart took Chester back to Toronto tonight. I miss him.

Monday, June 25, 1934
I had a fair sleep. Wrote a *Pat* chapter but could put no heart in it. The mail brought a note from Ewan. He had to take "sleeping pills" two nights. Is "a little better"—the old refrain of his 1919 letters. I feel upset and worried. I fear sometimes that I am going to break down. Suppose Ewan does not recover in a reasonable time. Then we must break up our home here and go where—do what? A minister's family is in a peculiarly unhappy position if he has to give up work for the manse is not their own and they cannot stay in it....

Tuesday, June 26, 1934
I could not sleep till 12 and woke again at three with an attack of coughing. I hope I am not going to have asthma again this summer. Oh, for *one* good night's sleep. My heart is like lead in my breast. I wrote a little at *Pat II* and made strawberry jam and painted a floor. I felt better after supper and went out and walked about the lawn. There had been a nice rain in the forenoon and how cool and velvety the grass felt under my burning feet. It *felt* green.

Wednesday, June 27, 1934
A poor night. I took a tablet of chloral but even so couldn't sleep. My nerves were very bad all day. I am afraid I waited too long before taking Ewan to Homewood. I cannot rest even now when the burden is removed. I tried to write a *Pat* chapter but couldn't.

After dinner Stuart and I went to Guelph. I dreaded it—and dreaded hearing from the doctor that Ewan might have some physical trouble, as they were to give him a thorough examination. Nothing like this developed but I found E. in the throes of a very bad spell. He had felt much better Saturday, Sunday and Monday and had slept without drugs. But now he was in despair. I got him to his room and let him "talk it out." At once he was better. We took him for a drive and left him comparatively cheerful. I felt a little better coming home. At least he does not seem to have any organic trouble.

Charlotte MacPherson called this evening. I cannot help squirming in her company. She and her sisters have always been kind to me but they are such bitter and malicious gossips.

The night mail brought a letter from Dr. Clare, head of Homewood—a sort of official report that was fairly optimistic. There was a letter from Myrtle Webb with all the flavor of home. Perhaps I shall sleep tonight.

Thursday, June 28, 1934
The Manse, Norval

....It has been a terrible day and evening of muggy heat. Mrs. Thompson and I managed to get the stair carpet down—E. and I always did it. It is a hard task owing to the twist in the steps but we managed it.

In the afternoon I went with Charlotte MacP. to a tea on the United Manse grounds and enjoyed it a little but with worry gnawing under all. In the evening I painted floors. For twenty-two years it seems to me I have been painting floors!!....

Friday, June 29, 1934

I slept fairly till five. I think I am getting back to normal slowly. It was a hot day and Mr. and Mrs. Sam Kennedy from Leaskdale came for dinner and stayed till four. Normally I would have been glad to see them but as it was every moment seemed tortured. They told a bit of news about our old friend, Mr. Fraser, which I was sorry to hear. A few years ago he married again—a woman who had been divorced. An unwise choice for a minister even if she was, as she claimed, the innocent party. Now she has left him. He has not deserved that. What a twisted world it is!

I had a letter from E. but the news was poor. He had not been able to sleep Wednesday night even with pills. A second letter came tonight. Last night he slept ten hours after a bromide and is "a little better." Ah, me!

I am tired and discouraged tonight—perhaps because of the dreadful heat. "My heart is smitten and withered like grass." How the *Bible* puts things! There is no emotion of our passion-wrung humanity that is not expressed perfectly in that amazing old book....

Saturday, June 30, 1934
The Manse, Norval

I had a bad night. I had hoped when Ewan was not here that I would be able to sleep but I seem to be past that. Last night as I lay sleepless Stuart came in—got me some toast—kissed me. It helped—he fed my starved soul. Stuart does not often kiss me now—he who never used to pass me without a kiss in the old days. He has grown very undemonstrative these past two years and it hurts me.

After he went out I tried to sleep but could not. A bromide did no good. At two o'clock in desperation I took a chloral tablet and slept an hour or so. I felt exhausted when I rose but the day has not been so bad. I got a little of *Pat II* done. The evening mail brought a letter from Ewan. The writing looks good—I can always tell to a certain extent how he is feeling by his writing—but I have decided not to open it till the morning. It might upset me and I dare not risk it.

Had to make a "duty call" tonight and listen to a lot of silly and malicious yammering. Faugh!

274

Sunday, July 1, 1934
The Manse, Norval
....Mr. McKinnon preached a ruthlessly long sermon today—the afternoon was hot and at times I felt as if I could *not* sit still until he made an end. When I came home I opened E's letter. It was just the same old story—it might have been written in 1919. He had a terrible nightmare Friday night and "thought he was dying." But was "a little better" at time of writing.

After reading it I went out and sat on the lawn to seek a little coolness. Our pet black squirrel "Slim" came into my lap and ate nuts out of my hand. We have tamed him this summer—it was not hard to do. He was so friendly from the start. He will eat out of our hands and loves nuts and bits of stale cake. If he cannot eat them he buries them on the lawn. There are several other gray and black squirrels about but he is the only one who will make friends.

I have had a rather dreary evening. No company—not even anything fresh to read. My thoughts seem to prey upon me. I am really frightened lest I have a total nervous breakdown.

Monday, July 2, 1934
The Manse, Norval
Last night I had the first *good* sleep I have had for weeks. As a result I felt almost well all through the day until three. Then I began to feel nervous and was not so well the rest of the day. In the evening I managed to write a little. It was better than brooding. Then I re-read *The Woman in White*—worth a million of today's mysteries. I never tire of it. And I adore "Count Foscoe." He is the most fascinating villain I ever met.

Tuesday, July 3, 1934
I had a bad night with asthma. Slept only two hours and wakened with it. I can't understand what gives it to me. I've no cold. I have suffered with it now for several summers, always in July and August. I took one of the tablets Dr. Paul gave me for it and in half an hour was relieved but could not sleep at all the rest of the night. That is what the tablet does. It seems it is an old Chinese remedy well-known in Europe a thousand years ago and since then forgotten—it is not known why. Now it has been rediscovered and is used again. One feels so blessedly *at peace* after taking one. It is a wonderful sensation....

This forenoon I wrote but found it hard. In the afternoon Stuart and I went to Guelph—and had an experience which has left me wondering just how much sense some doctors have!!!

When I arrived I saw nothing of E. so went to his room and knocked on door. After some delay an orderly came out, shut the door quickly behind him and said in an agitated way that I "couldn't go in just then as the doctors were with him." Then, before I could frame a question he exclaimed jerkily that he would "see what Dr. McKinnon said" and rushed around the corner of the corridor. I waited, expecting his return, for a full half hour which seemed as long as a year. *What* was wrong with Ewan? Horrible suppositions presented themselves to me.

Had he tried to kill himself? I dared not enter the room. I could hear no sound from it. Presently the orderly came back and asked if I would wait in the office until Dr. Clare could see me. I went there, feeling convinced, since everybody was so mysterious, that something dreadful *had* happened to E. I waited in the office for nearly an hour, half mad, walking the floor. Then Dr. Clare wandered casually in and said, "Oh, are you here? We've been having a dreadful time with Mr. Macdonald."

I thought, "Ewan has gone insane." I *said*, rather sharply, "What *is* the matter, Dr. Clare?"

Then he told me. They had discovered that Ewan had an impacted bowel and they had been trying to get it cleared out by enemas and that was what had been going on in the room. They had succeeded and all was well again. Dr. Clare thought the condition had been there for a long time. I knew it had not. He got like that after going to Homewood and it betokened great carelessness on the part of the staff that it should have happened. Or if it were true that he had been like that when he went there that they had not discovered it when they gave him that "physical overhauling."

I was very angry. Why on earth could not the orderly have told me what was the trouble when he came out of the room? Why couldn't he have said, "Mr. Macdonald is having injections for an impacted bowel and cannot be seen until it is over"? I would not then have spent such an hour of worry and suspense. The whole thing has made a most unfavorable impression on me.

I did not see Ewan as Dr. Clare thought he had better be allowed to rest after his ordeal but I came home in somewhat better cheer. With this poison out of his system perhaps Ewan's recovery will be hastened.

Thursday, July 5, 1934
Slept till four and then had asthma the rest of the night. Stuart and I went in to Toronto and I shopped and got very tired. Went up to see Chester at his new flat. I don't like the flat or the locality. I think it would be better if Chester were boarding. I am worried about him. I had no word from Homewood today and felt a cold chill whenever the phone rang.

Friday, July 6, 1934
Another bad night with asthma followed by a horrible day of heat and clammy mugginess. Quite the worst day this summer. It was hard on the nerves and at night came a letter from Dr. Baugh. It was not encouraging save for the fact that the bowel had been thoroughly cleaned out and Ewan was feeling better yesterday morning....

"Slim" came back today after two days' absence. We rejoiced over him for we feared that something had happened him.

I don't know what I would do if it were not for Stuart. We were both disappointed in May that he could not get any work for the summer but now I thank God he didn't. What I would do here alone I shudder to think.

Saturday, July 7, 1934
The Manse, Norval
I slept a little better, waking at five to cough an hour and sleep again. Nothing I take for this cough seems to help it at all. Today however was blessedly cooler and Stuart and I went to Guelph in the afternoon. We found Ewan on the grounds quite recovered from his disagreeable bowel experience but not well. His head was bad and he looked pale and sad. I felt disheartened but tried to dwell on some few encouraging signs. He is sleeping without drugs and feels better some days. But there is no *real* improvement.

Nora phoned this evening. She is coming out tomorrow. I don't know whether I feel glad or not. It is so hard just now to plan for visitors or do anything outside routine. How I long for *one* good night's sleep!

Sunday, July 8, 1934
....After service was over Nora came. At first I could not enjoy her visit but after awhile I forgot *temporarily* and found pleasure in her companionship. We went up the river to our "log" and sat and talked. I felt soothed and strengthened. We had a nice dinner in the evening and then Nora went....

Monday, July 9, 1934
I had last night the first real sleep for weeks. I slept from ten to seven unbrokenly and though I coughed badly when I woke I have felt much better all day and able to write.

I got out the silver mug Aunt Flora sent Chester when he was born and polished it up for Pussy. It seems so short a time when it came for him.

As usual this evening I walked down to the office for the mail, as usual hating the ordeal of going in and through the store and the ranks of loafers, who stare and talk. There was a letter from E. A little more cheerful than previous ones. He is sleeping better but is still tormented by his phobias. Poor Ewan! He has never in his life suffered much over anything real. But over the *un*real!!!

Wednesday, July 11, 1934
....I had a very curious dream. I was on a steep barn roof covered with snow out of which iron spikes were sticking at various angles. The snow was sliding down and carrying me with it. I clutched wildly and despairingly at the spikes but each pulled out as I grasped it. I was almost over the edge and in despair I thought that the next moment I would slip right off the roof and be dashed to pieces on rocks which I seemed to know were below. Then all at once I found my feet firm on a flat porch roof from which a staircase led easily to the ground.

It was one of my vivid *meaningful* dreams. I believe it foretokens some kind of escape or good news. I *would* like something of the sort just to make life a little less dreary. I wrote a little but felt very tired. After dinner Stuart and I went to Guelph. If it were not for the dread of what I may find at the end I would enjoy these drives. But for the first time I found E. really better. He was outside, chatting with Eva Winfield (Mrs. Barraclough's niece who is a nurse in Guelph) and was quite cheerful and smiling. His head was much better. He came for a drive and asked interestedly about everything. He has not been so well since his first attack and I came home encouraged but too tired. It is very close and muggy tonight and I am rather breathless—a nasty feeling.

Thursday, July 12, 1934
....Nora came today for a short visit. We will not have the beautiful time we had last summer—*that* was too beautiful to be repeated—but I am greedily looking forward to a little real companionship. We just rested and talked in the afternoon. It is delightful to have someone to talk to. There was a letter from Ewan in the evening mail but I decided not to open it till the morning. Nora and I went for a walk down the town-line for a couple of miles. But I found it rather a nightmare coming back. The air was dreadfully close and oppressive and I felt an attack of asthma coming on. When I got home and into my room I had the worst attack I have ever had. I really thought I was going to die right there for lack of breath. It was a most dreadful feeling. I never experienced anything like it. The tablet was so long in taking effect and every moment was torture. But it *has* taken effect at last, thank God, and I am lying in bed at peace. Nora is asleep in the guest room. The house is quiet. I have the heavenly sense of rest and repose and relief those tablets give. Was there a time when I always felt like this? I have forgotten it!

Friday, July 13, 1934
The Manse, Norval
The world seems a little less hostile tonight. I slept fairly well. Opened E's letter this morning. He seems much better. I made currant jelly, did a little writing and gossiped with Nora. Then after supper, as we were sitting on the veranda, I opened the evening paper and saw a bit of news that was very unexpected and cheering.

Four years ago I put $14,000 into the Robert Simpson Co. For a year or so they paid dividends of 6½ per cent. Then the depression struck them and they passed the dividend. This meant over $900 cut from my income. This is why we have been so pinched these past two years. But there was still worse to it.

For a year rumor was busy with the impending crash or reorganization of Simpson's. The stock went down from $100 to *$6*. My $14,000 shrank to *$840*. I was worried about this as about so many other things.

Recently the stock has been climbing again but nobody seems to have been expecting a resumption of dividends. The announcement in the paper was they were going to pay $1 on each share for the quarter. This was only 4 per cent but it was much better than nothing. Besides, it meant Simpsons were getting on their feet again.

This was what my dream foretold!

After I had read this Nora and I went for a walk up the station road. I felt light-hearted with relief and some power of enjoyment came back to me. There was a wonderful sunset, with great headlands of gold and purple in the west. Once again the first star was a miracle as it always was in the years before the world grew dark. It was not so muggy as last night and I had no trouble with asthma. But now in my room I feel it somewhat. How I wish I could get rid of it. I am haunted by the fear that it will become chronic and I will be a gasping nuisance.

Saturday, July 14, 1934
....Nora went back to town today and Stuart took me...for a day's boredom with Isobel—who bestowed upon me a framed and colored picture of herself which I had neither asked for nor desired. Stuart came for me in the evening and we had a pleasant drive home....

Tuesday, July 17, 1934
The Manse, Norval
Another poor night. They come with monotonous regularity now. I slept from 12 to 2. Then awoke with asthma. Took a tablet. This cured the asthma but the other effect of this tablet is to prevent sleep. So I lay awake the rest of the night. Had a letter from Stokes today. There is another possibility of the *Blue Castle* being dramatized. A Hollywood playwright, a Miss Jerry Dean, has asked for an option on it. I wonder if anything will come of it.

I went to the Gollops' for eggs tonight and had to listen to a long account of the Gollop-MacPherson "row" which has been raging for two years and made a lot of unpleasantness in the church. We have tried our best to patch matters up between the two families but both sides are bitter and unreasonable and *petty*.

A letter from Ewan tonight said he was keeping better and the doctor's report was also good. I worked at *Pat II* this evening but felt very bad. What a dreary, makeshift sort of life this is!

Wednesday, July 18, 1934
....At breakfast I had a blow. Mrs. Thompson said abruptly, "I might as well tell you I will be leaving in a month's time."

I admit I was thunderstruck—though I took care not to show it.

"Mr. Gollop's House"

Ever since Mrs. T. came here she has been studying shorthand and typewriting. She had the idea that she would like office work better than housework. At first she studied by herself but for the last two years she has been taking lessons from a Mrs. Baker who lives in Norval and was a stenographer before her marriage. But judging from some specimens of Mrs. T's work I have seen lying around she is yet very far from being expert enough at it to have any chance of getting a stenographer's position in Toronto. So, although I knew she would probably be leaving sometime when she became capable of holding an office job, I never dreamed of her going so soon.

I might have pointed out to her that she had practically no chance of getting such a position in a city where scores of college trained girls can't get any kind of a job. I might have told her that if she could not get an office job she would have a very hard time to get a place at housework where she could have June with her. But I held my tongue. Not likely anything I could say would influence her. She would think I was only playing my own game. Or, if she were induced to stay, she would always be wishing she had gone and imagining she could easily have got a position if she had.

So I only said I was sorry to lose her but I would not want to stand in the way of her bettering herself. I did, however, ask her what she proposed to do with June if she got a job. Her answer rather appalled me. She was going to rent a room and leave June—a child of four—in it alone during office hours!!

"You could never do that!" I exclaimed. "She would break her heart."

Well, Mrs. T. thought her mother wouldn't see her stuck. She would likely come in and look after June. I could have said—but did not—"Do you think you will be able to pay room rent and board yourself and mother and June on an inexperienced stenographer's salary?" I knew my lady. She is very stubborn when she has once decided on a thing.

But I felt it keenly that she should elect to go now of all times when I am ill and in such trouble. It is not as if she had a job secured and must go at once or lose it. A few weeks or months more or less would make no difference. She came here with her baby and herself almost in rags. We have all been very kind to her. She has been like one of the family. And it seems to me a very ungrateful course of conduct....

Stuart and I went to Guelph this afternoon. Ewan is *much* better. Laughs and chats naturally and is beginning to be homesick—a very good sign. This is encouraging; but it is evening now and I am alone and very lonely and disheartened. I have no idea where to look for a girl and the thought of breaking in a new one just now is peculiarly unpleasant. I shall miss Mrs. Thompson. She is the most competent maid I have ever had and very pleasant to work with. She took an interest in everything—the plants, the cats, the garden—almost as much as I did myself. In my lonely life she was a bit of company. I shall miss June too—I have become very fond of her....

Friday, July 20, 1934
The Manse, Norval
This was the hottest and muggiest day of the summer so far. At 12 last night I took veronal and so got some sleep. I hate taking the stuff but it is a choice of evils. I

can't do without some sleep. I had no letter from Ewan and was worried but a nice one from Nora helped a little.

I am all alone tonight except for Luck. The house is stifling—I can hardly bear to stay in it but I can't go out and wander about the village alone.

Later. Twelve o'clock
Stuart has been in and talked to me for an hour. This has helped me much.

Saturday, July 21, 1934
....A letter from E. was not so good. He has had to wear the ice-cap again. It is the same old story—temporary improvement followed by relapse. I really do not think Homewood is helping him in the least. But it is helping *me*. I could not, under present conditions, look after him as I once did.

Sunday, July 22, 1934
Last night I slept well till six and today was fine and clear with none of that horrible "mug." I went up to Pinecrest Camp and talked to the girls there and had dinner with them. I don't know whether these things help or not. At the time they force worry into the background but the reaction always follows.

Monday, July 23, 1934
I wonder what it would be like to sleep again—really sleep as I used to do. I woke at two with asthma and cough. I got up and went down cellar to get a glass of wine. When I returned to my room I had a most terrible and indescribable moment or two. I could *not* get my breath—I felt as if I were dying. Sipping the wine presently relieved the asthma but there was no more sleep for me. I passed the day doing routine jobs of various kinds. Several times that awful feeling of *desperation* came but happily passed quickly.

After several false hopes I have got the promise of a maid—Ethel Dennis, the sister of Mrs. Robinson, the butcher's wife. I don't know what she will be like but Mrs. R. wants me to give her a trial. I would have preferred an older one—Ethel is very young—but must take what I can get. At least I know she is respectable and honest. It is a relief to have the matter settled.

There was a letter from Ewan in the evening mail but I have decided not to open it till the morning. I need sleep so badly I cannot risk being upset.

In the *Globe* this morning there was a letter in the Home Maker's page from a certain "Eve" who reads my books when she gets discouraged and always finds strength to go on in them. But there is no one to help me.

I worked all day but after I stopped work tonight I went to pieces. Cried and walked the floor and felt that fearful flood of desolation....

Tuesday, July 24, 1934
The Manse, Norval
I slept till three last night. Then asthma awoke me. I sipped a glass of wine and the asthma departed but I could not sleep. I took one of the Chinese tablets after breakfast and as a result felt restful and calm all the forenoon. I opened E's letter after

breakfast. It was not encouraging. He has had "five days of intense experience." I know too well that this is simply his way of saying that his phobias have returned.

In the afternoon, the effect of the tablet having worn off, I had several of those indescribable attacks of desolation and despair. At six I took another Chinese tablet and it calmed me. Then I went for a walk through the lovely moonlit night and tried to summon up enough strength and courage to go on. Go on! I could go on if I could see any way to walk on. But I don't know what to do.

Wednesday, July 25, 1934
....The world seems so upset. Drought and strikes everywhere—Europe seething—war talk unceasing. The poor old planet has a very bad attack of stomach ache.

Thursday, July 26, 1934
....A certain Miss Dean of Los Angeles has signed a contract with Stokes and me for an option on the dramatic rights of *Blue Castle* for a year. She seems to think she can place a play written on it. I haven't much hope of it after the former fiasco. But I get $100 for the option and that is a help just now.

If this terrible heat wave would pass I think I could "carry on."

Friday, July 27, 1934
I had a fair sleep till six but today was hot and I had a very disheartening letter from E. But when Stuart and I went to Guelph in the afternoon we found him bowling and feeling fine—another of the lightning changes that characterize his strange malady.

Chester and Luella and Pussy were here when we got home. Pussy is beginning to be very cunning.

I had a slight return to that terrible feeling tonight but it quickly passed. Since I gave up taking a tonic with strychnine in it I do not have these spells so often or so badly.

Sunday, July 29, 1934
....Luella and Chester and Pussy were here to supper. Pussy is very sweet. To touch her little face is like touching a roseleaf. She slept all the evening in Chester's bed and I tiptoed in now and again to imagine time had turned back twenty-two years and I was watching baby Chester in the old manse at Leaskdale. Ah me!

The vacation Sundays have come to an end. I got Rev. Mr. McKenzie of Woodbridge to preach today but I am

Luella, Baby, and Chester

282

worried regarding supply for future Sundays. The elders might—and should—attend to this but they never try to help me in any way.

Slim is storing nuts in the steeple of the church against the winter. It is fun to watch him running up and down the drain pipe. I can't imagine how he does it. It is of zinc and as smooth as ice.

"Luck"

Monday, July 30, 1934

....I read over what I have got written of *Pat II* today and find it better than I expected. It has been so hard to get it written.

Tuesday, July 31, 1934

....I had an encouraging letter from E. He is much better and says he will be ready to come home in two weeks. I was so frightened to open the letter and it was such a relief.

I went over this evening for a call at the MacPhersons. Luck went with me but would not go in. When I came out an hour later he was waiting for me at the corner of the honey house. I picked him up and carried him in, all fluffy and purring and loving. Dear little cat! He and Stuart are all that have pulled me through this summer.

Wednesday, Aug. 1, 1934
The Manse, Norval

....I wrote some at *Pat II* this morning and got on fairly well. In the afternoon I went to the W.M.S. at Mrs. Fred Lyons. A stranger—Mrs. Watson—was there and called across the room to me, "How is your granddaughter?" This did not add to the pleasure of the occasion because I feel sure she did it to hurt me—or at least out of curiosity to see how I would take it. I do not think she saw much. I have not been hiding my feelings from the public eye all my life to give myself away to a Mrs. Watson.

A letter from E. says he is sleeping pretty well and has less headache. The doctor's report is also good.

On the whole I have been feeling better lately—no more of those dreadful "spells."

Thursday, Aug. 2, 1934

....Today the news was that Hindenberg is dead. Back in the war time we would have rejoiced. Now we are all sorry because everyone is afraid of what may happen in Germany now. What changes time brings!

I am all alone this evening and a thunderstorm is going on but I do not mind. Being alone is not so hard as trying to behave normally in company. Ewan's letter today seemed quite normal. But years ago he would improve like that and then slump as suddenly.

Saturday, Aug. 4, 1934
I had a fair sleep and today was blessedly cool. Chester came home for his vacation and he and Luella and Pussy and I went to Guelph. Ewan didn't seem quite so cheerful as last time. But he wants to come home next Friday and I think it best. We cannot afford any more time there and they are doing nothing for him that I cannot do at home.

Mr. Thompson, who is to preach tomorrow, came tonight. A talkative chap. Entertained me with many tales of answered prayer. Looked at my picture of Mona Lisa and said, "Is that intended as a representation of Christ?"

I said I thought not!!!

Sunday, Aug. 5, 1934
I had a fair sleep but a nasty dream—one of my "predictive" dreams—of that I feel sure. I was walking on a street in Toronto when a man suddenly attacked me with a knife. I screamed and tried to beat him off. I succeeded in escaping him but was arrested by a policeman on the ground that I had been creating a disturbance. I awoke crying and vowing that "It wasn't my fault—it wasn't my fault." More trouble is coming I know.

Monday, Aug. 6, 1934
The Manse, Norval
I had a really good sleep last night. I tried to write at *Pat II* but my brain isn't up to it yet. I got so very tired after an hour's work.

I put in an evening of boredom at a U.F.O. meeting tonight.

Tuesday, Aug. 7, 1934
Had another good sleep—two in succession—a record for this summer. I wrote some, painted a floor, did several routine jobs and am tired. I have no *heart* in my work now and that makes it all hard.

Friday, Aug. 10, 1934
....Chester and I went to Guelph to see E. and had a very hot drive. Ewan is not at all well. I went to pieces from nerve strain and heat and cried all the way home. The heat this evening is terribly oppressive. I feel exhausted.

Saturday, Aug. 11, 1934
The Manse, Norval
I slept till five and then wakened with a slight asthma. A glass of wine banished it and I slept again. Today was cooler and I was able to work. In the evening I went to Brampton to see *The House of Rothschild*. It helped me. When I came out I felt that I was captain of my soul again. I am too much alone with nothing pleasant in the days to divert my thoughts from worries and dreads.

Sunday, Aug. 12, 1934

....Mr. Chapman, a retired United minister, preached today and had dinner and supper here. He is a very nice man. It is pleasant to have cheerful folk around.

Monday, Aug. 13, 1934

....As Stuart was going in to Toronto for gym practice I went in and spent the evening with Mary. A nasty tight feeling in the head troubled me. It has bothered me off and on for two years now.

Wednesday, Aug. 15, 1934

Last night I had a veronal sleep. Managed to write a little but my head felt queer all day. I am afraid I am going to break down myself. *This must not be.* What would become of us all if I did?

I had a gloomy letter from Ewan today and one from Isobel. I dread the coming of the mail nowadays as much as years ago I used to welcome it. Isobel's screed was full of yowls of "love." Asks me in all seriousness if I will take her as my maid!!! Says she is jealous of Chester's baby. (Luella and Pussy were here a little while the day she was and I was petting Pussy.)

Mrs. Thompson and June went tonight. I shall miss little June. But I feel bitter in regard to Mrs. T. for more reasons that I have mentioned here. No use going into details.

I was all alone in this big house after they went and for a little while I had a bad time with a return of that terrible *buried* feeling. I had to go out finally into the dark silent night. I walked about the lawn for a long time. The pines on the hill were carrying out their mystic ritual. Luck came padding along in the dark and purred about my feet. I regained control of myself.

> From the cool cisterns of the midnight air
> My spirit drank repose.

Thursday, Aug. 16, 1934

I had a fair sleep till six and got up early to make a batch of cookies. Ethel Dennis came today and the first day of breaking in a new maid is always a bit of a strain. She is very crude and seems to know hardly anything about cooking.

Chester and Luella and Pussy were here to supper. Pussy is getting to be a sweet thing. In the evening we went to a local "pageant" in Brampton. I had to stand all the evening and was also bored to the point of desperation but had to hide it because many of the performers were our church people. I am, as usual, very tired....

Friday, Aug. 17, 1934

I had a good sleep but the day has not been easy. In the afternoon we had a hot drive to Guelph and brought Ewan home. He seems quite fair—laughed and talked with some evening callers and played solitaire. I think if he has no setback he will soon be able to take up his work again. He is really quite well enough now if he only thought so but he insists he "*dare not* enter a pulpit," so of course his mind is not normal yet. If he would only *do it* and find he is *not* "struck down by heaven" for presumption he would likely be all right. I am very tired tonight but hopeful.

Ewan was really on a fair way to recovery when he came home that night. I do not attribute this to Homewood. I do not think they did one thing for him that could not have been done at home, except that they taught him to *bowl* and *play solitaire*. This may not seem much in return for the outlay but I have often wondered in these last two years what he or I would have done if he had not learned these two things. I think that the solitaire especially was all that saved our reason and our lives in the weeks that were to come.

Yes, I was "hopeful" that night. And I was just on the verge of the most hideous experience of that terrible year—one of those experiences that have finally convinced me that some malign fate was actually dogging my steps in everything. I had had a hard bitter winter, spring and summer. But Ewan's homecoming from Guelph ushered in an autumn that for sheer misery surpassed anything I had yet experienced in life. Even yet I can hardly endure to think of it—write of it.

When I went to Guelph that day I had a talk with Dr. Clare to find out just what to do for Ewan. He said it was most important to keep his bowels open and told me to keep on giving him the mineral oil he had been taking—a tablespoon every morning. I remembered that in those years at Leaskdale I had found that a weekly "blue pill" had good effects. So I asked Dr. Clare if it would be advisable to get some and give him one occasionally.

"Capital," said Dr. Clare. "Get some and give him one once a week. They will be good for him."

I can never feel thankful enough that I asked Dr. Clare about it. If I had given Ewan the pill off my own bat!!!

On the way home I went into a Georgetown drugstore and asked the clerk for a box of blue pills. He said they had none made up and it would take half an hour to make them up. But first he would go to the drugstore across the street and see if they had any. He came back in a few minutes with a small cardboard box marked "Blue Pills."

That night Ewan slept till five and awoke with a bad headache. We got up and I gave him his tablespoon of mineral oil and then suggested his taking a blue pill. I got out the box. It was full of round grayish tablets. The "blue pills" I had had in the past were either black or white according as they had been coated with chocolate or sugar. So I supposed the color of these was due to their coating. Ewan took one and swallowed it. Immediately he complained of a "burning sensation." Now, Ewan has often complained of a burning sensation after eating and I thought little of this so I do not know just what made me go to the phone and ring up the Georgetown druggist. I told him what Ewan had complained of and asked him if he was sure he had given me blue pills. No suspicion of the horrible truth occurred to me but I did think he had given me something other than a blue pill. He said he would make sure. I then ran upstairs where Ewan had gone without taking any breakfast except a cup of tea. He suddenly began to vomit and vomited a panful of what seemed altogether liquid. I concluded that the pill and the oil together had turned his stomach and now that he was rid of them there would be no more trouble. He seemed to feel all right, said the burning had stopped and lay down on the bed. He wanted me to run down to the P.O. and get the morning paper.

I went. I was gone I suppose about ten minutes. As I came through the lawn on my return the recollection popped into my head of the curious dream I had had shortly before and I thought, "Nothing has come of it. It was only a dream, not a forerunner."

I noticed a car at the front door and when I entered the kitchen I asked Ethel who it was. "The doctor," she said composedly—and said no more. I at once thought it must be Dr. Clare or some of the other Homewood doctors who might be going through to Toronto and had called to find out how Ewan had got home. I ran into the library, expecting to find them there. Then into the parlor. No one there. With a sudden curdling fear I ran upstairs and stopped at the door of my room to stare in horror at the scene before me.

Ewan was lying unconscious on the bed. I thought he was dead. He will not look more corpse like when he is. Dr. Paul, with coat off and his shirt sleeves rolled up, was jabbing a hypodermic into his arm.

"What has happened?" I gasped.

This was what had happened. Mr. Watson, the druggist, had gone across the street to find out what kind of pill had been given to his clerk by the clerk there— the latter, by the way, being a raw youth who had had no training whatever in pharmacy. Then Mr. Watson found that what had been given was the *deadliest germicide* on the market—a "bug killer," composed of strychnine, bichloride of mercury and some other deadly drug with a long scientific name which I cannot now recall. Half a tablet would have been a fatal dose and Ewan had taken a whole one!

As soon as Mr. Watson discovered the horrible truth he 'phoned Dr. Paul at once and told him what had happened, adding, "For God's sake get up to Norval manse as soon as you possibly can."

Dr. Paul lost no time. He reached up and snatched from the shelf above his desk a bottle which had sat there for *fifteen years*, unopened and uncalled for. It contained an antidote to the poisons and if it had not been there he could never have got it in time. He was at the manse almost before I had disappeared from view down the street. He was just in time to get a dose down Ewan's throat before the latter collapsed from shock.

Dr. Paul briefly told me what had happened and said he had given him an injection of some powerful drug, the name of which I cannot now recall—a heart stimulant.

"It should take effect in fifteen minutes if it takes effect at all," he said.

It did not take effect in fifteen minutes. It did not take effect for half an hour. That half hour seemed like a hundred years. The only thing that helped me through it was the remembrance of my dream. In my dream I *had escaped*. I believed this meant that Ewan would not die but as the minutes passed with no response from the inert figure on the bed I fought panic. With ghastly clearness I seemed to see the days and weeks ahead. Ewan *dead*—dead by poison which *I*, however innocently, had been the means of giving him! All this would be dreadful beyond words. And not only that, but all the horror and publicity of an inquest!

At the end of that endless half hour Ewan rallied. His pulse became perceptible again and he was able to speak faintly. Before very long he was fully conscious and surprisingly strong. Dr. Paul went away, leaving tablets and directions and I got Katherine MacPherson, who is a retired trained nurse, to stay with me for the day.

Four things contributed to save Ewan's life and prevent any bad after effects of the poisons.

My strange feeling that something was wrong which led me to telephone at once. The fact that Dr. Paul had the antidote at hand.

The fact that Ewan had taken a double dose which made him so sick that he vomited almost immediately.

The fact that just before taking it I had given him the dose of mineral oil which coated the stomach and prevented the bi-chloride of mercury from burning the lining of the stomach. Dr. Paul was afraid of this and said Ewan might have digestive trouble for some time. But he never had the slightest. There were absolutely no *physical* after-effects from the poison.

Ewan seemed pretty well all the afternoon. But at six he took a weak spell and seemed to be so near collapse that we sent for Dr. Paul. He came but by the time he got here Ewan was quite over it. After the doctor had gone Ewan told me that the cause of his weak spell was his "thoughts"—the awful conviction that he had been so near the death and *hell* he had been dreading for so many months. This had affected his heart just as a shock of bad news or terror might have.

Dr. Paul left sleeping tablets for Ewan and he slept well. I, in Chester's room, could not sleep. Even if I could have, I was too frightened to sleep lest Ewan awake and have another attack of heart weakness. After such a day, coming on top of the wretched summer I had spent, I was almost on the point of collapse myself.

Sunday, Aug. 19, 1934
The Manse, Norval
Today was hot and windy. I did not go out to church and Luella left Pussy here while she went. She lay and cooed and laughed on Chester's bed all the time and I delighted in her. In the afternoon we had a lovely rain. I lay down, worn out, and had a refreshing sleep. Ewan slept most of the afternoon, too. Tonight I feel a strange peacefulness which is probably only the reaction from the dreadful strain of the preceding days. But it is nice to feel so even for a few hours.

This was the first Sunday that certain vague suspicions I had been feeling for some time began to crystallize into a definite conviction that something was wrong in Norval congregation in regard to us. The news of Ewan's poisoning had spread all over and we expected that some members of Norval church, especially the session, would be over after service to see him, or at least inquire after him. *Not one came.* Their minister, whom for eight years they had professed to love so devotedly, had just come home from the Sanatorium and had nearly lost his life through poison and not one member of Norval congregation came to the manse to inquire how he was or to ask how I had got through—not one, woman or man.

As I have said, I had felt for some time that they were not taking the interest in us that Union was. I felt a *chill* everywhere. I could not think of any possible cause for it, except impatience over his slow recovery and I felt very bitterly over it. We had both worked almost slavishly for them for eight years and surely they need not grudge him time to recover. They were not suffering in any way. We had arranged for good supply and I entertained them and the boys drove them, so that nobody was put to any trouble.

And when, later—too late—we discovered the real reason for their behavior I was—and am—still resentful. Even if Ewan had done what they were believing he had done, that did not justify the way they acted. It was not such a very awful thing even if he had been guilty of it and some of those men and women, with whom we had worked so long might have shown ordinary human interest in a sick and worried fellow creature. I shall never as long as I live forgive Norval congregation for the way it used us, even if it was misled by an unfortunate mistake and bedevilled by two men.

When we first went to the charge of Norval and Union, we found that the Union people welcomed us kindly and generously but did not make any particular fuss. But, as the years passed, we found that they were true as steel. At the bitter last, "every man, woman and child"—to quote one of the elders—was behind us.

Ewan and I often said to each other that Union was an ideal congregation. It was small but it was a solid block of well-to-do, well-bred and intelligent people, loyal to their church and to their minister. The Session was composed of men worthy of their eldership, the Board of Managers were business-like and took their duties seriously. I am not saying this because of what came later. That was our opinion from the first and time only confirmed it. We found the Union people sympathetic, friendly and congenial. I enjoyed every evening I spent in their homes, every afternoon in their W.M.S. The Union W.M.S. was a wonderful bunch of women, who would have died of shame, I verily believe, if they had failed in any year to overtake their "allocation." There was a splendid lot of young people in the church and it was a pleasure to work among them. We always felt thoroughly at home among the Union people. The salary was always paid promptly on time. If they did not have it on hand they borrowed it from the bank.

Norval, even from the first, was a cat of another color. When we went there they made far more fuss over us than Union did—they were really rather ridiculous in fact. They had just come through a bitter "Union" crisis. Half of the members had left the church and gone to the United church—the best half financially rated; and they bitterly assured the continuing Presbyterians that they would never be able to get anything like a decent minister because none such were left in the Presbyterian church! So when they got us (with L.M. Montgomery thrown in!!!) it rather went to their heads. (In passing, I may say that Ewan was the first minister ever called to that charge that both Union and Norval wanted to call. Always before one section or the other had been averse to calling the ministers they did, and agreed only under protest.) Norval bragged about us ceaselessly. Never, so Garfield McClure loudly averred, in season and out of season, had there been such a couple in

Norval manse. At the induction supper at Union Church the said Garfield made a very flowery speech of welcome, winding up by vowing amid great applause that "the Irish McClures would be loyal to the Scotch Macdonalds."

Loyal! Humph! And again humph!!

Norval congregation, as we soon recognized was a very different type from Union. For one thing it was composed of two very distinct and separate congregations. The church at Mt. Pleasant had voted narrowly into Union and the Presbyterians had left it and come in with Norval, thereby making it as strong numerically and financially as before the split. The Mt. Pleasant people were, on the whole, a fine group of people, well-to-do and nice. In fact, all the families in Norval church, with four or five very marked exceptions, were nice in themselves and in their homes. It was only as a church they failed to measure up. They never seemed to cohere into a real church. The Mt. Pleasant people were always rather unwisely talking of how they had done things in Mt. Pleasant church and this aggravated the old Norval section. Still, they all liked us, times were "good," they were all full of "I'll-show-you" after their Union fight—for a while things went swimmingly.

Ewan soon found the men of Norval church were, for the most part, weaklings. There was a striking difference between them and the men of Union. In the whole session there was only one man, Mr. Cook, worthy of his office. Of the rest, two were nice men with no backbone, one was a cipher, and one, Andy Giffen, an ignorant crank. Nevertheless, one good man on a session is a power and at first Ewan and Mr. Cook together were all that were needed.

The Board of Managers was in a similar condition. Only one man on it—Mr. Laird—was really any good. But again one man was enough. As long as they had such a leader they functioned well.

I was more fortunate as regards the women. While they did not rate as high as the Union women they were quite a good lot to work with. There were two or three nasty old cranks but the rest were pleasant. When I took hold of the W.M.S. it was almost moribund. But by the end of my first year it was in good shape, with a large membership, and so it continued, though it never attained to the Union standard. It never worried *them* if they saw they were not going to raise their allocation. It was I who had to scurry round and get up a "pie social" or something of the sort—at which I admit they worked valiantly—to raise the deficit.

But by far the worst feature of Norval congregation and the thing that made our work hardest was the "touchiness" of the members. I never saw such a "touchy" combination of people. Always in any congregation there are a few who have to be handled with gloves but in Norval this type was in the majority. Somebody was always getting "peeved" over a meeting, or offended at something somebody else had done or said. And then Ewan—whose strong point was certainly patching up quarrels and soothing wounded feelings—had to get busy and coax them back to church. Andy Giffen was furious because at a congregational meeting he hadn't attended it was voted to sell the clumsy and inconvenient old seats in the basement and replace them with chairs. He resigned from the session and stopped coming to church. Ewan had a hard time smoothing him down but finally managed it and he came back. Mrs. Sam McClure quarrelled with Mr. Capps, the man whom the managers had engaged to give the choir a musical training and she and Sam were going to leave and go to Brampton church. They only relented "because," Mrs. Sam told Ewan, "of you and Mrs. Macdonald." Jim Russell got offended at something old Mr. Gollop said to him and stopped coming to church. Nor would he ever come back, although he always remained a good friend of ours. Then the MacPhersons and the Gollops had a bitter personal quarrel which no one could patch up and which made certain things difficult during our last years in Norval. And so it always was—every few months somebody having to be pacified or smoothed down. But up to the summer of 1934 they all liked us—one can always *feel* those things—and in spite of everything things went on pretty well. When "the depression" struck it was harder. Union stood up to it but Norval went to pieces. Mr. Laird was laid aside by ill health and the rest were useless. The worst year they never held a single meeting. The salary was always hundreds of dollars behind. But we never dreamed of complaining or saying a word about it to anyone. What we would have done if I hadn't had some money I do not know. But I had, so we never opened our lips about the delays.

Life in Norval was in many ways pleasanter and much easier than it had been in Leaskdale. The manse had conveniences. Shops, etc. were nearer, also Toronto. I had a little more real social life—not, of course, in Norval itself, which was the usual collection of gossips and derelicts, but in the surrounding towns. Above all, we had the Barracloughs and the many wholly delightful evenings spent in the Glen House. Even had we had nothing else that would have been enough. Yes, until Chester's behavior and Ewan's breakdown we liked our churches and our people and our work. Our people liked us and our churches were doing as well as any of the rural churches and much better than most. So we—or I, for Ewan troubled himself about it not at all—simply could not understand the atmosphere I felt in Norval church and people from the midsummer of that year on.

Monday, Aug. 20, 1934
The Manse, Norval
Ewan slept well after taking two of Dr. Paul's tablets and I had a wonderful sleep and felt so much better all day. Ewan complained a good deal of his head but was able to eat three good meals, so his stomach cannot have been injured. Chester's brief vacation being ended he went back to Toronto today. Ethel remarked when he went that she had "heard he had lost his job and that was why he was home!!!" I suppose this is typical of the yarns that are bandied about among ignorant and malicious gossips. It makes me grit my teeth that I and my family should be the butt of them. But what matters it?....

Tuesday, Aug. 21, 1934
The Manse, Norval
Ewan slept after taking two tablets. Today his head seemed better than any day yet but he had a brief wild spell at noon. Dr. Paul says he can get up for a little while tomorrow. He also gave him some "nerve tonic pills." I shall have to give

them to him but I really do not want to. All those "tonic" things seem to excite Ewan's nerves and make him worse. None of his doctors seem to understand this and Dr. P. seems very pettish if I venture to differ from him on any point.

Wednesday, Aug. 22, 1934
Ewan awoke at six this morning. When I went in his face was as red as fire and he was literally writhing in the grip of all his worst phobias. It has been a hard, hard day. He had several crazy spells and several "sinking" spells—these last being just the same hysterical kind he had so often in Leaskdale. I knew those "nerve pills" would work harm. I did not give him any today. This evening he was calmer and able to play solitaire.

Anne of Green Gables is to be made into a talking picture. An actress named "Dawn O'Day"—probably a stage name—is to play the part of "Anne," instead of Mitzi Green as at first reported. As I get nothing out of it I have only an academic interest in it. But I suppose it will do me some good by way of indirect advertisement....

Thursday, Aug. 23, 1934
I have had a dreadful night and a hellish day. Ewan could not sleep at all last night, even with three of Paul's tablets. Then, at three, he took a "sinking" spell. As in these attacks his pulse is always strong I know they are not dangerous but nevertheless they always alarm me and furnish him with complete proof that he is dying! I got him a hot drink and then he slept for three hours. He got up at eleven, declaring he would not stay in bed. We had an awful afternoon. I have never seen him worse. In the evening Stuart and I took him for a drive and it seemed to help him a little. I played casino with him all the evening and now I have given him veronal. He *must* have some sleep tonight and Paul's tablets are no good when he is like this.

Friday, Aug. 24, 1934
Ewan slept for eight hours last night but woke groaning about his head. This has been another terrible day. He lay on the bed and groaned. "He was dying—I might as well be prepared for it—he was lost—God hated him—he was outcast." Once or twice he tried to get up and rush out, declaring he was going to throw himself in the river. I dared not leave him alone for a moment. Twice he broke into tears and cried maudlinly. In Leaskdale this used to help him but today it did not. Stuart advised me to agree with him that he was dying. I risked it and it seemed to work. In a few minutes he said, "I know it is all in my mind." Then he cried and sobbed. "I am a very sick man. You do not realize it."

At four o'clock callers came. I locked the door and went down. Smiled and talked to them for half an hour. Oh, I am a good actress—and I have had plenty of practice.

When I went back Ewan was in a terrible condition. I remembered how I used to give him potassium bromides. I gave him one and in a short time he was much calmer—ate his supper, played casino and even made a joke! It would all be comic if it were not so tragic!

In the evening mail I had a bit of good news—the first for a long time. I had sent a short story—"I Know A Secret"—to my new agent, Miss Elmo of New York and she has sold it to *Good Housekeeping* for $400. This is more than welcome just now. The joke is—I had sent it to *Good Housekeeping* a few months ago on my own and they rejected it!

Ewan was restless again this evening and again hinted at suicide. Yet with all his "worries" he can eat three hearty meals a day while I can hardly force down a bite. It is sometimes rather difficult to be patient with him.

Saturday, Aug. 25, 1934
The Manse, Norval
A bad night. Ewan could not sleep and at last had to take veronal. He said he was no better when he woke and we had a bad forenoon, with all the usual goings-on.

After dinner I made him get up for I knew it would be much better for him and we drove to Brampton and then over to Union to call on Verne Thompsons. This was Ewan's own suggestion and as the drive had made him feel much better I consented, though I was nervous about it—with good reason for, as we were sitting talking on the veranda Ewan took one of his "sinking" spells. Everyone made a great fuss and probably thought I was very heartless because I took it so coolly but in a little while he was all right and seemed much better on the drive home. As long as Ewan has his hands on the wheel he is practically well. He has to concentrate on driving and his mind cannot torture him with conviction of damnation. Yet I think people think I am crazy to let him drive and lost to all sense of rational fear when I get in with him. I am not one bit afraid. I know he will be all right as long as he is driving.

After supper he took one of his sudden turns for the better and wanted to go up and see Joe McClures. We spent the evening there and nobody would have thought there was one thing wrong with Ewan. He laughed, chatted, joked. The McClures were delighted to see him so well. I am always tortured by the hope that he will stay well—because it *did* happen so many times in Leaskdale.

Sunday, Aug. 26, 1934
Ewan slept well last night—he said it was the first *restful* sleep he had had for months. I went to church, taught my class and played the organ. I think some of them might have offered to play for me when they know what a strain I am under but no one did. Ethel was away and I had Mr. Chapman to dinner. He said this was one of the pleasantest homes he had ever stayed in—so restful—so considerate etc. And all the time I was listening tensely for any warning sound from the room above!

Ewan got up for supper and talked to Mr. Chapman fairly well. Then we drove to Hornby and up to Mt. Pleasant. Called at Arthur McClures and Lairds. Ewan was pretty well at Arthur's but not nearly so well at Lairds'. Talked about his symptoms all the time and worked himself all up.

They have been making some alterations in the house to fit it for *two families.* I think Murray is going to P.E.I. in September to bring Marion back with him.

I am so tired of telling the poison tale to everyone who inquires. It is bad for Ewan to hear it—it would be so much better for him if he could forget it.

Monday, August 27, 1934
The Manse, Norval
....We drove to Georgetown and spent the evening with Pat and Ken Langdon. They had some friends in, we played Euchre and Ewan seemed absolutely jolly. The vagaries of his malady are beyond me.

I signed the contract today with the agent for the stage production of *The Blue Castle*, giving her a year's option. I wish something would come of it but I don't suppose anything will.

And dear little "Slim," our pet black squirrel, has been killed. He was walking happily across the street and a brutal car ran over him. I feel terribly over it—he was such a pet and so cute and delightful. His little hoard of nuts and cones in the church steeple will never be eaten.

Today I happened to be looking over the faded old scrapbook wherein are pasted the first stories and poems I ever had published. What thrills those acceptances gave me—what delight to see what I had written in print. Ah, well, that far-off youth is something the gods cannot touch. It is forever mine even in these hideous days when it is hard to believe I was ever young and in love with life.

Thursday, Aug. 30, 1934
Ewan had to take two Paul tablets and then chloral last night and even then slept fitfully. I slept hardly at all. But this has been his best day yet. He does not have any of those sinking spells now. But there are times when I fear his mind will never really recover its normal poise. He seems so *childish* in many respects.

Friday, Aug. 31, 1934
Ewan had to take veronal last night and then slept only four hours. He had a bad day but not as bad as last Friday. He would not get up and had several bad spells. This is eating my life out. I seem gnawed by so many worries and I cannot decide what is best to do.

Stuart was in Toronto today for the gymnastic contest at the Ex. and came home still Junior Champion of Canada.

Saturday, Sept. 1, 1934
Ewan slept naturally and seemed fairly well through the forenoon. He was able to read a good deal. After dinner he got up and played solitaire. In mid-afternoon I went down to the store and heard there that Edith McKane had died. She was one of our Union girls, a bright, nice thing in her teens. She has been ill for over a year with some disease which no doctor has been able to diagnose or understand. I hurried home to prevent Ewan from hearing of it, if possible, until he was fitter to receive it. But I was too late. Ethel had already heard it over the phone and had blurted it out to him. I found him in the library, terribly upset, moaning that he wouldn't be long behind her. He went to pieces so badly that I got him off to bed before Mr. MacKay should come.

Mr. MacKay is a retired minister whom we have got to preach for some Sundays. He is a Scotchman by birth, very courteous and intellectual and a great talker. If my mind were at rest I would enjoy his conversation but as it is I wished a great many times during the evening that he would get tired and ask for his room.

Speaking of Stuart's gymnastic success he said one of Stuart's classmates had told him that Stuart was far and away the most graceful gymnast on the field. "None of us can hold a candle to Macdonald."

As a summary of this week—Ewan has slept *one* night without drugs. Has not had any one day as bad as Thursday and Friday of last week. He has had no "sinking spells" and his mind spasms seem to pass more quickly. Nevertheless, I have had many bad moments trying to fight discouragement. I can only live by not thinking of the future at all—just living for the day.

Sunday, Sept. 2, 1934
Ewan had to take chloral last night and this has been a hard, hard day. Sundays are always his worst days. I went to Sunday School and church. Margaret Russell, home from Toronto, offered to play, saying that she thought it terrible no one had offered to play last Sunday when they knew I had been under such a strain. But she herself has made things hard for me in the Sunday School Christmas work more than once.

I went to Union Church with Oliver Hunter because I wanted to go to see McKanes. The service seemed endless to me—Mr. MacKay is a good preacher but his sermons *are* too long. Edith looked lovely and young and peaceful. There was the usual talk of how sad it was for anyone to die so young. I have never felt so. I believe in the old saying "Those whom the gods love die young." They have had the loveliness and happiness of youth. They go out of life—they are born over again to another reincarnation and a second youth. It is like having two springs together, with no winter between.

When I got home I found Ewan, as I had feared, in a terrible state. He was crying and so on and so on. I gave him a bromide—and a sound talking to. It did him good, too. After supper he was quite rational. I hate to be severe with him but at certain times it seems to be the only thing that does him any good. He spent the evening talking to Mr. MacKay on the veranda but had a haunted look all the time.

Monday, Sept. 3, 1934
The Manse, Norval, Ont.
Again a hellish day—Ewan slept only three hours despite three Paul tablets. They are losing what little effect they ever had. He was as bad all day as any day yet. He was "lost"—"dying"—"fated"—all the old drivel I have heard so many hundred times. I tried during the forenoon to reason him out of it but in the afternoon I was too tired to try so I sat in silence by his bed and did mending while he groaned and maundered ceaselessly. I kept up till the evening when I had to let go in a moment of panic and rush away to Chester's room for a burst of tears.

This evening I talked things over with Stuart. He will be leaving for college in three weeks' time. What shall I do then if Ewan is no better?

Lucky knows I am troubled and follows me round anxiously, looking at me with his bright sympathetic eyes. Darling little cat!

Tuesday, Sept. 4, 1934
I slept till 1.30. Woke and found that Ewan had not slept at all. I let him have a veronal and he slept till eight. In the morning he was dull and moody and refused to get up. At dinner time he took what is undoubtedly the worst spell he has had yet. Cried—threatened suicide—would not eat his dinner. After dinner—at which I could eat nothing either—I had to leave him, my mind racked with anxiety, and go to Edith's funeral. Mr. Howard of Georgetown conducted it. It was an ordeal. Everyone was asking about Ewan. I wonder what they would have said if I had blurted out the truth. I repeated the old patter about his "nerves." I went over with Oliver and Margaret Hunter and had an hour's wait after the service while they gossiped with everyone. And each minute seeming to me a year! When I did get home I found Ewan in bed in a dreadful state of mind. He declared he had been "unconscious"—which was all nonsense, of course. He had heard a voice saying, "The Wrath of God abideth on you." He is the prey to all kinds of odd delusions just now. I told him some compliments the Union people had paid him and got him to supper. He ate a good meal and was a little better in the evening. Charlotte MacPherson came over and made an interminable call while I wondered what Ewan was doing upstairs. History repeats itself. I remember just such an evening in Leaskdale with Lizzie Oxtoby. Charlotte is a dreary companion. Even at the best of times she always blows my candles out. Yet she and her sisters have been very kind to me and are really faithful friends.

I got a photo today of Dawn O'Day, who is to play Anne, of O.P. Heggie, who is to be "Matthew" and of Helen Westley who is to be "Marilla." Dawn really looks like my idea of "Anne" and "Matthew" is good though beardless but Helen Westley is not the Marilla type at all. She would be a perfect "Mrs. Rachel Lynde"....

The next two days were written in my notebook as a sort of hourly log.

9 o'clock A.M. Ewan had a broken night with some sleep from chloral. He was restless when he woke. Ate a good breakfast but was grouchy. Up to now he has been playing solitaire and reading novels. At least, he can read a good deal of the time now. In spring he could not read at all. I am thankful for this.

Ten. I went for the mail and got a little fresh courage from the pine hills. "My help cometh from the hills." A phone call came from Toronto saying a man would be out to interview me for the *Star* re screen appearances of *Anne*. I got ready with a sick heart. During this past hour Ewan has been alternately reading, playing solitaire and brooding. He is very quiet and does not talk. He seems to resent my dressing up and curling my hair. His attitude in regard to this seems to be, "I am dying, etc. She should not be thinking of vanities." It is all absurd but it hurts me.

Eleven. Ewan has brooded all this hour and will not talk. I made him take a glassful of Vip. He looks terrible—sullen, unshaved, vindictive. The change in Ewan's appearance during these spells is almost unbelievable. Normally, he is a fine looking man, with clear-cut features and friendly dimples. But in these spells he seems almost bestial—hideous. I can't bear to look at him. Nobody has ever seen him in one of them—I have always been able to prevent that. They could never forget it.

Twelve. E. brooded till 11.40. Since then has been making an attempt to play solitaire.

Two o'clock. The *Star* man came at twelve and stayed an hour. I was in torture all the time, not knowing what Ewan might be doing or feeling. He asked so many ridiculous questions I would have liked to throw something at him. When he finally went I relieved my feelings by a few italics and came up to Ewan. I found him dreadful. Cranky and hateful. This is a new development. He says he won't eat dinner—won't get up—won't shave. He fairly glared at me. I told him if he would not eat his dinner he would have to get up. If he did he might stay in bed. He then ate everything on his plate—a hearty meal. Then he raved for an hour. He is furious with me because I won't believe he is dying and lost. Now he has begun to play solitaire again. I have not been able to eat a mouthful.

Eight thirty. Ewan ate a hearty supper. After supper I got him to get up and dress and we went for a drive. He was very grim at first but as we drove along he became better as always. We went south along a lovely new road—new to us. It had hardly a house along it and in many ways it reminded me of an island road. It was secretive and yet friendly. It had many moods and all beautiful. I got some spiritual satisfactions from its loveliness that helped me over the evening. When we came back Ewan was quite normal and played solitaire till eleven. "I was possessed today," he said. "It was not I who was speaking."

No? But who was it? What demon inhabits his body at such times? I can understand the old belief in devil possession.

Thursday, Sept. 6, 1934
Ten o'clock. Ewan slept well after a Dr. Paul tablet and seems fairly well this morning. It is a muggy drizzly day. At present Ewan has dressed, shaved and is reading on the verandah. What a blessed change from yesterday. If it would last!

Twelve. Ewan has been pretty fair all the morning. Has read and played solitaire and has made no complaint of body or mind.

Two o'clock. Ewan came down for dinner. Was quite normal and even joked.

Five o'clock. Ewan went to see Dr. Paul and has come home pretty well. He seems to enjoy reading and playing solitaire. It is like heaven after hell.

Seven thirty. At supper Ewan said he wasn't feeling as well as through the day. We went for a drive to Victoria and home by way of Terra Cotta. He was very quiet all through the drive, merely saying that he was "resigned." When we came home he went to see the MacPhersons.

Ten thirty. Ewan has been fine all the evening. Plans to go into Toronto tomorrow. This has been his best day since coming home.

Friday, Sept. 7, 1934
Ewan took a Dr. Paul tablet and slept but not so well as last night. He wakened several times and moaned a great deal in his sleep. We went into Toronto but he was very grim. When we got in he complained of "feeling like falling" and I got

him a bromide. He then went to have a Turkish bath and I shopped and ached
with worry lest he take some kind of a spell on the street or in the store. When
he came back he was still very gloomy but at lunch one of his sudden changes
came over him and he has been fine ever since—the best yet. It is all very mysterious. He had a good evening and read a magazine. But I am so tired I don't
know what to do.

Saturday, Sept. 8, 1934
The Manse, Norval, Ont.
Ten P.M. Ewan slept from eleven to eight last night without any dope but somewhat brokenly. He was all right till eleven A.M. but from 11 to 5.30 none too
good. At 5.30 he took one of his spasms in the middle of a game of checkers. I
brought him up to our room and kept him here. The same old story—it was the
end—he was fainting—dying. I gave him a bromide and a good talking to besides.
In a short time he was all right and we went back to our checkers. I haven't played
checkers since I was 18 but anything to amuse him and divert his mind.

We went to Georgetown after supper to see Dr. Paul and had an awful drive
home through a thick fog that had come up. Yet Ewan did not seem to mind it and
drove quite coolly through it.

Mr. MacKay came and I compelled myself to talk to him. He recommended
"quiet" for Ewan. Well, I think we are quiet enough outwardly. If he could suggest how Ewan's mind is to obtain "quiet" I should be obliged to him.

I *cannot* face another time like last Tuesday and Wednesday. Or so I feel. Of
course if it comes I shall manage to face it. It is only in prospect I cannot face it.

Four o'clock at night. Ewan has not slept in spite of two veronals. Neither have
I. I am in Chester's room, feeling that life is too awful to go on with. Everything
is always so much worse at night. I dread tomorrow. But when has there been a
tomorrow I have not dreaded?

Sunday, Sept. 9, 1934
In spite of his sleeplessness Ewan has had a fair day. Indeed, it is a curious fact
that his bad days generally come after he has slept well—as if something, balked
of its prey for a time, descended on it in redoubled fury. He was quite easy till ten,
after that not so well. I went to Sunday School and, as ever, forgot my anguishes,
or drove them into the background while I taught the young men's class. The lesson was a very dull one from the Old Testament. I wonder just what the people
who select the lessons mean by some of them. The lesson today was on some of
the ceremonial of the old temple law, about which none of the boys cared or could
be made to care. After Sunday School I ran over to see how Ewan was. He was
fair but the service was one long torture to me. I thought it would never end. Mr.
McKay, whose prayers are really as long as his sermons, prayed for Ewan until I
thought he would never finish with it. And I *feel* the people are *not* at one with him
while he does it, though I can't imagine why. I came home and, as it was Ethel's
Sunday off, got dinner. Ewan was fair. Stuart took Mr. McKay to Union service
and I sat down, hoping for a little rest and breathing space. No use. A car load of
people arrived. Mrs. Oxtoby and Mary from Leaskdale with Leslie and Ruth Hart.

The afternoon was a nightmare. Ewan came down and acted and talked quite well but I never knew from one minute to another how long it would last. I got supper and then they went. Then Ewan and I went for a drive to Acton. He was better than any night yet. He hardly mentioned himself or his symptoms and spoke of plans to be carried out "when we got better." When we came home he went to bed but I washed the supper dishes. I am woefully tired but a little more hopeful. But it is a dreadful see-saw. I know not what a day or a night may bring forth.

Tuesday, Sept. 11, 1934

Ewan had a very bad night. Took two Dr. Paul tablets but could not sleep. They have no effect on him at all. Then he took veronal but it did not make him sleep. Neither of us slept—for I never dare go to sleep before he is sleeping—but Ewan read most of the time and did not seem distressed. We went into Toronto this morning and while I shopped E. had his Turkish bath. When we met he was very bad and continued so till after dinner—when he was very well again and has been so ever since. But I cannot see that he is making any *real* progress. He is bad one day and better the next. It was always so. He never recovered by degrees but always suddenly.

I am very tired tonight, after my sleepless night and day of shopping. My head aches.

Wednesday, Sept. 12, 1934

Ewan slept naturally and well from ten to seven but has had none too good a day. His head and his phobias bothered him considerably.

I had a good sleep, too, but have felt very tired all day. I am feeling the strain of these past dreadful weeks very severely. And I am not getting any writing done. I don't see how I am going to get *Pat II* finished in time and if I don't things will be serious financially.

Tonight I got a letter from Mrs. Thompson which has worried me. She writes that she has not been able to get a situation and wants me to take her back.

Now, I can't do this. I told Ethel when she came that it would be a permanent place if she could fill it and she is doing fairly well. If I sent her off Robinsons, who are very touchy, would leave the church probably. So I had to write and tell Mrs. Thompson so. I feel badly over this. I know what trouble she will have in finding a place at house-work where she can have June with her and how hard the world is for a woman in her position. I suppose I am foolish to let this worry me. *She* left *me* in my serious trouble and did not worry over it. Still, I would not let that weigh with me if I were free to take her back.

Thursday, Sept. 13, 1934

A bad night for both of us again. Ewan didn't sleep at all, despite drugs, and had a pretty bad day. Had several spasms, the worst coming on at supper time, though it passed quickly. After supper he went to Toronto with Stuart. I had been in a state of terrible though concealed despair all day and when I found myself alone I permitted myself the relief of breaking down and having an hour of tears. This calmed me and I could appear to be my usual self when Ewan came home. He seems a little better tonight. But what will I do when Stuart goes back to college? Can I continue to endure this hideous life without him?

Friday, Sept. 14, 1934
Again a bad night. Ewan took veronal but could not sleep. At two o'clock he was in such a state I gave him another dose and he slept the rest of the night. Dr. Paul does not approve of veronal but what is one to do? The tablets Paul gives have no effect at all most of times and if Ewan goes for two nights without sleep the result is terrible.

I had to take a tablet myself to get any sleep at all.

This night was followed by another dreadful day. Ewan was as bad as his worst day. Stayed in bed all day—howled and wept—declared he was dying and lost etc.—vowed he couldn't eat dinner or supper but cleaned up everything both times. And this was the day I had to entertain the Union Missionary Auxiliary. I spent the afternoon literally in torture. I would smile—talk—answer all questions regarding Ewan's condition by saying it was one of his days for bad nerves and he had decided to stay quietly in bed! Every quarter of an hour I would make some excuse and slip up to our room to make sure that Ewan was still there and hadn't rushed away to do something dreadful, listen to his raving for a minute, beg of him to try to control himself until the guests got away, compose my face and return to the parlor. The meeting over I gave them all supper and afterwards saw them off smilingly. Then, after our own supper, I made Ewan get up and go for a drive. For the first mile or so he was very bad. Talked of himself and his destiny unceasingly and warned me darkly that I was going to have a terrible surprise—his meaning being that, since I wouldn't believe he was dying, I'd get a bad jolt when he did. Then, as ever, the driving took effect. He became quite calm, admitted he was enjoying the drive, and when we came back was quite rational all the evening.

An added pleasure of the day was a distracted letter from Ella yowling about Maud's marriage.

Ever since Maud Campbell's father died I have provided for her. I bought her clothes and paid for her music lessons, her tonsils operation etc. I sent her to P.W.C. When she failed there the first year I sent her back. The second year she succeeded in getting though. She had been promised the home school but when she passed a new set of trustees had come in and they refused it to her, both last year and this year. As there are now far more teachers in P.E.I. than there are schools it is very difficult for a girl to get one unless she can get her home school. I did not blame Maud for feeling a bit discouraged.

For a couple of years she has been engaged to Wallie Sims, a French River boy, who is well enough in his way, though there is a very bad streak of insanity in the family. He and Maud wanted to be married last fall but Ella managed to prevail on them to wait. Now Ella writes me that they have told her they are going to be married and nothing can move them. Maud is very stubborn when she makes up her mind (like her mother before her for that matter!) and will not listen to reason. Ella implores me to see what I can do.

I will not. I do not approve of it and I am deeply disappointed in Maud. She knows very well what I want her to do. She is only eighteen. Four years from now

300

she would be plenty young enough for marriage. I wanted her, if she could not get a school, to stay home and help Jim till he got on his feet. She could save him a hired man's wages for she is big and strong and likes working outside. But she will listen to no one and I have neither energy nor inclination to meddle in the matter. If she wants to cut her girlhood short and settle down on a farm with Wallie Sims she may, for all of me. I have other things to worry over....

Saturday, Sept. 15, 1934
The Manse, Norval
Ewan slept after two tablets of chloral last night but wakened with phobias galore. Still, he got through the day better than yesterday. He got up, shaved and dressed, and played sol. He had a bad spasm at twelve but it soon passed. We had a drive up to the Sanatorium in the afternoon but Ewan heard there of the death of Mr. Bruce who had been a friend of his while he was there and this depressed him terribly. His turn, he said, would be next. However, the Barracloughs called this evening after their return from England and this cheered him somewhat. One of the San doctors gave him a bottle of sleeping draught and I hope it will make him sleep. Chloral and veronal seem to be losing their power and I dare not let him have larger doses.

For myself, I have been very miserable with cold all day. The weather was muggy—slimy—oppressive, with rain at night. Mr. Laird—Murray's father—died today. He has been an invalid for two years and a terrible one. Murray is worn out waiting on him. It is a blessing and a relief that he has gone but if he had chosen of malice prepense an inconvenient time to die he couldn't have hit it better. Murray was all ready to slip down to the Island, marry Marion, and bring her back. Now he cannot go and leave his mother. I will wire to Marion to come up and be

"Lucky"

married here—she asked me some time ago if she might come, should it so happen that Murray could not get away. But I dread it under the circumstances more than words can say.

I have not told Ewan about Mr. Laird's death and won't till after the funeral if I can help it. I dread the effect on him. Any *thought* of death seems to drive him crazy with dread. Poor, poor man! What a curse he is under! And why?

Luck is curled up beside me on the table as I write, looking at me with his round, limpid eyes. Without Stuart and him this summer what would I have done? And Stuart has always been out in the evenings and I had only Luck. I've seen that cat, when I was crying, stand on my lap, and push my hands away from my face with his nose and rub his head against my cheek as if to say, "You've got *me*!"

Sunday, Sept. 16, 1934
The Manse, Norval

....It was a wild night of rain and thunder and noises. The trees around us seemed all to have gone mad at once. Normally, I like to look out into a storm. There is something in it akin to the deeps of my spirit. But at present it adds to my disheartenment.

Ewan seemed dull this morning and I dreaded the day but oddly enough it was his best day since coming home. He came to supper and said grace quite normally—that is, not in the mumbling, deprecating voice he uses when he is feeling "guilty"—and talked to Mr. McKay quite rationally. In the evening we went to the Glen House and had quite a nice evening. Ewan laughed quite a good deal—after assuring me on Friday that he would "never laugh again." We had one of the lovely Glen suppers and Ewan seemed quite normal coming home. But I feel very exhausted after the strain of the day and I dare not let myself hope again. It is better to stay down than be hurled down repeatedly.

I read today that the Sea of Galilee is being used as a storage reservoir for the "complete electrification" of Palestine!!!

Must this be? Should this be? Might they not have kept that one little land sacred to the highest of humanity?

Mon. Sept. 17, 1934
The Manse, Norval, Ont.

Ewan had a poor night. The Sanatorium medicine gave him only two hours' sleep. He took veronal and slept one. Then chloral and slept till 8. It is terrible—his taking so many drugs but he says he would go mad altogether if he did not sleep and I suppose it is a choice of evils. Dr. Paul says "no veronal" but the tablets he gives are of no use whatever, as I have told him repeatedly. He just changes them—or pretends to—for others no more effectual. It is a difficult situation....

Ewan was gloomy till three but had no bad spasms. I had to tell him of Mr. Laird's death. He took it fairly well but said he would "follow soon,"—he had "no hope of getting better." After three we went to Brampton for a drive and came home by Huttonville. Ewan seemed very well all the evening. We played casino and he has read quietly from nine to ten....

Tuesday, Sept. 18, 1934

Ewan slept naturally from ten to four and has had, I think, his best day yet. He was rather dull till three but got up and shaved and dressed of his own accord. After three he seemed *much* better and we went for a drive. It was a lovely day and Ewan was quite chatty. The roadsides were green after the recent rains—like a second spring. The hills were windy and golden.

Ewan really seemed quite normal all day except for two speeches—"I feel guilty"—"I have no right to be alive." But he played casino all the evening and seemed to enjoy it—laughed frequently....

302

How I dread the shortening days! Tonight is a lovely night. The river valley seems filled with a cold wine of moonlight. The dark moonlit pines on the hills— ten minutes of looking at them rested me. Beauty such as this has always been meat and drink to my soul. There has always been some subtle unbreakable bond between me and trees.

I am homesick tonight. Shall I ever see my Island again? Shall I ever watch a moon rise over the dark old hills of spruce there again?

If Ewan would get just a little better I would urge him to go down to the Island for a month. But he cannot yet go alone and we both cannot go, for a great many reasons. One of us must be here to "hold the fort." For I feel there are traitors in it.

Wednesday, Sept. 19, 1934
The Manse, Norval
Ewan *did* sleep well all night—the second night in succession. I do feel encouraged, even though he had only a fair day—dull, with spasms of unrest. We went to the Glen House in the evening and played Euchre. Ewan played well—laughed and talked normally but took two restless spells and had to go out a few minutes each time. He made some excuse and the Barracloughs did not notice anything wrong but I knew the significance and sat in tense misery until he came in. He has read since he came home and seems fair.

It has been a hard day for me, tense and strained, dreading the next lash of the whip. I tried to do some "spade work" on some short stories but did not do much. I am getting nothing done. And there is trouble brewing up over a note I signed for a friend—more fool I! If I have to pay it—as I fear I will—I don't know where the money is to come from. I can't sell out a single investment without heavy loss. I am terribly worried about it.

"If I could have one day free from bondage!" Ewan has just groaned.

I echo the wish with all my heart!

Thursday, Sept. 20, 1934
We paid last night for two good nights. Nothing could make Ewan sleep and he has been very restless all day, though without any very bad spells. I got no sleep and my nerves have been raw all day. Had an air mail letter from Stell raging about Maud's marriage. What does she think I can do about it?

I would be at the end of hope and courage altogether if it were not for Lucky. He is so lovely and affectionate and charming. Not an hour but he gives me some pleasure that sweetens life. In my sleepless nights he comes to me, purring encouragement and love. Dear beloved little cat!

Friday, Sept. 21, 1934
....Murray called re wedding plans. Mr. Taylor came re note. He has got it renewed and is going to England for a few weeks in a last endeavor to get a foothold under him again. Says he will be back in time to take care of note.

A silly fussy old maid came to see Ewan this afternoon and had a bad effect on him. But after supper we went for a drive on my "dear road" and he seemed like his old self. Physically he is really quite well and there is nothing to prevent him going back to work except that crazy conviction that he is "forbidden to preach." Nothing seems to have any effect on *that* phobia. It is terribly exasperating.

Saturday, Sept. 22, 1934
A bad night. Ewan could not sleep and insisted on taking a double dose of veronal. I was in agony lest he never waken and I sat on the rug outside our bedroom door most of the night. As I sat there in the dark worried and anguished, a warm fluffy body came creeping into my lap and a soft little head reached up and rubbed my cheek. Then the dear cat curled himself up in a ball and kept me company all through my dreary vigil.

Ewan had a bad day and a terrible spell at twelve. He came up to our room, lay down on the bed and cried. There was a score of different things the matter with him. He has, since Dr. Williams told him about his—supposed—heart condition become a hypochondriac as well as a melancholiac. A trifling twinge of rheumatism in his ribs—he has angina—a slight cough—he has contracted tuberculosis. It would be funny if it were not so dreadful.

We went for a drive after dinner but the first half of it was misery. When we got to a garage just out of Milton he told me solemnly he was "a very sick man and could go no further." I didn't see *how* we were to get home. Then, suddenly as ever, the change came. He was all right and we had a pleasant drive home by our wood road, scarfed with its golden rod and asters.

Ewan seems quite well this evening but I dread tomorrow. But when have I not dreaded it?

Marion is coming Saturday. If all was well how delighted I would be, fussing over her wedding and having things nice. As it is, I wish heartsickly that it was over. I have had a dreadful time convincing Ewan that he must marry them.

Sunday, Sept. 23, 1934
The Manse, Norval, Ont.
Ewan had some natural sleep and seemed better all day than any day yet. I find myself asking if the horror can be over but afraid to believe it. I took some of the San. dope myself last night and had a wonderful sleep. So the day has been a little easier in every way than usual. But I go in fear—always in fear.

> And if I laugh at any mortal thing
> 'Tis that I may not weep.

Monday, Sept. 24, 1934
Ewan had a bad night and again I feel the old sickening despair. I got up in the foggy, drizzly morning wondering how I could face the day.

Ewan had some pretty bad spells all day with the usual phobias. This afternoon I could not work and walked the parlor floor two hours in despair. This evening we went to the Glen House and Ewan seemed fine all the evening and said he felt better than for a long while. The old see-saw that is harder on the nerves than continued despair!

304

Tuesday, Sept. 25, 1934
....Stuart went to Toronto in the morning, having taken his trunk in yesterday. I saw him go with a kind of despair. I seldom saw him save at meals and bed time but that was a help. I fear the time between was spent in an environment I cannot approve of. There are some things I feel keenly worried over in connection with Stuart. But I feel I can do only harm by talking. He knows what my opinion of some of his associates is and I can do no more. But it all adds terribly to my burden just now.

Wednesday, Sept. 26, 1934
The Manse, Norval, Ont.
....I got out *Pat II* and read over the chapters I have written. I *must* try to get some more done....

Thursday, Sept. 27, 1934
....A letter from Stokes says Miss Dean has signed the play contract and paid the option.

Friday, Sept. 28, 1934
Ewan had seven hours of real sleep last night—but was rather grim and restless all day. As soon as I had sat down to try to write a little he came up with the old palaver of never being well again etc. I lost patience and simply ordered him out but it spoiled the day. I worked doggedly till five, then went to pieces and walked the floor. To add to my unrest I had a disturbing letter from Mr. Starr, Taylor's lawyer, about that note.

Sunday, Sept. 30, 1934
A horrible night and dreadful day. Ewan didn't sleep and I was too worried over many things to sleep. Finally he took chloral. I was in my own bed as Marion had to take Chester's, when Mr. McKay was here, and I began coughing so I got up and went down to the parlor sofa where Luck and I lay till five. I went to Sunday School this morning, again wondering how I could teach, but as ever managed it. I played also but it is the last Sunday of my quarter for which I am devoutly thankful.

Mr. MacKay made his usual long prayer reference to Ewan and "his loyal people." His people, at least in Norval, are *not* loyal. I found it very difficult to sit quietly through the service. At supper Mr. MacKay talked almost continually of people dying and said everything he shouldn't say in Ewan's hearing. I knew what the effect would be on Ewan and nearly went mad with the strain. Now, at 7.30 I really feel as if I were going out of my senses. I have been walking the floor. If the wedding were only over!!!....

Monday, Oct. 1, 1934
The Manse, Norval
Ewan slept till seven without drugs and seemed fine this morning. It had been arranged that while I went to Toronto with the M's he was to spend the day at

the Glen House, so my mind was fairly easy and I enjoyed the day more than I have for a long time. We got home at five, when an evening sun was kissing the misty golden hills, and I found a Stokes report which was a pleasant surprise, as it was much better than I expected. But I soon paid the price of my enjoyable day. The Barracloughs brought Ewan home at seven with an alarming tale. They had taken him out driving and during the drive he had had "a heart attack." They had taken him to the Glen House, he had been "sinking" and Dr. Paul was summoned in a hurry. Paul gave him a stimulant and told him he must not go driving in a car again!!

I knew just what had happened and after the Barracloughs had gone I found I was right. If Ewan had been at the wheel he would have been all right but as he was not he had nothing to do but *think*. His phobias took possession of him and he became suddenly convinced that he was "dying and damned." This acted on his nerves exactly as a shock of bad news would do and brought about a collapse. Paul did not know this of course. But I am in despair over his forbidding Ewan to drive. His daily drive is his only salvation. Without it he would have been past help by now.

Ewan seemed very upset all the evening and I have just at bedtime found out the cause. Paul, the old idiot, told him he "might have anemia if he were not careful." Ewan evidently thinks anemia is very deadly—I think he has confused it with "pernicious anemia" and is all worked up. I *told* Dr. Paul never to tell him anything about his health that would alarm him, but to tell *me* and indicate the proper treatment—and this is what he has done! Ewan had a slight coughing spell this evening and said hollowly, "It would not take long to establish a consumptive cough in me." If he becomes a hypochondriac as well as a melancholiac God help us!

Tuesday, Oct. 2, 1934
The Manse, Norval
....Wiggins, the treasurer, called today and paid Ewan $450—the salary up to date. This was thoughtful of the people. Perhaps I have been too hard on them. It may be "just their way" when I have been thinking them cold and unsympathetic.

Simpsons Pfd. has crept back to $80. Last year it was $6. So my investment of $15,000, which I feared was a total loss, has come back to $11,000. Perhaps it will come back fully yet. But nearly all my investments are far below what I have paid for them. I could not realize on any of them without loss. And my biggest one *is* a total loss and I have said farewell to it....

Wednesday, October 3, 1934
This has been one of the days I am tired of calling hellish but it is the only adjective that applies. Ewan took only Paul tablets last night and slept poorly. Seemed fair this morning but as usual developed phobia at ten and by eleven was frantic. He declared he would not and could not perform the marriage ceremony— that he would be smitten by a curse if he did. At four he declared he was dying. I suddenly lost my patience and gave him a sound drubbing. All at once he began to smile and in a few moments was all right. His complaint is nothing but

neurasthenia or hysteria but as he is letting it ruin our lives it is as bad as if it really were insanity. He was quite cheerful at supper and all the evening and is calmly reading now. I told him flatly that there were to be no more tantrums—I wouldn't put up with them.

Apart from Ewan I had a miserable day, preparing for the wedding and trying to be bright and normal—or at least to appear so. I made cake, salad, jelly, mock chicken and layer cookies. Went to the MacPhersons' for flowers and decorated the parlor—and all the time I was in mental agony and gnawing worry. Oh, if it were only tomorrow night!

Thursday, Oct. 4, 1934
Well, it is "tomorrow night," thank God—

> The darkest day
> Live till tomorrow will have pass'd away.

Knowing Ewan must have sleep I gave him veronal and he slept all night and so did I. But when I woke worry rushed over me like a wave.

Ewan wakened with phobia and was bad all the forenoon. At noon my legs were simply trembling under me with worry and strain. I worked all the morning, getting the table ready etc., running up to our room every ten minutes to scold or comfort Ewan, and all the time waiting for the axe to fall—a flat refusal of Ewan to perform the ceremony. *What* would I do if that happened!!!

After dinner Marion dressed and Mrs. Laird and Murray came. Ewan dressed and looked all right but said he was "under a doom." Nevertheless he performed the ceremony as well as he ever did and looked all right. There are times when I lose patience with him. He *can* control himself when he tries and he could preach as well as he performed the ceremony if he would make the effort. I hope Marion will never know what a haunted minister married her, or what black despair was in my own heart as I watched the marriage, kissed and congratulated them and hurried off to give the last touches to the table. Finally they were gone—going to Muskoka for a week—and Ewan and I, in defiance of Paul's dictum went for a drive to Brampton. I know people will think it is dreadful of me to let him drive when they know what Paul said but I cannot help it. They do not know what I know. Ewan was quite well and cheerful during our drive and had his best evening yet tonight. Did not have the usual bad spell between seven and eight. By contrast, this evening has seemed almost one of peace and happiness.

Friday, Oct. 5, 1934
The Manse, Norval
....Chester and Stuart came home this evening. But Chester went to Reids' and Stuart went where I would not have him go so my burden is heavier instead of lighter.

Saturday, Oct. 6, 1934
....A Dr. Schofield spent the evening here. He...says that Isobel undoubtedly is a mental case.

Sunday, Oct. 7, 1934
....Mr. Barraclough told us Norval had asked for a "joint meeting" with Union. We feel something is in the wind but cannot guess what....

Monday, Oct. 8, 1934
....I tried to work at *Pat II* and wrote half a chapter but find it very difficult to settle my mind on it.

We drove to Streetsville and enjoyed it.

I heard today that Mrs. Thompson is home in Zephyr, not having been able to get a place even at housework. This made me feel very badly. Sometimes I feel like letting Ethel go and having Mrs. T. come back.... But I know Robinsons would be offended and just now I am particularly anxious not to antagonize anyone.

Ewan has been reading all the evening and enjoying it. And I noticed one thing tonight. For the first time since last spring Lucky has curled himself up on Ewan's body and gone to sleep. He has never done this all summer—a strange thing, for he was always very keen to do it any time he could not get on or near me. Darling Lucky! Many a time this summer and autumn he has been my sole companion and comfort in hours that without him would have been unbearable....

Tuesday, Oct. 9, 1934
The Manse, Norval, Ont.
....I tried to write at *Pat II* in the forenoon but found the strain unbearable. I cannot concentrate.

We went for our drive but it was of the nightmare variety. Ewan took a notion to go to Woodbridge to see Mr. MacKenzie, the minister there. But when we got there, by some devilish coincidence we found him in a terrible state—in the grip of real melancholia. This had a very bad effect on Ewan. Mr. MacKenzie was sure *he* would never preach again and Ewan at once decided *he* would not either. I had a dreadful time with him on the way home.

This evening I went down for the mail, hoping there would be something nice for me—perhaps a good letter from some old friend of happier days. Nothing at all. I came home in the dim cold twilight, feeling hopeless and broken.

Wednesday, Oct. 10, 1934
The Manse, Norval, Ont.
E. slept for several hours but seemed *possessed* when I went in this morning. He was violent and *abusive*—something he has never been before. We had a dreadful scene. Then he burst into tears and was very dull all day. We went for a drive but it was a miserable affair for both of us. I was in such despair.

And then he was quite well all the evening and read, while I could do nothing but play solitaire—for I've come to that, too. I have not played solitaire since the winters I was at home in Cavendish after Grandfather's death. But now there are hours when I can neither work nor read and I think I'd go crazy if it were not for solitaire. It is a curious fact—and it seems to be the same with Ewan—when I am so worried and restless I can neither read nor work I can play solitaire and find a certain escape in it.

We have not yet heard what they did at the congregational meeting last night. I feel certain there is something ominously significant about it and I am tortured by a dozen different suppositions as to what is the object of it. This is a terrible life—but it seems to be my predestined lot—I must bear it for the sake of my children.

Thursday, Oct. 11, 1934

....I tried to do something at *Pat II* but failed. I couldn't work or plan. There was no nice mail—only a crazy letter from some man in Guelph, named McLeod, who says he is from P.E. Island and wants to come to the manse for "a visit"—to beg when he gets here I suppose. Why must I be persecuted by maniacs like this. I have written him twice that my husband's illness prevents me from having guests and I shall ignore this letter.

It is all a hundred times harder than it was at Leaskdale. *There*, too, our people were so helpful and considerate. I am desperately afraid tonight that I am at the breaking point myself.

Saturday, Oct. 13, 1934

....Mr. Barraclough came over in the evening and told us what was done at the meeting. They decided to give Ewan "leave of absence" till the end of December and have student supply. This is equivalent to saying, "If he isn't well then he must go." Well, we know this. Some time ago I told Ewan that if he could not take up his work by New Year's he must resign. This was all Mr. Barraclough told us but I feel quite sure there is much he was not told. He is so strong a friend of ours that he would not tell us anything that would hurt us....

Sunday, Oct. 14, 1934

....I had to play again today as Mrs. Sam McClure had some excuse for not being there. *I*, of course, have no excuse—except that my husband is ill and that I am almost at the breaking point myself. I wonder what people think I am made of.

Monday, Oct. 15, 1934
The Manse, Norval, Ont.

Ewan had a rather bad night and had to take veronal. In the forenoon he went to Toronto on the bus to have a Turkish bath and got home at five. His mind seems much better.

I didn't sleep till two and then only by a dose of barbital. But today in Ewan's absence was very peaceful and I got a chapter of *Pat* written. But I am getting on so slowly with it. Sometimes I fear I'll never be able to write again.

Tuesday, Oct. 16, 1934

....We spent the evening at the Glen House and Ewan seemed jolly and normal the whole time. This is the first evening since April that I have felt at ease when out in company with him.

I did a bit of *Pat II* and found it easier. Life had a bit of savour today but I dare not let myself hope too much. But I *must* hope a little. I could not continue to exist otherwise. Yet I am afraid—afraid—afraid. If he slumps again.

Wednesday, Oct. 17, 1934
The Manse, Norval, Ont.
Ewan slept from 12 to 8 naturally and has been pretty fair all day. No bad spells. In the afternoon we went to Jean Giffen's wedding. She is one of our girls but was married by a relative of the family. I was thankful Ewan was not asked to do it. He seemed pretty normal all through the afternoon—laughed and talked. He had a slight restless spell while waiting for lunch but nobody but myself would notice it. He spoke to the toast to the bride quite well and pronounced the benediction. He seemed very well all the evening and has not had to take a sedative today in spite of all the excitement.

But the afternoon was a serious strain for me and I am very very tired. I could hardly summon up a laugh when "The M's"—Murray and Marion—came in.

I wrote a chapter of *Pat II* this morning but it dragged.

But oh, the difference between the Ewan of this day last week and today. Yet I go in terror of a return of the worst symptoms.

Thursday, Oct. 18, 1934
Ewan had to take medinal last night—a new sedative which we find much better than veronal or chloral. He seemed very well all day. We went in to Toronto. Ewan had a Turkish bath which always seems to do him a great deal of good. I think it soaks some poison out of his system.

"Jean etc. myself at back"

We got home at four and I wrote a bit of *Pat II*. I am very hollow eyed and nervous but my appetite has picked up a bit this week. I feel more like myself. I am able to take pleasure again in darling Lucky's beautiful curves and stripes. He is curled up on my bed beside me now as I write, in a fluffy, perfectly round gray ball. Before he went to sleep he lay for awhile on his back, spreading out his paws and weaving them in the air—*almost* perfectly happy. He would have been perfectly happy if he could have lain on my breast, his body against my face. Failing that, on my stomach,—or he could have been contented on my legs. Since I could not have him on any of these portions of my anatomy tonight he has curled up in the back curve of my knees. And the purrs of him! He is as warm as a little stove. I love to touch him—poke him. When I do he gives utterance to a delightful sound between a purr and a "Way-ow"—or unrolls himself and begs me to tickle his little abdomen.

There never was such an exquisite cat in the world!

I saw a sunset tonight—a fiery autumnal sunset, with sorrowful dark cedar spires against it—and further on dark pines tossing. I cannot express the strange exquisite pleasure which dark pine or fir boughs tossing against a night sky always give me. It goes to the deeps of my being. Ah me, how little it takes to make me in love with life once more, in spite of all. But that little is lacking. I wonder if I will ever be able to abandon myself to beauty again—I wonder if a feeling of permanence and ordered living can ever be mine again. I have forgotten what it is like.

And I am so tired. As soon as the strain relaxes at all I realize how tired I am. I know what I would like to do. Go to bed for a month—a warm, fluffy bed with a hot water bottle and be *waited* on. I feel cold and tired all the time.

Saturday, Oct. 20, 1934
The Manse, Norval, Ont.
I could not write last night.

For a long time now I have noticed this. If I begin to feel a little bit encouraged or allow myself to feel a bit of my old joy in life it means that some new blow is coming—some new worry is going to pounce on me.

Ewan slept naturally Thursday night but I slept poorly—too tired and nervous. Ewan was pretty well all day. I wrote some at *Pat II* but found it hard. This is one of my worries just now. If I become unable to write what will we do? It haunts me in the dark hours of the night.

I raked and burned some leaves in the afternoon. It would do Ewan good to take some exercise like this but he simply will not do it. After supper I went down for the mail in the chilly October dusk. I wished wistfully that I might get some nice mail that would cheer me up.

Instead—I got a letter for Ewan from Mr. Geggie of Knox College in regard to Stuart. I will not go into details. It nearly drove us both crazy. We had a dreadful evening. "The M's" dropped in and I tried desperately to laugh and chat but they must have seen that I had been crying. And I was wild with fear that this would set Ewan back again. *What* demon is persecuting us? And Stuart, who is a general favorite and never gave us any worry of this kind before!

Of course we had a bad night and though both of us took veronal we did not sleep. This morning we went into Toronto and saw Stuart. We discovered to our indescribable relief that the whole thing was absurd—the exaggeration of an officious old maid. At least, that is Stuart's story and that of the other four boys involved and he has never given us any reason to doubt his word. But Mr. Geggie evidently believes the whole concoction. If Ewan were well I would have insisted he go to Geggie and have it all out but as he is not I cannot. We came home. I was much relieved but worn out and my nerves were in a dreadful condition. Fate might have spared us this at such a time.

Sunday, Oct. 21, 1934
The Manse, Norval, Ont.
It rained nearly all day and has been dull and dark. Ewan slept naturally but had a headache this morning. He seemed pretty normal all day however, and this evening and said, "I feel pretty well. If I keep on I will soon be back to work."

But it was a hard day for me. I was so nervous that it was only with the utmost effort I could pretend to be calm and cheerful. I got through Bible class but I could hardly sit out the service. In the evening I felt a little better and was able to read. I thought of the days long ago, before 1919, when on a Sunday evening my little lads would be cosily tucked up in bed and I would have a lovely Sunday evening of reading, with no gnawing worries and recurring fears. That seems a century ago. Now I never know a really peaceful evening and my boys are away and I am alone.

No, not alone. I have my dear pussy, looking at me with those deep soft loving eyes. Forgive me, Lucky.

Chester has neither written nor come home for some time. This worries me. I can never feel sure of Chester again, after the past....

Monday, Oct. 22, 1934
Ewan had to take medinal last night and has been very dull all day. His phobias have returned. This may be the result of our worry Friday night but it may have come anyhow. It has before. I couldn't sleep, despite veronal, and have had a wretched day. The weather has been dark and dismal. I wrote two hours at *Pat* but found it impossible to work the rest of the day. From four to six I shut myself in a room where no one could see or hear me and walked the floor.

The Thank-offering meeting is tomorrow and I must lead it!!

Tuesday, Oct. 23, 1934
Ewan had a bad night in spite of medinal but seemed fair all the forenoon. I wrote at *Pat II*. It came a little easier but I can find none of the old pleasure in it. Ewan went alone to Toronto in the afternoon to have a Turkish bath and I prepared for the meeting, fixing up the table in the basement with ferns, candles etc. But I could not feel the old interest in it. I went down for the mail before the meeting but felt very weak and short of breath. Still no letter from Chester. But we had a good meeting and it did me good—dragged my thoughts away from the torture

for a little while. Mrs. Smith of Toronto spoke and was very interesting. Some of the speakers we have had at our meetings have been pitiable.

Ewan came home at six and has seemed pretty well all the evening.

Wednesday, Oct. 24, 1934
The Manse, Norval, Ont.
....Dr. Howard called with another MS. of a "novel" he wanted me to "criticize," of which I cannot say one good thing. It was ghastly—in plot, conception and treatment. The man must be crazy....

Tuesday, Oct. 25, 1934
A bad day. Ewan did not sleep well and was very restless all the forenoon. As bad as ever—all the old rot about "being Judas" etc. The day was dark and dull and I couldn't work or think.

Friday, Oct. 26, 1934
Ewan slept pretty well but was very bad all the forenoon and refused to get up, saying he was dying and would be in hell before the day was over!! I tried to work but couldn't. He got up for dinner—he can always eat a hearty meal which I know is something to be thankful for but feel is a little peculiar, considering what he believes and seemed fair all the afternoon. In the evening he said he "felt fine"— better than for a long time etc.

I had a terrible day. That dreadful, indescribable "solar plexus" feeling which attacks me when I am worried beyond a certain point was present all day.

But the evening brightened life a little. Stuart came home and the matter of the Geggie letter has been finally cleared up. One of the other five boys who got a similar letter went to Geggie about it—and found that Geggie had never written the letters or even seen them. His secretary, Miss Irwin, had written them and signed his name to them. He told the boys, "Those old maids get queer notions into their heads sometimes."

Very fine!!! But why does Mr. Geggie allow his secretary to send such letters under his name unless he knows what is in them is justified? His easy-goingness has given me a week of hell when I was already bearing all I could bear, and probably given Ewan a bad back-set.

Saturday, Oct. 27, 1934
Ewan slept well and was fair all day. No bad spells. We were in to Toronto. I called at McClelland's, got some books, and felt cheered up by a chat with rational minds. I have, it seems, got to the stage of which Emily Dickinson speaks in her tragic poem—I only ask of the Grand Inquisitor—"those little anodynes that deaden suffering."

We brought Chester out. He looks well. Perhaps my recent worry in regard to him has been without foundation. But I don't like the way or place he is living— in the small "apartment" to which he removed when Luella came home. It isn't the kind of place he should be in. I wish he would go back to Knox. He doesn't want to—perhaps because of his situation—perhaps—but it is idle to speculate....

Sunday, Oct. 28, 1934
The Manse, Norval.
....A hard day, as Sunday always is now but a little easier than hitherto. Mr. MacKay preached for the last time. I am thankful I'll hear no more long screeds about Ewan from the pulpit but I'll miss Mr. MacKay's weekly visit. He is a pleasant conversationalist and a gentleman—which all ministers are *not*, in my experience.

Monday, Oct. 29, 1934
Ewan slept for the fourth night naturally but seemed dull and depressed all day. He went to Toronto for a bath and I wrote at *Pat II* and found it easier as I always do when Ewan is not around....

Wednesday, Oct. 31, 1934
Ewan had to take medinal last night and was dull all the forenoon. We went to Toronto in the afternoon and I had a short visit with Nora. It helped for a time but underneath it all I was full of unrest. We called at Chester's flat on the way home. He is ill again with a bilious attack and was not in the office.

Ewan seemed well all the evening but I was so nervous and restless I had to play solitaire to keep an even keel....

Thursday, Nov. 1, 1934
Ewan slept naturally and was quite fair all day. He played solitaire and read. The day was fine and cold. I went to the Institute meeting and it was cheerful and helped me a little. We spent the evening at the Glen House and up to ten Ewan

"The Glen House"

was quite normal. He talked to Mr. Barraclough about politics and church matters and played euchre. At ten he had a restless spell but it soon passed. We had a nice lunch and talked and laughed around it as of yore. They are *such* dear people. On the way home Ewan remarked that he was "getting his confidence back."

Friday, Nov. 2, 1934
Ewan slept for three hours and then I was awakened by his groans. He was as bad as ever and continued so all the forenoon. I could get nothing done and I had a good deal to do. After dinner we went to Toronto and had an *ugly* drive. Ewan was not only neurotic but *disagreeable*. I had no shopping to do so I read in Simpson's rest room while he had his bath. Or I tried to read. In reality I was aching with worry. But Ewan turned up smiling and normal. We left for home—the car developed trouble—we had to go back and put car in garage till 8.30. Meanwhile we had supper and saw a movie. Coming home Ewan seemed in good spirits but I was tired and discouraged. There was bad news, too, from the Dominion stores, in which I have quite a bit invested. They have passed dividends and there are gloomy reports about them.

Saturday, Nov. 3, 1934
The Manse, Norval.
Ewan had a bad night. Took veronal but couldn't sleep. So neither could I. Even if I shut myself in Chester's room I heard his groans. He was in bed till 11.30 today—dying etc. Then he picked up and by four was feeling all right. We went up to Marion's for supper. Ewan was all right till ten and was playing checkers with Murray when he took a sudden bad spell. I was watching and seeing it coming on made some excuse and got him right away. As we left in the car he said he had had "a vision of himself in hell."! By the time we got home he was all right. This case is beyond me. I have never heard or read of anything like it. No wonder Dr. Garrick found it "hard to diagnose."

Not having had any sleep I had found the day very hard. I tried to write but had to give it up. Tried to sew and go on one of my "dream voyages" which have so often given me a little escape from intolerable realities. But in vain.

"The M's" seem very happy. I do not grudge them their happiness but I cannot help feeling a little bitter when I see it—a bitterness I never before felt at any time. I used to find compensation for everything in my children. But I can no longer do that.

Sunday, Nov. 4, 1934
The Manse, Norval
....We had the first student preach—a Mr. Dunn. He gave a good sermon but was crude and flippant. He was here to dinner and patronized Ewan very amusingly. Mr. Davies of Willowdale, an old friend of Ewan's, came to supper and spent the evening. It helped Ewan, I think. Very few of the ministers of the Presbytery have troubled themselves about him....

Monday, Nov. 5, 1934
Ewan slept fairly well and has been fairly well all day. He went to Toronto on the bus to have a Turkish bath and some electrical treatment he is trying. The bath is good for him—I wish he could have one every day—but I doubt if the other is. He always seems worse after it. It stimulates when what his nerves require is something soothing.

I got a chapter of *Pat* written but had no pleasure in it—or in anything else for that matter. I am very thin and strained-looking.

The Choral Society, which flourished for two winters, has petered out this fall. Dr. Fletcher tried to start it up but failed—probably because Ewan could not go about to round them up and get them to join. So this bit of brightness will be wanting in the church life this winter. I, of course, went only on social nights but I enjoyed them and the final concert very much.

But I doubt if we would be here for it this year in any case. I doubt if Ewan will be able—or rather will think he is able—to take up his work at New Year's. I know if he made the effort he could do it but the problem is to get him to make the effort. And if he cannot he must resign. There is no other solution.

The thought of leaving Norval hurts me horribly. I love it so—my hills, my trees, my river, my garden, the beautiful church I've loved and worked for, the pretty roads all around. And go—where? To Toronto I suppose, to live in some dreary cramped house on a street where scores of exactly similar houses stand cheek by jowl. The thought is intolerable. I have always had space and openness around me....

Tuesday, Nov. 6, 1934
Ewan has had *thirty* consecutive hours of almost normality. This is the longest period since he came home....I wrote a little and got on fairly well....

Norval Manse in November

316

Thursday, Nov. 8, 1934
....The wind is waking far off in the pines on the hills. Luck is squatted at my side, gazing at me with his limpid round-eyed look. The room is peaceful; but I would I were at peace in my soul....

Friday, Nov. 9, 1934
I slept till four when I was awakened by Ewan's groans. Going in, I found he had had a sleepless night and he has felt badly all day. I could not write but did a little spade work. After dinner we went to Toronto. I had a wretched worried afternoon. Mr. Taylor is not back yet and I doubt if he will be in time to take care of the note. Then I wandered around Simpson's in a daze of misery until Ewan came. We had a miserable drive home.

I went to Brampton with the M's this evening to see the *Count of Monte Cristo* but I was too gnawed with worry to enjoy it. I recalled the first time I read *The Count* years ago in the old home. Uncle Leander had brought it with him in his batch of vacation books. It has never been any great favorite of mine.

I came home dreading what I might find but Ewan was better and says he is feeling all right.

Mr. Gollop and Mr. Morgasen called this morning about the Old Timer's concert. I sensed something a little odd in the wind but cannot decide just what it is.

Odd, indeed! Had I known what was behind that call I would politely have shown Mr. Gollop to the door and told him with equal politeness that he could take himself and his "Old Timers' Association" to limbo as far as I was concerned.

In the second winter I was at Norval, the executive of the Young People held a meeting to draw up the season's program. Among other things I suggested that we have an "Old Tyme" night, with old-fashioned costumes, songs, readings etc. The idea was adopted. In due time the "Old Tyme Night" came off and was a huge success. The big audience was delighted and it was unanimously decided to make it a yearly event.

When the executive met the next year someone suggested that it be only the older married folks who should give the Old Tyme program and that later on there would be a night at which only the young people would take part. "We will see which will put up the best program," it was said. The "Old Timers" had their night, which was held in the Parish Hall and it was even a bigger success than the first one. Later on the young folks put on theirs, but it fell rather flat and was never repeated. But from then on the "Old Tyme night" was held every winter, expanding and becoming more elaborate each time until it became "the" event of the season and drew crowds from far and near. Last year so many were turned away that we had to repeat it. Three years ago we cut loose from the Y.P. society altogether, formed an "Old Timers Association" with an executive of our own and divided the profits equally between the two churches.

The second year I got up a dialogue with Ewan, Mrs. Mason and myself in it, which was a hit. Next year I put on a one act play with an all-woman cast. By this time the "pattern" of the Old Tyme night was set and never varied. It was an understood thing that I was to put on a play, choosing the cast and directing the production. Apart from this, a committee was appointed to get up a program of music and readings. With this I had little to do, save hunt up readings and stunts, and I never attended the musical practices, which were held on different nights from the play practices.

After the concert the Association held a business meeting, at which a new Executive was appointed, whose duty it would be to start the affair up again in the fall. It was an understood thing that I was always on the executive and I was always notified of the fall meeting along with the others.

I always enjoyed getting up the Old Tyme play, in spite of some difficulties. The cast, being older, did not fool away half their time, as the younger casts did, but settled right down to business and we always had a pleasant social hour and lunch after the work. Garfield McClure was in his element. He was in every play (it was never easy to get a willing and suitable cast. So many of the older folks didn't want to be bothered) and always had the comic part. He gloried in it and was very good, only that he invariably clowned his part. There were times a-plenty when I could have boxed his ears. It was of no use to tell him anything—he "knew it all" and was impervious to hints. I could not "tick him off," because I dared not risk offending him. But I shall never forget my secret delight when Mrs. Boyd, the Anglican minister's wife, did it. I had no reason to care much for that lady but I forgave her all for the sake of that.

We were at a practice and Garfield was just a little more clownish than usual. Suddenly Mrs. Boyd lost her temper and turned on him. I never heard anyone get such a combing down. The mildest thing she said was that he was ruining the play and throwing everybody else out.

The rest of us stood with our mouths hanging open. I expected Garfield would leave the play in air. But he was too fond of it to do that. He simply sulked for three nights—just moved like a stick and repeated his lines like a robot. Then he snapped out of it and seemed to forget all about it—also he gave up clowning. But when we put the play on he broke his record for clowning—whether to "spite" Mrs. Boyd, or whether in the intoxication of the public performance he lost his head altogether I can't say.

Last year Garfield did what a good many of the Association disapproved of— he went outside our bounds and asked several strangers to take part. Their numbers were effective but I knew there was a good deal of grumbling among the real "Old Timers." As it did not matter to me, I said nothing. I got up the play, gave a recitation, wore a very handsome "period" dress, and worked like the proverbial slave generally.

Last spring Mr. Gollop was elected President of the Association and this fall it was his duty to call a meeting and notify all executive members.

When he and Mr. Morgasen (who is one of the Anglican members and a very nice man) came to the manse this morning I naturally thought they had come to consult with me about a suitable night for the meeting. Mr. Gollop seemed rather ill at ease but at last said they had come about the Old Tyme night. I said, "Oh, yes, I suppose you will soon be having the meeting."

I saw Mr. Gollop shoot a glance at Mr. Morgasen but Mr. M. preserved a rigid silence, so Mr. G. had to say,

"We had the meeting last night at Mrs. Webster's."

This was the point where I should have arisen and said, "In that case I do not see where I come in, in regard to the matter." I really felt as if I had been struck in the face. The Executive meeting had been held and I, a member of that Executive, had not been notified!

"It was decided to have a Scotch night this year," went on Mr. Gollop—in the light of what I learned later I realize how exquisitely uncomfortable he must have been, the old hypocrite—"and would like to have you help."

As I had been "helping" for nine years, without any special request to, I thought this seemed peculiar. But I said pleasantly, "I'll be glad to get up a play as usual."

Again Mr. Gollop's eyes sent an S.O.S. to Mr. Morgasen and again the good Jake ignored it.

"Well," hesitated Mr. G. "we don't know if we'll have a play this year or not. Some thought we might have something else."

I am glad to say, for the sake of my own self-respect, that when I heard this I stiffened up.

"In that case," I said coolly, "I don't see what assistance I can be."

Mr. Gollop mumbled something about "nothing being decided" and got himself away. I was both hurt and puzzled. But I had too many other and far more pressing worries to give it a great deal of thought. I decided that possibly no insult had been intended—I *could not* believe it had been. Mr. Gollop was old and had quite possibly forgotten to send me word or thought someone else had sent it—and when he discovered I had not heard of it, felt uncomfortable over it. As for the play, quite likely they had thought a change would be better and, as matters were, I would not be sorry to be rid of the drudgery of it. So I dismissed the matter from my mind.

Not very long afterwards I discovered what had happened in regard to that meeting. Garfield had called on Gollop and they had selected a night for the meeting. Nobody knows what went on between them but it is certain that the insult to me was decided on then and there. *I was not to be notified of the meeting.*

The rest of the Executive assembled at Mrs. Webster's and when it became evident that I was not coming Mrs. Hewson and Mrs. Brown demanded why I was not there. (They were Anglicans. From first to last, I understand, the Anglicans one and all stood up for me!) Mr. Gollop hemmed and hawed—tried to evade the question—but Mrs. Hewson would not be denied and he had to admit that he had not notified me. Then every Anglican on the Executive declared that they would have nothing to do with it if I were left out. (I daresay they had heard rumors and smelled several large and odorous rats. So poor old Gollop had to say he would see me about it next day and I suppose he asked Jake Morgasen to come with him because he was scared to face me alone. Otherwise, there wasn't the slightest need for anyone but himself coming.

If I had known this—but I didn't know it. I knew I had been slighted but it never occurred to me that the slight could be deliberate and intended. I thought I had been simply overlooked and I considered *that* insult enough from a group with which I had worked in perfect harmony and accord for eight years and an association of which I was the founder.

Sunday, Nov. 11, 1934
Ewan slept fairly well but was very restless a great deal of today. However, he began to write a sermon and wrote for fifteen minutes at it. This is an advance.

I went to Sunday School and church and found it hard to sit through the service as the student, Mr. Richie, was very flat.

In the evening we called at Arthur McClure's. Ewan behaved very well but I felt a sense of strain all the time—"watchful waiting" is hard on me. But I feel better tonight than I have for a long time. Two weeks ago Ewan wouldn't have dreamed of trying to write a sermon. But I am so tired—I slept only four hours last night.

Monday, Nov. 12, 1934
A hard day. Ewan did not sleep well and from morning on was very bad. He threatened to go and drown himself—a threat he has not made for quite a while. Then he took a notion he wanted to go to the Island and stay till New Year's. I agreed. I believe it will be a good thing for him. He is, I think, able to travel alone now and Aunt Christie will look after him. The change will be just what he wants, now that he has begun to enjoy things again at times....

I told Ewan if he went to the Island he must promise that when he came home at New Year's he must make an effort to take up his work and he said he would "if he were living!"

In the afternoon we went to Toronto. I spent a little while with Nora and then we met the Barracloughs and the four of us went to see the pre-view of the *Green Gables* movie. It was a dreadful experience for me. Ewan sat in front of me and I knew all the time he was almost as bad as he had ever been. Afterwards he told me he "thought all the time he was dying and that hell was waiting for him."

I had looked forward to seeing the screen presentation of my book with interest. But it was just one of the nightmares with which my life abounds—two hours of misery. And then to have reporters coming up to ask "what I thought of it etc." I don't know what I said. My one desire was to get Ewan away. We had a miserable drive home. It is now late and Ewan has had to take medinal—the first time for nine nights. I feel terribly discouraged. And yet he *has* improved. Till today he has had no bad spasms for some time—he sleeps *much* better—he takes an almost normal interest in things a great deal of the time. I must not let myself despair.

Thursday, Nov. 15, 1934
I slept well last night and so did Ewan but he was dull and moody all day. Not quite so bad as yesterday, however, though he had one spasm when he declared "a hand had caught him."

But I got a slap in the face tonight that almost stunned me. I simply cannot understand it. I am too sick at heart about it to mention any details.

A slap in the face! I should think so. The scar of it is on my soul to this day. And my blood still boils with indignation whenever I recall how two men, whom I had for years regarded as my friends, inflicted on me such humiliation. Well, I think that perhaps today they feel more regretful over it than I do. Yes, I think both Mr.

Gollop and Garfield McClure would be very glad if yesterday could be tomorrow as far as that incident is concerned.

That Thursday morning Ewan had gone down for the mail and when he came back he said he had seen Mr. Gollop and the latter had told him to tell me that the Executive were meeting at George Brown's that evening and wanted me to be there to see about a play!

Well, I decided to go. I supposed there had simply been an oversight on Mr. Gollop's part in regard to the first meeting and that his embarrassment when he called was due to his shame over the fact. So in the evening I took the three plays I had selected after hunting for one all summer and went down.

The rest of the executive arrived in due time. I and some more were in the "den" and the others were in the living room with the folding doors between open. Finally, the secretary, Prairie MacGuire, was asked to read the minutes of the former meeting.

Knowing what I know now I realize that this must have been a very uncomfortable moment for two men there.

I heard the minutes read with a sense of stupefaction. *At that meeting a committee had been appointed to get up a play!* Mrs. Hewson and Mr. Morgasen were on it, and either one or two more. I am not sure which and at this distance of time I cannot recall their names. *But my name was not on it.*

Moreover, I knew then and there that Mr. Gollop had told me a deliberate lie when he had said that they did not know if they were going to have a play or not. At the very moment of speaking he knew that they had decided to have a play, that a committee had been appointed to get one up and that I was not on it!!

And Mr. Gollop, sitting there and hearing those minutes read must have known that *I* knew him for a liar.

I was hurt to the core—and I was bitterly angry as well. But at least I knew what I had to do and I took the only course open to me with dignity and self-respect.

I sat there, quiet and smiling; and presently the "committee" came into the den, sat down in the corner around me and proceeded to "meet." Garfield was there, too, though his name was not on the committee (he had been cute enough for that!) and he asked me what I thought about it. I took the opportunity. Politely and coldly I said that since I was not a member of the committee I did not see that it was necessary for me to think about it at all!

The result was very visible consternation. Garfield muttered something about not being on the committee either. Poor Mrs. Hewson said that she understood that I was to be play director as usual and the "committee" was simply appointed to "help" me. "Wasn't that so?" she appealed to Mr. Morgasen. He squirmed and said nothing. Evidently *he* was not going to lie out of it. As I did not then know how Mrs. Hewson and the other Anglicans had stood up for me at the first Executive meeting, I thought they were all in the plot to insult me and I did not thaw. After a few uncomfortable moments Garfield rushed into the breach and asked Mrs. Hewson *if she had read the plays he had given her?*

This gave away something else. I grasped the thing at once and later found out I was right. Garfield had spent the day after the executive meeting scouring the country for plays. He had gone to people in Georgetown and Huttonville. *But he had never come to me*, the person who always had plenty of plays on hand.

And when he got some plays he had taken them to Mrs. Hewson to read and report on!

Mrs. Hewson cleared her throat desperately and said she had read the plays but didn't think any of them would be suitable.

Another silence. Finally Garfield in desperation—and it must have been a pill for him—turned to me and asked me if I had a play.

I flicked an airy finger at three plays, lying on the table.

"The ones I chose are there," I said. "The committee is very welcome to them."

Nobody took up the plays. Nobody did or said anything. I was mistress of the situation and I kept on being mistress. Garfield must have hailed the invitation to lunch which came presently as a providential happening.

After lunch I picked up my plays, excused myself courteously and went home. As soon as I found myself on the dark street, where sombre trees were tossing against a pale sky my pride failed me and bitter tears filled my eyes. I had never been treated so—insulted so—by any organization in all my life. I raked my memory for some cause I must have given the Executive to use me in this fashion. I could not recall anything—I had never had any dispute with any of them—we had parted in the preceding spring on the best of terms.

I stopped at the manse gate and bowed my head on the post and cried bitterly. Then I opened the door and went into the house where no help or companionship awaited me.

No, I must not say that. "Is thy servant a dog?" said Luck—or would have said it, as he came to meet me in the dark hall. I scooped him up and pressed him to my face. He rubbed his head against my cheek, he licked it with his tongue. Here was a faithful, loving little creature who would never hurt or forsake or betray me. A fig for the Old Timers. Let them stew in their own juice. I was through with them.

I should have adhered to that resolution.

Friday, Nov. 16, 1934
Ewan and I both slept well last night but he was dull all the morning. He made some visits in the afternoon and seemed better all the rest of the day. It is an advance that he feels like visiting. He seemed well all the evening. But I found the day very hard. I couldn't write and was very nervous. In the afternoon I went to the Anglican bazaar in the Parish Hall—something I have always enjoyed. But I felt "out of it"—as if my pain and worry made a wall around me that shut me off from human companionship. After supper I went to pieces and spent most of the evening in the spare room where Ewan could not see me walking the floor. I could not even play solitaire. *Everything* seemed to hurt me. All my old hurts and sorrows seemed to come up and hurt again. This has been my worst evening yet. I *must* get a grip on myself.

Saturday, Nov. 17, 1934
The Manse, Norval, Ont.
....I had a fair sleep but Ewan had to take veronal and was very miserable all the morning, going on about being "lost" and going to die. I could not write but held myself to routine tasks. After dinner we went to Toronto and I shopped while Ewan had his bath. The Christmas crowds are beginning and I felt like a hunted

creature among them. Ewan seemed better when he met me and has as usual been well all the evening.

Marion dropped in for a call and bent over Luck, curled into a ball on my bed. "Oh, Lucky, you are such a *satisfying* cat," she said.

I realized that out of all the adjectives of the world she had hit upon the right one. Luck *is* satisfying—entirely and absolutely....

Monday, Nov. 19, 1934
Ewan slept naturally and was fair all day. A little grimmer some hours than others. He had one bad spell in afternoon. Cried and threatened the river again. But this passed and he was quite normal again.

I had to take veronal to get any sleep at all and up to five o'clock today was really the most unbearable day I ever spent. I could not write, my hand shook and trembled so. I could not read or do anything but walk the floor. I am worried over Ewan going to the Island—over the Taylor note—over Chester—and over this tumor. It has been the last straw. It is sore now and bled quite a bit today. I suppose I must see a doctor about it and I hate to. Suppose it is something really serious—how can I face it now, on top of everything else? At all events, I won't see a doctor until Ewan is off to the Island. He has to wait until he can get his permit to travel half fare and that is a matter of some red tape. I wish it would come. Since he is going the sooner he goes the better.

Tuesday, Nov. 20, 1934
The Manse, Norval, Ont.
Ewan is sleeping better again. He had a pretty good night and wakened without groans. I had to go to Toronto this morning to see about that note, so I went by bus. The bus broke down and we had to wait two hours on the road. The woman on the seat by me insisted on finding out who I was and talking endlessly. She seemed to think I was a very *enviable* person because I had written "so many delightful books."

Enviable!!!

I went to see Mr. Taylor's secretary but got no satisfaction there. He is not back from England yet. Then I saw Starr. I managed to get the note renewed for three months by paying interest and thirty dollars of the principal. So I have a breathing space as far as that is concerned. But I needed that money.

Coming home the driver drove furiously through a thick fog. Not a very soothing thing for nerves. I walked home from the corner in a blanket of fog filled with dread. It is bitter to *dread* returning to your own home. There was no one to meet me but Lucky. That dear cat is all that makes life tolerable. Once there were two little boys always glad to welcome mother back.

Ewan seemed quite bright and said he had felt better than any day for a long time.

My heart has been very *fluttery* this past week. And there has been a good deal more bleeding from the tumor.

Wednesday, Nov. 21, 1934
....I called to see Mrs. Hewson today and gave her the plays to take to the committee. I said I felt I could do nothing in regard to it after such a slap in the face.

She said as far as she could find out "Garfield and Gollop" were behind it. I knew they were but I could not discuss any members of my husband's congregation with an outsider. She told me what had gone on at that first Executive meeting and said she was not going to have anything to do with the play either. Well, among them be it!

We spent the evening at the Glen House. Ewan *seemed* well and deceived the Barracloughs who spoke of how well he was. But I knew the signs of inward unrest too well to be deceived and the evening was one of great strain.

Thursday, Nov. 22, 1934
Ewan had a very restless disturbed night and a bad day but is all right this evening. It is curious how he is always worse in the day and better at night. With me, when I am worried or neurasthenic it is the other way round. I always feel better in the morning, begin to feel worse around five and very miserable in the evening.

I found it very hard to keep up today. I couldn't write or read or eat. I have such a terrible feeling of despair and *aloneness*. Every night I feel I *cannot* endure another day.

Friday, Nov. 23, 1934
Ewan slept six hours and was fair today, improving as usual towards night. He spent the evening with a Union family and came home in real good spirits.

I felt very miserable all day. Stuart came home tonight and brought a breath of sane life into this tormented house.

The *Anne* picture is reviewed in *Liberty* and given three stars.

After I had written the foregoing entry and was ready for bed the phone rang. It was Oliver Hunter, demanding agitatedly if I were not coming to the Old Tyme practice at his place. I said, no, I had not thought I was needed, as it was a musical practice. Oliver, seemingly much upset, urged me to come. Besides a practice, there was much to be discussed concerning the program, etc. I *must* come—he would send someone down for me.

I decided to go. Oliver and his wife were good friends of ours and I certainly did not want to antagonize any friends just then. So I agreed to go and re-dressed. Murray came down for me. When I reached Hunters' I found literally a houseful of people, more than half of whom were total strangers. This meant nothing to me. But afterwards I found it meant a good deal to most of the Old Tymers.

At that famous executive meeting, it seems there had been much discussion as to whether they would ask outsiders to help or stick to the real Norval people. It was put to a vote. By a large majority it was decided *not* to have any outsiders. And then, in the face of that, Garfield McClure had asked all these strangers. He did it—and got away with it. Oliver and his wife could not insult them by turning them out, although they were staggered when they began to arrive. Everybody was resentful but nobody wanted to start a fuss which would probably end in smashing up the Old Tymers altogether. So Garfield had his way unchecked.

Garfield and Mr. Gollop greeted me almost fawningly. I sat me down and continued sitting for the evening, talking smilingly and diplomatically to everyone who sat near me, and offering *no* opinion whatever on any question discussed.

But I used my eyes. I saw that not one of the "Play Committee" was present. But the plays I had given Mrs. Hewson were lying on the table. Later on I found that Mrs. Hewson had sent them to Mr. Morgasen to take to the practice, saying she couldn't go. He had sent them by someone else, saying *he* couldn't go. This was the last that was heard of the "Play Committee."

Several times through the evening I saw Garfield and Mr. Gollop holding agitated conferences. At last, about eleven, they came to me, saying could we have a conference about the play and asking me to choose and direct it. I wanted to refuse—and refuse stingingly. But I had been thinking. If I did there would be a lot of scandal—perhaps a smash-up of the whole affair—and it might make things more difficult for Ewan if and when he was able to take up his work again. For his sake I did not want an open quarrel with Garfield and Mr. Gollop. And for his sake I decided to ignore what had happened and grant their request.

We picked one of the plays—a very amusing little farce with five characters. Garfield was cast for the comic part, Mrs. Hewson, Marion, George Brown and Mr. Morgasen for the others, and we decided on a night for practice. That done, I came home, feeling very unsatisfied over it all but resolved to do my best gracefully.

Saturday, Nov. 24, 1934
The Manse, Norval, Ont.
....Ewan's permit came at last today. He is leaving tomorrow night.

Sunday, Nov. 25, 1934
This has not been quite so hard as some Sundays have been, though it couldn't exactly be called a pleasant day....A very dull and savorless Mr. Gowland preached. At the last minute Mrs. Sam McClure phoned that she couldn't play and I had to take the organ.

Ewan left for Toronto on the 7.30 bus, then to take the ten o'clock train to Montreal. I watched him go across the dark lawn and around the corner of the church wondering if I would ever see him again! Would the trip make him worse or better? I felt terrible—and yet there was a dreadful *relief* in his departure.

Monday, Nov. 26, 1934
The Manse, Norval, Ont.
This has been my first *livable* day for months. I had a glorious unbroken sleep. Stuart went back to town this morning. It was hard to see him go. I am alone now—except for Ethel and she is rather worse than nobody....A score of times I have wished I had let her go and taken Mrs. Thompson back, no matter who was offended.

This is the first time I've ever been alone when Ewan was away. Always before I would have at least one of the boys with me.

I wrote a whole chapter of *Pat II* this morning and found it quite easy though as yet I cannot take pleasure in it. But it was wonderful to be able to write without Ewan coming in every few moments with some bogey to be laid. And such a relief to my mind to find I can really write again when the strain is lifted.

I was hungry at dinner and supper and enjoyed them as I haven't done for weeks.

I had a few bad moments just at dark. A phone call—a telegram from Montreal! My heart seemed to turn over. Was it about Ewan? But it was only a business wire from the Radio Commission.

A card came from Ewan on the night mail. He had reached Montreal in morning and was "feeling well now." I got the impression that he had had a bad night.

Tuesday, Nov. 27, 1934
I hoped for another good sleep but did not get it. Several worries kept me awake. So the day was not as good as yesterday. I got a chapter of *Pat II* done but didn't find it as easy as yesterday. Went to W.M.S. in church. In the afternoon I had a very bad attack of neurasthenia but felt calmer this evening. But I am finding the loneliness ghastly. Nobody ever comes in to see me. I can't understand it. Why am I treated so? If they don't want us here any longer why don't they tell us instead of trying to freeze us out like this? It is inhuman. I have never known anyone in trouble in our congregation that I did not go to see them and offer sympathy and help and this is my return.

Lucky is my one comfort—but he *is* a comfort, the darling!

A crokinole social in aid of the Sunday School funds is looming up and I have had to do a lot of phoning in connection with it. No matter how they use me they expect me to work for them, it seems. And people everywhere keep writing me for help of some kind—advice—plays—speeches. There are times when my mail "gets on my nerves."

Wednesday, Nov. 28, 1934
I had a fairly good night and felt better all day. Wrote a *Pat* chapter—"Judy's" death—and did it rather well....

Thursday, Nov. 29, 1934
The Manse, Norval, Ont.
....The Barracloughs came in the afternoon and took me to Toronto. Mrs. B. and I went to see *Anne* in one of the theatres. This time, not being racked with worry over Ewan, I enjoyed it and could form an opinion on it. On the whole, it is not a bad picture. At least the first two thirds. The last third is a silly sentimental commonplace end tacked on for the sake of rounding it up as a love story. The scenery is California, not P.E. Island, except for the opening scene and another scene midway where "Matthew" is fencing. Dawn O'Day, who played "Anne Shirley's" part was good. (By the way she has taken "Anne Shirley" as her stage name. She is a good little actress but I fear she isn't "pretty enough" to become a popular star). She really looked very like my idea of Anne, especially in regard to her eyes.

While I was writing *Green Gables* my idea of Anne's face was taken from a picture I had cut from a magazine, passe-partouted, and hung on the wall of my room—a photograph of a real girl somewhere in the U.S., but I have no idea who she was or where she lived. I wonder if she ever read of *Anne*, never dreaming

326

Model for Anne's face

that, physically, she was the original! I lately came across the picture in an old scrap-book and I am putting it here.

"Marilla," played by Helen Westley, was in no respect whatever my tall, thin, Puritan Marilla. She was, indeed, my perfect conception of "Mrs. Rachel Lynde" (who was not in the picture at all). But her performance, judged on its own merits, was capital. "Matthew" was very good also, though he had no beard. "Gilbert," at least in the earlier scenes, was much too crude and "Diana" was a complete wash-out. However, on the whole, the picture was a thousandfold better than the silent film in 1921.

I am pestered to death by questions as to "how I like it" and "what I feel like" seeing my characters "come to life" like that. I liked it well enough but I had no sense of seeing my characters come to life because they were *not* my characters as I saw them, with the partial exception of "Anne." The whole picture was so entirely different from *my* vision of the scenes and the people that it did not seem *my* book at all. It was just a pleasant, well-directed little play by some-body else.

O. Heggie flew from New York to Los Angeles one afternoon on a hurry-up call to take the part of "Matthew." If, when I was writing those first two chapters of *Green Gables* that spring evening in the old home so long ago someone had told me that such a thing would one day happen—well, I would just have wondered why they hadn't taken the poor soul to Falconwood long ago!

I went down for the mail this evening in dread. I suppose this will be the ordeal of the day again as it was all summer. There was one which I thought was a let-ter from Chester and I opened it in fear but it was only a birthday card. This cheered me a bit. Nobody else has remembered my birthday. It hurt me that Stuart hadn't—but what matter. Everything hurts now. And perhaps his greeting will come tomorrow.

I went with the M's to the Old Tyme practice at Garfield's and got through the evening comparatively well, though I felt tired and sad. For the first time in my life I *felt old* among the others. I feel a million years away from their interests.

Mr. Morgasen refuses to go in the play and I fear I will find it difficult to get anyone to take the part.

Friday, Nov. 30, 1934
Today is my sixtieth birthday! And what a day! For the first time on my birthday no human being I love is with me.

I slept fairly well and felt better this morning. I got the last chapter of *Pat II* done. Such a relief! I thought so many times this fall I should never get it done. I never wrote a book in such agony of mind before.

It poured rain all day and was so dark we had to have the lights on all the time. At four a heavy fog blotted the world out. I had a nasty sensation of being smothered—I felt as if I *must* get out of the house but couldn't go out in that reeking fog. My loneliness was awful. I had a bad neurasthenic spell at 8 but feel better now. I am in bed, with Luck purring beside me. He is certainly sealed of my tribe....

Saturday, Dec. 1, 1934
I slept from ten to five but could not sleep any more for worries. There were letters from Stuart and Ewan in the morning mail. Stuart hadn't forgotten my birthday after all. He wrote but the letter which should have come yesterday did not get here till today. He wished me "a happy birthday." And what a day of misery it was. Such wishes hurt me now. Long ago, when I was still young enough and hopeful enough to look forward to what I believed was "the unspent joy of all the unborn years," such a wish would not have seemed so full of sarcasm as it does now.

Ewan's letter was not very encouraging. I revised *Pat II* all day till four. Then I could work no longer and passed an evening gnawed by a certain worry that is torturing me just now.

Sunday, Dec. 2, 1934
The Manse, Norval, Ont.
I took chloral and got some sleep. When I went to Sunday School Chester came in with Reids', having gone there on the bus last night. I think he might have dropped off to see how I was. However, he seems well and happy, so I concluded my worry had no real foundation and was only born of fear, the consequence of bitter experiences in the past. I felt easier but found it hard to teach my class. It was difficult to concentrate on the lesson.

I ran up to see Marion in the afternoon and in the evening had a good read. Now I am very tired and thinking almost happily of bed and a hot water bottle and a dear pussy purring beside me.

We had a Mr. Weir preaching today—a nice fellow and a good preacher—a welcome change from the nonentities we have been having.

It is a year today since Chester and Luella came to me and confessed their marriage. What a year!!

Monday, Dec. 3, 1934
I had a lovely natural sleep of nine hours—nothing like it since last April. I revised *Pat II* all day. The weather was cold and sunless and I got a little neurasthenic again about four. The evening mail brought a letter from Ewan that upset me. He said he would not be back till "after New Year's." This is what I have feared all along—that once he got down there it might be impossible to get him back. He is quite indifferent to what might be the result of delaying—nothing matters in the slightest degree to him except his own morbid preoccupations....

Tuesday, Dec. 4, 1934
I had a veronal sleep, followed by a cold sunless day. Revised *Pat II*. Mr. Taylor's secretary called me up to say that Mr. Taylor had returned, had attended to the note and had had a "very successful trip." This was a huge relief and I almost enjoyed the rest of the day....

Thursday, Dec. 6, 1934
I took medinal and had some sleep so today was bearable. I began typing *Pat II* today. I cannot afford to have it done but it is a tedious job....

I have been having hard work to get a cast for the play but Mr. Morgasen telephoned today that he would take it rather than see me stuck so I suppose I must go ahead with it.

Friday, Dec. 7, 1934
Had a fair sleep and felt a little better all day. I typed *Pat II* all the morning and part of the afternoon but could do nothing in the evening. I was a prey to unrest and dread of the future. If I could only get out for a good long walk! But that is impossible. It is too cold and there is nowhere one can go after dark this time of the year. One can't stroll on the highway. These long lonely evenings are very hard to endure. I am all alone in this big house except for dear Lucky.

Sunday, Dec. 9, 1934
....Mr. Andrews, a very crude and flat student, preached. I got through the day without any attacks of neurasthenia, but after Stuart went away in the evening I had a few moments of feeling "smothered." This sensation is an indescribably dreadful one. I wonder if this hideous existence will *ever* end....

Monday, Dec. 17, 1934
The Manse, Norval, Ont.
I slept till four last night but could not sleep again. I typed *Pat* most of the day. There was no letter from Ewan today and that upset me. This evening I went with the M's and the Oliver Hunters to the S.S. concert at Union. It was a lovely moonlit night and they were four gay and happy young people—as I myself was once, though it seems an incredible thing to me now. I did not grudge them their happiness but it made me feel very lonely and apart—and bitter. Yes, I am getting bitter. I perceive it without being able to help it.

But the evening was pleasant. I always feel so "at home" with the Union people. And they had *such* a chicken supper! They do love a good bite, bless their hearts. And everyone was so nice and so interested in knowing how Ewan was getting on. I felt quite cheered up.

But as we drove away I looked back at the beautiful old church against the moonlit sky and all at once the thought came to me that I would never be there for another Christmas concert. When I came home I found a letter from Ewan that had come on the night mail but I am not going to open it till the morning. I dare not risk being upset tonight.

Union Church

I think I *am* getting better. I can read again and my appetite is picking up. But I am dreadfully *shaky*....

Tuesday, Dec. 18, 1934
I had a good sleep and this morning read Ewan's letter. There was nothing alarming. He said little about himself—which is a good sign—and seems to be sleeping well and without dope at that.

This has been my best day yet but I feel weak and "wavy." I had no heart flutters today. I typed all day and in the evening went to the MacPhersons' where Charlotte and I did up the presents for the Christmas tree.

I was alone when I came home but I did not feel lonely or neurasthenic. It is a blessing to be able to work again and darling Lucky is on the bed beside me, kneading and spreading his claws in an ecstasy of happiness and contentment. When Luck can snuggle up against someone he loves he asks no more. Whatever would I have done without him this terrible autumn?

Wednesday, Dec. 19, 1934
The Manse, Norval, Ont.
....I spent the afternoon in the church basement, decorating it and the tree for the concert. It was a stormy night and we did not have a good crowd. There was not

even a card on the tree for me and it seemed the last straw. I kept up till it was all over, smiling gaily and helping the tots through their numbers. Then I came home alone and cried in this big empty house. I was alone, of course. Ethel was out as she always is. Not that *that* mattered. I am always glad when she hangs up the supper dishpan and takes herself off. But I am too much alone here.

Thursday, Dec. 20, 1934

....Stuart came home tonight for the holidays, so things will not be quite so unbearable for a time. I had to go to a play practice at Geo. Brown's tonight. At first I thought I *couldn't* do it. But finally I set my teeth and went and got through the evening fairly. Everyone is talking of Christmas. I hate the thought of it. What a Christmas it will be for me! Well, no doubt, it will be just as bitter for a great many other people.

If I can just *keep going*! I seem to have so little reserve strength. Everything upsets me.

"Chester and Pussy"

Sunday, Dec. 23, 1934

I had a poor sleep and the day was dull and dark—threatening rain. I slept a little in the afternoon—it is very seldom I can sleep in the daytime—and supper was quite a cheerful meal as Chester, Luella and Pussy were here. It is really funny to see how *jealous* Lucky is of the baby. He can't bear to see me fuss over it or nurse it. He will go away into a corner and sit with his back to me, once in a while stealing a look at me over his shoulder out of very reproachful eyes to see if I am taking any notice of him.

Monday, Dec. 24, 1934

....There was no letter from Ewan. It is a bitter Christmas Eve. I have felt smothered all the evening and craved to get out but walking is impossible. My head feels as if a tight band was around it.

Tuesday, Dec. 25, 1934

....A letter came from Ewan but I dared not open it. We had dinner in the evening and Chester and Luella and Pussy were here. It is the first time Ewan has been away on Christmas Day.

In the evening when I was alone I had one of those nasty smothering spells. Stuart was out—I knew too well where—and Chester had taken Luella and Baby home. I am alone—alone. But I would not mind being alone if I had peace of mind.

Friday, Dec. 28, 1934
The Manse, Norval, Ont.
....I opened Ewan's letter which came last night and found better news than I expected. He says he will be home on Jan. 9th and will preach the next Sunday. This is wonderful—if he doesn't slump again. And I am thankful he is coming back. They are having it very cold and stormy on the Island now and I am so afraid of his catching cold.

His letter changed everything and I had a day of peace. I typed all day but found it rather hard to stick to it. I have such a queer feeling in my head. But my appetite came back today. I know I would soon pick up if I could be free from worry.

Sunday, Dec. 30, 1934
....We had the last of the student series today. Somehow, I am inclined to wonder, "what of the church of the future?" We have had seven. One was a good preacher and a gentleman. One was a fair preacher but of unpleasing personality. The remaining five were hopelessly crude and futile. The ministry of today offers no inducement to young men of brains or vision. The salaries are inadequate—there is no proper provision for old age—and a deadline for nine out of ten at fifty. They cannot be blamed for passing it by.

The announcement was read that Ewan would take his pulpit two weeks from today. God grant it may be true. But not one person in Norval church said a word to me about it. I cannot understand it. Is it merely indifference or is there something behind it? I cannot imagine what it would be. Up to the time of Ewan's breakdown everyone seemed our friend and we had no reason to think that anyone was dissatisfied over anything connected with us. Surely illness is not a crime. Well, if Ewan is able to take up his work we can soon pull things into shape again and all may be well.

We had a rather pleasant afternoon. Chester and Luella and baby were here for supper and I found myself actually enjoying what I ate. My head gave me no trouble today and for the first time in months I felt that I had a normal outlook.

Monday, Dec. 31, 1934
The Manse, Norval, Ont.
It was 15 below zero today and the house was very cold. But I had a fair sleep and was able to work all day. A letter came from Ewan and I hardly dared open it. I shook like a leaf. Suppose he had slumped again! But all was well. He says that he will be home next Saturday night.

Nora 'phoned out that she and Ned were coming out for a call. I flew happily round, prepared afternoon tea and had a fire in the grate. We had a nice chat and I felt quite cheered up.

Nora told me that Chester had been up and spent an evening with them recently. An engineering friend of Ned's had been there, too. Chester had talked well and after he went the visitor remarked, "A wonderful boy—he will go far."

This is the impression Chester makes on some people—and yet look at what has happened! I *know* Chester has ability—but will he use it? He is lazy—*talking* brilliantly is not *working* brilliantly.

This is the last day of 1934. What a year! What a year! I have lived through many hard and bitter years but all of them put together would not have equalled this....

1935

Friday, Jan. 1, 1935
Dear God, what will this year be like? Surely it cannot be as bad as last year was....

Today was a much pleasanter day than Christmas. I knew that Ewan was better and will probably be home soon. Chester and Luella and Pussy were here to dinner. We had a turkey. Stuart won one in a raffle!! Robinson, the local butcher, had a turkey left from his Christmas market so he raffled it off—twenty-five cents a ticket. Stuart bought one and his was the winning number.

Chester went back to Toronto in the evening and I spent it with the M's. We had a bit of amusement making the table rap. But I was so tired I was glad to come home to my bed and my pussy cat. I seem to have so little strength.

I had a letter from Laura Carten today—the girl who followed me as proofreader on the *Echo*. She has been there ever since and is editor of a department for Young People in the Chronicle. She wrote, "How proud Halifax is of its brilliant sister, the creator of *Anne*." That sounds very Laura Cartenish—she was always given to gush. I grinned cynically over it. Halifax, indeed! Never shall I forget the loneliness of that year I spent on the *Echo* staff. I thought Halifax was the coldest place in the world for the stranger.

I feel that I would like to spend a month in bed!

Wednesday, Jan. 2, 1935
....I finished typing *Pat II* and then started in to give the house a good overhauling to get it into order for the New Year and Ewan's return. If the worst is really over I do so want to get back into a gracious and ordered way of living again. Everything has been such an effort and a compulsion so long.

I went down to George Brown's to go with them to practice at Morgasen's, when to my great surprise—for I wasn't expecting him till Saturday—Ewan telephoned that he was at Georgetown station and could I get someone to go for him! As our car was in Toronto (Chester was to meet his dad and bring him out Saturday) I didn't know what to do but George Brown said he would go over for him. I went, too. Ewan seemed real well, though he had a bad cold. There had been a huge storm on the Island and he had thought it best to come away at once before the trains might be blocked. When we got home I told Ethel to get him some supper and I had to hurry off to the practice. When I got home at 11.45 Ewan was in bed sound asleep. He looks well but has a bad eruption of spots over his face. He has often had this during his attacks. There must be some poison in his system but whether it is a cause or an effect I know not.

Thursday, Jan. 3, 1935
I could not sleep well but Ewan did, with very few nervous jerks or twitches. I see a great change for the better in this respect. He seems quite cheerful—reads and talks naturally and spoke of taking the services on Sunday week as a matter of course. The Barracloughs 'phoned over inviting us to supper. The afternoon was cold and stormy but their chauffeur Albert North came over for us. We had a lovely turkey supper and an evening of euchre. It was such a blessed relief not to have to watch Ewan for symptoms of mental unrest. He seemed well and quite free from evil thoughts. I was glad to find I could still laugh and find sweetness in life's little things again....

Friday, Jan. 4, 1935
The Manse, Norval
We both had a fair sleep. Ewan was absorbed in a book all day, even bringing it to the table as of yore. He has some headache yet but no phobias. It was always thus when he was recovering—the headaches would linger for some weeks after the phobias had disappeared.

It has been wickedly cold today—15 below. I really suffered from it as I went for the mail through the dim snowy twilight. It was nice not to feel afraid of getting letters in the mail.

I have begun correcting the typescript of *Pat II*. I begin to feel so differently. I have a good appetite—we both have, and Ewan is quite cheery at meals.

Saturday, Jan. 5, 1935
Ewan slept well. His head bothered him a bit today but he seems quite cheerful. In the afternoon he wrote a notice to be read tomorrow in the churches. "Your pastor will take the services next Sunday." I felt so relaxed—almost happy.

But the day was not to pass without its meed of worry. I had expected Chester home but he did not come and the evening mail brought a letter saying that the car had skidded into a truck on an icy street and was in a garage. This means more expense at a time when every cent counts. But this is a minor detail if only Ewan keeps well.

Sunday, Jan. 6, 1935
....Dr. Rochester came to take the services and Ewan talked to him quite normally. The service here was in the afternoon today and for the first time since May I felt at ease and enjoyed it. Could it really be possible, I thought, that Ewan would be in his pulpit again next Sunday? Are my awful Sundays ended? I cannot believe it till I see it. But to hear Ewan talking—laughing—joking—after seven months of crazy speeches! It just seems unbelievable—heaven after hell.

But I noticed one thing—not one in Norval church came to me to say they were glad he would be back next Sunday. I felt bitterly hurt over that. Dr. Rochester said that Union people were delighted.

Monday, Jan. 7, 1935
A very dark day, with a thick fog coming up at 4.30. I do not like the Ontario fogs. I remember how I used to love fog on the Island—coming in at evening from the sea—dim gray mist floating along the woods and over the fields. Here it is stagnant and heavy, like a moist gray blanket.

Ewan is fair. His breath seems short but his head is better than yesterday.

I finished revising the MS. of *Pat Second* and did it up. I have at last decided to call it *The Chatelaine of Silver Bush*.

We had a play practice at Mrs. Hewson's tonight and during the evening I heard Garfield saying he would not be at the annual meeting as he had an engagement for that evening. This mislikes me much. Garfield is chairman of the Board of Managers and should be there above all others. He *must* be offended about something. As soon as Ewan is really well he must try to find out what is wrong and put it right. He is as nice as pie to me at the practices now. But I mistrust my Garfield very much.

Tuesday, Jan. 8, 1935
....The annual meeting was to have been this evening but was postponed because of the downpour. I have been dreading it for I feel sure something is brewing and it may come to light there.

And another worry has come up. The night of the Christmas concert Robert Reid, who is Superintendent of the S.S. and was chairman of the program, insulted John Ismond in a quite unjustifiable fashion. I don't think Mr. Reid meant it as it sounded but he is a very tactless man and John Ismond is a touchy boor always looking for slights. Now we hear that the family is going to leave the church and go to Georgetown. Will there never be an end to these explosions in the church for which we are not in the least to blame but the consequences of which are visited on us?

There is a blank of two days in the notebook record—two awful days and nights. I could not write a line in that tortured time. But every moment of it is branded on my memory.

For years life has been thus with me: when I have allowed myself to think that the worst of something was over—whenever I dared to cherish a faint hope that there would be no more of such things—invariably some terrible thing has happened. When I wrote that entry of Jan. 8 in my notebook I was letting myself hope. And the malignancy that has dogged me struck again.

The next day, Wednesday, Jan. 9, was a rather hard day. I had not slept the night before and I had the Executive of the W.M.S. meeting at the manse in the afternoon. Charlotte MacPherson came over, too, in a sputter about John Ismond's leaving and worried me a little more. I was very tired by supper time and I thought I would go down for the mail and then go to bed. It was a dark foggy evening and I walked dispiritedly down to the office.

There was a letter for Ewan with the firm name of Ernest Bogart in the corner!

All the fall and winter I had been vaguely worried over Chester. Somehow, I *felt* that things were not just right with him. But I never could find out anything definite, only that he seemed to be suffering again from the headaches that have so often bothered him. So I tried to tell myself I was foolish and was only worried because I was run down and haunted by the shadow of the past.

The moment I saw the letter I felt sure there was some bad news in it. I hurried home and opened it in the library, thinking if it were something I could deal with I would not let Ewan be bothered with it at all.

There was in it a letter from Mr. Bogart, and also the copy of one he had sent to Chester.

Bogart's letter stated that Chester had not been in the office since Christmas, that he did not know what he was doing and that he had sent him a letter, copy of which he enclosed.

The copy told Chester that Mr. Bogart was through with him and that he was to return his articles to Mr. B. at once, as he, Mr. B., did not wish to be associated with him any longer.

There is no use trying to describe what I felt like. I took the letters up to poor Ewan who had to be told, though I knew what effect it would have on him. We decided that we would go into Toronto at once on the night bus and see Chester. Ewan got up and dressed and we started.

Oh, that nightmare drive! I kept seeing all that might be before me—Chester coming home—another horrible failure—no way of hiding it—all openings closed to him—and him with a wife and child on his hands. I could not face it—especially after the horror of the year just passed. It was too much. When we reached Chester's flat we found he had not seen Bogart's letter, not having looked in his mailbox that day. He said that ever since Christmas he had been ill with stomach trouble and constant headaches and that he had told Mr. Downey (the lawyer who shared Mr. B's suite of offices) that he was ill and asked him to let Mr. B. know. He had intended to go back the next day.

Next day Mr. B. remarked scornfully to Ewan that anybody who had had headaches that long would be dead. That was a foolish thing for anyone to say. But we have found out a few things about Mr. B. since that we did not know then.

As for these attacks of Chester's, he had many of them in boyhood. He used to be ill with them for six weeks at a time, able to take only liquid food. I used to put him on a diet and eventually he would get over them. After he had his tonsils out he did not have them so frequently but occasionally they came. He had been getting his meals out in various places and something had upset his stomach.

The thing about these attacks that had always worried me was a curious *indifference* to his work which seemed to possess him in them—exactly like the indifference that Ewan has in *his* attacks. I have felt worried lest C's would eventually develop as his father's have done, though so far he has been free from all phobias in them.

I had to take veronal to get any sleep for I dared not go another night without sleep, in regard to the ordeal that faced me on the morrow. I wondered dully as I sank to sleep what life would be like if I did not have to be always wishing that ordeals were over. I had forgotten what it had once been like.

Thursday morning we all went down to Bogart's office. I did not go in—I had never met Mr. B. and Chester thought it was better I should not. Ewan and

Chester went in. I walked the corridor in dreadful anguish and suspense. Eventually they came out—Bogart had agreed to let Chester stay on for a month "on probation" and see if he had "learned a lesson."

This was a slight relief. I went and did a little shopping and we came home early. Home! What a home is mine! I thought bitterly as I entered it. Even the joyful purrs of a dear cat could not charm away my heartache. Never had life looked blacker and more hopeless to my tired eyes. Yet it had to be gone on with. And all must be hidden from the world. *That* has been the gnawing worm in so many of my miseries. They were not such as could be openly acknowledged and justify me in going up for a little rest and release from outside duties while I strove to rise above my suffering. I had to hide them and carry on, with false smiles and forced calm.

Friday, Jan. 11, 1935
The Manse, Norval, Ont.
I had a fair sleep last night and worked hard all day to keep from thinking. Ewan went to see Ismond's this evening to see if he could smooth them down. No good. They are going—although Robert Reid, it seems, went to them and apologized. The church would be better off without a man of John Ismond's type if it could afford to lose a family but it cannot....

Sunday, Jan. 13, 1935
Ewan had a poor night and a nervous fit at six. It was a cold stormy day. I had so hoped it might be a pleasant day for him to start in on. I had hard work to get him off to Union but I managed it and he came home feeling quite fair. He had got on all right with the service and the Union people had crowded around him and welcomed him back. One woman said, "It's like getting home again to have you back."

But the Norval service was rather dismal. Ewan read his sermon and got on all right. *But not one soul went up to speak to him or welcome him back.* I *can't* understand it. The more I think of it the more it puzzles me. Even if Garfield has got offended at something the whole congregation can't have. They are not so fond of Garfield as all that. They were all friends of ours up to last spring. Even if they think Ewan is not physically fit to keep his work up that is no reason for their not being decent. *What* is the explanation?

When I came home I felt dreadfully after the day's strain and could not keep back the tears. Ewan seemed much better in the evening. It has been a hard day in one way but it was lovely to see Ewan in his own pulpit again and no stranger. Once the congregation see he is able to carry on his work they will likely be all right. But they have not behaved to us as they should have.

I wrote Chester this evening and sent him a box of pills that have always helped him in his previous attacks.

Monday, Jan. 14, 1935
The Manse, Norval, Ont.
Ewan had a bad night and eventually had to take medinal. He has taken a notion that the feeling in his head is the precursor of a stroke of paralysis. These hypochondriac notions of his are very hard to confute but are not to be compared

to his theological ones. I had a fair sleep and a nice day. I had to give a paper at the Literary Club in Brampton and I had lunch with the Hodgins and enjoyed it. Mrs. Coulter, the wife of the new Brampton minister, was there also and is very nice. She and her husband motored me home. I dreaded to come home—it's so bitter to dread coming to your home. I used always to *love* coming home from anywhere in the years when Ewan was well....

Tuesday, Jan. 15, 1935
A poor night and a hard day. Ewan was bad all day with his head and nerves. But thank God his mind keeps all right. Yet I walk in dread of the return of his phobias. Dread! Dread! I eat and drink dread—I lie down with it at night and rise up with it in the morning. It is the constant Dweller on my Threshold.

The day was cold and raw. The house was uncomfortable and there was no nice mail or news. The annual meeting came off tonight. It passed quite well. But Garfield and Sam McClure and Andy Giffen, the three "leading" men(!) *were not there. What* is the reason? Sam McClure has always been a good friend of ours. This must be found out as soon as Ewan is able to grapple with it. Ewan presided and did very well but said when we came home that he had not felt well....

Wednesday, Jan. 16, 1935
....I had letters from Myrtle and Fan, telling me about seeing *Green Gables* in Charlottetown.

It's like a taste of home to get letters from the Island. If I could just find myself for a few hours dropped into a June day on P.E. Island—preferably in the 90's— where I could taste a sort of ghostly happiness again—walk in green wood lanes and look at old beloved farms—catch a sudden sapphire glimpse of sea through the trees—follow my little brooks, drink wine of white clover—trace out a magic of twisting red roads with little ferns growing out of their dykes—and at evening see the sheen of the moon on a full-bosomed sea.

But no such wish fulfilment is possible alas!

I dreaded a letter from Starr. Surely it must be all right or I would have heard.

Friday, Jan. 18, 1935
....It is very cold and I could not get any writing done. Stuart came home on the bus, so I must brisken up, that his week-end may not be too grim.

Saturday, Jan. 19, 1935
....Chester and Luella and Baby were here this evening. Chester doesn't look well. I can't get anything out of him as to how he is getting on in the office and sometimes my heart misgives me.

Sunday, Jan. 20, 1935
This has been my easiest Sunday for a long long time. We both had a good sleep and Ewan was fairly well and cheerful all day and got through both services pretty well. He went to the Glen in the evening and came home in good spirits. I had

a serious talk with Chester before he left on the bus and hope he will take it to heart. But unfortunately impressions don't seem to be lasting with him.

Monday, Jan. 21, 1935
Both of us slept well. I did spade work on stories and prepared for the play practice here. I find I can't take my old interest in it. I can't forget the way I was used in November, though everyone is very nice now, Garfield especially. Ewan chatted for half an hour with the cast before he went to bed. Later on he remarked to me how nice it was not to dread seeing people any longer. If Ewan can only go along with his work he will soon be quite well I believe. If—if—if!!!

But one cannot go on without a little hope.

Tuesday, Jan. 22, 1935
Ewan didn't sleep well. His head bothered him all day but his mind is normal. He still thinks and talks too much about himself and his symptoms.

I dread going for the mail every evening now, lest there may be a letter from Mr. Bogart, saying that Chester is not measuring up. I suppose I'll really not hear anything until the month of probation is up, as long as he doesn't slump but if he does we might get a letter any time. But what is one dread more or less in my gay life?

I wonder if I'll ever cease to dread the coming of the mail. All through my childhood and girlhood I used to look eagerly for the mail every day—I never thought of being afraid of it. But I began to dread it during my unhappy engagement to Edwin Simpson. That passed. The next time was the winter Ewan was in Glasgow—and not again till the war broke out. From then on there have been few years when, for some reason or another, I was not afraid of what might come— bad news from the front—a gloomy letter from Ewan if he were away—worrying screeds from Rollins about the law-suits—and of late years, Chester.

The date when the Taylor note fell due is passed. I have heard nothing—so I am daring to hope all is well there.

Wednesday, Jan. 23, 1935
The Manse, Norval, Ont.
....I had a letter from Mrs. Thompson in reply to one I had sent her asking for a certain knitting pattern. She has gone back to her husband!!! A line of exclamation points couldn't do justice to my reaction. After all she said to me of him! After the way she said he used her!

I am afraid the poor soul was "up against it." She said she could not get a place where she could have June with her. I wish I had let Ethel go and taken Mrs. Thompson back when she asked me to.

Tonight was so cold I felt I could not face the east wind so did not go for the mail. Oh, well, life is very dreary—but when I think of what it would be if Ewan were as he was two months ago I realize I ought not to complain.

Today sixteen years ago Frede died. Happy Frede! Would I could have gone with her.

How plainly I can see her before me at this moment—the blue black hair—the brilliant eyes—the mobile, expressive face. Frede was not pretty but no one ever asked if she were pretty or not—she was so vital, so wholesome, so joyous. Well, perhaps some still sadder star—if such there be—needed her. Somewhere she exists—sometime, somewhere we will meet again. I know it.

Meanwhile—if I could hear her laugh, feel her hand-clasp for one moment, life would not be the horror it is.

Thursday, Jan. 24, 1935

....I went down for the night mail, as usual dreading it. But there was a nice letter from Stokes who say they are "delighted with the new Pat." They don't like the title though—they think people will be afraid to try to pronounce "chatelaine"— so we'll have to find a new one....

Friday, Jan. 25, 1935
The Manse, Norval, Ont.

We both had a good sleep but Ewan was very dull all day. The cold continues. And at eleven the 'phone rang. The Bank of Montreal in Georgetown saying that note had been sent to them protested!! In a panic I 'phoned the Taylor office. He was not there but his secretary said it would be all right—Mr. Taylor had "waived protest." I don't know what that means but I don't like the situation at all. I feel very bitter towards Taylor but it is all due to my own foolishness. I drudged away at spade work till five and then had a cry. It has been a bitter day. *What* is persecuting me so relentlessly at every turn! Whenever I pluck up a little courage a new blow or worry comes.

Saturday, Jan. 26, 1935

We both slept badly. It was again below zero and so cold I could not write, so I devoted myself to clearing the cellar and getting out all the ashes.

Ewan was very dull all day and did nothing but play solitaire. The thought that he is *slipping back* comes to me and unnerves me. There has certainly been no improvement lately. But it has been a hard week for both of us. We have been housed up ever since last Sunday and it is as cold as ever tonight.

Sunday, Jan. 27, 1935

We had a fair sleep but it was 25 below zero this morning and the house like a barn. Ewan was none too well. Talked again of having "no message" and "no freedom" as of yore. I fear the phobias are returning. He had trouble getting the car started because of the cold and that upset him. He can't as yet stand the least worry. All through the Norval service he looked so distressed and I sat in misery. But we spent the evening at the Glen House and Ewan seemed quite jolly and normal. It was so nice to get out and see our friends but there was a dull ache of worry under everything.

Mrs. Hewson has broken her wrist. This means that someone must be found to take her place in the play.

Monday, Jan. 28, 1935
The Manse, Norval
....Ewan went to Toronto with the Barracloughs in the afternoon. I spent the forenoon scouting round in the cold trying to get someone to take Mrs. Hewson's part. Finally Mrs. George Brown agreed to take it. I also had a letter from an unknown *German* in Winnipeg coolly asking an unsecured loan of $600 to pay for his college course!

I took a nap this afternoon—a very unusual thing for me—and feel better this evening.

Wednesday, Jan. 30, 1935
Coldest night yet—27 below zero. It all makes life harder. Ewan had to take medinal before he could sleep. I feel discouraged. And the house was so cold when I got up that I sat down and cried. I was ashamed of myself. But I hadn't slept and everything seemed so dreary and I am worried to death. "Oh but for one short hour to feel as I used to feel!"

No use wishing that!

Thursday, Jan. 31, 1935
A little milder but still below zero. Ewan went to Toronto with the Barracloughs and Mr. Taylor came at last. He and Mr. Gibson have managed to build up some good connections in England and believe this will eventually put them on their feet again but just now ready money is not to be had and he can't take up the note. The bank won't renew without good security. Finally I agreed to put up my last $1000 bond as security. I suppose I may never see my bond again—but something must be done to secure a little freedom from recurring worry about that note.

I went with the M's to Brampton and saw the "Barretts of Wimpole Street." Escaped for a time from my prison. Then I went to Mrs. Greenwood's, who was having the Old Tyme practice that night. I dreaded coming home because Ewan had said something about going to Bogart's to see how Chester was getting on and I dreaded bad news. But he is in bed sound asleep so probably there is none.

Tuesday, Feb. 5, 1935
Ewan had to take medinal and was grum all day. I slept little and today has been a cold untamed winter storm. We had planned a trip to Toronto but had to give it up. The house was cold. It was really funny to see the poor cats sitting humped up on the rads.

Tonight we had a practice at Browns' and I came home tired, but I have been sojourning for a delightful hour in *The Flower Patch Among The Hills.* That book gives me something new every time I come to it.

Wednesday, Feb. 6, 1935
....It was twenty below zero and the house too cold to write. But the W.M.S. met at Clarence Anderson's this afternoon and I enjoyed it—the friends, the nice

supper. It was for me a great contrast to the last meeting. Ewan was there and seemed quite jolly, laughing and joking.

There was no nice mail today but no dreaded letter either.

Thursday, Feb. 7, 1935

....The Institute met at Mrs. Joe Hunter's and I had quite a nice time. I am beginning to be able to enjoy little social affairs again. But the practice at Webster's tonight tired me out. Then, when I came home, a letter from Chester was lying on the table. I opened it, shivering. The first sentence leaped at me like a blow. "I might as well tell you the bad news at once."

My heart seemed to stand still in frozen horror. "He has been turned off," was my thought. Then I took in the rest of the paragraph at a glance.

He had had his pocket picked in a street car of $28.00.

The letter fluttered from my hand. I turned faint and would have fallen if a chair had not happened to be behind me. I cannot stand these shocks now. It was such a relief that the loss of the money seemed a blessing in comparison with what I had feared. But it is no light thing just now when money is so tight. I shall have to give up the idea of getting a new coat. My old one is on its fourth winter but it is warm enough and if it is shabby what matter? I would dress in sackcloth for the rest of my life if I could have peace of mind in it.

Friday, Feb. 8, 1935
The Manse, Norval

I had a fair sleep and today was mild and snowy. We went to Toronto and had a bad fright with the car skidding on ice. I had a hard day shopping with a sore foot. Had a talk with Mr. McClelland over the title of *Pat II*. He and Mr. Stewart said I looked very tired and run down and advised me to take a trip!! Little they realize the circumstances of my life. But I had a nice dinner with Mr. and Mrs. McClelland in the Round Room at Eaton's. We saw Chester and all seems right so far. We had a dreadful drive home with snow freezing on the windshield. Our defroster wouldn't work so we had to drive with the windshield open and were nearly frozen.

Saturday, Feb. 9, 1935

We both slept fairly. Ewan does not jerk and twitch in his sleep now as he used to. We spent the evening at the M's. Marion is going to have a baby. I am sorry. It is too soon. Murray seems quite pleased over it. His old horror of babies seems to have vanished. "Ain't life queer?"

Sunday, Feb. 10, 1935

Good sleep for both. Ewan took the Bible Class today for the first time since his recovery—and got a nice insult from Garfield.

The men did not come into the class and Ewan thought it was perhaps they did not care to be in the same class with a lot of rather dowdy old ladies. So after Sunday School he went up to Garfield and suggested that the men have a Bible Class of their own with a teacher chosen from themselves. Garfield's answer was, "A good idea. *We might get somewhere then*."

Ewan was almost stunned. Never had anyone insulted him so. And Garfield who used to be, or pretended to be, our greatest friend! *What* is wrong? Garfield and his wife (who is Luella's aunt) have never been quite the same I think, since Chester's marriage but that can't account in full for his behavior to us. I wish Ewan would get well enough to have a talk with him. There must be some misunderstanding as we have never done or said anything to justify such an attitude.

This ruined the day for me. We went over to the Glen House for the evening. Mrs. Barraclough is not well. She has anemia and a heart condition and we were all worried. I had been fighting off a cold with soda all day and so life seemed a bit drearier even than usual.

It is a month today since Bogart's letter. In two or three more days we will know if C. can go on there. If he can't—

Tuesday, Feb. 12, 1935
It was 15 below in the morning but got milder. We both slept well. Ewan had a funeral today—the first since his recovery. He did very well, too. But all the evening he has been harping on his "numb" finger and worrying lest he is going to be "like your Uncle Leander." This is absurd, of course. Uncle Leander never had numb fingers. But almost every day he imagines he is going to fall victim to some new ailment. It would be funny if it were not pitiful. It really got on my nerves tonight. Ewan worries constantly about his own imaginary complaints but he never worries over Chester. He has apparently forgotten the whole affair....

Wednesday, Feb. 13, 1935
I feel a bit better of the cold today but still not well. Ethel went down for the mail this morning and brought up a letter from Chester. I never in my life felt such dread and horror of opening a letter. When at last I forced myself to do it I learned that all was well. I have no words to describe my relief. But a terrible tiredness came with the reaction.

It seemed so wonderful to go for the evening mail tonight with no particular dread.

Ewan is away at a Session meeting tonight in the church. He isn't home yet. Somehow I have been feeling a little dread of this meeting.

There is no entry for Feb. the 14th. I could not write even a few lines in a notebook. The end came that night after I had written the entry of Feb. 13.

Ewan was very late coming home from the session meeting. When he came in I knew by the look on his face what had happened.

"I don't like to tell you but I have to," he said.

"The Session has asked you to resign?" I said.

They had not done anything half as manly and decent as that. They had just been incredibly insulting—at least Andy Giffen and Rob Reid. The others, Sam McClure, Mr. Wiggins, Arthur McClure and Albert Hunter said nothing—but they sat in silence and allowed their pastor to be insulted—they, who had always posed as warm friends of ours. And yet, when it came to the point, all they could allege against Ewan was that "people were not coming to church because of him."

Ewan asked who these people were. And all they could scrape up were five—Percy Leslie, Graydon Chester, Jim Russell, John Ismond and George Ismond.

Percy Leslie, when we came to Norval, was living near Oakville. He was a bitter Unionist and was an elder in Oakville United Church. He quarrelled and left the church. Then he sold his Oakville farm and bought a farm in Norval about three years ago. He married one of our girls and in the marriage license described himself as a member of the United Church. He rarely came to our church but his wife came regularly and was a good friend of ours. It was absurd to say it was Ewan's fault that Percy Leslie did not come to our church. Graydon Chester also came to Norval a few years ago. He had been an Anglican and had just married a girl who went to a United Church. They had agreed to compromise on the Presbyterian but they very seldom came to church. We had found that he had never gone to church before he came here but they were always nice and friendly when we visited them. Jim Russell is one of our best friends. Everyone knows—Giffen and Rob Reid know it as well as anyone—that Jim Russell stopped going to church because of his quarrel with old Geo. Gollop and for no other reason. And it is equally well-known that John Ismond left because of the way Rob Reid insulted him the night of the Christmas concert. George Ismond never came to church after a certain election of elders in which he was *not* elected. Perhaps he blames Ewan for that. But only *one* man with a grievance against his pastor is a pretty good record for any church after nine years, as I know churches.

Ewan met the situation calmly and properly. He told them he certainly would not stay a day longer in a congregation that did not want him. And he also told them, without mincing matters, the truth—that never since he came here had either they or the managers co-operated with him in anything he had wished to do for the good of the church.

Well, we had a bad night. We did feel heart stricken. We had both worked so hard for this church, sparing ourselves in no way. To be rewarded with such ingratitude—such unprovoked insult! If they wanted us to go surely they could have asked him to resign without insult. Is illness a crime? We had nothing else to charge ourselves with. And up to last spring everyone was our friend and no word of complaint had ever been uttered to us by anyone. It was un-understandable. There seemed, Ewan said, to be such *malice* in what they said.

We were in a hard position. Of course we must go—and at once. Any other procedure was impossible. But Ewan could not possibly go "preaching for calls" in his condition, even if a minister of his age could hope to get a decent place. The only thing to do was to rent a house in Toronto and move there. I hated the thought of living in a city—I hated the thought of leaving Norval. I had never loved any place so well except Cavendish. I knew we could not hope to stay there as long as we had stayed in Leaskdale. But I had hoped we could stay three years more, till Chester would be through his law course and Ewan eligible for retirement and a little pension. I sometimes dreamed of buying a certain very beautiful river lot not far from the manse, building a nice home on it and spending the rest of our days there, helping the church and the community.

I was worried lest this make Ewan worse mentally. But I don't think it did at all. On the contrary, his anger over the way he was used seemed to "pep him up" and he was really much better from that on, as long as we remained in Norval. It was I who felt the worst. Ewan did not mind at all leaving Norval or the manse. He never feels the slightest attachment to places or houses. But it nearly broke my heart.

By morning we saw our way and were resolved to walk in it proudly. We had done nothing to be ashamed of and we would keep our flag flying. I tried to reckon up our consolations. We would have the boys with us again for a few years at least. We could choose our friends. What someone has called "a life-time of self concealment" would be ended. We would not have to "visit" any more—oh, heavenly freedom! And I might have a little more time for my own work.

But at first nothing alleviated the anguish of humiliation and pain. Coming on top of all that had gone before it was almost unbearable. And it *spoiled* all that had gone before—"stained back" over all our happy years and pleasant associations in Norval church. We could never look back on them with pleasure. We could never come back to revisit the church—for we could never again associate ourselves in any way with a people who had used us so abominably. For we know it could not have been the session only—the managers and the whole congregation must have been behind them.

To leave Norval with its pines—its river—its hills! To leave the beautiful commodious old manse—the lovely tree-shaded grounds—my garden—the church I had loved and worked for. This was the bitterest drop in a very bitter cup. And to be torn away from them in such a cruel fashion, not knowing where we could go or what sort of a home we could get added to the bitterness of it. I often wonder why I was born to love places so deeply and passionately when my whole life was to be a continual tearing up and uprooting.

That dreadful night passed and a day of fog and rain followed. I spent most of it in the garret *beginning to pack*. I worked feverishly all day, pausing now and then to cry bitterly. I had loved my garret so. I always loved garrets—I suppose

"The Manse"

because of the fun long ago in the old Park Corner garret. I always wanted to live in a house with a garret and when we came to Norval and I found such a lovely big one I was as delighted as a child. It was such a *convenient* place—and apart from that there was something about it that enchanted me. There was such a lovely view up the river and across to the West Branch hill from its little dormer window. And it was so shadowy—and how the rain pattered on its zinc roof when it did rain! And how the cats loved it, turning immediately into prowling jungle tigers whenever they entered it!

I worked till dark and then broke down. I felt as if my heart were actually broken. I had stood up to blow after blow—but this treachery and ingratitude overcame me. *Everything* hurt me—I was just one great *bruise*.

And I had another attack of that *imprisoned* feeling. I know now what it was—a certain degree of claustrophobia. I have often called it a "smothering" sensation but that was not the right word. I felt imprisoned—as if I were buried alive—as if I *must* push the walls away and escape into the open. Once I got out the feeling passed. But on this day it was pouring rain and I could not get out, and for a few moments it was indescribably awful. I know exactly how I would feel if I went into a trance and woke to find myself buried alive.

But the day and the claustrophobia passed, as all days do, and night came.

Feb. 15, 1935
The Manse, Norval
I have written "The Manse, Norval" very proudly and happily at the beginning of my journal entries for nine years. Well, I shall not write it very often again.

We both took medinal and slept. Today has been fine and mild—a rare combination this winter. Ewan went to Toronto. I bore up all day and worked, keeping the tears resolutely back because I would not have Ethel see me crying. In the afternoon I went to play practice in the hall—went through the motions of directing it and took absolutely no interest in it. Ewan came home and in the evening we went over to the Glen, longing for a talk with sympathetic friends. But the Barracloughs were away and the house was dark and empty. I cried all the way home. But I might have known something like this was coming up when I dared to feel happy last Wednesday because my fear about Chester had been removed. For many years now I have been a mouse in the claws of destiny. For a few moments now and then she lets me alone—just long enough for a little hope of escape to rise in my heart. Then she pounces again. For a long time I have thought I would welcome the final crunch.

I feel the bitterest resentment at the treatment meted out to us by Norval congregation. And, puzzle over it as I will, I *cannot* understand it....

Saturday, Feb. 16, 1935
Tonight we know all. The great mystery is solved at last.

This afternoon Ewan went to see Robert Reid and asked him point blank why it was that Norval had turned against him, when everyone in Union was on our side.

"Well," said Reid, "it was that letter."

Ewan stared at him.

"The letter! What letter?"

And then the truth came out—the ridiculous truth. I could shriek with laughter over the absurdity of it all, if the outcome of this absurdity had not been such bitter suffering for us.

Back in late August or early September—just around the time I began to feel the chill in the Norval atmosphere—Sam McClure, as clerk of the session, got a typewritten screed from the clerk of the Toronto Presbytery—a Presbytery, by the way, which, as at present constituted, is not noted for discretion or wisdom. This letter stated that "some congregations" in the Presbytery were behind hand with their minister's salaries, and were paying other bills before said salaries. And consequently the Presbytery solemnly reminded the congregations that the minister's salary was the first charge on the funds and must be paid before anything else.

Now, this was simply a circular letter, mimeographed at that, which the Presbytery had decided to send—and *had* sent—to every congregation in its bounds. It was a very unwise procedure but see above my comment on said Presbytery. And of course anyone but a fool would have realized it was only a circular and have thrown it into the kitchen stove. But Sam McClure took it into his head that it was meant for and sent to Norval alone—because, I suppose, he knew Norval *was* hundreds of dollars behind in its payment of the salary and a guilty conscience takes things to itself.

Sam had always been one of our good friends but our deadliest enemy could not have injured us more. No wonder Proverbs is harder on the fool than on anybody else.

Sam took the letter to the session. They referred it to the board of managers, of whom Garfield was the chairman! Then the fat *was* in the fire. Of course Garfield would be furious. When, at a meeting of the managers to consider the situation— or rather the *supposed* situation—the rest all voted to borrow money from the bank and pay the arrears of salary. Garfield alone voted against it. The motion carried, and the money was borrowed and paid to us. And we, knowing nothing of all this, thought it was very kind of them to pay up so unexpectedly!!

When Ewan told Robert Reid that we had never dreamed of such a thing as mentioning the salary to the Presbytery or any member of Presbytery, and that the letter was merely a circular sent to all congregations alike Reid said, "Well, if you can prove this it will be all right"—a true Reidian speech. Ewan laughed and said, "I do not *prove* such things. I expect my word to be taken."

This discovery has made an enormous difference in our feelings. The sting of humiliation is gone. If the Norval people believed Ewan had done such a thing I can understand their being angry and sore. But I *do* blame them for believing such a thing of us and never giving us a chance to prove our innocence.

Everything is explained now—all that has puzzled and hurt us. I suppose even the insult of the Old Tyme Committee is to be referred to this.

Chester came home tonight and we all went to the Glen House. We called at Reids', meaning to drop him there but no one was home. I have a pretty good idea that Robert Reid went to Garfield McClure's tonight to discuss this new development.

It was a relief to relax in the sympathetic atmosphere of the Glen House. We found out a great deal—especially certain things that were said and done at that mysterious joint meeting in Union Church. Moreover, just before Christmas the Norval session asked for a joint meeting with the Union session (something they should not have done, since no such meeting of session can be held without being summoned by the minister or moderator). The Norval Session, through Andy Giffen, demanded that the Union session back them up in getting Ewan out. The Union session was furious. Jim McKane told Giffen, "You Norval people have driven away three of our ministers but you are not going to do it again. Every man, woman and child in Union is behind Mr. Macdonald."

It is a fact, which we did not know before, that the last three ministers had to leave because of dissatisfaction in Norval, while Union had no fault to find.

The curious thing is that neither at the session meeting nor the church meeting did the Norval men make any reference to the letter. I suppose they were too ashamed to have Union find out that they had been so far behind with the salary when Union always pays on the dot. If they had mentioned it they would have found that Union had got a similar letter and had thrown it in the discard where it belonged.

Union, Mr. Barraclough says, is furious over it all. He did not want Ewan to resign—"stay and fight it out—Norval will be all right when they find out you were not responsible for that letter."

They may be—but we *can't* be. Ewan could never go on working with men who have behaved to him as the Norval Session has.

I am overtired tonight but I feel far far better than I have felt any time since that dreadful Wednesday night. I imagine Andy Giffen and Garfield McClure will feel pretty cheap when they find out how they have been persecuting an innocent man. When I told Ethel we were leaving she said, "An awful lot of people are down on Garfield McClure." This reveals that Garfield has been very active and is probably responsible for the whole trouble. Andy Giffen has been as wax in his hands. Garfield made the balls and Andy fired them. Garfield's self-love would be tormented to frenzy by the thought that the congregation had been complained of during *his* regime, after all the blowing he did when he became chairman. How could even he believe that *we*, after years of service and comradeship would do such a thing? Poor Ewan was not thinking much about such mundane things as salaries last summer. Only the other day I found in his desk drawer a check for $75.00 Mr. Wiggins had given him last June and which he had never cashed.

Sunday, Feb. 17, 1935
This has been a bitter day. Ewan went to Union in the morning and announced his resignation. The result was rage and consternation. The whole congregation buzzed in protest but, as he told them, there was nothing else he could do.

I went to Sunday School and taught my class. I was outwardly calm but found it hard to suppress tears I would not weep for the sake of my self-respect. Norval shall not see me in tears.

Garfield and Giffen were both there and went into the Bible Class. Evidently they have heard the truth from Reid. They are too late. Also John Ismond and family were there. We have learned that they are coming back because Robert Reid resigned as superintendent at the Annual Meeting and Albert Hunter was appointed in his place. So much for the yarn of him not coming because of Ewan.

Ewan preached very well—and then announced his resignation and the reasons therefore. He told them the letter had been a mere circular and that Toronto Presbytery had never heard a complaint of Norval from him.

The congregation seemed stunned. I heard one manager say to another as I went out, "Well, this *is* a surprise."

After the service, for the first time since I came to Norval, I did not linger to shake hands and chat with the women. I walked out, looking neither to the right nor to the left. Ewan had asked the Session and the managers to meet him in the vestry. From the manse window I watched them finally come out, walking slowly in groups of two or three. Never have I seen people who more closely resembled whipped dogs slinking off with their tails between their legs. I suppose they all at once realized what their conduct had been and what fools they had made of themselves.

When Ewan came home he told me that he had asked them how they could think he would do such a thing after knowing him for nine years. Every man, even Garfield, hung his head in shame. Ewan said, "Why did you not tell me about this letter?" Sam McClure muttered something about "not wanting to bother him when he was ill." Very considerate!!

This evening we went to the Glen House. My heart overflowed with bitterness when I thought of how few more visits we would have there. It has always been a Mecca to us.

Mr. Barraclough says Union is furious and declares it will separate from Norval etc. Of course it can't. It cannot stand alone and there is no other congregation it can be joined to. In time it will cool down and make the best of it. But at present feeling is red-hot.

Poor Kate MacPherson died tonight of internal cancer. In her own queer distorted way she was a good friend of ours. Charlotte sobbed, "I knew Kate was leaving me but I thought, 'I'll always have the Macdonalds anyway!'" She says there are two men in the congregation who are responsible for it all—Garfield and Andy Giffen. That may be true—but if the rest of the congregation had been loyal to us they could not have done us any real harm.

Monday, Feb. 18, 1935
....Ewan saw the clerk of Presbytery in Toronto and found out about the letter. It seems one city congregation and one country one somewhere *had* been complained of. The Presbytery "did not like" to single out the delinquents for warning so decided to send an admonitory letter to *every* congregation. A wise procedure! Insult all alike, innocent as well as guilty. Though for that matter, Norval *was* guilty, though Presbytery didn't know it, and that was why the letter struck home and they believed it was meant for them alone. I can't help feeling bitterly towards Presbytery. If this had not happened Ewan and I could have gone on with our work here and Ewan would soon have fully recovered. Now I doubt if he ever will.

Friday, Feb. 19, 1935
The Manse, Norval, Ont.
This evening the play practice was at Marion's. Garfield did not come till late—not until we sat down to lunch in fact. We were at the table when he came in, beaming and talkative as usual. I ignored him. I chatted to all the others casually and naturally but I never looked at Garfield. And in a few minutes he realized that he was being ignored. For the first time since I knew him I saw Garfield McClure without a word to say. He was silent during the whole meal. We had a practice after it and I spoke to him courteously when necessary, addressing him as "Mr. McClure." The friendly "Garfield" days are gone forever. I rather think Garfield felt pretty rotten as he took himself home. He knows he is *found out* and while I don't think he has a particle of conscience I believe his self-conceit will absolutely writhe under the knowledge of being "found out."

Ewan was up to see Sam McClure today. Sam has found out that Brampton church got the same letter from Presbytery and that has not made him feel any happier. Sam was an elder—but he never came or went to see his pastor after his being poisoned or while in the San. He must feel pretty sick over his conduct now that he knows the truth.

Wednesday, Feb. 20, 1935
Kate MacPherson's funeral was held today. After the service was over I saw Garfield scurrying around talking to several elders and managers. I wonder what he was saying. Trying to whitewash himself no doubt.

Ewan seems much better. Sleeps normally and laughs heartily. Today I took a certain satisfaction in dumping down the toilet and washing away bottle after bottle of useless sleeping tablets which he has at different times tried and found wanting in the past months. I hate the very sight of them. Thank God, he no longer needs anything of the sort.

Thursday, Feb. 21, 1935
The W.M.S. met at Robinsons' today. I coolly told them that they must bear in mind the fact that it would be necessary for them to elect another president at their next meeting. Mrs. Garfield and Mrs. Will McClure (Garfield's sister) looked very uncomfortable I noticed. I found it all bitter—bitter. I have worked with them all for years and liked them all. I have brought the Auxiliary up from something that was almost moribund to a vital and flourishing society. And now we must part like this.

Friday, Feb. 22, 1935
The Manse, Norval, Ont.
Cold again—below zero. We had play practice in the hall. Garfield was very quiet on the stage and very noisy off it—like a schoolboy who had been publicly rebuked and wanted to display his indifference. Mr. Morgasen was very angry and remarked at the close that it was no wonder the rehearsal was a failure since there was so much noise off stage.

Ewan was at Dr. Paul's funeral today—poor old Dr. Paul who undoubtedly saved his life last August—and had a talk with Ed Townsend of Union. He told him the Norval men were in a panic and didn't know what to do.

There is nothing they can do. They can never undo what they have done—and they know it.

Saturday, Feb. 23, 1935
....Packing goes on apace. It is very bitter to be packing up with no idea where we are going. When I have packed before I had always a home in sight. What a difference when we packed in Leaskdale! I was sorry to tear up our home there but I knew I was going to a nicer one and though there was sorrow there was no bitterness.

And I hate the thought of living in Toronto—on one of those terrible streets where the houses are all alike and all cheek by jowl with each other. It will be so ghastly lonesome there at night with miles of houses around me in whom I will not know a single soul.

Ethel is going with us. I hoped she would not, for I did not think she would want to leave her friends here and her beloved Gordon. But it seems she does. If Mrs. Thompson had not gone back to her husband I would let Ethel go and get her back. But as it is, I don't want a new maid just now, as well as a new place and a new life. But there are times when her everlasting and invariable "For the Land's sake" gets on my nerves.

Sunday, Feb. 24, 1935
It is amusing to see how all the men crowd into the Bible Class now. It is as if everyone was afraid to stay out for fear of being a marked man. It is all a little too late....

Monday, Feb. 25, 1935
The Manse, Norval, Ont.
A dreary day of snow and sleet. I packed and wrote to several house agents in Toronto. We have decided we can afford only fifty a month for rent. I fear in the present acute housing situation in Toronto we will not get anything like we want for that.

I had a letter from Mrs. Warren today and she tells me Mrs. Thompson has left her husband *again*. It is aggravating that this word should come just too late—when I have agreed to take Ethel to Toronto with us.

We had dinner at the Glen House tonight—a lovely dinner, spoiled by talk of the trouble. The Barracloughs are so indignant they can't talk of anything else. I would prefer to forget it temporarily. But their sympathy is very sweet. We hear the Norval people are in a terrible stew over what has happened.

When we came back dear little Luck came running to meet us, as usual. Dear cat, what will become of him in Toronto, with nothing but a dismal back yard to range in?

He had evidently been over in the MacPherson barn for his thick fluffy coat was full of the fragrance of clover hay. He will have no clover barns in Toronto.

In daytime I feel fairly confident we can manage to make both ends meet but at night I grow despondent. I fear Ewan will never be contented there. He has no friends in Toronto and has no hobbies to fill his time.

I am thankful I feel so much better physically than I did a few weeks ago. My appetite is picking up and I sleep pretty well most nights. Occasionally a dreadful feeling that everything has come to an end, good as well as bad, sweeps over me. But if I had a little rest and ease of mind I believe I could win back to myself even now.

Tuesday, Feb. 26, 1935

Ten below. It has certainly been a bitter winter. We had dress rehearsal in the hall this afternoon. Mr. and Mrs. Garfield were more than friendly and insisted on driving me home—I had trudged home alone over the icy streets many a night this winter and no one offered to drive me.

This was the last play practice I will ever hold. I *should* be glad—but I am not. There has been much pleasure mixed with all the hard work—and just now I feel myself so cut off from all those people who were once my friends and with whom I have jested and chatted and planned for years. They all liked me before that wretched letter. I suppose they would like me yet if they did not feel they had been such fools and worse. I think they hate the very sight of me when it must be a reminder to them of their folly and treachery.

Wednesday, Feb. 27, 1935
The Manse, Norval.

Last night we both slept well. Once it never occurred to me to note down whether we slept or not. Good sleep o'nights used to be a matter of course. And now a good sleep is a rarity.

It was 20 below zero and the house was cold all day. Forlorn and upset, too, in packing disarray. Ewan was very dull and grim all day. I felt no heart for anything. In the evening I called upon the MacPhersons, who are sad and broken over their bereavement....

Thursday, Feb. 28, 1935

I had two letters from real estate firms today—rather encouraging. They have "nothing listed" that would suit us but will inform us if anything turns up etc.

The Old Tyme concert came off tonight—the first night. They are going to have two nights in succession this year. I did not dress or join the procession but sat down in the audience. I no longer felt one with them and could not pretend to. Garfield clowned his part in the play so absurdly that it spoiled the whole performance. The rest of the cast were very indignant and Oliver Hunter told him bluntly that he had ruined the play.

They presented me with a bouquet! If I could have thought Garfield had not contributed to it I would have appreciated it. The rest of the cast are my friends and sympathize honestly with me in the difficult situation in which I have been placed. I am thankful tomorrow night will see the last of it.

355

"MacPherson House"

Sunday, Mar. 3, 1935

I have had no good news from the real estate men. Have had only three replies to all my letters and none has anything to offer.

Friday night the second Old Tyme performance came off. I hated having to dress up and go. I gave a recitation and as I left the platform I thought drearily, "I suppose this is the last time I will ever recite in public." And my thoughts went back to that night so long ago in Cavendish Hall, when I "recited in public" for the first time at a Literary Society program—Nov. 22nd, 1889. I recalled what a tremendous event it seemed to me, my getting up there before the little audience of Cavendish people and schoolmates to recite "The Child Martyr," lifting my right hand dramatically at the last line—"In *that* fair upper fold." I was very nervous—I had the strangest sensation that I had swelled to huge proportions and that my voice was coming to me from some incredible distance and didn't belong to me at all. Every detail came vividly back. And Nate Lockhart walking home with us afterwards!

All the years between I have been "reciting." Soon after I came to Norval I recited my own poem "The Watchman" at the St. Patrick concert in the church and some visitor said it alone was "worth the price of admission."

Well, it is all over now. It is extremely unlikely that I will ever "recite in public" again. And I'm sorry. Because I've always enjoyed it. It always satisfied some dramatic urge in me.

I spent yesterday...with Isobel, and Chester and Luella came for me at night. I do hope when I go to Toronto I will not be pestered with Isobel—at least, to the same extent. That would be some slight compensation.

I had a good sleep last night but I never feel rested. Today I got through Sunday School and church but I was so neurasthenic in the evening that I couldn't bring myself to go to the Glen House with Ewan. I feel hopeless and without courage and I dread the next two months so terribly. I wish since we have to go we could go at once.

At the Glen House tonight Mrs. Barraclough's sister, Mrs. Winfield, said some friend of hers had got a letter from Mrs. Watkins—one of our Norval people—in which she wrote indignantly that—"we are losing our beloved minister soon. A couple of ill-mannered fellows in Norval having driven him away!" Jim Russell, too, is reported as boiling over with rage because of the way Mr. Macdonald has been treated. So much for the yarn that *he* wouldn't come to church because of Ewan.

Tuesday, March 5, 1935
The Manse, Norval, Ont.
I had a good sleep and so feel better, though it has poured rain all day. Ewan went to Presbytery with Mr. Barraclough. I had a depressing letter from the LePage Real Estate Co. They say there are very few desirable houses to be got for a reasonable rent.

Mr. Morgasen phoned down tonight re the Old Tyme business meeting. I said I did not think it was necessary for me to go. He became very urgent—oh, I must go—"You have a lot of friends in that Association, Mrs. Macdonald." I suppose the fact is they are going to give me a farewell present—and I wish they wouldn't.

Ewan came home. His resignation was not accepted by Presbytery but was tabled, pending the result of a "Committee of Inquiry" to be sent out. Ewan did not want this but the Presbytery insisted. They seemed to think the affair could be ironed out and Ewan induced to stay. They should realize that is impossible. Too many festering wounds have been made. And it will mean more humiliation and misunderstanding for us. The congregation will probably think we asked for it and will resent being hauled over the coals by Presbytery. Will there never be an end to this nightmare?

Wednesday, March 6, 1935
The W.M.S. of Union met at Mrs. Young's today. I felt terribly all day with a ghastly weariness of soul. Old Gollop came in this evening to make me promise to go to the Old Tyme business meeting. I said I would go. What does it matter? If they are going to "make a presentation" I can't make a scandal by refusing to attend.

Thursday, Mar. 7, 1935
Ewan had a nervous chill at one last night and seemed very short of breath. I gave him sal volatile and he slept the rest of the night but I could not, so had to take veronal in view of the hard day ahead. It was very cold and the house was cold. I was busy all the forenoon preparing for the Institute which was to meet here. Twenty-three came. It was, I suppose, the last time I will entertain an organization of the kind and I was sad. I've always enjoyed such affairs. I like to make out a nice menu and get out my pretty linens and dishes and give everyone a pleasant time. "I'm awful, *awful* sorry you're going," said Miss Smellie, a sweet old thing who always came to our doings though not one of our people—she is, I believe, a "Christadelphian," whatever that may be. I've always been very fond of her.

Tom Macdonald told Ewan today that everyone in Norval is down on Garfield McClure. It is funny, if one felt like being amused. They all want to get out from under and put the whole blame on Garfield. He deserves most of it but not quite all—oh no, not quite all.

The "business meeting" of the Old Timer's Association came off tonight. I sat back demurely while they adopted reports and elected an executive for next year. Then I was called to the platform and Mr. Morgasen read an address and Oliver Hunter presented me with a very nice floor lamp in the name of the Association.

I made a speech in reply. It was a very nice, smooth, graceful speech and no outsider would have smelt any rats. But there were quite a few rodents around. I made my speech with a good deal of satisfaction to myself.

It had come to my ears that Mrs. Hewson had said something to that old hypocrite of a Gollop about the way I, the founder of the Association, had been treated and Mr. Gollop had told her a deliberate lie. He said I was *not* the founder—that they had started the Old Tymers back in Mr. Ferguson's time!

Sweet as honey and roses I smilingly remarked that I would always feel a special pride and interest in the Old Tyme Association since I was the founder of it. I sketched its rise and progress from the beginning—the meeting of the Young People's executive in my second year here—my suggestion that we have an Old Tyme Night on our program. I described the good evening that was the result, the old songs and costumes and the amusing skit "Why We Never Got Married" that wound up the program. And I wound up by wishing them all the success possible in the future and many more merry programs etc. and Mr. Gollop had to sit there and take it. Well, he deserved the dose.

I felt sad to think it would be my last evening in the Parish hall. I've always loved that place somehow. We have had a lot of fun and good fellowship there since it was built. It is not probable that I shall ever be in it again....

"The Parish Hall, Norval"

Friday, March 8, 1935
We went to Toronto with the Barracloughs after dinner. I called on several real estate firms but could get no satisfaction. They all seemed very indifferent. There is a house famine in Toronto and they don't need to bother trying to please people. One firm said they had a house on Inglewood Drive for $50 and if I would call next day I could get the key to it. I went out and took a street car to Inglewood Drive rather hopefully. I knew it was a nice street and I hoped the place would be possible. I found it eventually away up at the old end of the street. My heart sank like lead. Live there! A mean little house jammed in between two other mean ones. A narrow driveway leading to a tiny grimy back yard where there was a garage and nothing more. I looked in the kitchen window. The kitchen was terrible. I looked in through the glass of the front door. A tiny dark hall and a steep dark stair. Two miserable rooms with dreadful paper. I felt as if I were in a nightmare. Fifty dollars for *that*! I could not dream of trying to live in such a place. And it would not have held a third of our belongings.

I was so sick at heart that I felt as if I could do no more house-hunting that day. But—fortunately—I decided to go to one more place—the A. LePage Co. Here I found a different atmosphere. They were interested and understanding. I made an appointment for Tuesday to see some of their houses. Then Mr. LePage said, "Why don't you buy a house, Mrs. Macdonald"?

"I haven't the ready money to pay for it," I said.

"If you could manage a few thousand cash down you could put a mortgage on for the rest and the interest would not be as much as rent would be, even if you could get a house for $50. And I do not think you can get any house you would really like for less than nine hundred a year."

The idea suddenly took hold of me. It seemed a happy solution to my problems. I *could* raise two or three thousand by selling some securities that have recently come back to their former value. And in four years time one of my insurances would come in and clear the mortgage. We would own our home—we would have some choice of location—it could never be sold over our heads at any time and another quick move forced on us.

And to live in my own house—something I had never done. To own a bit of land—to stand on it and say "This is *mine*." A house one could do as one liked with, never having to care what "the congregation" thought or think, "What is the use? We may have to move on in a year or two and leave it."

I felt like a new creature when I left the office. Hope and encouragement flooded warmly over my bleak heart. Everything seemed changed. We drove home with the fiery orange of a winter sunset before us on the hills and I felt for the first time in a long while that it might be possible to go on with life graciously after all. I was very tired when I got home but I feel so much better tonight. A door seems to have opened in what was a blank wall.

Saturday, Mar. 9, 1935
The Manse, Norval, Ont.
Today I started in to do spade work on a new *Anne* book, having succumbed at long last to the urgency of publishers and "fans." I mean to try to fill in the gap

between *Anne of the Island* and *Anne's House of Dreams* when she was teaching school in Summerside. If it proves possible to "get back into the past" far enough to do a good book it ought to do well commercially after the film.

I had a strange feeling when I sat down to my work. Some interest seemed to return to life. The discovery that I may still be able to work heartens me. So often lately I have been afraid I never could again.

Mr. Wiggins' funeral was held in the church today. Ewan spoke well and looked well. I am fighting a froggy cold tonight and the discomfort makes me feel rather neurasthenic. I cannot reconcile myself to living in the city. I want my pine trees—my river—my garden—my friendly chats with neighbors—the stars over all. I shall miss the stars. One can never see them properly in a city. Humanity in its great lighted cities is shut out from the stars.

Sunday, March 10, 1935
I slept well but when I wakened this dark, wet, icy morning bitterness rolled over me like a wave.

One of the Dolson boys from Union, who was visiting friends in Norval, was in my class today and after it was over he came up to me and said, "If we only had a teacher like you in Union, Mrs. Macdonald!"....

We spent the evening at the Glen House. The sympathy and understanding we meet there are a great help to us in our difficult position. We have discovered that several Norval families have been very resentful of our intimacy with the Barracloughs. Jealousy and stupidity really do most of the harm that is done in the world. But we no longer care a penny whether they are jealous or not.

Monday, Mar. 11, 1935
I had a good sleep and worked three hours this forenoon at the new *Anne* book. Marion was here for supper and we had a nice time. When she came to Norval to live I thought how pleasant it would be to have someone of my own so near me. And now I have to leave her....

Tuesday, March 12, 1935
The Manse, Norval, Ont.
I am very tired tonight but much happier than I have been for a long long time.

Last night I had a lovely dream—the first nice dream I have had for a long long time. I dreamed that I was home again in my dear old room in Cavendish. I seemed to know that I was going to stay there. It was clean and fresh with a nice new window in it. The furniture was strewn about and parcels were lying everywhere but I thought, "I can soon bring everything into order and have my own dear room again." Grandma was there, too, smiling and kind. I felt so happy and the influence of the dream stayed with me when I woke. I thought, "This dream means that we will find a house today that we like."

Ewan and I went in to Toronto. We had an appointment with Mr. LePage at his west office at the end of Bloor for ten o'clock. We got in at 9.30 and I said, "Let us drive up along Riverside Drive and put in the time till ten looking at the nice homes along it."

Mossom Road and Riverside Drive, which is all one long winding street, going along the top of a curious ridge extending along the Humber from Bloor Street to the Lake Shore. It is one of the prettiest, if not *the* prettiest, of the new suburban developments of Toronto. It has been building up rapidly the past few years. We have always driven through it on our way to the business section and I used to say jestingly, "When we retire I'd like to live here," but I had no idea that dream would ever come to pass. The homes were all nice, set in nice gardens with lots of trees. I *must* have trees about or near a house I would love. A house without some trees to veil it is an indecency like a too naked body.

We drove slowly along until all at once I saw a new house with a "for sale" placard on the lawn. I liked the look of it at first sight. There was a couple of oak trees in front and behind it was a group of pines. Pines!! I said, "I am going to get out and look through the window."

I did not need to do this, however, for as I went up the little stone flagged walk the owner and builder came along and took us in. I fell in love with it at once. The front door opened into a little vestibule. A glass door led into a nice paneled hall. On the right was a dining room with a large beautiful casement window in the end. A breakfast nook and pantry separated it from a darling bright compact and convenient tiled kitchen. On the left was a beautiful living room with fireplace. It ran across the whole end of the house, with two large casement windows at each end and another on the side. The front one looked out on the drive but the back one looked out on a lovely ravine full of oaks and pines, where they told me the ferns were to your waist in summer. Below it was the Humber River and beyond open country of green wooded hills. Off to the left was a glimpse of the Lake. I think it was when I saw the ravine I knew I must have the house. What a place for the cats to prowl in! What a lovely series of rock gardens could be made down the slope! And how lovely those big dark pines were behind our garage!

"The New House" [210 Riverside Drive]

The stairs went up to a landing with a glass door opening on a nice square balcony. On the upper floor were three lovely bedrooms. A tiled bath was off the hall and another was off the large "master bedroom." There was also a darling dressing closet with built in wardrobe. The large window to the south overlooked the ravine, the river and the lake. On the third floor was a darling room, a trunk closet, another bath room and a nice hall. In the basement was a nice "recreation" room with fireplace, a laundry, furnace cellar and two closets.

I asked the price with fear and trembling and when he said $14,000 I felt a shiver of disappointment. I could not go so high. But as I went away I felt that I was leaving "my" house behind me.

We went to the LePage office and Mr. LePage took us all over the Kingsway district. It is a very nice district and we looked at houses until my head whirled. They were all nice and new and convenient: but not one of them did I feel was "mine." Finally I asked Mr. LePage about the one on the drive and he said he was the agent for it too and that we could get it for a good deal less than the listed price if we could pay $3000 down. We went back and looked it over. I liked it better than ever. We decided to go home and think it over for a few days, but as we drove home I *knew* I was going to buy that house—that it had been built for me. My dream had come true....

Wednesday, Mar. 13, 1935
The Manse, Norval, Ont.
Today my packing had so far advanced that it became necessary to tear up my parlor and use it as a basis for further operations. It hurt me terribly. I've always loved this big shadowy room. And I like a *parlor*. I am sorry to think I shall never have one again. They have become hopelessly out of date. There are only "living rooms" now and a living room can never have the kudos of a parlor—that sacred room which was only opened up when company came. To be sure, I have "lived" in my parlors in Leaskdale and Norval as much as in any other room in the house. I always wrote in the Leaskdale parlor, while my pussy slept curled up beside me and dear little Stuart lay down on the hall floor outside and threw kisses under the door to mother, who was not to be disturbed while she was writing, unless for some absolutely necessary reason. He would poke flowers under the door for me, the darling.

In Norval I have always written in my room, finding it the best-lighted and most convenient—finding inspiration, too, in the wooded hill of pines beyond. But we have always used the parlor a great deal, as we had the fireplace in it. It was roomy and had a big bay window—which to be sure looked out on a rather drab little side street but had a view of pine hills and the sunsets beyond them. I have walked its floor in bitter anguish many a time these past five years—but I have loved it and I hated to dismantle it—take down the mirror and the pictures and the curtains—roll up the carpet—pack away the cushions and bric-a-brac. The poor forlorn room seems to reproach me whenever I go into it.

We brought the trunks down from the garret too. They have never been down since we took them up when we came.

We had supper at the Glen House and then I went to the Play contest in the hall and gave the judges' report. The last time for the old Glen Hall too, I suppose. But there is no need to waste much sentiment over that.

Today when I was unpacking a box of point lace in the garret I found my gold thimble, to my surprise and delight. I got that gold thimble over thirty years ago—to commemorate getting into some important magazine. I have always used it. It was a very pretty one and never discolored my finger as ordinary thimbles do. Two or three years ago it disappeared. I had reason to think it had dropped out of my work bag as I crossed the lawn and I searched for it for days but never found it. And today it rolled out of a folded lace bertha. I cannot imagine how it got there, but I was delighted to find it again....

Friday, Mar. 15, 1935
Today was lovely and springlike. We went in to Toronto and conferred with Mr. LePage and Mr. Small, the builder. I walked up and down the living room. I looked out on the ravine and the pines. They decided me. I said I would buy the house for $12,200.

Am I a fool? I don't think so. The neighborhood is excellent. If I find I can't carry the house it should be easy to sell it. I *do* want a nice home to end my days in—"Journey's End" I am going to call it. I hope it *will* be "journey's end" and that I will never have to "move" again.

I went all over it again, liking it as well as ever. There is a curious *impersonality* about a house that has never been lived in. It has no memories, no traditions, no ghosts. It seems to be *asking* for a soul.

But there was an unpleasant surprise awaiting me when I went to McClelland's. Hodder and Stoughton have refused *Mistress Pat*. This slap in the face was entirely unexpected and I cannot understand it. They were "delighted" with *Pat of Silver Bush* and did quite well with it. I think the sequel is quite as good as *Silver Bush* and Mr. Stokes wrote me that they were "delighted" with it. Mr. McClelland said they gave no reason for it. He thinks Harrap will take it—they handle a lot of the reprints of my books and seem a good firm. But I came away feeling down-hearted. Hodder has published all my books since *Rilla of Ingleside* and I have always liked the firm and found them honorable and pleasant to deal with. I hate changing—and my pride has suffered a bit, too, though that is of small moment among all the other worries of life....

Saturday, March 16, 1935
The Manse, Norval, Ont.
....I packed all the books in the garret today. It all seems bitterly different from the Leaskdale packing with the kind neighborly women there coming in and out with offers of help and meals, telling us how sorry they were etc....

Sunday, March 17, 1935
The Manse, Norval, Ont.
I had a good sleep and went more cheerily to Bible Class and Church. Ewan for the first time since his illness preached extempore and did very well. In the moonlit

evening we went to see Joe McClures', who are very indignant over the way we have been used. I laughed and chatted the evening through wondering if the ache in my heart would ever turn to a merciful numbness.

Tuesday, Mar. 19, 1935
I have been packing all day and am terribly tired. Had a letter, too, from Isobel, begging for another visit before I go. In the afternoon I wandered down to the river for a breath of air and mourned there over leaving my lovely stream. The Humber is not nearly so beautiful....

My garden is coming up—the Madonna lilies are pushing above the ground. Shall I ever have a garden again? I have had to leave three.

Germany has announced her intention to re-arm and the papers are full of war talk. What a world!

Wednesday, March 20, 1935
I could not sleep last night for nervous unrest until I took a bromide. Today I stripped Chester's room for packing and remembered fixing it up when we came.

Ewan was in to see the MacPhersons this afternoon. By all accounts everybody in the congregation is terribly sorry and everyone is blaming the other.

Ewan was away this evening and I have been in bad shape. I never minded being alone before—I even liked it. Now I cannot endure it. I had a terrible attack of claustrophobia. I felt as if I *must* get out—that I could not bear walls around me another moment. I was filled with such a terror of the future that I couldn't face it. I took the jitters whenever the phone rang. In those awful moments I feel exactly as I did in that terrible dream of nearly a year ago when I was the only living thing in a dead universe. I am nothing but an incarnate *fear*. I wonder if this

"MacPherson Group"

362

tortured haunted creature can be *me*—the once merry light hearted girl who could find a joke in everything, and who now feels like a beaten cringing dog. Will life ever be anything but a nightmare again?

I read *Anne of The Island* and *Anne's House of Dreams* today. Since my new book is to fill the gap between them I want to get back into the spirit of them. And I thought longingly of that sweet, simple olden day when I found it so easy and pleasant to write.

Thursday, March 21, 1935
The Manse, Norval, Ont.
I had a wretched night with sciatica. Had to take one of Dr. Paul's tablets to get a little sleep. I dismantled my spare room today—my pretty, sunny room, with its outlook of pine hills. I felt fairly well until four when an attack of claustrophobia came on and persisted. I had to go out and walk up and down our little side street for half an hour before I could get the better of it. In the evening I called at MacPhersons'. As I walked back the night was lovely—stars in soft silvery skies, pines dark against them. But I can no longer feel the old divine communion with these things.

There was a letter from Stuart in the evening mail. There was no reason on earth why I should fear to open it but I just couldn't bring myself to do it. So I'm leaving it till the morning.

I received word today that I have been elected a member of "The Literary and Artistic Institute of France!!!"

I wish the honor would cure my sciatica, banish neurasthenia, and take away all the bruises of my soul and spirit!

Friday, March 22, 1935
A lovely day. I really never remember such a beautiful March as we have had. I had to take medinal last night but had a good sleep and felt better all day. Did not have any attacks of nervous restlessness but felt instead a strange immeasurable sadness.

I read Stuart's letter this morning and it had a bit of bad news. His new overcoat has been stolen. Our ill-luck seems to pursue us in everything.

I took all the pictures in my room down today. I papered the room soon after I came and planned to paper it again this spring. Somebody else will do it now. The unfaded spaces where the pictures hung stare down like reproachful ghosts.

We were at the Glen this evening and had our game of euchre but a fresh shadow hung over us. Mr. Barraclough has high blood pressure and a bad heart condition and this news made us feel very worried and upset.

Saturday, March 23, 1935
....I packed all day—the house is beginning to look terrible. In the evening I read the proofs of *Mistress Pat*. I used to enjoy reading proof but it gave me no pleasure tonight. Ewan keeps pretty well but I notice he gets tired very easily. I have been bitterly lonely and *homesick* tonight.

Sunday, Mar. 24, 1935
The Manse, Norval, Ont.
....Church was hard to bear. I could hardly keep the tears back. Next Sunday will be our last. How will I be able to bear it? I wish we could get away right after it but our house will not be quite finished for a month yet, so we cannot go till it is.

I have a nasty pain in the back of my head a great deal of the time and I am getting very thin. If I could get a real rest and freedom from grief and worry I believe I could soon pick up even yet. A doctor once told me I had wonderful recuperative powers. But there seems no chance. If I dare perk up a bit another blow comes. I'm getting very superstitious about it.

Monday, Mar. 25, 1935
I began packing my dishes today and packed a barrel full of my good dinner set. I have always been fond of those dainty delicate dishes. They have been used a good deal since I was married and there are a few nicks caused by careless maids but only one piece is missing.

....The Presbytery Committee had its meeting here today and Ewan had the news for me when I came home. They aired things thoroughly and told the Norval people some things it was good for them to know. After all, I think it was well they came, though I did not think so at first. But the cream of the news came after the meeting. Outside Garfield came boldly up to Ewan and demanded of him why "you and Mrs. Macdonald don't speak to me." Of course, this was not the case. We always speak to Garfield, very politely when it is necessary. What Garfield really meant was, "Why do you not speak to me in the old friendly hail-fellow-well-met way?"

Ewan said briefly that Mrs. Macdonald could speak for herself but he understood that she had been insulted by the Old Tymers Association. "I had nothing to do with that," cried Garfield. "That was *Morgasen* and Gollop."

If I had not known already what Garfield was that lie would have revealed him. Gollop *was* in it, of course, but only as the puppet whose strings Garfield pulled. Mr. Morgasen had nothing to do with it. When he found out what had been done he refused to have anything more to do with the Old Tymers and only came back into the play to help me out. If I had been there when Garfield said that I would have said, "Oh? Well, will you please tell me which of them it was, Mr. Gollop or Mr. Morgasen, who drove all over the countryside next day looking for plays and took what he had found to Mrs. Hewson to read and decide on?" I wonder just what answer he would have made to *that*. And I wonder what Mr. Morgasen will say when he hears Garfield has put the blame on him. *I* will not tell him; but I will mention it to a few of my friends and I think it will get to him in time. He *should* know it—he should know just what falsehoods Garfield is telling about him.

"As for me," Ewan went on, "when I spoke to you about forming a Men's Bible Class, with their own chosen teacher, *you* said, 'A good idea. We might get somewhere then.'"

"I never said it," cried Garfield. "Who told you I said that?"

"I was not told it," said Ewan. "You said it to me."

And he turned and walked away. My conceited Garfield would go home with a flea in his ear.

Tuesday, Mar. 26, 1935
The Manse, Norval, Ont.
The W.M.S. met at Marion's this afternoon—my last W.M.S. as a minister's wife! I felt very sad and fought with tears all the time, for I would not let those women see I cared. They read me a flattering address and gave me a nice table lamp. Well, we have always got on well together and I have enjoyed my work among them. But it was the husbands of these women who hounded my husband when he was ill and I was distracted with worry. I cannot forget that.

Old Mrs. Early came up to me crying after lunch. "I'm so sorry you are going," she sobbed.

"So am I," I said quietly, "but there was nothing else we could do."

She said nothing—there was nothing she could say.

I stayed after everyone had gone to help Marion wash the dishes and heard another funny thing. Garfield has been to Murray with a tale of woe. "Everybody was making him the goat," he wailed. He did not get much sympathy. Poor Garfield would give a good deal if some things could be blotted out.

But the *ugliness* of it all hurts and bruises me. To think of Ewan's ministry ending like this, after all the other congregations who mourned so much to see him go!

Thursday, Mar. 28, 1935
....We went to Toronto today and took the MacPherson girls along. We called to show them the new house on the way home. When I am in it I love it and think I can be happy in it, but when I come home my love for the manse reasserts itself and then I feel a queer hatred of the town house. I know with my *mind* that I shall like "Journey's End" when I am living in it but my *heart* does not yet know it.

The lady who lives next door to us on the right—Mrs. Cowan—came over and spoke to us. She seems very nice and friendly.

We spent the evening at the Glen House and felt better mentally. But I got so horribly tired and sciatica tortured me all the time.

Friday, March 29, 1935
I had a good sleep and did not feel so tired today and had none of those awful fits of bottomless despair. They are so dreadful. I cannot describe them. It seems for just a moment that a black empty gulf of terror opened at my feet, and that moment seems like a century. Fortunately it never lasts longer than a moment. If it did I don't know what would happen to me. I packed all day and in the evening we went to a euchre party in Union. I have always felt so *at home* with those people. They all seemed like one big pleasant family.

Tuesday, April 2, 1935
The Manse, Norval
It would be idle for anyone to tell me that a malignant fate is *not* pursuing us.

Last Saturday Ewan and I, with others, had the narrowest escape we have ever had in our lives from sudden death or dreadful injury. I can't imagine how we did escape. It must simply be predestination.

Saturday morning I spent packing but in the afternoon Mr. Barraclough came along and wanted us to go for a drive with them. He had bought—or got on trial— a magnificent new car and was taking it out to test it. He wanted us to see what we thought of it before he committed himself definitely to the purchase of it. We went, picked up their niece Eva Winfield, who was on a case in Guelph and drove as far as Elmira. We enjoyed it—pleasant and congenial companionship always helps me—for a space I felt uplifted and courageous. We turned at Elmira and came back through Kitchener. The superstitious can read what omen they like in the fact that on turning a corner we found ourselves involved in a funeral procession just behind the hearse! We had to keep on till they turned up a side street to a church. Mrs. Barraclough was quite upset over it.

We had left Kitchener behind and were travelling at a very moderate rate of speed. On one side was an embankment fully twenty feet high, quite unguarded by even a railing. All at once it happened. I can hardly describe it. Nobody knows what went wrong—I suppose we never will know. That car seemed suddenly to go crazy. It made one wild bound to the side of the road, bounded back to the other side, shuttled back and forth two or three times as if possessed by a demon. "What is the matter, Ernest?" cried Mrs. B. "I can't do a thing with it," he replied. And as he spoke the car went over the embankment!

When I felt we were going over I was conscious of no fear or alarm whatever. But I did think quite clearly, "This is the end for some of us. Some of us will certainly be killed or horribly injured. What will the boys do?"

The car rolled over and over like a shot rabbit down the slope which fortunately was not sheer but slightly inclined. After two and a half revolutions it came to rest on its side, also fortunately in a soft mud puddle.

Characteristically I was the first to find my tongue. "Is anyone hurt?" I cried. And every voice answered "I'm all right."

It was a miracle—we will have to let it go at that!

Everyone of the five of us had glasses on, two of them pince-nez, and not even a pair of glasses were knocked off.

Followed a pretty nasty half hour however. Mr. Barraclough got the door above him opened and he and Ewan scrambled out that way. In the back I was lying curled up in an indescribable heap on the glass door of the down side. Mrs. Barraclough, a woman weighing well over 200 lbs. was lying on me, with a trembling little Boston bull between us. Eva was lying on top of her.

When we had gone over not a soul or a car was in sight. But by the time the men got out the usual crowd had collected. They got the door above us opened and with the aid of men pulling her Eva managed to get out. But Mrs. B. was too heavy to be thus dragged out and when I tried I found that I had strained some muscle in my back that made every movement an agony. So they had to send to a nearby house for a step-ladder. Meanwhile the oil was running over the hot engine and beginning to send out black smoke. We could not see this but we could hear people outside saying, "She's going on fire!!" And there we were like rats in a trap!! It was the strain of this that did us more harm than the plunge over. But after what seemed ages the ladder was brought and we both got out, were lifted down and assisted up the bank. The car was covered with mud but otherwise was but little hurt. The steel top and the unbreakable glass no doubt saved us from death or mutilation. That glass *was* unbreakable. Mrs. B. and I stood on it for half an hour and there was not a crack in it.

Eventually we were all assembled in a Kitchener hotel and took stock. Mr. B. and Ewan had neither scratch nor bruise, though I could not help feeling anxious about the after effect on Mr. B.'s weak heart. Eva had cracked a rib (as we found out later), Mrs. B.'s knee was badly bruised and I could hardly move for pain in the aforesaid muscle. But our escape from all serious injury was something incredible.

Eventually we got a taxi and were all taken home. The drive was agony for me because of my back but at last we got home. When I got into bed and lay down my back did not hurt me as long as I did not move. But when I tried to get up in the morning Ewan had to pull me up by my arms. Once up I contrived to dress. Of course I should have stayed in bed. But it was our "farewell" Sunday. I was resolved to go to church. We did not want the news of the accident to leak out just then and give satisfaction to certain people who have been jealous of our intimacy with the Barracloughs.

I had meant to go to Union but I gave up that idea. Ewan went alone. After the service the whole congregation, men and women alike, sat there in tears. After dinner I went to Bible Class and when it was over I said goodbye to the boys. They seemed to feel very badly. I did, too, but not as badly as I would have done three years or so ago. When I came to Norval there was no class for the bigger boys from seventeen up, who were being lost to the Sunday School when they grew too "big" for the intermediate class. So I organized a Young Men's Bible class. It has always been very successful. We controlled our own finances and always raised about forty dollars a year. We gave a contribution to the budget and to the Sunday School funds and spent the rest as we liked. Among other things we got the lantern and hymn slides, the hymn boards, and another piano for use in the basement. In class we always had interesting times for the boys were old enough to have opinions of their own and discuss them. Then, a few years ago these boys had all gone—moved away or married. The ones that came in from the intermediate were much younger—from thirteen to sixteen. It was hard to get them to discuss questions—indeed, they seemed a much more *stupid* lot and did not seem to have any opinions. Still, they were most of them nice boys and I was sorry to part from them. I wound up my little speech of farewell by wishing them all possible good and success in the future and one of them responded, "We wish the same to you, Mrs. Macdonald."

So nine years' work is over. I don't know who they will get for a teacher. There is no suitable one in sight. But the next minister's wife may carry it on.

Then I went upstairs to hear Ewan preach his farewell sermon. It was a hard ordeal for me, for besides my grief and sorrow I was in physical agony from my back. But I sat upright and gave no sign. There were a great many outsiders there, United and Anglican. Some of them came no doubt out of friendliness, but some came from curiosity. They did not get much for their pains. Ewan looked well and preached well and any significance was in what he did *not* say, rather than in what he said. He referred briefly and in good taste to his nine years' pastorate and thanked the Young Peoples', the Sunday School Executive, the W.M.S. and the Ladies' Aid for the way they had co-operated with him in all things—which was

Interior of Norval Church

perfectly true. He did not even mention the Session and the Board of Managers. They all knew why.

I thought sadly that I would never see Ewan in his own pulpit again.

When the service was over I rose quickly and went right out. I knew that I would never enter Norval church again if I could avoid it. And I have loved it so. I recalled the last Sunday in Leaskdale when I could hardly get out for the crowd of weeping women around me. I knew the women here were just as sorry but there was an insurmountable barrier between us.

We went to the Glen in the evening and spent it talking our accident over and comparing sensations and impressions. We cannot understand our escape.

Yesterday, having a fair sleep I felt a little better but at times a dreadful feeling of absolute exhaustion would come over me. As I couldn't pack I did the sensible thing and stayed in bed most of the time. It was a dark day and some snow fell. Snow in April is abominable—like a slap in the face when you expected a kiss.

Today I got up and packed and rested alternately. My back makes any packing very painful but packing the barrels is absolutely impossible. Ewan was in Toronto and Mr. Bogart told him Chester was doing fine now. If it only lasts! I got my royalty report from Stokes today and it was a good one—much better than I expected. Which is a relief for I've been worrying a bit over finances. I have sold out all the stocks I could sell without a loss in order to make the payment on Journey's End and I shall have to depend on my earnings now for everything.

Wednesday, April 3, 1935
The Manse, Norval.
....I packed all the forenoon and tore up Stuart's little den. He has slept there for a couple of years. Lucky loved it too. Many a night when I hunted all over the house to make sure Luck was in before I went to bed I would at last find him rolled up into a ball on Stuart's little bed.

Thursday, April 4, 1935
I went to Georgetown today and got a tonic from Dr. Paul. He does not however sell peace of mind or relief from a sore heart in bottles. This evening we went to the farewell reception in Union Church to which Norval was also invited. There was a representative present from every Norval family except Garfield McClure's and Will McClures!! As I was there early I was helping Mrs. Dick arrange the plates and she said bitterly, "There was no need of this. But you are not the first Norval has treated like this and you won't be the last."

It was a hard evening. We had to sit on the platform and listen to many speeches of praise from the Union men. The poor Norvalites were invited to speak and were in a sad predicament. *They* could not get up and praise us, when Union was blaming them for sending us away. Poor old Andy got up and stammered that he was "very sorry this had to be." Perhaps he knew what he meant himself. Oliver Hunter, who *has* been our friend right through and stood up for us, made the only good Norval speech. We were presented with a purse and the Dramatic Club gave me a pen and ink-stand. We called in a few moments at the Glen House on our way home and talked it over.

Friday, April 5, 1935
The Manse, Norval, Ont.
I managed to get a barrel of jam packed today but it was very hard. It almost kills me to bend. Then we went to supper and an evening of euchre at the Glen House. Mr. Barraclough is better and his blood pressure is down. We had a lovely time as always.

Saturday, April 6, 1935
I got another barrel packed as well as several boxes. Then we went to supper at Joe McClure's. His brother Dave McClure was there, a member of the Brampton congregation. He was talking about Mrs. Coulter—the new Brampton minister's wife, who is a very charming woman. He praised her to the skies for every good quality—"an ideal minister's wife"—"in fact from all I can hear, just like your own good lady here," with a bow in my direction. Humph! Wonder if Garfield would subscribe to that!!

The sad part is—he would have once. He used to sing my praises in season and out of season. And *I* have not changed. It all hurts me.

Sunday, April 7, 1935
A dreary day. I felt dreadfully when I saw the cars arriving for Sunday School. If we had been "retiring" of our own free will and going as we went from Leaskdale I would have kept on with the Sunday School as long as I was here but under the circumstances it could not be. Ewan, too, seemed to suddenly realize the new "emptiness." He was dull and complained of his head. I am so afraid he will have another attack of melancholia now. He has been so well during these "fighting" weeks.

Nora and Ned were out this afternoon. Nora was full of gay plans for our life in Toronto. But I couldn't *feel* them. They dropped into my heavy heart like pebbles in a sullen pool.

We went to the Glen House in the evening. Mr. B. said there had been very few out in Union. Mr. Kaye of Boston and Omagh preached the pulpit vacant and also let it be understood that he was a candidate. But I don't think he stands any chance.

When we came home I saw the new moon over the branch hill as I came in to the house. I have seen it often so—I shall never see it so again!

Monday, April 8, 1935
The Manse, Norval, Ont.
We went into Toronto this cold raw morning. I met Mr. Bogart for the first time, as he is fixing up the mortgage. I did not take any great fancy to him. Perhaps because he said to me, "I am glad you are coming to Toronto. You will be able to keep check on Chester." No doubt it was true but it hurt. He had just found out that I was "L.M. Montgomery" and said he hadn't "known Chester had such a famous mother." It might have been better for Chester if he had—in some ways.

We left at 12 and stopped in Brampton to have dinner with the Coulters. Dr. and Mrs. McKerroll of Victoria Church Toronto (where we will probably go) were also there. I should have enjoyed it but I was too tired. I went to the Literary Club and read a paper as I have done every year since coming to Norval. They presented me with a bouquet of roses.

I am so tired tonight I feel as if I could never get rested and I cannot believe anything good will ever happen to me again. People keep telling me I ought to go to bed. I never complain to anyone but they are beginning to notice how I look. How can I go to bed?

Tuesday, April 9, 1935
I had a fair sleep and felt fairly well all day. We took Mrs. Hoare of Union to have dinner with a sister of hers and baptize a grandchild. As we drove along Mrs. Hoare said that we had been nine years in Union and they wanted us for nine more. Also that all the countryside was "down" on Garfield McClure....

Wednesday, April 10, 1935
I had a fair sleep and today was fine and warm. I thankfully packed the last barrel. Ewan remarked that he was "not feeling any too well." I know what that phrase means and at five I broke down and cried. We were to supper at Verne Thompson's and came home at ten. The Y.P. were having a social in the basement tonight and Luella had phoned over asking me to go. I said I couldn't because I had a supper engagement. She then asked me to go over when I came back—"I must." I knew by this another presentation was in the offing so I went over reluctantly. The Y.P. and my Bible Class together gave me a glass relish plate on a silver tray. Claude McLaughlin whom I have never liked presided. He has never been in my class and this is the first year he has been a member of the Y.P. He certainly doesn't suffer from an inferiority complex. He very condescendingly informed the audience that he was sure Mrs. Macdonald would always be welcome in Norval church!!! I would have liked to have stood up and told the insufferable creature that Mrs. Macdonald had not the slightest intention of ever revisiting Norval church, whether welcome or unwelcome.

Thursday, April 11, 1935
The Manse, Norval, Ont.
A hard day. I have felt so heart-broken and Ewan has been very dull and grim all day. Mrs. Davies called and had no precisely cheerful effect. She said Jean (her daughter) had said it hadn't seemed like Sunday School or Sunday without Mrs. Macdonald! Well, I have worked very hard for that Sunday School ever since I came and got little thanks for it.

Sunday, April 14, 1935
Today was lovely. We were at the Glen in the afternoon and at Mr. Dick's to supper. These affairs are always spoiled for me by the persistent talk over the whole ruction. I want to forget it. Ewan is dull and moody and just wants to lie around all the time. Complains of "that burning sensation" in head and abdomen again.

For myself, my back is better at last and I can get in and out of a car again without trouble.

Monday, April 15, 1935
A pouring rain that turned to snow, with a high wind. After dinner we went to Toronto with a car load of stuff. I felt dreadfully as I carried them out. Ewan was very dull all the morning but seemed better in the afternoon. We stowed the stuff away in the closets of Journey's End and the house at once began to seem "lived in."

We spent this evening with the McKanes. My head felt funny and *tight* all the time. When Ewan was out in the kitchen talking to the boys Mr. McKane said to me, "Mr. Macdonald will be a hard man to follow with the young people. My boys think there is nobody like him."

Tuesday, April 16, 1935
Bitter cold, with a wailing wind blowing around the eaves. The house was wretchedly cold and Ewan was dull. My head felt very queer all day and I was haunted by that "homeless" feeling which I cannot conquer. We were at Arthur McClure's for supper tonight. There is a curious difference between our Union and Norval visits now. In Union they all talk about our going away and what has led up to it. But in a Norval household there is absolute significant silence about it all.

Wednesday, April 17, 1935
The Manse, Norval, Ont.
I had a fair sleep and the day was fine but cold. I was busy all the morning preparing for a sale of certain bits of furniture and odds and ends we are selling off. I hated it. When the time came I shut myself in Chester's room and stayed there till it was over. In especial I hated to see my wardrobe and cedar chest go. The wardrobe is really a very handsome piece of furniture. I had it made from my own design when I went to Leaskdale because there were no closets in any of the rooms and I always liked it. But Journey's End is well closeted and there is no room for such a big article. There is also a cedar closet and my chest is so big it is unwieldy and would not fit in anywhere....

Tonight I stood on the back platform and looked for a long time at the moonlight behind the church. And I said good-bye to my echo. How often I have stood there calling "Puss-puss-pussy" and back it would come to me from the far pine hill in most delicious mockery, as if some fairy were calling some frisking kitten of elfland in out of the moonshine.

Thursday, April 18, 1935
We took another load of stuff into Journey's End today. Then we went to the Glen House for supper and afterwards to Union Church where Ewan was Chairman for a play the Cheltenham Young People put on. I gave a recitation, so my Norval "appearance" was not my last one after all. Stuart came home tonight for his last week-end in Norval manse.

Friday, April 19, 1935
Today was a June day dropped into April. I went to my last W.M.S. of Union at Andrew Macdonald's. They presented me with a very nice packaway and an address which pleased me very much, because it referred to "my oneness" with them. They had always felt me as one of themselves. We all cried bitterly. I have never felt more poignant pain at parting from any organization than I felt at leaving Union W.M.S.

This evening we had supper and a boring evening at Robinsons'. Stuart seems very distrait. He says he is worried over exams. I don't like this.

Saturday, April 20, 1935
We took a car load of stuff to Journey's End. I carried my old Woolner jug on my lap and locked it carefully up in a closet. We had supper with the Fred Lyons tonight and spent an evening of terrible boredom. My eyes seemed to be pulling out of my head. They have been like this since the car accident.

Mr. B. has had his car completely overhauled and no reason for its behavior can be discovered. Something must have jammed temporarily about the steering gear.

Two or three times today one of those dreadful "waves of despair" rolled over me. I cannot describe how terrible they are. When they come on I feel *hungry for death*. That expresses my feeling exactly. It is well they never last long. If they did—

Sunday, April 21, 1935
The Manse, Norval, Ont
Sunday is always a bitter day now. A Mr. Boyle came to preach. Nobody met him or provided transportation for him so he came here and Ewan took him to Union and brought him back for dinner here. I am not inhospitable but I do think Norval might provide for its own candidates!....

Monday, April 22, 1935
This morning I took my ferns and cats to Toronto. We put each one in a burlap bag. Pat yowled bad temperedly the whole way in but darling Luck never uttered a cry. What must he have felt! I hated to come away and leave him. And

Cats

I missed him so when I came home. Never to see him again on the window sill, or trotting under the maples—never to find him curled up asleep in the vacant lot!....

This is Stuart's last night in the Norval manse. He was a child of ten when we came here—he is nineteen now.

Wednesday, April 24, 1935
The Manse, Norval

Stuart went back to college yesterday. Never again will I hear his footsteps in these rooms.

Tonight I went down to the office for the evening mail for the last time. It is a prosy little village street but I have always loved walking down it because of the enchanting bits of beauty visible in the distance—lovely hills everywhere and the river and the pines—the beautiful trees around the church.

I had little to do today so lay down for a while in the afternoon. My back is quite well but my nerves have not yet recovered from the shock of the accident....

We had supper and spent the evening at the Glen House and had our usual euchre game. But we were all sad. When we came away Mr. and Mrs. Barraclough stood as they have always done at the window of the living room to see

Barraclough's House in Glen Williams

we got started all right and waved their hands to us out of sight. I cried all the way home at leaving them. For, though we hope for other visits in the future, they cannot be so often and nothing will be quite the same. They have been wonderful friends to us from the night we came here. And we have had many many delightful times together. The gods themselves can't take that away from us.

And this is our last night in Norval manse. Our first one nine years ago was not a particularly happy one. We were worried over the Pickering affair. I was homesick for Leaskdale, and it was a terribly cold night. But all that passed and our first four years here were very pleasant.

This time tomorrow night the cold windows will shine no more with welcoming lights. All will be dark and still. We shall be gone and the closed doors and empty rooms will be left to the ghosts of our pains and pleasures. I have written "The Manse, Norval" at the head of an entry for the last time.

Maud and Pussy

At last, in this "writing up" of my journal I have finished with our life in Norval. And I am glad. It has been hard: all the old wounds have been torn open afresh from day to day. But, as always, it has done me wonderful good. Writing it all out seems to have taken some poison out of my soul. I think the wounds will heal up wholesomely now. The scars will always be there but the old ache will disappear. It will just be something over and finished with—a page turned—a book closed.

Notes

1929

August 11 ZINC ROOF. The bluish-white metal, zinc, was commonly used as a coating on galvanized sheet iron. Sometimes wrongly referred to as "tin roof". One of the world's largest zinc mines was in Sudbury, Ontario. PAS SEUL. A solo dance in ballet. CHESTER. LMM's oldest son, Chester Cameron Macdonald, now aged 17, was working at a Georgetown garage during summer holidays from St. Andrew's College, a private boarding school in Aurora, north of Toronto, Ontario. BRAMPTON. The nearest town to the east, between Norval and Toronto. **August 24** MAGIC FOR MARIGOLD. LMM's 15th novel, completed October 17, 1928. STOKES. The Frederick A. Stokes Company had held the American rights to reprint LMM's books in the USA since 1917. FAN MUTCH. Fannie Wise Mutch, a friend from Prince of Wales College days (1893-4) in Charlottetown, Prince Edward Island. THE EX. The Canadian National Exhibition, held in Toronto each year at the end of August, had developed from an agricultural fair. Housed in handsome permanent buildings, it now also featured a midway and a spectacular grandstand show. STUART. Ewan Stuart Macdonald, LMM's younger son, now aged 13, at home for summer holidays from St. Andrew's College. MRS. MASON. Mrs. Margaret Ruth Checkley Mason (1900–1993) was raised on a large farm near Arthur, Ontario, one of ten children in a prominent family; she married William Mason (perhaps originally named William Sowerby?), a handsome English-born farm worker from a nearby farm, and became a widow after her husband died of cancer when their baby, Helen (b. June 21, 1925), was four months old; apparently estranged from her parents, she became Montgomery's housekeeper in 1927, but later remarried, to Tony Korbelas of Kitchener, with whom she had three more children (Georgina, John, and Paul). Helen Mason married Ed Schafer of Kitchener. MRS. MILLS. A Leaskdale farm woman to whom the boys' black Airedale terrier had been sent, after being found chasing sheep. Mrs. Mills had earlier taken in Barnardo children. **September 2** GUELPH. 41 km (25 mi) to the west of Norval, the Guelph General was the nearest hospital. CHLOROFORM ETHER. LMM confuses two anaesthetics in common use since the 1840s: ether (diethylether: $CH_3CH_2OCH_2CH_3$) developed as an anaesthetic in dentistry and chloroform ($CHCHl_3$) developed in veterinary medicine from the 1840s in the United States and Britain. In the 1920s chloroform was the preferred drug for operations about the mouth. W.M.S. Women's Missionary Society. Interest in foreign missions among church women began in the Maritimes as support for the Geddies, missionaries in the New Hebrides. In 1876, the male-dominated Foreign Mission Committee (FMC) of the Presbyterian church accepted the Women's Foreign

Mission Society (WFMF) as an auxiliary. Similarly the Women's Home Missionary Society (WHMC), concerned with service in western Canada, began in 1903. The two women's groups amalgamated in 1914 as the Women's Missionary Society and continued to operate as the WMS after Church Union. "HEART'S DESIRE". The home of Fannie and R.E. Mutch, in Brighton, PEI, now a suburb of Charlottetown. TO HEAP COALS OF FIRE. From the Bible, Proverbs 25:22 and Romans 12:20—to return good for evil. EWAN. The Rev. Ewan Macdonald, LMM's husband, now 59 years old, had moved from his first dual Ontario charges in rural Leaskdale and Zephyr to the larger charges of the Norval Presbyterian Church, located in the hamlet of Norval, and the Union Presbyterian Church, located just outside the nearby town of Glen Williams, both west of Toronto. SIMPSON'S. The Robert E. Simpson Company, one of the two major department stores in Toronto until 1978 when it was bought by the Hudson's Bay Company, was situated on Queen Street at Yonge opposite its rival, Eaton's. Simpson's elegant restaurant was the Arcadian Court. ROYAL YORK. Prestigious hotel in Toronto, opposite the Union railway station. "TALKIE". Silent moving pictures had been replaced in 1928 by versions with sound tracks. The slang term "the movies" remained in use from silent picture days. CAVE OF THE WINDS. The passage underneath the Falls. A "KICK". Slang term for sharp stimulus, in use in USA since 1903. MILTON. Village in PEI. "SOMETHING ATTEMPTED...". Henry Wadsworth Longfellow, "The Village Blacksmith": "Each morning sees some task begin, / Each evening sees it close; / something attempted, something done, / Has earned a night's repose." **September 11** THE WEATHER MAN. Since 1909, the Meteorological Service of Canada had had its headquarters in Toronto, in the Observatory at 315 Bloor Street at the northern edge of the University campus. Its main role was forecasting daily weather probabilities, based on observations received from all over the American continent and maps prepared in Toronto. Forecasts were distributed by telegraph and then by teletype. After the early 1920s some forecasts were transmitted by commercial radio stations and the forerunner of the CBC, but the major distribution until after World War II was by newspapers. Forecasts remitted by the trans-Canada chain covered the whole country except British Columbia. THE ISLAND. Prince Edward Island, the Canadian province where LMM was born and raised. **September 17** Between the entries of September 11, 1929, and September 17, 1929, an entry dated October 17, 1929, tells us that she is transferring "into this volume the notebook entries scribbled while I was away". THIS VERACIOUS JOURNAL. LMM habitually made rough notes day by day, later transcribing and editing them for formal entry into her permanent journals, kept in legal size ledger books. These ten handwritten volumes, with pictures pasted in them, are now in the Archives of the University of Guelph. She apparently destroyed her rough notes. Late in life, she typed a shortened version of her handwritten journals, and these are also in the Montgomery Collection in the library archives at Guelph. RAMESES I. Pharaoh of Egypt, 1324?–1258 B.C. A PICTURE. Elliptical reference in use since 1912 to moving pictures (cinematographic). ANGIE DOIRON. Descendant of the Acadian francophone settlers of Ile-Saint-Jean (Prince Edward Island). In LMM's youth they were relegated to a low social status. Attitudes toward bi-lingualism and bi-culturalism later changed; one of the Doiron descendants became Lieutenant-Governor of the Province in the 1990s. ABOVE-KNEE HORRORS. "Flapper" dresses, with hemlines at the knee, had been in vogue in Britain, Europe, and eastern United States since the early 1920s. Canadian women's magazines in 1929 were featuring the longer skirts that would dominate in the 1930s. ARTY CLARK. Artemas Clark, son of J.C. Clark and Margaret Anne Simpson, who was sister to Samuel Simpson, Edwin's father. REV. EDWIN SIMPSON. In 1897–98, LMM had been engaged to marry Simpson, and this remained a painful memory. QUARTET OF MINXES. Mary Campbell (Mrs. Archie Beaton), Nell McGrath (Mrs. Dingwall), Ida McEachern (Mrs. George Sutherland) and LMM had been friends at Prince of Wales College. WINSLOE. Mary Beaton's village, four miles north of Charlottetown. The Dominion Experimental Farm is on the road to Winsloe. AUNT CHRISTIE. Kinross, 20 miles east of Charlottetown, was in the home territory of LMM's husband Ewan. His father had brought the family from Scotland in 1841. Ewan's sister, Christie Macdonald McLeod, had lost her husband and was in straitened circumstances. Ewan's well-to-do brother, Dr. Angus Macdonald, lived in Warsaw, Indiana, where he ran a successful private medical facility. KIDIDOES. Slang: "silly tricks". **September 22** MONTAGUE. A scenic town in the eastern section of PEI, where Rev. John Stirling was the United Church minister. Stirling's acceptance of Church union had caused some coolness in LMM's long-time friendship with Margaret Ross Stirling. "ALL LIFE IS BONDAGE, SOULS ALONE ARE FREE". Edward Bulwer-Lytton (1803–73) was LMM's favourite author in girlhood years, and she knew much of his novel *Zanoni* by heart. DORIS. John and Margaret Ross Stirling's daughter; they had two children, Doris and Ian. John Stirling was descended from Lowland Scots who came from Ayr, and Margaret from the Ross clan of Inverness in the Highlands. Only Ian Stirling left descendants, John and Glenn Stirling of Rosedale and Willowdale (Toronto). ALBERT AND MAUD MIDDLETON. Mary Campbell Beaton's daughter and son-in-law. MYRTLE (Webb). Granddaughter by adoption of David Macneill and his sister, Myrtle and her husband Ernest Webb now lived in the house described as "Green Gables". **September 25** LIZZIE STUART LAIRD. A classmate in Cavendish school. **September 26** MAMMOTH CAVE. Natural marvel in Kentucky, a tourist mecca since 1809, visited by LMM and her family in 1924. LMM's interest in Kentucky was perhaps spurred by early reading of James Fox's best-selling *Trail of the Lonesome Pine* (1908) and Hal Standish's *Fred Fearnot in a Death Trap; Or, Lost in the Mammoth Caves* (1905). In 1912, she had quoted from Eliza Obenchain's *Aunt Jane of Kentucky* (1907). INSTITUTE. The Women's Institutes were rural organizations, founded by Adelaide Hoodless in 1897, with the motto "For Home and Country". The Provincial groups amalgamated in 1919, becoming the Federated Women's Institutes of Canada. Their membership has diminished in the face of urbanization. ISLAND HYMN. This commissioned hymn, with music by Lawrence Watson and words by LMM, had first been performed in 1908. NATE LOCKHART. A schoolmate, later educated in Law at Acadia University. CHESLEY CLARK. The Clarks had helped LMM through her final restricted days in Cavendish, 1900–1910. **September 28** UNCLE JOHN. Eldest brother of LMM's mother, Clara Macneill Montgomery; John Macneill had inherited the Macneill farm and added it to his own adjacent farm. The "olde home" where LMM was raised was torn down; in the 1980s, John Macneill (grandson of LMM's Uncle John Macneill) and his wife Jennie developed this site, restoring the foundations of the house, rebuilding the dug well, and establishing a garden full of the flowers that LMM loved next to the old orchard; this site is now open to visitors. *Mistress Pat* (1935) uses the motif of a beloved house destroyed. FRANK. Franklin Macneill (1882–1963), son of Uncle John and Aunt Ann Maria. CH'TOWN. Charlottetown, capital of the Province of Prince Edward Island. BLACK FOX. Fox farming became the most lucrative enterprise for many PEI farmers during the 1930s. Black fox deviated from the dominant red fox colour, and breeders developed a strain of black fox with white frosting known as "silver fox", producing the most stylish and expensive fur. The market for silver fox broke suddenly in the 1930s. PIERCE'S FIELD. Pierce Macneill was a Cavendish cousin of a generation older than LMM. NEW LONDON LIGHT. The lighthouse on the point north of French River, PEI, thought to be the model for Captain Jim's lighthouse in *Anne's House of Dreams*. **September 29** GARTMORE FARM. Childhood home of Pensie Macneill and her family, now owned by her brother Alec Macneill (1870–1951) and his wife May. CECIL SIMPSON. A distant cousin, son of Walter Simpson and Mary Ada Macneill; the Simpsons lived on the shore road west of Cavendish toward Bayview. TRYON. A port on the south shore of PEI, halfway between Charlottetown and Summerside. **October 2** PENSIE. Cousin and childhood friend, Pensie Macneill Bulman now lived in New Glasgow, a village on the road between Cavendish and Charlottetown, founded 1818. RUSTICO HARBOUR. Nearest harbour to the east of Cavendish. **October 3** THE ROAD WAS TOO SLIPPERY. The red-dirt roads of Prince Edward Island turn greasy when wet. **October 5** HAMMOND AND EMILY [Mackenzie]. Cousins through the Woolner connection of LMM's grandmother Lucy Woolner Macneill. **October 13** GEDDIE MEMORIAL. Named for pioneer missionaries, the Rev. John Geddie and his wife Charlotte, who served in the New London and Cavendish congregation in 1838 before going in 1845 to Aneiteum, an island of the New Hebrides located in the South Seas and since 1980 the Republic of Vanuatu. In the graveyard of the church, members of the Campbell family, including Frederica, LMM's cousin and dearest friend, were buried. AUNT EMILY [Macneill Montgomery]. Sister of LMM's mother Clara, and widow of LMM's father's cousin, John Montgomery. ELLA. Widow of LMM's first cousin George, Ella Johnstone Campbell was a second cousin on the Montgomery side. THE SPEAR AND THE SPINDLE SIDE. Colloquialism for family connections on the father's side and the mother's. PARK CORNER. Home of the Campbell cousins, children of George and Ella Campbell and grandchildren of LMM's Uncle John and Aunt Annie: Jim and Dan, Maud, Georgie, and Amy. In LMM's youth, Park Corner was home to her cousins George, Stella, Clara and Frederica. AUNT ELIZA [Johnson Montgomery], AUNT MARY [McLeod Montgomery]. Sisters-in-law of LMM's father, Hugh John Montgomery. The Montgomery homestead was now occupied by Heath Montgomery, LMM's cousin. "HOW STRANGE IT SEEMS...". From J.G. Whittier, "Snowbound", 181–2. KENSINGTON. Nearest railway station. HELEN LEARD. Sister of Herman, with whom LMM had been in love at the time she was teaching at Lower Bedeque, 1898. WIGS ON THE GREEN. Colloquial expression, originally Irish: coming to blows, wigs being pulled off in the fray. PUFF. Feather-filled comforter or duvet. MARY MILES MINTER Born in 1902, this silent screen favourite made 50 films between 1912–1923. Her career ended after the unsolved murder of her lover, W.D. Taylor, in 1922. MARY PICKFORD (1893–1979). Toronto-born movie star who became "America's Sweetheart" through a long series of silent films. PAGES. Louis and George Page, Boston publishers of LMM's first eight books, and antagonists since 1919 in a long series of legal battles. WILLIAM DESMOND TAYLOR (1877–1922). Irish-born actor and director. It was suspected, but not proved, that he was murdered by Mary Minter's mother. ROLLINS. Boston lawyer W.A. Rollins successfully pleaded LMM's cases against the Page Company, including her suit against their publication of her rejected version of *Further Chronicles of Avonlea* in 1920. (Rollins's current information was misleading: Page did not die until 1956.) MAY JACKALS SIT ON HER GRANDMOTHER'S GRAVE. A proverbial saying, still in use fifty years later by LMM's son Stuart (1915–1982). **October 22** GUARDIAN. A long-established Charlottetown newspaper. In 1894, the paper published LMM's prize essay on "Portia", read at the PWC graduation exercises. "CLOCHES". Stylish, tight-fitting bell-shaped hats. **November 5** RUSSELLS' HILL. From the writing table in her bedroom, LMM looked across the Norval main street toward the Russell hill farm. **December 1** PYORRHEA. Discharge of pus from the gums. DR. BAGNALL. Dr. John Stanley Bagnall, of 117 Fitzroy Street, had a dental office on Richmond Street, Charlottetown. His son, John Stephen Bagnall, also became a dentist. The Bagnall family once owned the entire Sidney/Richmond block. NORA. Nora Lefurgey Campbell (1880–1977), now living at 24 Wilburton Road in Toronto, and one of LMM's best friends, had boarded with the Macneills while teaching in Cavendish, 1903. The daughter of Thomas Lefurgey (of French Huguenot descent) and Janet McMurdo (of Scottish descent), Nora (one of five children) was born in Summerside, PEI, where her father was a school teacher. A spirited, adventuresome, and fiercely intelligent young woman, she had in 1907 written Civil Service examinations in Ottawa, and gone west in 1910 to marry Edmund Ernest Campbell (1880–1937) of Belmont, PEI. After graduating with an MSc from McGill in 1910, Edmund ("Ned") went into Mining Engineering. Early in their marriage, the Campbells moved extensively, including to South Dakota and Arizona; they eventually moved back to Toronto. (See note of June 16, 1930.) YOUTH'S COMPANION. This American magazine published "Fisher Lassies" by M.L. Cavendish (LMM's pseudonym), on 30 July, 1896. **December 21** "LIVING AMONG ALARUMS AND EXCURSIONS". Lytton Strachey, "Queen Victoria". GEORGE-TOWN. The nearest big town, 10 km (6 mi.) to the west of Norval, with medical and veterinary services, shopping, and the area High School. RADIAL. An electric railway line ran from Guelph, 25 miles to the west, to Toronto, 20 miles to the east, through 200 stops, 74 kilometres, and $2\frac{1}{2}$ hours of year-round travel. Begun in 1923, it had been taken over by the Canadian National Electric Railways. It ceased operation in 1931, partially a victim of the automobile. CREDIT. Norval is situated at the forks of the Credit River, as it flows from the height of land near Orangeville toward Lake Ontario. DR. ROYCE. Gilbert Royce, M.D., a distinguished ear-nose-and-throat specialist in Toronto. A VOLUME OF MY JOURNAL. In 1919, LMM had begun copying her earlier journals into legal-sized volumes, each covering roughly a year. **December 27** LEASKDALE The village 35 miles north-east of Toronto where the Macdonalds had lived from 1911 to 1926. "ICICLES". Christmas decorations: tinfoil in 12-inch lengths, to hang from branches of the Christmas tree. COLORED BALLS. Christmas ornaments made of blown glass. SPINNING WITH THE BIG WHEEL. Traditional women's work involved spinning with two different wheels. The great wheel, also called a walking wheel, was more than 3' in diameter, and was rotated by hand, in order to turn a spindle mounted horizontally on an upright post. Holding the raw wool on a distaff, the spinner walked away from the wheel, attenuating and twisting the wool or flax fibres into long strands, then walked back to wind the spun yarn onto the spindle, ready for knitting or weaving. A spinner walked 100 miles to spin enough wool for a day's weaving. The small wheel was turned by foot-pressure on a treadle, both hands of the spinner being left free to manipulate the yarn. EATON'S. Founded in 1869 by Timothy Eaton (1834–1907), the Timothy Eaton Company became an institution in Canada and one of the largest department stores in North America. After Eaton came to Canada about 1854, he lived with his sister Margaret (1824–1896) who was married to her first cousin, Robert Reid (1815–1896); Reid had emigrated from Ireland in the 1830s and obtained a large farm in Esquesing Township in the Halton-Peel Region. Timothy began work in Lyon's Store in Glen Williams, later moved to Kirkton, Ontario, to St. Marys, and then to Toronto, locating his store on Yonge Street. After he was established in Toronto, he purchased farmland in the Georgetown area, where some of his relatives lived. AMANDA [Robertson]. A Macneill cousin, and school friend. **December 30** OLD TYME CONCERT. Shortly after her arrival in Norval, LMM had organized and subsequently directed an annual theatrical entertainment involving members of all three churches in Norval (Anglican, United, and Presbyterian), and presented in the Anglican Parish Hall.

1930

January 2 CANADIAN ASSOCIATE CO. An insurance company based in Toronto. OCTOBER STOCK PANIC. During the post-war economic boom of the 1920s, sales in the stock exchanges had soared in Montréal and Toronto as in London, New York, and Chicago. Stocks and bonds were sold on margin in many cases. In October 1929 the boom ended when heavy selling led to panicky unloading of holdings, and the market "crashed" in November, heralding financial ruin for many investors. As capital dried up, many companies were unable to pay dividends. **January 5** GLEN HOUSE The home of Ernest Barraclough (1874–1938) and his wife, Ida Stirratt Barraclough (1874–1967), dear friends who lived in the nearby village of Glen Williams. Mr. Barraclough was an Englishman managing the Glen Williams woollen factories and was a major supporter of Union Presbyterian Church. Ida Stirratt was the first cousin of the grandfather of Luella Reid (b. 1911), Chester Macdonald's first wife. UNION. The second church in Ewan's charge, established in 1834, and from its first years affiliated with Norval church and sharing a minister's services. **January 18** MRS. ARTHUR MCCLURE. Wife of an elder in the Norval church living on a farm near Mount Pleasant, mother of Harold, Clarence, and Edna McClure. BLUE. Slang phrase, current since the 16th century, but in vogue from the 1870s: as in the song by F.L. Stanton, "Just a-wearyin' for you — / All the time a-feelin' blue". **January 23** GRAPHIC PUBLISHING CO. Established in 1925 by Henry C. Miller, an Ottawa printer committed to publishing Canadian authors. Frederick Philip Grove, whose work had impressed LMM, served as editor 1929–1931. Raymond Knister and Madge Macbeth were among noted Graphic authors. Graphic went out of business in 1932, largely because of Depression conditions. **January 27** BLAND'S IRON AND ARSENIC PILLS. Probably Blaud's pills, not Bland's pills, were a common source of iron to treat anemia; the iron carbonate was sometimes combined with arsenic or strychnine, both of which were used in small quantities for their bitter or tonic or appetite-stimulating qualities. **January 28** BIG OLD MILL. Flour and saw mills, erected at the fork of the Credit River, formed the nucleus of Norval, established by James McNab, the first mill proprietor, in the 1820s. After years of successful business by its later proprietors, the Noble family, the operation declined, and was taken over by the Bank of Nova Scotia in 1923, management being turned over to Gord Browne. During the disastrous fire of 1930 recorded here, 100,000 bushels of grain were lost, and the mills extensively damaged, devastating the village's whole economy. KOBOLD. In German folklore a brownie inhabiting a mine or haunting a house and helping inmates. **February 11** QUEEN OF SCOTS COSTUME. Queen Mary (1542–87) was usually depicted in black with white standing ruff at the neckline. **February 15** A. GIFFEN. Andrew Giffen had become an elder of the Norval Presbyterian church in 1926. ALBERT HUNTER. Appointed Superintendent of the Norval Presbyterian Sunday School in 1927, and elected elder that same year, Mr. Hunter eventually served on the church Session for over 50 years, and beginning in 1939, was clerk of the session for 32 years. The Hunter house was on the main street of Norval, near the bank and the hardware store. WIGGINS. John Wiggins, who had become an elder of the Norval Presbyterian church at the same time as Andrew Giffen (1926), was now Treasurer. "BILLY". The Willys-Knight car, purchased in 1927. MRS. BOYD. Wife of the Rev. R.W.S. Boyd, who had come to Norval the same year as the Macdonalds. Mrs. Boyd had a reputation for free thinking and acting: she sat on her porch reading novels and smoking while others went to church. BILLY GRAY. A young Englishman, a carrier who lived across from the manse. **March 1** ISOBEL. An elementary school teacher in her 30s, remembered locally as a poet and a witty elocutionist, she was first mentioned in the journal entry for July 17, 1926. ROCKWOOD PARK. In Rockwood village, west of Georgetown, quarries and caves constituted a favourite regional picnic place. SINBAD. Hero of *The Thousand and One Arabian Nights*; in one of his adventures he is tricked into carrying the Old Man of the Sea on his shoulders. "SEX PERVERTS". The term "perversion" appeared in American dictionaries of the 1930s as applied to "sexual practices departing from what was considered normal"; contemporary English dictionaries offered only the meaning of "turning away from accepted religious beliefs", and "pervert" was there defined as "apostate". MALODOROUS WORKS OF FICTION. Novels about Lesbianism before 1930 included [Margaret] Radclyffe Hall's *The Well of Loneliness* (1928) and Compton Mackenzie's *Extraordinary Women: Theme and Variations* (London: Secker, 1928). Morley Callaghan's *No Man's Meat* came out in a limited edition from the

Paris publisher "black mannekin" in 1931. SCRAPBOOKS OF REVIEWS. The large scrapbook of LMM's review-clippings (from a clipping service) is held at the University of Guelph in Ontario. The reviews start in 1910. At this point in her journals, LMM copies 20 or so phrases from reviews of each of her works to date. ALICE HEGAN RICE, KATE DOUGLAS WIGGIN... This list includes most popular children's books of the late Victorian period and early twentieth century: ALICE CALDWELL (HEGAN) RICE's *Mrs. Wiggs of the Cabbage Patch* (1901); WIGGIN's *Rebecca of Sunnybrook Farm* (1903); FRANCES HODGSON BURNETT's *The Secret Garden* (1911); Louisa May ALCOTT's *Little Women* (1867–8); George MARTIN's *Emmy Lou* (1902); John HABBERTON's *Helen's Babies* (1876); J.M. BARRIE's *Peter Pan* (1904); "GYP" (Sybille de Mantel de Janville's) *All About Marriage* (1884); LEWIS CARROLL's *Alice in Wonderland* (1865); Kenneth GRAHAME's *The Wind in the Willows* (1908); Annie JOHNSTONE's *The Little Colonel* (1896). LMM capitalizes the names of writers she considered most important. Others in the list of writers to whom critics compared LMM include older but still popular authors of gentle books for adults: Jane AUSTEN's *Pride and Prejudice* (1813), Mary MITFORD's *Our Village* (1830), Elizabeth WETHERELL's *The Wide, Wide World* (1851), Elizabeth GASKELL's *Cranford* (1853), Margaret DELAND's *John Ward, Preacher* (1887), MARY S. WILKINS' [Mary E. Wilkins Freeman]'s *Pembroke* (1894), Sara Orne JEWETT's *The Country of the Pointed Firs* (1896), and Edward WESTCOTT's *David Harum* (1898); and contemporary authors of sentimental romances such as ZONA GALE's *Romance Island* (1906), MYRTLE REID's *Lavender and Old Lace* (1902), ALICE BROWN's *Country Road* (1906). **March 6** THE "WILLIES". American slang (not in British dictionaries): a state of nervousness or jitters. **March 17** "THERE IS NO UNION...". From James Montgomery, "Friends", stanza 1. FLUPNEUMONIA. Influenza with side effects attacking the lungs. THE BOOK. *A Tangled Web*, eventually titled *Aunt Becky Began It* in Great Britain. WOOLNER JUG. LMM's grandmother Macneill was a Woolner; the jug had come with her family from Dunwich in England in the 1830s. **April 9** UNITED CHURCH IN WOODBRIDGE. LMM's Young People's theatre group had performed each year in Woodbridge, a village 15 miles north-east of Norval. MARION CRAWFORD'S GHOST STORIES. Crawford (1854–1909) produced a series of best sellers in the 1890–1910 period. *Uncanny Tales* appeared posthumously, 1911. SIR JAMES JEANS' *The Universe Around Us* [Cambridge University Press, 1929]. Jeans (1877–1946), a prominent British scientist, summarized and popularized cosmology. Astronomy had been LMM's hobby since her girlhood days. **April 26** MRS. HORACE QUIGLEY. This parishioner is not named in the journals covering the years at Leaskdale. GEO. LEASK. Lived in the old Leask homestead, in view of the Leaskdale manse. He and his wife were great friends and supporters of the Macdonalds during Ewan's ministry in Leaskdale. MR. MCINNIS. Rev. P.W. McInnes was Ewan's successor in 1926 as Presbyterian minister. He died in 1949. In the Presbyterian Church pension book his name is spelled MacInnes. JAS. MUSTARD. The Mustards, pioneer families in Scott Township since 1831, may have been instrumental in bringing the Rev. Ewan Macdonald from PEI to the parish which had a strong concentration of Scots-Presbyterians. The Mustard farms lay south of the village of Leaskdale. James was the son of Alexander Mustard, from Cromarty, Scotland,

and Marion Smith Mustard, from Carluke, Scotland, and the brother of Hugh Mustard, Isabella Mustard, and the Rev. John Mustard from LMM's Prince Albert year. James is the grandfather of Dr. Fraser Mustard. KATE MACNEILL. LMM's first cousin, daughter of Uncle John Macneill. **April 30** REV. JOHN MUSTARD [1867–1950]. LMM's teacher and suitor at Prince Albert, now minister of Oakwood Presbyterian Church in Toronto, had a distinguished ministerial career, becoming Moderator of the Toronto Presbytery and of the Toronto and Kingston Synod of the Presbyterian Church. After his graduation from the U. of Toronto in 1889, he had taught in Prince Albert; in 1908, he graduated from Knox College, then spent time in pastorates in Colorado, New Mexico, and Iowa, returning to Canada in 1906. From 1909 to 1928, he was minister of The Dufferin Street Presbyterian Church, and pastor of Oakwood Church until his retirement in 1937. From 1943 until shortly before his death, he was the Presbyterian chaplain for the Toronto Hospitals. In 1946, Knox College conferred on him the honorary doctorate of divinity. Married to Catherine MacFarlane, he left one son, Gordon A. Mustard, who became a mining engineer in Northern Ontario. JUDGE JEFFREYS. In 1685, Judge G.J. Jeffreys tried and mercilessly condemned supporters of the Monmouth rebellion against James II. Kneller's portrait in the National Gallery of London, according to the *Encyclopedia Britannica*, 11th edition, "shows a refinement of features and expression". MACAULAY. Lord Macaulay's biased and hostile treatment of Jeffreys in his *History of England* (1849) was based on untrustworthy sources. LMM had been taught to regard Macaulay as a model of style but here and elsewhere she misspells his name "MacCaulay". [Lion] FEUCHTWANGER'S *Ugly Duchess* (London: Secker, 1927). Part of a revival of serious historical fiction leading to best-sellers *Anthony Adverse* (1931) and *Gone with the Wind* (1936), though without the standard cast of strong men and beautiful women. **May 24** QUEEN VICTORIA. May 24th had been celebrated as "The Queen's Birthday" in Ontario since 1845. Renamed "Empire Day" in the 1890s, it was again retitled "Commonwealth Day" in 1934, but now again appears on Canadian calendars as "Victoria Day". EMIL LUDWIG'S *Son of Man* (New York, 1928). A new rationalist version of the story of Jesus. In 1928 LMM had recorded re-reading Ernest Renan's *Life of Jesus* (1863); she also admired David Friedrich Strauss's *The Life of Jesus Critically Examined* (translated by George Eliot, 1846). POINT LACE. Made with a needle, following patterns set out on sheets of parchment mounted on linen. "Battenburg" lace, commonly used as inserts in solid fabrics, was named in honour of Queen Victoria's youngest daughter who married the Count of Battenberg. A "bertha" is a deep-falling collar; a "bolero" is a buttonless, short-cropped jacket, usually without sleeves. Examples of LMM's needle-work are in the University of Guelph archives. **May 28** BERTIE. Alberta McIntyre, LMM's first cousin on the Montgomery side. **June 9** THE PRESBYTERIAN. Founded 1848: one of several Church publications, including *The Canada Presbyterian*, *The Presbyterian Review*, and *The Westminster*. The *Presbyterian Record* was the official organ. JOHN A. PATERSON, K.C. His entire article is pasted in Montgomery's journal. "DO GOOD BY STEALTH AND BLUSH TO FIND IT FAME". Alexander Pope, *Epilogue to the Satires*, Dialogue 1, Line 136. FORBES. Leaskdale and Zephyr sent $1200 in four instalments to support Forbes in his mission. Of this, the Macdonalds donated $400. Forbes, born in 1886, served in China from 1914–1940, except for the years he was on active service during World War I. He retired in 1954. HONAN. Presbyterian mission work in North Honan, China, had begun in 1888 but had been dramatically interrupted during the Boxer Revolution of 1900. During Forbes's time, there was a large contingent of missionaries, including 20 women missionaries. **June 16** DR. PAUL. Dr. Reginald Paul was the medical man in nearby Georgetown; at this time no doctor had replaced old Dr. Webster in Norval. An injection for asthma probably consisted of epinephrin or adrenalin. KATE MACPHERSON. A nurse, working in Toronto at this time. The MacPherson family, living next door to the Presbyterian church, consisted of Charlotte, Katherine, Florence, Margaret, Andy, and Bob. Margaret MacPherson had been the church organist from 1875 to 1915. STRYCHNINE TABLETS. A poisonous vegetable alkaloid, used in medicine as stimulant and tonic. MRS. BUCHANAN. Dr. Mary Mackay Buchanan (1864–1935) originally from Pictou, N.S., served in India in 1888–9, married a fellow missionary and raised a family there, and after her return from India continued her ministry as a speaker. EDMUND [ERNEST] CAMPBELL. Nora Lefurgey's husband "Ned" (1880–1937) was a distinguished mining engineer, at this time in business as a Toronto consultant, where he held Directorships in numerous international corporations. From Belmont, PEI, "Ned" was the eldest son of Eva Compton (Campbell) and Daniel Campbell whose United Empire Loyalist ancestors had fled from North Carolina in 1775, settling first in Nova Scotia and then obtaining a large grant of French land in Belmont, PEI. When LMM had taught at Belmont, Edmund, who, like his wife Nora, was six years younger than Montgomery, had been a pupil in her school. (See note of Dec. 1, 1929.) THE GRASSHOPPER [shall be] A BURDEN. Ecclesiastes 12:5. **June 22** MR. AGNEW, BARRISTER. In English law, a lawyer entitled to plead in court (as distinct from "solicitor"); the American equivalent is "counselor". REX VS. BEATON. Legal formula for referring to a Canadian court case brought by the crown (the government) against a defendant. SUTHERLAND BEATON. Son of LMM's friend and cousin, Mary Campbell Beaton of Winsloe, PEI CABINET TEA COMPANY. This company is not listed in the Toronto Business Directories for 1930–35. STREETSVILLE. A town 7 miles south of Norval. THE PEN. The penitentiary. The slang term is recorded from 1884, and was in common usage by 1900. **June 25** *THE STAR*. This Toronto evening paper, established in 1892, was directed by its publisher, J.E. Atkinson, toward emphasis on local issues and human interest stories, such as the "Beaton Case". By 1930, with a circulation of 178,012, it had become the dominant paper in the Toronto area. **June 29** MR. GRIER. The Rev. James C. Grier was Minister at Campbellford. His pension ended in 1946. **July 4** HAYHOE TEA CO. This company, situated at 7 Front Street, is first listed in the Toronto Business Directory of 1921. **July 5** REN [Lorenzo] TOOMBS. Married to LMM's cousin Minnie Macneill, sister of Pensie and Albert. **July 14** CUTH. Cuthbert McIntyre, a first cousin, brother of Bertie McIntyre and Laura Aylsworth. **July 18** MURRAY LAIRD (July 24, 1904 – Dec. 28, 1987). James Wilfrid Murray Laird was a member of a pioneer Norval family; Murray's grandfather had played a leading role in building the Norval Presbyterian Church. The Laird family farm and homestead was at the top of the hill east of Norval village.

MRS. LESLIE. The Stirratt Leslie family were important parishioners in Union. Both Stirratts and Leslies were among the pioneers who settled the township in 1815. **July 26** LAURA. Laura McIntyre Aylsworth, LMM's first cousin on the Montgomery side, had visited Leaskdale and Norval since moving to Ontario. BERTIE. Laura's unmarried sister, Alberta McIntyre. THE PRICK OF THE FAIRY'S SPINDLE. In the folk tale, "The Sleeping Beauty", the princess pricks her finger and falls into an enchanted sleep. **July 28** THE LIBERAL GOV'T. In 1930 the Conservatives, led by R.B. Bennett, defeated the Liberals, led by Prime Minister W.L. Mackenzie King. **July 29** MUSKOKA. Cottage country north of Toronto. In 1922 the Macdonalds had spent a family holiday at Bala in the Muskoka area. **July 31** HYPODERMIC. An injection against asthma and hay fever, probably adrenalin (UK) or epinephrin (USA). "BUSTER" BLACK. Mrs. Black had a candy store on the main street of Norval. BIGNALL GIRLS. The Bignalls lived on Adamson Street across from the Anglican church. **August 7** ERN MACNEILL. LMM's first cousin, Ernest (1884–1965) was the younger son of Uncle John and Aunt Ann Maria Macneill. His wife had been ill since the birth of her first child. **August 11** PORT PERRY. Village on Lake Scugog, 10 miles east of Uxbridge. THE R-100. A dirigible, on a tour of Canada in the summer of 1930. **August 23** MIDLAND. A city on Georgian Bay, 85 miles north of Toronto. PRINCE ALBERT. LMM had lived in this Saskatchewan town with her father and stepmother in 1890–91. **August 30** JOURNEY'S END. A movie based on the long-running tragic play by J.M. Priestley, set in an underground bunker in the trenches during World War I. MARIE CORELLI'S *Sorrows of Satan.* Corelli (1855?–1924) became a best-selling novelist in the 1880s with *A Romance of Two Worlds* (1886) and *Thelma* (1887). *The Sorrows of Satan* (1895) presents Lucifer as tragic hero, and the narrator as being in love with him. **September 2** MY NEW BOOK. *A Tangled Web.* Except for a reference on March 17th, the journal contains no allusions to the work of writing this novel, all through a summer of depression and illness: her silence differs from earlier notes on the progress of her manuscripts. BESS (COOK) WALKER. Daughter of Mrs. Albert Cook, one of the women who helped LMM dismantle the Leaskdale manse. LAURA. Laura Pritchard Agnew, sister of Will Pritchard, had been LMM's best friend in Prince Albert. **September 11** PREDESTINATION. The belief that all events are fated, having been pre-ordained by God. **September 30** KNOX COLLEGE. Presbyterian residential college, affiliated with the University of Toronto, established 1844. In 1915 the new building on St. George Street opened. GRANDFATHER MONTGOMERY The Hon. Donald Montgomery was a Senator in the Dominion Government when he travelled with LMM to visit his son Hugh John Montgomery at Prince Albert. SIR JOHN AND LADY MACDONALD. LMM as a girl of fifteen was presented to the Prime Minister and his wife by her grandfather at the outset of their trip to the west. C.P.R., C.N.R. Canadian Pacific Railway and Canadian National Railways, rival transcontinental Canadian lines. JOHN O'LONDONS. Copies of a popular English literary magazine. MR. [George Boyd] MACMILLAN. LMM's long-time pen friend was the recipient of the letters published in *My Dear Mr. M.*, edited by Francis Bolger and Elizabeth Epperly. CROSS WORD PUZZLES. The term was coined in 1924. By 1930 doing crosswords had become a popular pastime. The Toronto *Star* was among many papers featuring a daily crossword puzzle in the 1930s. LMM and her son Stuart were both addicted to them. A VERSE OF POE'S The lines are from Edgar Allan Poe's "To One in Paradise" (1834). LMM misquotes slightly: the first lines should run: "And all my days are trances / And all my nightly dreams/ Are where thy gray eye glances,/ And where thy footstep gleams —". **October 1** HARRY MCINTYRE. LMM's first cousin, son of Aunt Mary Montgomery McIntyre, brother of Bertie, Laura, and Cuthbert. SASKATOON. Not on the map when LMM went west for the first time. Incorporated in 1906 by the merging of three villages, Saskatoon by 1930 had become a major city in Saskatchewan. **October 2** WATROUS. Saskatchewan railroad town where the time zone changes from Eastern Time to Central Time. "THERE IS A PLEASURE...". From John Dryden, *The Spanish Friar*, I, 1. KOH-I-NOOR. A superb Indian diamond belonging to the British Crown since 1849. EMERSON. Ralph Waldo Emerson's essays were among LMM's lifelong favourites. The correct quotation from "Friendship" is: "A friend is a person with whom I may be sincere. Before him, I may think aloud". ANNIE MCTAGGART A half-sister of Mary Ann McRae Montgomery, LMM's step-mother. The McTaggart house was next door to the Montgomerys' in Prince Albert, where Mr. McTaggart was Dominion Land Agent. **October 3** "SCREAM". American slang for a hilariously entertaining person. THE BREEDS. Several of LMM's school-mates in Prince Albert were of mixed blood, French-Indian or Scottish-Indian, scorned as "half-breeds" in 1889, when LMM went to school in Prince Albert. The Métis leader Louis Riel had made his headquarters 35 miles from Prince Albert, at Batoche, during the North West Rebellion of 1885. "THE SECOND COMING". Like Seventh Day Adventists, Laura held the belief that Christ's return to earth is imminent. WOMEN'S CANADIAN CLUB. A national organization founded in 1907 to introduce speakers on intellectual and social topics to audiences in Canadian towns and cities. "SPOONERISMS". Named for an Englishman, the Rev. W.A. Spooner (1844–1930), noted for transposing initial letters of two words, as in "a blushing crow". "I MUST WORK IT IN SOME BOOK...". This appears in *A Tangled Web*, apparently worked in during revision. **October 6** LONG DRESSES. Hem-lengths, lowered from knee-length to mid-calf during the first Depression years, were lowered again for evening dress to floor-length. AIR MAIL. In Canada, postal service by air began in 1927 with experiments in Québec, Montréal, and Ottawa. In 1929, bush pilots were flying mail north from western centres such as Saskatoon. Trans-Canada air service was not established until 1937. "GREAT LONE LAND". Title of a book about the northwest by W.F. Butler, published in London in 1872. RED DEER. Frede Campbell taught Household Science at Red Deer College from December 1912 to September 1913. EDITH SKELTON. Edith had acted as household help for LMM's stepmother. The two girls shared a room when LMM first arrived in Prince Albert. **October 10** THE OLD PRINCE ALBERT. Founded in 1866 as a Presbyterian mission, its brief boom had ended when the Canadian Pacific Railway chose to by-pass it for a more southerly route. The La Colle Falls plant, opened in 1904, promised a revival of prosperity, and the town was incorporated that year; but when LMM revisited Prince Albert, it was suffering from the Depression that hit most western towns with terrible force. ALEXENA AND FRED [Wright]. Alexena MacGregor was a school and Sunday School friend in

Prince Albert. A CHAIN DRUG STORE. Liggett's drug store occupied part of the Macdonald Block, built about 1912. THE OLD MCTAGGART HOUSE. The home of John McTaggart, stepfather of LMM's stepmother Mary Ann McRae Montgomery. The Montgomerys moved into this house in 1898 when Hugh Montgomery became warden of the jail. MRS. M. Mary Ann McRae Montgomery, 27 years old at the time her stepdaughter LMM lived with her. MADE WHOOPEE. Slang: having a gay noisy time. DUG OUTS. Canoes, hollowed out of tree trunks. INDIANS AND SQUAWS. Members of the Sioux tribe, indigenous to this area of Saskatchewan. ALEXENA'S HOME. A family home, still standing in Prince Albert. The house was demolished in 1994. EMPRESS HOTEL. Built about 1912, and considered one of the two "better" hotels in Prince Albert, the Empress was destroyed by fire in 1967. MRS. GEORGE WILL. George Will came to Prince Albert as a member of the Mounted Police. He later became wealthy in real estate, built a mansion in 1914 and owned one of the first automobiles in Prince Albert. NEW PROVINCIAL SANATORIUM. A treatment centre for tuberculosis, opened early in 1930, one of the "show places" at the time of LMM's visit. After the Sanatorium closed in 1959, the building housed a branch of the Saskatchewan Training Schools for the handicapped. The main building is now demolished but the power house is still used as a summer theatre. MISS MONTGOMERY. Perhaps she was the superintendent of nurses: the medical superintendent was Dr. Kirby. **October 11** LUCY BAKER. In 1879 Lucy Margaret Baker went to Prince Albert as a teacher working in the Presbyterian Mission School. When it closed she worked with a band of Sioux Indians north of the town and helped them get a reserve (which still exists). In memory of her, the Lucy Baker Home for girls was established by the Presbyterian church. THE NEW "CHURCH". The church being built while LMM was a school girl was demolished in 1968. It had been replaced by St. Paul's Presbyterian Church, built in 1906 and now used as an auditorium. **October 12** MAIDEN LAKE. At one time a popular picnic spot 3 or 4 miles south of the city limits, Maiden Lake dried up later in the 1930s. JOSEPHIAN. "Of the tribe of Joseph": a pet saying of Frede Campbell's, derived from Genesis 42:8 and Exodus 1:8, which refers to a new king of Egypt, who "knew not Joseph". LAUREL HILL FARM.. The Pritchard farm was 9 miles north of Prince Albert. "Ochil" is a Scottish family name, sometimes spelled "Okill". "THE SKIRTS OF THAT FORGOTTEN LIFE...". From "A Mystery" by John Greenleaf Whittier, st. 8. "HEART-THROBS, NOT IN FIGURES...". Lines from P.J. Bailey, "In a country town" (1855): "We live... / In feelings, not in figures on a dial. We should count time by heart-throbs". ROYAL HOTEL. Once a multi-purpose building, housing the Town Hall, the high school, the Mounted Police, the Board of Trade office, and a Town Council meeting room, the Royal Hotel was demolished in 1946. **October 13** THE PENITENTIARY. Established in 1911, the Federal prison at Prince Albert was in 1930 the newest in a chain of 8 fortresslike prisons across Canada. It now has an inmate population of 500–600 but is no longer rated as a maximum security prison. The Warden's house was set back behind trees. **October 15** BATTLEFORD. This town, 130 km northwest of Saskatoon, incorporated 1910, had been the capital of the North West Territories 1876–1882, in the period when LMM's father began his western career there as a settlement agent. Its importance diminished after the projected railway line of the CPR went to southern Saskatchewan, and the capital to Regina. WEBERS. Ephraim Weber (1870–1956) had been a long time correspondent, recipient of the letters published as *The Green Gables Letters,* ed. Wilfred Eggleston. He published two valuable articles on LMM in *Dalhousie Review* (1942 and 1944). IRV HOWATT. A friend from Park Corner and Prince of Wales College days. LMM had loaned money to him in the 1920s. KATE AND ILA. LMM's half-sisters, Kate Montgomery McKay and Ila Montgomery MacKenzie, daughters of LMM's stepmother, Mary Ann McRae Montgomery. "FAREWELL". The poem was published in *The Saskatchewan,* 2 September 1891. **November 2** "ALL FAREWELLS...". From Lord Byron's *Sardanapalus,* Act V. NORTH BATTLE-FORD. A newer community, created after the Canadian Northern Railway bypassed Battleford, lessening its importance. EDMONTON. LMM's most westerly stop, still a small city in 1930, would achieve major growth in World War II and become a metropolis, "gateway to the North". DAISY [Williams McLeod]. One of the "sewing circle" when LMM taught in Bideford, 1894–95. JIM MCIN-TYRE. A first cousin, son of Aunt Mary Montgomery McIntyre. BERTIE HAYES [Arnett]. One of LMM's pupils when she taught in Bideford school. UNCLE DUN-CAN [McIntyre]. The estranged widower of LMM's Aunt Mary of Charlottetown, sister of Hugh John Montgomery. WINNIPEG. Capital of the Province of Manitoba, incorporated 1873; a centre of prairie trade and transportation, although at the time of LMM's visit the city was suffering severe effects of the Great Depression. PRESS CLUB. Established in 1888 as the oldest Press Club in Canada, the Winnipeg Press Club met separately from the Women's Press Club once a month, generally in a private dining room in Eaton's department store. In the 1930s, the Women's Press Club had 25–35 members, half of them working for the *Tribune* or the *Free Press,* the other half being free-lancers. The Women's Press Club joined the Winnipeg Press Club in 1964. CARL [Montgomery]. LMM's half-brother. THE "PIT". The impressive Grain Exchange Building, constructed in 1908 at the corner of Lombard Avenue and Rorie Street, with major additions in 1922 and 1928, housed an open cash market for buying and selling prairie wheat. The "Pit" was the sixth floor room where prices of grain were established by competitive bidding—a hectic place in 1930 because of the crash in wheat prices since 1929. KILDONAN. Site of the Selkirk settlement, in 1930 a small city about 5 km northeast of downtown Winnipeg. Kildonan has since been amalgamated into Winnipeg. St. John's Anglican church in Kildonan was the Cathedral Church of Rupert's Land. LMM might also have visited St. Andrew's Presbyterian Church in Kildonan, one of the oldest small churches still in existence in Manitoba. MRS. FITZGERALD. Adele Constance (Mrs. Desmond) Fitzgerald (1883–1967), second cousin of Will and Laura Pritchard, and daughter of Archbishop Matheson. She lived on O'Meara Street near St. John's Cathedral. ARCHBISHOP MATHESON The Rt. Rev. Samuel Pritchard Matheson, D.D., D.C.L., Anglican Archbishop of Rupert's Land in 1930, later became Primate of All Canada, Chancellor of the University of Manitoba and Chancellor of St. John's College. POINTE DU BOIS. In 1926 Winnipeg City had reached maximum output of hydroelectric power from Pointe du Bois and secured the rights for Slave Falls. The new plant being built there would augment the hydro power supplied to Winnipeg. LAC DU BONNET.

Augmenting the train connection, regular commercial air flights between Winnipeg and Lac du Bonnet had started in 1926. ROYAL ALEXANDRA. A hotel (now demolished) constructed in 1906 at the corner of Higgins and Main streets. FORT GARRY. The Hudson's Bay Company fort, constructed in 1822, and situated in Selkirk, about 8 km northeast of downtown Winnipeg. The old fort was being restored in the 1930s. In 1951 the Hudson Bay Company gave it to the government of Canada. DOING THE STORES. Eaton's department store had been at the corner of Portage Avenue and Donald Street since 1905, and the Hudson Bay Company had opened their store at Portage and Memorial in 1926. **November 4**. JUDGE EMILY MURPHY (1868–1933). Prominent defender of women's rights, and one of the plaintiffs battling for legal standing as "persons" who convinced the British Privy Council of injustices to women. Judge Murphy had published a children's book with LMM's old publisher Page (*Our Little Canadian Cousin of the Great Northwest*, 1923); she had also published a novel, and four travel books "by Janey Canuck". JEAN LESLIE. Daughter of the Leslie family in Union; through Mrs. Mason, she met and married Mrs. Mason's brother, Wilbert Checkley. SHAW'S *Back to Methuselah*. In this 1921 play, George Bernard Shaw examines the causes of civilization's failure, as demonstrated by World War I. **November 7** MARSHALL PICKERING. A Zephyr man, member of a pioneer family in Scott Township, involved in a motor car accident with the Macdonalds, leading to traumatic litigation. See *SJLMM* III. **November 9** MR. REID. Robert F. Reid had acted as Sunday School Superintendent before 1927; he was elected elder in 1927, together with Albert Hunter. Mr. Reid was a descendant of Esquesing pioneer Robert Reid, and the family had had extensive holdings in the area since the 1840s. MARGARET RUSSELL Daughter of the family on the hill farm visible from LMM's window, Margaret (d. 1996 in her 94th year) was the church soloist. MRS. GEORGE DAVIS. Annie Kay Davis is remembered for her work in the Women's Institute as well as in the Presbyterian Church, where she fought to get gowns for the choir. ELSIE McCLURE. Daughter of the Elder, Sam McClure. LUELLA REID. Born in 1911, aged 18 at this time, Luella Agnes Reid was the daughter of Robert Reid and Ella May Hyatt. Luella had left high school and was helping on her father's farm, west of Norval. See note for EATON on Dec. 27, 1929: Luella Reid's father, Robert Reid, was a direct descendant of the first Robert Reid (1815–1896) who had married Timothy Eaton's sister Margaret, his first cousin. Luella's mother was of German descent, but the Reids, the Eatons, the McClures, the Craigs, and the McGills—all settlers in this area—were from Country Antrim in Ireland. The Reids were devout Presbyterians and helped establish the Presbyterian Churches of Union and Norval. The extended Reid family farmed in the Georgetown area until Heslop Developments purchased farms in 1955 to develop the Georgetown area. They orginally held most of the land that is now in the eastern part of Georgetown. **November 10** "WEE SMA'S". Scotticism: the hours before dawn. **November 18** SHAW'S *Joan of Arc*. *Saint Joan*, George Bernard Shaw's controversial dramatization of Joan and her voices (1924). LMM had seen a production in 1924. EINSTEIN. Albert Einstein (1879–1955), who developed theories of relativity, of the equivalences of mass and energy, and the photon theory of light, had begun work on relativity in 1905. He received the Nobel Prize for

Physics in 1929 and in 1931 was a visiting professor at Oxford, quoted in news-papers world-wide. **November 19** "OH, FOR A LODGE...". From William Cowper, *The Task*, Book II, 1; the poem continues "Where rumour of oppression and deceit / Might never reach me more". **November 27** MR. GREENWOOD. L.F. Greenwood, a veteran who had lost an arm during the war, was manager of the Norval branch of the Bank of Nova Scotia, located at the crossroads near the mills. GARFIELD MCCLURE. Member of a large Norval Presbyterian family, includ-ing Joe, Arthur, Sam, and Clarence. Unlike his more dignified brothers, Garfield had not been chosen to be an elder. NONE SO DEAF AS THOSE WHO WON'T HEAR. Matthew Henry, *Commentaries*, Psalm LVIII: originally "those that will not hear". ALF SIMPSON. Brother of Rev. Edwin Simpson; a friend from Belmont days. **December 2** [W.F.] GREIG, LITTLEJOHN. Lawyers in Uxbridge who had represent-ed Marshall Pickering in the 1922 lawsuit over the car accident. Willard F. Greig (1890?–1964), Q.C., from Uxbridge, practised law from 1915 and was town solicitor of Uxbridge from 1919 until his death. Willard Greig's sister, Florie Greig, married Bert Gould; Florie and Bert were the parents of Glenn Gould. **December 3** CRONAN. Gerald F. Cronan, President of the Insurance Investments Ltd. of Toronto, was arrested Dec. 2 for conspiracy. He had asked clients who purchased insurance to exchange their holdings for stock of National Liberty Insurance Company. Instead of purchasing the stocks, however, he had put funds into a general banking fund to keep the company afloat. He had previously worked for the Ontario Equitable Insurance Company; in 1926 he became acting Secretary-Treasurer, and in 1930 President and Secretary-Treasurer of Insurance Investments Limited, 1910 Bloor West. LMM had been interested in insurance companies since the days of her friendship with Edwin Smith. **December 6** MARION WEBB. Marion (b. 1907) was the daughter of Myrtle and Ernest Webb, the family living in the "Green Gables" house in Cavendish; LMM and Myrtle Webb were both descended from "Speaker" Macneill. A DRIVER. An ambitious person, often an employer, who pushes ("drives") others to work hard. **December 14** THEODOLITE. Surveying instrument for measuring horizontal and vertical angles. **December 20** LILY [Leila Macneill] BERNARD. Sister of Minnie Toombs, and of Pensie, Albert, Bob, Alex, and Russell Macneill. **December 28** "CHRISTMAS WAS LAST WEDNESDAY". The 25th was on Thursday. **December 30** BROMIDE. Potassi-um bromide or elixir of triple bromide was formerly used for daytime sedation of psychotics, to lower demonstrative symptoms, especially sexual drives. A com-pound of bromine, which is a poisonous substance, bromide is no longer pre-scribed, because of its toxic qualities and its creation of chronic spots on the skin.

1931

January 7 ILIAD—POPE'S TRANSLATION. Homer's epic poem concerns the war between the Greeks and Trojans. In 1715–20 Alexander Pope published a charm-ing though inaccurate translation, rendered in heroic couplets. **January 9** PRAYER SERVICES. Personal testimony about experiences of sin and salvation was part of an evangelical revival of the 1930s, perhaps stirred by economic depression. MISSION BAND. Organization designed to involve children in concern for foreign and home missions. MRS. DICK OF UNION. Mr. and Mrs. Peter Dick lived between

Glen Williams and Georgetown. MRS. SINCLAIR OF GEORGETOWN. Ada Sinclair and her husband had a farm between Norval and Georgetown. "I GUESS AND FEAR". Robert Burns, concluding lines of "To a Mouse": "An' forward though I canna see / I guess an' fear!" **January 14** CONGREGATIONAL MEETING. In the Presbyterian church, decision-making begins at the local level. Ministers are "called" by the congregation, church business affairs are run by the Managers, and the Church Session, consisting of the Elders, oversees the church services. **January 15** LEWIS LAW. Lived at Huttonville; eventually became a guard at a correctional centre. CHELTENHAM. A village north of Glen Williams. $10 A MONTH. Relief hand-outs were $19 a month per family. **January 19** HAMMOND MACKENZIE. LMM's second cousin on her grandmother Woolner's side. LMM had visited him October 5, 1929. **January 31** SEVENTH OF FEBRUARY. There is no record of this dream in the July entries. CANADIAN ASSOCIATED COS. A fire and life insurance company, based in Toronto. LMM was not alone in the 1920s in believing insurance companies to be good investments. Post-war insecurity had increased awareness of the desirability of insurance, and in the beginning of the Depression years life insurance held up well as security for borrowing. Investments in insurance companies turned sour as the Depression deepened and companies reneged on payments. GIBSON & TAYLOR. James C. Gibson, President, and Allan B. Taylor, Vice-President, were officers in Organized Trade Limited, with its head office in the Federal Building, in Toronto. **February 3** FIFTEEN BELOW ZERO. Minus 15 degrees fahrenheit equals minus 28 degrees centigrade. **February 6** JAMES BENTLEY. LMM's second cousin Tillie Macneill had married a Bentley and lived in Kensington. This news is entered again, three days later, on February 9, with "Bentley" spelled differently. **February 8** VARSITY. Slang term for "university". COUNCIL ON DELINQUENCY. Probably the Committee on Discipline, of which Professor Allcutt was Chairman and Professor Wilson Secretary at this time. The Committee was dissolved around 1960. Journal entries during Christmas holidays do not mention the first letter from the Council. DEPT. OF ENGINEERING SURVEYING AND DRAWING. Both courses were required for all first year students in the School of Practical Science (Engineering). In 1930–31 there were 850 students in SPS. A CERTAIN GIRL. Presumably Luella Reid. CODEINE PILLS. Alkaloid derived from opium used as a sedative; not as addictive as morphine. MR. WILSON. William Stewart Wilson (1896–1965) became secretary of the School of Practical Science in 1927. He was appointed Assistant Dean in 1945. PROF. ALLCUT. Edgar Alfred Allcut (1888–1979) was an Associate Professor in 1930; made full Professor in 1932. He became head of the department of Metallurgical Engineering, 1944–56. PROF. WRIGHT. William James Turnbull Wright (1890–1989) was on the Staff of the School of Practical Science from 1912–1959. TECHNICAL ENGLISH. A composition course for science students, required since 1922. **February 15** MY NEW BOOK. *A Tangled Web* is a sardonic story about an elderly woman who tries to control the lives of the younger people in her clan. AUTHORS' ASSOCIATION. Formed in Montréal in 1921, the Association worked for improvements in the copyright law and for extension of the reading public through Canadian Book Week and *The Canadian Author and Bookman*. LMM had been a member of the Toronto branch since its inception. GARVIN. John Garvin, now 72 years old, edited

Canadian Verse for Boys and Girls, 1930. See entry for February 12, 1928, *SJLMM* III, 363–4, for an anecdote about him. **February 18** DOLSON. A Mount Pleasant family that had come to Norval Church after the Mount Pleasant Presbyterian Church voted to enter the United Church. Dolson was a common name in the Norval-Georgetown area. "FORGOT BECAUSE I MUST". Matthew Arnold, "Absence", ["we forget because we must..."]. QUADRILLE. Square dance for four couples. EIGHT-HAND REEL. More commonly called an eightsome reel: a Scottish dance for eight people. FRENCH HIRED BOY. An allusion to the fact that long-established French settlers of Prince Edward Island suffered social inequity because of language and religious barriers. STANTON MACNEILL. See entry of February 27, 1890. **February 20** JARVIS ST. COLLEGIATE. A large secondary school in downtown Toronto, founded 1807. LMM recorded reading there in 1921 (*SJLMM* II). THE CAT CREEPS. This 1930 re-make of the silent film *The Cat and the Canary* (1927) is the story of an escaped maniac, as told by the asylum keeper. SATURDAY NIGHT. A journal of essays and reviews, established in 1887, edited at this time by Hector Charlesworth. **February 27** "ON THE AIR". Commercial radio broadcasting, begun in Montréal in 1919 by the Canadian Marconi Company, had grown to over 60 Canadian stations by 1928. A Commission on public broadcasting had been set up in 1928, but action in establishing the Canadian Broadcasting Corporation was delayed because of the Depression. PRESTON. This town is now part of the city of Cambridge, 47 km (30 mi.) southwest of Norval. Its radio station was CKPC, with a studio at 265 Guelph Street, Preston. **February 28** VIOLET LAW. Daughter of the indigent Mrs. Law, remembered in Norval as a nice little girl with long braids. **March 2** HELEN. Mrs. Mason's daughter. After her marriage, Mrs. Mason moved to Kitchener. (See note August 24, 1929.) "A MIGHTY STONE...". The original lines run: "A mass enormous! which in modern days / No two of earth's degenerate sons could raise". *Iliad*, tr. Pope. XX, 337. **March 9** *Anne's House of Dreams*.... INTO POLISH. Translated as *Wymarzony dom Ani* by Stefan Fedynski (Warsaw: Wydawnictwo Arcyziel Literatur Obych, 1931); see *CCL: Canadian Children's Literature* issue #46 for information about the reception of LMM's works in Poland. **March 22** KEITH. Marion's brother, son of Myrtle Webb of the "Green Gables" house. **March 24** JENNIE HARRISON. The Harrisons had a farm north of Leaskdale, and Mrs. Harrison kept the local store. MRS. SHIER. Lily Harrison Reid had left service at the manse in Leaskdale to marry Rob Shier of Zephyr. MRS. THOMPSON. Faye Doak Thompson was born in Goodwood near Zephyr. **April 4** MARK TWAIN'S *Roughing It*. This book of sketches, which began selling through subscriptions in 1871, concerned MT's life as a writer and prospector in the American West. **April 8** JAUNDICE. Morbid state caused by obstruction of bile. Yellow jaundice affects the appearance of the patient; a "jaundiced eye", medically discoloured, is the source of much literacy allusion. **April 13** HODGINS IN BRAMPTON. John Hodgins was the choir director of the Presbyterian Church in Brampton. BRAMPTON LITERARY SOCIETY. The Literary and Travel Club of Brampton, founded around 1910 by eight Brampton ladies as a "reading club", devoted itself during World War I to community service. In the 1920s, members supplemented their own literary reports and reviews by inviting faculty members of the University of Toronto to speak. LMM was a valued associate member of the club from 1926 to 1936, presenting papers annually to the group of twenty-odd women, assembled monthly in a member's home. In January 1931 she had given a paper on "The Cat"; over the years her other topics included her trip to Mammoth Cave, a PEI poet, mackerel-skinning, and abnormal characters in history in the light of modern science. **April 14** "HERE HATH BEEN DAWNING...". From "Today", by Thomas Carlyle. The poem continues "Think, wilt thou let it / Slip useless away?" MIMICO. A village south of Norval, now in the greater Toronto area as part of Oakville. "COP". From "copper", slang for policeman: one who cops or catches. In use since 1859. FROOD MINE IN SUDBURY. First opened in 1889. Discovery of a major lode at the Falconbridge Mines in Sudbury in 1928 had led to renewed activity in copper and nickel mining. In 1931 the Frood Mine produced about 3000 tons a day. The mine is still operated by INCO. **April 18** PERITONITIS. Inflammation of the lining of the abdominal cavity. **April 21** SUPPLEMENTALS Make-up examinations set to permit a second try at passing university courses. **April 26** DR. NICKELL. Veterinarian in Georgetown. ON HIS OWN BAT. Slang, alluding to cricket: doing it by himself. **May 2** MR. [W.] CAPPS. The choir director was the father of three musical daughters. SUDBURY. Major city in the mining area north of Georgian Bay; about 241 miles (390 kilometres) north of Toronto. PRECIOUS BANE. From John Milton, *Paradise Lost* I, 679. "[R]iches grow in hell: that soil may best / Deserve the precious bane". The phrase had been used as title of a best-selling novel by Mary Webb in 1924. **May 8.** WINTER GRIME. When houses were heated by coal furnaces, a sooty coating accumulated over the winter. Spring cleaning involved washing woodwork, carpets, drapes, and windows. **May 9** ENGINEERING PASS LISTS. University of Toronto results for all faculties were published in Toronto papers. **May 10** MISS FERGUSON. J.K.F. Ferguson of Napanee had been "saved" in China. She was connected with George Ferguson, Premier of Ontario. **May 11** P.W.C. MAGAZINE. Publication of Prince of Wales College, in Charlottetown, attended by LMM in 1893–94. DR. RAMSAY. Ernest Herbert Ramsay, born in 1875 in Hamilton, PEI, attended Prince of Wales College, Dalhousie University and Pine Hill Divinity Hall, and became a Presbyterian minister. Acadia University conferred the degree of Doctor of Divinity on him in 1921. After Church Union he became a United Church minister. His article in the PWC *College Times*, VII, 2 (March 1931) was entitled "Pictures of Old PWC". DR. [Alexander] ANDERSON. Principal of Prince of Wales College, 1868–1902. **May 16** CLIFTON. Crossroads village, LMM's birthplace, six miles from Park Corner. **May 18** YAKIMA, WASH. A small city, founded in 1885, 100 miles southeast of Seattle, Washington, in the centre of a valley named for the Yakima Indians. **May 26** REV. MR. PAULIN. Rev. J.B. Paulin was Housemaster of Memorial House at St. Andrew's College, and on the staff from 1927. **May 31** [Henry] HOLT'S *[The] Cosmic Relations and Immortality* (New York, 1914/15). A new edition of *On the Cosmic Relations*, a study of psychical research, thought transference, and spiritualism. **June 2** AUNT MARY LAWSON. This sister of LMM's grandfather Alexander Macneill was the famous story-teller to whom LMM dedicated *The Golden Road*. Her 1919 letter appears also in H.H. Simpson's *Cavendish, Its History, Its People* (1973). LMM provides a gloss on the letter. DOCKENDORFF. LMM spells the name with one "f". PORTRAIT

OF THE SPEAKER. The portrait of "Speaker" William Macneill is still in the Charlottetown legislative chamber. GEORGE MONTGOMERY. George and John Montgomery were not descendants of "Big Donald", LMM's grandfather, but of "Little Donald" Montgomery, his cousin. **June 8** [Francis] HACKETT'S *Henry VIII and His Wives*. The actual title of this book of popularized history (New York, 1929) does not mention the wives. In a contemporary letter, LMM asked her publisher, Mr. McClelland, to send her Paul Rival's *Six Wives of Henry VIII*. **June 16** ISABEL[le] COCKSHUTT PRIZE. The St. Andrew's College Prize for History was donated by Mrs. F.A. (Jocelyn) Schulman, former President of the St. Andrew's Ladies Guild. It is still being awarded. **June 27** ART GALLERY. The Art Gallery of Ontario, established in 1900 as the Art Museum of Toronto (renamed Gallery in 1919), was situated just south of Dundas, near the University. MARSHALL SAUNDERS. A woman of 70 at this time, Saunders had become a best-selling novelist in 1893 with *Beautiful Joe* (Charles H. Bane). Her later books were published by L.C. Page, LMM's publisher and antagonist. Saunders had since produced animal stories and romances annually. OPTIMIST'S CLUB. The Toronto branch of an international community service club, first organized in Buffalo, N.Y., in 1911, with headquarters in St. Louis, Mo. HART HOUSE. Built between 1911 and 1919 by the Massey family and named for Hart Massey, with a memorial Soldiers' Tower added in 1924, Hart House is a centre of student activities at the University of Toronto. LUCKOVICH, M.P. Michael Luchkovich, B.A., Member of Parliament for Vegreville, Alberta, was born in Pennsylvania, USA, the son of Ukrainian immigrants. He came to Canada at 15, graduated from University of Manitoba, and was elected to the House of Commons in 1926 and re-elected in 1930, representing the United Farmers of Alberta. TORONTO HUNT CLUB. Established in 1843 and situated east of the city at 1355 Kingston Road, is at present a "golf club and fine dining establishment". MRS. SHEARD. Virna Stanton Sheard (1865–1943) had published 5 novels at this time, the latest being *Fortune Turns her Wheel* in 1929. MISS DENNIS. Clara Dennis, author eventually of 3 travel books on Nova Scotia, beginning with *Down in Nova Scotia, My Own, My Native Land* (1934). KING EDWARD. An elegant hotel located at King and Victoria, built in 1903. WILSON MACDONALD (1880–1967). This prolific poet published *Caw-caw Ballads* in 1930, and *A Flagon of Beauty* in 1931. TAGORE. Rabindranath Tagore (1861–1941), a much-admired poet from India, made extensive lecture tours during the 1930s. He was a vegetarian on religious grounds. WHITMAN. Vegetarianism was perhaps the least notable of the unconventional attitudes of Walt Whitman (1819–1892). PI-JAWS. School slang, from 1870: pious exhortation. PRESS CLUB. The Toronto Press Club, in sporadic existence from 1882–9, 1902–9, re-established in 1926, was a going concern in the 30s, with hundreds of members. NAPIER MOORE. An Englishman who as editorial director of *Maclean's* since 1928 oversaw the magazine's increasing emphasis on Canadian nationalism, politics, and fiction. MACLEAN'S. "Canada's National Magazine" had developed from a series of business magazines. *Busy Man's Magazine*, bought by J. B. Maclean in 1905, was given its current name in 1911. It had published or re-published 15 stories by LMM between 1915 and 1929, 2 poems in 1915; it would publish "Secret Knowledge", a new poem, 29 October 1931. **July 10** NELLIE MCCLUNG.

Active feminist and author of popular novels and autobiographies, Nellie Mooney McClung (1873–1951) had most recently published books of short stories in 1930 and 1931. "JANEY CANUCK". Judge Emily Ferguson Murphy. WYLIE GRIER. [Sir] Wylie Grier [P.R.C.A., O.S.A., D.C.L.]. This distinguished artist was also on the executive of the Canadian Authors Association. CANON [H.J.] CODY (1868–1951). Clergyman and imperialist politician, Cody was Chairman of the Board of Governors of the University of Toronto, 1923–32, and became President of the University 1932–1944 and Chancellor 1944–47. LIEUT. GAGNON Lt.-Col. Henri Gagnon was Managing Director of the Québec City newspaper Le Soleil. He was also in 1931 Vice-President of the Canadian Press, past President of the Canadian Daily Newspaper Association, and active in the Canadian Legion and in many charitable and patriotic causes. He had been decorated by the Pope and was a member of the French Legion d'Honneur. LMM mistakenly refers to him at first as "Lieutenant" but subsequently changes the reference to "Colonel" Gagnon. MACAULAY'S Life. The author, Sir George Trevelyan (1838–1928), was Macaulay's nephew. The Life and Letters of Lord Macaulay (1875) was the first of Trevelyan's major works of social and political history. July 11 HODDER AND STOUGHTON. LMM's British publishers since Rilla of Ingleside (1921). AUNT BECKY BEGAN IT. LMM repeats the news about the English name at the end of this entry. TAMASHA. Anglo-Indian: a show, entertainment, or noisy commotion. In Pat of Silver Bush, LMM assigns this term to Judy Plum, who pronounces it "tommy-show". THE CHATELAINE. This Canadian women's magazine had published three of LMM's stories since it was established by Maclean-Hunter in March 1928. It was edited first by Anne Elizabeth Wilson, with Napier Moore as Editorial Director. LMM's "The House" in the May 1932 issue would be her final fictional contribution to the magazine; her article "Is This My Anne?" would appear in January 1935. WINTER OF 1892. Items in this entry connect with LMM's next novel, Pat of Silver Bush. THE STORM WRACK. A wrack normally means wreckage, but LMM is using the term metaphorically. "WATERLOO". A wood stove, like the "Franklin" stoves in the United States. THE BLUE CHEST. Parts of The Story Girl and The Golden Road centre around this family chest. July 18 "WHAT FOND AND FOOLISH...". Wordsworth, in "Strange Fits of Passion Have I Known", described "fond and wayward thoughts" about the possibility of his beloved's death. July 28 "WHAT THE CONGREGATION EXPECTS...". Published as "An Open Letter from a Minister's Wife", October 1931. August 2 A TYPEWRITTEN COPY. This typescript, digesting material from the journals until September 29, 1936, was partially edited by LMM's son, Dr. Stuart Macdonald. It is now at the University of Guelph. August 5 MAC'S OFFICE. John McClelland, of McClelland & Stewart, LMM's Canadian publisher, had an office at 215–219 Victoria Street in downtown Toronto. MR. STEWART. George Stewart had been a partner in the publishing firm since 1914. D[OCTO]R. THORNE. Anthony Trollope's novel (1858) concerns the efforts of a family to separate an obscure and penniless orphan from the young man she loves. RED RUSSIA. In 1922 the USSR had emerged, with Moscow as its capital and Josef Stalin as General Secretary, bent on adherence to the principles of the Russian Revolution of 1917. The use of "Red" in relation to Russia, particularly to its army, derives from the red flag of revolutionary socialism. August 21

STOKES. As with all the LMM novels since 1917, this New York publisher brought out the American first edition simultaneously with the Canadian McClelland & Stewart one. **August 31** FRAMLEY PARSONAGE. In Trollope's novel (1861), Lady Lufton tries to prevent her son's marriage to Lucy, the sister of a young clergyman, Mark Robarts. Archdeacon Grantley, his daughter Griselda, the wealthy Miss Dunstable, and Mrs. Proudie the Bishop's wife, fill out the cast. U.F.O. United Farmers of Ontario, a political party founded in 1914. WILL COOK, LILY MEYERS. Lily had been LMM's maid at the manse, 1918–25; she had been keeping house for widower Will Cook since 1927. ROB ANDERSON, ELSIE. Elsie Bushby replaced Lily Meyers in 1925–6. She eventually married Cliff Davidson and lived in Uxbridge. **September 6** EARL GREY. Governor General of Canada in 1911 when LMM was presented to him. See *SJLMM* II. DUKE OF DEVONSHIRE. Governor-General 1916–1921. Sir William Cavendish (1505–1557) was the father of the first Earl of Devonshire. PROHIBITION. Sale of alcoholic beverages had been prohibited by law in PEI in 1901, and in the other Canadian provinces during World War I. Immediately after the war, provincial laws cut off imports of spirits and wine, closed drinking establishments, and consumption except in private dwellings. In the USA, even stricter prohibition was legislated between 1922 and 1933. Canadian provinces began easing legislation on prohibition before the Americans did: Québec "went wet" in 1919, British Columbia in 1920, and Ontario in 1927, although individual counties had the local option of maintaining prohibition. **September 10** A NEW JACKET. Edna Cooke designed the dust cover for *A Tangled Web*. **September 13** ETHEL MAYNE'S *Life of Lady Byron*. This much-discussed book, properly titled *The Life and Letters of Anne Isabella, Lady Noel Byron* (London: Constable, 1929), analyses marital troubles between Lord Byron, the dashing and enormously popular poet and the intellectual and unworldly Annabelle Milbanke. The marriage ended in legal separation after a year. **September 16** GUELPH. A city 25 miles (41 km) west of Norval, with well-established shopping facilities. The shopping trip marks the publication of *A Tangled Web*, and preparation for a book tour to publicize it. Founded in 1827 by John Galt, Scottish entrepreneur and novelist, Guelph in 1931 was the site of Ontario Agricultural College (founded in 1874, the first English-speaking agricultural college in Canada), Ontario Veterinary College, and Macdonald Institute of Household Science (founded in 1903 and, like Macdonald College at Montréal where Frede Campbell had worked, it was named for its principal benefactor, the PEI-born Scottish-Canadian Sir William Christopher Macdonald, the greatest Canadian educational philanthropist of his generation). All these colleges, plus others, were amalgamated in 1965 into the University of Guelph. Guelph was also the site of Homewood Sanitarium, a famous private establishment for the treatment of alcoholism and mental illness established in 1883 and significantly expanded in 1907, which drew private patients from all over North America, and treated, among others, the Rev. Ewan Macdonald. The Ontario Reformatory, established in 1915, was also located in Guelph. **September 29** "SOMETHING LOST BEHIND THE RANGES". Rudyard Kipling, "The Explorer", Stanza 2. HECTOR CHARLESWORTH [1872–1945]. Editor of *A Cyclopaedia of Canadian Biography in the Twentieth Century* (Toronto: Hunter Rose, 1919). His more recent works included *Candid Chronicles* (1925) and *"The Canadian Scene" Sketches: Political and Historical* (1927). **October 10** GLOBE. This Toronto morning paper, established by George Brown in 1844, now carried the phrase "Canada's National Newspaper" on its masthead, and was very widely read. **October 15** WAR BETWEEN CHINA AND JAPAN. Japan invaded Manchuria September 18, 1931, as part of the rise of military power in Japan. In the typescript of the LMM journal, a handwritten comment is added at this point: "But compared to now!!!—1942." **October 21** THE AURORA HUNT. In Canada several hunt clubs established in the nineteenth century continued the British habit of wearing "pinks"—the traditional red coats of English hunters. **October 22** EDISON AND HENRY FORD. Thomas Edison (1847–1931) American inventor of the electric light bulb, the phonograph, etc.; Henry Ford (1863–1947) American inventor and mass manufacturer of automobiles. **October 31** NATIONAL GOV'T. British Conservative, Labour, and Liberal cabinet members from previous governments took office in a new Coalition government in 1931. THE "DOLE" SYSTEM. The cost of maintaining support for unemployed Britons was blamed in Canadian newspaper stories of the 1930s for a collapsing British economy. **November 7** "MOVIE" CAMERA. The term "movie" for a moving picture originated in America in 1913. PROFESSOR HAULTAIN. Herbert Edward Terrick Haultain (1869–1961) was the widely respected head of the Mining Engineering Department. The Haultain Mining Building at University of Toronto is named for him. ABERFOYLE. A village 8 miles south of Guelph in Puslinch township. **November 9** ALBERTON. A harbour town on the north shore of PEI, in Prince County, in the most easterly part of the Island. LUCY L. MONTGOMERY. An American writer of essays and verse. See *SJLMM* II, 29, 288, 409. **November 10** BLACK BULL. See S. R. Crockett's "The Black Douglas". **November 18** "DEPRESSION". American dictionaries include an economic definition: a period marked by slackening of business activity, much unemployment, falling prices and wages. The term was not used in this sense in Great Britain. Because Canada's economy depended so largely on exports, the country felt the impact of worldwide economic depression in the 1930s. Between 1929 and 1933, the gross national export dropped by 42% and unemployment was climbing to 30% by 1933. Stock market prices continued low and many companies were unable to pay dividends. **November 27** MONTREAL MARITIME CLUB. Probably the Maritime Provinces Club, which had headquarters at the Windsor Hotel. MARITIME WOMEN'S CLUB. This club met in down-town hotels to hear speakers, and held an annual bazaar until 1968. FLORRIE SUTHERLAND. LMM's first cousin, daughter of her Uncle Robert and Aunt Margaret Montgomery Sutherland. T.B. MCCAULAY President of the Sun Life Insurance Company and a major figure in the Montréal and Canadian business community. MONTREAL BRANCH OF THE AUTHORS' ASSOCIATION. Led by Stephen Leacock and Murray Gibbon, this group had instituted the national Association in 1921. **December 4** *The Wind in the Willows.* Kenneth Grahame's whimsical animal story (not a fairy tale), published 1908. MISS MAPP. E.F. Benson, son of an Archbishop of Canterbury, began his series of popular satires with *Dodo* (1893); his stories of Lucia and Miss Mapp, though not particularly successful in the United States, were best-sellers in England. **December 11** PEACE OF VERSAILLES The terms of the peace treaties that ended World War I were established at international conferences beginning January 1919 in Versailles, near Paris. Major concessions of territory and financial reparations rendered Germany temporarily powerless, but also disturbed and resentful. **December 13** LADY INTO FOX David Garrett (b. 1892) first published this book in 1931, and re-issued it in combination with his *A Man in the Zoo* (London: Chatto, 1932). **December 19** TO WRITE A LITTLE. This is the first reference to the composition of *Pat of Silver Bush*. AUSTRALIA. Australia was particularly vulnerable to the Great Depression: unemployment now stood at over 25% and social misery was general. J.H. Scullin's Labor Ministry was elected in 1929 but in June 1931 the Premier's plan for reducing government spending led to the disintegration of the Labor Party, and its defeat in the November election. Lyons, the new premier, led a coalition government, the United Australia Party. **December 26** NEURASTHENIA. Nervous debility: the term was first used in 1856.

1932
January 2 BAYFIELD WILLIAMS. A friend from 1894–5, when LMM taught in Bideford. **January 2** HYDRO. Hydroelectric power. In the 1920s, Ontario Hydro took over most local power companies, including the Georgetown Hydro; in 1924 Ontario Hydro brought electric power to Norval. **January 10** KATE DOUGLAS WIGGIN. Author of *Rebecca of Sunnybrook Farm* (1903), often compared to *Anne of Green Gables* (1908) since its story centred on a little girl sent to an unsympathetic older foster family. PARTHIAN SHAFT. Horsemen from Parthia, in western Asia, flung their missiles backward while in real or pretended flight. RIDEAU HALL. Official residence of the Governor-General in Ottawa. **January 24** AGLEY. Scotticism: awry, as in Burns's lines "The best laid plans of mice and men / gang aft agley". RED MENACE IN SPAIN AND GERMANY. In Spain, a coalition of urban workers and agricultural labourers joined a small communist movement to establish a republican government, headed by socialists. During the subsequent Civil War, this group would be aided by the USSR, Mexico, and France, and set against General Franco and the Spanish Nationalists, aided by Germany and Italy. In the early 1930s, fear of international communism was one of the forces fuelling the rise of Hitler's power in Germany. [Beside] THE BONNIE BRIER BUSH AND [The Days of] AULD LANG SYNE. Two very popular novels of the Kailyard school, both published in 1895 by "Ian Maclaren" (Rev. John Watson). WILLIAM MACLURE. A sentimentalized "doctor of the old school" in *Beside the Bonnie Brier Bush*. ELMER GANTRY. An evangelical preacher, anti-hero of the novel by Sinclair Lewis (1927). STATIC. Reception on early radios was often disturbed by the interference of static electricity. HITLERS. Adolf Hitler (1889–1945) became internationally known after the Munich rising of 1929 and the publication of *Mein Kampf*. He opposed von Hindenberg in the election for the German presidency in 1932. **January 31** "FORWARD THOUGH I CANNA SEE...". Final lines of Robert Burns's "To a Mouse". THE WAY OF ALL FLESH. Samuel Butler's novel, published posthumously in 1903; an exposé of bitter relations between parents and children. "TO EACH SAINT HIS OWN CANDLE". A French proverb. JACK COOKE. Son of W. Cooke, who had been clerk of the session at Union in 1925. Jack later became a member of the Board of Management. WILL TOWNSEND. Son of another strong Presbyterian family: his

father was on the Union Session. ERINDALE. A village south-east of Norval, now absorbed into metropolitan Toronto. MARY RINEHART'S *TISH* BOOKS. Rinehart's successes began with *The Circular Staircase*, which shared the American best-seller position with *Anne of Green Gables* in 1908. Her comic novel *Tish* (1916) was followed by *Tish Plays the Game* (1926) and *Tish Marches On* (1929). "BELIEVE THEM WHEN THEY AUGUR CHEER". From Walter Scott, "The Lady of the Lake", canto 4, v. 11. **February 7** OLD MAN OF THE SEA. In classical legend, Proteus, old prophet tending the seals of Poseidon, changed shape in order to thwart his captors. **February 11** EDGAR WALLACE (1875–1932). Among his most popular thrillers were *The Four Just Men* and *Sanders of the River*. NATE. Nathan Lockhart, stepson of the Baptist minister in Cavendish during LMM's schooldays, perhaps a source for Jingle in *Pat of Silver Bush*. SHINDIG. A lively social affair: derived from "shin dig": a kick in the shins. GEORGE MACNEILL AND ARTHUR SIMPSON. Arthur married Clarinda Macneill, sister of "Big George", and Arthur's sister Agnes married George's brother Artemas; see H. H. Simpson's *Cavendish: Its History, Its People*. TRIG. Trim, tidy, and neat. THE NEW BOY. See *SJLLM* I, 2 (entry of Sept. 24, 1889). She seems to be quoting from the diary she says she has destroyed. The Rev. Spurr came to Cavendish in 1885. ACADIA COLLEGE. Chartered in 1841, named "Acadia University" in 1891, the year Nathan Lockhart entered it. This Baptist institution in Wolfville, Nova Scotia, had accorded a degree to its first woman graduate in 1884. SYDNEY. Major centre of Cape Breton Island, N.S. "PASTOR FELIX". The Rev. A.J. Lockhart, a Nova Scotia cleric, poet, and essayist. LMM included many of his poems and cards in her journals and scrap-books. **February 25** FRED LYONS. The Lyons family were among Union pioneers. MARGARET LESLIE. Descendant of a family who were charter members of Union Church. When World War II broke out, Margaret joined the Canadian Navy. **February 26** ELLA CAMPBELL. Widow of George, one of LMM's cousins of Park Corner, brother of Stella, Clara, and Frederica. Donald (Dan) was the eldest son of Ella and George. The Campbell descendants have a copy of this letter, which is dated March 7, 1932 (and is missing the last page). There are a few differences between the original letter and LMM's journal transcription of that letter. She changes the occasional word, removes some small redundancies, sharpens a few points, and deletes several paragraphs. The sentence in the letter which reads "Prices for farms are low now and a run-down farm like Park Corner would bring next to nothing" becomes simply "Prices for farms are low now". Two sentences later, she tacks "and Georgie" onto the line "how much would be left and how long would it support your mother?" To the sentence in the letter which begins "Now, I have told you plainly what I think" she adds "as you have asked me to do". The three omitted paragraphs are as follows: (1) "As for his [Jim] not being of age I thought 18 was of age as far as an estate is concerned. But if not, why shouldn't a guardian be appointed? It would only be a matter of form, since Jim is quite old enough and shrewd enough to paddle his own canoe. Life Howatt or that Johnstone at Long River (I forget his name) who is a good friend of your mother's would no doubt be willing to be guardian for a year or two, since the duties would only be nominal and involve no real responsibility". (2) "If the farm were Jim's own he could borrow a few dollars on it now and again if he got temporarily stuck but of course nobody would lend him money if it wasn't [his own]". (3) "As for you, I again repeat—you'd be *free* of all claims and encumbrances. This depression can't last forever and you will get a job and be able to support yourself with a clear mind, knowing that the others are provided for and have a home at Park Corner". HEATH MONTGOMERY. Heath (1893–1962) was LMM's first cousin, son of Uncle James and Aunt Eliza Montgomery. For LMM's comments on Heath's wife, Mary Ella Hogan, see *SJLMM* III, 142. **February 28** [W.P.] CROZIER'S LETTERS OF PONTIUS PILATE. An historical novel (London: 1928), based on imaginary letters from Pontius Pilate purportedly written during his governorship of Judaea. **March 24** CENTRAL Y. The Young Men's Christian Association had its central Toronto building at 36 College Street. **March 30** CONDITIONED. Given a conditional pass, to be removed by a supplemental exam. **April 2** PAT OF SILVER BUSH. Set in a house reminiscent of Park Corner, the novel centres on a girl who devotes herself to maintaining the family home. HINDENBERG. In the German election of 1932, World War I General Paul von Hindenberg (1847–1934), President of the German Republic since 1925, ran against and defeated the Nazi party led by Adolf Hitler. In 1933, however, while government scandals erupted, Hitler rejected offers of various ministries but emerged as Chancellor of the "Third Reich". **April 16** FLORA KLICKMANN'S FLOWER PATCH. LMM's Scottish correspondent, George Macmillan, had sent this series of books to her as yearly Christmas presents, beginning with *The Flower Patch Among the Hills* (N.Y: Frederick A. Stokes, 1916). **April 20** SIMPSON COMPANY. Stock in the Robert Simpson Company plunged during the Depression. Simpson's heads the list of LMM's holdings. The rest of the companies on her "blue chip" list of stocks are Teck, McColl-Frontenac, Dominion Stores, Agnew-Surpass, Ford, and Imperial Tobacco. **April 30** BASEBALL. This entry ends with a very detailed explanation of the rules governing baseball games, Cavendish style (*Appendix D*). **May 1** MR. MACMILLAN. Hugh Alexander Macmillan (1892–1970) was a missionary in Formosa (now Taiwan), 1924–1932. PACE. By leave of, or with all deference to. The Latin term does not appear in American dictionaries of the 1930s. **May 3** MRS. STEWART. Wife of Rev. Alexander Clark Stewart (1875–1950), minister at Acton 1921–30, then at Chalmers in Toronto, 1930–37. AGATHA CHRISTIE'S PERIL AT END HOUSE (London, 1931). One of a shelf-full of mystery stories to be enjoyed by LMM during the 1930s; she particularly admired Agatha Christie. **May 11** GOING INTO THE LIBRARY FOR PRAYERS. The old-fashioned tradition of collecting everyone in the household for prayers and readings from Old and New Testaments, led by the man of the household, was less widely practised in 1932, but still part of the manse regime. **May 13** THE LINDBERG BABY. Newspapers around the world followed the kidnapping of baby Charles A. Lindbergh Jr., first of the six children of Charles Lindbergh (1902–1974), famous as the first aviator to fly the Atlantic Ocean solo (1927). Bruno Hauptmann was subsequently electrocuted for kidnapping and killing the two-year-old baby. **May 30** ELEANOR AGNEW. Laura Pritchard Agnew's daughter. She eventually moved to South Africa. MARY SLESSOR OF CALABAR. LMM's account of this strong-minded Scottish missionary emphasized the discipline she maintained in the African principalities where she taught, preached, nursed, settled tribal and domestic disputes, and "fought witch-doctors to a finish in their own stamping grounds". JOAN OF ARC. LMM's treatment of Joan is based largely on the Bernard Shaw play. FLORENCE NIGHTINGALE. LMM presents an idealized story of the "Angel of the Crimea", and underscores her effect on army barracks and hospitals. "FAMOUS GIRLS". Eventually published as *Courageous Women* (1934), the volume includes the three brief biographies by LMM and 15 by the other two authors, Marian Keith and Mabel Burns McKinley. **June 5** MR. ROBB. Reverend Edward George Robb (1878–1949), minister at Beaverton, moved to Kimbourne Park Church, Toronto, 1926–1933. **June 24** MONDAY. Monday was on June 20. **July 2** EBBIE. Nora Lefurgey Campbell's son, Edmund, the only one of their four children who survived childhood. Y CAMP. The Noble family, former owners of the Norval mills and proprietors of the large mill-owner's house across the Credit from LMM's home, now lived in Toronto. In the late 1920s they rented their property to the United Church, which in cooperation with the Young Men's Christian Association used the house as billets for young English immigrants en route to farm jobs in Canada. As local unemployment halted this scheme, the grounds were used more frequently by the YMCA for short-term camping trips for boys and girls from Toronto. LMM had read to groups of girls camping there. ANDRE THEDON'S PSYCHOANALYSIS AND LOVE. LMM mistakes the name: André Tridon (1877–1922) published a number of books on psychoanalysis; this one was published in N.Y. and London by Brentano's in 1922. "ALL THE WORLD IS QUEER [SAVE THEE AND ME, AND EVEN THOU ART A LITTLE QUEER.]" From Robert Owen's *Correspondence*, 1828. **July 14** KENNETH LANGDON. A lawyer in Georgetown who later became a judge. His son is now a Judge in Brampton. **July 18** BENSON'S NEW BOOK. E.F. Benson, author of the *Miss Mapp* series, published *Charlotte Brontë* (London: Longmans Green, 1932), focusing on the Brontës' brother Branwell. MRS. GASKELL'S BIOGRAPHY. Elizabeth Gaskell's biography of her friend and contemporary was published in 1857. LMM recorded reading the book in 1911 and 1925. **July 21** KINGSTON. Ontario city, 168 miles (280 km) east of Toronto; home of Queen's University and the Royal Military College. GRAND LODGE. Ernest Barraclough was a leading figure in the Masonic Order. THOUSAND ISLES. From the 1830s on, tourists had enjoyed boat trips through the labyrinth of some 1149 islands in the St. Lawrence between Brockville and Kingston. Many of the Islands were named after military places, as well as after officers who had distinguished themselves in the War of 1812–14. EWAN'S CONDITION. In 1919 Ewan Macdonald had gone to Boston to consult a psychiatrist about his depressions and his obsessive thoughts of damnation. **August 20** WORDSWORTH. LMM spent her first royalty money on buying books of poetry, including a volume by Wordsworth. "THOSE WHO FEEL THE THRILL...". Slightly misquoted from Bliss Carman, "At the Making of Man", 89–90, "For these were they who feel the thrill / Of beauty like a pang". Quoted also in *Mistress Pat*. HER DAUGHTER DIED. Nora Campbell's daughter Jessie had been stricken with polio and died; her other son, Donald, who survived polio but had to wear heavy iron braces, drowned when a boat overturned and he was pulled down by the weight of his braces; Nora had also lost a baby at birth. Ebbie (Edmund Ernest, b. April 14, 1918) was left as Nora's only child. MILTON SIMPSON (1879–1952). In 1932, head of a college English Department at Kalamazoo,

Michigan. "DAYS THAT ARE NO MORE". Alfred Tennyson, "Tears, idle tears", from *The Princess*, IV, 5. GEORGETOWN GREENHOUSE. The Dominion Seed House had large premises at the eastern edge of Georgetown. **August 25** This entry is mistakenly dated August 25, 1933, in the handwritten copy. MY OWN WEDDING. The journal entry becomes confusing at this point: LMM shifts from meditation on a fly to memories of Park Corner, and pastes onto the page a Christmas card, dated 1921. THIS WILL BE THE LAST. Pat Aylsworth died when her children were young. **September 11** THE HOSTEL. The Noble house, a country estate across the river from the Norval manse. "LIFE'S UNLIT DECEMBER". From an Ethelwyn Wetherald poem. BESSY LAIRD. Murray Laird's sister Elizabeth married Charles Lorimer. **September 14** "THERE IS NO UNION...". From James Montgomery's "Friends", stanza 1. LMM had quoted this in her journal of December 16, 1912. **September 18** "THERE ARE NO FIELDS...". From Walter Savage Landor's *Imaginary Conversations*, "Aesop to Rhodope", I. LMM omits the original punctuation. MR. HAMMOND. Melville Ormond Hammond had joined the *Globe* in 1895 and rose to become City Editor, Financial Editor, and Magazine and Literary Editor. In *Who's Who in Canada* he listed his recreation as "amateur photography". ENGLISH "SUNDERLAND"' WARE. Porcelain dishes manufactured in the English seaport on the North Sea, at the mouth of the River Wear: the general area from which LMM's grandmother Lucy Woolner Macneill had emigrated. **September 24** ARDATH. Corelli's 1889 novel, subtitled *The Story of a Dead Self*, was mentioned by LMM in 1924. **November 13** "NOTHING IN EARTH...". From "A Song of the Unreturning" by Wilson Macdonald, from *Out of the Wilderness* (Ottawa: Graphic Press, 1926). "AS MOONLIGHT UNTO SUNLIGHT...". From Alfred, Lord Tennyson, "Locksley Hall", 153. THE LAW OF PSYCHIC PHENOMENA. LMM first mentioned reading this book by Thomson Jay Hudson (1834–1903) in 1906; its subtitle is *A Working Hypothesis for the Systematic Study of Hypnotism, Spiritualism, Mental Therapeutics, etc.* WILL HOUSTON. Husband of LMM's friend and second cousin Tillie McKenzie. In 1911 he made unwelcome advances to LMM. (See *SJLMM* II, 46–51.) THE SECRET FIELD. As described earlier, October 2, 1929, this "exquisite little nook" would become a central motif in *Pat of Silver Bush*. "LIVING GREEN". From Isaac Watts' "There is a land of pure delight". "THE FUTURE LIKE THE GATHERING NIGHT". Henry Glassford Bell, "Mary, Queen of Scots". **November 18** PAULINE, ANITA. Daughters of Myrtle and Ernest Webb, sisters of Marion Webb Laird. The Webb children were Marion (b. June 6, 1907); Keith (born Dec. 8, 1909); Anita (Dec. 13, 1911–March 5, 1997); Lorraine (b. May 28, 1917); Pauline (b. March 14, 1920).

1933

January 13 THE ROUND ROOM. Elegant Art Deco dining room in the College Street branch of Eaton's Department Store. **January 28** GUADALLA'S *PALMERSTON* (London: Benn, 1926). One of a series of studies of Victorian statesmen by the historian Phillip Guedalla (1889–1944). **February 5** IT HAS HAPPENED. The explanation of this sentence is given later in this volume in the retrospective entry dated September 16, 1936. **February 7** VERONAL. A sedative which was prescribed in the treatment of melancholia and insomnia. Veronal (now Barbital) was a barbituate first formulated in 1903. LMM took it regularly in 1922 at the time of the Pickering trials. It is dangerous if over-used. **April 8** April 8 was a Saturday, not a Wednesday. AN AUTOGRAPH QUILT. Each member of the quilting group embroidered her name on a square to make a community memento. BRITISH PROOFS OF *PAT*. The British version contains some variations in spelling from the Canadian version. TACITUS (A.D. 54–119). Roman historian, author of *Annals, Histories*, and *Agricola*. GRAND HOTEL. Establishing the tradition of all-star casting, this movie starred Greta Garbo, John and Lionel Barrymore, Charles Laughton, Joan Crawford, Wallace Beery. Set in Berlin, it was based on a best-selling 1930 novel by Vicki Baum. FROISSART (1338–1410). His *Chronicles* deal with the Medieval period of chivalry in Europe and England. **May 10** CAVALCADE. Noël Coward's serious movie about a British family from the Boer War to the Jazz Age emphasizes the love between a couple who cling together through the years. **June 15** THE MUSEUM. The Royal Ontario Museum in Toronto, Canada's largest museum, was established in 1912. In 1933 two new sections were opened: the East Wing and the Centre Block. UR. An ancient city on the Euphrates River. **June 19** THE ETIENNE MEDAL. The George-Etienne Cartier Medal in French, named for the French Canadian statesman, G.-E. Cartier (1814–73), was established by W.A. (Jack) Beer, a former St. Andrew's College student, and Bursar at St. Andrew's in the 1930s. The Medal is still being awarded. "DID YOU EVER...?" As a child, Stuart Macdonald recited this poem at a Leaskdale Young People's meeting honouring his mother, March 22, 1922. **June 27** DR. HOWARD. Rev. Allan Leslie Howard (1873–1959) was Minister in Georgetown from 1931–1935. LIMEHOUSE. A village west of Georgetown, toward Rockwood. AGNES MACPHAIL, M.P. (1890–1954) The only woman elected to Parliament in 1921, the year that women first had the vote in Canada, Macphail was then a member of the "Ginger Group" of the Progressive Party. In the 1926 election she represented the United Farmers of Ontario. She was interested in agricultural issues, prison reform, antimilitarism, and women's rights; she helped form the CCF party. After losing a federal election in 1940, she ran for the Ontario Provincial Legislature, and served there 1943–45 and 1948–51. **July 6** "FROM THE COOL CISTERNS...". From Henry Wadsworth Longfellow, "Hymn to Night", 13–14. "ABOVE THE SMOKE...". John Milton, *Comus*; originally "which men call earth". **July 7** "SPLENDIDLY NULL". From Tennyson's "Maud II". **July 15** DROUTH. Archaic form of "drought": a common localism in Ontario. "NOTHING WORTH". Echoes line 39 of Tennyson's "The Epic" (poem introducing "Morte d'Arthur"). ANTHONY HOPE'S PRISONER OF ZENDA (1894) and RUPERT OF HENTZAU (1898). Romantic fiction in rococo style about the mythical Balkan kingdom of Ruritania. **September 1** AN ELSIE BOOK. Martha Finley's *Elsie Dinsmore* (1867) was the first of a long series of stories about a pious young girl. SELAH. A Hebrew word, appearing in the Bible version of the Psalms; its meaning is unknown but it is presumed to be a musical direction indicating a pause. LMM uses it in the sense of "so be it". **September 3** C.G.I.T.'S. "Canadian Girls in Training": a youth group established in 1915 by the Young Women's Christian Association and the major Protestant denominations to promote Christian education of girls ages 12 to 17. **September 12** HEART GNAWED BY WORRY. Probably a reference to Chester's growing interest in Luella Reid.

September 27 RASPUTIN AND THE EMPRESS. Irving Thalberg's movie brought John, Lionel, and Ethel Barrymore together in a superb historical epic. **September 30** THE BENNIES. Rev. Herbert Law Bennie (1887–1953) had moved from Uxbridge Church in 1924, to Mitchell, 1925–28, Knox Church in Halifax, 1929–30, and Acton 1931–41. **October 14** PUCK OF POOK'S HILL. Rudyard Kipling's book for children (1906) incorporates stories from British history into a modern fairy tale. **October 31** LORD AND LADY BESSBOROUGH. Governor-General of Canada, 1931–1935, and his wife. **November 8** "THE KINGDOM OF HEAVEN...". Luke 17:21; the King James version has "the kingdom of God". "THE FOUNTAIN OF PERPETUAL PEACE...". Also from Longfellow's "Hymn to Night", 15–16. **November 11** A GRUE. Scotticism: a shudder. **November 24** ANDROCLES AND THE LION (1912). Shaw's irreverent portrait of early Christians, their martyrdom and their pride. **November 25** HAROUN AL-RASCHID. Caliph of Baghdad, in many of the tales of the "Arabian Nights". GEORGE SIMPSON, JUNIUS, HOWARD. George and Howard Simpson were brothers, sons of John Simpson and Nellie Montgomery. Junius (1835–1915) was a cousin. The Simpsons, with the Macneills, were the first settlers of Cavendish, and distantly connected with LMM. "WALKED BY HIMSELF". The cat in Rudyard Kipling's *Just So Stories*: LMM had been accustomed to applying the phrase to Frede Campbell. **November 26** LAURA'S LETTERS. LMM fills out the last pages of volume 8 of her hand-written journals with reminiscences about Laura Pritchard Agnew, putting in many pictures, snips of Laura's wedding-dress, and newspaper cuttings, including Laura's obituary.

1936 *[As in her journal for 1911, LMM interrupts the flow of entries with a later-written explanation, and then resumes the chronological order.]*

September 16, 1936 JOURNEY'S END. LMM's house in Toronto was perhaps named from the quotation "Journeys end in lovers meeting", from *Twelfth Night*. See also the entry August 30, 1930, for her comment on J.B. Priestley's play *Journey's End*. SECRETLY MARRIED. The marriage record shows that Chester and Luella were married November 25, 1933, not in 1932, as they told Montgomery. THE ASHTON MEDAL. The Charles Ashton Medal for English was established in honour of a St. Andrew's College graduate of 1920. It is still being awarded. DR. MACDONALD. Dr. Donald Bruce Macdonald (1872–1962), son of J.K. Macdonald who founded St. Andrew's College in 1899, was Headmaster of the college 1900–35, and Chairman of the Board of Governors, 1938–47. THE FROOD MINE. In her manuscript, LMM here misspelled the name as "Froude", echoing the name of a Victorian sage, disciple of Thomas Carlyle. HAULTAIN LIED. Probably Professor Haultain avoided telling the Macdonalds the truth about their son's misdeeds: gambling, and theft to cover gambling losses. STUDY AT HOME. There is no reference in the contemporary journals to Chester's presence in the manse from February 1933 until September 1933, except for LMM's recurring allusions to worry and distress. ERNEST BOGART. About 45 years old at this time, Ernest Charlton Bogart eventually became a K.C. (King's Counsel). He was listed in *Who's Who* until 1949. HOBSON'S CHOICE No choice at all: named for an English liveryman who gave riders no choice in the horses they leased from him.

1933

December 2 LUELLA IS OLDER. Luella was born in May, 1911, Chester in July, 1912. "COMPANIONATE MARRIAGE". In the late 1920s, according to the OED, this term meant that people could contract a legal marriage without intending to have children, and they could divorce by mutual consent, without payment of alimony, if there were no children. Many people saw it as a threat to the traditional marriage. **December 2** WISH I COULD DIE. The original phrase, crossed out, was "wish I were dead". **December 6** GEORGETOWN *HERALD*. Established as the *Herald* in 1867 on the base of earlier Halton County papers, the weekly paper was edited in the 1930s by Joseph Moore. The *Herald* was taken over by Thomson Newspapers, and closed in 1992. **December 7** "THIS DAY THAT SEEMS SO STRANGE...". Slightly misquoted from the Indian poet Sarajini Naidu's "Transience", published in her 1912 collection *The Bird of Time: Songs of Life, Death, and the Spring*. The original runs "To-day that seems so long, so strange, so bitter...". LMM had sent copies of this poem to G.B. Macmillan and Ephraim Weber. She also quotes it in *Mistress Pat*. **December 12** "NEVER MORNING WORE TO EVENING...". Alfred Tennyson, *In Memoriam*, section 6, stanza 2, lines 7, 8. **December 13** THE SIGN OF THE CROSS. A florid spectacle of decadent Rome, complete with Christian martyrs, lions, gladiators, sex, nudity, homosexuality, lesbianism, mass murder and orgies. Cecil B. DeMille employed 4,000 extras in the scene where Rome burns. **December 18** GROTE'S HISTORY OF GREECE. As a young woman LMM read the 12 volumes of George Grote's account of Greek legends and history; she re-read them in the spring of 1921. **December 23** POOR SPLENDID WINGS. Frances Winwar's study of the Pre-Raphaelites (Boston, 1933). LMM misspelled Rossetti as "Rosetti" in her journal. **December 25** MR. AND MRS. MACKINNON. The Rev. Neil MacKinnon (1856–1937) ended his Presbyterian affiliation when he became minister of the United Church of Norval, formed when many Presbyterians joined with Methodists in the Church Union of 1926.

1934

January 6 SHAW STREET. In Parkdale, an older area in the west end of Toronto. **January 8** CAN. LIT. CLUB. Not listed in contemporary Toronto directories, either under its name or under "clubs" or "societies". **January 15** A SEQUEL TO SILVER BUSH. First mention of *Mistress Pat*. **January 16** "THE NIGHT". *Canadian Magazine* published "Night" in January 1935. **February 25** ALBERT OF BELGIUM. King Albert I (1903–1934) had been considered a hero during World War I because he remained in Belgium with his troops in 1914 after Germany occupied much of his country. PUNCH. An English illustrated periodical, running from 1841–1992, was famous for its trenchant caricatures and cartoons. THE KAISER. The militant Wilhelm II, German Emperor (Kaiser) and King of Prussia (1859–1941), a grandson of Queen Victoria, transformed the Balkan crisis of August 1914 into a worldwide conflict. At the end of the war he fled to Holland and finished his life in exile. BACON. Francis Bacon, Lord Verulam (1561–1626), Lord Chancellor of England, essayist, and philosopher. In LMM's college days, Bacon's polished, aphoristic style was taken as a model for polished prose. RENAN. Joseph Ernest Renan (1823–1892), leader of the French school of critical philosophy, contributed to mid-Victorian religious scepticism. His *Vie de Jesus* (1863), presenting Jesus as "an incomparable man" (but not a God), was denounced by churchmen. LMM re-read *The Life of Jesus* several times, and referred to it as "one of my favourite books". **March 31** SECOND PAT BOOK. The entry for January 15, 1934, also mentions beginning work on this book. **April 6** SIRIUS. Chief star in the Greater Dog constellation. **April 9** TRAVEL CLUB OF BRAMPTON. Another name for the Brampton Literary and Travel Club. Their minutes record that on April 8 LMM gave "a humorous Scotch paper". **April 10** DR. WILLIAMS. Dr. C.V. Williams lived in a handsome Georgetown house, since converted into a tearoom. **April 17** GLEN HALL. Glen Williams town hall, down the hill from the Barraclough house. **April 18** LITTLE WOMEN. This movie, which competed with *Cavalcade* for the 1933 Oscar, starred Katharine Hepburn, with Paul Lukas as Professor Bhaer, the shy older man who marries Jo the writer. Set in the American Civil War period, it buoyed Depression spirits. **April 28** HYDERABAD. City in South Central India. EXAMS TO CAMBRIDGE. As elsewhere in the British Empire, students could take the Cambridge entrance examinations in their home countries and, if they passed them, follow the Cambridge course of study. MITZI GREEN (1920–1969). A child star, who played Becky in *Tom Sawyer* (1930); retired at 14, returning in the 1950s to play minor adult roles. **May 9** RELIGIOUS MELANCHOLIA. Medical term used to describe an emotional mental disease marked by clinical depression and unfounded fears of damnation. **May 13** READ HIS SERMON. Presbyterian pride eschewed reading a sermon from a prepared text. **May 21** A BABY GIRL. Luella Macdonald, LMM's first grandchild born May 17. **May 22** MYRLE EARLY. Wife of Tom Early, a farmer near Norval. Chester Early played a part in the Norval drama productions. **May 26** SCARBORO[ugh]. Village at the eastern edge of Toronto, on the Lake Ontario bluffs. **May 29** CHLORAL. Chloral hydrate, or Chloralol, a sedative, used by psychiatrists as a safe hypnotic, relatively nonaddictive. **May 30** W.A. Women's Auxiliary of the Anglican Church. **June 11** DR. BRYDON. W.H. (Bill) Brydon (1881–1962), a prominent and much respected Brampton doctor, who had been in medical school with the Dr. Dafoe who delivered the Dionne quintuplets. Dr. Brydon had married the daughter of the founder of Dale Estates, an important horticultural enterprise in Brampton. His son, also William H. Brydon, later served for a time as Brampton's mayor. ELECTRIC HEAD TREATMENT. Electro-static therapy: little jolts of electricity applied to the skull; not electric convulsive therapy, which is popularly known as "shock treatment". Electric convulsive therapy was not introduced until around 1940, and not introduced into Ontario until 1947. "WHO CAN MINISTER TO A MIND DISEASED?" Shakespeare, *Macbeth*, V, III:41: "Canst thou not minister to a mind diseas'd?" **June 14** PUSSY-GIRL. Pet name for baby Luella; the same pet-name Ewan had used for Maud early in their marriage. HOMEWOOD SANITARIUM IN GUELPH. Established in 1883 as a "Private Asylum for the Insane and an Asylum for Inebriates", The Homewood Retreat was renamed "The Homewood Sanitarium" in 1902. Although provincially licensed and inspected to assure that it met the same standards as the Ontario Provincial institutions for the mentally ill, Homewood was privately owned and operated, and was more expensive than Ontario asylums such as those in Toronto or in London, Ontario. The term "Sanitarium" is an

American alternative to "Sanatorium". Homewood prefers the former spelling. **June 15** HUTTONVILLE. A village south east of Norval, on the way to Brampton. **June 17** VERNE THOMPSON. Lived on a Union farm. Fred Thompson was on the Session at Union. **June 18** VAUGHAN. The township of Vaughan is north-east of Norval, beyond Brampton Township. JIM MCKANE. James McKane was on the Session and the Board of Management of Union Church. **June 19** HIS MEMORY. Loss of memory is a symptom of clinical depression. **June 21** DR. MACKINNON. Dr. Archie L. MacKinnon came to Homewood in 1923 as a University of Toronto medical student, and returned as a full-time physician in 1925. He acquired psychiatric specialty and in 1951 he would become Superintendent. A centre in the present-day Homewood is named after him. In the 1930s most of Dr. MacKinnon's work was with women patients. **June 22** JOHN ISMOND. The Ismond house was in Norval village, west of the bridge over the Credit. **June 27** DR. CLARE. After five years as Superintendent of the Ontario Hospital in Toronto, Dr. Harvey Clare had become Medical Superintendent of Homewood in 1925 and in 1930 was also head of what is now the Ontario Psychiatric Association. In 1933, Dr. Clare had welcomed members of the scientific community to Golden Jubilee celebrations of Homewood's founding, showing them the dining-room, gymnasium, farm, library, music room, treatment rooms and residences, as well as fine sports facilities: bowling alleys, curling rink, and billiard room. Ewan Macdonald was staying at a fine facility, rather under-used in the 1930s because of the Depression. **June 29** SAM KENNEDY. A farmer on the Uxbridge-Leaskdale line. MR. FRASER. Rev. J.R. Fraser, a college friend of Ewan's, was the Presbyterian minister in Uxbridge until 1921; he outdid Ewan in preaching for a call to Columbus, where he remained until Church Union in 1926; he then became a United Church minister. "MY HEART IS SMITTEN...". Psalm 102:4. **July 2** THE WOMAN IN WHITE. Count Fosco is a fat and devious man, foiled and killed in the conclusion of Wilkie Collins's mystery novel, published 1860. **July 3** ASTHMA TABLETS...AN OLD CHINESE RECIPE. The root of Ma huang was used to extract ephedrin, used for asthma. It is still used for bronchial dilation, and to some extent as a heart stimulant. AN IMPACTED BOWEL. Acute constipation is another frequent accompaniment to clinical depression. **July 6** DR. BAUGH. Coming to Homewood from the Ontario Hospital in Brockville, Dr. F.H.C. Baugh served as physician until 1942, when he succeeded Dr. Clare as Superintendent, with Dr. MacKinnon as Assistant Superintendent, until 1951. Dr. Baugh was interested in dietary experiments and took a particular interest in utilizing and beautifying the 55-acre grounds of Homewood. **July 9** AUNT FLORA. Ewan's older half-sister, Mrs. Amos Eagles of Braintree, Mass. The Macdonalds had stayed with her during Ewan's 1919 visit to Boston "nerve specialists". **July 17** JERRY DEAN. Hollywood writer. GOLLOP-MACPHERSON "ROW". Still remembered in Norval as the "War of the Hollyhocks" as the two families competed for supremacy in gardening. **July 22** PINECREST CAMP. The YWCA camp across the Credit River. **July 23** ETHEL DENNIS. The maid at the manse came from Campbellville. She later married Gordon Curry. **July 25** WAR TALK. In Germany, Adolf Hitler had become Chancellor in 1933, and President in 1934. His expansionist, pro-German extremism led to premonitions of the renewal of war between Germany and the Allies—France, Great Britain, and by extension, the British Commonwealth countries. **July 27** A TONIC WITH STRYCH-NINE. Possibly the medication first mentioned in June, 1930, but it could have been anything to stimulate the appetite, which strychnine was used for as well. **July 29** REV. MCKENZIE. Rev. John McKenzie (1874–1949) was Minister at Woodbridge, just north of Brampton, 1930–35. **July 31** THE HONEY HOUSE. One of the McPherson brothers raised bees; the little shed in which he processed the honey was in the back yard, near the Manse garden. **August 2** HINDENBERG (1847–1934). Paul von Hindenberg, German Field Marshal and Chief of Staff WWI; second President of the German Republic since 1925. **August 4** MR. THOMPSON. Rev. James Elmer Thompson, a graduate of Knox College in 1909, served after ordination in Orangeville, Wiarton, and Yorkton, Sask. In 1926 he became an insurance agent in Barrie, but continued to fill in for occasional services. **August 6** U.F.O. United Farmers of Ontario, a political party founded in 1914. LMM had voted for them in provincial elections in the 1920s. **August 11** THE HOUSE OF ROTHSCHILD. George Arliss played a double role in this movie, as the Jewish banker fighting anti-Semitism in the Napoleonic period, and as his descendant, the urbane Baron. **August 12** MR. CHAPMAN. It was common for a retired minister, or a minister from another denomination to fill in, especially during summer, and especially in small towns. **August 15** "FROM THE COOL CISTERNS...". Quoted again from Longfellow's "Hymn to the Night". **August 17** The entry about the blue pills seems to have been interpolated when LMM recopied these entries in 1936. "BLUE PILL". Tablet of blue paste used as a laxative, usually coated with white sugar. An old-fashioned remedy, likely a bile salt compound, no longer in pharmacists' books. MINERAL OIL. Oil derived from petroleum, widely used as a laxative, until physicians realized that, being oily, it dissolved the fat-soluble vitamins in the gut. Now rarely taken by mouth, although occasionally used in enema form. **August 19** MT. PLEASANT. The rural area just east of the Credit valley in which Norval is situated. The Presbyterian churches at Norval and Union were originally served by the Mount Pleasant minister. MR. LAIRD. Murray Laird's father, Alfred Laird. JIM RUSSELL. From the farm whose "hill o' pines" delighted LMM as she worked, writing in her bedroom. See entry of March 1, 1926, in *SJLMM* III. **August 21** MAKE HIM WORSE. Pharmacologists in the 1990s judge that many of the medications would indeed have had a rebounding effect. **August 22** DAWN O'DAY (1918–1993). A movie actress from the age of five, born Dawn Evelyeen Paris, and known successively as Lenore Fondre, Lindley Dawn and Dawn O'Day, she changed her name to "Anne Shirley" after the success of the new movie version of *Anne*. **August 24** CASINO. Cassino is a card game for 2, 3, or 4 people, dating from the 15th century, very popular in the 1930s until eclipsed by gin rummy. "I KNOW A SECRET". Published in *Good Housekeeping*, August 1935, pp. 22–5, 137–9. The story was later adapted for chapters 30–31 of *Anne of Ingleside*, and reprinted in *The Doctor's Secret and Other Stories*, ed. Catherine McLay (Toronto: McGraw-Hill, Ryerson, 1979). In 1982 it was made into a film by Atlantis Films, Toronto, directed by Bruce Pitman from a screenplay by Amy Jo Cooper. MISS ELMO. Ann Elmo worked for the A.F.G. Agency on 5th Avenue, New York. The firm had connections with a Hollywood agent. GOOD HOUSEKEEPING. LMM had sold a story to *Good Housekeeping* in 1900, a poem in

1914, and another poem "Friend o' mine..." in 1936. **August 26** MR. CHAPMAN. An example of a minister from another denomination filling in during summer in a small town. HORNBY. A village 10 km due south of Norval. **August 27** OLD SCRAPBOOK. Now in the Confederation Museum, Confederation Centre of the Arts, Charlottetown. **September 1** EDITH MCKANE. Edith McKane's father was one of the elders at Union Church; her sister later married Ewan's successor, Rev. Norman McMillan. MR. MACKAY. This is likely the Rev. James R. McKay, born in Scotland, who studied at Knox College 1892–4, was ordained in Prince Edward Island in 1894, and served in a number of Maritime parishes before retiring. **September 2** OLIVER HUNTER. The Hunters' house was on the Ashgrove Sideroad. Oliver would be elected elder in 1955, and would remain on the Session for over 30 years. "THOSE WHOM THE GODS LOVE...". From Plautus, *Bacchides*, IV, 7; quoted in Byron as "Whom the gods love die young", *Don Juan*, IV, 12. **September 4** LIZZIE OXTOBY. Member of a farm family in Leaskdale. Their home was next to the Leaskdale manse. See index *SJLMM* II, and the entry for Sept. 24, 1911. O. P. HEGGIE (1876–1936). In the same year as *Anne* he also played in *The Count of Monte Cristo*. HELEN WESTLEY (1879–1942). She had also played in *The House of Rothschild* in the same year. **September 6** VICTORIA. A village about 15 miles north of Norval, in the Caledon hills. TERRA COTTA. A picturesque village on the Credit River, between Victoria and Norval. **September 7** A TURKISH BATH. After a period in a room full of hot air or steam, the bather is massaged. Commercial establishments in Toronto duplicated a form of therapy used at Homewood. **September 9** LESLIE AND RUTH HART. These parishioners are not mentioned in the Leaskdale sections of the Journal. **September 14** WALLIE SIMS. In 1892, Jack Sims of French River was among the young men who formed LMM's circle of friends during her happy time at Park Corner. **September 23** "AND IF I LAUGH...". From Byron, *Don Juan*, Canto IV, 4. **October 2** SIMPSONS PFD. Preferred shares of the company: holders of these shares had a priority for receiving dividends. **October 4** "THE DARKEST DAY...". From William Cowper (1731–1800), "The Needless Alarm", line 132. **October 15** BARBITAL. The first hypnotic barbitate, Diethyl barbituric acid, was introduced in 1903 under the trade name "Veronal". This long-lasting, habit-forming drug in the form of a white powder was replaced by shorter-acting barbiturates. **October 17** JEAN GIFFEN. Daughter of Robert Giffen. **October 18** MEDINAL. It was a prescription drug manufactured by Schering which was used then as a "hypnotic and sedative in nervous insomnia, neurotic state of anxiety, apprehension, melancholia and hysteria". The patent name is acetaminophen, now sold as Tylenol. **October 20** MR. GEGGIE. Knox College. NEWS ABOUT STUART. According to his contemporaries and his own accounts, Stuart at first spent too much time gambling and playing bridge for money in his college residence, and because of his lack of studying, he failed his anatomy examination. LMM was accustomed to having reports that Stuart was a brilliant student. **October 23** MRS. SMITH OF TORONTO. Probably Charlotte Madill Smith, a former missionary, and wife of Rev. David Smith, who served in India from 1906–1937. **October 26** MISS IRWIN. As secretary of the college, Miss Mary Irwin (known to the students of the day as "Black Mary") acted as administrative assistant, dealing with student affairs. **October 27**

EMILY DICKINSON (1830–1886). "THOSE LITTLE ANODYNES...". In "Heart not so heavy as mine", Emily Dickinson uses the phrase "An anodyne so sweet". **November 2** DOMINION STORES. A chain of grocery stores with headquarters at 2 Phoebe Street, established in 1919 with the simultaneous opening of two Toronto stores. It was modelled on the Atlantic & Pacific chain based in New Hampshire. **November 3** DR. [Nathan] GARRICK (b. 1885). Boston nerve specialist, consulted by Ewan Macdonald in 1919. **November 4** MR. DUNN. James Dunn, in his third year at Knox College, class of '36, was born in India and eventually served in British Columbia. **November 5** DR. FLETCHER. The director of the Choral Society came from Nova Scotia. **November 9** THE COUNT OF MONTE CRISTO. Based on the Dumas novel of 1846, the film starred Robert Donat as a man wrongly imprisoned, but returning to wealth and power. MRS. WEBSTER. Widow of the long-time Norval doctor, Dr. William Webster (1842–1928). **November 11** MR. RICHIE. James Moore Ritchie was a student at Knox College, 1933–36. He later went on to become a missionary in Nelson, B.C. **November 12** THE GREEN GABLES MOVIE. *Anne of Green Gables*, an RKO movie, directed by George Nicholls, produced by Kenneth MacGowan from a screenplay by Sam Mintz, previewing in November 1934 and released in 1935. **November 15** GEORGE BROWN. Not a member of the Norval Presbyterian Church. In 1928 Stuart Macdonald had witnessed the terrible accident in which the three Brown children were killed. PRAIRIE MACGUIRE. Adopted daughter of Dr. and Mrs. Webster. The nickname came from Dr. Webster calling her his "little prairie rose". MRS. HEWSON. Bess Hewson (Mrs. Thomas Hewson) was an Anglican, and a member of the Old Tyme group. **November 19** TUMOR. On November 17, she found a swollen lump on her rectum, but it drained and was gone by December 4. PERMIT. Ministers, priests and rabbis (and also journalists) were entitled to apply for a half-price pass on the railways. **November 23** LIBERTY. An American magazine, founded 1924 to join *The Saturday Evening Post* and *Collier's* as a large circulation five-cent weekly; sold in 1931 to the publishers of *True Story* magazine. OLIVER HUNTER. An elder for 30 years who lived on the Ashgrove side road, married to Margaret Townsend of Union. **November 25** MR. GOWLAND. Arthur James Gowland, born in 1913, was a student at Knox College 1934–37. **November 26** THE RADIO COMMISSION. The Commission on Radio Broadcasting, chaired by Sir John Aird, had been appointed by Prime Minister W.L. Mackenzie King in 1928, but its work was delayed by the economic crash of 1929, and opposed by the privately owned Canadian Association of Broadcasters. The Conservative Government, led by R.B. Bennett, passed the Canadian Broadcasting Act, which led to the formation of the Canadian Broadcasting Corporation as a Crown Corporation in 1936. **November 27** CROKINOLE SOCIAL. Crokinole is a game for several players, involving checkers on an octagonal table-sized board. **November 29** PASSEPARTOUTED. Passe-partout is a picture mounting in which glass, matting, picture, and backing are bound together by strips of gummed paper along the edges. FALCONWOOD. The Prince Edward Island Hospital for the Insane (commonly called Falcon Wood, after the family home previously on the property) opened in Charlottetown in 1879. In 1931, fire destroyed all but the east wing of the hospital. The remodelled complex on the site is now called Hillsborough

Hospital. **December 1** "THE UNSPENT JOY". Quoted from "Transience" by Sarojini Naidu. The poem is also quoted December 7, 1933. The poem continues, "Will prove your heart a traitor to its sorrow / And make your eyes unfaithful to their tears". **December 2** MR. WEIR. William Weir, 29 years old at this time, but not yet ordained, became minister at Huntsville in 1936 after ordination. **December 9** MR. ANDREWS. David Keith Andrews (1912–1967) attended Knox College 1933–36, and was ordained as a missionary at Olds and Innisfail, Alberta, 1936. He later did graduate work at Edinburgh and University of Chicago (Ph.D.) and became a Professor at Knox, 1945–67.

1935

January 1 TABLE RAP. Experiments with extra-sensory phenomena had been very popular in LMM's youth in PEI. See *SJLMM II*. THE ECHO. Halifax daily paper, where LMM worked as a proof-reader in 1901–02. **January 6** DR. ROCHESTER. Dr. William M. Rochester, ordained in 1891, did not have a parish at this time. He was an Assembly Officer in 1933, and Editor of *The Presbyterian Record* 1934–35. **January 8** ROBERT REID. Luella's father owned a farm on the outskirts of Georgetown. (See notes for Dec. 30, 1929, and Nov. 9, 1930.) MR. DOWNEY. Donald F. Downey (1903–1964) who practised law in Toronto from 1930 to 1958 and in Newmarket from 1960–64. He later let Chester "buy into" his practice. **January 14** MRS. COULTER. A member of the Brampton Literary and Travel Club, 1934–35. The Rev. Mr. Coulter had served in Neepawa from 1928–33, moved to Brampton 1933–38 and then to St. Catharines 1938–52. **January 15** DWELLER ON MY THRESHOLD. From Edward Bulwer-Lytton's *Zanoni* (1845), a novel LMM read over and over as a child. **January 30** "OH BUT FOR ONE SHORT HOUR...". Recalls Tennyson, "For one short hour to see / The souls we loved...". *Maud*, II, iv, 3. **January 31** THE BARRETTS OF WIMPOLE STREET. Frederic March, Norma Shearer, and Charles Laughton add psychological subtlety to this excellent film version of the Browning story. LMM misspelled the name as "Barrets". **February 5** GRUM. Perhaps a spelling error, or perhaps a deliberate combination of "grim" and "glum". **February 6** CLARENCE ANDERSON. A Union family, connected with the McKane family. **February 7** MRS. JOE HUNTER. The Hunters were a Union family. **February 8** MR. MCCLELLAND. John McClelland (1888–1951), senior partner of the publishing firm McClelland & Stewart of Toronto, had been LMM's friendly and supportive publisher since she broke with L.C. Page and Co. of Boston in 1919. WINDSHIELD OPEN. In early cars, the windshield could be cranked up so as to let passengers enjoy fresh air. **February 12** "LIKE YOUR UNCLE LEANDER". Leander Macneill developed a serious nervous disorder (characterized by tremors) at the end of his life. **February 13** OAKVILLE. A village on the shore of Lake Ontario, west of Toronto, now fused with Metropolitan Toronto. **February 16** PROVERBS IS HARDER ON THE FOOL. In the Bible, the Book of Proverbs mentions fools in chs. 1, 10, 12, 14, e.g., "The way of the fool is right in his own eyes", Proverbs 12:15. **March 3** THE CHILD MARTYR. A recital piece by May Anderson, about a child who dies to protect her father. "THE WATCHMAN". First published in *Everybody's*, December 1910, this was the title poem in LMM's book of poetry, by the same name, published in 1916 by McClelland & Stewart.

March 5 LEPAGE REAL ESTATE COMPANY. This firm, established in Toronto in 1913, became a national realtor in the 1930s. LMM misspells "Lepage" as "Lepage". **March 7** SAL VOLATILE. An aromatic solution of ammonium carbonate and ammonium bicarbonate, used as smelling salts to prevent fainting, or as a general stimulant. MISS SMELLIE. Lived with her brother on a farm on the 6th line outside Norval. CHRISTADELPHIAN. An evangelical sect whose members practised speaking in unknown tongues, like the Apostles after Pentecost. MR. FERGUSON. Rev. J.A. Ferguson was the minister in Norval/Union, 1913–1920; he moved on to Duff's Church in Seaforth. TOM MACDONALD. Thomas F. McDonald was on the Board of Management at Union. PARISH HALL. The Anglican Parish Hall opened in 1928, with a concert and an old time dance. The Hall was used by the whole Norval community for joint entertainments. **March 8** MR. LEPAGE. Albert E. LePage was born in Charlottetown in 1887. He became one of the Macdonalds' neighbours on Riverside Drive. Lepage is credited with revolutionizing real estate sales by taking people around to see houses, as against simply listing available properties. **March 9** A NEW ANNE BOOK. First mention of *Anne of Windy Poplars*, published the next year. **March 12** THE HUMBER. This river rises north of Toronto and empties into Lake Ontario, cutting a ravine through the western section of Toronto. BLOOR. A major east-west road in Toronto. **March 15** HODDER & STOUGHTON. LMM's British publisher since 1921. Her first British publisher was Pitman, followed by Constable. **March 21** LITERARY AND ARTISTIC INSTITUTE OF FRANCE. *L'Institut de France* is made up of 5 academies, including *L'Académie des inscriptions et belles lettres*. In being made a member of this academy, LMM was receiving one of France's highest honours. It was an even greater honour for a foreigner to be made a member. In 1997, there were 45 members of this academy (3 of them women), including the most revered of French authors. **March 28** MRS. COWAN (of Toronto). Wife of an executive of the Loblaw grocery stores. **April 2** ELMIRA. A village 37 miles north-west of Norval, in the Kitchener area dominated by German immigrants. **April 4** DR. PAUL. The son of the late Dr. Paul who was buried on Feb. 22, 1935. **April 7** MR. KAYE OF BOSTON AND OMAGH. Rev. Horace Kaye, born in Yorkshire, England, was in Egypt during World War I as a mechanic. Ordained in 1927 at Auburn Theological Seminary, he ministered in Boston and Omagh and later in Dromore, Normanby, Colborne, Lakeport, and Brighton. He retired in Peterborough. **April 8** DR. MCKERROLL OF VICTORIA CHURCH TORONTO. Rev. Donald Thomas McKerrell (1870–1943) was at Victoria Church in the Swansea district of Toronto 1910–37, and in Niagara 1937–41. **April 9** MRS. HOARE. Mrs. Joseph Hoare was a Sunday School teacher in Union Church. **April 10** CLAUDE MCLAUGHLIN. A farmer who lived 1½ miles below Norval village on Adamson Street (now Winston Churchill Boulevard). **April 11** MRS. DAVIES. "Wee Annie" (Mrs. George Davis) was a Sunday School teacher and caretaker, and took part in the plays. JEAN. Mrs. Davis's daughter later went to Wheaton College and moved to the United States. **April 14** RUCTION. Colloquialism: an uproar or quarrel. **April 15** MCKANES. The McKanes were among the first settling families in Union. James McKane was on the Board of Management. **April 18** CHELTENHAM. A village 10 miles north of Norval. **April 19** ANDREW MACDONALD. Andrew Macdonald was on the Session at Union. PACKAWAY. Localism: a small valise. ROBINSONS. Laura and Nelson both took part in Old Tyme Concerts. Nelson had been an Anglican, but he turned Presbyterian when he married. **April 21** MR. BOYLE. Rev. Alexander McKenzie Boyle (1876–1950) was at Knox College 1900–04. He was at St. Matthew's Church in Toronto 1927–37, moving to Blythe, Auburn, Belgrave, and Smith's Hill 1937–42. CANDIDATES. The successful candidate was Rev. Norman McMillan, who remained in Norval/Union 1935–1938.

List of deletions

All the entries that have been deleted, either in part or in total, are listed below. (The last entry of Volume 3 was August 6, 1929.) In this list, an asterisk after the date indicates that the deletion is only partial. In the text, three dots indicate a deletion of less than a sentence, and four dots indicate a compete sentence or more has been deleted. When four dots come at the end of a paragraph, this usually means that a subsequent paragraph, often on a different subject, has been deleted.

Volume 7 ends with the entry of Dec. 21, 1929. Volume 8 ends with the entry of Nov. 26, 1933. This is marked in the text.

1929: Aug. 17; Sept. 17; 22*; 23, 24* 27, 28*, 29*; Oct. 2*, 4, 13* **1930**: Jan. 15, 29; Feb. 15*; Mar. 1*, July 2; Aug. 2, 3, 7*, 18*; Dec. 31 **1931**: Jan. 10; Feb. 3*, 8*, 9, 27*; Mar. 2*, 3, 21, 27, 29, 30; Apr. 4*, 7*, 14*, 17, 18*, 20*, 26*; May 19*, June 1*, 2*, 8*, 29; July 11*,18*, 19*; Aug. 31*; Oct. 10*; Nov. 21, 27*; Dec. 4*, 19*, 20 **1932**: Jan. 9*; Feb. 7*, 11*; Mar. 12; Apr. 16*, 20*, 30*; May 3*; June 7, 10*; July 10*: Aug. 27*; Sept. 14*, 15*; Nov. 13* **1933**: Jan. 22*, 28*; Feb. 8, 10, 17*; Mar. 19; Apr. 8*, 19*; July 6*, 12; Aug. 28; Sept. 27*; Oct.10*, 29, 31*; Nov. 24*, 25*, 26*; Dec. 14*, 16, 24*, 29* **1934**: Jan. 5, 9, 11*, 12, 13, 14, 17, 21, 22, 24; Feb. 11*; Mar. 30; Apr. 1, 11*,12, 24; May 9*, 12, 15, 23, 24*, 27, 30*, 31*; June 1, 4*, 5, 7, 8, 9*, 11*, 14*, 16*, 18*, 25*, 28*, 29*; July 1*, 3*, 4, 6*, 8*, 10, 11*, 12*, 14* , 16, 18*, 19, 21*, 23*, 25*, 26*, 28, 29*, 30*, 31*; Aug. 1*, 2*, 3, 8, 9, 10*, 12*, 13*, 16*, 20*, 22*, 27*, 28, 29; Sept. 4*, 10, 14*, 16*, 17*, 18*, 21*, 25*, 26*, 27*, 29, 30*; Oct.2*, 5*, 6*, 7*, 8*, 9*, 11*, 13*, 14*, 16*, 21*, 24*, 27*, 28*, 29*, 30, 31*; Nov. 4*, 5*, 6*, 7, 8*, 10, 12*, 13, 14, 17*, 18, 21*, 24*, 25*, 26*, 28*, 29*,30*; Dec. 3*, 4* 5, 6*, 8, 9*, 17*, 19*, 20*, 21, 22, 24*, 25*, 26, 27, 28*, 29, 30*, 31* **1935**: Jan. 1*, 2*, 3*, 6*, 8*, 11*, 14*, 15* 16*, 17, 18*, 19*, 23*, 24*, 28*, 29; Feb. 1, 2, 3, 4, 6*, 7*, 11, 12*, 15*, 18*, 23*, 24*, 27*; Mar. 3*, 4, 7*, 10*, 11*, 12*, 13*, 15*, 16*, 18, 19*, 23*, 24*, 25*, 27, 28*; Apr. 3*, 9*, 12, 17*, 21*, 22*, 23, 24*.

Mistakes in Montgomery's date-headings:

The first date below is the date Montgomery gives for an entry; the second is the date that it actually was, according to a perpetual calendar.

Monday, Aug. 11, 1929, should have been Sunday, Aug. 11, 1929.
Friday, Oct. 22, 1929, should have been Tuesday, Oct. 22, 1929.
Wednesday, Mar. 6, 1930, should have been Thursday, Mar. 6, 1930.
Friday, Mar. 8, 1930, should have been Saturday, Mar. 8, 1930.
Wednesday, Feb. 11, 1932, should have been Thursday, Feb. 11, 1932.
Monday, Feb. 28, 1932, should have been Sunday, Feb. 28, 1932.
Sunday, Mar. 24, 1932, should have been Thursday, Mar. 24, 1932.
Monday, June 24, 1932, should have been Friday, June 24, 1932.
Friday, July 10, 1932, should have been Sunday, July 10, 1932.
Tuesday, Sept. 24, 1932, should have been Saturday, Sept. 24, 1932.
Tuesday, Dec. 23, 1932, should have been Friday, Dec. 23, 1932.
Tuesday, Jan. 6, 1933, should have been Friday, Jan. 6, 1933.
Saturday, Feb. 17, 1933, should have been Friday, Feb. 17, 1933.
Wednesday, Apr. 8, 1933, should have been Saturday, Apr. 8, 1933.
Friday, Sept 12, 1933, should have been Tuesday, Sept. 12, 1933.
Sunday, Dec. 2, 1933, should have been Sunday, Dec. 3, 1933.
Tuesday, Dec. 22, 1933, should have been Friday, Dec. 22, 1933.
Monday, Jan. 2, 1934, should have been Tuesday, Jan. 2, 1934.
Tuesday, Oct. 25, 1934, should have been Thursday, Oct. 25, 1934.
Friday, Feb. 19, 1935, should have been Tuesday, Feb. 19, 1935.

Appendix A

Summerside, P.E.I.
July 8, 1909

My dear nephew:—

Having met your dear mother on a visit to her native home after an absence of twenty years you can scarcely imagine how delighted we all were to see her and to hear of all her family. I think that she is wonderfully preserved after all the different phases of life that she has been called upon to pass through. Her children must have been very good and kind to her, or she would not look so well, and retain her old happy, cheery way as she does. As a bride she was the prettiest creature I ever saw and your father a very fine-looking man. This I write by way of making acquaintance with you. In the course of our talk your mother said you had often expressed a wish to hear something of your mother's family history and so far as my old age will allow me I will go back for five generations and give a short and very imperfect sketch of your mother's ancestors on her father's side.

My Grandfather John Macneill, came to the Island with the first Chief Justice. His ancestors had followed the house of Stewart till their defeat at Culloden and when one of their adherents got the appointment of Judge of the Island he cast in his lot with them and came here from Argyllshire. The Island was then almost a forest. He married Margaret Simpson, daughter of William Simpson, who had emigrated from Morayshire, Scotland, a man of rare ability and Christian character, whose descendants filled a large space in the moral, intellectual and religious development of the country, and who were strongly impressed with the idea that they were above the common herd. So this being a family failing, you will pardon my egotism, seeing from whom I have descended.

They had a family of nine sons and three daughters, of whom my respected father, your great grandfather, was the eldest and I think the most talented in the connection. Pardon my egotism. You see I have warned you and you will be prepared for all that follows.

At that time in the history of the Island schools and teachers were very scarce but by dint of study and perseverance he fitted himself for teaching which he did first in Nova Scotia and on the Island. Then he went to study law in Haliburton's office in Halifax. But money in the early days of our history was hard to get so he abandoned the idea of law and came to the Island and went into shipbuilding and trading in partnership with Mr. Townsend, a gentleman from England who had received from George the Third, King of England, a grant of land for his services in the British army.

My father married his granddaughter, a daughter of Captain John Townsend, who had distinguished himself by an act of bravery for which he had received from the King a gold medal about six inches in circumference on which was inscribed his services to his country. He had been employed by the British Government to carry gold from the coast of Africa to the Bank of England. Getting short of water he sent two men on shore for water. The savages took them and cut their tongues out and swam out in hundreds and climbed up the sides of the ship. He had no firearms but stood on the quarter deck with his cutlass and killed them as soon as they reached the deck and took two of the savages captive. He put them in irons and brought them to England. This was all stamped on the medal. Before this he had been taken prisoner and his ship run down at the time of the war by a French privateer and during his imprisonment he had his picture painted by a French artist which is still in the family. Then came an exchange of prisoners and he got his liberty and followed his father to P.E. Island where he got into business with Mr. Cambige (?) going as Master of his ships to England and the West Indies. He took the yellow fever and died and was buried on the island of Antigua. The ship, with all his nautical instruments and gold medal, was run down by a French privateer. It was a great loss. His descendants would have prized it very much. My mother and her two brothers were then brought to New London by their grandfather where he had this grant of land, which he had named Park Corner after their estate in England.

My father was called in early life to take an active part in political affairs. He served twenty years in the local legislature, sixteen of which he was Speaker. He served without pay for a number of years as we then had no revenue or very little. That was the time we had patriots. That time has passed away and the loaves and fishes seem to have taken the place of the love of country. He was the Commissioner of Public Works for all the north side of Queen's county and he presided over the county for twenty years as a magistrate. He married all the people in the vicinity, wrote all the wills, settled all the disputes, and was an elder in the church where his advice was very much prized.

But I must speak of my sainted mother, left at home with six girls and five boys to manage, to clothe and send to school. The task was Herculean. She had splendid sons. There was none of them born tired. How could they be with such a mother? She encouraged them all in their work, went to the fields with them, helped them in all their labor and play, recited poetry to them, told them tales of England that she had heard from her mother, wept when they wept, laughed when they laughed.

> She tried each art, reproved each dull delay,
> Allured to brighter worlds and led the way.

She, as I have told you, had two brothers, whose families have left their mark in the country for many ideal traits of character, two sons in one family being clergymen.

I have now brought you down to your grandfather's place in the family. If you have been able to follow me through all the windings you will see that your great-great grandfather was John Macneill of Argyllshire, Scotland, and your great grandfather William Macneill of Cavendish and your grandfather W.S. Macneill, and as you have the Mac on both sides you will be able to appreciate the tale of your mother's ancestors.

My oldest brother was John Macneill, father of "Captain John" of Michigan. He married Anne Simpson, still keeping up the relationship. He was a most beautiful character. He left home when very young, was apprenticed to a ship carpenter, went to Upper Canada and settled on the Canadian side of the river that divided the countries. Could not be persuaded that he could do better on the other, so he was a true Briton. Of his family your mother will be able to tell you. He spent part of his age in California. I know that he was a man of sterling character, highly respected in the community where he lived. Then comes your grandfather W.S. Macneill, a man popular with all classes and loved in his home. His mother when dying, in bidding him farewell, said, "You never said worse to me than 'mother' " He left home when very young and went to the lumber woods of New Brunswick, made money, came home, bought a farm, and went into farming and ship-building, trading to Newfoundland and the different provinces. He was a born Liberal and when the country threw off the Family Compact he took up the side of the tenant league and helped to free this country from the tyranny of landlordism. He was returned four times, but the Opposition started the question of having the Bible put out of the schools and the Liberal Government was broken up, the Catholics all going on the one side. When very young he had been sent to the Charlottetown Academy which was then but an inferior seat of learning, out of which has grown our efficient Prince of Wales College, second to none in the Provinces. But with what he learned there, and his own natural ability, he was able to take his place among the best. He then gave up politics, sold his farm and you know the rest.

He married Anne Maria Jones, whose father had emigrated from Wales and his wife from England. Their daughter, your grandmother (A.M. Jones) still lives, at a very advanced age, a very clever woman, the mother of four sons and seven daughters, all living but two. Your two uncles in Dakota and Colin in Ottawa will have historians long after I have ceased to write, and among them I will expect my nephew, Harold MacDougall, to take a prominent place.

My next brother is Thomas, a man of great strength of character and strong religious convictions, and very rigid in his condemnation of any deviation from the paths of truth and uprightness. He was a very apt scholar and learned all the district school teacher could teach him. He was then sent to the clergyman of the district to learn the languages but the good old man was too indolent to take any trouble with him and he left and went into a store at the age of 14. The merchant did a large business in buying up grain and shipping it to New Brunswick and Halifax in the fall. Money was scarce at that time. There were no factories and very little business done. My brother used to relate a little incident which will show you the state of the country at that time and the pluck of the boy. Having (word in original undecipherable) all the accounts, the grain shipped and the money received, now the returns for the goods must be sent. There were no banks and no way of sending it only by (another indecipherable word) and that involved a trip to Charlottetown, a distance of some seventy or eighty miles, as there were at that time no bridges over the different streams of the country. The merchant did business at the harbor of New London and by crossing there you shortened the journey by twenty miles. The boy got the merchant to write to the officer in charge, got a canvas bag and put the money in it, got across the harbor in a canoe, walked six miles, got a horse from his father and got on the horse's back with the money. We had no paper money in those days. He arrived in time, handed the letter to the officer in charge, who read the letter, looked at the boy and said, "Down with your dust." He counted his treasure. There were in the bag about 6,000. I write this to give you a little idea of the state of the country at that time but everything has changed since then and business can be transacted without any trouble. But I proceed with my account, trusting to your patience and good breeding to read.

My brother after a time went to work in the lumber woods of New Brunswick as there was a very large business down there by two large rich firms from Scotland. The Cunards of line steamer fame and the (name indecipherable) brought large ships from the old country and loaded them with lumber and it was a boon to the young men of the Island who got work they could not get on the Island.

He came back, went to farming, and married Charlotte Simpson, a granddaughter of the first Simpson I have mentioned. He filled a great many important positions in his country. He was a magistrate, employed in settling up the land after it had passed out of the hands of the proprietors. He was a very successful farmer, an elder in the church in which he took an active interest, and left money to pay his share in the salary for several years after his death. He left a family of two sons and one daughter. His other son and daughter died.

I now take up the history of my fourth brother James. He was a little different from the others, possessed of a very sensitive and retiring disposition. He shunned publicity. He had a great brain, wanted to know the ins and outs of everything and often expressed his opinion in poetry of no mean order. He had a great desire to go to sea. He got books on navigation and often studied by the firelight in the kitchen when the rest of us were amusing ourselves in another room. When a boy he would climb to the top of the main mast of any ship he put his foot on. He knew the name of every rope and spar on the ship and taught me how to box the compass when I was only five years old. I have often thought what a pity that they did not try to get him an education which would have fitted him to carry out his natural love for the sea, for there was no doubt it was inherent in him, his grandfather being such a navigator. But my mother, having lost her father in childhood on account of his seafaring life had such a horror of it that she discouraged it altogether and I have thought that it blighted his life to a certain extent but I think he lived a happy life. He and his wife, Jane Harker, the daughter of an honest Scotchman from the land of the heather, had a family of two sons and two daughters, very clever and talented women, one the wife of a member of parliament. The one son living was proposed for a member but refused to act, but is the coming man. Of my brother I will just say that he lived where his fathers lived, died where they died and was saved.

Next comes my youngest brother Alexander, playmate of my childhood, friend of my riper years. Oh, how everything good and kind comes up before me as I go back to the scenes of childhood's happy hours. He tried to make you feel happy and contented and never was it my lot to find in him "a deed ungentle or a word unkind." I was very much attached to my brothers. He and my brother James often carried me to school when I got tired, as we had almost two miles to walk, and I think that physically, morally and mentally they were above the average. But I have left my subject. You will please excuse a childish old woman!

Alexander lived at the old home, took charge of his father and mother, and kept them comfortable in their old age. They lived to be 89 and 82 years. He married Lucy Woolner, sister to your uncle Benjamin, a very clever woman who had been educated in England. They had a family of three sons and three daughters. The eldest, the Rev. L.G. Macneill was a very talented man but from overwork is a complete wreck of his former self (so very sad). His second son is a successful farmer. His third son is a very talented lawyer in Vancouver. His granddaughter, L.M. Montgomery, whom he brought up, is a very talented author and poet. She has achieved a niche in the temple of fame. His oldest daughter married John Campbell a descendant of the Townsends. Two of her girls are teachers. The youngest married John Montgomery, a member of Parliament who died, and left her a widow with six children. She has educated two of them, being very successful teachers. I have now given you a little history of my brothers and I will conclude this with the words of a great poet.

My brothers these, the same our native shore,
One house contained us and one mother bore.

Mrs. Mary Lawson

Added from another letter:—
....My eldest sister married the honorable Jeremiah Simpson, a grandson of the first Mr. Simpson. They had seven sons, all married but one and have large families. There are ten clergymen in the family. All are men to be trusted and respected and who take their place in everything that is for the moral and religious development of the country. One son has a son who is a minister in a Baptist church in Chicago, another a professor in a college in Arkansas. The eldest daughter married John C. Clark. They have a family of seven who are all graduates of colleges. Two are missionaries in India. One is a medical missionary in the northwest and another a professor of forestry in a large company in Vancouver.

My second sister Helen married Alexander Macneill, no relation of her own but a man of a big soul, kind and generous. He scorned meanness and would almost lay down his life for a friend. He was a very successful man in his business and died comparatively young. His wife, my sister, had the beauty and brains of the family but she had a large family and it required all her exertions to attend to them which she faithfully did and left behind her a family of six daughters and two sons who have all been distinguished for honesty and uprightness of character and have helped to make the world better for having lived in it.

My sister Anne died unmarried in early youth, much regretted. Then comes my next sister Jane, who married Duncan McKenzie and moved to Michigan. She died there years ago and left three daughters and two sons. Of her family I knew very little as they left the Island in childhood. She was a person of rare kindness of heart, gentle and retiring. She never did an unkind action or suspected anyone of such, she was so good herself. Then comes your humble servant, myself, a widow for the last twenty-five years, baffed about from the storms of misfortune. Once having a good husband and a good home I reached out my hand to help many. I am now in my eighty-fifth year and will soon be where tempests cease to beat and billows cease to roar.

Mrs. Mary Lawson

Appendix B

The Montgomerys of Prince Edward Island

There is no name more closely identified with the early settlement, development, political and social history and educational progress of Prince Edward Island than that of Montgomery. The family traditions assert and the claim is well authenticated by history that the Montgomery's came from France in the train of a French princess who married a Scottish king and soon spread over the United Kingdom. The name is a French name.

The first English speaking settler in Princetown, P.E. Island, was Hugh Montgomery, who with his wife, Mary (MacShannon) Montgomery, settled there in the year 1769. He settled at Fox Point and proceeded to carve out a home. His family consisted of six, three sons and three daughters. John married Miss Anne Hooper and founded the Bedeque family, where James, Thomas and Norman, three of his grandsons, still reside, prosperous and intelligent farmers and enterprising citizens, loyal to the church of their fathers, the Presbyterian, as well as to the state. Hugh married Miss Christy Penman of Port Hill and was the father of "Little Donald," a successful farmer and prominent public man who represented the first electoral district of Queen's County for a number of years in the provincial legislature of Prince Edward Island.

Helen married Archibald Ramsay of Beech Point and to them were born eight children, five sons and three daughters; John Ramsay, the oldest son, bought Rose Hill from his uncle and moved across Richmond Bay. He represented Prince County for a number of years in the Provincial legislature, was a prominent magistrate, filled the office of high sheriff and other important positions, and was highly respected. Donald Ramsay, the fourth son was for years a member of the Legislative Council of the province. Mary and Margaret both married MacEwens of Campbellton, New London, and Helen married R.S. Patterson, a Presbyterian minister of Bedeque.

Margaret Montgomery married Capt. McLeod by whom she had one daughter. The Captain was drowned and she married Thomas Archibald, a Scotch merchant and ship-builder, of Rose Hill. The latter sold Rose Hill to his nephew John Ramsay, and went to Lisbon, Portugal, where he died. The other daughter of Hugh Montgomery died young.

Donald Montgomery married Nancy Penman, oldest daughter of George Penman, Paymaster of the garrison who under Colonel Rollo took possession of this Island (then named St. Jean) after the fall of Louisburg in 1758. He afterwards moved to Port Hill where he continued to reside till the time of his death. Donald Montgomery was renowned as the first magistrate appointed in Prince County and represented the county for over thirty-five consecutive years in the House of Assembly of the colony. He always resided in the ancestral home in Fox Point, a home famed far and wide for its unbounded hospitality. Governor Fanning during his term of office made Fox Point his summer resort, and during one of his visits the inhabitants built a new school and called it the Fanning Grammar School in honour of the Governor. He made the district a present of two valuable lots of land and his daughter, Lady Cumberland, in her will bequeathed the school district of Princetown several valuable properties in Charlottetown from which a comfortable revenue is received annually, the bequest having been made on account of the school having been named after her father.

To Donald and Nancy (Penman) Montgomery were born seventeen children, nine sons and eight daughters, sixteen of whom grew to maturity, and they had one hundred and eighteen grandchildren. Of their children, Archibald married Mary Ramsay and settled in Port Hill where his grandson resides on the old homestead, an intellectual and prosperous farmer. Hugh married Miss Ann Owen and John married Miss Eliza Hamilton of Scotland. Those two brothers moved to Dalhousie, N.B., where they established a large ship-building and lumber business. John represented Restigouche county in the New Brunswick legislature for a great number of years and his son after him.

George married Miss Ramsay and moved to Miramichi, N.B. where he died soon after the great fire of 1825. James Townsend Montgomery married Rose McCary, first daughter of Rev. John McCary, first missionary to Newfoundland, having been sent there by John Wesley. After seven years spent in Newfoundland he returned to Ireland and there was married. He with his family sailed from Dublin on board the ship "Hannah" bound for Quebec. The ship was cast ashore in a gale on Cape Rossier, Gaspé Peninsula, and became a total wreck. The captain chartered a schooner and put the passengers and their luggage on board and again started for their destination but encountering another storm in the gulf was again stranded at "The Ponds," a place midway between Malpeque and New London Harbours.

Donald married first Miss Annie Murray and second Mrs. Louisa Gall (née Cundall) of Charlottetown. He represented Princetown in the local legislature of the Province from 1838 to 1862 when the Legislative council became elective. He then resigned his seat in the Lower House for the first district of Queens in which body he sat as president until 1874. When the Island entered the confederation he was appointed to the Senate of Canada, which position he held till the time of his death, having served his country faithfully for fifty-four consecutive years in the legislative bodies, never missing one session, a record that is unbroken in the annals of the Dominion. "Big Donald," as he was lovingly and familiarly called, is still honored and remembered and will continue to be for the years to come, his name a household word. He had the courage of his convictions, was a staunch and consistent Liberal-Conservative, a true friend, a good citizen and a devout and practical Christian. He had no superiors and very few peers.

Edward married Miss Campbell of Lot 16 and always resided in Malpeque, following farming as his chosen profession. Robert and William, twin brothers, and the youngest of the family, moved in early life to New Richmond, Quebec, and established a large lumber business which is still carried on by R.H. Montgomery, Robert's son, who was also a successful farmer and merchant.

Mary married Rev. Mr. Pidgeon, the first Presbyterian (Query, Congregationalist?) sent to the Island from the mother country, he having been sent out by the London missionary society.

Helen married first Mr. Woodside of Malpeque and second George Owen of Little March.

Barbara married Archibald Woodside of Malpeque. Christy married William Cuthbert, a merchant of Scotland who carried on business at New Richmond. Ann married William Murray of Bedeque, a farmer and prominent elder in the Presbyterian church. Elizabeth married James Campbell of New London, father of Hon. William Campbell, for many years a member of Parliament and executive councillor, Commissioner of public works and incumbent of other important offices for a long period. Jane married Benjamin Murray, a farmer of Bedeque, and Margaret died young. There being as above stated one hundred and eighteen first cousins it would make this sketch entirely too long to follow them any further in detail and reference will be made only to the family on the old homestead which is occupied by the children of the fifth generation.

Fox Point has been the scene of many happy and historic events. The Tuplin family landed there from England over seventy years ago and accepted the true Highland hospitality extended to them by James T. Montgomery and family, whereby a lifelong friendship was established. In the great gale of 1851, known as "the Yankee storm," thirty-eight fishing schooners were cast on shore in front of the old farm and out of them all not a life was lost. The crews not only took possession of the old home but literally filled the large barns and outbuildings and were fed and cared for without charge until they could get away from home.

To James T. and Rose Montgomery were born ten children, eight of whom are living but scattered all over the world, from far-off Persia in the east to the Golden Gate in the west....

[George Montgomery next lists, without dates, the births, marriages, and deaths of the families of Hugh and Mary MacShannon Montgomery, Donald and Nancy Penman Montgomery, Donald and Annie Murray Montgomery, Donald and Louisa Gall Montgomery, Hugh John and Clara Macneill Montgomery, and Hugh John and Mary Ann McCrae Montgomery.]

Appendix C

The Haunted Spring

Gaily in the mountain glen
The hunter's horn did ring
As the milk-white doe escaped his bow
Down by the Haunted Spring.
In vain his silver horn he wound
'Twas echo answered back,

For neither groom nor baying hound
Was on the hunter's track.
In vain he sought the milk-white doe
That made him stray and 'scaped his bow,
For save himself no living thing
Was by the silent Haunted Spring.

The purple heath-bells blooming fair
Their fragrance round did fling
As the hunter lay at the close of day
Down by the Haunted Spring.
A lady fair in robe of white
To greet the hunter came.

She kissed a cup with jewels bright
And pledged him by his name.
"Oh lady fair," the hunter cried,
Be thou my love, my blooming bride"
A bride that well might grace a king
Fair lady of the Haunted Spring.

In the fountain clear she stooped
And forth she drew a ring
And that loved knight his faith did plight
Down by the Haunted Spring.
And since that day so minstrels say
The hunter ne'er was seen.

And legends tell how he doth dwell
Among the hills so green.
But still the milk white doe appears
and wakes the peasants' evening fears
While distant bugles faintly ring
Around the lonely haunted spring.

[Author unknown]

Appendix D

Speaking of playing "ball"—what fun we had. The game was somewhat complicated. It was not baseball nor was it like any of the ball games played today. Perhaps it is no longer played anywhere. But this was the game as we played it on the old school playground in the last decade of the 19th century.

Two "captains" were chosen. These captains picked their sides, turn about, choosing the good players first, and so on down. Nate and John were never on the same side. They were the best players when it came to sending a ball flying wide with a mighty "crack." So if Capt. A picked Nate Capt. B snapped up John. For the same reason Annie Stewart and I were seldom on the same side. We were both experts in "shifting hands"—a manoeuvre to be described later –and we were generally picked next to Nate and Jack.

When the sides had been picked it must be settled which side should be "in" first. Captain A. took the bat by the handle and tossed it to B who caught and held it by the handle. Then A clasped it above B's hand. B removed his hand and placed it above A's. This was repeated until there was no room for another hand. Then the one whose hand was uppermost—say A—had to swing the bat three times around his head without dropping it. Occasionally he dropped it, the last space on the handle having been too narrow to permit a firm grip. In that case "B's" side went in.

The players then took up their position on the ground where four "stops" have been marked thus:—

2

3   X   1

Y

O

The captain took the bat first. He stood on Y, with the bat—a flat one with a blade about three inches wide and a foot and a half long, made out of hardwood— held at an angle over his right shoulder. The bowler stood at X. Behind the batsman stood one of B's side to catch missed balls; the rest of B's men scattered over the ground as "scouts."

Each batsman had three balls. He did not have to "try" for any of the balls if they did not suit him. If he "tried" for the ball and missed the scout behind might catch it and if he caught it the batter was "out." The scout might catch it "on the fly" or on "the bounce," when it rebounded from the ground. "First" and "second" bounce but "third" bounce was not. The same rule applied to balls caught anywhere by any of the scouts. Long and bitter were the disputes which often took place as to whether a ball had been caught on the 2nd or 3rd bounce.

If the batter did not attempt to strike the ball he could not be caught out but if the ball struck his bat anywhere when he had not tried he was "out."

The bowlers always tried to give good balls. There was no object in their doing anything else, since the batsman did not have to try for a ball he did not like it merely prolonged the time. Some balls were too low, some too high; some too far to one side; but these were accidents. The bowler did his best to throw a straight ball.

When the batsman saw a ball he thought he could hit he struck at it. Most of the players, holding the bat at the right shoulder, sent the ball to the left or straight ahead. But Annie Stewart and I could "change hands like a monkey" as Everett Laird used to say. That is, we could change the direction of bat and blow at the last moment by a quick turn of the wrist and send the ball flying to an entirely unthought of place—we could even step aside and send it flying backwards. As we always chose to send it where scouts were few or unready we were rarely caught out.

If the ball was caught on the fly or bounce the batsman was out. If it were not he could, if he liked, drop his bat and run to the first "stop." If he got there safely he might continue on to second, stop, then to third, then possibly home. But he must keep on running to do this. If he "stopped" at any "stop" he had to stay there. If between stops he was struck by the ball thrown by a scout he was out. If he were not struck but the ball passed in front of him he was "crossed." He then had to return to the preceding stop and run to next stop again. If the same scout could salvage the ball in time to "cross" him a second time from the same stand he was "out." This last happened seldom but sometimes it did. If he escaped all these dangers—as he did seven times out of ten—and got safely to a stop he stayed there unless he was lucky enough to get clear around "home." This only happened to players like Nate and Jack who could send the ball so far that they could run clear around the diamond before the scouts could get the ball. If they did this they retired into the background until their turn came around again, for a side was "in" until every player was out.

The danger in striking a ball too vigorous a blow was that it might go over the fence—either the fence of the playground to the right or the fence of Grandfather's field across the road. This was "out"—*unless* the ball could be reached by a scout lying flat down and stretching his arm under the fence. Again there were many bitter disputes when a too zealous scout was suspected of having given the ball a little push to send it further on!

The illogical part of all this was that, there being no fence across the road, a muscular batsman might send the ball flying down the hill and yet not be "out." He would then have time to *walk* insultingly around the diamond before the breathless scouts returned the ball. Nate and Jack were able to do this repeatedly; it was not easy to strike the ball directly down the road. The slightest curve and it went over the fence. Many a ball was lost altogether in the wood or field.

These balls, I may say, like our bats were home made. We took a cork and wound home-made yarn tightly around it until the ball was the right size. Then we took needle and yarn and "darned" it all over tightly until it was solid and would not ravel or unwind. There was a "knack" in making balls. I could make a very good one. These balls were very resilient and "bounced" beautifully.

To resume:—

If the first ball struck, even if not caught, did not go far enough to make a run safe the batsman waited for the second. If he escaped being caught out in this he could wait for the third. Then he *had* to run whether he hit it or not, as long as he had tried. If he did not hit it he was generally balled out by the scout behind him. So a batsman very seldom risked waiting for a third ball but ran as soon as he had got a fair clip at first or second "try."

We will suppose he has escaped all risks and reached first stop. No. Two takes the bat. He hits a ball. The moment it is hit No. One can run to the next or as many stops as he has time for, taking the risk of being struck or crossed out. If the ball is not hit he must wait until it is. Or even if it is hit he can remain where he is if he thinks the risk too great. But at the third "try" he must run willy-nilly because now No. Two is running to first stop. If the ball has been hit he can run as far as he dare, but if it was not hit he can run only to the next stop. There will soon be players on all the stops, waiting for a lucky hit to run on. The fun grows fast and furious. The unskillful players were soon caught or "balled" out but there were always a few tough ones whom it was hard to get out. Oddly enough "runs" were not counted at all. It did not matter how many runs your side had. The thing was to keep the other side out as long as you could. I have seen Nate Lockhart alone keep his side "in" for an hour. I have done it myself while perspiring scouts cursed the trick of the wrist which sent the ball precisely where a scout was not and enabled the solitary player to make a home run. But the end always came and with a glad whoop the outs went in and the ins went out and it was all to be done over again, with a bitter difference that now *you* were out and had to run after flying balls until you were out of breath while the disdainful "ins" careered from base to base.

Oh, it was fun! The thrill of it has come back to me as I write—I tingle with it—I long to be back on that old diamond with the bat in my hand. Well, wake up! Those players are scattered over the world. Annie Stewart was in the Klondike the last time I heard of her!

Chronology

1874   Lucy Maud Montgomery is born on November 30 to Clara Macneill Montgomery (age 21) and Hugh John Montgomery (age 33). Both the Macneills and the Montgomerys had emigrated from Scotland in the late 18th century. By 1874, they are old, established families on Prince Edward Island who have been prominent in Island politics and history.

1876   Clara Macneill Montgomery dies of "galloping consumption". Lucy Maud is raised by her maternal grandparents, Lucy Woolner Macneill and Alexander Marquis Macneill, in Cavendish, Prince Edward Island, a rural village founded in 1790 by three clans (the Macneills, the Simpsons, and the Clarks), all of Scottish descent. LMM's grandparents have already raised six children, and she grows up having many relatives in this rural village and elsewhere.

1890   LMM travels with her grandfather, Senator Donald Montgomery, to Prince Albert, N.W.T. [now Saskatchewan], to stay with her father and new stepmother. She becomes close friends with Laura and Will Pritchard and achieves her first publications in the Charlottetown *Patriot* and the Prince Albert *Times* during this year. She rejects a suitor, John Mustard, her high school teacher, who comes from Leaskdale, Ontario. [John Mustard and Laura Pritchard both reappear in this volume of her journals.]

1892   Back on the Island, LMM finishes school and studies for the entrance exams at Prince of Wales College, in Charlottetown.

1893   She passes her entrance exams, ranking 5th highest on the Island. She completes the two-year teaching course in one year, places 6th in the certification examinations, and gets a First Class certificate. In September, *The Ladies' World* accepts her poem, "The Violet's Spell", and gives her two subscriptions as payment.

1894–5 She spends her first year teaching in the rural school at Bideford, PEI. She rises early to write each day, and she begins publishing poems and stories in newspapers and magazines.

1895–6 She attends Dalhousie University in Halifax for one year, all she can afford, with earnings from teaching and help from her grandmother. She receives her first cash payments for writing from Philadelphia's *Golden Days* and Boston's *Youth Companion*. She also wins a Halifax newspaper contest for poetry with feminist themes.

1896–7 Montgomery teaches school in Belmont, PEI, and becomes engaged to her cousin, Edwin Simpson, in June 1897.

1897–8   Teaching at Lower Bedeque, PEI, she is attracted to a young farmer, Herman Leard, with whose family she boards. She continues writing and publishing while teaching. She breaks her engagement with Ed Simpson.

1898   Her grandfather Macneill dies suddenly and she returns to Cavendish to live with her aging grandmother. There she learns of two more deaths, Herman Leard's in 1899 and her father's in 1900.

1901   She is written up in the PEI's *Daily Patriot* as one of several promising Island poets in the spring. In September she moves to Halifax to work on the *Daily Echo*.

1902   In June, she returns to Cavendish where her grandmother needs her. Her close friendship with two people begins: with her younger cousin, Frederica Campbell, and with Nora Lefurgey, the new teacher in Cavendish school.

1903   The Reverend Ewan Macdonald becomes the new minister in Cavendish, PEI. Nora Lefurgey moves to board with LMM and her grandmother. [Nora reappears in this volume]. In December 1903, LMM begins a life-long correspondence with George Boyd Macmillan, a journalist in Alloa, Scotland. LMM is making a good income from publishing stories and poems in many American and Canadian magazines.

1905   The Rev. Ewan Macdonald moves to Cavendish to board there. LMM begins writing *Anne of Green Gables* in the spring.

1906   The Rev. Ewan Macdonald resigns in order to take further theological training at Glasgow, Scotland, and proposes before he leaves: LMM keeps her engagement a secret.

1907   L. C. Page offers LMM a contract for *Anne of Green Gables* and urges her to begin a sequel.

1908   *Anne of Green Gables* is published in the spring. Favourable reviews pour in from England, the USA, and Canada, tourists start descending on Cavendish, and the book is reprinted six times, selling over 19,000 copies, in its first five months. LMM must furiously produce sequels to satisfy the public.

1909   *Anne of Avonlea* and some 50 short stories and poems are also published this year. First of a sweep, *Anne of Green Gables* is translated into Swedish in 1909—then into Dutch, 1910; Polish, 1912; Norwegian and Danish, 1918; Finnish, 1920; French, 1925; Icelandic, 1933; after LMM's death in 1942, it is published in Hebrew, 1951; Japanese, 1952; Slovak, 1959; Spanish, 1962; Korean, 1963; Portuguese, 1972; Turkish, 1979; Italian, 1980. [In this volume, a young Muslim woman in India writes her after reading *Anne of Green Gables*.]

1910   *Kilmeny of the Orchard* is published. The Rev. Ewan Macdonald moves to Ontario to accept a charge in rural Leaskdale. In September, LMM is honoured by an invitation to meet Lord Grey, 4th Earl Grey, Governor-General of Canada. In November, she visits Boston, a personal guest of Mr. and Mrs. L.C. Page.

1911   Her grandmother, Lucy Macneill, dies at age 87 in March. *The Story Girl* is published in May. LMM (age 36) marries the Rev. Ewan

Macdonald in June, and they take a two-month honeymoon to Scotland and England, visiting literary sites that LMM loves and her grandmother's ancestral home in Dunwich, Suffolk, England. They return and set up house in the Leaskdale Presbyterian Manse, northeast of Toronto.

1912   *Chronicles of Avonlea*, a collection of earlier stories revised to make references to Anne, appears just before the birth of LMM's first son, Chester Cameron, born July 7, 1912.

1913   *The Golden Road* is published. LMM returns to the Island for a visit.

1914   LMM gives birth to a son, Hugh Alexander, who dies at birth on August 13. The beginning of World War I adds to her personal sadness, but Montgomery's fiction turns to the happy days of college and romance, and she finishes *Anne of The Island* just before her 40th birthday.

1915   LMM is traumatized when her cousin, Frede Campbell, almost dies of typhoid. *Anne of the Island* is published in July. On October 7, a healthy baby son, Ewan Stuart, is born.

1916   *The Watchman and Other Poems* is published. LMM's growing dissatisfaction with her publisher, L.C. Page, ends in a rupture, and she shifts to Canadian publishers: McClelland, Goodchild and Stewart of Toronto.

1917   *Anne's House of Dreams* is published in 1917, by Frederick Stokes in New York and McClelland, Goodchild and Stewart in Toronto. LMM publishes an autobiographical essay in a magazine series which is later published as *The Alpine Path: The Story of My Career* (Fitzhenry and Whiteside, 1975). Frede Campbell marries Lieutenant Cameron MacFarlane.

1918   Legal battles with L.C. Page intensify. LMM vacations in PEI.

1919   In January, LMM is devastated by the sudden death of her cousin Frede during the influenza epidemic. In May, the Rev. Ewan Macdonald has a nervous breakdown. Treated in Boston during the summer, he improves in autumn. *Rainbow Valley* is published. Right after LMM settles her lawsuit with Page, selling him rights to her novels, the publisher sells movie rights to *Anne of Green Gables*, which is made into a silent movie with Mary Miles Minter as "Anne". All the income goes legally to L.C. Page. LMM begins recopying her handwritten journals into uniform legal-size volumes, making her own "life-book".

1920   Page publishes *Further Chronicles of Avonlea*, a collection of LMM's earlier stories which turned up in the Page vaults. LMM warns him not to publish them and sues him when he does. He brings a countersuit for malicious litigation. *Rilla of Ingleside*, LMM's story about women's lives in the years of the Great War, is published at year's end.

1922   A car accident involves Ewan in an acrimonious local lawsuit, launched by Marshall Pickering of Zephyr. The judgement goes against Ewan, who disputes it, and refuses to pay. The Macdonalds vacation in Bala, Ontario, in the Muskoka lake district.

1923   Montgomery wins another case against Page in American courts. Page launches an appeal. *Emily of New Moon* is published. LMM is the first

Canadian woman to be made a Fellow of the Royal Society of Arts in Great Britain.

1924   Ewan Macdonald works to persuade his Leaskdale and Zephyr congregations to vote against "church union", the uniting of the Presbyterian, Methodist, and some other Protestant denominations into the United Church of Canada.

1925   *Emily Climbs*, the second in this trilogy, is published. Chester goes to St. Andrew's College, a boarding school in Aurora.

1926   *The Blue Castle*, an adult romance set in the Muskoka Lake District, is published. Ewan accepts a new ministerial position in Norval, Ontario, where he will have two charges, at Norval and Union. They move in February.

1927   *Emily's Quest* ends the Emily series. LMM is presented to the Prince of Wales, to Prince George, and to the Prime Minister of Britain, the Honourable Stanley Baldwin, and Mrs. Baldwin at Chorley Park in Toronto.

1928   The Macdonalds again vacation in the Muskoka lake district. LMM's younger son, Stuart, leaves for boarding school in Aurora. She meets Ephraim Weber, a schoolteacher from Alberta, with whom she has corresponded since 1902. The long series of lawsuits with L.C. Page ends successfully, and LMM invests the settlement.

1929   *Magic for Marigold*, featuring a little girl younger than Anne or Emily, is published. LMM makes an autumn visit to PEI. The stock market crashes, affecting LMM's investments.

1930   LMM travels to re-visit friends in Prince Albert, Saskatchewan.

1931   *A Tangled Web*, the second of her adult novels, is published. Her elder son, Chester, enters the University of Toronto.

1932   Church work involves LMM in directing plays. LMM's friend Nora Lefurgey Campbell moves to Toronto.

1933   *Pat of Silver Bush* is published. Stuart enters the University of Toronto.

1934   Ewan spends several months in Homewood, in Guelph, Ontario. A first grandchild, Luella, is born to Chester and his wife. Montgomery helps produce a book of biographies called *Courageous Women*.

1935   *Mistress Pat* is published. In March, LMM is elected to the Literary and Artistic Institute of France. The Macdonalds move to 210 Riverside Drive in Swansea Village, on the west side of Toronto. LMM is made an Officer in the Order of the British Empire.

1936   Stories about Anne as a young teacher appear in *Anne of Windy Poplars*. The Canadian Government purchases and designates part of Cavendish as a national park.

1937   *Jane of Lantern Hill* is published, set in Toronto and PEI. The Green Gables site in PEI is officially opened in April.

1939   Grosset and Dunlap begin reprinting all of LMM's early works. She visits PEI and uses Island scenes for *Anne of Ingleside*.

1942   Lucy Maud Montgomery dies on April 24.

Index

Acadia College, 170, 376, 392, 398

Actors: Lionel Barrymore, 231, 402, 403; Mitzi Green, 260, 291, 405; O. Heggie, 295, 326, 408; Katherine [Katharine] Hepburn, 259, 405; Dawn O'Day ("Anne Shirley"), 291, 295, 325, 407; Mary Pickford, 20, 263, 378; Helen Westley, 295, 326, 408

Agnew family: 70, 200; Andrew, 69, 75, 80; Christine, 69; Eleanor, 69, 183, 188, 200, 399; Laura (Pritchard), 66-81, 83-7, 98, 180, 183, 188, 200-3, 218, 236-7, 384; Willard, 68, 82, 98

Air mail, 71, 385

Air travel: R-100, 63

Albert of Belgium, 255, 404

Anglican Church: in Norval, 27, 32, 93, 154, 317-18, 320-1, 344, 366, 379, 384, 405, 409, 412; Parish Hall, 321, 411; in PEI, 194; in the West, 387

Anne of Avonlea, 37, 41-2, 213

Anne of Green Gables, 20, 28, 36-7, 41, 79, 107, 136, 171, 194-5, 235, 291, 295, 325-6, 394, 398, 428-9; editions of, 195; illustrations, 194-5; the movie, 20, 260, 291, 295, 323, 325-6, 333, 407-9, 429

Anne of Ingleside, 356, 407, 430

Anne of the Island, 38, 41, 357, 362, 429

Anne of Windy Poplars, 356-7, 411, 430

Anne's House of Dreams, 42, 109, 357, 362, 377, 391, 429

Aurora, Ontario, 25-6, 87, 106, 115, 120, 153, 232, 374, 396, 430

Australia, 21, 32, 39, 41-2, 44-5, 48, 159, 397

Authors cited: Alcott, 40, 381; Austen, 40, 381; Bacon, Francis, 255, 404; Barrie, 40, 381; Benson, A.C., 158, 187-8, 257, 396, 400; Bronte, Charlotte, 187-8, 257, 400; Brown, Alice, 40, 381; Browning, 341, 410; Bulwer-Lytton, 8, 375, 410; Burnett, 40, 381; Butler, Samuel, 163, 397; Butler, W.F., 71, 385; Byron, 84, 150, 387, 395, 408; Carroll, Lewis, 40, 381; Christie, Agatha, 181, 399; Corelli, 65, 202, 384, 401; Crawford, Marion, 46, 381; Crozier, 177, 399; Deland, 40, 381; Dickinson, 312, 409; Emerson, 70, 385; Feuchtwanger, 49, 382; Froissart, 219, 402; Gale, Zona, 40, 381; Gaskell, 40, 187, 381, 400; Grahame, Kenneth, 40, 381, 396; Grote, 247, 404; "Gyp", 40, 381; Guadalla, 214,

401; Habberton, 40, 381; Hackett, 135, 393; Holt, 121, 392; Homer, 99, 109, 389; Hope, Anthony, 226, 402; Jeans, James, 46, 381; Jewett, 40, 381; Johnstone, Annie Fellows, 40, 381; Kipling, 232, 395, 403; Klickmann, 179, 399; Ludwig, 49, 382; Macaulay, 48, 139, 382, 394; Martin, George Madden, 40, 381; Ethel Mayne, 150, 395; Mitford, 40, 381; Nicholson, Meredith, 43; Poe, 67, 385; Pope, 99, 109, 382, 389, 391, 394; Reid, Myrtle, 40, 381; Renan, 49, 256, 382, 404; Rice, Alice Hegan, 40, 381; Rinehart, 164, 398; Rossetti, 248, 404; Saunders, 136-7, 393; Shaw, 89, 91-2, 233, 388, 400, 403; Tacitus, 219, 402; Tagore, 137, 393; Thedon [Tridon], 186, 400; Trevelyan, 139, 394; Trollope, 146-7, 394, 395; Twain, Mark, 43, 113, 391; Wallace, Edgar, 164, 398; Wetherald, 401; Wetherell, 40, 381; Whitman, 137, 393; Wiggin, Kate Douglas, 40, 161, 381, 397; Wilkins, Mary S., 40, 381; Wordsworth, 143, 190, 394, 400

Auto accidents, 365

Aylsworth, Laura (McIntyre), 61, 98, 99, 138, 187, 251, 384; Pat (Mrs. Ken Langdon), 187-8, 192, 401

Banks: Bank of England, 416; Bank of Montreal, 340; Bank of Nova Scotia, 115, 380, 389

Barraclough, Ernest and Ida, 30, 64, 94, 135, 153, 188, 218-21, 223-4, 245, 248, 257, 259, 261, 265, 267, 276, 290, 300, 302, 305, 308, 314, 319, 323, 325, 334, 341, 343, 346, 348-9, 351, 354, 356-7, 362, 365-6, 368, 372, 379, 400, 405; Glen House, 22, 28, 62, 78, 94, 138, 143, 160, 218, 220, 245, 248, 259, 290, 301-3, 305, 308, 313, 323, 340, 343, 347-9, 351, 353-4, 357, 360, 364, 368-9, 371-2, 379

Battleford, 72, 83-5, 386; *people*: Mr. and Mrs. Clouston, 85

Beaton family (PEI): Archie, 55-6, 60, 113; Mary (Campbell), 6, 8, 23, 55-60, 63, 113, 157, 376; Roland, 59-60; Sutherland, 55-60, 63, 89, 110, 383

Bentley, James, 103; Tillie Macneill, 103, 207-9, 390

Bernard, Lily Macneill, 97, 389

431

Credit River, 25, 61, 185, 189-91, 197-8, 203, 226, 229, 263, 265, 276, 302, 315, 322, 344-6, 361, 372, 378
Crewson's Corners, 186

Dalhousie University, 171, 387, 392, 427
Davis, Mrs. George, 90-3, 95-8, 114, 155, 157, 388
Dean, Miss Jerry, 278, 282, 305, 406
Dennis, Ethel, 280, 284, 286, 290, 292, 293, 297, 298, 307, 324, 330, 333, 339, 343, 346, 348, 351, 406
Depression, The, see economic depression
Devotional Guild, 162
Dingwall, Nell, 6, 199, 376
Doctors: Baugh, 275, 406; Brydon, 268, 405; Clare, 273, 275, 285-6, 406; MacKinnon, 271, 406; Williams, 258, 303, 407; Royce, 26, 379; see also Paul
Doiron, Angie, 5, 375
Domestic help in the manse, see Dennis, Harrison, Mason, Meyers, Shier, Thompson
Dramatic Club, 154, 256, 368
Drugs and medications: 279, 290, 298, 300; barbital, 308, 401, 408-9; blue pills, 285-6, 407; bromide, 98, 267, 268, 273, 291, 294, 297, 361, 389; chinese tablets, 280-1, 406; chloral, 266, 268, 270-3, 293-4, 300-1, 304, 309, 327, 405; codeine pills, 104, 390; cold remedy, 158; Dr. Paul's tablets, 262, 274, 277-8, 287, 290-1, 293-4, 296, 298, 299, 301, 305, 362; iron and arsenic pills, 29, 380; medinal, 309, 311, 313, 319, 328, 337, 341, 346, 362, 408; Sal Volatile, 354, 411; "San. dope", 303; sleeping pills, 272, 287; tonic with strychnine, 53, 281, 380, 383, 407; veronal, 215, 243-4, 246, 262, 279, 284, 291-3, 295, 297-301, 303, 306, 308-9, 311, 314, 321-2, 328, 336, 354, 401, 408

Earl Grey, 147, 162, 395, 428
Eclipse, 196
Economic depression and falling dividends, 28-9, 91, 97, 100, 102, 110, 155-8, 176, 179, 183, 211, 221, 228, 277, 290, 380, 385, 387, 389-91, 396-7, 399, 405
Edison, Thomas, 153-4, 396
Edmonton, 83, 85-6, 89, 387; *people*: Daisy McLeod, Bertie Hayes Arnett, 86, 387
Einstein, Albert, 96, 388
Elmo, Miss (agent), 292, 407
Emily Climbs, 39-40, 430
Emily of New Moon, 38, 227, 429
Emily's Quest, 40, 430
England, 129, 133, 139, 142, 154, 220, 259, 267, 300, 302, 322, 341, 382, 396, 402, 405, 416-18, 420, 423, 429-30; *see also* Great Britain

Films: actors, Mary Miles Minter, 20, 194, 378, 429; Mary Pickford, 20, 263, 378 (*see*

also actors); director, William Desmond Taylor, 20, 378
Food, 4, 65, 100, 103, 246, 306, 325, 336; cheeses, 140-1; cookhouse, 140; jelly, 139; turkey, 333
Forbes, Rev. Stuart, 51-3, 382-3
Ford, Henry, 153, 396
French people, PEI, 6, 123, 375, 378, 383, 391
Further Chronicles of Avonlea, 21, 378, 430

Gagnon, Lt., 138, 151, 394
Games: checkers, 297; crokinole, 325, 409; euchre, 293, 302, 314, 334, 362, 364, 368, 372; solitaire, 284-5, 291, 293, 295-6, 307-8, 313, 321, 340; table rap, 333, 410
garden parties, 223-4
Gardens, 6, 16, 43, 59, 62, 116, 119, 140, 154-6, 170, 178, 180, 182-3, 220, 222, 226, 254, 260, 264, 266, 269, 358-9, 361, 377, 406
Garvin, John, 107, 390
Geneva, 152
Georgetown, 25, 32, 42, 50-1, 65, 99, 157, 187, 192, 223-4, 226, 228, 241, 243, 246, 258, 267, 271, 285, 293, 295, 297, 320, 333, 335, 340, 368, 374, 378-80, 383, 388, 390-2, 397, 401-2, 404-5, 410; Bank of Montreal, 340; Georgetown High School, 241; Presbyterian church, 246; *people*: Dr. Howard, 223-4, 296, 312; Mrs. Howard, 223-5, 226; Mrs. Sinclair, 100, 390; druggist Watson, 286; *see also* Dr. Paul
Germany, 158, 162, 179, 282, 341, 361
Gibson & Taylor, 102, 107, 119, 162, 180, 302, 304, 316, 322, 328, 341, 390
Giffen, Andy, 31, 95-6, 98, 100, 289, 338, 343, 348-9, 380; Jean, 309, 408
Glasgow, 339, 429
Glen Williams: 32, 259, 367, 375, 379, 390, 405; Glen Hall, 259, 360, 405
Golden Road, The, 38, 392, 394, 430
Gollop, Mr., 278, 290, 316-18, 319-20, 323-4, 344, 354-5, 363, 406
Governors-general: Bessborough, Lord and Lady, 232, 403; Duke of Devonshire, 148, 395; Earl Grey, 147, 395
Graphic Press, 401
Graphic Publishing Company, 29, 380
Great Britain, 154, 381, 396, 406, 431; *see also* England
Greenwood, Mr., 93, 114-15, 143, 161, 341, 389
Grier, Rev. James C., 383
Grier, Wylie, 138, 151-2, 394
Guelph, 2, 25, 150, 186, 269, 271-2, 274, 276, 279, 281, 283-5, 308, 365, 374-5, 378, 382, 394-6, 405, 430; *people*: McLeod, 308; *see also* Homewood

Halifax *Echo*, 42-3, 333, 410, 428; *people*: Laura Carten, 333; Miss Clara Dennis, 137, 393

CPSIA information can be obtained
at www.ICGtesting.com
Printed in the USA
BVOW10s0932040817
491141BV00001B/61/P